THE SOUTHERN WAY OF LIFE

THE
SOUTHERN
WAY OF
LIFE

Meanings of
Culture and Civilization
in the American South

Charles Reagan Wilson

THE UNIVERSITY OF NORTH CAROLINA PRESS

CHAPEL HILL

*This book was published
with the assistance of the William R. Kenan Jr. Fund
of the University of North Carolina Press.*

Design by April Leidig
Set in Minion by Copperline Book Services, Inc.
Manufactured in the United States of America

Cover photo: View of the town of Odum in Wayne County,
Georgia, in 1993. Courtesy of the Library of Congress.

A NOTE ON LANGUAGE: This book contains quoted material that includes
upsetting racial language, including the N-word, "colored," and "negro."
Commentators in the past used these terms to describe African Americans
of African descent. These demeaning terms were part of a cultural strategy to
disrespect and marginalize African Americans, who were oppressed in the
various expressions of the southern way of life. These terms are disturbing,
but including them illuminates the importance of language in
buttressing the southern racial system.

Library of Congress Cataloging-in-Publication Data
Names: Wilson, Charles Reagan, author.
Title: The southern way of life : meanings of culture and civilization
in the American South / Charles Reagan Wilson.
Description: Chapel Hill : The University of North Carolina Press, [2022] |
Includes bibliographical references and index.
Identifiers: LCCN 2022023740 | ISBN 9781469664989 (cloth) |
ISBN 9781469664996 (ebook)
Subjects: LCSH: Southern States—Civilization. | Southern States—
Social life and customs.
Classification: LCC F209 .W563 2022 | DDC 975—dc23/eng/20220521
LC record available at https://lccn.loc.gov/2022023740

To Marie
and to the graduate students I taught
at the University of Mississippi

CONTENTS

PART II
SOUTHERN WAY OF LIFE

Chapter Three
Agrarian Way: Regional Consciousness
and Southern Tradition

Chapter Six
Revolutions and Counterrevolutions:
Challenging and Defending the Southern Way
in the Civil Rights Era 297

ILLUSTRATIONS

THE SOUTHERN WAY OF LIFE

INTRODUCTION

A FTER JOKING ABOUT his sister's psychosis, a character in Pat Conroy's novel *The Prince of Tides* (1986) tells his physician, "It's the southern way, Doctor." He explains that this is his "mother's immortal phrase. We laugh when the pain gets too much. We laugh when the pity of human life gets too . . . pitiful. We laugh when there's nothing else to do." The doctor asks, "When do you weep . . . according to the southern way?" The reply is "After we laugh, Doctor. Always. Always after we laugh."[1]

This phrase, "the southern way," has a long genealogy, and South Carolina native Conroy is one of many modern southerners who have thought and written about the region's ways, who know that joking and crying are somehow both involved. Earlier observers of the South have long attached passionate rhetoric of good and evil to the construct of a "southern way of life." These earlier ways of thinking remain woven into the fabric of the idea, but dramatic changes in southern history and life over the last fifty years have affected the rhetoric. When observers employ the term today, sometimes it evokes the southern past and sometimes it centers on features of a new future for the region. Whatever the underlying purpose, however, it is clear that the core idea of this "southern way of life" runs as a strong current in the cultural life of the region, from the eighteenth century to the present.

After a career spent reflecting on and writing about the South and its regional consciousness, I have come to believe it has evolved around three concepts: southern civilization, southern way of life, and southern living. Each grew out of changing contexts, with both people in the American South and outsiders contributing to the concepts. From the colonial period to World War I, observers of the South spoke of southern civilization in discussions that touched on complex meanings of civilization itself, in both American and global contexts. From the 1920s to the mid-1960s, commentators on the South shifted to produce and wrestle with various meanings of a southern way of life. That term could mean a segregated and hyperracialized way of life, but it could also mean an agrarian way of life, a well-mannered way of life, an interracial way of life, a spiritual way of life, a leisurely way of life, a business way of life, or a workers' way of life. White southerners used their power and privilege to define these understandings, but African Americans were a formative countercultural force, persistently criticizing the segregated way of life and revealing its costs while defining and living out a "Negro civilization" distinctively rooted in the South.

With the end of Jim Crow legal segregation in the mid-1960s and the decline of agrarian life by the same period, a final major expression of the concept appeared. "Southern living" expressed the new dominance of a suburban, more prosperous South that began to reshape the region by the 1980s. Cultural forms such as music, literature, food, sports, and regional magazines would express this commodified South. The contemporary South also began to divide along ideological lines between a conservative, individualistic "southern living" and an interracial, progressive, and increasingly multicultural one. This new attention to diversity reflects a basic conceptional change from the long search for the unitary southern way.

The historically dominant concept of a unitary southern way of life, or a southern civilization, suggested the grand aims of its advocates in positing a sweeping, all-encompassing view of the region's culture. Attention to changes over time provides a way to unravel how the term evolved as an expression of regional consciousness. A sharp focus on this construct offers insights into how it arose, how it changed over time, and how it was simultaneously challenged and buttressed at particular times.

The term "southern way of life" appears often in scholarship on the U.S. South. It was a chapter title in literary critic J. V. Ridgely's survey of nineteenth-century southern literature, and it also appeared as a section descriptor in a chapter of a John B. Boles book. Sociologist Howard Odum titled a book *The Way of the South* (1947) and used the term to define the folk culture of the region. Historian Drew Gilpin Faust was among a growing number of later scholars who pointed out the racial, political, and class interests inherent in the term, assessing Confederate ideology as "the dominant class's effort to protect its cherished way of life from the challenge of American national control." Other scholars have demonstrated that religion was inherent in the term's meaning as well. "Southern church leaders could easily think of themselves as the first line of defense for the South and its way of life," wrote C. C. Goen in a study of antebellum religion. W. Fitzhugh Brundage applied the term to describe part of the southern social memory: "The predominant postwar white memory dwelled on loss—of battles, loved ones, a way of life, prestige, power." James C. Cobb concluded that by the 1960s many white southerners could not face change because they had believed for a long time "that their racial system" was the heart of their "way of life."[2]

"If there is such a thing as a Southern way of life," said the main character in Walker Percy's *The Thanatos Syndrome* (1987), "part of it has to do with not speaking of it." Percy is undoubtedly correct that naming the way also transforms it. The term "way of life" can mean an actual, functioning culture, which is implicit in Percy's comment. David Harvey, in his Marxist geographical critique of contemporary capitalism, notes that most people experience life within the particularities of localism: "For most people the terrain of sensuous experience and of affective social relations (which forms the material grounding for consciousness formation and political action) is locally prescribed by the sheer fact of the material embeddedness of the body and the person in the particular circumstances of a localized life." Harvey points to the need to look at "the preservation and production of cultural diversities, of distinctive ways of life," in the context of "both non-capitalist and capitalistic modes of production, exchange, and consumption." As Raymond Williams argues, politics is always "embedded in 'ways of life' and 'structures of feeling' peculiar to places and communities."

The South has indeed had, and still has, such a functioning culture; southern claims to a distinctive "place" are legendary. But such a functioning culture can be reified and take on a conceptual life that becomes an agent in history. "An assumed way of life, in other words," writes literary critic Lewis P. Simpson, "displaced by history, is converted by mind into an idea of this life." Naming a way of life may signal that society has changed, but that is only the beginning for understanding its cultural history. Naming is becoming, the foundation of cultural identity.[3]

Anthropologist Clifford Geertz describes culture as, in one sense, a socially constructed web within which people in a society live and move, and the idea seems particularly appropriate to consideration of the southern way of life. The metaphor of the web has been a recurrent one in discourse on southern civilization, the southern way of life, and southern living. The South, W. J. Cash wrote in 1941, lived "under the sway of a single plexus of ideas of which the center was an ever-growing concern with white superiority and an ever-growing will to mastery of the Negro. And of which the circumference was a scarcely less intense and a scarcely less conscious concern with the maintenance of all that was felt to be Southern, a scarcely less militant will to yield nothing of its essential identity." Cash's analysis came during the interwar period of the mid-twentieth century, and it reflected a regional society at a crucial point in its development from the end of Reconstruction to the civil rights movement. Race was a crucial component, but so was "all that was felt to be Southern." The South was more than just an idea; it had the emotional power typical of those "primordial ties" that bind a group of people together.

Writing about the same time, William Faulkner saw southerners trapped in history, with yesterday always present in today, creating a historical web of meanings. Gail Hightower in Faulkner's *Light in August* (1932), to take but one example, was a Presbyterian minister who could not get the hoofbeats of his heroic Confederate grandfather's horse out of his head, as he blended his Christian message with the religion of the Lost Cause in the modern South. Meditating on Faulkner's insights in the 1990s, decades after the end of legal segregation, African American writer Anthony Walton observed that "freeing oneself from this psychic and cultural web can take superhuman effort." He added that "few manage to do so."[4]

Grounded in the interdisciplinary field of conceptual history, this book will trace "the thread of life and language that connects past and present." Conceptual history considers the evolution of ideas and value systems and how they seem to become commonsensical, natural, and normal over long time periods. A central tenet of this approach holds that ideologies are not unchanging processes but contingent cultural values and practices that have to be seen in their particular contexts over time. So the historical meaning of the terms "southern civilization," "the southern way of life," and "southern living" will be central to my arguments, with special attention paid to the cultural contexts in which the concepts were developed and to moments when they faced crises or gained clarity in expression.[5]

This book builds on a great deal of recent interdisciplinary scholarship on the American South, which is often gathered under the idea of a "new southern studies." Those engaged in this work include literary scholars, historians, social scientists, documentarians, religious studies scholars, environmentalists, and gender studies scholars. Collectively they show how the long-established southern context has influenced, and still does, the predominant patterns of thought and action among people in the American South. Importantly, these scholars see the South now as part of national and global narratives, as do I.[6]

One of the most important areas of new southern studies is critical realism, and its approach anchors this study. It argues that the term "region" does not refer to a specific site "but to a larger network of sites," as it is always a relational term. Talking about a region is not "talking about a stable, boundaried, autonomous place but a cultural history, the cumulative, generative effect of the interplay among the various competing definitions of that region." This approach is especially valuable in structuring the conceptual history of the South as it puts in conversation the various meanings of civilization, way of life, and living, including national as well as southern viewpoints. Critical regionalism shifts away from a focus on the products of regional culture to "the processes by which ideas about regions come into being and become influential" so that the core idea of critical regionalism, and of this study, is that "a region is not a thing so much as a cultural history."[7]

The "southern imaginary" is a fertile idea within critical regionalism relevant to the southern way. Scholars define it as "an amorphous and sometimes conflicting collection of images, ideas, attitudes, practices, linguistic accents, histories, and fantasies about a shifting geographic region and time." Attention to the southern way and its social relations and to the ways white southerners idealized them will range widely to suggest how they embodied a southern imaginary. Conceptual history explores the ways that people use concepts politically; the term "political imaginary" can include "the public shapes of power, representation, and possibility." The imaginary can reveal how ideologies mobilize power to control mental frames, which is vital to understanding how social practices form. Power is hidden in and mobilized through apparently neutral structures and cultures. But part of the story is that viable opposition to it does happen by challenging what seems a commonsense view of social reality—such as the segregated southern way of life.[8]

This book does not intend to offer a comprehensive story of southern history, then, but rather a sharp focus on the concepts that reveal an ongoing southern regional consciousness. Abstract concepts, their behavioral expressions, and their materialistic manifestations are embedded in the historical narrative that follows, as events and forces drive the adaptations that have enabled southern regional consciousness to survive into the twenty-first century. It is not a static story of an essential South but one of contestation, contingency, and change as groups and individuals claimed the authority and social power of southern civilization, the southern way of life, and southern living.

The concept of a "southern way," clothed in political and religious rhetoric and the passion of ethnicity, came to have a life of its own in the nineteenth- and twentieth-century South. It was far more than an idea. It came to be virtually synonymous with a civil religion that tied the region's cultural values to intense evangelical religious faith and produced a structure of institutions, rituals, myths, beliefs, ideologies, and identities, which encouraged white southerners to invest enormous meaning in the southern identity. The term "southern way" often evoked moral meanings, whether of belief in the moral superiority of white southerners surrounded by allegedly savage Black people, the moral virtues of victimized Blacks, the potential salvation associated with the region's identity, or, alternatively, the region as a peculiar moral problem for the nation. The "southern way" involved behavioral expectations for everyone living in southern society, and the term generated social rituals, typologies, representations, and styles that made performance an essential element. Critics engaged the concept, whether they were African Americans in the South or elsewhere, northerners, or white southerners who had escaped from the mental strictures of what James Silver called the "closed society."[9]

The concept of the southern way has had several specific expressions. By far the dominant one through most of southern history was white supremacy. Another specific focus was agrarianism, receiving its most important expression in the symposium *I'll Take My Stand* (1930), which first used the term "southern way of life" extensively and defined it not explicitly around racial issues but in terms of a besieged southern rural society in the early twentieth century. The Agrarian writers were among those southerners who saw spiritual and philosophical meanings in southern life. William Alexander Percy, a twentieth-century planter and poet, did not identify with the Vanderbilt Agrarians. He gave, though, one of the fullest examinations of the South with spiritual meaning in his 1941 memoir *Lanterns on the Levee*, as he wrote of the "old Southern way" and the "simple wisdom of the South." Another usage of the term evokes manners and proper cultural etiquette. There was a "proper" way, in other words, of behavior, a mannered southern way of life that emphasized the importance of form as a governing mechanism in the biracial society. Although analytically different versions, all of these expressions of a southern way overlapped, generally taking for granted the segregated society.[10]

A different expression of the southern way emerged full-blown in the late twentieth century, as reformers challenged Jim Crow segregation and finally overturned it in the 1960s. This version of the southern way of life was one of biracial redemption, with race again central to the southern way. This version embraced a biracial culture that had emerged from centuries of Black and white presence in the South, with culture as the possible source for not only southern salvation but national and even international redemption as well.

Another version of the southern way is one of the most tenacious varieties: the South as a leisurely—lazy, in its negative connotations—society. This reflected the foundational issue of work in southern society. The exploitation of the labor of African Americans from slavery to domestic work and the contemporary service economy has provided an ongoing social context for discussion of a southern way. At the same time, African Americans' work was said to provide the leisure for the highest type of civilized living by whites, especially elites. This concept united ideas of white privilege and philosophical understandings of the good society.[11]

Most of this study focuses on the dominant, white supremacist version of the southern way of life, which operated at the intersection of social status, cultural authority, and regional identity. It represented a form of power that buttressed the peculiar (in the American context) arrangements of a regional society and reinforced the economic and political dominance of whites within segregated society and, one should add, of Black elites within African American society. The concern is to see how social arrangements came to be at the heart of regional identity. The predominant southern way was social separation of the races, based on the intermingling of privilege and power, with a moral justification of racial superiority based in the discourse of civilization.

The history of the southern way of life is significant because it offered social and cultural legitimacy to its advocates. They used it to gain and maintain social status, political power, and moral authority. It was one of those cultural artifacts that worked to establish the normalization of a biracial, hierarchical society dominated by white power. Mississippi writer Elizabeth Spencer spoke for many white southerners in recalling her twentieth-century childhood in Jim Crow society. She "had subscribed to the 'Southern way of life,' had thought that my parents and grandparents could not be wrongheaded, that they had lived a correctly reasoned approach, had died in clear consciousness of having done the right thing during the time of slavery and war and all the difficult years that followed." Looking back on it in the 1990s, she realized that "it was an ugly system, of course," but growing up, "in that childhood time of enchantment and love, it never seemed to me anything but part of the eternal." She wrote that one "might as well question why the live oaks were there, or the flowers in Aunt Esther's garden, or the stars in the sky," as to say that their farm could "be run any way but the way it was, always had been, always would be."[12]

Dorothy Walton, a native Black Mississippian who was part of the Great Migration out of the South after World War II, came back to the state in the 1990s and reflected back—at about the same time as Elizabeth Spencer—on the meanings of racial segregation for whites. "No matter how poor or corrupt their families were," she said, "it seemed they felt they were better than any black person." She understood that the whites of her generation had inherited their southern ways from their ancestors. "They had been taught by the generation before them that white ways and white skin were better than anything that was black." She related this white perception partly to the social realities of work, of Blacks performing service jobs: "*And* we'd always been their servants. . . . I think they were taught not to question it." She speculated that much of the feeling for segregation was based in the desire for social separation. "They didn't want any *real* socializing. It was okay to spend a bit of time together," but "it was just the southern way. You don't mix." For Walton growing up in Jim Crow Mississippi, "I was never raised to think I was second class, even when I was waiting behind the white folks' bus." Whites might be "mean and they wouldn't let us ride, but we were taught we were good as them."[13]

Nothing was more important than religious sanction to the development, evolution, and adaptation of southern civilization, the southern way of life, and then southern living. Evangelical Protestantism emerged as the dominant religion of the South in the antebellum era, the same historical period during which southerners and outsiders defined a distinctive sense of southern identity, and religion extended a sacred canopy over the region's social relations. It resulted in a southern civil religion, a common religion of white southern culture that gave providential sanction to white dominance of the region and that reflected a belief in peculiar southern missions to the world. In earlier writings, I have argued for a southern civil religion around the white memory of the Confederacy and its defeat. Religious sanction for this memory implied the possibility of redeemed, reborn Lost Cause conservative values of virtue and order. One sociologist argued that civil religion is not about salvation, though, but about achieving "the good life," a term that resonates in discussions about the southern way of life. This study examines how various southerners used the concept of "civil religion" to mean the sense of providential missions that became attached to the South and that southerners and others used to explicate understandings of the good life.[14]

"The southern way of life" is a twentieth-century term, as in Walton's use, but the origins of the concept go back to the colonial era. The earliest reference I have found to a "way of life" in the context of the U.S. South was in Hugh Jones's *The Present State of Virginia* (1724). The book showed, said the subtitle, Virginians' "religion, manners, government, trade, way of living." The author noted particularly that the "common Planters" had an "easy Way of Living" that made them, in the summer heat especially, seem "climate-struck." The journal of John Woolman, who traveled through Maryland, Virginia, and North Carolina in 1746, offered another, more troubling early use of the term. "I saw in these southern provinces so many vices and corruptions, increased by this slave trade and this way of life, that slavery appeared to me as a dark gloominess hanging over the land; and though now many willingly run into it, yet in future the consequences will be grievous to posterity." Woolman was an early Quaker critic of slavery; few American colonists at the time seemed to take his words to heart. He nonetheless understood that the South by the mid-1700s had become a distinctive American place based in part on slavery but more broadly on "this way of life" in the region.[15]

By the early nineteenth century, white southerners and other Americans talked of "southern civilization," which typically summoned images of a hierarchical, paternalistic, racially conscious society and became the nineteenth-century version of "the southern way of life." After 1830 a heightened southern self-identity made white southerners defensive about not just slavery but all aspects of their peculiar system within the United States. The antebellum South's cultural distinctiveness existed ultimately in myth and ideology, but it also appeared in very tangible ways. The Civil War tested the region's ideology of being a distinctive civilization and having a southern way, and Confederate defeat threatened the region's separate identity and customs. Reconstruction may have been an even more important challenge than the Civil War, not to the region's political independence but to its cultural identity. The war and Reconstruction represented dramatic change, but the specter of lost regional identity led southern whites to assert the southern identity with a vengeance. With slavery's destruction at the end of the Civil War, the drastically altered southern social system resulted in a turbulent postwar period as the formerly enslaved, former enslavers, and nonsoutherners who came south struggled during Reconstruction for control of the region's politics, society, economy, and cultural understanding. Black southerners typically embraced an American ideology of democracy and egalitarian ideals, while whites constructed the beginnings of a Lost Cause sensibility that would dominate the South's public culture and social expectations for generations.[16]

The late nineteenth century saw a struggle to control the South's future. Social class and racial tensions heightened as the region redefined itself in the aftermath of slavery and modernity's stirrings. The white Redeemers who overthrew Reconstruction governments represented a dominant prewar elite who, joined by postwar new elites, struggled with discontented farmers, industrial workers, and African Americans in general for political and cultural dominance. White elites enforced their dominance through violence, economic intimidation, electoral chicanery, racial baiting, and outright usurpation of power by any means available. Disfranchisement, social segregation, a predominant tenant economy for Blacks, a spike in racial violence, and the daily racial etiquette of submission by Blacks to whites established the context in which antebellum southern civilization as a concept was revivified after the war. Southern civilization now rested on advantages that accrued to white southerners from racial segregation. W. E. B. Du Bois called these the "wages of whiteness," advantages earned simply from having a white skin. Sociologist John Dollard, in a 1930s study of social life in the Mississippi Delta, argued that racial segregation resulted in privileges for whites in terms of social position, sexual advantage, and economic position.[17]

The concepts of traditionalism and modernity provided the intellectual terminology for evolving discussions of the southern way. "Southern civilization" remained a term in use, but most observers after 1930 used "the southern way of life." Folklore emerged as a key force in shaping the South's understanding of itself as a place of traditional ways, while such icons as the railroad, the textile mill, and the automobile represented the forces of modernity invading the region. The forces of modernity—urbanization, industrialization, consumerism, mass culture—provided a new context for discussions of the southern way and the need to adapt it to the new society. Interracial organizations and social reformers emerged to witness for a new biracial ethic, as they drew from religious/philosophical understandings of a southern way that looked radically different from the hegemonic white supremacy version or the agrarian traditionalist version.[18]

The interwar years were thus important ones in recognizing a biracial ideal in the South. This biracial concept was about power, and white southerners used the concept as a powerful ideological tool to try to dominate African Americans, who were a sizable presence in the South and on whom white people relied for labor. The language of biracialism suffused the southern way of life. That said, this study recognizes the multicultural nature of southern society. White southerners created concepts of the southern identity at the same time—the 1830s—that the federal government removed most of the South's Indigenous people to the West. Before that, Indians were a foundational element in the creation of southern cultures, and their legacy would remain through the remnants of tribes who remained in the region. The colonial era had a diverse population of peoples from western Europe whose interactions in the cosmopolitan coastal cities and in the frontier backcountry would lay the basis for hybrid New World cultures. The South had fewer large ethnic communities than other parts of the United States, but Italians in New Orleans, Irish in Savannah, Greeks in Birmingham, and Jews in Atlanta are only a few of the groups who became associated with southern places. In the twenty-first century, multiculturalism became a leading concept associated with the South, but the diversity of ethnic and social groups was quite apparent earlier in southern history.[19]

The term "southern way of life" was key to political discourse at the end of World War II, with the rise of the Dixiecrat political movement and the white reaction to the *Brown v. Board of Education* (1954) Supreme Court decision requiring the desegregation of public schools. White supremacy was the defining feature of the term, with agrarianism reduced to a supporting role. Demagogic politicians found the term a useful one in conveying emotion and clarity of vision in resistance efforts to ending the legally mandated social separation of the races. An August 1964 editorial in Mississippi's *Meridian Star*, for example, vowed to fight integration to "keep up the sacred obligation to . . . fight for our precious Southern way of life." Most nonsoutherners accepted the same dominant usage of the term. A polemical, ideological rallying cry, it seemed to evoke the deepest social memories of white southerners. Civil rights activists countered its rhetorical usages with evocations of American democratic and Christian egalitarian values associated with what Gunnar Myrdal called the "American Creed." Black southerners, and whites who became activists, appropriated the concepts of a southern way. They claimed historical legacies and cultural representations and styles to frame a new biracial version of the southern way, one that would be central to the region's public culture in and after the 1970s.[20]

Despite many changes in the contemporary South, "the southern way of life" is still an oft-used term and concept, and the last chapters explore the sometimes surprising recent developments. Some commentators use it on occasions when the dark segregationist past seems still alive. In 2002 Senate majority leader Trent Lott, a Republican from Mississippi, praised retiring senator Strom Thurmond and speculated that the nation would have been better off if Thurmond's 1948 Dixiecrat segregationist campaign had succeeded. Lott earned considerable disdain, both from other Republicans and from Democrats. One letter writer to the Jackson, Mississippi, *Clarion-Ledger* noted that Lott was not simply praising an old politician "but giving credence to an old political way of life, a way of life that upheld discrimination, bigotry, violence, and murder." By this time, few people wanted intentionally to claim the white supremacist version of the southern way. The phrase "way of life" is now used, as well, in a South that is the new center of Latino immigration to stir anti-immigrant feelings, much as George Wallace and his supporters used the phrase to warn of Black integration. In a February 2002 rally in Siler City, North Carolina, David Duke, a contemporary white supremacist political leader, implored the audience to complain to public officials about the presence of immigrants. If the immigration tide was not stemmed, "you'll lose your homes, you'll lose your schools, you'll lose your way of life."[21]

The use of the term "southern way of life" dramatically declined after the 1960s and the end of Jim Crow segregation. But the concept has remained, redefined as southern living, an adaptation of the concept to the changed economic, social, cultural, political, and demographic contexts of the contemporary South. Nicholas Lemann suggested the current dominant usage in a review of V. S. Naipaul's book *A Turn in the South* (1988). "White people talk about 'the southern way of life,' it actually isn't any longer a code phrase for white supremacy; it connotes the 'totally planned community' around a golf course, cheese grits and honey-baked ham at the pre-game brunch, a five-year subscription to *Southern Living*." Welcome to the newest South. As the region's middle class grew, moved to the suburbs, and became a well-defined social group with increasing Sunbelt prosperity in the 1980s and after, it became the locus for southern identity, which included reflecting on the concept of a southern way, now understood as a southern style and lifestyle: southern living.[22]

Race is not far, though, from reflections on southern living. In one of the most significant developments in the recent South, African Americans since the 1970s have been returning to the region in large numbers, and the attraction of the region can sometimes evoke a mental construct very different from that of the past. Taylor Wilson, a Black Chicago electrician returning to the South in the 1980s, said of leaving the North, "I'm moving South for the same reasons my father came here from Mississippi. He was looking for a better way of life." The understanding of that way of life is very different today than it was 100 years ago, but Wilson's words suggest that places, north or south, are associated with ways of life that shape understandings of experience. In terms of the southern way of life, African Americans, like middle-class whites, are among the prime narrators of a particular version of southern living in the contemporary South, the newest version of the southern way.[23]

The southern way of life takes on its greatest significance when seen in relationship to the term "civilization." "Civilization" in the South both connected the region to Western civilization, as an extension of it, and indicated a specifically regional way of life, a southern civilization. The tensions between these two regional meanings of "civilization" took dramatically different configurations at differing times. In addition, white southerners helped foster understandings of an exceptionalist American civilization in the early national period, but then in the antebellum South they came to see a distinctive southern civilization as the true heir of the founders of American civilization and went to war in part to defend that concept. White southerners into the twentieth century were ambivalent about American civilization. Some of them embraced its technological and economic progress, others endorsed its democratic and egalitarian values, and many resented its centralizing role in wearing away at traditionalism and spirituality.[24]

White southerners refined their idea of southern civilization through encounters with Indigenous peoples and enslaved Africans, people in their midst representing savagery and its developing racialization in the eighteenth century. From the colonial period, observers saw southern North America as a meeting ground of Black and white people, with nascent southerners embodying a negative—from the European perspective—creole identity. A New Englander, Jonathan Edwards the younger, wrote that white people in the West Indies and the southern colonies should expect their intermixing with the enslaved to produce "a mungrel breed," or else they should leave their land and houses to "the Negroes whom they have hitherto holden in bondage." He imagined that whites in those southern places, representing advanced civilization, would one day have to "make in one way or another compensation to the Negroes for the injury which they have done them," including possibly "giving them their own sons and daughters in marriage." Edwards thus linked the Caribbean and the South with a fearful prediction for those in colonial places struggling to maintain a toehold on civilization, and it remained a potent apocalyptic fear for white southerners thereafter.[25]

The modern usage of the term "civilization" dates to the mid-eighteenth century, a key period of the maturing of the American colonies, preparatory to the Revolution. The noun "civilization" emerged out of the previous century's verb "civilize," which suggested a process of uplifting to a higher state of humanity. The moral code of the dominant elites was the aristocratic ideal of the gentleman, with his economic independence, supposed selfless paternalism, and honor-bound value system that became a symbol of civilization. This ideal would take deep root in the plantation culture of the South and become an enduring one for the future southern way of life.[26]

The Enlightenment defined an enduring understanding of a universal civilization, with civilized standards of behavior, that would lead in the nineteenth century to European and American imperialist ventures throughout places deemed savage, including the U.S. South. The modern meaning of the term "progress" entered the language at the same time as that of "civilization" and reflected the emergence of the scientific method and the confidence in reason that marked the Enlightenment worldview. Thomas Jefferson could embrace this, to a degree, yet he was also very much the self-conscious Virginian, aware of his society's local and customary realities. As part of an emerging South, an abiding feature of southern thought, seen in southern civilization and later in the southern way of life, is the belief that the South represented civilization better than other parts of the United States or even Europe, which had evolved over time.[27]

The early nineteenth century saw a romantic reaction against the expansive claims of the possibilities of a universal civilization, and observers identified the idea of "culture," which was strongly rooted in German thought, as an alternative. Romanticism, one expression of culture, promoted the appreciation for particularities of place that included national cultural identities, and white southerners' rising regional self-consciousness in the early nineteenth century led to increased exploration of southern society's distinctiveness and supposed superiority. All of these factors undergirded talk of a southern civilization.[28]

The Victorian era of the mid and late nineteenth century would define ideas of civilization that would be particularly influential in the U.S. South. Darwinian evolution, a new factor, refocused Enlightenment interest in the unity of humanity into a new concern with the origin of human civilization. Cultural differences became embedded in ideas of racial heredity. American anthropologist Lewis Henry Morgan proposed a series of stages in human development, showing with scientific authority the particular levels of human racial evolution. Civilization thereby became an explicitly racial concept, signifying not just Western societies or industrially advanced economies. Humans advanced from simple savagery through barbarism to advanced civilization. Morgan concluded that only the white race had reached that stage. The refinement of high culture became a signifier for civilization. Cultural and intellectual elites in the South as elsewhere appropriated what they saw as civilized activities such as the enjoyment of Shakespeare, traveling opera companies, fine paintings, and classical music. White southerners adapted the antebellum gentleman and lady, the cavalier myth, into the context of the New South in the late nineteenth century, a particularly southern contribution to the idea of civilization.[29]

This evolutionary view rested on the understanding of gender relations. A Victorian litany of traits defined manhood: self-reliance, strength, resoluteness, restraint, courage, and honesty. The lady, the complement to the Victorian gentleman, embodied gentility, spirituality, and purity. These middle-class virtues grew shaky in the late nineteenth century in England and North America, under challenge from immigrants, the working class, and suffragettes. Middle-class men and women used "civilization" to connect male dominance to white supremacy. Gender is an important category in this study, which will explore the variety of roles that women have played in the history of southern regional consciousness. Writers made them the preeminent symbol of an elite southern civilization in the antebellum years through the myths of the southern belle and southern lady. Women were teachers of the southern way, whether in the domestic world or as members of organized women's groups that led campaigns to teach about and memorialize the Lost Cause. They could also be critics of the excesses of the southern way, as in the Association of Southern Women for the Prevention of Lynching. And they could be victims of the southern way as well. Black women faced sexual exploitation growing out of the privileges given white men in the slave, and later Jim Crow, society. White women were victims of the restricted roles required by the patriarchal expectations of the southern way of life. Women such as Rosa Parks were heroic figures in challenging the segregated southern way of life.[30]

The discourse on civilization declined after World War I, and white intellectuals in the South generally moved away from defending southern barbarities such as lynching, but moderation remained the norm, as white critics understood the social, economic, and physical threats that awaited anyone questioning the predominant social arrangements of southern life. Many southern intellectuals could not help but see themselves as being out of touch with modern civilization. R. C. Collingwood's lecture on "what 'civilization' means" in the 1940s pointed to a decline in the West of the idea of "standards of civilization" as dividing the civilized and uncivilized. "To accept it in the middle of the twentieth century," he insisted, "is a sure sign of retarded development, of being a century and a half behind the times in your habits of thought."[31]

By the 1940s, "way of life" had replaced "civilization" as the defining moniker of regional self-consciousness; first used to mean agrarian traditionalism, as in *I'll Take My Stand* (1930), it later signified the defense of Jim Crow racial segregation in the 1950s. Beginning in the 1960s, "southern living" was the concept used to express an evolving southern identity. The text is divided into three parts that explore this evolution.

———————

Part 1, "Southern Civilization," explores how civilization and the South became mental constructs linked in the popular and intellectual imagination up to World War I. Key topics include the appearance of an identifiable southern society in the colonial era, frontier settlement, the sectional conflict, the elements of an antebellum southern civilizationist ideology, the Civil War and Reconstruction, the memory of the Lost Cause and the Old South, New South economic diversification, efforts to assert a rural southern civilization, Populist reform, and the binary between a South of economic and social problems and a South achieving a considerable amount of sectional reconciliation with the North and accompanying claims of progress toward American norms.

Part 2, "Southern Way of Life," covers the years from 1920 to 1970 and analyzes how agrarian writers in 1930 first used the term in defense of rural traditionalism, before defenders of racial segregation seized on it in the 1950s as a term in their violent and emotional defense of southern racism. Chapters in this section examine the reform efforts of the New Deal and organized labor in the South, the role of moderates in trying to manage social change, the range of racists from moderate paternalists to racial extremists, and the creative and powerful role of civil rights activists in countering the segregationist southern way of life and championing a biracial model. The section concludes with the portrayal of the end of Jim Crow segregation and the adaptation to new realities.

Part 3, "Southern Living," considers the decades from the 1970s into the twenty-first century. Chapters in this section argue for the tension in southern regional consciousness between backward-looking white supremacist understandings of the South and more dynamic and progressive versions based in interracialism. The section shows that economic transformation accompanied changes in race relations and southern society in general, and these developments produced a new middle-class, suburban South that became the locus for discussions of southern ways. This section concludes with the argument that the twenty-first-century South has become increasingly multicultural and cultural issues are now central to a reimagined southern living.

This Thomas Satterwhite Noble painting, *The Price of Blood*, shows a slave trader bargaining on the sale of the mixed-race son of a slave owner, a moral quagmire that long haunted understandings of southern civilization.
Morris Museum of Art, Augusta, Georgia.

PART I

SOUTHERN CIVILIZATION

CIVILIZATION EMERGED as a concept from the Enlightenment in early modern Europe, became a driving force in Europe's expansion around the world in the following centuries, and in time came to define broad thinking about the American South. The concept in the Americas and elsewhere helped foster nationalism and the accompanying growth of democratic processes and humane values. Alas, powerful people and institutions used the concept of civilization to carry out some of the worst features of modernity: colonialism, racism, imperialism, xenophobia, and capitalistic exploitation. Reformers, however, also spoke the language of civilization to counter such practices. As leading French thinkers explored meanings of civilization in the early nineteenth century, their influence was palpable among white southern intellectuals.

The latter also were familiar with German thought, which saw civilization as institutional and public, often within a political and economic framework. White southern intellectuals learned from German thinkers who emphasized the development of culture within this structure; "culture" here refers to inner, spiritual values and traditions of thought and feeling. Germans saw themselves as people of culture, while Anglo-Saxons and the French were specialists in civilization. This tension was at work in the United States' North-South relationship, generating questions about the superiority and inferiority of each region's civilization in the nineteenth century and up to World War I. In this outlook, the South seemed backward and underdeveloped in some respects but saw itself as more spiritually advanced. Another key concept, civil religion, appeared in the antebellum era to express a southern sense of God-ordained mission that reflected the belief of southern white people in their defining spirituality, and it would grow stronger after the Civil War as white southerners tried to understand divine providence in Confederate defeat.

Chapter 1 examines the perceptions that shaped early observations of the southeastern part of North America as a particular spot in the global imagination, one on the margins of civilization. The climate and landscape inspired lush descriptions and the promise of productivity. Contact and interaction among Europeans, Indigenous peoples, and enslaved Africans, meanwhile, disturbed European-descended observers but contributed to the cultural exchanges that came to characterize the region. Whites in the emerging South saw themselves as the emissaries of Western civilization, struggling to achieve order while interacting with peoples they saw as savages and barbarians. The founding of the United States, which southern leadership helped achieve, proclaimed an exceptional identity, a civilization focused on republican institutions, but white southerners and northerners came to see opposing free and slave versions of republicanism. The Five Civilized Tribes (Cherokee, Chickasaw, Creek, Choctaw, and Seminole) aspired to features of civilization by the 1820s, but the land hunger of white pioneers and American expansionist ideology overwhelmed democratic procedures and humane values and led to the tribes' expulsion by the 1830s. White southerners made slavery and white supremacy the centerpieces of their regional civilization, with romantic sentiments ennobling it and a southern civil religion investing sacred meaning in it. Northern and midwestern abolitionists, including prominent African Americans, relentlessly exposed the brutalities and injustices of southern slave civilization. The Civil War was, in part, a contest with other parts of the United States for control of the meaning of national identity, to determine whether the New England version of American civilization or the southern ideal of civilization would dominate.

Chapter 2 shows that civilization became an even more powerful idea in the late nineteenth century. British thinkers and institutions were then at the forefront in asserting an expansive "discourse of civilization," a term describing that time period's ideology of Western progress. Victorian thought became crucial to thinking about civilization, and it saw the culture within it in two ways. One was the highest, most idealized refinement that humans could achieve. The second view saw culture in an evolutionary sense, with human societies ranked in an ordered progression from savagery to civilization. Both views justified Britain's—and Western nations' in general—powerful role in the world. Racism was at the heart of it, and the white southern segregationist outlook fit easily with this ethos. The memory of the Confederacy and the Old South and the proclamation of a New South of economic development shaped the post–Civil War assertions of a distinctive southern civilization. African Americans contested these meanings of civilization throughout the nineteenth century, but they also claimed civilization as their ideal. Into the twentieth century, they asserted their claims to an African civilization they saw as having once been mighty. Accommodating to the realities of Jim Crow racial segregation led to African Americans' efforts to embody a "Negro civilization" separate from, yet intertwined with, white southern society.

CHAPTER ONE

Southern Civilization

Imagining the Southern Way
through Reconstruction

A FTER A Massachusetts Bay Colony minister, Nathaniel Eaton, moved
to the Virginia Colony in the 1630s, New England founding father
John Winthrop noted his rapid decline. Eaton, Winthrop reported,
"was given up by God to extreme pride and sensuality" and prone to drunken-
ness, "as the custom is there." Winthrop's observations were secondhand rather
than ethnographic, but he was among the earliest of British colonists to note
that people to the south behaved differently from folk in New England. Winthrop's words lead into the world of southern stereotyping—can the hillbilly
with his moonshine jug be that far in the future? But this is not, in any event,
a comical image. The "difference" noted by Winthrop was of profound moral
significance; there were dangers to the south. Reverend Eaton, at the least, had
fallen in with a bad crowd. This early "northern" judgment became a standard
American view of the American South in the colonial era and through the
nineteenth century. The abolitionists emerged in the early nineteenth century
to sharpen the moral critique of southern civilization over slavery, but the nonsouthern critique of the region was broader than that issue. It indicted, more
broadly, any claims of civilization in the region.

Nearly three centuries later, Henry Adams, in his memoir, *The Education of
Henry Adams* (1907), recalled going with his father in the 1850s to visit Mount
Vernon in Virginia, a trip that would give "him a complete Virginia education
for use ten years after," referring to the coming of the Civil War. They had traveled by carriage over poor roads, and in his New England mind, "bad roads
meant bad morals." He would generalize, as well, about white southerners from
his college days with Robert E. Lee's son Rooney, whom he judged "an animal"—
using imagery reserved by the "civilized" for the "barbarian."[1]

Elite white southerners had from the colonial era asserted their claims to
civilized values, represented especially by the supposed civility and gentility of
a gentry class that identified with English civilization and its own grand claims

to represent the highest attainments of human society. But white southerners also aspired to civilization, and they came to claim slave society as its basis, far above the mongrel society of the free North. "There are no people in the world who have a higher opinion of themselves and of their surroundings than the inhabitants of certain districts of the South," noted novelist John Pendleton Kennedy in 1863. They claim, said the writer who had helped to create the cavalier image of the South through his novel *Swallow Barn* (1832), to have achieved "the very highest type of civilization," to be preeminent in the traits of "generous manhood," and to be "hospitable, frank, brave beyond all other people." They were "quick to resent dishonor," sensitive to "what is great or noble," and "refined and elegant in manners." Kennedy, a Unionist who was critical of secession and much of the southern character he observed, referred only to the people in "certain districts of the South," but his sketch of character traits had become identified, by the time of the Civil War when he wrote, as the essence of the southern character, the expression of a distinctive and distinguished southern culture. This image of the southern gentry asserted a regional identity associated with the planter class.[2]

"Southern way of life" is a twentieth-century term, but "southern civilization" was its predecessor that southerners and nonsoutherners used to conceptualize the American South. This chapter traces how "southern" and "civilization" became linked, from early imaginings in the colonial era, through the self-conscious depictions of an antebellum ideological civilization, to the postbellum sense of crisis.

Southern Civilization in the Colonial South

The Europeans who came to what became the American South brought with them preconceptions about that area. They included images of a tropical climate, of fertile land, but also of exploitation of African and Indigenous labor. Although Europeans often portrayed all of North America in these colonial terms, the colonies of the emergent American South especially evoked imagery of a Garden of Eden. If the Puritans established New England as a city on a hill, the white colonists in southern areas drew from earlier European imagery to portray their region as a southern paradise. English adventurer Sir Walter Raleigh had predicted that Eden would be found in the New World on the thirty-fifth parallel of latitude—a line now between Fayetteville, North Carolina, and Memphis, Tennessee. A recurring religious dimension to the images of the southern colonies was noted by observers of early Georgia, who described it as a "land of Canaan" and "a promised land." If the story of the biblical Israelites provided religious imagery, the sensual vision of the Song

First Mass, Celebrated when Menendez Founded St. Augustine, Florida, Sept. 8, 1565

Spanish settlers planted Western civilization in La Florida in 1565, several decades before the English came to Jamestown, Virginia, in 1607. Charles Reagan Wilson Collection, Archives and Special Collections, John Davis Williams Library, University of Mississippi Library, Oxford, Mississippi.

of Solomon was another inspiration. According to one historian, the images in the southern colonial garden myth are "overwhelmingly sensual," with "a pronounced emphasis upon smells, tastes, textures, and a visual stimulation."[3]

Robert Beverley's *The History and Present State of Virginia* (1705) developed the idea of the Virginia plantation as a paradise. He described "the climate, and air, so temperate, sweet, and wholesome; the woods, and soil, so charming, and fruitful, and all other things so agreeable, that Paradise itself seemed to be there, in its first native luster." Beverley's readers embraced the idea of climatic determinism. They saw the southern colonies as having a semitropical climate like in the Caribbean, with contradictory expectations of rich agricultural productivity and the decay and interracial interrelationships that did not bode well for people representing the civilized West. Beverley pictured early Virginia as an Arcadia as in classical times, with all the positive implications of that heritage, but confronting as well the special circumstances of enslaved people in the garden, he foreshadowed the efforts of nineteenth-century southern writers and intellectuals to see how a paradise could contain African slaves.[4]

An initial southern environment-based outlook accompanied an emerging inferiority complex toward the northern colonies. The differences had already been perceived before the Revolutionary era, but the racial issues that would one day spark southern defensiveness and a sense of grievance did not alone cause this attitude. Northern colonists already harshly judged southern places as failing to live up to civilized standards—as understood especially in New England. After a trip through the Chesapeake, for example, New Englander Josiah Quincy observed that the majority of farmers he saw "were a vastly more ignorant and illiterate kind of people than with us." The colonial era's sense of southern difference represented a general sense of inferiority based on moral laxity, particularly a climate-induced laziness. Even southern colonists argued that ease of environment could promote decline in moral character. These emergent white southerners described themselves using such terms as "soft," "slothful," and "sensual and selfish," while they described northern colonists as "diligent" and "enterprising."[5]

In the eighteenth century, planters consolidated their political, social, economic, and cultural power, including the definitions of cultural icons identified not just with the region's elite but with the image of the emerging southern region itself. By the end of the colonial era, outsiders saw the mansion of the southern elite, whether in the Virginia Tidewater or the South Carolina Low Country, as a distinctive emblem of a plantation world. The white southern gentry pictured themselves in relation to the achievements of English civilization. The English style was favored in buildings, furnishings, gardens, and other cultural features. The idea of the English country gentleman became identified in the 1700s with the southern colonies, as white southerners adopted pastoral imagery and travelers sometimes saw places in the colonial South through that lens. An English traveler, Nicholas Cresswell, visited George Washington and described him as living like a "Country Gentleman," noted for his hospitality, agricultural knowledge, and resourcefulness.[6]

One of the most notable colonial southerners, Virginia's William Byrd II, represented an important landmark in the southern context of the English gentry's cultural identity that represented civilization in North America. Lewis P. Simpson notes that during the 1700s, Byrd idealized "a unique historical community, the paternalistic, patriarchal, hierarchical, agrarian community of masters and slaves and yeoman farmers" that had become identified with southern areas of British North America. In 1736 Byrd characterized the "saints of New England" as "foul traders." Although Robert Beverley in 1705 might have pictured his enslaved people as agrarian tillers in a pastoral world, Byrd a generation later foresaw "bad consequences" as a result of the growing numbers of enslaved Africans in Virginia. Byrd devoted most of his attention, though, to

separating himself and civilization from the plain folk. His account of surveying the dividing line between North Carolina and Virginia sketches what he
sees as the differences between his "people" and frontier plain whites. For Byrd,
Carolina was a frontier "Lubberland," lively but troubling. The men there were a
worthless lot, leaving hard work for their women. This land and its people were
thus beyond the pale of civilization, and Byrd's imagery established enduring literary images for southern elites and outside observers viewing the plain
white folk in the later South and worrying whether they would undermine their
aspirations for civilization.[7]

Thomas Jefferson and Civilization

In the late eighteenth and early nineteenth centuries Americans learned what
civilization represented from French writers steeped in the concept coming
out of the European Enlightenment, including Henri de Saint-Simon, Jules
Michelet, Jean Charles Léonard de Sismondi, François Marie Charles Fourier,
and, especially, François Pierre Guillaume Guizot, the French historian who
directed the French Parliament under Louis Philippe. Guizot's *The History
of the European Civilization* went through endless reprints until the end of
the nineteenth century. Collectively, these thinkers presented civilization as
a comprehensive worldview, with history a progressive conflict between civilizing and barbaric forces. The civilized advocated ideals of human equality;
embraced a creative spirit that used science, mechanical inventions, and arts
and letters for human betterment; and appreciated the finer qualities of beauty
and truth. Enlightenment thinkers placed the savage in a dichotomy with civilization, though members of primitive societies could be "noble savages," free
from the corruptions of civilized life. After the discovery of America, Europeans had often portrayed Native Americans as children of nature; later, Euro-
American colonists were described as primitives of sorts as well. The American
Revolution presented early American thinkers the opportunity to see their new
nation as a virtual laboratory for civilization with their own colonial history
and geographic isolation from Europe creating a distinctive world destiny for
the new nation. The idea of an American civilization became a shaping force in
everything from politics and the law to education and plantation agriculture.[8]

Thomas Jefferson knew of ideas about civilization from his close links to
French thinkers of his era, and in the 1780s it became an important theme in
his *Notes on the State of Virginia.* Jefferson himself embraced Enlightenment
thought, the highest level of European civilization, rooted in rationalism and
natural laws. Civilization's ethical qualities appealed to him, as it was what
"first teaches us to subdue the selfish passions and to respect those rights in

others which we value in ourselves." Nurturing civilization would bring the
progressive realization of the humane values inherent in the rights he presented
in the Declaration of Independence. Like other eighteenth-century thinkers,
Jefferson fretted over the standards of civilization, but in his inquiry on manners in *Notes* he put forward good etiquette as the expression of civility, an
important expression of what became the mannered way of the later South.
"It is difficult to determine on the standards by which the manners of a nation
may be tried," he wrote, "whether *catholic* or *particular.*" His was a universal
intelligence, yet he was a particular Virginian and emergent southerner as well
as a visionary American. *Notes* shows him putting forward the civilized yeoman farmer as the quintessential American figure, the new man of the western
world who had escaped from the corruption of Old World aristocracy, monar-
chy, and feudalism to define an exceptionalist understanding of the new United
States in world history. The American Revolution produced a civil religion that
saw providential meaning in American destiny and promoted the seeming
necessity through the antebellum era for territorial expansion—the nation's
Manifest Destiny—to spread democracy.[9]

Native Americans and Enslaved Africans

Southern colonists, including Jefferson's forebears, had been on the periphery
of Western civilization at the beginning of settlement, but they self-consciously
came as predominantly English people who carried civilization into the New
World, in opposition to the savagery of Indigenous peoples and Africans. To
be sure, Indians of the early South sometimes appeared to possess their own
virtues, those of ennobled primitives, and were capable of progressing toward
civilization. English colonists saw a hierarchy of people of color, with Indigenous people ranking above Africans. Jefferson's *Notes on the State of Virginia*
emphasized the Native American's natural virtue and worried over the institution of slavery. Unable to justify the latter, he saw it as incompatible with the
new republic's stress on liberty and equality. The innate inferiority of Africans
prevented a vision of his plantation South with freed Blacks as equals to whites.
He stressed slavery's harmful effects on white slave-owning families who experienced tumultuous emotions of interracial wrangling.[10]

In the first decades of the nineteenth century, the development of the cotton
gin, the development of steamboat transportation, and the growth in scale of
cotton mills in England and New England promoted large plantations in what
became known as the Old Southwest, or later, the Deep South. A rising racism
would after the War of 1812 spread into what had been Native American lands.
Issues of civilization had been attached to Native Americans in the South since

George Washington's presidential administration outlined a "civilization policy" designed to provide Native Americans the resources to change their culture and adopt white ways in order to become civilized.[11]

American presidents, government agents, and Christian missionaries offered a model of American civilization for Native Americans in the early nineteenth century: written laws, individual property rights, farming for men and the weaving of civilized clothing for women, and education for children that would teach the value of money and the Bible. For the Five Civilized Tribes in the South, models of civilization lay with nearby planters. The model of civilization in the South was plantations, staple crops, and enslaved labor. The Cherokees adopted a constitution in 1827, modeled after the federal Constitution, and their legal code reflected the influence of the state of Georgia. A planter/merchant elite dominated tribal councils. The elite owned stores, saloons, mills, and other features of a diversified economy, but a plantation culture predominated. The log, frame, or brick house was typical among Natives as well as whites, and the gardens, orchards, stables, barns, large outdoor kitchens, and slave cabins of Cherokee farms copied plantation places of their white neighbors. The Cherokees followed their models of American and southern civilization well, as they made much progress in English language literacy, many converted to Christianity, some men became farmers rather than hunters, and they accumulated property—the material evidence of civilization as it had taken root in the American South. Such property included enslaved people. By the mid-1820s, enslaved African Americans represented 10 percent of the Cherokee nation.[12]

Intimidation and violence led most of the tribes to sell their lands in exchange for lands in the West by the 1820s, but the Cherokees fought removal through the legal and political system that expressed contemporary understandings of civilization. Nonetheless, white settlers on the southern frontier coveted remaining Indian lands, and their political hero, Andrew Jackson, implemented the removal policy in the 1830s. He justified it in terms of the economic development of the fertile land of the Deep South and as the only way to prevent total elimination of Natives should they remain in contact with white civilization. Cherokee leaders lamented that whites saw the issue as one of race and not culture, a significant departure from the earlier Enlightenment understanding that Indians could become civilized by adopting white culture. Hardening racial views in the 1830s had led to whites categorizing Natives as racially inferior and impossible to change. As they became a part of white-dominated southern civilization, one Native leader said, "We are not more favored than the poor African."[13]

Those same white racial sentiments affected attitudes toward African Americans as well. Although descendants of Africans had lived in North America for centuries by the early nineteenth century, whites still saw them often in terms of the savagery they identified with Africa. This view was especially prominent after the Haitian Revolution at the turn of the nineteenth century and, even more fearfully for southern whites, after the slave plots of Gabriel Prosser and Denmark Vesey and the slave insurrection led in 1831 by slave preacher Nat Turner. The proslavery argument that defended the institution as the basis of the best of all possible societies sometimes portrayed the enslaved in savage terms. But the effort to idealize southern society also promoted views of all Black people as "savage children," with slavery having the potential to advance enslaved people, under benign white influence, toward civilization.[14]

Abolitionism

During the antebellum years and the Civil War, defenders of southern interests went beyond economic and political concerns to articulate a broad interpretation of the white southern way of life as a civilization different from that in the North. The official ideology of the region, that view put forward by the intellectual and cultural elite in southern society's most esteemed forums and institutions, did not exhaust the meanings of southern civilization in the formative era of the mid-nineteenth century, but it offered a clear view of southern public culture as perceived by its most self-conscious promoters.

This ideology developed partially in response to the northern abolitionist movement's view of the slave South as a corrupt society in which white southerners abused their enslaved workers physically, sexually, and morally and exploited their labor and their bodies in general. One of the most influential compendiums of the horrors of slavery was Theodore Dwight Weld's *American Slavery as It Is* (1839), in which Weld wrote at the outset that "we will prove that the enslaved in the United States are treated with barbarous inhumanity," a charge that positioned the South outside civilization. Weld's sweeping condemnation of the South included examples from across the region that helped create the construct of a regional civilization with interrelated, evil parts. Slave South images undercut those of an appealing leisurely, premodern South, which had already become popular among some northerners and white southerners.[15]

Frederick Douglass had been born in slavery and escaped it; his testimony against the institution was one of the most powerful ones in the antislavery movement and cast into doubt any assumption of a benign pastoral South. His extraordinary oratory and rhetorical sophistication, along with his inside knowledge of the workings of the slave system, enabled him to cast white enslavers as demons outside of civilization, with a special scorn for the hypocrisy of Christian owners of enslaved people. By the 1850s, he was using the term "Slave Power" to help convince northern white audiences of the aggressiveness of southern civilization, dominated as he saw it by slave owners who instinctively reached for mastery not only of their region but of the nation. Harriet Beecher Stowe's *Uncle Tom's Cabin* echoed these themes of southern slavery's immorality, reaching a vast popular audience and portraying the South as beyond the pale of civilization.[16]

African American protest in this era drew from biblical religion, with the enslaved having a redemptive mission that challenged exceptionalist understandings of the nation as the New Israel. Whites since the Revolution had seen the United States as a Christian nation, with a millennial world destiny. African American leaders argued that slavery corrupted white American Christianity and eroded any claims to civilization. Black Americans insisted that they were the old Israel, waiting for freedom from the southern slave owner Pharaoh's bondage. David Walker's antislavery appeal in 1820 warned that "God rules in the armies of heaven and among the inhabitants of the earth, having his ears continually open to the cries, tears and groans of his oppressed people."[17]

Southern white defenders of slavery constantly evoked the image of Africa as a barbarous and uncivilized continent as a justification for the "civilizing mission" of enslaving its people to Christianize and civilize them. African American abolitionists took the lead in trying to vindicate Africa as a source of civilization. Their central argument was that ancient Egypt, a source of Western civilization, was home to people with "Negroid" features. "The ancient Egyptians were not white people," insisted Frederick Douglass, "but were, undoubtedly, just about as dark in complexion as many in this country who are considered Negroes." Prominent African American thinkers such as William Wells Brown and Martin Delany echoed such claims, drawing on evidence from ancient historians Herodotus and Diodorus Siculus.[18]

Abolitionism's moral and religious attack on the white South and Nat Turner's slave rebellion forced defenders of southern ways to examine and justify their slave civilization and to promote the emergence of a well-defined southern regional consciousness by the early 1830s. The southern identity emerged gradually, with society and culture in the southern colonies already differentiating themselves from those in New England and the Middle Atlantic colonies. A "first South" emerged during the years of the American Revolution as southern colonists recognized their shared economic and political interests. Although social and cultural differences existed earlier, a self-conscious embrace of the southern identity, as the foundation for a southern civilization, occurred in defensive reaction to the antislavery attack, which undercut white southern claims to civilization itself. William Lloyd Garrison's *Liberator* launched in 1831 with a call for immediate emancipation of enslaved people, and the antislavery movement grew over the next three decades. Nat Turner's insurrection in southern Virginia in 1831 represented a visionary Black preacher's

assertion of God's justice in the overthrow of slavery and led to white southerners strengthening slave laws and contributing to a newly refined regional
self-consciousness.[19]

The defense of slavery as a positive good after 1830 thus intertwined with the
new assertion of a southern identity, marking one of the most significant moments in the white embrace of a southern civilization. Writing in 1857 George
Fitzhugh said, "Until the last fifteen years, our great error was to imitate Northern habits, customs and institutions," even though southern conditions were
"so opposite to theirs, that whatever suits them is almost sure not to suit us."
Until that time white southerners, he admitted, had "distrusted our social
system," thinking slavery "morally wrong, we thought it would not last, we
thought it unprofitable." With abolitionist attacks, white southerners had examined their slave society and "became satisfied that slavery was morally right,
that it would continue ever to exist, that it was as profitable as it was humane."
With a new self-confidence and self-reliance, Fitzhugh claimed, "we are the
happiest, most contented and prosperous people on earth."

John C. Calhoun, in a speech protesting congressional reception of abolitionist petitions in 1836, said that the slave system in the South could not be
"subverted without drenching the country in blood, and extirpating one or
the other of the races." Whether good or bad, slavery had become so interwoven with southern institutions "that to destroy it would be to destroy us as a
people." Calhoun thus posited that social death would be the result for southerners if slavery was abolished.[20]

After this dramatic change in consciousness around 1830, southern institutions came under increasing criticism from the North, and the southern response was to defend southern culture itself. Many white southerners came to
believe they had a civilization, indeed "the very highest type of civilization."
Southern nationalists in the three decades before the Civil War conveyed the
vision of a separate South, with white southerners as a distinct people. But not
all white southerners embraced this vision before the war. "We are heartily sick
of this everlasting twaddle about the South," said a writer in the North Carolina
Argus in 1850 during the debate on the sectional crisis. "The South—that word
of talismanic charm with southern demagogues." Southern politicians, as well
as ministers, were in the forefront of those constructing "a South" with deeper
and broader meanings than before.[21]

A Southern Civil Religion

Events of the mid-nineteenth century created a crisis for white southerners.
In response, they drew together political and cultural ideas of the South to
forge a southern civil religion—in this case imbuing cultural and civil rituals

and ideas with religious ideology—as the foundation of southern civilization. Although bitter North-South conflict appeared first in politics, it produced its first decisive organizational divisions in religion. Protestant churches provided major institutional support for the development of a regional culture, with the separation, beginning in the 1840s, of white Christians into the three largest American Protestant groups: the Baptists, Methodists, and Presbyterians. In each case, slavery was a cause of the North-South division. After this, as white southerners worked to build their new churches and accompanying educational and missionary institutions, they became ever more committed to regional folkways and the ideology of a southern civilization.[22]

In the process, white southerners moved toward rejection of the civil religion that had given spiritual meanings to American nationalism. This was a crucial step in seeing southern civilization as sacred and not merely distinct. Antebellum white southerners, like other Americans, inherited the belief in American Manifest Destiny. The idea of Americans as God's chosen people traces back to the New England Puritans, who saw their transcendent destiny as building a religious society. The American Revolution had redefined this idea into political terms when a civil, or public, religion emerged expressing the faith that Americans had a special mission to represent, and spread, republicanism through the world. White southerners shared the confidence that the American nation was under divine guidance, but in time their vision diverged, and white southerners did not participate equally with northerners in a major expression of the antebellum civil religion—the quest to build a Christian America. They concentrated their efforts instead on soul saving.[23]

Although white southerners used the civil religion's rhetoric of American destiny through the antebellum era, two qualifications appeared to their commitment to it, which showed how emerging religious nationalism contributed to the regional consciousness of difference from other Americans. First, white southerners invested religious meaning in their states as well as in the nation. Virginians and South Carolinians, especially, continued after the Revolution to see their states with special significance in the American federal system, and the simultaneous rise of states' rights politics and evangelical religion joined the rhetoric of the two to attribute special spiritual meanings to the southern states. Beverley Tucker, for example, worked to make Virginia a sacred place, "a kind of cult." Tucker urged students at the College of William and Mary "to turn their hearts toward the Muse of Virginia in devotion as the Moslems turned their faces toward the tomb of the prophet in prayer." Northerners at times also attributed such meanings to their states, but this sentiment grew weaker in the antebellum era, as the union itself grew stronger as a force for religious patriotism. In addition to seeing their states in transcendent terms, antebellum white southerners drifted away from the American civil religion as they came to see their region as under divine guidance. For them, no other factor was more important in legitimating southern civilization. Racial fear may have been the psychological wellspring of "southernism," but religion provided its positive and ennobling justification. From the nullification crisis around 1830 onward, white southerners saw the union less in mystical, organic terms and more in terms of material efficacy, as the citadel of freedom, the protector of local rights and individual liberty. The union came to be John C. Calhoun's political mechanism for preserving minority rights, not a spiritual force beyond politics.[24]

Southern nationalist piety was transferred to the region instead. Attachment or even love of the union continued among many white southerners through the Civil War itself, but by the time of the war, "the South" had taken on rhetoric and imagery once reserved for the nation. White southerners before the Civil War began to see their destiny increasingly in regional terms that focused their thoughts on slave owners as the epitome of the southern faith. William Brantley wrote in 1837 that "the Baptists of the South . . . are now in many respects a distinct and separate people"; Leonidas Spratt wrote in 1853 of "a great destiny" awaiting slave owners, "the chosen people of the South"; and William H. Holcombe predicted early in the Civil War that "future ages will appreciate the grandeur and glory of our mission." The sense of mission once applied to Americans in general now was adapted to strengthen the belief that southern nationalism was divinely ordained.[25]

A Distinctive and Distinguished Civilization

If the emergence of a regional civil religion suggested the spiritual basis of an evolving antebellum idea of southern civilization, the term "civilization" itself came into widespread use to refer to the formal southern understanding of a regional way of life, of the "one South," in the antebellum era. "Civilization" evoked images of the highest cultural achievements in literature, art, and music. The triumphs of the classical era and the Renaissance defined it; religion, and more specifically Protestantism, provided the moral philosophy undergirding it; Western Europeans exemplified it. Part of this essential humanist understanding of civilization as the high point of human culture was an early social science influence suggesting that peoples went through different stages in the civilization process. Americans in general saw themselves as the carriers of civilization from a Europe that often seemed decadent, although Americans continued in fact to admire European culture. Southern intellectuals adapted ideas of Western civilization to a regional context as part of an effort to enhance intellectual order in a developing society.[26]

"Civilization" was also used to suggest a distinctive culture rather than the highest cultural achievements or the evolution toward them. "By the civilization of a nation," wrote Jesse Burton Harrison in 1832 in the *Southern Review*, "we desire here to express the sum of those results which constitute the character, intellectual and moral, public and domestic of that nation." He believed that a "Linneaus of the intellect" could categorize the characteristics separating Europeans from Africans, Americans, or Asians. This was the fundamental belief for cultural nationalists.[27]

White southerners were part of an American civilization that tried in the early nineteenth century to define its distinctiveness within Western civilization. Emerson celebrated self-reliance as the American character, and other writers of the American renaissance used local materials to fashion an American literature. The Hudson River school of painters and the genre painters of democratic life each, in their own ways, similarly executed works that drew on American locales and themes to assert the existence of distinct American culture. Popular culture and vernacular culture exhibited the peculiar ways and forms that would be celebrated as the basis of a new national culture. Throughout the period of growing sectional division, southern efforts to build a culture were a part of this broader national movement. Americans embraced romantic views of the South, which they saw as in counterpoint to a diverse, turbulent, and conflicted northern society enmeshed in the growing market economy. That market economy, and its modernizing influences, were affecting the South as well, but mythic views arose of a literary South characterized by leisurely and honorable planters, subdued and satisfied slave workers, an orderly society, and nonmaterialistic values.[28]

This view was reinforced by one of the most influential examples of popular culture in the antebellum North: minstrelsy. That musical genre nurtured enduring stereotypes of a South that defenders of southern civilization would have encouraged. Early minstrels such as E. P. Christy and Dan Emmett spent time in the Mississippi River valley, where they saw enslaved people and their culture and transposed behavioral traits under the slave regime into popular entertainment in circuses, sideshows, and theater saloons popular among the northern white working class. Minstrel music emphasized innovation, spontaneity, sexual and moral permissiveness, and ridicule of upper-class pretensions. Its imagery and narratives also reproduced southern white defenses of slavery, portraying the love of the enslaved for their masters and their fear of having to leave the security of the plantation at the heart of a southern civilization that, in some ways, white northerners could embrace as an escapist fantasy. Minstrelsy became embedded in the Jacksonian era's democratizing spread of mass periodicals, mass revivals, and mass politics, solidifying this particular image of the South in the nation's mind.[29]

Southern civilization—and the conscious attempt to define what would later grow into the southern way of life—developed in the context of all these antebellum meanings of civilization. White southerners began thinking about their society and its role not only in American life but in Western culture as a result of the sectional crisis of the three decades before the Civil War. Southern social theorists, in developing an ideology of defense for the region, stressed that southern culture was not only different from that elsewhere but also distinguished in its cultural accomplishments. Northerners had, in fact, long seen southern culture as different in a backward sense, and white southerners argued now that a southern civilization not only should be different from northern culture, embodying characteristic features, but should aspire to be a bastion of high civilization itself in a world in turmoil.

Southern intellectuals saw their age as dangerous because of social tensions associated with revolutions in Europe and industrial and urban changes in the North. The 1840s and 1850s saw political turmoil roiling such emerging nations as Italy and Germany and liberal political rebellions in France failing, bringing people from those countries to the South, while the potato famine in Ireland had brought desperate immigrants to the region through ports in Charleston, Savannah, and New Orleans and seemed to represent a destabilizing force to traditionalists. George Frederick Holmes claimed that these trends endangered "the whole fabric of the social system." George Fitzhugh argued in 1857 that western Europeans were "suffering intolerable ills" and were "ripe, at any moment for revolution." The South, "the only conservative section of Christendom," was the only American "section satisfied with its own condition," according to Fitzhugh, and thus had an important destiny in preserving a besieged civilization in the Western world.[30]

If civilization itself was at stake, in this rather feverish vision of southern destiny, then a southern civilization had to be not only distinctive but distinguished. As an ideological construct, southern civilization was about the good society, and its defenders argued that the South's leisured gentry had achieved heights of cultural glory. After all, southern elite ideology predicted as much. According to the logic of the proslavery argument, the enslaved were the "mudsill" for the high-achieving aristocracy. A lively intellectual world indeed existed, not only among the elite on the plantations but among middle-class lawyers, teachers, physicians, ministers, and a few professional writers in such southern cities as Charleston, New Orleans, Baltimore, and Richmond. Southern cities and towns established such cultural institutions as museums, schools, theaters, art galleries, opera houses, churches, and Chautauqua. A network of periodicals, institutions, and personal relationships drew them together. Southern high culture was a provincial one, on the margins of Western civilization, but its members knew of the wider world and related their concerns to it.[31]

The movement for southern nationalism in the thirty years before the Civil War led to increased promotion of a specifically regional high culture. Regional periodicals for the first time provided an outlet for southern writers. Artist John Antrobius, in proposing a twelve-painting series on "Southern life and nature," hoped "to vindicate the claims of the scenery of the South to the consideration of artists." He complained that artists turned out hundreds of paintings of the North yearly, "but none come to glean the treasures with which the grand and beautiful country of the south and its peculiar life abound." Implicit in his words was the belief that the South, in pursuing cultural independence and distinctiveness, could also achieve cultural greatness. Antebellum southerners did not occupy an intellectual wasteland, as they were part of transatlantic intellectual discussions. Southern periodicals showed wide-ranging interests in cultural matters, with issues of slavery not at all dominating. The most significant achievement of the Old South's high culture was in theology, where James Henley Thornwell, Benjamin Morgan Palmer, and other divines developed a consensus of evangelical groups around a conservative, orthodox theology that would long outlive the Old South itself.[32]

The southern dream of cultural grandeur was, of course, outrageously unrealistic to begin with, given the region's position as a mostly rural colony in the Western world. Colonies produce individuals of creative genius, but southern theorists asserted that the South itself should not only produce them but also nurture them. The southern populace should marshal popular support for a high culture for the few, but white southerners' lack of support for their cultural institutions and creative artists frustrated this hope. They bought few books and persisted in seeing writing as an amateur affectation rather than a profession. Few art patrons wanted anything beyond family portraits; Antrobius was only able to complete two of his planned dozen paintings. In August 1834, an editorial in the first issue of the *Southern Literary Messenger* noted that hundreds of periodicals succeeded in the North. "Shall not one be supported in the whole South?" it asked. Were southerners "to be doomed forever to a kind of vassalage to our northern neighbors?" White southerners refused to borrow political, religious, or agricultural ideas from "the other side of the Mason and Dixon's line," the editor noted, so why "should we rely on the North for literature?" Nonetheless, they did.[33]

Anxieties about Southern Civilization before the Civil War

The increasingly belligerent assertion of a southern civilization in the antebellum era masked the concerns of the educated elite about the nature of regional life. Ministers often worried about the moral health of the region's whites and the souls of the enslaved, the white upper classes were uncomfortable with the culture of the region's plain folk and periodically anxious over slave revolt, and everyone saw the poor whites as barbaric. Reform achieved limited results in the South compared to the North, but anxiety over society led to efforts toward temperance, improvements in education, establishment of asylums for the handicapped, and, above all, missionary efforts to the enslaved.[34]

Expansion west typically raised issues of whether the South's ways, on the frontier, were really so civilized and fed into the social unease about the region's future. The underlying issue was the role of the folk culture, displayed with least restraint on the frontier, in a distinctive and distinguished southern civilization. August Baldwin Longstreet and other southwestern humorists defended genteel southern culture by writing satirically of frontier people. They were patricians uneasy about this new South of the antebellum frontier. William Gilmore Simms portrayed the frontier as the home of the "bold, reckless adventurer, the dissolute outcast, the exile from crime . . . who goes forth to contend with the wild beasts, the stubborn forests, and the savage tribes who prowl among them." The assertion of civilized ways must counter frontier ways, the southern folk culture. Southern ideology, in this regard, represented settled agrarian life against the wilderness and the civilized aristocracy against the lower classes.[35]

The concerns of the elite paled, however, next to the increasing criticisms of the South by northerners. The level of civilization in the South became a prime source of contention between northerners and southerners. When antebellum northerners used the term "civilization" in regard to regions, it typically signified the differing characters they saw in the sections. But implicit in this was an evaluative dimension. Was the character of southern civilization up to a "civilized" standard? The question became an accusation in antebellum America. William Gilmore Simms reflected white southern irritation when he complained that southerners were "taunted by Englishmen and Northern men" as being inferior in culture. One of the most insightful travelers in the Old South, Frederick Law Olmsted, dissected the failures of southern society in comparison to that of the North. He admitted that the wealth of a few widely scattered plantation owners brought some tokens of civilization, such as "comfortable houses, good servants, fine wines, food and furniture, tutors and governesses, horses and carriages, for these few men." However, that concentrated wealth in the few would not bring "good roads and bridges," nor would it bring "such means of education and civilized comfort as are to be drawn from libraries, churches, museums, gardens, theatres, and assembly rooms." More generally it would "not bring thither that subtle force and discipline which comes of the myriad relations with and duties to a well-constituted community which every member of it is daily exercising." He identified, in short, "a vast range of advantages which our civilization had made so common to us that they are hardly thought of, of which the people of the South are destitute." The reason was the greater concern for community and the wider distribution in the North of the benefits of civilization. The "advantages of our civilization," he concluded, came mainly from "acts of cooperation, or exchanges of service; they are therefore possessed only in communities, and in communities where a large proportion of the people have profitable employment."[36]

The level of high culture became an issue signifying deeper issues. Simms saw the literature of a people resting upon their manners and civil institution. The northern attack on culture in the South was a critique of the southern way altogether. "What book has the South ever given to the libraries of the world?" asked the *Atlantic Monthly* in 1857. "What work of art has she ever given to its galleries?" New England's famed Unitarian minister Theodore Parker, in an 1848 sermon, asked, "Who writes the books—the histories, poems, philosophies, works of science, even the sermons and commentaries on the Bible? . . . Who builds the churches, who founds the Bible societies, missionary societies, the thousand-and-one institutions for making men better and better off?" The presumed answer to his rhetorical barrage did not point south.[37]

This recurrent dissection by nonsoutherners of sick southern ways was the key to the appearance of a defensive regional ideology. New England was the South's accusatory, the center of a persistent suspicion and dislike of southern civilization. The cultural tension between the two regions went back to the colonial era, but it became a cold war after 1830 and the rise of the militant abolitionist movement. By the early 1840s, before denominational divisions, a Methodist writer in the South, William Smith, could attack the South's "New England enemies," and other editors of church journals could in seemingly good conscience ridicule their northern brethren. Writer August Baldwin Longstreet observed that New England was "responsible for the ills of an otherwise happy nation." The sentiment was not limited to an educated elite. John Pendleton Kennedy, writing during the war, noted that nothing was clearer than "the dislike of the common masses of the Southern people—I speak more particularly of the untraveled portion of them—to the natives of the New England states."[38]

New Englanders focused especially on slavery as an evil institution making the South dangerously different, but beneath that specific moral criticism was the deeper worry that southern culture and white southerners themselves were outside the magic circle of civilization. White southerners responded with a moral defense of their peculiar institutions, but this defense of their society led them to prize cultural independence altogether as a way to assert a distinctive and distinguished civilization. When comparing their region to New England, white southerners feared they were provincial. A writer in *Russell's Magazine*, published in Charleston in 1857, suggested that "the philosophy of a people must concentrate itself in their metropolis . . . and all that portion of the people which is not represented there must be regarded as provincials." In the United States, New York City and Boston were the cultural centers, and southerners could "never be other than dependents and inferiors" to them. "Our place in the Union is provincial," the author concluded, "and as such our peculiarities will have to be defended, excused, ridiculed, pardoned."[39]

The Southern Creed

A particular set of cultural ideas and influences defined what advocates for southern civilization portrayed as a distinctive and superior South. They took very real differences—some substantive and others only a matter of degree, not kind—separating the South from the North in that era and elevated them into an unsystematic but ringing defense of the region's culture and people. The southern creed was a list of cultural values that defined southern civilization.

Agrarianism was long near the top of any effort to understand the South. While the Northeast was well along in the process of industrialization by the time of the Civil War, the South remained overwhelmingly agricultural and rural. The movement into the Old Southwest and the establishment of the cotton kingdom strengthened the white southern commitment to the farming economy. White southerners outside of the cash crop economy, such as the large body of plain farmers who combined herding with subsistence farming, as well as planters, fell within the agrarian framework that defined the good life as being far from cities and factories. Cities did grow in the antebellum South, but the urban economies remained dependent on the rural countryside and on agrarian values. As many historians have argued, though, pressures for modernization came not only from the North but from within southern society as well, especially during the 1850s, when increasing numbers of yeomen participated in the market economy. Southern staple crops drove much of the world's economy at the time, and southern planters and factors operated in international realms. These changes did not, however, transform the southern commitment to agrarianism as a driving economic force and distinguishing trait.[40]

White southerners especially feared such changes because their society, including racial and social class stability, seemed to rest on agricultural dominance. As symbolized by the country gentleman or the yeoman farmer, agrarianism suggested Arcadian images deeply engrained in the high culture of Western thought. Antebellum southerners claimed them as now distinctively southern because of changing Western culture that was moving away from an agrarian society. Writers made the southern planter into a unique version of the ancient pastoral patriarch, unique because he was surrounded by his slaves on the plantation, which became the central image of southern agrarianism.[41]

Agrarianism offered southern culture an image of itself as antimaterialist, a place where the spiritual needs of humanity were superior to all others. This pastoral humanism traced back to Hebraic and classical Roman thought that stressed virtuous behavior over materialism. Surely, it was not a deeply imagined belief among the hardscrabble yeoman farmers of the South, yet as a central belief of southern public culture it differentiated all those who toil in the soil from materialistic Americans—the stereotypical Yankees. Agrarianism offered virtue as a central tenet of the southern civil religion. Southern agriculturalists developed a ritualistic jeremiad in agricultural orations reminding white southerners to abide by the old agrarian ways.[42]

Promoters of antebellum southern civilization often linked it with republicanism and made that political philosophy a foundation of the southern creed. White southerners had inherited a belief in republican theory from the American Revolution, which defined liberty as the essential political value. Republicanism taught that citizens must be ever vigilant against government power as a constant threat to liberty. The "country republicanism" that influenced South Carolinians and other white southerners in the antebellum era taught that a variety of institutional structures had to be maintained as checks on government power. White southerners obsessively talked about abstract liberty partly because they had around them the tangible symbol of its absence: the slave. Moreover, the antislavery movement and the federal government seemed concrete threats to southern slaveholders' definition of liberty as the right to dispose of their property as they wished.[43]

Jacksonian democracy reinforced republicanism's stress on liberty and on virtue as the ultimate defense against political corruption. Southern public culture embodied the self-interest and philosophical self-image of the elite, but it also included arguments stemming from the democratic impulses within white southern culture. These beliefs ultimately traced back to Jeffersonian ideas, but the Jacksonian movement of the 1820s and 1830s ensured that the majority of the region's people, the plain folk yeoman farmers, would be represented. Constitutional changes made a more democratic system, and the wide ownership of land brought influence. Aggressive, self-made politicians attacked special privilege, concentrated economic power, and the evil of political opponents. The rights of the common folk became as effective a rhetorical strategy as any for political success. Although intellectuals such as George Fitzhugh were overtly antidemocratic and the elite remained socially and culturally dominant, the

inclusion of democracy as part of southern attempts to defend society represented the success of the plain folk in having their voices at least heard.[44]

By the 1850s, southern ideology was portraying the North as a lost civilization, as the betrayer of the American Revolution. The northern populace had
become corrupted by materialism, urbanization, religious experimentation,
and the immigration of foreigners. If the virtue of republican citizens was the
last protection of liberty, then, southern writers claimed, northerners had failed
the test. A distinct civilization in the South, composed of virtuous citizens,
was thus the last best hope for liberty in the United States. Southern political
thinkers, in helping to define the regional vision of a civilization, stressed a
conservative interpretation of republicanism that would become central to the
definition of a Confederate and, more broadly, southern sense of mission. They
claimed the legacy of the Revolution as theirs. Moreover, the South's notion of a
lost northern moral consciousness rested in a biblical typology that made white
southerners the saving remnant of the nation.[45]

Republicanism traced back to ancient Greece and Rome, with classical civilization providing themes and images that functioned to ennoble the region
and influence southern public culture. The classical tradition was well known
throughout the American colonies, and the political philosophers of the American Revolution constantly used references to the ancients. The Greek Revival
style became the unofficial architecture of the young republic. In the early
nineteenth century, though, such northerners as Noah Webster and Benjamin
Rush argued that the classics represented outdated, undemocratic European
influences and should be abandoned for modern philosophy. Antebellum white
southerners saw such rejection of classical thought as more bad judgment by
Yankee culture.[46]

The proslavery argument and the critique of northern capitalism embraced
classical references that gave intellectual heft to the southern creed. Basil
Gildersleeve, a Virginian who became one of the nation's most accomplished
classical scholars in the nineteenth century, urged southerners in 1854 to study
classical thought because it was "a harvest untouched by the sickle" of northern
intellectuals, thus making it a sectional issue. Fire-eater Robert Barnwell Rhett
would tell the South Carolina secession convention that a southern nation
could achieve a neo–Greek democracy, southern universities would remain
devoted to the classics into the twentieth century, and orators would study
Cicero and Demosthenes. Stoic philosophy would shape upper-class white
southerners from Robert E. Lee to twentieth-century poet William Alexander
Percy, and public buildings and private residences would long display the ubiquitous Greek Revival columns as symbols of southern regionalism. The Greek
features attributed to southern life enabled white southerners to claim a high
philosophical legacy.[47]

The climate was an early signifier for southern civilization, as seen in this
nineteenth-century depiction of a southern summer day. The Historic New
Orleans Collection, acc. no. 1980.202, New Orleans, Louisiana.

Philosophy and architecture thus were southern expressions of classical
civilization, and advocates for antebellum southern civilization could also
draw from the natural world in sketching their superior South. According to
its antebellum defenders, that regional civilization came from a semitropical
climate peculiar to North America. Observers had long seen climate as a basis
of southern differences, usually in a negative light. But the new element in the
antebellum discussion was the connection that climate gave southerners to
Mediterranean civilization, a significant validation for a southern civilization.
"Civilization is an exotic in all cold latitudes," said a commentator in *DeBow's
Review* in 1861. "It belongs naturally to temperate climes." He insisted that the
"Mediterranean latitudes" of Europe, Asia, and Africa "and the country south
of Mason and Dixon's line" were the "true and only seat of high civilization—
the only region in which man ever did, or ever will, arrive at fully developed,
intellectual, moral, and physical maturity."[48]
     The English word "south" comes from the old German word *sunth*, meaning
"the sunned region," and white American southerners persistently identified
themselves as sharing culture with the Mediterranean peoples in a worldwide

sun belt. Southern intellectuals went off to Italy, in fact, to find their identities. Closer to home, when southerners moved into Texas before the Civil War, they portrayed it not just as a new frontier for slavery but as a land particularly congenial to the traits of Mediterranean civilization. The Caribbean was a dynamic context for southern slave owners seeking to maintain their economic power, similar to the Mediterranean in southern Europe. Historian Matthew Guterl argues that southern planters were cosmopolitans connected to the ethos, institutions, cultures, and structures of feeling that nation-states could not contain. Their aspirations toward a distinctive civilization rested along "a messy, complicated borderland" between North America and the Caribbean. The independent Confederacy during the Civil War allowed white southerners to see themselves as a superior civilization in a unified, maritime system of economic, social, and cultural exchange centered to the south of their South.[49]

The cultural value system put forward by defenders of southern civilization was a peculiar combination of honor and faith. Honor was a system of beliefs that made an individual's worth dependent on reputation. Individual prestige and self-respect came from a community's evaluation, which meant that one defended honor as an essential means to preserve the respect of the community and one's power within it. Bertram Wyatt-Brown argued that the South's honor culture was a transhistorical sensibility that had roots in traditional societies going back to Mediterranean places. South Carolina congressman Preston Brooks's caning of Massachusetts senator Charles Sumner in 1858 was widely hailed in the South as an appropriate defense of the region's honor, while northerners dismissed it as simply a barbaric act.[50]

This belief system portrayed white southerners as the peculiar bearers of honor in the American nation. Northerners not only had lost their republican virtue but lacked the essential honor that was the mark of a good society. In the South, the good society was a hierarchical one, with one's position defined clearly by those above and below in the class and caste system. Southern country life was a world of face-to-face relationships where one dealt with the same people throughout a lifetime. Defense of honor was a life-or-death matter. Honor rationalized not only violence but also the pride that nonsoutherners often identified as an essential feature of the southern white temperament. Southern politicians embodied this style to the nation.[51]

Evangelicalism was, however, a competing value system to that of honor in the rural South. Few factors were more important than religion in producing a self-conscious southern civilization. Methodists and Baptists would come to be the South's predominant evangelical denominations, and they spread throughout the rural South as a result of the Great Awakening, dominated the region's religious life by 1830, and became a feature of the southern white belief system. Evangelicalism taught that all individuals had value as children of God. Each was responsible to God, not to the community that dictated honor. A highly individualistic faith that nurtured inner guilt as a central psychological mechanism, Evangelicalism also produced a closely knit community of souls who cared for each other. Religion in the North was changing, as northern society became more diverse and modern. Although Evangelicalism dominated Protestantism in other parts of the nation by the Civil War, southern whites came to see their religion in this period as distinctive and essential because it had become embedded in southern civilization. They identified with the biblical typology of the chosen people and saw themselves at that point as the saving remnant of the nation.[52]

Although camp meetings and revivals were vital institutions, and preachers became influential leaders, evangelical defenders of southern civilization in this era made only one aspect of southern religion into a central symbol of regional culture: the Bible. As the Reverend Thornton Stringfellow said in a proslavery essay, he hoped that "we shall be seen cleaving to the Bible and taking all our decisions about this matter from its inspired pages." He, like other white southerners, made the contrast with the North, insisting that he knew only a few northerners who made "the Bible their study" on the issue of slavery. Ministers often contrasted the southern faith in the authority of the Bible with the northern faith in Jefferson's equalitarian ideas expressed in the Declaration of Independence, which represented, said the Charleston Presbyterian minister Thomas Smyth, an "infidel, atheistic, French Revolution, Red Republican principle."[53]

The defense of the Bible and southern religion and the religious attack on the North went beyond religious spokesmen. Politician-planter James Henry Hammond complained that with abolitionists, "it is no end of the argument to prove your proposition by the text of the Bible, interpreted according to its plain and palpable meaning." Despite his attempts to show them the biblical support for slavery, "they deny the Bible, and set up in its place a law of their own making." He concluded that "our religion differs as widely as our manners." Hammond blamed the changing northern society for religious divergence that produced "a transcendental religion" that was "a religion too pure and elevated for the Bible." Drawing the distinction with the North even more sharply, he also noted that "few of the remarkable religious *Isms* of the present day have taken root" in the South, as southerners were so irreverent "as to laugh at Mormonism and millerism, which have created such commotions farther North."[54]

An anonymous writer during the Civil War identified as "Sigma" captured the southern confidence that the character of the region's people produced by the paradoxical ethics of honor and Evangelicalism reflected the truest southern civilization. He insisted that each contributed to a "heroic individuality," an identifying southern trait that "blazed to a mighty splendor that dwarfed the boasted 'culture' of the North to microscopic worthlessness." He saw education as the institution most shaping northern character. Although "the myriad schoolhouses of the Free States" did influence the masses of people for the better, such community institutions would not match "Honor, co-equally with Piety," which formed the essence of the southern individualist ethic by creating "a true nobility of heart." The South's combination of two value systems based on diametrically opposed assumptions of religious faith and secular etiquette rested on shaky foundations. For white southerners, though, they both were useful in legitimating their social institutions.[55]

Romanticism was another feature of the southern creed, a special influence on the southern public culture's understanding of its distinctive civilization, shaping its expressions of honor and Evangelicalism, among other values. With their defensiveness aroused by northern attacks, white southerners used Romanticism to differentiate themselves from northerners by cultivating what seemed like appealing features and thereby claim a distinctive and distinguished civilization. White southerners relished playing within American civilization the role of nonconformists, who were always heroic figures in Romanticism. This outlook thus gave dignity and stature to the very peculiarities that New Englanders so bitterly attacked. As an ideological feature, southern Romanticism validated the region's society through tradition. Drawing from the writings of such cultural nationalists as Germany's Johann Herder, England's Thomas Carlyle and Samuel Taylor Coleridge, and Scotland's Sir Walter Scott, southern Romanticism provided a conservative image of the organic society as the good society, in which everyone had a place. Romanticism was useful as an intellectually respectable influence that sanctioned the status quo to hold back the changes that southerners were quite aware of in the world. Like other ideas in the southern intellectual armor, Romanticism entered the region's intellectual life through reprints of European and northern essays and book reviews and through original pieces by southern intellectuals. Such periodicals as the *Southern Literary Messenger* and the *Southern Quarterly Review* fostered a lively interregional debate that kept white southerners aware of Western culture's latest ideas.[56]

Few aspects of antebellum southern Romantic ideology were more tenacious than the image of the cavalier. The cavalier myth that writers and essayists made into a vital Romantic story of antebellum southern culture concerned the ethnic differences of white southerners and northerners. Southern ideologues recognized that not all people living in the South were of one ethnic stock, but they asserted a unified white racial type as the "southern character." By "the *Southern* people," wrote William H. Holcombe in 1861, was meant "the *representative* blood of the South." By "Southern people," he continued, "is not meant *all* the people of the South, but that controlling element which exists with every people, and gives character to the whole." Ethnicity separated white southerners from northerners, but it also separated true Southrons—to use a word from Sir Walter Scott that became popular among white southerners—from people just living in the South. Holcombe and other spokesmen for southern civilization believed that the Norman barons of William the Conqueror, who had mastered England, a race "renowned for its gallantry, its chivalry, its honour, its gentleness and its intellect," had been the progenitors of white southerners. Southerners, according to the cavalier myth, had been Royalists during the English Civil War, with clear differences from Puritan-descended northerners.[57]

Ideologues thus insisted on the most prestigious English stock of their white citizens and saw the planter as a southern gentleman whose heroic character established order and brought culture to those around him. He was the principal symbol of a refined agrarian South. Plantation families found the feudal parallel a particularly pleasing one, as it cast them in the role of all-powerful lords and ladies harking back to a time when it all seemed so right. Southern Romantic trappings drew from a culture of honor that included the love of florid oratory, the ritualized violence of dueling, the beauty and grace of the stereotypical belle and the athletic prowess of the cavalier, and the cult of chivalry seen in the pageantry of jousting tournaments. This world was never an accessible one for most southerners, and little evidence suggests that the plain folk ever aspired to jousting. Together these ways did reflect, though, a Romanticism that prized the physical rather than the contemplative. The obvious fantasy and unreality of this southern Romantic world makes it difficult to take it seriously as social philosophy; but its mythic representation of the region's "feudal" past clothed the region in glory and tradition at a crucial point in its cultural history and proved surprisingly durable in popular culture. Romaticism gave a final flourish to the southern creed.[58]

Defense of Slavery

Slavery presented special problems for southern claims to a high civilization. The proslavery argument utilized religious, scientific, and historical arguments to justify the peculiar institution. Ministers saw slavery as being God ordained, Josiah Nott portrayed biologically inferior Blacks needing slavery's discipline, and the historically minded cited slavery in ancient Greece and Rome. Through these arguments, white southerners insisted that slavery was, as Thomas Dew noted in the 1830s, "the principal means of impelling forward the civilization of mankind." This brazen claim for slavery tried to position the South at the forefront of civilized societies.[59]

Religion was an especially significant ingredient in the abolitionists' condemnation of slavery's role in southern civilization. The southern way, said northern critics, violated the brotherhood of man and the spirit of uplift that marked northern Evangelicalism. The biblical defense of slavery, citing specific passages that recognized slavery and bondsmen in biblical times and that cast Blacks as the outcast people of Ham, was especially popular with southern whites and unusually influential in the formulation of a lasting southern way. Postbellum defenders of southern race relations would trot out the biblical legends, which later became the heart of the defense of segregation in the 1950s and 1960s. This mythic view pictured slave owners as religious benefactors of their enslaved workers. Under God's providence, proslavery writers claimed, Africans had been brought to America, white southerners had evangelized them, and they would someday take the gospel to the Dark Continent. Slavery was thus essentially a religious institution for the conversion of Africans. The biblical defense did more, then, than simply justify slavery. It asserted the noble motives of slave owners and defended their virtue as civilized Christians.[60]

The southern civil religion fused cultural and religious values in the South that would come to embody the concept of a spiritually blessed, distinctive, and distinguished southern civilization, and it emerged as a result of white southerners coming to believe that God had ordained their regional ways. The defense of slavery was a landmark in its definition. The central concept was the sense of a regional mission under providence. The proslavery stance asserted a peculiar purpose for the South that enabled white southerners to see their destiny in regional terms.[61]

In February 1861, William Holcombe admitted the South's besiegement, as "the sympathies of the civilized world are united against us." He looked more to the future than the past and argued that if white southerners were "faithful to our sublime trust" of benevolent rule over the enslaved, then "future ages will appreciate the grandeur and glory of our mission." Writing at the start of the Civil War, Holcombe outlined the southern mission as nurturing a slave republic: "The government of the South is to protect it," he wrote, "the Church of the South is to Christianize it; the people of the South are to love it, and improve and perfect it." From the 1850s, southern ideologues saw expansion as essential for the slave society, and Holcombe agreed that a Caribbean empire was the South's manifest sectional destiny. The ringing conclusion to his wartime article was that the South would succeed in establishing "a vast, opulent, happy and glorious slave-holding Republic, throughout tropical America," and "future generations will arise and call us blessed!"[62]

The proslavery argument thus pictured righteous slavery as the foundation for the distinctive and distinguished southern civilization. Although recent scholarship emphasizes the cold-blooded exploitation of slave labor and denigrates any supposed tendencies toward paternalistic benevolence, the self-conscious southern ethos of the time suggested that masters and their enslaved workers lived in a reciprocal world, each having responsibilities toward the other, that masked the brutal realities tainting such southern claims. Enslavers provided food and protection, said the ideologues, while their workers toiled for their owners—overlooking the latent violence, sexual brutality, and economic exploitation the institution represented.[63]

Efforts to define a noble and providentially blessed southern civilization would mean little if the plain white folk, most of whom had no slaves, did not support the antebellum southern social system and, later, march off to defend it in battle. Their votes and, during the war, their bodies would protect southern civilization. The editorial fire-eater J. D. B. DeBow found it "easy to show that the interest of the poorest non-slaveholder among us is to make common cause with, and die in the last trenches, in defense of the slave property of his more favored neighbor." Urban nonslaveholders were connected to the slave system by economic necessity because urban "mercantile interests are so interwoven with those of slave labor as almost to be identical."[64] The nonslaveholder understood, as DeBow put it in another fundamental text of the southern way, that "as soon as his savings would admit, he can become a slaveholder, and thus relieve his wife from the necessities of the kitchen and the laundry, and his children from the labors of the field." The large slaveholder began as yesterday's yeoman.[65]

In this regard, antebellum southern civilization, the nineteenth-century precursor of the southern way of life, was about the dream of achieving privileged status. The plain folk resented forms of special privilege that excluded them, and Jacksonian democracy showed their willingness to attack such forms. They questioned but ultimately accepted, though, a peculiar belief system that combined social class and racial appeals suggesting that southern civilization allowed them a higher spot on the societal hierarchy than would have been the case in northern free society. "No white man at the South serves another as a body-servant," noted DeBow, "to clean his boots, wait on his table, and perform the menial services of his household! His blood revolts against this, and his necessities never drive him to it." In 1858, South Carolina's James Henry Hammond had made high civilization itself dependent on Africans who had the needed docility, vigor, and fidelity to perform the "drudgery of life," while southern whites devoted themselves to "progress, civilization, and refinement."[66]

Thomas Jefferson once recalled that his earliest memory was of being carried, as a baby, on pillows by enslaved workers. That pampered image represented the southern way of life, but it was not accessible for most white southerners. Clean boots—that is, having someone to clean your boots while you never had to clean another man's boots—were a very tangible symbol of the southern way for the plain folk. The southern civilization, in this essential form, involved the shared white dream of a lifestyle based not in escaping work but in the dignity coming from escaping the "menial work" of life.[67]

Arguments about Civilization

The pressures toward conformity in the South in this period were immense, but Hinton Rowan Helper nonetheless offered an alternative view to that of a civilized South in *The Impending Crisis of the Union* (1857). He portrayed it as a backward society and undercut southern white claims to civilization's highest aspirations. Using statistics, quotes, and other evidence, he showed the socio-economic and cultural gap between the southern states and the rest of the nation. His indictment of the region breathed class resentment. He claimed to be "a true-hearted Southerner" and noted that his hardscrabble farmer father had owned slaves, yet he lambasted slave owners as "knights of bludgeons, chevaliers of bowie-knives and pistols, and lords of the lash." In effect, Helper judged northern and southern societies in a trial of civilization and found the South wanting. He measured what might be called the trophies of civilization and found more of them in the North than in the South in material and intellectual realms. "Whence come our geographers, our astronomers, our chemists, our meteorologists, our ethnologists, and others, who have made their names illustrious in the domain of the Natural Sciences?" he asked. The answer was not from the South; thus he concluded that "we are under reproach in the eyes of all civilized and enlightened nations." He self-consciously spoke for non-slaveholders, but few rose to befriend him. His views led him to move north. By the 1850s, Cassius Marcellus Clay of Kentucky and Benjamin Hedrick of North Carolina were among the few white southerners to still openly question slavery, and they endorsed Helper's work. Most of his support came, though, from the North. Abraham Lincoln used the study in his House Divided speech in 1858, and Republicans raised funds to print and distribute 100,000 copies of the book during the 1860 presidential campaign.[68]

By the time of the Civil War, civilization had thus become a defining issue between the North and the South. The idea of civilization itself, widely disseminated in the nation, made a deep impression on popular opinion and suggested the centrality of progress to the concept. In 1857 *Harper's Weekly* launched with its subtitle, "A Journal of Civilization." In the same year, another key journal of opinion appeared, the *Atlantic Monthly*, under the editorship of New Englander James Russell Lowell. As the Civil War approached, the journal published an article entitled "Barbarism and Civilization," making clear that the South rested outside the magic circle of civilization while New England represented its American essence. A second article on civilization, "American

Civilization," appeared in 1862, written by another key New England writer, Ralph Waldo Emerson. As early as 1851, Emerson had posited New England as the national norm, parallel to London for global importance, and insisting that "it is confounding distinctions to speak of the geographic sections of this country as of equal civilization."[69]

White southerners agreed with those north of the Mason-Dixon Line that the two regions represented differing civilizations. William Harper's *Memoir on Slavery* (1837) had insisted that "the institution of slavery is a principal cause of civilization" and went even further to claim that "perhaps nothing can be more evident than that it is the sole cause"—a bold claim indeed. The reason was that the "coercion of Slavery alone is adequate to form man to habits of labor," and without that discipline "there can be no accumulation of property, no providence for the future, no taste for comforts or elegancies, which are the characteristics and essentials of civilization." The end of this slave-based civilization was not to be contemplated either. A writer in *Southern Quarterly Review* in 1851 warned that "Negro emancipation would be inevitably the death-blow to our civilization."[70]

Such were the warning messages of defenders of southern civilization to American northerners, who increasingly seemed a foreign people. A July 1859 essay in *DeBow's Review* showed the white southern belief that history had created two differing civilizations of the North and South. "We seem designed for a separate people," wrote "A Mississippian" about white southerners. "Climate, pursuits, tastes, and even our common language, all proclaim that the laws of nature will direct and control the will and laws [of] man." His view reflected the prominence of racial thinking in the South and cultural nationalism's tendency everywhere to see the members of a distinct culture as "a people." J. Quitman Moore, writing in June 1860, claimed that as far back as the American Revolution, "two systems of civilization" and "two distinct peoples" had existed in North America. The two civilizations were "separate, distinct, antagonistic, and repellant," because the two peoples were so different. White southerners who developed this argument saw northern civilization as composed of two primary groups: the original Anglo-Saxon settlers of Puritan New England ("the common people of England") and a polyglot mixture of recent immigrants, who had made northern cities uncivilized wastelands.[71]

Confederate Civilization

The Confederate States of America represented the nationalization of the concept of southern civilization. One of the most confident promoters of secession, the notorious fire-eater Robert Barnwell Rhett of South Carolina, imagined a historian in the year 2000 writing of the great achievements of the southern

Confederacy: "And extending their empire across this continent to the Pacific, and down through Mexico to the other side of the great gulf, and over the isles of the sea, they established an empire and wrought out a civilization which had never been equaled or surpassed—a civilization teeming with orators, poets, philosophers, statesmen, and historians equal to those of Greece and Rome—and presented to the world the glorious spectacle of a free, prosperous, and illustrious people." Rhett's audaciously grand vision acknowledged the importance of defending not only slavery but also self-determination, states' rights, constitutional authority, virtuous morality, and righteous holiness—all marks of an emergent civilization. A writer in *DeBow's Review* in 1861, admitting that all the prewar talk about southern civilization masked the difficulties of actually achieving it, noted that white southerners would now not only resist Union aggression and assert their political independence but devote "our minds also to brood over and develop the seeds of a new and original civilization, which have hitherto striven in vain to burst through their native soil." The Confederate mandate should be extended so that, "in the name of every dear and sacred tie which binds us to each other and to our State, let us also resolve that we will not be *provincials* in the world of intellect and civilization." Those words represented both aspirations and awareness that the South had earlier failed to achieve the civilized standards that the future might bring.[72]

In the midst of war, white southerners further defined the symbolic content of their civilization in documents, institutions, legends, heroes, and other cultural artifacts that marked not only the achievement of nationalism during the war but also contributions toward a future southern way of life. The Confederate myth combined the intertwined concepts of the Worthy Southron, the Demon Yankee, and the Silent Slave, and a belief in a common history that represented Confederate Americanism. Confederates understood their new nation as the authentic American nation, the nation of the American Revolution, whose heroes—especially southerners such as Jefferson and Washington—had defined a constitutional government, which the Union had deserted.[73]

The Confederate Constitution closely resembled the American federal Constitution, but, unlike the 1787 document, in appealing directly to the "favor and guidance of Almighty God," it reflected the centrality of religion to the predominant idea of southern civilization. The Reverend Thomas Smyth captured the importance of naming the divinity when he wrote in the *Southern Presbyterian Review* that the Confederate Constitution was "sealed in the chancery of Heaven." Southern ministers became the celebratory priests of the southern way in war. Preachers applied the rhetoric of the American redeemer nation, the civil religious language, to the South. Benjamin Morgan Palmer's influential sermon "National Responsibility before God," delivered June 13, 1861, near the beginning of the war, placed southern political culture under God's protection. A Presbyterian, Palmer was comfortable with the concept of the covenanted relationship between God and society, an idea once associated with the New England Puritans. "At the moment when we are crystalizing into a nation, at the very opening of our separate career," he preached, "we bend the knee before God—appealing to his justice in the adjudication of our cause, and submitting our destiny to his supreme arbitration."[74]

Despite this sacred sanction, the hoped-for unity across southern regions and groups did not materialize fully. Confederates tried to identify elite class interests with national interests, but the effort was not altogether successful. Banking resources were inadequate, inflation rose, citizens refused to submit willingly to heavy taxes, and food shortages and protests about them occurred. With conscription not popular, desertion became a major problem for the military. Further class conflicts appeared as the burdens grew heavier for the plain folk, while some plantation families away from the fighting managed to do well and speculators clearly profited. An uninspiring leader, Jefferson Davis could not make an eloquent case for national unity. War also dramatically undermined the predominant southern ideology through the emancipation of the enslaved. Although the Emancipation Proclamation issued in 1862 did not immediately free those people in slavery in Confederate-controlled areas, it was a landmark for Black southerners—the Day of Jubilee. The actions of enslaved peoples had helped bring freedom. Most of them stayed on the plantations during the Civil War, but many left as soon as Union armies approached. In Virginia, Alabama, Arkansas, and Mississippi, plots and conspiracies by the enslaved worked to undermine the institution, while thousands of African Americans fought for the Union army against slavery.[75]

Confederate cultural nationalists, nonetheless, expected the Confederacy to survive, and they worked to develop a Confederate civilization. Imbued with the Romantic nationalism of the age, they wanted to produce books, plays, poems, songs, and other cultural items that would express the new nation's distinction and distinctiveness. The new nation's capital, Richmond, was the center for newspapers, textbooks, and religious pamphlets and books, and the developing railroad system of the Confederacy distributed such works widely. Confederate culture made few significant contributions to high culture, however, such as novels, paintings, sculptures, or even political discourse. And notwithstanding the future hope of cultural nationalists, defeat in the Civil War was a severe setback to advancing southern civilization. The postwar era's poverty, isolation from national life, and ideological attachment to older ways was traumatic for the maturing of the region's culture.[76]

Reconstruction's Clarification of Civilization

The war's end brought a dark mood to white southerners, as outside observers and southerners themselves talked of their despondency, depression, and apathy. They had to face the central cultural question of whether their southern civilization had died along with the Confederate nation. A Georgia Baptist periodical warned in 1866 that "the victory over Southern arms is to be followed by a victory over Southern *opinions*," and the perception of such a danger spurred on white southerners to be suspicious of northern ways, even before Radical Reconstruction began in the late 1860s. Richmond editor Edward A. Pollard insisted in 1866 on the need for a "war of ideas" against the North. He predicted that "the worst consequence of defeat" would be for the South to "lose its moral and intellectual distinctiveness as a people, and cease to assert its well-known superiourity [*sic*] in civilization, in political scholarship, and in all the standards of individual character over the people of the North."[77]

Such postwar intellectual recalcitrance was a preview of the tenacity of the concept of southern civilization in the face of traumatic social changes for white southerners. Rhetoric from northerners such as the minister Nathaniel Hall did not lessen such fears. After a trip through Kentucky and Tennessee Hall observed, "It seems indeed to the Northern stranger that he has fallen back generations from the civilization he has left." He felt he had come "upon a different age; among those who have been slumbering, while the rest of the world has moved on." During the war, Ralph Waldo Emerson also pointed to the issue of civilization, or rather the lack of it, in the Confederacy. "Why cannot the best civilization be extended over the whole country," he asked, "since the disorder of the less-civilized portion menaces the existence of the country?"[78]

Observations from occupying Union troops added to the image of the Confederacy as a backward, ignorant place. A New York soldier stationed near Richmond, Virginia, wrote that "the country is behind the times 100 years." Another from New England smugly predicted that "it will probably be more than one generation before any of these slave-cursed states will rival New England in those elements which have made that little corner of the world of so much importance as affecting the human race." One Massachusetts soldier wrote home, "Honestly, papa, I do not see how anyone can say that the Southern people are civilized."[79]

In 1865, James Russell Lowell, writing in the *North American Review*, pondered the importance of the Civil War in global terms; he noted that through "the glory of conquest" the United States now stood at the front rank of nations in the world. The victory would be "trifling and barren," though, unless it cleared "the way to a higher civilization," with the advancement of an

American civilization now extended across the nation. Another northerner, E. P. Whipple, also writing in 1865, envisioned the defeated southern population in terms of the markers of civilization. With Union victory, the nation now had power over "the masses" in the South, a biracial population "unfitted for self-government." He wrote of the "humble, quiet, hard-working negro" and the "worthless barbarian whites," the latter who were "ignorant, illiterate, vicious, fit for no decent employment on earth but manual labor." Northern writers who expressed their latent racism in seeing the "Africanization of the South" as a threat to the nation portrayed Reconstruction as an effort comparable to European nations gaining dominion over the backward continent of Africa in the same period.[80]

Southern writer William H. Holcombe had coined the term "Africanization of the South" during the early days of the war. He saw the alternative of a separate nationality for the Confederacy or the dominance of a freed African American population in the South. He predicted that if the North had its way, it would "be ready to reduce the South to the condition of Hayti and Jamaica, and expect the approval of God upon the atrocity." With Confederate defeat, this frightening vision for southern whites seemed all too possible. Images of desolation were rife in the immediate postwar South. During Reconstruction, white southerners came to see white supremacy as the essence of their southern civilization. "Everybody talks about the negro at all hours of the day, and under all circumstances," wrote Boston reporter Sidney Andrews after his postwar tour of Georgia and the Carolinas. "Let conversation begin where it will, it ends with Sambo."[81]

Race had always been a central concern in the South, but when Radical Reconstruction granted political rights to freedmen and when the development of public schools in the region threatened to bring white and Black children together in classrooms, the evolving southern white belief crystallized that white supremacy was essential to the region's social system. Reconstruction never offered social equality of the races as public policy, but "Negro rule" became the phrase suggesting to whites their deepest fears of losing control of the South. It was civilization versus savagery, with southern civilization now taking on new clarity. In the postwar years a revised proslavery argument appeared to justify not slavery but African Americans' subservience appropriate to their alleged inferiority. Reconstruction thus became synonymous in the southern white memory with the assertion of African American rights. It also became synonymous with the idea of outside intervention, of northerners and the federal government trying to change southern civilization.

The Reconstruction years witnessed a ferocious contest for control of the South's public spaces and the memory of the southern past. Confederate widows honored wartime southern heroes in graveside rituals in the year after the Civil War ended, as the religion of the Lost Cause emerged and, by the end of the century, would give sacred sanctuary to the Confederate memory and become the focus for large commemorations. African Americans and some northern whites staged hundreds of commemorative celebrations in the Reconstruction years, a sign of their new rights of citizenship and voting power. In the new postwar circumstances, African southerners paraded, posted banners, waved American flags, said an "amen" to prayers of thanksgiving, and applauded speeches in city public spaces. Black churches and civic organizations also became important sites for Blacks in a new southern public culture. Whites waved the Confederate battle flag and sang "Dixie" at their rallies, while Black southerners waved the U.S. flag and sang spirituals that told of freedom. The Lost Cause rhetoric spoke of the tragedy of Confederate defeat, while Emancipation Day commemorations spoke of the blessedness of freedom that came as a result of that war.[82]

The southern white view of Reconstruction as a period of a savage threat to southern civilization itself survived for generations through the South's official history books, family stories told generation after generation, literature such as Thomas Dixon Jr.'s *The Clansman* (1905) and D. W. Griffith's film *The Birth of a Nation* (1917), and the academic histories produced in the early twentieth century by William A. Dunning and his Columbia University students. Southern political conservatives would dramatize the events of Reconstruction for decades and use them to put the fear of the federal government devil into southern whites. The memory of Reconstruction would be especially valuable to the normalization of white supremacy in the late nineteenth century, when white Democrats forged the Solid South in politics and excluded Black voters from participating. African Americans refuted this mythic view of the past, as they saw Reconstruction as the most democratic era in the nation's history, a time when two African Americans from Mississippi were U.S. senators; when Black politicians represented their districts in legislatures throughout the region; and when those legislatures established the South's first real public school systems. Mississippi's former U.S. senator John Lynch wrote a book on Reconstruction to counter Dunning's "superficial and unreliable" views. But he failed to overturn the Dunning school of historiography.[83]

The Ku Klux Klan emerged from Reconstruction as a major embodiment of the concept of southern civilization and showed the lengths to which white southerners would go to defend their understanding of its racial basis. A new mystical, racially oriented terrorist folk institution, the Klan claimed for itself the right to define southern civilization and to enforce its understandings through vigilante violence. Former North Carolina governor Zebulon Vance insisted that the 1868 campaign against the Republicans, which included the

In this Thomas Nast drawing, members of the White League and the
Ku Klux Klan shake hands over a shield labeled "Worse Than Slavery"
and a scene depicting an African American couple with
their dead baby and a man hanging from a tree.
Library of Congress, Washington, D.C.

efforts of the Klan, was a "struggle for the rights and liberties of our race, for
constitutional government and for Christian civilization." Defenders of the
Klan argued that it stood for civilization itself against the threat of rule by
Black barbarians—a racial and cultural orthodoxy at the heart of a southern
civilization. It reappeared whenever the perception of change in southern society came to haunt white southerners.[84]

"Redemption" was a familiar term in the southern evangelical vocabulary
that stressed the need for personal salvation, and white southerners used this
religious term to describe their violent retaking of southern politics from those
reformers trying to reconstruct the South. Between 1868 and 1876, white men
devised strategies to regain control of state governments and the Black labor
force. The political activities of the Democratic Party, of agricultural reform

movements, and of tax-protest conventions worked together, along with the Ku Klux Klan and other paramilitary groups, to impose an intimidating new order on the South. The willingness of white elites to use their wealth and power to evict or deny supplies for mostly impoverished freedmen and freedwomen, and their lack of hesitation to use violence, led to the loss of considerable African American political and economic power. In South Carolina, Confederate war hero and wealthy planter Wade Hampton's campaign for governor used reactionary supporters known as Red Shirts to conduct a massacre at Hamburg as well as violence in other places. In response, South Carolina governor Daniel Henry Chamberlain asked for federal troops, as he condemned the "atrocity of barbarism, the triviality of the causes, the murderous and inhuman spirit which marked it in all its stages." He pointed to the troubling spiritual nature of what happened and anguished, "What hope can we have when such a cruel and bloodthirsty spirit waits in our midst for its hour of gratification? Is our civilization so shallow? Is our race so wantonly cruel?" These questions would arise for anyone contemplating the growing savagery of southern whites and increasingly radical racial attitudes by the end of the century.[85]

Writing in 1880 at the end of Reconstruction, Edwin L. Godkin, editor of the *Nation*, noted that the South had not, in fact, been changed despite war and its aftermath. "The South," he wrote, "in the structure of its society, in its manners and social traditions, differs nearly as much from the North as Ireland does, or Hungary, or Turkey." Godkin saw the region's needed transformation in specifically economic terms but as one that involved an ethnic reconstruction of white southerners. He called for "the conversion of the Southern whites to the ways and ideas of what is called the industrial stage in social progress." He was not hopeful, pointing out that this "is not a more formidable task than that which the anti-slavery men had before them fifty years ago."[86]

Mid-nineteenth-century white southerners were not unique in seeing their culture as both distinctive and distinguished as the basis for a good society. All societies develop myths and ideologies to justify themselves. The people of the American South, before roughly 1830, had seen their cultural destiny, though, primarily in terms of American myths and ideologies, affirming an American civil religion of the nation's mission to defend democracy. During the "First South," which lasted from the mid-eighteenth century through the early national period, some southern whites came to see "the South" as an identifiable place and "southerners" as a distinctive regional group, based in a peculiar community of people and interests in the American context.

After 1830 and when threats to slavery began to arise, the regional consciousness led to attempts to define a "southern civilization." By claiming "civilization" in the nineteenth century, white southerners asserted a moral authority that attempted to ennoble their society and assert larger meanings of particular social relations, cultural practices, and political behaviors. They clarified the meaning of their society through their encounters with Native Americans and African slaves. They saw these two groups as outsiders to civilization, as savages and heathens. They saw themselves as the bearers of Western civilization at the very time that industrialism, democratic revolutions, and other changes in Europe were promoting changing ideas about civilization itself. Well before the late nineteenth-century rise of Western colonialism and the white man's burden of civilizing darker races, though, white southerners had shown how to attach white supremacy to civilization. The experiences of Indians and Africans in the slave South showed the potential for the concept of civilization to justify the worst imaginable injustices. Native Americans embraced national and regional models of civilization, but the ruthless greed of white southerners closed off their aspirations. African Americans contested the image of savage Africa as they asserted that African civilization was once honorable and placed dark-skinned peoples in a civilization that served as an origin for Western civilization itself, but few whites in the South were listening.

The ideas advanced in the antebellum South about a regional civilization were often older ones, but they had new meanings in a southern context. Agrarianism, republicanism, classicism, honor, Evangelicalism, environmentalism, Romanticism, paternalism, patriarchalism, and racism represented basic influences that would shape the region's public culture in the nineteenth century and beyond, although not without considerable contestation and alteration to changing contexts. They were the region's own "isms." Other Americans clarified the new American civilization of the early nineteenth century by cordoning off white southerners and their slave civilization from it. They shared much in terms of white supremacy with white southerners, although the threatening nature of slave power to national ideals obscured that shared racism for a while. Northern attacks on antebellum southern culture ironically made white southerners ever more proud and assertive of the distinctiveness and achievements of their civilization, leading them often to exaggerate its achievements and to grasp at any glory.

By explaining the Confederacy in terms of its relationship to civilization, white southerners sought a moral authority that, in the end, could not inspire victory on the battlefield or support in the centers of nineteenth-century European civilization. The experiences of Reconstruction led white southerners to greater clarity on a primordial racial basis of their regional civilization, which they would see endangered for a generation. Through the dynamics of nineteenth-century events and movements, the southern philosophy became the basis for a civil religion focused on the spiritual superiority of southern civilization and on the ethnic identity of white southerners. The Civil War and Reconstruction promoted the idea of a providential destiny for a besieged "white civilization," one that would evolve with new meanings as the region worked to maintain a social identity and a society that observers could see as a civilization.

CHAPTER TWO

Reimagining Southern Civilization

Adapting Civilization to New Regional, National, and International Contexts

O
N APRIL 1, 1917, at a Palm Sunday evening worship service the day
before Congress would assemble to decide on the issue of war against
Germany, the Reverend Randolph McKim, rector of the Episcopal
Church of the Epiphany in Washington, D.C., summoned the United States to
what he believed was its destiny. Congress should, he concluded, "declare war
against Germany in self-defense," and "it will not only be a justifiable war . . .
but beyond and above all this, it will be in the highest sense a holy war, a war to
save all that is best and holiest in civilization. . . . Germany was lacking humane
and merciful instincts" and "the principles of morality recognized among civilized nations." McKim thus saw civilization itself at stake in the conflict with
Germany, a nation that southern religious people had come to identify as the
home of a modernist theology that threatened traditional Americanism. To
white southerners, that nation represented materialism and murky rationalism
as seen in its theologians developing the dangerous, to them, higher criticism of
the sacred southern text, the Bible. The result was the moral decline of a once-
high German civilization and the need for southerners to join the nation in a
new crusade against evil—a holy war.[1]

McKim thus articulated the crusading spirit with which the United States
entered the Great War, anticipating the rhetoric and idealism of another southerner, President Woodrow Wilson. McKim was a Confederate veteran who
had served in Robert E. Lee's Army of Northern Virginia and remained active
in Confederate veterans' groups throughout his life. He made clear that the
Americans fighting in World War I would do so out of the same concern for
the principle of democratic self-government and self-rule that he believed had
motivated the southern movement for independence in the 1860s, a belief that
had become conventional wisdom of the Lost Cause narrative. McKim was in
1917 rector of a great national church, the embodiment of an American religious establishment. In his rhetoric of a holy war, he drew on a long Christian

tradition, but one with specifically American and southern regional meanings. It drew together an American civil religion—which spoke of providentially extending the blessings of democracy—with a southern civil religion—which began with the defense of slavery, became synonymous with the Lost Cause after the war, and spoke of extending the virtues of a conservative, orthodox social order. The differences between the two civil religions blurred as the lines between them faded. Southern civilization now seemed an intimate part of the American civilization that it had not long before tried to destroy, an American civilization that had long lingered on the savagery of the South's supposed civilization.[2]

This blurring would have seemed unfathomable forty years earlier, as Reconstruction ended and the South entered a new stage in its conceptualization of a southern civilization. Memories of the defeat in war, the humiliation of military occupation, and the attempted remaking of southern society during Reconstruction were primal. New England thinkers had hoped to destroy southern civilization and rebuild the South in an image of the North, but that effort went nowhere after Reconstruction ended. The belief in the concept of southern civilization did not vanish, although white southerners feared their social death would result from Confederate defeat and efforts to remake the region. Instead, southern opinion makers and intellectual elites reimagined southern civilization, as the South's relationship with the nation and the world evolved.

This chapter outlines the dominant Lost Cause and New South ideologies that arose after 1880, analyzes the agrarian movements that challenged that dominance, considers how Victorian sensibilities took root in the South, examines the varieties of white racism that existed, and surveys the intellectual contours of the two race-based societies that appeared by the turn of the twentieth century. Race and religion became anchors of adaptation of antebellum southern civilization to new, more modern ways. Sectional reconciliation was one key theme of the South's role in American culture, but so was the "problem South" that saw southern civilization as a backward threat to a modernizing nation. Meanwhile, African Americans played a growing role in challenging the segregated southern civilization.

The Lost Cause

In the post-Reconstruction period, new ideologies crystallized that would shape the public culture and private mentalities of people in the South for generations. Especially prominent was the memory of the Civil War that became enshrined in legend and ideology as the Lost Cause. Mourning for the

Confederate dead immediately after the war gave way, by the 1880s, to a spirit of celebration of the Confederate war effort, and the 1890s saw the institutional flowering of the Lost Cause social movement in groups such as the United Confederate Veterans, the Sons of Confederate Veterans, and, most influential of all, the United Daughters of the Confederacy. They staged huge Confederate reunions in major southern cities between the 1890s and the 1930s that drew some of the largest crowds for public events in the South. The Daughters, and members of the Ladies' Memorial Associations, put up hundreds of monuments honoring the Confederate heroes, visual expressions of the memory of the war as a fight for southern civilization.

Although the proslavery argument and the Confederate secession ordinances made crystal clear that slavery was the cause of sectional conflict and the Confederate war effort, the Lost Cause ideology insisted on the legality of secession and the centrality of constitutional issues to secession. States' rights, in short, were the cause of the war. Still, many southern white commentators admitted the centrality of race. Just after the war, Edwin Pollard had used the term "lost cause" to describe the failed Confederacy's efforts right after the war, and he insisted that "the supremacy of the white race, and along with it the preservation of the political traditions of the country," had been the real issue of the war. The Lost Cause ideology launched a movement that solidified in the 1890s at the same time as southern states codified racial discrimination through disfranchisement, Jim Crow segregation laws, racial violence, and economic marginalization of African Americans, all part of the same worldview that sought to normalize southern civilization as a white-dominated world rooted in the supposed virtues of white Confederates.[3]

Southern white ministers had seen the conflict from beginning to end as a holy war, but the Lost Cause asserted that God had not abandoned white southerners in defeat; rather it was preparation for a greater destiny. The Civil War experience had led white southerners to see their historical experience in transcendent, cosmic terms, and the ideology of the Lost Cause provided cultural materials to revitalize the idea of southern civilization, one now seen absolutely rooted in the memory of the Confederate effort. The religion of the Lost Cause became one of the movement's most important dimensions. The Lost Cause had icons, including pervasive images of Robert E. Lee, Jefferson Davis, and Stonewall Jackson—the Lost Cause Trinity. Presbyterian theologian Robert Lewis Dabney claimed the South needed "a book of 'Acts and Monuments of Confederate Martyrs,'" and he added that it should also "paint the picture skillfully of Southern martyrdom under ruthless abolition outrages" during Reconstruction. White southerners indeed portrayed the Confederate heroes as saints, prophets, and martyrs. Their images appeared in schools and on stained-glass windows in churches. From the 1890s into the 1930s, white southerners participated in regional rituals such as Confederate Memorial Day, dedications of Confederate monuments, funerals of Confederate veterans, and reunions of living veterans. Most importantly, remembering the Lost Cause promoted a continuing southern white consciousness that the region would always have a providential mission.[4]

The Lost Cause movement celebrated not just the white southern war effort but also the mythology of the Old South, which became another foundation for the vision of a revitalized southern civilization. The pastoral perfection of the plantation-based antebellum civilization gleamed in the words of novelist George W. Bagby, who wrote in 1884 that prewar Virginia had "a beauty, a simplicity, a purity and uprightness, a cordial and lavish hospitality, warmth and grace . . . a charm that passes all language at my command." Bagby evoked the combination of aesthetic appeal and moral idealism that became attached to the legend of the Old South. Another Virginian with aristocratic lineage, Thomas Nelson Page, became the ultimate celebrant of the Old South in his fiction and memoirs, building on earlier southern literary traditions and portraying southern civilization as "the purest sweetest life ever lived," whose men were "noble, gentle, and brave" and its women "tender and pure."[5]

Page, the most successful literary romanticizer of the southern past, undoubtedly saw his writings on the Old South and the Lost Cause as part of a broader assertion of "tradition" at the center of a revitalized postbellum southern civilization. He lamented, in an address published in 1892 but delivered earlier, that "there is no true history of the South," which was an urgent issue because "in a few years there will be no South to demand a history." In this, he echoed most white southerners' belief that they were living in an era of dramatic, radical change that threatened their group identity. Even as late as the 1890s, the lingering effects of Confederate defeat might still lead to the dissolution of southern culture and social death of white southerners, but Page proposed using history as a basis for preserving a true understanding of the antebellum southern civilization as inspiration for the future. "By the world at large we are held to have been an ignorant, illiterate, cruel, semi-barbarous section of the American people," he complained, "sunk in brutality and vice, who have contributed nothing to the advancement of mankind: a race of slave-drivers, who, to perpetuate human slavery, conspired to destroy the Union, and plunged the country into war." White southerners "stand charged at the judgment bar of history with these crimes." The reason for this sorry state of affairs was that the South had "left the writing of her civilization" to the North. In seeking to remedy this wrong, Page appealed to southern pride in regional achievement and its history. White southerners had "crowded into two

N-831 MOSS COVERED OAK TREES SHADING A SOUTHERN HIGHWAY

W-9 ROAD LEADING TO WRIGHTSVILLE BEACH FROM WILMINGTON, N. C. E-4832

A postcard presenting a romantic image associated with the moonlight-and-magnolias version of southern civilization, in this case, live oak trees hanging with Spanish moss. Charles Reagan Wilson Collection, Archives and Special Collections, John Davis Williams Library, University of Mississippi Library, Oxford, Mississippi.

centuries and a half a mightiness of force, a vastness of results, which would have enriched a thousand years."[6] Page then made a correlation. "Reverence for the greatness of its past, pride of race," he said, "are two cardinal elements in national strength." These qualities "made the Greek; they made the Roman; they made the Saxon; they made the Southerner." The people of the South were in danger of losing those qualities, however. The tie connecting sense of tradition, precarious regional group identity, and racial pride at the heart of southern civilization became clear. Page seemed to see white southerners as still a race apart: "We are not a race to pass and leave no memorial on our time."[7]

The southern plantation rendered in literature by writers such as Page had considerable national appeal to Americans in the late nineteenth century, not only for white southerners seeing in it a verification of their cultural superiority and civilized society but also for northerners who were in the throes of an economic revolution and facing news of labor unrest, immigrant challenges to white Protestant dominance, and Gilded Age corruption. The southern cavalier's graciousness, breeding, and moral idealism offered a stark contrast.

James C. Cobb argues that "part of the appeal of the Old South legend may actually have been not its 'otherness' but its quintessential Americanness," presenting an appealing image of "the ultimate and complete fulfillment of the American dream."

One definition of the civil religion has relied on the values of the "good life" associated with the American dream; Rollin G. Osterweis noted that post–Civil War white southerners embraced the Lost Cause and Old South because they represented "every man's dream of the good life." He saw that southern whites' "willingness to perpetuate the Southern system, to help keep Blacks in perpetual if not legal bondage, to resist stoutly all liberal efforts at social reform," stemmed not just from bigotry but from the belief that white supremacy represented southern civilization's "means of achieving the leisure and enjoyment which a beneficent climate and bounteous land made possible." That southern version of the American dream, though, rested on the exclusion of southern African Americans from the hopes of that dream.[8]

Frederick Douglass was a lion in fighting that exclusion, from his days as a leading abolitionist and continuing into the postwar world. The emergent Lost Cause troubled him, and he devoted considerable time to countering the sentimentalized southern legend. "The spirit of secession is stronger today than ever," Douglass wrote in 1871. "It is now a deeply rooted, devoutly cherished sentiment, inseparably identified with the 'lost cause,' which the half measures of the Government towards the traitors has helped to cultivate and strengthen." Lee's death in 1870 and the praise of the general's character that appeared in print had appalled Douglass. "Is it not about time that this bombastic laudation of the rebel chief should cease?" he asked. "We can scarcely take up a newspaper . . . that is not filled with *nauseating* flatteries of the late Robert E. Lee." The Lost Cause memorialized the single event that had given southern whites a separate history from northerners, and Douglass saw dangers in its idealization. "The South has a past not to be contemplated with pleasure," he wrote in 1870, "but with a shudder." He added that the South had "been selling agony, trading in blood and in the souls of men." White southerners should look at their past and embrace "repentance and thorough reformation."[9]

New South

The New South complex of thought seemed the opposite of the Lost Cause— a forward-looking movement that sought to northernize the South in terms of an increasing prominence of capitalist values and industrial/business leadership. This booster sentiment sought closer ties with business in other parts of the nation and made economic development a new mantra for state governments and cities. Journalists were at the forefront of the movement, and the "New South Creed" of economic diversification, harmonious race relations, and educational improvements became the South's dominant ideology. This New South movement embraced, though, the Old South and Lost Cause and used their mythical appeal to suggest that the South could advance economically without disturbing the values of Page's "tradition" and the racial, social class, and gender hierarchies that had survived the war. Atlanta newspaper editor Henry Grady, for example, praised the "exquisite culture" of the Old South, insisting that "the civilization of the old slave regime in the South has not been surpassed, and perhaps will not be equaled, among men."[10]

Early critics of the New South nonetheless saw it as the embodiment of materialistic values, anathema to the underlying spiritual foundations of southern civilization. Presbyterian religious leader Albert Bledsoe saw materialism as the "great defect of Northern civilization," one that contradicted the "spirit of Christianity." For southerners to adopt this outlook would destroy the "fine sense of honor which formed the beautiful enamel of Southern character." To blunt this charge, New South advocates romanticized the southern past, virtually inventing the legend of the Old South.[11]

The businessman as hero became a new part of the folklore of southern civilization, often pictured in heroic terms to counter the materialistic charge. Business leaders were typically self-made men from the middle class. The railroad, lumber, textile, tobacco, furniture, iron and steel, and mining industries expanded in the 1880s, generating wealth and a new privileged class. Lawyer-politicians were powerful figures in the New South, dominating courthouse rings, monopolizing public offices, and supervising public expenditures. If the nature of the New South version of southern civilization can be conveyed through these social types, its meaning can also be seen through the appearance of newly important institutions on the landscape. The textile industry defined manufacturing in the South after the Civil War. It made geographic sense to have mills near the cotton fields that continued to spread throughout the region. The industry had begun before the war in the Piedmont of Virginia, North Carolina, South Carolina, and Georgia, but it developed quickly after 1880, and the South surpassed New England as the nation's textile center. The extensive waterways of the Piedmont supplied power to the mills, and the region's extensive labor willing to work cheap furthered the industry's growth. Recruitment of textile factories from New England became a crusade intended to give jobs to the region's poor whites. Employers excluded African Americans from working on textile production, although Black men unloaded cotton bales and served as janitors and Black women were domestics in the homes of mill managers.[12]

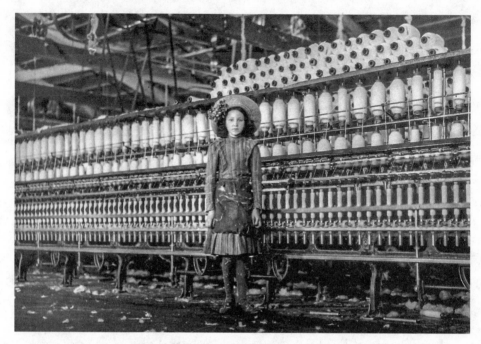

This Lewis Hine photograph shows a child laborer in a North Carolina textile mill.
Albin O. Kuhn Library and Gallery, University of Maryland,
Baltimore County, Baltimore, Maryland.

A culture of paternalism pervaded mill villages, with owners and managers seeing workers as like children who needed oversight, not only on their work but on the quality of worker life in general. Broadus Mitchell portrayed early textile mill builders as philanthropists, "far-seeing, public-minded, generous natural leaders," latter-day cavaliers who transferred southern paternalism from the plantation to the factory. The mills sponsored social events such as dances and baseball games, provided health care, and oversaw schools. This paternalism became wedded, though, to the harsh economic logic of capitalism. Managers fought the unionization of workers, kept them dependent on mill town services, and nurtured suspicions of "outside agitators."[13]

The isolation of rural mill sites led to mill houses being built in remote locations, along with schools, churches, general stores, recreational facilities, and primitive health-care facilities. The mills used child labor, required long and often grueling workweeks, and paid low wages. The housing was generally better, though, than what many workers had known on the farms many of them came from, and cash payments were a tangible benefit. Mill life was likely a better one than many had known as sharecroppers or hardscrabble small farmers. The late nineteenth-century mills continued to reflect such southern cultural features as rural ways, religious attitudes, and racial obsessions. Mill village people suffered social disrespect from nearby townspeople, who denigrated them as "lintheads" not good enough for respectable work, adding to the plethora of stereotypes of poor southern white people. Still, a notable sense of community marked life in the villages. Although the industry as a whole grew in the years after 1880, individual factories remained small and personal.[14]

The New South movement was an optimistic one, embracing an ideal of progress that united it with the broader Western civilization ideology of the late nineteenth century. One of its leading advocates, Richard Edmonds—editor of the *Manufacturer's Record*, which endlessly promoted economic development—claimed in an 1890 pamphlet, *The South's Redemption: From Poverty to Prosperity*, that the South would soon become the "richest country upon the globe"—an expansive cosmic claim, indeed—because of its previously untapped resources and a new ethic of hard work suited to an industrial ideal that would envelop the South. Northern business leaders, eager to reap the profits from a developing colonial economy, agreed. Richard A. McCurdy, president of the Mutual Life Insurance Company in New York City, traveled through the South and boasted that the region's resources "ought during the next generation to experience a development which will place them among the foremost communities of the civilized world in health and happiness." Again, such observers fit the South into an international web of nineteenth-century civilizationist development.[15]

New South promoters had the zeal of new converts, and the region's religiosity seemed to influence their claims, as they asserted a southern industrial civil religion of providential destiny. The New South rhetoric enhanced the long representation of the South as a Garden of Eden. Richard Edmonds wrote that "a harmonious relationship between industry and agriculture would make the South . . . the garden spot of the world." He saw nature endowing the South with so many resources that their development would "make 'Dixie' the Canaan of the new world." Wilbur Fisk Tillett, a Vanderbilt theologian, urged southerners in 1881 not to worry about materialism coming to predominate in the New South. "The South is morally better than before the war," he wrote, and added that the region's people also had "neater and finer churches than they ever did." "Neater" and "finer" were not typical terms in the evangelical lexicon, but they fit religious folks aspiring to a higher civilization, with good churches a marker. Leading Methodist minister Atticus W. Haygood was quite specific about the providential nature of material improvement in the New South, thanking God for the "mattresses, stoves, lamps and parlor organs," citing these as evidence of the growth of a middle-class civilization in the South, which God smiled upon. Soon, New South advocates came to believe that their goals had been achieved, despite the evidence they overlooked of widespread poverty and other social ills.[16]

Agrarian Movements

The rural South nurtured the most influential counternarrative to the dominant Lost Cause/New South ideology of southern civilization. Farmers faced a crisis in the late nineteenth century, based in declining economic fortunes for many of them but more broadly in a sense of losing out in a modernizing nation. To be sure, southern planters and farmers still affirmed the national agrarian myth that had ennobled rural life since before the nation's founding. One Baptist after the war highlighted the continuing faith in this myth, observing that "God is at all times in love and sympathy with the toiling tiller of the soil." But a growing urban-rural divide affected the South in this period, as well as the rest of the nation, seen in the marginalization of rural life in American culture, politics, economics, and finance. Town and city types used newly minted derogatory terms such as "hayseeds," "rednecks," and "hillbillies" to dismiss the backwardness of rural people, with civilization increasingly understood to be located in towns and cities.

From the 1870s to the turn of the century, high interest rates, scarce currency, and low commodity prices characterized the national economy, conditions that threatened the livelihood of farmers, especially those in a South recovering from the devastations of war and suffering from a severe cash and credit shortage. An exploitative sharecropping and tenant farming system had settled into the rural South after the war and became the normative organization of farm life for many farmers, with the crop lien keeping many tenants in perpetual debt or at least barely able to survive, much less get ahead. The two existing political parties appeared hopelessly unable to deal with these problems. One Populist complained that both parties were plutocracies, and under their tyranny "the tree of liberty will wither" and the "light of Christian progress and civilization will be darkened," using terms that evoked an urgency for the fundamentals of the "good society."[17]

People in the countryside responded with cooperative action, beginning with the social and emerging political activities of the Grange, then the Farmers' Alliances of the 1880s, and culminating in the electoral successes of the People's Party—the Populist movement. This movement affirmed the ideals of an American civilization that believed in democratic participation and a roughly egalitarian society, and it railed against the injustices of the financial system that left them devastated. The movement's proposals included programs to lower interest rates, raise commodity prices, and expand the money supply. Their social base was not the poorest whites and Blacks but the middle- and lower-middle-class plain white folk and African Americans. Populists saw their plight in terms of a larger story of the 1890s, a sacred narrative that imagined their economic problems and the need for political reform as parts of an attempt to reclaim the nation from corrupt and centralizing forces. The South, and its evangelical religious tradition, were at the center of agrarian protest, which affected the Midwest as well as the South. "Populists' reform agenda rested," writes historian Joseph Creech, "on a cluster of evangelical patterns of thought foundational to what most southerners thought it meant to be Christian, southern, and American." Populists wanted to restore Jeffersonian democracy, which they equated with what Creech calls "Christian liberty."[18]

Southern Populists dismissed the appeals of the Lost Cause/Old South mythology as irrelevant to their pressing needs, remembering the antebellum South without the nostalgia that had become a foundation for the dominant concept of southern civilization after the war. They ridiculed appeals to the bloody shirt, refused to support Democratic and Confederate heroes as the region's best models, exposed Democratic charges of "Negro rule" as ridiculous, and refused to honor anyone who did not support their plans. Populists also admitted that the war had been in defense of slavery, Lost Cause ideologues notwithstanding, benefitting the planter class and not the plain folk. One North Carolina Populist insisted he had "no drop of secession blood in his veins," although he, like others, did not regret the "humble part" he took in fighting Yankees. In 1895 Populist leader Marion Butler urged the North Carolina legislature to not fund a $10,000 loan to the Ladies' Memorial Association for a memorial to the Confederate dead, believing that no monument should "be built on either side to perpetuate the memories of our unnatural war." To oppose women supporting the Lost Cause in the 1890s was a bold move. Populists criticized appeals to sectional loyalties by both Democrats and Republicans as ploys by elites to prevent western and southern farmers from uniting against the moneyed East; the Civil War and the abolition of slavery were thus most significant for their connection to the making of a new wage slavery that was afflicting both white and Black people.[19]

Populists nevertheless saw issues of civilization swirling about the region. Connecting "the South" with the concept of "Christian civilization" was one of the movement's most notable contributions. "We are rapidly drifting from the moorings of our fathers," proclaimed Populist leader Leonidas L. Polk in an 1890 lecture, "and stand to-day in the crucial era of our free institutions, of our free form of government, and of our Christian civilization." He spoke of the "holy mission" of the farmers' movement to restore "the equipoise" between industrial interests and agrarian interests. Religion was, indeed, crucial to the farmer's revolt, providing institutional, rhetorical, and ideological resources, growing out of the South's dominant evangelical Protestantism. The Baptist, Methodist, and Presbyterian Churches had grown enormously after the Civil War, making them a part of the cultural establishment of the South. While the dominant urban and small-town churches were conservative, Evangelicalism rested on a belief in spiritual egalitarianism, which became an important component in the support of rural Evangelicals for the cooperative work of Populism.[20]

Religion provided a sense of mission and meaning to Populist efforts, giving their narrative cosmic overtones for believers in the cause. They did not affirm a southern civil religion that saw transcendent meanings in the South's experience alone, but they did affirm the American civil religion's claim that the nation, including the South, had providential destiny. They talked of "patriotic millennialism"—the notion that God had a special destiny for the United States as a beacon for democracy to the world. As Joseph Creech notes, they believed the nation was "Winthrop's city on a hill" and "the culmination of all that was good in Western Christian civilization." Disciples of Christ laywoman Mattie Harn wrote expansively, for example, that because of its resistance to British tyranny, "the American Government more fully embodies the principles of Christianity than any other political system on the globe." These agrarians saw that destiny endangered, though, by the economic and political crises of their age. Polk recounted the decline of such past civilizations as Carthage, Tyre, Greece, and Egypt because they departed from their principles and fell into tyrannical rule, and he warned that Americans were on the brink of the abyss. He warned his listeners in one speech that they might "live to see our God-favored land transformed into one vast mausoleum, in which shall be buried forever the splendid wreck of our past and prospective glory, and with the world's last hope for civil and religious liberty."

Reformers offered a critique of the materialism of the Gilded Age by imagining Jesus in their time. Baptist J. F. Click said, "The doctrine of the equality of man was good enough for Christ to preach 1800 years ago, but in the glory of the present civilization it is [out] of place, and the new Christ must wear a plug hat, smoke 25 cents cigars, take fine whiskies freely for the stomach's sake, and faithfully vote for the old party tickets arranged by the grace of Wall Street." He lamented that "the new Christ must be a millionaire, ride in palace cars, own land enough to make a couple of states, operate several thousand miles of railroad, get up a supper worth a thousand dollars a plate, and dictate to a congress of millionaires." Populists saw the problems facing the nation not just in economic or political terms but as moral and religious issues.[21]

The Populists had to confront the realities of a biracial South in trying to put together a movement that could take political control of the region. African Americans were still voting in many places in the 1890s, and their leaders were a part of the agrarian reform coalition. White Populists included African Americans in their version of southern civilization, combining older paternalistic attitudes toward Black southerners with white supremacy and authentic conviction that racial harmony could help promote reform. One of the leading Populist politicians, Tom Watson of Georgia, made explicit a biracial, class-based appeal when he noted in 1892 that "the accident of color can make no difference in the interest of farmers, croppers, and laborers." He urged white Democrats and Black Republicans to vote for him, arguing that "you are kept apart that you may be separately fleeced of your earnings." Watson's sentiments did not represent racial enlightenment so much as political strategy, seeing the biracial coalition as an essential one to achieving electoral success. Southern Populists did denounce lynch laws and convict leasing, but the decision of white Populists to fuse with the Democrats in 1896, as well as a general unwillingness to support broader efforts to assist African Americans beyond the Populist agenda, led many Black Populists to return to the Republican Party.[22]

The seriousness of the Populist efforts and their successes terrified the white establishment in the South, who saw this agrarian uprising as a threat to the dominance of New South economic goals, the Democratic Party and its achievement of a "Solid South" in national politics, white supremacy, and, not coincidentally, the powerful mainstream evangelical Protestant denominations. Those people who could vote under growing restrictions of the ballot probably cast their ballots for some combination of white supremacy, states' rights, memories of the Civil War and Reconstruction, traditional morality, and preservation of a stable social order. Such people perceived the agrarians as lower-class incendiaries who threatened southern civilization itself. The agrarians fed this fear with rhetoric that talked of "the impending Revolution" and the fact that it was "not a revolt; it is a revolution." As political scientist John C. Green adds, "For many deeply religious southerners, opposing sin and supporting Jim Crow were unconsciously bound together." Populism seemed to its critics a threat to the values of orthodoxy, social stability, economic development, the political dominance of the Democratic Party, white supremacy, and religious conservatism—all of which had come in mainstream culture to represent southern civilization.[23]

Katharine Du Pre Lumpkin, who grew up in an elite Georgia family that fell on harder times after the Civil War, observed of the years of Populist insurgency that "no years since reconstruction's overthrow had been filled with so much belligerence and anxiety to Southerners of my people's kind." Even after the Populist Party dissolved in the late 1890s, Lumpkin said, "a tumultuous residue" of fear remained. Conservative men, as she called her father and his colleagues, feared that Populism's appeal to Black voters threatened white solidarity in politics, which they believed had prevented a return to what they saw as the horrors of Black assertiveness during Reconstruction. "It seems they saw white solidarity as their source of strength," she wrote, adding that "they did not intend to let it be sapped away." She remembered that time as one when "violence, bitterness, invective, hatred, became the almost daily portion of those Populist years," with "white Southerners pitted not against outsiders, but battling among themselves."[24]

After the defeat of the Populist Party in 1896, the agrarian movement was in effect finished. Democrats in that election drew the color line to prevent Blacks from winning political offices. As the editor of a local North Carolina paper had written earlier, "The civilization of the white man must not be scotched." In 1896 and the following years, Democrats used intimidation, voter fraud, violence, appeals to white manhood, and any other methods deemed necessary to capture elections. Wilmington, North Carolina, was the site of one of the most notorious examples of white vigilantism violently removing Black officeholders and establishing total white control of governmental power. Afterward, southern legislatures completed the work of devising new methods of restricting not only African American voting but also that of poorer whites. The dominant Lost Cause/New South narrative of southern civilization had been seriously challenged and its contingent nature made apparent, yet in the end, its advocates ensured the dominance of that account of civilization in the South for generations.[25]

Reforming the Countryside

After Populism, the rural South continued to produce ideas to address the blight of the countryside and drew from linkages between region and civilization in different ways. The progressive Country Life Commission, for example, sought to help modernize agriculture and rural life, and the South was a major focus for its effort. Led mainly by middle-class city and small-town professionals, editors of farm journals, officials in the U.S. Department of Agriculture, teachers at land grant colleges and agricultural institutions, and social reformers, the commission's final report concluded that American farmers had not adjusted to the modernization of the national economy. As a result, "contemporary civilization" did not affect rural life as much as that in urban areas. Reformers wanted to uplift the countryside's people, but they still idealized farm life as the ideal society, romanticizing the small, self-sufficient farmer.

Born in the Midwest, Seaman Knapp was particularly important, through his leadership role in the U.S. Department of Agriculture, in thinking about the rural South and its problems as part of that movement. He insisted that scientific agriculture would make farming more profitable and country living more appealing to those who had the resources to move to cities seeking the material and cultural advantages of civilization. He saw the South experiencing a farm disaster after the Civil War, a general depression in rural living, and believed nothing valuable had replaced the ruins of what he called "the old civilization." Nonresident landownership had increased, resulting in poor farming habits. He and other reformers in the country life movement advocated crop rotation and diversification, use of new plows for deeper plowing, better use of fertilizers, and improved breeds of livestock. He viewed women and mothers as central to moving farm families ahead, seeking to liberate them from "the burden of housekeeping" and "the slavery of cooking," through scientific management and more use of technology that would enable them to furnish additional farm income through their gardens, poultry, and dairy.[26]

The U.S. Department of Agriculture, colleges of agriculture, extension services, and demonstration farms all encouraged improved farming techniques, yet many of these improvements were not within the reach of typical southern farmers. Most farms had only one mule, few modern implements, a handful of chickens, a few pigs, and a cow or two. Landowners and merchants controlled credit and made the decisions to maximize staple crop production for reliable market sales; fertilizers were more expensive than small farmers and tenants could afford; and no marketing mechanisms existed for crops other than cotton or tobacco. The result was limited success for this vision of reformed rural life that would provide the accoutrements of civilization in the countryside and keep a diverse population there.[27]

Historian U. B. Phillips's 1904 article "The Plantation as a Civilizing Factor" put forward a different model to address the modernization of southern agrarian life, insisting, in view of "the ignorance of the great laboring class in the South, that a system for the organization of labor under skilled management is desirable in agriculture as well as in mining, commerce, and manufacturing." He brought a historical perspective in advocating a revived patriarchal plantation system that would nurture better farming techniques under the wise management of elite southern whites. Race was at the forefront of his plans. "A century or two ago," he wrote, "the negroes were savages in the wilds of Africa." As slaves in the South, they and their descendants "acquired a certain amount of civilization" via their association with whites, making them "in some degree fitted for life in modern civilized society." The issue was how to provide for their continued progress and avoid a regression to barbarism, which Phillips claimed was happening in some places with a concentrated African American

This postcard portrays the emblems of the cotton South—a wooden house,
a church building, an ox-drawn wagon, and farmworkers. Charles Reagan Wilson
Collection, Archives and Special Collections, John Davis Williams Library,
University of Mississippi Library, Oxford, Mississippi.

population. His solution involved sympathetic oversight of African-descended
laborers on his newly energized patriarchal plantations.[28]

Phillips framed his article in terms of what he thought best for African
Americans, rejecting both their movement to cities as creating social disorder
and their forced return to Africa as abandoning them to savagery again. He
rejected Jim Crow segregation as well, at least in the countryside, claiming that
"from the point of view of morality, industry, intelligence—of everything that
civilization means—the segregation of the negroes must work for their detriment." Instead, "the continuance of the interracial association" was essential
to uplifting African Americans and saving the rural South. He acknowledged
that "the exceptional negro" had an important role to play in that uplift, being
capable of "borrowing and adapting the white man's ways of life"; he insisted,
however, that the oversight of "average and exceptional white men" was essential because they possessed "their civilization and their capability as a natural
inheritance." Phillips pointed to large problems, though, namely the need for
substantial capital to invest in a new plantation system and the necessity for the

"better class" of whites to return to the land. Phillips's plan did not advance far in practical application.[29]

Those same problems stymied another ambitious plan for development of the rural South. Clarence Poe proposed what he called a "Great Rural Civilization" in the South, and he got further than Phillips in trying to put his ideal into practice. Poe was son of a Populist leader and publisher of an important farm journal, the *Progressive Farmer*. His commitment to social reform led him to support many Progressive Era good causes, and he was a founder of the Southern Sociological Congress, which spearheaded discussions of how to improve southern civilization. As a Jeffersonian Democrat, Poe worried about the fate of those whom Jefferson called "God's chosen people" in the early twentieth-century blighted southern countryside. On a trip to Europe in 1912, he saw thriving rural villages based in cooperative agricultural practices, and they became his model for a renewed southern civilization. To revive rural life, he called for a dramatic reorganization of the countryside, encouraging people to move into well-planned villages on the European model. He foresaw credit societies, cooperative storage and marketing facilities, recreational halls and renovated church buildings, community-owned banks, and well-funded schools teaching practical agricultural knowledge.[30]

Poe concluded that the greatest obstacle to his southern dream was the growing number of Black farmers in the South, people he believed were unfairly competing with whites by working and living cheaper than they did. A white supremacist, he also feared that white racial prejudice would be a barrier to the cooperative activities necessary for his version of southern civilization. While in England, Poe had met Maurice S. Evans, a South African writer who advocated the apartheid system that would eventually rigidly segregate South African spaces into "white" and "colored" areas, and Evans, after hearing Poe talk about the South, recommended the segregation of white and Black farmers there. Poe accepted Evans's belief that this solution would bring racial peace with fewer contacts across racial lines and also encourage white leaders to provide paternalistic oversight in areas peopled by African Americans.

Poe's three-year campaign for his plan saw him using his positions with the North Carolina Farmers' Educational and Co-operative Union and the North Carolina Committee on Rural Race Problems and his editorials in the *Progressive Farmer* to energetically work for his reform. He believed that segregated Black farmers would develop their own "black civilization," as he was probably thinking of the work of Booker T. Washington at the Tuskegee Institute. His plan would have required whites to give up their reliance on African American labor, but he assured planters with larger plantations that white European immigrants who were coming to the United States at the turn of the century would find the "Great Rural Civilization" of the South an appealing place and provide a new labor supply. Other agricultural leaders, however, criticized the plan, country store merchants showed no interest in giving up Black farmers as customers, absentee landowners did not want to give up renting land to Black tenants, and farm managers and owners generally expressed a preference for Black farmhands because they believed them easier to manage than whites. Poe's ambitious vision of the rural South represented another failed attempt to imagine a rural civilization that could deal with the combined economic and social complexities of the biracial South in that era.[31]

Workers in the New South

In the new industrial vision held by New South leaders, laborers were essential to success. Work had always been a defining issue for southern civilization, from the early colonial reliance on the labor of enslaved people, and its growing centrality in the southern economy with the emergence of the antebellum Cotton Kingdom, to the Old South defense of slavery as the best of all possible labor forces and the rejection of free labor. Emancipation was a devastating disrupter of southern society, requiring the reorganization of work. After an unstable immediate postwar period, planters, country merchants, and freedmen fell into the sharecropping tenant system that would be the long-term new labor system for the neoplantations and small farm operations of the New South. The debt and economic vulnerability that characterized the tenant system kept workers poor and costs low for the neoplantation owners. The industrial world of the New South also required a large-scale, cheap labor supply, in this case to run the mills and factories and compete with industries in other parts of the nation. Owners exploited workers in the late nineteenth and early twentieth centuries through low wages, long hours, sometimes dangerous work conditions, child labor, and other means. Women and children provided crucial work for New South industrialization, as they were forced into mines, factories, and mills because pay was so low for men that a family could not survive without additional family wages. Labor unions emerged as part of the industrial system, although they were vigorously opposed by industries themselves and often politicians, legislators, and the criminal justice system.[32]

Biracial union activism took root in the mining industry and among timber workers for a while, but by the turn of the twentieth century, observers less often noted it. Where unions did arise, critics brought furious charges that the work of labor organizers—who became prime examples of the "outside agitators" who would long be devil figures in southern culture—threatened southern civilization itself. Historian Glenn Feldman cites a 1908 Alabama coal strike as an example. The United Mine Workers housed striking Black and white workers under the same tents, nursing the fear, as one journalist said, of "social equality horror," alleging that striking African American men had raped two white women in the camp. Governor Braxton Bragg Comer, who was a prominent progressive politician, agreed that the camps were a threat not just to social order in general but to the "integrity of our civilization." Newspaper editor Dolly Dalrymple raged that white women and Black women were "meeting on the basis of 'Social equality' indeed!" She continued her tirade citing "white men holding umbrellas over negro speakers!" and "white miners eating side by side with black men!" Her overall judgment: "It is monstrous!"[33]

Observers flashed back to the remembered nightmare of Reconstruction's supposed enforcement of social equality. One Alabama editor urged the vigilant maintenance of the color line among laborers or "a silent tragedy, more terrible than that of the torch and sword would fill our fair Southland," namely "the decay and obliteration of our white civilization." Such language pictured the threats of biracial interaction as a danger not just to local communities or particular industries but to the very idea of what made southern civilization. In this case, deputies broke up union meetings, arresting Black and white miners and killing several people; eventually the governor sent in the Alabama state militia to tear down the tents and evict the families living there. He charged that the miners had been "badly advised" by "carpetbaggers and scalawags," linking labor activism to Reconstruction's attempted remaking of southern civilization.[34]

Victorianism

By the late nineteenth century, ideas about the "South" and its "civilization" came to evoke issues of morality, social order, cultural identity, race relations, and religiosity. Nonsoutherners dwelled on the cruelty of southern race relations; white southerners saw themselves as African Americans' best friends; African Americans brought special saliency to their critique of southern racial ways; yet the South, in many ways, was the Black American homeland. Nonsoutherners could also appreciate the legendary lifestyle of a region often represented with a premodern appreciation of cultural values and attitudes that seemed admirable but long lost to more enterprising northerners. Predominant southern opinion makers aspired to the achievements of Western civilization, although they often identified ideologically with medieval or eighteenth-century European outlooks. Few doubted that, for good or bad, an orthodox, predominantly evangelical, and surely tribal religion rested at the center of southern white civilization, positioned often against the supposed materialism of the rest of the nation. The New South, to be sure, looked to the future and represented a different ideology from the one that had been dominant before the war, but advocates of the new way also embraced the legends of the Old South and the Lost Cause, establishing considerable continuity in viewpoint.[35]

In the late nineteenth century, discussions of civilization in general shifted in Western society, the United States, and the American South. Victorian England represented the ideal for civilization for southerners in this period, as for most others in Western society. Its particular sensibility rested in a rising middle class, an energized religion of Evangelicalism, and the wealth generated by a dynamic industrialism. Victorian culture saw a bifurcated world of civilization and savagery, and it insisted on the need for moral discipline to nurture civilization. Civilization combined the refinements of gentility and the ideal of progress befitting a successful industrial juggernaut. This culture of refinement encouraged the arts, the "sweetness and light" of Matthew Arnold's search for the highest thoughts and behaviors. It was a world of rigid gender roles, with gentlemen to be masculine and ladies feminine, and everyone knew what that meant. It also routinely seemed the exclusive possession of white people, and not all whites were equal here—Anglo-Saxons stood at the forefront of civilization.[36]

Science left a mark on the Victorian sensibility as well. Charles Darwin's evolutionary theory dominated intellectual inquiry, and it led cultural anthropologists and ethnologists to develop influential ideas of the hierarchies that structured civilization. They generally agreed that natural growth was from simple to complex, and that differences in human development resulted from the varying cumulative interactions of human groups across time. They argued that human control over nature was the prime measurement of advancement as well, insisting that human groups could be classified by the state of society's use of technology and their states of knowledge. They willingly judged nineteenth-century groups as "savage" and "barbaric" based on being at the lower end of a ranked series of stages of human development, with surviving remnants of lower forms of social life still existing in that time period. When Lewis Henry Morgan's *Ancient Society* appeared in 1877, his opening discussion spelled out the belief in progressive development that underlay the most advanced intellectual understanding of civilization. "Mankind commenced their career at the bottom of the scale," he wrote, "and worked their way up from savagery to civilization through the slow accumulation of experimental knowledge." This knowledge had important social implications, of course, with Victorian elites seeing themselves as the civilized ones; anyone they disliked—laborers, lower classes, foreigners, people of color—represented the survival of the savage and barbaric.[37]

All of these sentiments tied in directly with the expansion of Western power through the world at the turn of the twentieth century. Led by Britain, European nations entered a new imperial age. Protestant missionaries went abroad, bringing Christian justification for overseas involvement, and white supremacy gave a justification of superior over inferior races. But economics drove this new imperialism. As historian Matthew Frye Jacobson notes, "The very idea of 'civilization' implacably ranked diverse peoples' way of life according to a hierarchy of evolutionary economic stages." In this context, extending the "blessings of civilization" had the added advantage of enriching the civilized by drawing on the forced labor and the natural resources that typically characterized the coming of the civilized to the less civilized peoples.[38]

These developments underscored late nineteenth-century linkages between the South and civilization. The image of the cavalier as the dominant southern "type" was a particularly regional contribution. Antebellum thought had made the cavalier the crucial linkage to a Romantic worldview about the plantation with the cavalier the source of order and honor, and New South writers embroidered the legend even more, with the supposed superiority of aristocratic lineage a psychological benefit to a defeated and economically depressed population of white southerners. They could especially identify with the Victorian dichotomy of civilized and savage, as they insisted that freed slaves remained brutes in need of the discipline and direction the white race could provide to get the work of the South done. The southern gentleman as a type became modernized, with new middle-class managers, businessmen, and others now capable of embodying it. New South ideologues did adjust the gentleman image, though, to distance themselves from the leisure ethic of the Old South legend, in favor of a new ethic of hard work and acquisitiveness, appropriate to a new regime. Although modeled after the Yankee, the new southern gentleman of the late nineteenth century embodied the morality, honor, and paternalism that seemed so sadly lacking among northerners.[39]

New South commentators typically saw the region's people in two categories relevant for thinking about southern civilization. The first embraced planters and a growing middle-class elite. The second included mill workers, hardscrabble farmers, sharecroppers, and mechanics. Those opinion makers constructing the dominant version of southern civilization saw these masses in terms of bigotry, superstition, ignorance, and poverty. A prominent Atlanta minister and progressive Southern Baptist, John E. White, wrote in 1909 that the South's population was "twelve million strong but eighteen million weak." He used a military metaphor in describing the challenge to progressive, reform-minded southerners. Twelve million might be soldiers in the army of the New South, but trailing behind them were the greater number of "undrilled, undeveloped, uninstructed, raw recruits of civilization, who do not know the rules of the march and who easily riot among themselves." Among these he counted poor whites, mountaineers, and a "thick and sluggish mass" of African Americans.[40]

Racism

Emancipation of the enslaved had created a need for a new stable social order. Reconstruction, meanwhile, resulted in the polarization of southern racial views. Postbellum white racial attitudes after that time came from several sources. Some recycled proslavery arguments, to which they added ideas and stereotypes from European science and anthropology. The natural and social sciences offered a new "science of race," one that reified long-standing ideas about African Americans' low intelligence and deficient brainpower. As historian Mark Smith has shown, white southerners constructed a view of the Black person as inferior through all of the senses: bad smells, frizzled hair, prehensile big toe, ugly color. Thomas Pearce Bailey's *Race Orthodoxy in the South, and Other Aspects of the Negro Question* (1914) was a seminal text in outlining the South's racial creed: "blood will tell," the Black person will always remain inferior, the South is white man's country, social equality is wrong, political equality can never happen again after Reconstruction, whites should be given all advantages in matters of civil rights and the law, the prestige of the white race may not be disturbed, Black schools can have only second-rate materials, industrial training for Black people can be provided only to the extent that will enable them to serve white people, white southerners should have all the say on the "Negro problem," Black people should be kept as peasants, the lowest white man must count for more than the highest Black person, and, finally, this creed reflects the leanings of providence. This was a stark summarization, but one that most whites would surely have understood. A popular view, north and south, was climatic determinism, which gave scientific authority to the belief that the environment had stunted the evolutionary development of Africans as a result of their abiding in the hot, stultifying climate of Africa. Those in the invigorating northern temperate zone (read: Europeans and North Americans) had stimulated the Caucasian's advanced development in physical appearance, emotional stability, and mental ability.[41]

As if those origins were not enough to satisfy white racists' need for justifying white supremacy, the late nineteenth century saw the popularity of theories of racial degeneration that suggested freed slaves had immediately begun a descent from the moral discipline, physical health, and psychological satisfaction the slave regime had supposedly instilled. After emancipation, white southerners feared at first that freed slaves would rapidly increase in numbers, overwhelming society. By 1892, though, Joseph Le Conte, one of the most distinguished natural scientists in the South, presented a social Darwinist view of race relations, arguing that Black people would inevitably decline because of their inferiorities in the struggle for survival. German-born insurance statistician Frederick Hoffman authored *Race Traits and Tendencies of the American Negro* (1896), presenting seemingly insurmountable statistical data showing Black degeneracy and impending extinction.[42]

Still, white southerners debated throughout the late nineteenth and early twentieth centuries whether southern civilization should try to include or exclude the large numbers of African Americans throughout the South. Paternalists favored inclusion, based sometimes on Christian responsibility for the weaker race and sometimes on a related paternalism. Planters and businessmen saw the need, as well, for cheap Black labor to drive the rise of the New South. Southern Baptist religious leader Victor I. Masters in 1918 described the southern civilization as one of "two separate races, one advanced and the other not long from barbarism and only recently from slavery, living permanently in the same environment under conditions that shall provide for the welfare and progress of both races." He argued that "fundamentally it is a question of Christian faith and of doing right because it is right," with the "right" being fair treatment of southern Black people. "Most of us really want the Negro to stay in the South. He understands us and we understand him. We would not know how to get along without him." He ruled out "social equality" as any kind of issue, assuming the races would not engage in "social intermingling."[43]

Charles Edward Robert was a journalist in Tennessee, Kentucky, and Indiana, and his earlier *Negro Civilization in the South: Educational, Social and Religious Advancement of the Colored People* (1880) made a strong case for African American advancement in the South, seeking to "show the world what has been the advancement of a race of people who less than a generation since were in ignorance and bondage—in darkness and slavery." Speaking optimistically at the end of Reconstruction, he praised African Americans in the South for "making brave, manly steps toward refinement of morals, mind and manners." Robert asserted his southern credentials in making his case, pointing out he was "a Democrat and a Southerner, with warm-hearted love and fidelity for the South ever aglow in his bosom." He defended the idea of African civilization, based on the belief that "Phoenicians had descended from the Canaanites, and Ethiopia presented cultural achievements in architecture and the arts and sciences." African American politicians, ministers, attorneys, teachers, merchants, scholars, and others of accomplishment appeared in Robert's account.[44]

A virulent "Negrophobia," to use a term from the times, came, on the other hand, to a violent and extreme point by the late nineteenth century, partly as a reaction to a belief in the degeneration of the "Black race" since the end of slavery. The image of the "Black beast rapist" was a compelling one that affected cultural and political expressions of southern civilization. Right after the Civil War, Hinton Rowan Helper, the prewar abolitionist, spoke of Black people as "pernicious," "inferior," and "impure and revolting," and he proposed that after July 4, 1876, they should be banned from the United States. Such white racism affected politics at the turn of the century with the rise of demagogues such as Cole Blease, James Vardaman, and Ben Tillman. The latter made frequent trips across the nation, giving lectures with his extreme racial views and helping to shape national attitudes to support white dominance in the South. He insisted African Americans "must remain subordinate or be exterminated." When Booker T. Washington dined with President Theodore Roosevelt at the White House, Tillman raged that "entertaining that n——will necessitate our killing a thousand . . . in the South before they will learn their place again." Tillman, meanwhile, embraced civilization as "the product of white Christian cultural evolution." Anglo-Saxons were "the superior race on the globe; the flower of humanity; the race responsible for the history of the world; for the achievements of the human family in a large degree." At best, Black people might acquire "a little of the veneer of education and civilization, but this only misled and frustrated people who were destined to be laborers." He spread lurid images, saying the "poor African became a fiend, a wild beast, seeking whom he may devour, filling our penitentiaries and our jails, lurking around to see if some helpless white woman can be murdered or brutalized."[45]

Tillman stoked white fears across the South and the nation, yelling in a 1908 address to the South Carolina legislature of the dangers of racial amalgamation, warning that, if white southerners did not maintain strict racial lines, the "traveler in the second century from this will find a breed of mongrels here!" Black efforts at racial intermingling activated the white man's instincts, Tillman insisted, to preserve white purity and supremacy. In the rising racism of the time, he saw civilization itself at stake and worth every effort of racial preservation. "If you scratch the white man too deep, you will find the same savage whose ancestry used to roam wild in Britain when the Danes and Saxons first crossed over." Abolition, emancipation, and Reconstruction had threatened white civilization with "amalgamation," thus forcing, notes historian Lawrence J. Friedman, "the white savage to emerge." White people might descend into their own savagery to blunt "amalgamation" with African Americans but did so, ironically, in the name of preserving a racial purity underlying southern civilization. Tillman's rhetoric and the rise of lynching after 1890 displayed the "white savage" as a turn-of-the-century southern type.[46]

Writers had long been shapers of the idea of southern civilization, and one of them, Thomas Dixon Jr., was one of the most influential postbellum figures in inculcating a southern racial radicalism throughout the nation. Born in the North Carolina Piedmont near the end of the Civil War, Dixon was a Baptist minister, lawyer, state legislator, actor, real estate speculator, and movie producer, as well as a novelist who wrote twenty-two novels that sold so well that he became one of the most popular fiction writers in the nation. His Ku Klux Klan trilogy—*The Leopard's Spots* (1902), *The Clansman* (1905), and *The Traitor* (1907)—depicted racial struggles between Black and white southerners as struggles involving the future of civilization itself. He presented some of the starkest, most dramatic images of the "Black beast rapist" and warned of the evils of miscegenation, which he insisted would lead to the end of the traditional family. In *The Leopard's Spots*, Dixon's hero, Charles Gaston, tells his prospective father-in-law that he had had to be involved in politics during Reconstruction because of the enfranchisement of African Americans—"it was a matter of life and death." The novel portrays scenes that suggest the disintegration of the life of freedmen and freedwomen in general and, in particular, the lust Black men had for white women. Dixon's plot justified the exclusion of African Americans from southern civilization. Gaston insists that a nearby textile mill had succeeded "because you have got rid of the Negro." To Dixon, the fear of the Black man and the violent resistance to him by southern white men had aided the nation, shoring up, as historian Harilaos Stecopoulos notes, "the importance of Dixie as a bulwark of white fraternal ideology." Southern men had shown how Anglo-Saxon men could master an inferior race, a lesson, Stecopoulos adds, "capable of sustaining the nation as it entered new global arenas." Dixon understood that the region's people wanted to play a role in the new turn-of-the-century imperialism that expressed Western civilization's advanced power and that brought a shared white supremacy among white southerners and northerners to the American role in the world. One Montgomery mother told her teenage daughter to read Dixon's writings "as you would read your Bible" and undoubtedly inculcated a religiously authorized hatred and fear of African Americans in the process.[47]

Segregated Society

The underlying issue for Dixon and for most white southerners was the need for white dominance and social distance from African Americans in the South. Black people would not, by the turn of the twentieth century, be totally excluded from southern civilization, but white southerners had established a racially segregated society, leaving African Americans virtually powerless.

Southern governments codified racial segregation in the 1890s—the result of the decline of northern support for protecting Black rights, the rise of a virulent white racism, and the growing assertiveness of African Americans. Cultural historians put particular stress on the last factor. A generation of young African Americans had grown up in freedom and challenged attempts to impose second-class citizenship on them in the 1880s. What historian Grace Elizabeth Hale calls "a culture of whiteness" became a new way to deal with a modernizing society that threw whites and Blacks together in urban and town settings that challenged older racial folk customs. The New South thus evolved at the expense of Black Americans. Life for southern Black people sank to its lowest point between the end of Reconstruction and the beginning of World War I, an era that became known as "the nadir." Economically, they were prisoners of a sharecropping system that kept them in near bondage to the land. They lost political power as disfranchisement came through poll taxes, residency requirements, literacy tests, "understanding the Constitution" tests, grandfather clauses that based the right to vote on ancestors having voted, and whites-only primaries. Jim Crow laws—named for a stereotypical Black minstrel figure— sought to establish a rigid caste system. Unwritten customs of racial etiquette also hardened. The economy segregated "Black" jobs from "white" jobs. The Supreme Court case *Plessy v. Ferguson* (1896) gave federal approval to southern actions by declaring "separate but equal" facilities to be legal. Railroads, schools, theaters, hotels, restaurants, restrooms, water fountains, parks, public offices, and even cemeteries were segregated by the early twentieth century. State legislators strengthened laws against interracial marriage and sexual relations between white women and Black men. Taboos opposed to sharing food and drink with Black people remained pronounced. "If anything would make me kill my children," one white woman said in 1904, "it would be the possibility that n——s might sometime eat at the same table and associate with them as equals." Her angry sentiment overlooked the frequency with which African American women and men prepared food for white families—one of the white privileges that white racial dominance demanded.[48]

Southern civilization rested on the exclusion of African Americans from many public and private places and the overall demeaning of Black people. Black southerners went to schools separate from whites, and on Sundays they worshipped in their own churches, separate from whites. They lived in parts of town deliberately denied resources, resulting in second-class physical living conditions for Blacks. Black southerners used separate water fountains and restrooms; had different waiting rooms from whites; had to sit in the back of trolleys and in Jim Crow train cars; could not use parks, playgrounds, and recreational facilities in general; could not eat in restaurants that served whites;

often could not try on clothing in department stores; and could not stay in hotels, except those few dedicated to Black customers. When they died, African American funeral directors embalmed Black southerners, and they were buried in separate sections of cemeteries. That list does not exhaust the legal separation of Black and white southerners, but it indicates the sweep of southern legislative attempts to cordon off Black southerners from white.[49]

The landscape itself reflected a newly reordered southern society—"white" and "colored" signs were soon pervasive. The signs made visual and tangible the concept of a segregated southern civilization. Katharine Du Pre Lumpkin later recalled the "deadly serious . . . signs and separations" that hit the South in the 1890s, rigidifying racial divisions that were "all so plainly marked." On a childhood visit to Columbia, South Carolina, white southerner John Andrew Rice recalled his first sighting of the new racial order and how striking it was: "The main entrance to the town was the depot, and here was something new, something that marked the town as different from the country and the country depots." He observed two doors to two waiting rooms and on these two doors arresting signs, "White" and "Colored."

Trains and train stations became the first contested places as public authorities enforced new segregation laws, and Black southerners tested the limits of the new rules. African American writer Charles W. Chesnutt, in *The Marrow of Tradition*, conveyed the experiences of a mixed-race train passenger, the mulatto character Dr. William Miller, on a return trip from New York City to North Carolina. The fictional Miller recounted the indignities of train travel under the circumstances, emphasizing that the complaint was less the inferior facilities than the evil of being "branded and tagged and set apart from the rest of mankind upon the public highways, like an unclean thing." If a Black person forgot "his disability, these staring signs would remind him continually that between him and the rest of mankind not of his color, there was by law a great gulf fixed." From early on, though, mixed-race, well-dressed, middle-class African Americans who rode the trains were able to buy first-class tickets but were sometimes forced to move to the Jim Crow car, which complicated attempts at rigid racial separation. Midwestern journalist Ray Stannard Baker, who traveled throughout the South in 1906 and 1907, saw no firm boundaries on streetcars, no curtains or even signs to demarcate precisely where the racial separation should be. Here, he said, "the color line is drawn, but neither race knows just where it is. Indeed, it can hardly be definitely drawn in many relationships, because it is constantly changing." That uncertainty, he noted, was "a fertile source of friction and bitterness." The same was true for small-town shopping districts where merchants wanted African American shoppers and might give some leeway on spatial issues in order not to offend customers.[50]

By the turn of the twentieth century, new media were spreading racial stereotypes nationally, as popular magazines such as *Harper's Weekly,* the *Atlantic
Monthly, Century Magazine, Puck,* and *Judge* published short fiction, poetry,
travel accounts, and cartoons that showed Black people as crude and grotesque.
Gross humor made laughing at Black people a norm. Popular culture depicted
Black people as savage, bestial looking, dishonest, idle, and criminal. Fiction
depicted Black people as petty criminals, dishonest and ridiculous preachers,
corrupt lawyers, and sexually promiscuous men and women. Southern weekly
newspapers, the main source of news for many country and small-town people,
were even worse than national publications, depicting African Americans as
animallike and uncivilized. Minstrel shows were another pervasive feature of
early twentieth-century popular culture, and they continued purveying pernicious images of Black people. "Coon songs" emerged in this era as a favorite
minstrel show segment, with actors delivering racist lyrics to the applause and
laughter of audiences. Businesses sold racist images on knives, glasses, cookie
jars, doorstops, and countless other items that normalized stereotypical views
of African Americans as part of everyday life.[51]

The Birth of a Nation (1915) represented perhaps the most influential use of
new media to reinforce and extend existing racist representations, drawing
from southern history to dramatize for national film audiences the chivalry of
white southerners in the Civil War era and the savagery of Black southerners.
D. W. Griffith had grown up in Kentucky hearing glamorous stories of the war
and Reconstruction, and this brilliant filmmaker pioneered such modern film
techniques as the long shot, close-up, flashback, and montage. He based the
film on the popular novels of Thomas Dixon Jr., using the power of the visual
to reinforce Dixon's racist narratives. The film focused on two families, the
Camerons of South Carolina and the Stonemans of Pennsylvania, whose children marry, resulting in a family-based sectional reconciliation, long a popular
theme of theater. Images of an idyllic antebellum plantation served by happy
slaves evoked the pastoral southern image, but the film showed bloody battles
and the tragedy, for the white plantation family, of Confederate defeat that
destroyed the beauty of the Old South civilization.

The second half of the film dwelled on Reconstruction, conveying the teachings of the Dunning school of historiography on the postwar period, which
emphasized the failures of Black southerners to govern the South effectively
and the need for a Ku Klux Klan to rescue the white South. A key scene showed
a young woman in the Cameron family being pursued by a lecherous Black
man, Gus, and then throwing herself off a cliff to escape sexual assault. The
film's Klan, like that in southern white memory in general, restored the proper
southern social order, disempowered freedmen, protected white southern

womanhood, and promoted the reunification of the nation. The film became one of the most profitable of all time, spreading its racism widely. It was boy-cotted and banned in some nonsouthern cities, but its influence was apparent in inspiring the rebirth of the Ku Klux Klan in Atlanta in November 1915.[52]

By the first decades of the twentieth century, southern states had put into place laws and practices to create a biracial segregated society, one that popular culture reinforced. The fiction that the South contained only two important so-cial groups—segregated white people and racialized Black people—was compli-cated by the ethnic diversity that increased at the same time that whites tried to define the South as biracial. It was an age of immigration to the United States, and although most immigrants went to other parts of the nation, enough came south to complicate the narrative of a biracial society. Jews, Italians, and Greeks came from eastern and southeastern Europe, Syrians and Lebanese from the Middle East, Mexicans from Latin America, and Chinese from Asia.[53]

Some of these ethnic groups entered into regional consciousness more notably than others. The history of the Jewish population of the South goes back to such colonial coastal towns as Charleston and Savannah, where Jews provided a cosmopolitan influence in the often-provincial South. Like other ethnic groups, Jews both assimilated into southern society and remained sep-arate from it. They became southern by sometimes changing their names or switching to Episcopalian or Presbyterian religions. Joining a fraternal group made a person part of a small-town community, and Jews were prominent civic and even political leaders in some cities and towns. If they ran successful busi-nesses many people knew and respected them. They became not just southern but white as well. There were Jewish slave owners; Jews fought for the Confed-eracy; Judah P. Benjamin was secretary of state of the secession government; Jews undoubtedly took part in lynchings of African Americans; their children attended white schools in the segregated South; and they had no recourse ex-cept to support segregation. In the course of a long history in the South, Jews found a home, as many memoirs suggest. Eli Evans titled one chapter of his The Provincials "Kosher Grits" to suggest his dual southern and Jewish identity. Most Jews did not change religion but built temples and synagogues, albeit sometimes to look like Baptist churches. They kept their sacred rituals, and their food reflected, as much as possible, kosher traditions.[54]

Italians and Syrians/Lebanese used many of the same survival tactics, blend-ing an impulse to become a part of the white community with the preservation of their cultural ways when possible. They often lived in houses side by side, in neighborhoods between "white" and "Black" housing areas. They often were merchants whose customers were Black people, but they rigorously avoided any social connections with low-status African Americans that might taint their children's futures. These dark-skinned people were sometimes targeted for violence, as were the eleven Italians lynched in New Orleans in 1906 and the Jewish mill manager Leo Frank lynched in Georgia in 1914. The Ku Klux Klan persecuted all three of these ethnic groups in the 1920s and later. Another group that contributed to the South's diversity in this time period was people of Mexican heritage who had been in Texas for generations and provided foundational cultures in that state. After the Mexican Revolution in 1910, new waves of Mexicans would come into not only Texas but parts of the Deep South to serve as seasonal migrant farmworkers. Mexicans suffered discrimination like the other groups, often classified as "mongrels" because of their intermingled heritage with Black and Native people. They built their own schools, worshipped in Roman Catholic churches they generally controlled, and joined mutual aid and insurance societies to see them through hard times. Chinese also came to the South in the late nineteenth century, sought at first by planters who wanted to find an alternative labor source to African Americans, but they soon became businessmen and women who ran grocery stores.[55]

All of these immigrant groups had to navigate the stark racial dividing line that segregation represented. They were part of a multicultural south society, but the rhetoric of southern civilization marginalized them, as whites were obsessed with constructing a biracial society of two groups. The variety of skin colors gave the lie to such thoughts, but public policy did its best to force everyone into one of the two categories. Ethnic groups remained "foreign," people who upset the best-laid segregation plans.[56]

Native American peoples who remained in the South after removal in the 1830s also challenged the southern racial order underlying discussions of southern civilization. That removal had been a landmark effort in constructing the biracial South and reinforcing white power in the region. In the late nineteenth century, the key issue for southern Indians was preservation of tribal sovereignty. Remnant populations of the Cherokee, Chickasaw, Choctaw, and Seminole tribes, as well as smaller tribes that had survived, built separate communities of schools and churches and tried to keep their land from being taken, legally or illegally. They made alliances with supportive white people when they could for protection and fought designation as "colored" because of the restrictions that would produce. They represented a visually different separate racial identity that policy makers struggled to find a place for in the legally and institutionally "Black/white" worlds of schools, public accommodations, and transportation. Authorities generally forced them into "colored" institutions unless churches or outside groups provided separate Native facilities. They complicated racial boundaries and challenged the logic of a "Black/white" society. In the early twentieth century, Native peoples entered into the

Immigrants added diversity to the South's multicultural
society in the early twentieth century, as seen in this
photo of a young Lebanese boy and his goat in El Dorado,
Arkansas, circa 1910–20. Courtesy of Marie Antoon.

dominant southern white culture as symbols of a remote past. No longer an
obstacle to civilization, virtually invisible to most southerners because of their
geographical and social isolation, Native Americans could be romanticized.
The Seminole chief Osceola became admired for opposing the federal government in war—just as white southerners had done in the Confederacy. The sad
Native lost cause could merge with the white version, as seen in a monument
erected at Fort Mill, South Carolina, which commemorated Catawba veterans

of the Confederate army. "The loss of the Indian way of life," writes Theda Perdue, "seemed to parallel the demise of the Confederacy so closely that a single monument commemorated both."[57]

Lynchings

Racist fears about Black male violence against white women led to the white communal ritual of spectacle lynchings, one of the seemingly most dramatic expressions of the conflict between a regionally specific "southern civilization" and many of the beliefs and values of Western civilization and American idealism. Lynching raised issues of race, gender, social class, modernity and tradition, and religion—all long-familiar ingredients in configurations of southern civilization. But the sense of accelerating social change at the turn of the twentieth century intensified many of these factors that had long figured in imaginings of southern civilization. The South's positioning in this era, in terms of a more favorable national image because of rising national and international white racism, gave a peculiar new context to discussions of the "southern problem."

The lynchings of African American men became a flash point in the early 1890s for a virulent racism that made race more central and primal a force in the definition of southern civilization than ever before. In 1892, white mobs lynched 161 African Americans, whereas none had been lynched a decade before that year. Estimates are that between 1882 and 1955 white vigilantes murdered 4,739 Black people in the United States, with the number likely closer to 6,000. More than 80 percent of lynchings occurred in the South. By the 1890s, most white southerners, as well as many other Americans, believed in the myth of the Black beast rapist who displayed an insatiable lust for white women. That myth was a specific imagining of Black men that was relatively new, positing them as uncivilized, unmanly, violent sexual predators. This myth drew on Victorian-era dichotomies of civilized and savage, manly and womanly. The middle classes believed that powerful male sexual desires inhered in all men, and self-control became a defining feature of a man's strength and authority, enabling him to protect the naturally good women and children around him. The discourse of civilization insisted that Black men were the opposite of "the white man," a new trope in this era, as well as the opposite of civilization. Black men embodied, by definition, the most unmanly and uncivilized behavior, including a total lack of self-control. Gender imagery was pervasive in accounts of lynching, which defenders often portrayed as a conflict between manly civilization and unmanly savagery. As one article on lynching by a northerner put it, African Americans were "but a little removed from savagery," and they were "incapable of adapting the white man's moral code, of assimilating the white man's moral sentiments, of striving toward the white man's moral ideals." American opinion in general, while reiterating white views of Black savagery, also warned white men of the dangers of lynching. Midwestern journalist Ray Stannard Baker's "What Is a Lynching?" (1905) noted that lynchings resulted from heinous crimes by "worthless negroes" whose criminality made it "unsafe for women to travel alone." But "yielding to those blind instincts of savagery which find expression in the mob" represented for white southern men a danger of bringing "the white man down to the lowest level of the criminal negro." He insisted that "if civilization means anything, it means self-restraint; casting away self-restraint the white man becomes as savage as the negro."[58]

Lynching seemed to most of the nation, and to southern moderates and reformers who recoiled from it, as the holdover of an archaic cultural impulse toward vengeance, a practice that disconnected the region from modern civilization. Historian Amy Louise Wood notes, however, that lynching reflected the South's fraught connection to modernity at the turn of the twentieth century. The region was undergoing "an uncertain and troubled transformation into modern, urban societies," and most lynchings occurred in such settings, with Black men hanged from telegraph and telephone posts, symbols of modernizing technology, with white spectators riding streetcars and trains to see the excitement. A new social order was being born, and many white southerners feared that emancipation and urbanization had led to changes that threatened the racial hierarchies they had come to enshrine as the basis of southern civilization during Reconstruction. Such traditional forms of authority as the male-headed family, the old-time religion of the Protestant churches, and the planter elite now seemed under fire, with a new generation of young Black men assertive of their rights and thereby threatening the social order. The southern white imagination fastened on the belief in rising African American criminality and extended that conviction to view lynchings as justified retributions against abhorrent crimes, a way to ensure white dominance and "the larger social and moral order" that was undergoing traumatic change. In this context, violated white women were the center of pro-lynching rhetoric and brought the worst lynching tortures because they represented the loss of white male dominance over African Americans and the failure to protect white households.[59]

The rising middle class of newcomers from rural areas to cities and small towns was especially anxious about social stability and economic opportunities. These newcomers asserted the need for moral propriety and self-discipline as the foundation for respectability. Concern about their own personal and social vulnerability led them to strike out viciously against the objects of their fears. They had a profound investment in maintaining a strict racial hierarchy to

prevent African American work competition and to ensure white male authority in their communities. Lynchings were the most dramatic expression of white
supremacy and dominance, but, despite the efforts of white southerners, their
dominance was always contingent, unstable, and not immune to challenge.[60]

Religion was essential for seeing lynching's relationship to issues of civilization. The South's predominant evangelical Protestantism focused on sin in
this era of rapid change. To some degree, southern theology may have justified lynching as a ritual sacrifice of Black men, who represented fiendish embodiments of evil sinfulness, for southern white sins in general. More likely,
though, defenders of the ritual portrayed it, in Wood's words, as "a terrifying
retribution, ordained and consecrated by God, against the black man's trans-
gressions." Mobs were thus "messengers of God's wrath, summoning all the
tortures of hell for the black 'fiends' and 'devils' in their midst."[61]

The late nineteenth-century rise in lynching coincided with the growth
in evangelical church membership, public religiosity, and church-supported
moral reform movements. Religious rhetoric portrayed the modern world as
a threat to traditional understandings of sexuality and morality. Like that of
defenders of lynching, that religious language obsessively focused on the term
"purity"—bodily and socially under siege. Lynching narratives justified this
blood ritual and its awful tortures as necessary, divinely sanctioned retribution
for Black sins. "Retribution" thus entered the lexicon of southern civilization,
tying religious mindsets to white racial vengeance. One defender of the lynching of Henry Smith, for example, said, "It was nothing but the vengeance of an
outraged God, meted out to him, through the instrumentality of the people
that caused the cremation." An eyewitness to the 1895 lynching of Robert Hilliard in Tyler, Texas, tried to make sense of Hilliard's refusal to die under the
most horrific of tortures, asking whether it was decreed "by an avenging God
as well as an avenging people that his sufferings should be prolonged beyond
the ordinary endurance of mortals?"[62]

Lynchings were thus violent expressions of the southern civil religion, which
always portrayed missions of southern civilization under providential oversight. The outrages that marked the desecration of Black lynching victims so
horrified the broader world of the era, but what Wood calls "the spectacular
excess" of these spectacle lynchings "constructed a symbolic representation of
white spiritual and moral superiority." The region's whites had long insisted
on the superiority of southern civilization, and lynchings became a primal
way in this new era to assert and preserve southern civilization's superiority
against the contaminating Black threat to that civilization's white racial purity.
Given the contingent nature of white supremacy, the performance of lynchings
by a white community assured insecure white southerners of the stability of

that identity, making the term "performance" central to the lexicon of southern civilization. The mass participation of whites was also significant for the "witnessing"—another key term—of southern civilization's continued preservation. As Wood says, "The public ritual of lynching offered white southerners a certainty of their own grace and a sense of belonging to a virtuous and consecrated white community." Whites thus achieved a spiritual elevation observing the just torture and utter degradation of a contaminating Black presence. The logic of racism was thus made to support civilization.[63]

White moderates in the 1890s were often silent on lynching, as racism rose to a disturbing new intensity. By the second decade of the twentieth century, they affirmed the general southern white view of white racial dominance, but they condemned lynching. Baptist leader Victor I. Masters spoke from a Christian need to oppose the practice, condemning "the shameful lynchings which disgrace our civilization." He insisted that "an overwhelming majority of white citizens are opposed to lynchings and deplore them" but claimed that "the absence of a recognized community spirit" allowed the "few depraved and brutal men who lead the lynchings" to punish helpless Black men with impunity. He wanted to distance respectable members of southern civilization from the practice, although scholars know now that community leaders often took part in lynch mobs. Still, Masters asserted that "Christian men and women of the South cannot quietly acquiesce to such a solution as this," and they were "morally bound to work for even justice for all." He warned that if Christians did not oppose and end lynching, it would lead to "the dwarfing of the South's spiritual life."[64]

Andrew Sledd's article in the *Atlantic Monthly* in 1902 recounted horrific details of a Georgia lynching, with an African American man burned to death before a large crowd on a Sunday, church day. He argued that the awful spectacle of white savagery was not so much to achieve justice as to "teach the negro the lesson of abject and eternal servility," burning into "his quivering flesh the consciousness that he has not, cannot have the right of a free citizen or even of a fellow human creature." Sledd represented moderate white opinion, but the article stirred furious emotion among many vocal white southerners who saw Sledd as a race traitor. He had to resign his position at Emory College, and the whole affair registered as a shocking lesson in violating southern racial orthodoxy. Whites reinforced the orthodoxy of lynching by recounting stories of lynching at the dinner table and in the parlor. "I've heard about that lynching a hundred times," a young interviewee told a sociologist in 1944. He added that "every time the men at the store start talking about how uppity n——s are now, someone talks about that lynching."[65]

Nothing brought more disrepute to the idea of southern civilization than

lynchings, and no one articulated the uncivilized savagery of lynching better than African American journalist and activist Ida B. Wells (later Wells-
Barnett). Raised in Holly Springs, Mississippi, in a middle-class African American family well socialized into Victorian-era conventions, Wells became a
crusading journalist in Memphis, Tennessee. In 1892, a mob of white people
lynched three respectable African American businessmen because of their successful competition with nearby white grocers, although the charge of rape was
brought up to justify it. The viciousness of the killings and the fact that they
were downplayed by the political and legal establishment led the twenty-nine-
year-old journalist to editorialize that "nobody in this section of the country
believes the old thread bare lie that Negro men rape white women"—words that
exposed the raw nerve of white supremacy. Forced to flee Memphis ahead of a
lynch mob, she ended up in Chicago in 1894.

Right after the Memphis lynching, Wells wrote *Southern Horrors* (1892), her
first effort to appeal to a wide white audience to end lynching. Where whites
depicted the Black man as unmanly passion incarnate, she portrayed the Black
man as manliness personified. Black men who had been lynched for rape were,
she wrote, innocent victims, seduced into consensual sex with carnal white
women. Wells wrote that they were "poor blind Afro American Samsons who
suffered themselves to be betrayed by white Delilahs." Her effectiveness partly
came through naming thirteen white women, including prostitutes, she accused of seduction and betrayal of Black men. White narratives portrayed
lynch mobs as disciplined, restrained, and manly, but Wells showed them as
uncontrolled, vicious, and unmanly. She argued that southern white men were
actually enthusiastic supporters of rape—as long as the victims were Black
women or girls.[66]

In her pamphlet and other writings and speeches, Wells used the discourse
of civilization so common in that era, but she gave it a new interpretation that
made whites understand that the differences between civilization and savagery
were not so clear as they thought. Her greatest success as the preeminent enemy
of lynching came during two British tours she made, in 1893 and 1894, which
she conceived of as campaigns against lynching, trying to educate and ener-
gize British public opinion against a southern civilization that denied the fundamentals of Western civilization. She knew that white Americans were not
listening to Black protests about lynching, but she believed that they respected
and admired the British as the preeminent people of the civilized world—and
fellow Anglo-Saxons. As Wells told one British journalist, if the British told
Americans "the roasting of men alive on unproved charges and by a furious
mob was a disgrace to civilization of the United States, then every criminal in
America, white or black, would soon be assured of a trial under the proper form
of law." Her goal was to convince Americans that their tolerance of lynching

rendered them unmanly savages in the eyes of the civilized world. She skillfully built alliances with the British reform community. In one public address in Birmingham, England, she said, "I believe that the silent indifference with which [Great Britain] has received the intelligence that human beings are burned alive in a Christian (?) country, and by civilized (?) Anglo-Saxon communities, is born of ignorance of the true situation," and when that fact is known, "she would make a protest long and loud." Throughout her time in Britain, she hammered away at the myth of the Black beast rapist and promoted the idea that southern white men were lascivious and unmanly.[67]

Wells modeled herself as the proper Victorian woman in her dress, language, and style, appealing as a clearly civilized person to the British people she met. Her accounts of her travels appeared back home in a Chicago newspaper, filled with details of dinners given for her by members of Parliament, mass meetings engineered by prominent clerics and reformers, and private gatherings organized by British aristocrats. Wells convinced the British press and reformers that American tolerance of lynching undercut any claims to civilization in the United States. A *Westminster Gazette* writer said that he could no longer "regard our American cousins as a civilized nation." *Christian World* thought American lynch law would "disgrace a nation of cannibals." One British aristocrat, Sir Edward Russell, insisted on the need for "uplift" of white Americans, proposing to send missionaries there instead of to other parts of the world because saving Anglo-Saxons from savagery should be the highest priority. The southern reaction was as to be expected, with newspapers finally giving Wells's arguments a hearing but refuting them as hopeless because the true cause of lynching was the Black beast rapist.[68]

Wells failed to end lynching, but she contributed to the decline in the number of lynchings after the mid-1890s. When she returned from her British trips, she issued a pamphlet that noted that since her return, many political and public leaders had spoken out against the barbarism of lynching because "the entire American people now feel, both North and South, that they are objects in the gaze of the civilized world and that for every lynching humanity asked that America render its account to civilization and itself." Her claims were a stretch, but she had clearly used the discourse of civilization to show a brutal underside of southern civilization that the Western world could no longer easily ignore.[69]

Sectional Reconciliation

To understand the evolution of "southern civilization" as a concept in the late nineteenth and early twentieth centuries, one must examine its role in the national culture as well as the South. Three themes structured the national representation of the South with special importance for southern civilization. One was the sectional reconciliation that wore down the bitterness between the region and nation during the war and Reconstruction. Second was the portrayal of the "problem South," focusing on the region's environmental, social, and economic inadequacies in an American culture that attempted in an imperial age to unify the nation around racial and global assumptions. Here, the South appeared as "the Other" to not only the nation but Western civilization. Third was the formulation of the South in terms of "folkloric primitivism," which saw the "backward South" as actually a value to a nation that many people now saw at the turn of the century as "overcivilized," with the region representing the values of racial purity and cultural authenticity.

After Reconstruction ended, events promoted sectional reconciliation and a positive assessment by many northerners of the southern civilization they had perpetually scorned for generations. Abraham Lincoln had promoted such a reconciliationist sentiment in his second inaugural address, and the centennial in 1876 of the nation's founding focused on national unity. The Supreme Court declared the 1875 Civil Rights Act unconstitutional in 1883, making it easier for southern states to restrict Black rights and encouraging white southern embrace of a seemingly less hostile national government. Former Confederate generals were among the pallbearers for Ulysses S. Grant's burial in 1885, earning northern approval for the South. The blue and gray reunions of Civil War soldiers, beginning with the twenty-fifth commemoration of the Battle of Gettysburg in 1888, encouraged a stress north and south on the valor and honor of Confederate and Union soldiers, downplaying the causes for which they fought. Northern businessmen encouraged friendly feelings between the sections for investment purposes, and northern Republicans discovered they could win national elections without the votes of Black southerners, leaving the latter without significant political protection in the national government. The rise of the "white republic" in the late nineteenth century reflected a shared rising racism throughout the nation and a willingness to let white southerners deal with the "Negro problem" in an age nationally more dedicated to materialistic acquisition and global expansion than idealistic reform causes.[70]

The South continued to be of importance to the United States as the source of a major American economic resource through its cotton production, which also promoted sectional reconciliation. Cotton, in fact, appeared everywhere as "a great civilizer," in the words of James L. Watkins, a U.S. Department of Agriculture statistician who insisted the South had a moral duty to grow more of the crop so the world's people could become fully clothed, and with "fondness for dress" would come a desire for "other comforts of life," a basis for civilized living. In this view, the South was a carrier of civilization throughout the world. Clarence Poe wrote a series of articles between 1904 and 1906 celebrating cotton as the "life-blood of commerce," a crop that would help the "vanquished people" of the South rise to a new eminence and play a part on the world stage.

The Spanish-American War proved a perfect occasion for those wanting sectional reconciliation, as southern boys once again fought for the nation, and President William McKinley appointed two former Confederate generals to important posts in the war and the administration of Cuban affairs afterward. Some white northerners abandoned the Reconstruction-era memory of a defeated American region for a new image of an Anglo-Saxon and traditional American South. The experience of white southerners serving as, in effect, administrators of the region's backward African American peoples was now seen as a lesson to the nation embarking on a new empire of postwar colonies containing dark peoples to be conquered—and civilized.[71]

Contacts between northerners and white southerners promoted the ideal of sectional reconciliation as well. To be sure, not everyone bought into it. Oliver Wendell Holmes, right after the war, attacked an ultimate icon of southern civilization, writing to a friend that "the humbug of the Southern Gentleman in your mind" was a delusion, as "the Southern gentlemen generally were an arrogant crew who knew nothing of the ideas that make the life of the few thousands that may be called civilized." He gave away his class orientation in the process as well. Other northerners, in time, began to ennoble the white southerner precisely because of his upper-class style. One early postwar traveler, John DeForest, praised the white southerner's "suavity of manner" and regretted that the typical money-grubbing northerner had "not been better educated in such gentilities." A *Nation* writer urged northerners to travel south on holiday, saying they would appreciate southern manners, which had an "ineffable charm." Defenders of southern civilization from the region itself could have hardly framed the issue better—the mannered way was the southern way. Novels by Herman Melville, Henry Adams, and Henry James in the 1870s and 1880s similarly showed upper-class white southerners as appealing figures, commenting in their own way on the Gilded Age's materialism and corruption and its contrast with the spiritual values of the South.[72]

Albion Tourgee's novel *A Fool's Errand* (1869) recounted the fictional adventures of a northerner come south during Reconstruction on a civilizing mission, which he came to see as failed because the federal government had been halfhearted in its efforts. Tourgee's 1888 article "The South as a Field for Fiction" suggested that national literature had "become not only southern in type, but distinctly Confederate in sympathy." He had come around to the belief that Reconstruction had been important in giving to national culture the tragic figure of the disinherited southerner, and he included both the Black southerner and the white southerner. To the African American, the story of the Civil War and afterward was that "the past is only darkness replete with unimaginable horrors," but his life "as a slave, freedman, and racial outcast offers undoubtedly the richest mine of romantic material that has opened to the English speaking novelists since the Wizard of the North discovered and depicted the common life of Scotland." And the story of southern whites "must hereafter be run from the benchline of the poor white, and there cannot be any levelling upward," as "the dominant class itself presents the accumulated pathos of a million abdications" around whom "will cluster the hero of romantic glory." At this point, one sees the southern white elite once again reclaiming a sympathetic role in national culture. The white southerner now, in Gilded Age America, represented a counterpoint to the materialism and corruption of the national experience. All of this promoted national acceptance of the South, with the region representing a distinctive spiritual force in a material age.[73]

Problem South

On the other hand, many northerners came to see the South as a problem for the growth of the nation-state at a time of global expansion, a concern that focused on the readiness of the South for the requirements of modern civilization. The sectional reunification that occurred included efforts by the federal government, national corporations and foundations, and southern reformers to identify, with as much scientific precision as possible, the problems tainting the region and then impose solutions for reform. Health problems, educational problems, widespread poverty, high rates of violence, and other evidence of a backward society seemed far from the national expansion of capitalism, technological advances, and general modernization that now seemed the cutting edge of Victorian-era civilization. National anxieties grew around the turn of the twentieth century over the profound economic problems in the South, the supposed racial degeneration of African Americans, and a similar degeneration of poor whites. Observations about the South's lack of civilization recurred in travelers' accounts, medical assessments, journalistic exposés, and other intellectual pronouncements. A northern woman visiting the South concluded, for example, that what most struck her about the region was its people's "determined resistance to the inroads of civilization."[74]

Environmental factors were central to nurturing a negative perception of southern civilization in this period, reflecting the growth of science and its moral authority to command the need for reform. By the late nineteenth century climate had long been a major lens through which observers, southern and otherwise, viewed the region, and the tropical connection went back to early European views of what would become the American South. But the early twentieth century saw a newly compelling concern for the South's tropical positioning. As before, the imagery of the tropics evoked natural abundance and fertility but also landscapes of poverty and disease. Natalie J. Ring notes that "the question being asked was: Could civilization overcome the perils of the tropics?" From the perspective of the national culture, the South appeared to be "alluring and perilous, exotic, yet familiarly American." Observers did not hesitate to make moral judgments about the region, though, condemning it as "a diseased and degenerative space." In this light, the South appeared to be like a colony, and its colonial economy, in fact, positioned it as part of a colonial world.[75]

Ellsworth H. Huntington's *Civilization and Climate* (1915) argued for environmental determinism, seeing the South suffering from "climatic handicaps," with the region's "depressed climate" resulting in its failure to develop an advanced civilization to match that of the North. Southerners suffered the weakening influence of hookworm and malaria, were careless about "food and sanitation," and did "not feel the eager zest for work which is so notable in parts of the world where the climatic stimulus is at a minimum." Huntington saw that certain tropical diseases common to the southern climate had encouraged the South's penchant for laziness and had caused some southern white people to "fall below the level of their race" and become "'Poor Whites' or 'Crackers.'" Such people increased in numbers as one moved "from a more to a less favorable climate." The presence of large numbers of African Americans with notable health problems reinforced the idea that the South was disease ridden.[76]

What seemed new by the early twentieth century was the fear that Huntington touched on: that southern poor whites were degenerating. S. A. Hamilton, for example, writing in *Arena* in April 1902, noted that the southern poor white was a distinctive racial type whose history showed little contact with the institutions of civilization, so that the southern poor white had "degenerated from the beginning into a besotted, ignorant, and vicious class." Alexander J. McElway, a North Carolina opponent of child labor, saw textile mills harboring a backward people, lamenting that there was "no greater catastrophe than race degeneracy," which characterized "the little child slaves of our southern cotton mills." Observers worried that their illiteracy meant that education could not help them and that their tendency toward violence worked against good citizenship. Physicians pointed to distinctive diseases, seen as tropical, that debilitated them. All of this raised serious broader concerns about the place of a decaying lower-class group of whites in Jim Crow society. "Growing evidence of the possibility of a degenerate white race moving backward toward a state of barbarism rather than forward toward a state of civilization," Ring writes, "muted the distinctions between black and white and challenged the fiction embodied in whites' efforts to keep the races separated socially." As a result southern white elites, public health reformers, and their political allies included efforts to monitor and reform the lives of poor whites as a part of the new legally segregated society, and the short-comings of poor whites blurred boundaries of Black and white. The "savagery" of poor white behavior was sometimes generalized to that of white southerners in general, adding to a national image of the South's "otherness."[77]

Folkloric Primitivism

A third predominant view of the South in American culture in this period saw it as a repository of traits beneficial by counterpoint to a modernizing, anxiety-ridden nation. This "folkloric primitivism" gained definition in the late nine-teenth century and increased through the early twentieth century. Journalist Henry Childs Merwin spoke for a rising American middle class in his 1897 *Atlantic Monthly* article "On Being Civilized Too Much," arguing that his age in Western society was creating people who were "over-sophisticated and effete" and out of touch with the natural world. That world nurtured natural human instincts and skills, and yet those needed qualities had been "dulled and weak-ened by civilization." Advancements in civilization had surely led to American greatness, but "every step in civilization is made at the expense of some savage strength or virtue," features that still needed to be promoted. Primitivism was mostly a negative feature in the bifurcated Victorian sensibility of civilization and savagery, but here Merwin is asking for a better balance between them. He pointed his readers who were "sick with civilization" to "consult the teamster, the farmer, the wood-chopper, the shepherd, or the drover," whom one would find "healthy in mind," "free from fads," and "strong in natural impulses." He might have said to "look south" as well because he was speaking to the mostly northeastern middle-class magazine readers who seemed to embody his fears of overcivilization and who would have thought of the South as far from the embodiment of advanced civilization.[78]

A torrent of fictional and journalistic stories about the South appeared, be-ginning in the 1870s and escalating with the end of Reconstruction. Easier train travel facilitated visitors coming to the South, and their writings became part of the local color movement. Local color stories were typically sketches told by a metropolitan voice coming into isolated places, and the genre was a lit-erary analogy to American corporations coming into the South to exploit its resources and "backward" people. Sherwood Bonner's stories helped create the popularity of dialect tales and represented the centrality of race to this genre; Constance Fenimore Woolson came only briefly to the South, to St. Augustine, Florida, but her stories of Florida history and customs resonated across the na-tion. Local places could be the south Louisiana of George Washington Cable's semitropical Creoles or Thomas Nelson Page's moonlight-and-magnolias Old South. Local color was significant for southern civilization in converting folklore materials of local places into popular literature that nurtured images of the South as a quaint and exotic place. In 1873 physician Will Wallace Harney published "A Strange Land and a Peculiar People," a portrayal of life in the Cumberland Mountains, and it became the model for treatments of the South and its regions. The title told the tale, with its suggestion of an exotic place and inhabitants. The description drew from an ethnological stress on the physical differences of mountain people from other Americans and on a nostalgic picture of their everyday life. He emphasized features that suggested a homogeneity of people in the mountains and their differences from other Americans. He and later writers such as Mary Noailles Murfree, James Lane Allen, and John Fox Jr. established a popular image of Appalachia as a separate region of the United States whose people were Anglo-Saxon, close to the soil, and devoted to kin, individualism, and tradition—but they could also be violent, backward, and poor but happy with their moonshine. As one writer said, these "Appalachians" were "our contemporary ancestors."[79]

The seemingly positive and negative qualities of mountain people cohered into a distinctive world because, above all, the mountain people lived isolated lives, or at least that was the widespread assumption. In fact, by the late nineteenth century the mountain people had undergone a commercial and industrial transformation, like the rest of the South, with northern business and industrial companies operating coal mines, textile mills, and lumber camps. Mail-ordered goods brought modern styles into supposedly isolated hollows, and rising land prices, wage labor, union organizing, and expansive railroad lines represented a different Appalachia than that of these popular writers. Nonetheless, this local color portrayal of Appalachia was the beginning of a national representation of the South in general as a primitive source of wonder—or embarrassment. Folklore became a central idea in this regard in enduring portrayals of southern primitivism. E. C. Perow's "Songs and Rhymes from the South," an early collection of southern folk songs published in the *Journal of American Folklore* between 1912 and 1915, showed the influence on the developing academic field of folklore of this local color popular primitivism, with its stress on cultural isolation nurturing essential differences. Writing about the mountains, Perow said, "The relative inaccessibility of the country, as compared with the surrounding territory, had until very recently kept back the tide of progress, which, sweeping around this region, had shut up there a strange survival of a civilization of three hundred years ago." Isolation had led mountaineers to "preserve primitive ideals"; language was a prime indicator of this tendency, as their dialect marked "them as belonging to another age."[80]

National representations of African Americans in the late nineteenth-century

South showed similar tendencies. Travelers to the region often saw them as picturesque features of the landscape, as with one traveler who had gone down the Mississippi River and noted "the beautiful plantations that lined both sides of the river, the numerous boats passing, and the singing of the negroes as they discharged and took on cargo." A railroad guide reported that "a grinning, turbaned colored woman" standing in the doorway of her simple house "apprises the Northerner he is certainly 'right smart down South.'" "Picturesque" is an aesthetic focused on everyday life in foreign places; its use so often in terms of the South revealed American attitudes about the South as a place of this variety of the primitive. Some writers who claimed the status of folklorists at the turn of the twentieth century often did little fieldwork but instead drew from their own memories of the "old-time negro" and from their nostalgia for a supposed time when Black and white southerners lived in harmony, albeit with one group in bondage to the other.[81]

If "isolated" and "picturesque" were key terms in this national portrayal of the primitive southern civilization, so was "authenticity." The hustle and bustle of modern civilization seemed to include rapidly changing fashions and fads, but the search for the primitive in the South rested on the idea that the region's backwardness from advanced civilization had enabled it to preserve traditional folkways that should be valued. Folk culture, in this regard, did not typically appear as an ongoing process of adapting cultural ways to changing circumstances; rather, it represented a collection of cultural ways that connected other Americans to the past. John Fox Jr. wrote in *Scribner's Magazine* in 1901 that "the Cumberland range keeps the southern mountaineers to the backwoods civilization of the revolution," with no incentive to embrace technology or innovation. The result was "an arrest of development," in which "a civilization, with its dress, speech, religion, customs, ideas, may be caught like the shapes of lower life in stone, and may tell the human story of a century as the rocks tell the story of an age." Cultural reformers who came into the mountains to try to "uplift" their supposedly backward, if authentic, people decided that the traditions of spinning wheels, patchwork quilts, feather beds, and fireplaces represented an "authentic" mountain culture, and they worked to discourage certain cultural features of mountain life that did not fit this assumption of authenticity. This concern for mountain lore, crafts, and folk songs was developed in the context of early twentieth-century recognition both of the artistic value of naïve productions and of the social science interest in the material culture of primitive folk societies in tracing evolutionary, developmental processes.[82]

"Folklore" developed in this era as an academic project. The American Folklore Society formed in 1888, and scholars publishing in its journal saw "the folk" as people other than themselves in terms of geographical, social,

This revival scene in the rural South shows the fervor of evangelical religious worship, a key part of southern African American folk culture. Charles Reagan Wilson Collection, Archives and Special Collections, John Davis Williams Library, University of Mississippi Library, Oxford, Mississippi.

and cultural locations. Those studying music declared music they collected in southern places as "authentic southern music," tying "authentic" and "southern" together. Commercially produced songs did not qualify at that point as authentic southern music. This had racial implications in the Jim Crow South, as folklorists came to appreciate, at least in their professional activities, the segregation that blanketed the region by the early twentieth century because it enabled them to find isolated performers and communities who seemed to be especially valuable sources for understanding the origins of culture itself. Their practices regularly were implicated in support of the racially separate southern civilization, naturalizing distinct African American or white cultural traditions as "pure"; such judgments also extended to ethnic types and regional subcultures. For example, folklorists claimed the purest Anglo-Saxon blood had survived in isolated Appalachian communities, a fact of particular interest to readers of folklore studies, mostly northeasterners struggling to accommodate waves of new immigrants from places outside the Anglo-Saxon world.[83]

Critical Thinking

Southern critics emerged as an identifiable group of liberal reformers at the end of the nineteenth century, often working with nonsouthern reformers addressing the socioeconomic problems of southern civilization. Critics included progressive ministers, intellectuals, academics, journalists, and elite women social reformers who brought new doubts about conventional New South wisdom that progress was occurring at a rapid rate. These critics sometimes did not contradict New South goals but pushed for better implementation of educational reform, industrial progress, and sectional reconciliation. They often went further and criticized the sharecropping system, the chain gang, and child labor. Antebellum white southerners had ennobled slavery as the best of all societies and worth going to war to defend; postbellum southern white opinion insisted the war had been about states' rights, not slavery, but the late nineteenth-century southern critics blamed the extensive nature of southern ills directly on slavery. Atticus Haygood, president of Emory College in Georgia and one of the most influential of southern Methodists, insisted that "our provincialism, our want of literature, our lack of educational facilities, and our manufactures, like our lack of population, is all explained by one fact and one word—slavery." Critics saw a malaise hanging over the South, even decades after the end of the peculiar institution.[84]

George Washington Cable was an early postbellum critic, daring to openly criticize the hardening of race relations after Reconstruction, insisting that the call for racial separatism was really an effort to assert white power in all public realms. He said that the "simple *belief* in a divinely ordained race antagonism is used to justify the withholding of impersonal public rights which belong to every man because he is a man, and with which race and its real or imagined antagonisms have nothing whatever to do." In his fiction, Cable portrayed the harmful effects of slavery, showed masters as not always the benevolent cavaliers that plantation fiction portrayed, and wrote about the mixed-blood people in his south Louisiana. A white character, Honoré Grandissime, admitted the pervasiveness of racial mixing and claimed it was "the Nemesis w'ich, instead of coming aftah, glides along by the side of the moral, political and social mistakes!" He regretted that it affected not just families but "our whole civilization!" One critic in New Orleans said that Cable's book *The Grandissimes* was "an unnatural growth" and used imagery of disreputable African American folk culture to marginalize Cable as "a High-Priest of Negro Voodouism," who "reminds us of the chatty magpie, the cold, sleazy serpent, the slime-imbedded alligator shedding pitiful tears."[85]

Cable embraced the idea of a biracial southern civilization, noting that the "only way to make the South a good place for white men to come to is to make it a good place for black men to stay in." Cable's "Freedmen's Case in Equity" (1885) was the South's boldest proclamation in the late nineteenth century of the need to respect African American constitutional rights and citizenship. Devoting the region's intellectual energies simply to the proslavery argument had ignored meanings of any southern civilization in the larger realm of civilized thinking. He lamented that the defense of slavery had paralyzed southern thinking and the region "broke with human progress." In his commencement address at the University of Mississippi in 1882 he warned students that to identify as southerners was to relegate themselves to a secondary status in the world. "I trust the time is not too far away," he said, "when you shall say, 'Southerners? South? New South? Sir, your words are not for us.'" Instead, students should say, "We are American," and revealingly he added that if one was looking for the New South, "go you to Mexico." He maintained there was a "silent South" of progressive white southerners who were "coming daily into the convictions that condemn their own beliefs of yesterday as the out worn artillery of an outgrown past," and he hoped that "our traditionalist friends" might soon come to embrace "the promotion of this revolution that everyone knows must come," referring to the recognition of African American public rights.[86]

Cable came to define many of the basic parameters of southern critical thinking about the region. He couched his arguments in relation to his own southern identity and claimed that gave him inside expertise in assessing southern civilization, something that outsiders lacked. Although he lambasted the evil effects of slavery on the region, he referred to Reconstruction as a "dreadful episode" and dismissed the idea that the federal government could coerce the South into providing equal treatment for African Americans. He insisted that material prosperity—a great goal of the New South movement—was impossible as long as most Black southerners continued to live in poverty and face discrimination, thus appealing to white self-interest.[87]

Walter Hines Page also exemplified the southern critic of the New South after the turn of the twentieth century. In some ways his outlook fit easily enough with the goals of the New South ideology, believing in the region's need for industrial development and supporting the philosophy of "uplift" to promote the bourgeois values of respectability among the white and Black masses of southerners. From North Carolina, Page spent much of his life in New York City as editor of two prominent journals, *Forum* and the *Atlantic Monthly*, and head of his own publishing house, Doubleday, Page, and Company, and later his own magazine, the *World's Work*. Page could not abide the South's obsession with the Lost Cause and its backward-looking gaze, lamenting that slavery had "pickled all Southern life and left it just as it found it." He attributed every "undemocratic trait" in the postbellum era to slavery, which had stifled "free inquiry and free discussion," and that lack of intellectual criticism kept southerners from questioning traditions that held the South back.[88]

Page's novel *The Southerner* (1909) portrayed a main character, Nicholas Worth, son of a slave-owning family but one with Unionist sympathies. Worth returns south after getting an education at Harvard and struggles to reconcile his love of family and place with the South's problems. In one passage, he gives a litany of the misery of everyday life for many southerners, writing of having forgotten "the neglected homes visible from the cars, the cabins about which half-naked Negro children played and from which ragged men and women, drunk with idleness, stared at the train, the ill-kept railway stations where crowds of loafers stood with their hand in their pockets and spate at cracks in the platform, unkempt countrymen, heavy with dyspepsia and malaria, idle negroes, and village loafers." He sees the "hopeless inertia of the white man who had been deadened by an old economic error." He becomes disgusted with the South's intellectual stagnation, racist demagoguery, provincial clergymen, and allegiance to the ghosts of the past as well as the "gallant and pious non-sense" put forth by the United Daughters of the Confederacy. He contrasts the South's sorry condition with New England's "orderliness, thrift, frankness; a clean land, clean towns," and the intellectual result—"open minds." He con-siders going back to the North but decides it is his duty to remain in the South and try to better conditions.[89]

Page himself used his publishing bully pulpit to point to southern problems and the need for sharp criticism. He understood the South's situation to be one of civilization itself. In "The Last Hold of the Southern Bully," he indicted white southerners for their savage support of lynching and criticized the south-ern bully who threatened to pull the region back into barbarism. He used the words "civilization" or "civilized" eighteen times in a short article, charging that justice in the South had become "in civilized life the place that revenge held in savage life." He was especially critical of South Carolina, with its his-tory as progenitor of secession that left the South bereft of so much that would contribute to civilization, charging that the state had "lost the true perspective of civilization" and was antagonistic toward "the moral force of the nation." Southern problems to be criticized were not just economic or even social; they were essentially moral.[90]

A landmark in the South's self-criticism was the formation of organizations to provide ongoing institutional direction to reform efforts. The Southern Sociological Congress formed in 1912 and held annual conferences bringing together people who organizers believed were the region's "best people" ded-icated to the need to study and reform the South, identifying the essence of the region's ills as the "Southern problem of civilization." It was a paternalistic effort, one that valued insights from the nation and the world's experiences in identifying and ameliorating social problems common throughout the world. The collection of addresses at the 1913 meeting, published as *The Human Way*, suggested the need to see the South's experiences beyond regional platitudes. It would not be the last time that a "human way" was juxtaposed with the "southern way." In one talk in 1913, W. D. Weatherford proposed using welfare agencies of the southern states to address problems of African Americans as well as poor whites. He raised up the region's churches as of central importance in this regard: "The great social mission of the Church," he wrote, "is the bringing on of a new appreciation of the sacredness and values of the individual life." This mission meant, above all, "brotherhood," "equal safety of life," and "an equal chance to make a living and build a life." The social gospel was inherent in his citing of the principle of "the Fatherhood of God and the brotherhood of man." Religious belief and practice would thus be essential to advancing civilization in the South. Despising any group or person would lead to "destroying our civilization, giving the lie to our Christian ethics, and damning our own souls."[91]

Like many others in the group, he was particularly appalled by "the horrible lynchings that have been taking place in the South during the last few months," which were "enough to make our blood run cold with despair." But Weatherford insisted on the need to zero in on the deeper issue, the necessity to "cure the horrible cancer that eats at the heart of our civilization," which he identified as "the horrible lack of appreciation for the sacredness of the individual person." Weatherford thus diagnosed the South's ruptured relationship with the soul as the essence of its disturbing violence that threatened civilization itself in the region.[92]

Another talk at the 1913 meeting exemplified the pervasiveness of the discourse of civilization by southern critics. Mrs. J. D. Hammond of Augusta, Georgia, addressed "the test of civilization," outlining the requirements, as she saw them, of civilized life and identifying "justice and opportunity" as "the fundamental human needs, the necessary basis of human progress, the test of the measure of a nation's civilization." In this regard, the South was outside the pale of American civilization. "Our problem is not racial, but human and economic," the latter of which would become the mantra for racial liberals up to World War II. Despite the despair about racial violence in the era of the Southern Sociological Congress, its members held fast to the hope of progress, not only on race relations but in other areas of southern life as well. Theirs was a program of uplift, of targeting new resources of government, business, and individuals to bring education, health care, recreational opportunities, jobs, and safer neighborhoods to the region's needy people.[93]

Cable left the South after ugly intimidation, and Page lived most of his life in the North, albeit obsessed with southern affairs. Other native critics stayed in the region, such as Edgar Gardner Murphy, Julia Tutwiler, and Rebecca Felton, whose family status, religious affiliation, and basic acceptance of racial segregation enabled them to criticize the South's convict lease system, child labor, educational woes, and other problems. William Preston Trent's "Tendencies of Higher Life in the South," published in the *Atlantic Monthly* in June 1897, explored the critical spirit in the South in general, lamenting the southern public's "failure to recognize the transcendent importance of criticism and culture to the accomplishment of the political and economic reforms that are pressing upon us." He identified the "baleful intolerance, political, religious and other," that was widespread "whenever it becomes necessary to question, even in a tentative way, the importance, or the propriety, or the truth of any idea that has in any way been labeled Southern." He was particularly judgmental of the South's lawyers, who sometimes tolerated racial violence "in a fashion permissible only in countries where law has no sway," yet these same attorneys "will nevertheless claim that their civilization is of the highest grade." Southerners, he intoned, had to be more critical, realizing that when the authority of law "has been questioned or defied among a civilized people the wedge of anarchy has entered the social and political fabric." Trent's article was an important expression of a beleaguered critical spirit in the early twentieth-century South, one that with some urgency saw the need to apply critical standards to preserve civilization itself.[94]

"Negro Civilization"

Overlapping understandings of civilization existed in African American discourse in the late nineteenth and early twentieth centuries, all of them pivoting back in one way or another to their presence in the South. The hopeful period of Reconstruction with its new sense of citizenship and political participation gave way in the South to ever more restrictive laws and customs that created a segregated society. Some observers came to speak of a "Negro civilization" in the South that grew out of the institutional structures separating Black life from white. A sympathetic white journalist, Charles Edward Robert, wrote *Negro Civilization in the South* in 1880, at the end of Reconstruction, portraying with some astonishment the progress of African Americans, as he showed "the world what has been the advancement of a race of people who less than a generation ago were in ignorance and bondage—in darkness and slavery." Despite the end of Reconstruction, African Americans still had, he thought, "civil and religious freedom, and by virtue of these blessings are making brave, manly steps toward refinement of morals, mind, and manners." The latter language suggested not just a distinctive civilization but one striving toward high civilization. He admitted that some observers might think he had given "a rose-colored view of the Negro," but he insisted he had "written of Negro *civilization* and not Negro *degradation*." He praised the advancements of Black southerners in education, saw the growth of a Black middle class, discussed accomplished Black people in the United States and elsewhere, and defended the idea of African civilization tracing back to Ethiopia and Egypt. "Thus we see," he wrote, "ancient Africa is rich in history." He foresaw that "a glorious future is before these people," one that should produce a "splendid history" that "some of their cultured scholars" would one day write. By the turn of the century, the web of Black businesses, churches, social organizations, schools, and other forms of social and economic life had indeed produced many accomplished individuals and strong institutions that gave form to the idea of a "Negro civilization" in the South.[95]

Robert mentioned another key expression of civilization among African Americans: the importance of African civilization serving to link Black southerners with an old homeland and a possible future one. The relationship of African Americans to Africa in this period was complex. Southern whites continued to use Africa as a shorthand for Black savagery and heathenism. In 1901, for example, Tennessee's *Jackson Times-Union* summarized orthodox white southern wisdom on the connection between race and civilization: "Civilization and culture and decency and learning" were spontaneous products growing out of "the hard soil of experience and adversity." African Americans, the paper said, had made progress in acquiring the rudiments of civilization, "but the Negro has had centuries of independence within which to show the metal that is in him—what has he done in Africa but evolve monsters that put our monkey ancestors to shame?"[96]

White southerners periodically flirted with the colonization of Black people back to Africa. In 1890 Alabama's U.S. senator John Tyler Morgan proposed a massive removal project, giving particular attention to exiling the best-educated Black people because they were the most discontented with the realities of southern civilization. In 1892, the editor of the Charleston, South Carolina, *News and Courier* had similarly urged that Blacks go back to Africa so that, "by the end of the next quarter of a century, the South will be relieved from the black cloud which hangs over it." African American leaders such as Methodist bishop Henry McNeal Turner and theologian Edward Blyden supported African American return to Africa, and African American denominations identified Africa as their missionary field.[97]

Whether Africa was to be the future for African Americans or not, many of them lifted up that continent as providing a proud ancestry. Orators at such commemorative occasions as Emancipation Day, Juneteenth, and the Fourth of July countered the predominant white image of Africa, seeing it as a hearth for the development of Western civilization. "The Negro race in primitive ages," O. M. Steward of Richmond boasted in 1907, had enjoyed "a high degree of civilization and culture." Steward and others lauded the technological and cultural innovations that made possible all future civilizations, which had emerged first in ancient Egypt and Africa. "The Egyptians," Professor Joseph L. Wiley wryly observed in 1900, "found the Greeks wild and unclad, living in trees, subsisting on roots." Fraternal groups such as the Prince Hall Masons insisted that the roots of Black Masons went back to King Solomon, who integrated the knowledge of the ages into a new physical science that became the moral and intellectual basis for sustaining human civilization. The Black Masons' triumphant histories of Africa and African Americans gave members a proud conceptual tool in nurturing the idea that "Negro civilization" in the South had a distinguished lineage. Black intellectuals admitted that Africa had fallen behind Europe and North America, but they did not see innate racial inferiority as the reason. As Christians, they saw God at work in history. The Reverend C. C. Summerville, at an Asheville, North Carolina, ceremony, insisted that God had consigned Africans to the "furnace of affliction" so that they "might mount up to the highest of true Christian civilization." This narrative gave a providential meaning to Black history, one located in the United States.[98]

This providential African connection was one part of an African American embrace of the possibilities of American civilization. From Reconstruction to World War I, African Americans displayed the symbols of American nationalism, such as the American flag; celebrated such American patriotic holidays as the Fourth of July and the national Memorial Day (in pointed contrast to white southerners); and, above all, pointed to the egalitarian aspects of the national exceptionalist ideology that offered them hope of ultimate equality. The American civil religion had been born during the American Revolution, seeing the nation as under God's destiny to spread democracy, and Lincoln in the Gettysburg Address had renewed the claim that the United States had a special mission, as it was fighting to free slaves and extend the egalitarian promises of the Declaration of Independence to them. African American leaders such as Frederick Douglass had spoken before the war about African Americans heeding a divine call to purge and redeem the nation from its long toleration of slavery, thus helping to redeem the United States. The African Methodist Episcopal Church especially reflected a Black civil religion that included dual destinies for both the nation and its African Americans. God had thus called Black Americans to push the nation toward its national destiny, but the nation was failing, according to these critics, in its commission to redeem the world for democracy and Christianity. By criticizing slavery and then postwar discrimination, Black leaders gained moral authority, making African Americans the true exemplars of Christianity in the nation. By incorporating the Christlike virtues of suffering Black people, the nation might be able to construct a just civilization and redeem its mission.[99]

Crummell and Uplift

Alexander Crummell was one of the most influential Black nationalists in the late nineteenth century, and while he was not optimistic about African Americans' future within American civilization, he was most significant for his adaptation of the discourse of civilization to African Americans. Like other intellectuals of the Victorian era, he used civilization to indicate material as well as intellectual and spiritual concerns. To him, it meant liberation from heathenism, the valuation of the cultural ideals of personal responsibility, acceptance of Victorian-gendered concepts of manhood and womanhood, and the belief in progress. Crummell spent almost two decades as a missionary in Liberia and dreamed of an African future, but he had little good to say about Africa in his day. He thought of Black nationalism in cosmopolitan terms. As Wilson Jeremiah Moses notes, Black nationalists such as Crummell were "civilizationists" rather than "culturalists." They saw civilization as a process governed by universal rules, and they wanted African Americans to be accepted as a part of that process. They affirmed the dominant Western scientific view that evolving forms of civilization could be measured by one universal scale. National cultures displayed particular characteristics, but the achievements of any cultural group had to be measured against civilization's universal principles.[100]

In addresses such as "Civilization, the Primal Need of the Race" and "Civilization as a Collateral and Indispensable Instrumentality in Planting the Christian Church in Africa," Crummell dismissed the idea of forced colonization of Blacks to Africa, affirmed a Pan-Africanism as the future of the race, rejected Booker T. Washington's primary emphasis on industrial education, and embraced liberal arts education to nurture an African American intellectual class. He confidently saw African diaspora peoples advancing but asked, "Who are to be the agents to lift up this people of ours to the grand plane of civilization?" Anticipating W. E. B. Du Bois—and, in fact, one of his main intellectual influences—Crummell posited that transforming "the souls of a race or a people is a work of intelligence." Crummell believed in racial uplift and insisted on the need for the teachers and ministers, rather than the Gilded Age's businessmen and industrialists, as the idealists who would push the race forward.[101]

Crummell's stress on racial uplift fit well with the thinking of many Black intellectuals. In response to the hardening of white supremacy in the later nineteenth century, they advocated public protest, migration, industrial education, and higher education. Racial uplift was another strategy, with those who saw themselves as the "better classes" nurturing Black respectability as a way toward social advancement. This ideology called for Black elites to assume responsibility for working with the Black masses to encourage them to follow middle-class values of temperance, hard work, thrift, perseverance, and Victorian sexual restraint. The expectation was that as more Black people came to practice middle-class virtues, they would earn the esteem of white people. Racial uplift countered stereotypes of African Americans by stressing class differences among Blacks, with Black elites the symbols of racial progress and civilization. The outlook encouraged, however, intraracial class tensions and overlooked the deeply racist categories of civilization and progress in the age of empire and the white man's burden. By endorsing the idea of backward Black masses, racial uplift ironically seemed to endorse white racist representations of Black people. Advocates of racial uplift endorsed Western European forms of music and discouraged the raw emotions of blues music and Black gospel music, seeing them as survivals from a primitive age of Black culture. In a famous example, the Fisk Jubilee Singers converted the folk spirituals of slavery into a choral style that would appeal to white audiences, and they successfully toured the nation and Europe, raising money for Fisk University and projecting for white audiences an appealing, modern, middle-class version of African American culture.[102]

Atlanta Compromise

One can see racial uplift as an example of a "civilizing mission" that was so popular in the era of powerful discourse on civilization in the late nineteenth- and early twentieth-century age of empire. Booker T. Washington became the most influential Black leader from the time of his address in 1895 in Atlanta at the Cotton States Expositions. He seemed the embodiment of a leader of a social group working to advance civilization among his people, and his own life story represented progress in American and southern civilization. His autobiography, *Up from Slavery* (1901), presented him as a figure from the Gilded Age American civilization in a rags-to-riches story emphasizing self-reliance and hard work. Born a slave on a small farm in rural Virginia, he moved with his family after emancipation to work in the salt furnaces and coal mines of western Virginia. He received a secondary school education at Hampton

Church fan portraying the preeminent southern
African American leader of the late nineteenth
century, Booker T. Washington, who advocated
a "Negro civilization" separate from white
civilization. Charles Reagan Wilson Collection,
Archives and Special Collections, John Davis
Williams Library, University of Mississippi
Library, Oxford, Mississippi.

Institute, established after the war by Union general Samuel Armstrong, who
used the methods of his missionary parents in Hawaii to provide industrial
education for freedmen and freedwomen. Washington excelled at the school
and took it as a model when he established Tuskegee Normal and Industrial Institute in the Alabama Black Belt in 1881. He built on the existing work of northern philanthropists and southern educational leaders for vocational training to
prepare Blacks for work in the New South.[103]

Washington's seminal speech in Atlanta came on the opening day of the
exposition. The ceremony showed the complexity of the South's symbolic

configuration in terms of the nation at that point. The crowd cheered as a band played "The Star-Spangled Banner," exploded with enthusiasm on hearing "Dixie," and then fell quiet to the sounds of "Yankee Doodle." The organizers had included an exhibit on African American life, and Washington began his talk by thanking them for recognizing the achievements "and manhood"—a term many whites denied for African American men—of Black men through the exhibit. He spoke at a time when momentous legal and political changes had already happened, taking the vote from Black southerners and placing them under the rigid spatial strictures of racial segregation. Black leaders, including Frederick Douglass, had concluded after Reconstruction ended that there was a need for African Americans to focus on economic issues, and that was the key that Washington hit that day.[104]

The speech's core argument became known as the Atlanta Compromise because Washington downplayed the need for Blacks to seek political rights or social equality and stressed the necessity of focusing on economic advancement, a goal that fit the economic focus of the New South and American society in general. He told the audience that "whatever sins the South may be called to bear, when it comes to business, pure and simple, it is in the South that the Negro is given a man's chance in the commercial world." He emphasized practicality and insisted that Black southerners "shall prosper in proportion as we learn to draw the line between the superficial and the substantial, the ornamental geegaws of life and the useful." While touting, above all, the need for education, he dismissed liberal arts schooling, observing that "no race can prosper till it learns that there is as much dignity in tilling a field as in writing a poem."[105]

Washington laid out the makings of a "Negro civilization" in the South, one based in learning "to dignify and glorify" common labor and to put "brains and skills into the common occupations of life." He used the metaphor "cast down your buckets where you are," rejecting colonization schemes that would take African Americans out of the region and urging Black southerners to stay in "our beloved South" and build "a new heaven and a new earth"; he used biblical language to suggest the possibility of a millennial transformation of Black life and endorsed a generalized version of a southern civil religion that invested sacred meaning in the South. "Negro civilization" would come about when Black southerners cast down their buckets "in agriculture, in mechanics, in commerce, in domestic science, and in the professions." Segregation opened the way for a separate structure of Black institutions, including businesses, which would represent "Negro civilization," but Washington reminded everyone that the "Negro civilization" had to be intertwined with that of white southerners. He predicted that Black southerners would interlace "industrial, commercial, civil, and religious life with yours in a way that shall make the interests of both races one." He urged white southerners, in turn, to "cast down your buckets" among "the Negroes whose habits you know, whose fidelity and love you have tested in days when to have proved treacherous, in ruin of your firesides," evoking the Lost Cause trope of the loyal slave. He urged white southerners not to turn to the immigrant labor that was coming to the nation, predicting that in the future "we shall stand by you with a devotion that no foreigner can approach."[106]

The image Washington left the audience with was that "in all things that are purely social we can be as separate as the fingers, yet one as the hand in all things essential to mutual progress." "Negro civilization" and southern civilization stood to gain material benefits from such simultaneous separation and cooperation, the "blotting out of sectional differences and racial animosities," but Washington ended by hoping that his plan would include "the determination to administer absolute justice, in a willing obedience among all classes to the mandates of law"—words that pointedly but without belligerence addressed the precipitous rise in lynching of Black men in the early 1890s.[107]

At the end of the speech, Clark Howell, editor of the *Atlanta Constitution*, rushed to the stage and congratulated Washington, telling him the speech was "the beginning of a moral revolution in America." New South leaders praised Washington, welcoming his acceptance of the segregated South and generally blessing Washington's vision of a "Negro civilization" in the South that could be expected to provide workers for the South's economic advancement. Northern philanthropists blessed Washington's work, especially by donating millions of dollars to Tuskegee Institute and befriending the Alabama educator personally. The speech helped make Washington the instantaneous leader of African Americans. W. E. B. Du Bois congratulated him for a "phenomenal speech," and Pan-Africanist Edward Blyden declared it freed the "two races from the prejudices and false views of life and of their mutual relations which hamper the growth of one and cripple the other." Scholar Norman E. Hodges Jr. argues that it "contained the kernel of all subsequent black nationalism," in contrast to Du Bois's integrationist approach. Washington became associated with Black pride and solidarity and the independence of the "Negro civilization" in the South. As time went on and the African American situation in the South worsened, critics would berate Washington for accepting the segregated society, but his embodiment of that civilization appeared in the physical reminders of his influence, namely the hundreds of segregated schools, libraries, streets, and other memorials to him, as well as the thousands of Black men who came to be his namesakes.[108]

Despite his influence, many white southerners in this age of virulent racism suspected Washington and his vision of "Negro civilization" as undermining white supremacy. Tom Watson, the onetime progressive Populist reformer who became a strident racist, accused Washington in 1905 of thinking that "the black man is superior to the white" because Washington had cited statistics that suggested Black literacy rates were higher than those of whites in some European countries. Watson used civilization as a weapon against Washington's claims for the possibility of Black uplift, ranting that during the millennium when Europeans were building a civilization, "your people were running about in the woods, naked, eating raw meat"; they were "steeped in ignorance, vice and superstition, with an occasional lapse into human sacrifice and cannibalism." Watson ended his tirade that focused on undercutting any Black American claim to civilization, asking, "What does Civilization owe to the negro? Nothing! *Nothing*!! NOTHING!!!" Thomas Dixon Jr. was perhaps even more pointed in lambasting Washington's education mission as a cover for racial equality and racial amalgamation, claiming that Washington trained his students for a "Negro civilization" in which they aspired "to be masters of men, to be independent, to own and operate their own industries, plant their own fields, buy and sell their own goods, and in every shape and form destroy the last vestige of dependence on the white man for anything." In 1905, several southern newspapers called openly for his assassination and the destruction of Tuskegee, and his northern friend, Oswald Villard, wrote that he pitied Washington, for he was in "a desperate position and may yet prove a martyr to his cause."[109]

Washington's Materialistic Civilization

Washington's strategy for racial uplift in the Jim Crow South was a materialist one. Although a bourgeois religion based on the Protestant ethic was an essential ingredient in his efforts, he lambasted and ridiculed the emotional preaching and worship he often observed in Black churches and intoned often on the need to make religion of practical benefit. In an 1894 speech, for example, he claimed that three-quarters of sermons by African American preachers in the South consisted of an imaginary description of heaven. He pointedly observed that "our people like to talk about heavenly mansions, and at the same time are content to live in one-room cabins in this world." They liked to "talk about golden slippers, and too often go bare-footed here." He quoted the hymn "Give Me Jesus," with its lyrics about the otherworld, but explained that Black parishioners needed to understand that to have Jesus "in a substantial way" was to "mix in some land, cotton, and corn and a good bank account." Work, moreover, undergirded his materialist strategy. He promoted agricultural labor, citing as good examples his sponsorship of the innovative agricultural work of George Washington Carver at Tuskegee Institute and his annual agricultural conferences, but he also insisted that "no race that has anything to contribute to the markets of the world is long in any degree ostracized." In 1900 he began the National Negro Business League to promote business and highlight his friendliness to commercial activity. The importance of work intersected with his idea of the South. He insisted in a 1909 speech, for example, that "here in the South no black man worth his salt has to seek for labor—labor seeks him."[110]

Tuskegee Institute was a testimony to his vision of a "Negro civilization" in the South. Within seven years of its founding, he had expanded the school from virtually nothing to a dynamic institution with more than 400 staff. By 1905, the physical plant included thirty-three buildings, most made of brick manufactured on the campus, and almost 2,000 acres of land, devoted mostly to vegetable production, livestock, and cotton. It was one of the largest and best-endowed educational institutions in the nation; the names of such do-nors as Carnegie, Rockefeller, and Huntington appeared above building doors. It rested on acceptance of white power and separation of Black people from white people, but the school was also a challenge to white dominance, as an institution of Black power, one that white racists such as Watson and Dixon understood and disliked.[111]

Racial interaction was a foundational principle of Washington's materialist-based "Negro civilization" in the South. One of the most revealing stories that showed the combination of separation and interdependence of Black and white southerners told of early Black students at the school making bricks to be used in the Tuskegee buildings, persevering to overcome obstacles to make the bricks, and selling the surplus bricks to local whites, building interracial rela-tionships in the process. Washington realized that uplift of African Americans in the South depended to some degree on cooperation with southern whites. His visionary dream insisted that "friction between the races will pass away in proportion as the black man, by reason of his skill, intelligence, and character, can produce something the white man wants or respects in the commercial world." Thus, Black owners of sawmills, brickyards, printing presses, and tin shops would one day make whites dependent on Black men, and economic success would lead to property ownership. Washington's metaphor for Black success was one right out of the American dream, as he promised southern Black people that "a white man respects a negro who owns a two-story brick house."[112]

Washington was very much the southerner, which undoubtedly made his vision of an independent "Negro civilization" in the South easier for whites to endorse or at least tolerate, in spite of the vicious racism of the time. His rural southern cultural style showed in his earthy language, informal personal manners, distrust of cities and urban dwellers, joy in working with animals, pleasure in nature, and enthusiasm for hunting, fishing, and horseback riding and dressing in the countryman's overalls. He was every bit the agrarian. But he was also a bourgeois Victorian-era figure. As Norman E. Hodges Jr. writes, he "sought to embody in his very person—in his carriage and habits—the play of cleanliness, efficiency, discipline, hard work and practical, or industrial education." Washington often made favorable comments about the glories of the Old South and the gallantry of Confederate soldiers, affirming the romantic legend. In a 1909 speech at his alma mater, Hampton Institute, he used the language of the southern civil religion, admitting that "Virginia is sacred soil," and generalized from that state to say that "we have in the Southland opportunities not equaled by those of the same number of black people elsewhere in the whole civilized world—opportunities to get land, opportunities to get work." In 1903, a southern white professor, John Spencer Bassett of Trinity College in North Carolina, proclaimed him "the greatest man, save Robert E. Lee, born in the South in the last hundred years." This statement raised the ire of many white southerners but rang true, as he represented a transitional style of a South moving from an agrarian past to the New South future.[113]

Washington's version of a civilizing mission was often critical of what he saw as the shortcomings of African American character, which he traced to the dysfunctional and debilitating effects of slavery on work habits and ethical behavior, but he always combined such sentiments—which echoed those of southern whites—with the unbridled confidence in the progress and hopeful future of African Americans. But he failed to anticipate the depth of white racism, which became visibly apparent in white opposition to Black successes. Alabama senator John Tyler Morgan predicted in the 1890s, for example, that as the growing population of African Americans competed with white people, their increased prestige and wealth would be checked by "the jealousy of caste."[114]

Historian David Sehat suggests looking at Washington's civilizing mission as an example of what he calls the "indigenous collaborator" typical of colonial systems, individuals arising from subjugated populations and sharing the colonizers' system of values. These individuals gained esteem and prestige within the colonial system by being intermediaries between colonial rulers and subjugated peoples. Sehat shows the complexities and ambivalences of such a role, and one feels that is surely true in regard to Washington. The American South was both an economic colony of the North and a colonizer of African American communities in Washington's era. The South had been conquered in war and suffered military occupation and a civilizing mission from northern

reformers and politicians who came south after the war with dreams of uplifting the region's people, white and Black. White southerners were also, though,
in charge of a colony-like administration of African American southerners,
and it is here that Washington might be seen as one involved in implementing
the New South agenda of uplifting African Americans. Washington was as
shrewd an uplifter as one could imagine, working closely with northern philanthropists, being friends with President Theodore Roosevelt and patronage king
for the Republican Party in the South, negotiating with New South leadership
to augment his position of power, undercutting potential rivals to his authority
in the Black community, and supporting behind-the-scenes efforts to combat
racial injustices.[115]

Du Bois's Southern Veil and Western Civilization

Perhaps no one perceived more clearly than W. E. B. Du Bois what it meant to
live within the various embodiments of civilization in the late nineteenth- and
early twentieth-century South. Born a New Englander in 1868, he grew up on
the idealism of American civilization as that region expressed it, from abolitionism to support for Reconstruction. He went south to matriculate at Fisk
University in Nashville and then became one of the nation's most distinguished
scholars, earning a PhD at Harvard University and doing advanced training
at the University of Berlin, which exposed him to a Europe that embodied for
him, as for so many intellectuals, a Victorian-era Western civilization that he
regarded as the epitome of the world's achievement. His first trip to the South,
on the other hand, had appalled him, as he noted that the region's customs
were barbaric. Still, he taught in rural areas in the summers while studying in
Tennessee, beginning a life-long devotion to championing the African American masses. His account of riding on a segregated railroad car was rich with
ironies and frustrations. Books in hand, he sat in a Jim Crow car, a quarantined
space that existed to demean African Americans. "I sit with Shakespeare and
he winces not," he wrote, picking a writer who represented the era's high cultural achievements. "Across the color line, I move arm and arm with Balzac and
Dumas, where smiling men and welcoming women glide in gilded halls," he
wrote, evoking a scene from European high style. He also summoned Aristotle
and Aurelius and they came "graciously with no scorn or condescension." He
pondered that, "wed with Truth, I dwell about the Veil." In this passage from
The Souls of Black Folk, Du Bois alluded to such key ideas as the color line and
the Veil, his poetic image to describe the spatial and emotional separation of
segregation. He concluded from his train reverie that the African American

should strive "to be a co-worker in the kingdom of culture, to escape both death and isolation, to husband and use his best powers and latent genius." That last term put the high achievements of the greatest civilization within the reach of the African Americans he documents.[116]

In "Beyond the Veil in a Virginia Town" (1897), Du Bois reported on spending two months in Farmville, Virginia, in 1897, trying to understand the workings of Jim Crow. He began with an appreciation of the physical setting of the place, which he attributed, as he often did, to the "southern" quality of the environment and social life, noting "a certain southern softness and restfulness not to say laziness about it that gives a charm to its sand and clay, its crazy pavements and 'notion' stores." He evoked a stereotypical South in describing the town's "old brick mansions and tiny new cottages, its lazily rolling landscape and sparsely wooded knolls that beck and nod to the three-peaked ridge of the blue Alleghenies." But his vision was drawn to the "most curious thing" about the community, namely "its Veil." "The great Veil—now dark, sinister and wall-like, not light, filmy and silky, but every[where] a dividing veil and running throughout the town and dividing it: 1200 white this side and 1200 Black beyond the Veil." Addressing readers not in the South, he observed the difficulty in understanding "the double life of this Virginia hamlet." The idea of social class was not responsible for it, and even the term "caste" missed "the kernel of the truth." He understood the biracial interconnections here, as the society was "two worlds separate yet bound together like those double stars that, bound for all time, whirl around each other separate yet one." Every question seemed to revolve around race. He saw two little boys walking and heard one say, "Big execution in town today," and the other asked, "White or colored?" Two rural men on horseback met, and one said, "Big meeting at the county," and the other said, "White folks or n——s?" "And thus it runs through life: the Veil is ever there separating the two peoples." On one side of the Veil was country life as known many places, although it was flavored here with "war memories, and a strange economic experiment," but still much like life for white people in Illinois or Connecticut in business and gossip, church life, and the customs of courting, marrying, and burying. But on the Black side of the Veil lay "an undiscovered country, a land of new things, of change, or experiment, of wild hope and somber realization, of superlatives and italics—of wondrously blended poetry and prose."[117]

In his essay "The Spirit of Modern Europe," delivered as a speech around 1900 before African American teachers and students in Louisville, Kentucky, Du Bois presented a dazzling and sweeping meditation on European civilization and its meaning for African Americans. He took the audience on a grand tour of Europe, from its eastern edges, on the margins of civilization, he said, to Vienna and Budapest and the center of Teutonic civilization and "the beautiful half-corporeal Rome of the Spirit of Rome." He summoned "the unquenchable fire of civilization kindled in Egypt, replenished in Greece, scarred burning by Rome, and gathered conserved and augmented in the furnace of Europe," winding up in Berlin and Paris. His purpose in his verbal tour of Europe, he said, was to "make you realize that after all America is not the centre of modern civilization." He stressed that "the spirit of modern Europe," as "the organized life of mankind that we call Civilization," rang through in a series of ideas: continuity of organization, authority of government, justice between men, individual freedom, and systematic knowledge. These ideas were "after all the end and striving of all civilization, no matter how imperfectly realized in particular societies." Du Bois stressed the centrality of "this idea of social solidarity and social responsibility," which outweighed the individualism of the past.[118]

That day in Louisville, Du Bois applied lessons of his conception of civilization and its spirit to "the new race like this we represent here tonight that comes upon the world's stage in the morning twilight of the twentieth century." He placed the "African people" newly on the world's stage for their striving toward new levels of civilization in the coming century. "The African people sweep over the birth place of civilization, they dot the islands of the sea, they swarm in South America, they teem in our own land." He pointed to "the students of Louisville" as a "part of the advance guard of the new people," while "the teachers of Louisville" were training the minds and forming the ideals that would "guide their onward marching." Their "ideals differ in no respect from the ideals of that European civilization of which we all today form a part," so that "our watch word today must be Social Solidarity—Social Responsibility." Du Bois then offered a critical perspective on the Black culture of his age, pointing toward the need for uplift. "Young Negroes are today peculiarly tempted," he said, "to impose upon the ignorance of their people, to prey upon their weakness, to flatter their vanity." He insisted, though, that freedom meant "not the right to loaf and squander money on luxuries"; knowledge meant "the trained capacity for comprehending the truth: in this world men who can do nothing, get nothing to do." Young African Americans "who would serve the negro race must bravely face the facts of its condition: the ignorance, the immorality, the laziness, the waste, and the crime." All of this sounded like Booker T. Washington's uplift, and in fact Du Bois agreed on the need for such basics of uplift. He also, though, evoked his idea of the Talented Tenth in telling his audience that in response to the needs for racial uplift, his civilized ideal of authority meant "the recognition of the fact that all cannot lead because all are not fit to lead."

But he saw his student audience as those who should lead the race's striving toward civilization. He pointed to such institutions as Spelman, Atlanta University, Fisk, and northern institutions where African American leaders "are not to be trained for their own sakes alone but to be the guides and servants of the vast unmoved masses who are to be led out of poverty, out of disease and out of crime." Here, again, he shared Booker T. Washington's rhetoric of uplift, although his focus on ideals and the Talented Tenth suggested a different calculus in achieving the "civilized mission."[119]

Du Bois's Spiritual Civilization

If Booker T. Washington represented a materialist understanding of civilization and the attempt to work out a singular "Negro civilization" in the South within a broader biracial regional civilization, Du Bois expressed above all a spiritual understanding of civilization. Stephanie J. Shaw argued that Du Bois, in fact, saw a dissonance between the spiritual and material worlds in general. The inner world was the mind/soul with its great potential for idealistic accomplishment, while the external material world was one of constraints, including the color line, which always worked against a people's ability to discover who they were and to have the agency to embody that identity. She pointed out that, in good Hegelian fashion, he believed in the possibility of a synthesis: a major goal of his writing was "to encourage real democracy—a material world that supported the freedom (self-determination) of consciousness (soul) for all its members to and for the good of the whole society—a unity that would reflect (and contribute to) the wholeness and harmony of World Soul." Du Bois spared no detail in relating the plight of rural African Americans under southern civilization, noting that "in well-nigh the whole rural South the black farmers are peons, bound by law and custom to an economic slavery, from which the only escape is death or the penitentiary." Even in the "most cultured sections and cities of the South," African Americans were a "segregated servile caste, with restricted rights and privileges." The judicial systems placed Blacks on "a different and peculiar basis." His age, of course, saw a rising imperialism in Western society, and Du Bois condemned the "war, murder, slavery, extermination, and debauchery" that resulted from "carrying civilization and the blessed gospel around the world," adding that "we have in the South as fine a field for such a study as the world offers."[120]

Du Bois spoke easily and often about "soul" and "spirit." In *The Souls of Black Folk*, his seminal work of understanding the separate "Negro civilization" of the turn-of-the-century South, he wrote, "I have sought here to sketch, in vague, uncertain outline, the spiritual world in which ten thousand Americans live and strive." That word "strive" was a key one, and he identified the main goals of southern African American striving to be work, culture, and liberty, all of which worked "not singly but together, not successively but together, each growing and aiding each, and all striving toward that vaster ideal that swims before the Negro people." Shaw used the key phrase of this study in concluding that Du Bois showed "how the southern way of life could cost black folk more than votes, land, crops, houses, schools, and wages." It could also cost their "identity—their self-consciousness—their soul, their humanity." Although Washington and many modernizing African American religious leaders lamented and discouraged an emotional religiosity they saw among the masses of Black southern folk, Du Bois appreciated that the congregants in churches he saw still had "the deep religious feeling of the real Negro heart, the stirring, unguided might of powerful human souls who lost the guiding star of the past and seek in the great night anew religious ideals." The spirit of southern Black folk "sprang from the African forests, where its counterpart can still be heard . . . was adapted, changed and intensified by the tragic soul-life of the slave, until, under the stress of law whip, it became the one true expression of a people's sorrow, despair and hope."[121]

Du Bois's chapter on Atlanta pictured it as the opposite of the spirit-filled southern African American rural culture, expressing his regret at that postwar city's embrace of materialism, with its "vulgar money-getters" who lived lives of "pretense and ostentation." Warning that Atlanta "must not lead the South into dreams of material prosperity as the touchstone of all success," he lamented that the New South honored businessmen and technicians but not teachers and ministers. An ethic of acquisitiveness had captivated African Americans, but he looked to education in the liberal arts to arrest that development. His concept of the Talented Tenth highlighted the importance of the arts and sciences to a proper education, one that would produce leaders to advance the Black masses into civilization, and Du Bois contrasted this idea with Washington's focus on vocational and industrial education. Du Bois's idea was part of racial uplift and suggested his own version of a civilizing mission, with its brand of paternalism of Black leaders toward the masses.[122]

The important point in terms of civilization, again, was that he put stress not just on material uplift but on spiritual uplift. Conservation of the soul required college-trained teachers who could reach people "whose ignorance was not simply of letter, but of life itself." Black colleges and universities should resist the focus on "bread-winning" and instead should "be the organ of that fine adjustment between real life and the growing knowledge of life, an adjustment which forms the secret of civilization." He regarded education as essential for not just Blacks but whites in the South as well, as only that knowledge would enable the South to "catch up with civilization," pointing to the South's understanding of its civilization as a deficient one in the grander scheme. Du Bois's chapter on Washington similarly lamented that he was creating "a Gospel of Work and Money," but one that surrendered Black people's legal and political rights to determine how to go about their work and how to protect its achievements. He charged that Washington's materialist program prepared Black people for a lifetime of "industrial slavery and civic death" and a permanent "position of inferiority." Recounted in *The Souls of Black Folk* were tragic stories of Black southerners losing their struggles for land and public schools, their right to vote and express their citizenship, and their right simply to live "like folks," leading Du Bois to conclude that Washington's leadership had made the relinquishing of civil and political rights "into a veritable way of life" that Du Bois opposed.[123]

African Americans Look North and to Africa

African American intellectuals countered the reality of a racially oppressive southern civilization, but the most eloquent insights came from the plain folk, and voices from the Great Migration of African Americans out of the South that began around World War I are good examples. "I want to bring my family out of this southland," wrote one Black Mississippian to the *Chicago Defender*, the premier African American newspaper that chronicled the Great Migration that began in earnest during World War I. "I am sick of the south," wrote another; "We are anxs to get off southern soil," said another. "I'm tired of this Jim Crow," sang a bluesman, "gonna leave this Jim Crow town," saying he was "sweet Chicago bound." Migration out of the South became the most effective refutation of the social segregation of southern civilization. Southern whites and some Black leaders argued against migration out of the South, claiming the South was the "natural home" for African Americans. The climate had a supposed magical appeal; news accounts from Mississippi in the early twentieth century noted that Black migrants north were freezing to death in the "bleak and blizzardly" Yankee streets. One migrant from the Mississippi Gulf Coast wrote from Chicago, though: "They say we are fools to leave the warm country, and how people are dying in the east. Well, I for one, am glad that they had the privilege of dying a natural death there. That is much better than the rope and torch. I will take my chance with the northern winter."[124]

The loss of faith in Western civilization during World War I diminished it as a standard for many African Americans to aspire to achieve. Pan-Africanism had been long emerging as a vibrant cause, but the Pan-African Congress in 1919 dramatized new interest in it. It stirred hopes that the future of those people who were part of the African diaspora might be back in Africa. In the United States, the Universal Negro Improvement Association attracted hundreds of thousands of believers to its leader, Marcus Garvey. Although popularly identified with northern urban areas, the movement put down deep roots in the South, building on interest in places such as the Arkansas-Mississippi delta in the back-to-Africa migration in the late nineteenth century. Arkansas alone had some forty Universal Negro Improvement Association divisions, often organized in churches and led by ministers or sharecroppers. The group's newspaper, *Negro World*, circulated widely in the rural South, often brought into the region by African Americans who worked on north-south railroad lines. Garvey used the waning of the civilizationist ideology and the hope for African redemption to create the largest mass movement in African American history, founding the Universal Negro Improvement Association on principles of democracy and Christianity, which he hoped to further in an African republic that would attract Africans scattered around the globe. He despaired of achieving justice in the United States but remained loyal to what he saw as its universal ideals of freedom and equality. Garveyism inspired civic piety among the Black masses and promoted symbols of a Black civilization to inspire them. Historian Randall Burkett argues for a "black civil religion" represented by Garvey's ideology, one with its own hymns, creed, catechism, and baptismal ceremony, seeking to replace the American civil religion of national providential destiny with a Black civil religion teaching that people of African ancestry had their own providential mission to embody universal ideals in an African homeland.[125]

Progressive Era Triumphalism

In the early twentieth century, white southerners reached an emotional and spiritual place where they felt the long search for a distinctive and distinguished southern civilization had been virtually achieved. A New England traveler in the region, Albert Bushnell Hart, noted in 1910 that within the South, one found "a fixed belief that the South is the most prosperous part of the country, which fits in with the conviction that it has long surpassed all other parts of the world in civilization, in military order, and in the power to rise out of the sufferings of a conquered people." As historian Joel Williamson concluded of this period, white southerners "were deciding that they were a specially spiritual people with a high sense of ideals and personal honor." History books written by southerners and published in the region appeared bearing the label "southern," a token of regional self-consciousness. The Progressive Era saw the expansion and consolidation of schools in the South, and students in those schools read about the glories of the past for white southerners.[126]

Women played an essential role as symbols of southern civilization itself through the mythic representations of the Southern Lady, but they also actively witnessed for preservation and extension of the hegemonic southern civilization that rested on the Confederate memory. The United Daughters of the Confederacy had formed in the 1890s and led the way in putting images of Confederate heroes in southern schools, sponsoring awards for students to write about the southern past, and supervising the erection of Confederate monuments throughout the region's small towns and big cities. Invocations of civilization occurred in the speeches, minutes of organizational meetings, and publications of these women's groups and other clubs. Evelyn E. Moffitt told a North Carolina Daughters of the American Revolution meeting in 1911 that "for two thousand years, woman had gradually moved upward in the scale of civilization and now she is at the zenith of her power." The discourse of civilization made white men drivers of civilization's progress, but southern women used the need for improving society to assert their gender's contribution to civilization in the South. Sallie Southall Cotton, for example, in a speech to a United Daughters of the Confederacy group during World War I, proclaimed that "civilization and religion are menaced and organized womanhood will strive to save both." Genealogy became an obsessive white southern tradition in this period, and elite southerners fawned over antiques that tied them to a glorious aesthetic tradition. "Tradition" itself now seemed synonymous with "southern" only a few decades after Thomas Nelson Page lamented the lack of tradition in the South. State governments began funding new state archives that collected historical materials that would soon be used to produce the books that burnished the heroic and honorable history of white southerners—and to ignore the stories of African Americans in the South. The southern memory became enshrined in this time period, a powerful mythic presentation that would work against changes in essential southern ways and, incidentally, empowered upper-class white elites to embody the honor and idealism of the distinctive and distinguished southern civilization.[127]

The seventeen-volume *Library of Southern Literature* (1907) was one of the earliest efforts to codify the idea of writing in the South that reflected a regional consciousness, and the twelve-volume reference work *The South in the Building of the Nation* (1909) used history to further a proud southern sense of

superiority in matters of the spirit. Even the solution to the South's racial problem was, said one contributor to the book, "primarily one of spirit." "Spirit as a
sovereign genius" presided over the social process that would produce "a more
excellent way" of harmonizing the interests of Black and white southerners.
The series of books emphasized, as the title suggested, the region's significance
to the nation. In the preface to volume 10, Samuel Chiles Mitchell stressed how
dynamic the early twentieth-century South was—a place undergoing "shuttle-
cock changes" seen in the expanding energies and ideals of the region—but he
argued that sectionalism was, in fact, "in retreat before a revival of loyalty to
the nation." Mitchell's writings in the volume stressed the achievement of the
long-sought unity of southern whites, a unity that grew out of the "common
experiences in struggle and suffering" that produced "a community of feeling
among all Southern people, a type of local patriotism that has stood the test
of self-sacrifice and war." The South had been "welded by sorrow." That unity
led to the reference work itself, which, Mitchell said, compared to such well-
defined places as one saw in "a description of Tuscany or a history of Holland."
But again, his interest was in viewing the South "as a national asset," conceiving
the book in relation to "a national spirit."[128]

In 1903, Edwin Alderman, one of the most progressive forces in southern
education, made the connection between the South, the nation, spirituality,
and civilization in an address to a joint meeting of the American Historical
Association and the American Economic Association. The nation needed, he
said, the "intense idealism of the South, stamped into its life by its sad, strange
history," because the region represented "a spiritual force needed to help combat vulgar strength and coarse power, and a vast indifference to fine issues."
He foresaw a coming industrialism as part of a maturing New South movement and realized that development would "change the idealism"; however, he
insisted the southern spirit was "too deep for destruction or submersion," reflecting the confidence that the South's history of suffering had strengthened it
to master industrialism's challenge to the South's idealism. Southern idealism,
moreover, represented "a benign national asset," so that whenever "southern
idealism takes fast hold of the idea of national unity, of national destiny, of
national hope, the great Republic that we all love and count it a glory to serve,
will feel its buoyant power as men in a valley feel the tonic of upper altitude."[129]

Preparing to deliver the Commemoration Day address at Johns Hopkins
University that same year, Alderman corresponded with some of the South's
leading intellectuals. In a typical letter, one to classics scholar Basil Gildersleeve, Alderman said he was "trying to study the contributions made by southern stock and southern civilization to our American character," the latter term

again suggesting concerns beyond region and the materialistic realm. What "distinctive contributions," he queried the southern intellectual elite, had been made to "American character out of southern life?" What in American life had been made richer "by reason of the life and civilization of its southern half?" Those intellectuals who responded mentioned many southern contributions to the nation, including statesmanship in the early nation, Jeffersonian democracy, Jacksonian democracy, concern for individual freedom, a virtuous planter elite, the spirit of romanticism, and brilliant oratory. Alderman decided to present a collective biography of southerners, including such predictable figures as Robert E. Lee, Andrew Jackson, and John C. Calhoun (in a stretch, he argued the South Carolinian had been important to the nation in presenting its greatest challenge to be overcome). Alderman also insisted that "the South did the nation a great service by perpetuating this spirit of romanticism," relating its value in his era to the importance of the South's "demonic body of energy and achievement" and "the tradition of largeness of life, and the ideal of the general mind kept sane and catholic to the core" to "an over-nourished, over-specialized, nervous democracy." In the end, his major point was that the South had "something high and precious and distinctive in manhood and leadership to contribute to American civilization."[130]

Evangelical Missions

In the early twentieth century, evangelical faith was a main source for the belief among white southerners that the South was a special spiritual place with a special destiny. This belief was a renewal of the southern civil religion that had flourished in the religion of the Lost Cause and more broadly in the faith in southern civilization's moral superiority. Southern churches were pillars of regional life, as important to understanding conceptualizations of southern civilization as Jim Crow segregation and rural-influenced values. Evangelical religion was a hegemonic force in southern life, and religion came to shape the institutions, values, and outlooks of southern places. In 1900, 3.5 million whites out of 6.2 million church members joined the three historically southern denominations—Baptist, Methodist, and Presbyterian. An interdenominational evangelical religion of whites, augmented by an equally evangelical consensus among African Americans in the South, dominated the region as in no other society in the Western world.[131]

"Evangelical faith has had its best chance in the world to show what it can do for a civilization," wrote South Carolina–born preacher, writer, and editor Victor I. Masters of the South in 1918. The South's material deprivation after the Civil War had, Masters claimed, promoted in the region "a great gentleness of spirit which was worth more than all the billions we have now gained," and he went on to compare the spiritual legacy of the South to its relative New South prosperity. Because of the earlier sufferings and the qualities of spirit it nurtured, the South had a "peculiar responsibility" to show its "moral and spiritual superiority." Embedding the South's religious tradition in a larger Manifest Destiny, Masters wrote of spreading the "Anglo-Saxon evangelical faith uniquely preserved in Southern religion." Race was especially important, as "no race ever had more passion for liberty than the Anglo-Saxon." In the United States the freedom of whites had found its fullest expression, and "in the South their blood has remained freest from mixture with other strains," he wrote, constructing southern civilization as a distinctive space for making whiteness. In the South, Masters wrote, the Anglo-Saxon's commitment to evangelical religion had been "less interfered with than in other sections," so he could see the South as the nation's, indeed the world's, last best hope for an evangelical empire of righteousness. The South's awareness of its sorrows, of the gallantry of its soldiers, of its mistakes and sufferings, "of its superiority to the worst calamities which came of it, of its ability to build a civilization out of ashes, makes the present South worth far more both to the nation and to itself." Failure to live up to this responsibility would "mean farewell to the best traditions of the South, and to the high and sacred destiny for which our noblest and best have prayed the South should be made fit." He thus linked "tradition" and the southern sense of mission.[132]

Many southern evangelical leaders were reluctant to become involved in social and political issues. Progressive Era reformers who came out of evangelical backgrounds did see certain issues that required them to go beyond individual conversion to provide legal restrictions on behavior, mostly on issues of personal vice, such as gambling, drinking, and dancing, and on Sabbath observance, to preserve the moral integrity of the southern civilization they affirmed. They also justified reforms to improve society as moral imperatives to assist those in need, including initiatives to improve public life through better schools, improved sanitation, elimination of child labor, and women's suffrage. Women reformers, like ministers, used the civilizationist ideology and the Confederate memory to justify their involvement in social reforms of a broad range. Some southern church women supported women's suffrage, for example, but others opposed it as violating conservative norms of southern women's behavior and bringing the threat of increased federal government involvement in the South, always a concern for its potential effect on race relations. Southern politicians braked any reformist instincts, though, when it came to gender issues. When the U.S. Congress approved the Nineteenth Amendment to the U.S. Constitution authorizing women's suffrage in January 1918, 90 of

101 Democratic votes against the measure came from the South. The Senate
narrowly rejected the amendment, and only seven senators from the former
Confederate states voted for it, men affirming their commitment to the South's
belief in a hierarchical society, despite the challenges to traditional gender roles
by many southern women. Once states later approved the amendment, only five
southern states ratified it. Contrast that with southern support for the Prohibition amendment restricting the sale of alcoholic beverages. Prohibition was the
great moral cause for southern religious people in this era, and the passage of
the federal amendment owed much to southern congressmen, state legislators,
organizations, and public opinion. Southern congressmen, in contrast to the
vote on the women's suffrage amendment, voted overwhelmingly for the prohibition amendment, and all thirteen southern states approved it.[133]

Woodrow Wilson

Woodrow Wilson symbolized the overlapping of regional, national, and international understandings of civilization in the South in the early twentieth
century. Born on the eve of the Civil War and leading the United States through
its involvement in the trauma of World War I, Wilson represented the merging
of a southern and national civil religion. Wilson was the son and grandson of
prominent leaders in the Presbyterian Church in the United States, and he grew
up in Presbyterian manses in Virginia, Georgia, and North Carolina. Some
of Wilson's earliest memories were of the Civil War, and his father was a proslavery advocate. Educated at Davidson College and the University of Virginia,
he married a southern woman and practiced law briefly in Atlanta, observing
firsthand the leadership of the New South. His higher education and teaching
career were at institutions with pronounced southern ties—Johns Hopkins and
Princeton. He said in an address on Robert E. Lee at the University of North
Carolina in 1909 that "it is all very well to talk of detachment of view, and of
the effort to be national in spirit and in purpose, but a boy never gets over his
boyhood, and never can change those subtle influences which have become a
part of him, that were bred in him when he was a child." He affirmed his southern sensibility in noting that "the only place in the country, the only place in
the world, where nothing has to be explained to me is the South." Wilson thus
embraced a southern identity and affirmed the early twentieth-century sense
of southern moral superiority as the defining feature of a regional civilization
in the South.[134]

Wilson believed that southern history was important because it revealed a
concern for principle. White southerners before the war had cherished, he said,

an older idea of the union as dominated by the preeminent rights of the states rather than centralized power. "Even a man who saw the end from the beginning should, in my conception as a Southerner, have voted for spending his people's blood and his own, rather than pursue the weak course of expediency." Despite defeat, the South had "retained her best asset, her self-respect."[135]

Wilson believed the Confederate defeat had been a blessing, but the legacy of it was a concern for principle, touching on the common theme of a superior southern civilization based in idealism. This good Presbyterian did not doubt that God had used southern defeat to push the nation forward, preparing to meet its destiny in a world war where civilization itself seemed at stake. Wilson spoke to a Confederate veterans reunion in 1917, during the war, a symbolic moment that witnessed the blending of regional and national elements in a wartime setting that recalled a previous American conflagration. Wilson told the Civil War veterans that their region was "part of a nation united, powerful, great in spirit and in purpose." The United States was now "an instrument in the hands of God to see that liberty is made secure for mankind." Confederate veterans, one repository of the southern civil religion and regional identity, enthusiastically endorsed Wilson and this new crusade for civilization.[136]

Wilson saw himself as positioned to promote nationalism over southern sectionalism, and his election to the presidency brought many southern political figures into national prominence. Five of his cabinet members were from the South, and his closest adviser, Col. Edward M. House, was a Texan. Senators and representatives from the South now dominated Congress, and they sent unprecedented federal government funding into the South, despite their rhetoric of states' rights. They generally supported Wilson's agenda of banking and currency reform and antitrust laws. Southern leaders also extended segregation to the nation's capital, requiring racial segregation on public transportation facilities and opposing new appointments of African Americans to federal jobs. Southern congressmen supported Wilson's war measures that dramatically increased the power and reach of the federal government, and they vigorously supported his ill-fated ratification of the League of Nations. Southern political influence on a national scale only furthered white southerners' belief in the superiority of their civilization, which they saw now affecting the nation for the better.[137]

———————

"Civilization" was a term that, by the end of the nineteenth century, observers had long been using to identify the highest social, political, economic, and cultural development, with Europe the benchmark and such marginal geographical spaces as the American South the outliers from it. The post-Reconstruction South refashioned itself after the turbulent years of Civil War devastation and Reconstruction struggles among white southerners, African Americans, and nonsouthern whites. The ideologies of the Lost Cause/Old South and the New South framed thinking about a southern civilization, and the Populist reformers championed a counternarrative of southern civilization that almost changed history. The turn of the twentieth century saw white southerners firmly in control of defining and performing southern civilization as a white-dominated, future-looking but past-obsessed, and openly religious civilization. The discourse of civilization achieved an unprecedented prominence and influence at that time, tied in with the imperialism of Western Europe and the United States, which was justified in civilization's name.

The concepts of "the South" and "civilization" interconnected often, whether in assertions of the region's distinctive and distinguished civilization or as the problem South of critics, north and south. African Americans generally were a part of white visions of southern civilization. Radical racists saw only marginal roles for them, but paternalist racists saw them as useful in the South's Christian and capitalist society, which needed people of faith and people to work. African Americans dismissed the patriotic appeals of a Jim Crow southern civilization, with Ida B. Wells leading the way in reimagining for the British exemplars of civilization a white South of savages. African American leaders believed in civilizing missions to the African American masses, whether it was Booker T. Washington's materialistic "Negro civilization" that built institutions and values within a segregated society or W. E. B. Du Bois's understanding of the need for spiritual striving by the oppressed blacks in the South.

The South's assertion in the early twentieth century of a superior regional civilization grew out of its experiences in the decades after the Civil War. Despite the realistic critiques of Black and white intellectuals, white southerners came to believe that the sufferings of wartime defeat, the travails of racial conflict and rural dysfunction, and pervasive evangelical religious values had created the South as a redemptive community in history. The southern civil religion had been refurbished. With the decline of the wartime generation, the Lost Cause as a social movement honoring Confederate veterans had declined, but advocates of seeing the South's history and future in providential terms saw the region now as a national spiritual asset. Randolph McKim portrayed World War I as a war for civilization, and he could easily fit his Confederate heritage into that world-endangered civilization. That appeal was the end product of two generations of reflections on southern destiny—now seen as part of a nation that welcomed its white-dominated civilization as part of American civilization. The results of World War I nonetheless would bring a new critical focus to the South in terms of its civilization and provide the context for the reassertion of an agrarian-based, tradition-oriented southern way of life that would highlight newly rediscovered conceptions of southern civilization. The term "southern way of life" would begin in the 1920s to take center stage in ponderings of the U.S. South's society and role in history.

African American painter Romare Bearden paid homage to blues singer Bessie Smith in *Empress of the Blues*. The years from World War I to World War II witnessed a southern cultural renaissance that grew out of the customs and sensibilities associated with the southern way of life. Smithsonian American Art Museum, Washington, D.C. / Art Resource, New York. © 2022 Romare Bearden Foundation / Licensed by VAGA at Artists Rights Society (ARS), NY.

PART II

SOUTHERN WAY OF LIFE

I N THE THIRD DECADE of the twentieth century, commentators began to use the phrase "way of life" as a descriptor for societies that had become self-conscious in the face of social changes and challenges to their inherited identities, including the American South. Reference to an American way of life, for example, dates from the early 1930s, a time of crisis for American capitalism and threats from such new ideologies as communism and fascism, causing a reexamination of democratic beliefs. References to the South in terms of civilization persisted, but "way of life" gradually replaced them in thinking of a collective regional consciousness.

As elsewhere throughout the Western world, World War I was a watershed in the decline of civilizationist thinking, with the bloodshed and disillusionment of the war and its aftermath leading to questioning of Victorian-era certainties in the 1920s. Marxism revealed the high-sounding economic ideals of capitalism were a cover for economic injustices, Freudianism unmasked the hidden psychology whose sometimes dark instincts drove human behavior, biblical high criticism questioned the inspired and factually infallible Christian scripture, and Einstein's theory of relativity disproved Victorian claims of the coherence and solidity of culture.

Reliance on the language of way of life grew most directly, though, out of the emergence of cultural anthropology as a science in the early twentieth century. It showed that culture was a set of traits and practices that people created to adapt to the environments in which they lived. Earlier spiritual claims of culture lost influence. Cultural theory now dismissed previous belief in the racial basis of culture, with a new interest in the cultures that all societies possessed without using any racial hierarchy in assessing them.

In comparing themselves with other civilizations, some historical, others contemporaneous, southerners embraced foundational ideas of savagery and barbarism. Commentators who referred to the southern way of life in the twentieth century typically assumed that the South was a self-sufficient entity, marked by such concerns as agrarianism, white supremacy, leisure, manners, and spirituality. The agrarian writers who produced *I'll Take My Stand: The*

South and the Agrarian Tradition (1930) were among the first to use the phrase and concept extensively. They were modernist writers, poets, historians, and others who rejected the stale verities of the region's Lost Cause and its New South materialism, but most fundamentally, they dismissed the industrial and commercial values they identified as the American way of life. They overlooked the decline in southern rural life to assert a timeless ideal of agrarian living, one with spiritual qualities. They also egregiously ignored race as a category in southern life, with a focus on tradition that would endure in conservative thought.

A range of further influences shaped ideas about the southern way of life in the 1930s and 1940s: liberal reformism associated with the New Deal; a new cultural criticism that skewered the region's shortcomings; the importance of journalists, academics, and creative writers in revealing a suffering South the Agrarians ignored; a binary of racial thought between rising white racism and a cautious interracialism; and conflicting progressive, moderate, and conservative political reactions. This section of the book dwells on key intellectuals whose life stories and thinking illustrated the complexities of a region on the cusp of fundamental change. World War II was a crystallizing factor in pushing the region toward national and global worlds that would soon undermine the backward-looking regional perspective but not without determined opposition from traditionalists.

In the 1950s and 1960s, forces of progress and reaction clashed powerfully. Passionate defenders of white supremacy regularly used "the southern way of life" in support of their segregationist cause. The Supreme Court's *Brown v. Board of Education* decision (1954) helped spur civil rights activists, who became the driving forces of social change by the late 1950s. Massive resistance described political efforts to mobilize white commitment to white supremacy, seen in the Dixiecrat movement in 1948, the massive resistance movement in the late 1950s, the movement of conservative Democrats into the Republican party in the 1960s, and George Wallace's politics of white rage.

This era also reveals the intellectual sources of civil rights protest and critique of Jim Crow society. Readers will see at the end of this section how civil religion, both American and southern, offered spiritual sanction to both protesters and resisters, and they will glimpse the development of a biracial southern mythology that saw Black-white interaction as a source of possible national redemption. White reformers were an important part of the civil rights story, and they appear in the narrative as well. As always, the story of the southern way of life cannot be understood without consideration of national images of the region, as it struggled to adjust to a new social, political, and cultural order.

CHAPTER THREE

Agrarian Way

Regional Consciousness and
Southern Tradition

WORLD WAR I was a culmination of the turn-of-the-century discourse of civilization; disillusionment with its promise became a prominent postwar theme in Western society. But the era's intellectual and cultural changes promoted new concepts and frameworks to consider the broad meaning of national and international experiences. In the American South, writers associated with Vanderbilt University produced a seminal text on the region, *I'll Take My Stand*, in 1930, that advanced for the first time a concept of the southern way of life. Their image of the southern way came at a time when the confrontation between tradition and modernity seemed especially urgent in the region. The Vanderbilt writers, dubbed the Agrarians, saw the South as the last best hope to preserve the antique values of Western civilization.

H. L. Mencken would have none of it. He was the South's chief nemesis in the early twentieth century. Mencken's essay "The Sahara of the Bozart" first appeared in a New York newspaper in 1917, but it resonated throughout the 1920s as a sharp attack on the white South's pretensions. Growing up in Baltimore and knowing genteel Virginians, Mencken fancied himself an admirer of the best of the older South, which he praised for its high achievements. "It was a civilization of manifold excellences—perhaps the best that the Western Hemisphere had ever seen—undoubtedly the best that these States have ever seen." Antebellum southerners gave attention to "the art of living" and had the "vague thing that we call culture." But looking at the twentieth-century South, Mencken insisted, "gives one the creeps." Calling up an old stereotype, he noted that "the poor white trash are now in the saddle," with the region "fallen to the bombastic and trivialities of the camp-meeting and the stump." He saw a decline of the "best blood" of the Old South and the rise of the poor whites "with some of the worst blood of western Europe" flowing in their veins. Virginia was "the most civilized of the Southern states," but he saw its "mind" as simplistic and unimportant. Georgia, meanwhile, had "a culture that, at bottom, is but little removed from savagery." Mencken could not contain his disdain of the region's aspirations, noting that "it would be impossible in all history to match so complete a drying up of a civilization." He positioned the South's calamity globally by repeatedly making comparisons with other supposedly backward places. The South "is an awe inspiring blank—a brother to Portugal, Serbia, and Albania." Contemplating "so vast a vacuity" led him to write that "one thinks of the interstellar spaces" to find something comparable to the South.[1]

Having launched this celestial critique, Mencken came back down to earth in his specific indictment. He cataloged the region's civilization deficit in opera houses, theaters, prose writers "who can actually write," critics, musical composers, painters, sculptors, architects, theologians, historians, and scientists. The South of his time, Mencken wrote, rested on "the philistinism of the new type of town-boomer Southerner," who is indifferent to civilized ideals. He saw the North as "also stupid and obnoxious," but only in the South did one see such a depressing lack of civilized gestures and aspirations, "the almost pathological estrangement from everything that makes for a civilized culture."[2]

Mencken's diatribe symbolized the sharp departure from the previous north-south embrace of sectional reconciliation. The South had been an important part of early twentieth-century thinking about civilization, where race was prominent in a way that made the South's Jim Crow fit in well with the broader Western imperial world. But American culture in the decade after Mencken's essay produced a raft of critical works that fed the revitalization of a "benighted South" image that went back to the colonial era. Even more striking was the emergence of homegrown southern critics such as Gerald Johnson, a North Carolina protégé of Mencken's who skewered his own region for its racial violence, illiteracy, political demagoguery, and general backwardness.[3]

Crisis in Civilization

Mencken's essay appeared during World War I, which stands as a landmark in attitudes toward civilization throughout the Western world. The war's bloodshed and a general disillusionment with idealism fed the modern world's skepticism, encouraged along by the ideas of Darwin, Freud, and soon Einstein. The war eroded belief in inevitable progress, material and moral. French writer Paul Valery touched a broad Western concern when he wrote in 1919, "We modern civilizations have learned to recognize that we are mortal" and that "a civilization is as fragile as life."[4]

The agrarian writers of *I'll Take My Stand* feared industrial civilization's effects in the South, but they were also part of such broader concerns as Valery's after World War I. Many Americans were aware in the 1920s of a crisis in civilization. Warren Susman concludes that "the great fear that runs through much of the writing of the 1920s and 1930s is whether any great industrial and democratic mass society can maintain a significant level of civilization, and whether mass education and mass communication will allow any civilization to survive." One response was to popularize knowledge of civilization's achievements, with *Reader's Digest*, the Book of the Month Club, and numerous outlines of Western history and philosophy appearing among middlebrow people. Americans in the 1920s, including southerners, were aware they lived in a new age through the pervasiveness of such modern media as radio and motion pictures. But the Agrarians would come to echo philosopher Paul Arthur Schilpp's serious questions about the value of what the new media communicated—"stocks and bonds, football scores, World Series results, jazz music, and bedtime stories."[5]

To address the sense of crisis in civilization, hundreds of magazine and newspaper stories appeared, as well as books with such titles as *Whither Mankind: A Panorama of Modern Civilization* and *Toward Civilization: Recent Gains in American Civilization*. The editors of one such volume, *Sex in Civilization* (1929), suggested that the term "civilization" had once represented progress, but now the fear was that true human advancement as identified with civilization could only occur with the destruction of the old civilization that had led to world war. Like many other writers of the 1920s, the editors saw the solution to the threat through science, specifically the techniques of human psychology that could unveil the individual malaise that beset modern times. The debate over civilization in the 1920s, the decade when the Agrarians conceived their manifesto defending the southern way of life, came out of a new recognition among many Americans that collective human identities were "no longer constructed around the antagonisms between civilization and barbarism, but around the concept of a plurality of *civilizations*." New developments in archaeology, anthropology, philology, Oriental studies, and sociology suggested the West had no monopoly on civilization, with the war leading many observers to question whether European civilization was any more admirable or as unified as previously thought and to incline them to see it as one civilization among many. In 1918 Frederick J. Teggart deplored "that inevitable human propensity to classify all those who are in any way unlike ourselves, or who merely lie outside our own groups, as 'fiends,' 'aliens,' and 'barbarians.'" He saw an urgent need to understand how "civilizations have arisen and decayed, to be followed by other *civilizations*."[6]

German historian Oswald Spengler's *The Decline of the West* (1918, 1922) expressed a pessimistic take on civilization, a dark view that represented modernism's movement away from Victorian certainties and confidence in progress, and he influenced writers who asserted that agrarianism was the southern way of life. Spengler's central thesis was that civilizations were like living organisms, which were born, grew up, flourished, and then decayed and died. He saw the most creative phase of societies being the formative period of collective identities when they developed cultures. The second, declining period he called civilization. "The Culture suddenly hardens, it mortifies, its blood congeals, its force breaks down, and it becomes *civilization*." So civilization in this understanding was not a descriptor of a high point of collective achievement, or even just a distinctive embodiment of a people, but the fulfillment and finale of a culture. The broader point in the postwar period was the need to move beyond the parochial European story to a world historical perspective. Spengler outlined six culture-civilizations: Egyptian, Indian, classical, Chinese, Arabian, and Western.[7]

Several of the Agrarians read and embraced aspects of Spengler's thought. John Crowe Ransom noted in 1926 that Spengler reinforced his "idea that provincial life is the best." In the same year, Allen Tate, reviewing the first volume of Spengler's book, pointed out favorably that his philosophy "is Physiognomic (organic) as opposed to Systematic (mathematical)," so it reflected the centrality of organic thought to *I'll Take My Stand*. Inherent in Spengler's organism is "growth and decay," but the nature of organism "is that it unfolds according to its inherent properties, which are not *laws* but *forms*"—words that illustrated the importance of order to this future Agrarian's thought.[8]

The Agrarians were one of many groups and individuals struggling in the 1920s with dramatically different meanings of civilization. Ernest Elmo Calkins wrote of "Business the Civilizer," while socialist leader Eugene V. Debs saw socialism's role as to "civilize civilization." Marcus Garvey promoted a specifically African civilization that included Black Americans, while Lothrop Stoddard's *The Revolt against Civilization* was a white supremacist's warning against the appeal of the primitive in this new questioning of Western civilization. Harold Stearns's anthology *Civilization in the United States* (1922) saw itself as a "critical examination of our civilization . . . in order to do our share in making a real civilization possible." Stearns lamented that Americans had "no heritages and traditions to which to cling," a point the Agrarians reinforced in comparing southern agrarian society, replete with traditions, to the general American lack of heritage. Nonetheless, the 1920s marked a watershed in Americans coming to see themselves as evolving into the world's preeminent exemplar of Western civilization. One response to the crisis of Western civilization appeared in the title of Charles and Mary Beard's *The Rise of American Civilization* (1927). They suggested that "the history of a civilization may symbolize a certain coming to maturity in that civilization itself," and they saw

American civilization as having reached that maturity. The Agrarians fundamentally rejected the Beards' confidence in a mature American civilization,
characterizing it as a "pioneering" one that explicitly had never matured. The
Agrarians embraced, on the other hand, another leading book about American
civilization, James Truslow Adams's *Our Business Civilization: Some Aspects of
American Culture* (1929), which noted that "if the fundamental idea underlying
our civilization . . . is to become that of a business profit, it is inevitable that we
shall decline in the scale of what has hitherto been considered civilization as
contrasted with barbarism in the Greek sense."[9]

Richmond newspaper editor and award-winning biographer Douglas Southall Freeman noticed a crisis of confidence in the United States as a result of the
war, and he feared the South was coming to share in a general decline in spiritual and moral values. The growth of cities, industrialization, consumerism,
and mass culture all, indeed, pushed the South in the 1920s closer to modernity
and challenged the belief in traditionalism that the generation before the war
had come to see as having particular importance in the South. In the face of
changes, Freeman asserted in a 1924 *Nation* article that Virginia should be a
model for managing change through its "social gentleness, old ideas of home life
and religion," which could have "wholesome influences" on the entire nation.
Freeman's confidence in the South's moral and spiritual superiority reflected
the lessons of the Lost Cause, with southern spokesmen for two generations
before Freeman's time claiming that the South's defeat in the Civil War and
subsequent suffering had resulted in a spiritual superiority that made southern
civilization a national resource. No evidence suggests that Mencken and Freeman ever met, though the former would probably have admired the Virginian
as an anachronistic symbol of the best South. The context for their reflections
on the South would change rapidly in the two decades after they wrote, and
the interwar years would see the appearance of the term "southern way of life,"
with competing meanings for it. The term "civilization" would continue to be
used to talk about a regional society working out evolving understandings of
its relationship to American civilization and Western civilization.[10]

The Agrarians from the Lost Cause to the Modern Way

The writers who became the Vanderbilt Agrarians represented a conservative
effort to assert boldly a traditional vision of the region's culture that would be
relevant in a modernizing society that was generating a sense of crisis about
civilization. Middle-class white male southerners, mostly townsmen and
mostly from the hill country yeoman South, had grown up at a particular time
in southern history, hearing stories of the Civil War and noble Confederate

ancestors from respected elder family members. The world that produced the Agrarians was suffused not only with a Lost Cause outlook but also with a New South ideology that embraced material progress, an increasing regional reconciliation, southern racial separatism, and even violence. The 1920s were a time of transition, though, with increased regional prosperity, the growth of modernist ideas and modernizing influences on society, and escalating external and internal criticisms of southern ways. The perception of increasing industrialization would be especially important to the Agrarians, who would offer a new sharp focus on the concept of a southern way that was agrarian in values. One of the Agrarians, Robert Penn Warren, observed that "after 1918, the modern industrial world, with its good and bad, hit the South" and produced a cultural shock to a more or less closed and static society. He noted that it led to "all sorts of ferments" as southerners had "to 'relive,' redefine life." Other southern observers expressed concern over the growing materialism of southern life as well. Thomas Wolfe reported that the emergence of Asheville, his hometown, as a tourist center had brought increased prosperity to his family and community, but he doubted that "more Ford automobiles" and "more Rotary Clubs" necessarily meant progress. He dismissed the idea that "we are necessarily four times as civilized as our grandfathers because we go four times as fast in our automobiles."[11]

The agrarian writers of *I'll Take My Stand* have been provocative and controversial, then and now. Coming from privileged backgrounds, they presumed to speak for a South they believed to be endangered. They guarded "what they considered to be their exclusive rights to narratives of the southern past." Michael Kreyling argues that they launched "a willed campaign on the part of one elite to establish and control 'the South' in a period of intense cultural maneuvering" as they created a "fabricated South as the one and only real thing." They used their cultural power to diminish African American stories of the South, which were far different from theirs.[12]

The long conceptual context of this study makes clear that the Agrarians fit easily into older attempts to solidify the white southern identity, but the rejection of their immediate forebears was crucial to their significance as modern, twentieth-century defenders of southern civilization. The Agrarians would explore a southern way that rested in the conservative values they associated with earlier Western civilization and that they saw as distinct from the American way they identified as industrial society. But their real polemical targets were white southerners—both those associated with the moonlight-and-magnolias Old South and those driven by optimistic New South materialist values. When the Agrarians wrote, those groups were the ones with real power, and the Agrarians never really changed that fact. To be sure, they did gain considerable

authority, especially those Agrarians who became New Critics, in controlling
the study and teaching of southern literature. But their broader power in southern culture seems limited indeed, as their advocacy of agrarianism was more
or less dead on arrival in the Depression-era South and they had little impact
on the emerging group of writers in the region who would win acclaim in national circles. Before they became the Agrarians, many of these intellectuals
were poets identified as the Fugitives, viewing themselves as part of modernist
literature and disclaiming what had become a sentimentalized Lost Cause ideology best represented by the bad poetry of the women of the United Daughters
of the Confederacy. In the first issue of the *Fugitive*, John Crowe Ransom wrote
that the Fugitive "flees from nothing faster than from the high-caste Brahmins
of the Old South." The Fugitives dismissed the literature celebrating the Confederacy as romanticized, feminized, downright exploitive of the South, and
intended for northern audiences feasting on southern nostalgia. Instead, they
saw moral issues as central to their time of transition in the South. They were
still practitioners of the southern civil religion, who fashioned "an image of the
South as the good society, which could provide a moral if not always a concrete
social and political alternative to the modern world." To take the South seriously, they had to debunk the romanticized South that had defined southern
tradition to Thomas Nelson Page and others in the post-Reconstruction South.
Hoop-skirted southern belles, chivalric southern gentlemen, and "happy dar-
kies" loyally devoted to their "masters and mistresses" defined that South.[13]

If the Old South and the Lost Cause represented one target for the Agrarians, the New South ideology represented an even more important target. "Our
fight is for survival: and it's got to be waged, not so much against the Yankees
as against the exponents of the New South," wrote John Crowe Ransom. In the
1920s the promotion of southern industry took on aspects of a spiritual movement—a new expression of the civil religion, the idea of redemptive industry.
One speaker at a southern textile conference described industry as "a divine
institution" and the pioneers of southern industry as prophets of God. Broadus
Mitchell wrote that "industrialism was the instrument of Southern salvation."
New South advocates by the 1920s saw themselves as progressives who believed
the South's essential problems were economic, and "business progressivism"
became the term in the 1920s for conservative efforts to use state governments
to improve the South's infrastructure to promote economic development.[14]

Changing values came with industrialism, but as in the late nineteenth
century, the New South creed still affirmed southern traditionalism. Edwin
Mims was a genteel progressive counterpoint to the agrarian advocacy of a
rural southern way of life, as he embraced reforms in a changing South that he
thought could still hold on to such values as honor and faith. He insisted that

Cartoon of Donald Davidson, Allen Tate, and John Crowe Ransom on the cover of the Vanderbilt University humor magazine, 1933. Special Collections and University Archives, Jean and Alexander Heard Libraries, Vanderbilt University.

white southerners were more self-critical by the 1920s than they had been previously, and *The Advancing South* (1926) was an optimistic book, one which the
Agrarians dismissed as an outdated, rosy New South perspective. Written in
the aftermath of the Scopes trial and its ridicule of white southerners, the book
argued for southern progress. Mims accepted that problems such as lynching
and poverty were real, but he insisted the region was well along the path of industrial growth, educational improvements, and artistic accomplishments. He
was also an Evangelical and appreciated the South's religiosity; he advocated
for Black rights though not social equality. Mims offered a model for southern
advancement in the 1920s, but the Agrarians lampooned his approach. They
were tied to him, though, because he was chair of the English department at
Vanderbilt University at a time when many of them taught there. He was an
institution builder, talking with governors and mayors, dining with Nashville's
business elites, and giving talks to the Rotary Clubs that the Agrarians mocked.
Mims was a public intellectual who influenced public policy, while the Agrarians were alienated intellectuals using modern literary ways to try to protect the
southern culture they saw threatened.[15]

Planning the Manifesto

The key early figures in the planning stages of the Agrarian manifesto—John
Crowe Ransom, Donald Davidson, and Allen Tate—had in the early 1920s
shown varying degrees of interest in southern matters. Although some historians dispute it, the Scopes trial in the summer of 1925 likely caused them to
turn to the South as a subject for their aspirations to indict modern civilization. Fundamentalism was more an American than a southern phenomenon
in the 1920s, as leading southern denominations were already so orthodox that
modern theology was only a limited target for reforming fundamentalists in
the region. However, the teaching of evolution in schools did engage southern
fundamentalists, and the Scopes trial seemed to provide evidence to the national culture of the South's irredeemable backward religious life. Mencken
characterized religion in the South as "a cesspool of Baptists" and "a miasma of
Methodists," and he coined the term "Bible Belt" and gleefully lampooned its
imagery. The Agrarians were intellectuals who had distanced themselves from
evangelical experiential emotionalism, but they endorsed fundamentalism's
orthodoxy. In any event, they recognized the trial as an assertion of science as
the essential source of modern intellectual authority, a challenge to Protestant
religion associated with the South and an invasion of outside interference, especially through the role of the media in ridiculing the region. Davidson wrote
in 1957 that the trial "broke in on the literary concerns" of writers like himself

"like a midnight alarm." He said they "began to remember and haul up for consideration the assumptions that as members of the Fugitive Group, we had not bothered to examine." One of the assumptions they began to examine was that "the South still possessed at least the remnants, maybe more than the remnants, of a traditional, believing society." In March 1926 Davidson agreed with Tate and Ransom on the idea of a symposium on southern matters. Around the same time, Tate announced he had found "his Southern spirit," a revealing term for the spiritual dimension of "the southern way."[16]

On June 25, 1927, Ransom wrote Tate "about our joint Southernism." He observed the many "men of my acquaintance born and bred in the South who go North and cannot bring themselves to surrender to an alien mode of life." That sentiment suggested to him "something ineradicable in Southern culture." He also made a connection with the role of writers in Italy in stimulating "a genuine and powerful revival of Italianism (in a most advanced aesthetic sense) among the younger generations of Italians," and he asked, "Why can't we?" In the flush of enthusiasm, Ransom insisted that people at Vanderbilt were "just waiting to be shown what their cause is." The reference to aesthetics foretold a key Ransom contribution to the movement's attempt to define a southern way. In the late 1920s, Ransom published "The South Defends Its Heritage" and "The South—Old or New?," both of which contained ideas Ransom later developed in *I'll Take My Stand*. In the latter essay, Ransom noted that the South's key contribution to the nation might be to show "how an American community can really master the spirit of modern industrialism rather than capitulating to it." A sentiment drawn from the early twentieth-century rhetoric of the Lost Cause, it offered a deeper ideological view than the popular sentimentalism of the Lost Cause of the 1920s. In these articles, Ransom put forward "his model of the good life—a society aristocratic in its social relations and political leadership, traditional in its culture, and orthodox in its religion." Agrarian versions of the civil religion's good society would rest in European qualities of the eighteenth century, shared in modern times only by what Paul Conkin said were the "antique gentry in twentieth-century Britain."[17]

Davidson's response to the Scopes trial appeared in "The First Fruits of Dayton" in June 1928. He defended fundamentalists for placing "morally serious roadblocks to the new age, asking how far science, which serves human physical needs, should also determine one's philosophy." Davidson's use of the term "morally serious roadblocks" presaged the Agrarians' belief that moral concerns rested at the heart of the southern way. He feared the businessmen and boosters of local chambers of commerce who he worried would have the last word on the South's future. The Rotary Club indeed became a symbol in the emerging southern industrial civilization. The South should avoid business progress, Davidson insisted, and such accompanying problems as wage slavery, strikes, labor agitators, grafts, and monopolies, flashing back to the antebellum South's proslavery critique of northern free society.[18]

Tate brought the enthusiasm of a new convert in the last years of the 1920s by proposing in 1929 "a society or an academy of *positive* reactionaries" and the publication of a magazine or newspaper to advocate their ideas. Tate proposed a list of topics for the symposium. The first was "The Philosophy of Provincialism" but the next was—in the first reference in agrarian writing to the term—"The Southern Way of Life," nominating novelist Stark Young to write it "if he can be prevented from including anecdotes of his grandmother." Tate recognized here that the agrarian project needed a level of abstraction that might conflict with southern culture's storytelling specificities. He believed the volume had to address concerns broader than the South.[19]

The manifesto lacked unity in many ways, including discussions over a title leading up to publication. Tate disliked the proposed title because it pointed to a sectional patriotism that would limit the group's aspiration to address broad concerns in Western society. So, from early on, Tate at least saw the "southern way" as relevant to these broader interests. Davidson and Ransom favored the title. In a joint letter to the group in September 1930, they noted that the title united "Southernism with agrarianism, on grounds both historical and philosophical. The title-phrase is strong, clear, homely, and mostly Anglo-Saxon from the point of view of language and historically apt." The subtitle, "The South and the Agrarian Tradition," "could not possibly occur to a frenzied and uncritical patriot." Tate observed that "my melancholy is profound" in contemplating the title, which he felt limited the group's efforts to simply an agrarian revival and "reduces our real aims to nonsense." He feared people would think they really just wanted to be farmers.[20]

The emerging Agrarians of the late 1920s turned to the southern past, especially the Civil War, for inspiration. Davidson had heard stories of the heroic Confederates and the postwar federal occupation and supposed Black rule from his live-in grandmother, and that southern memory now stoked his writing. He abandoned an interest in poems on classical Greek and Roman times to explore regional history in his epic poem "The Tall Men" about Tennessee's frontier heritage. Tate, meanwhile, wrote a biography of Stonewall Jackson, inspiring him to become a neo-Confederate. Soon he was challenging a critic to a duel. His 1928 biography of Jefferson Davis further cemented his obsession with the sectional crisis, and he portrayed the North's brutality toward the South. Recognizing in the biography that the antebellum South had been a class society, he admired its embrace of orthodox Christianity and portrayed "a civilization based on Agrarian class rule, in the European sense." Tate saw the North in his age as reflecting a modern European, industrialized society, while the South still embodied an older Europe, closer to feudal Europe than to modern Europe.

Tate wrote to Davidson in 1929 that the planned symposium should rest "less upon the actual Old South than upon its prototype—the historical, social, and religious scheme of Europe." He added that the southern Agrarians had to be "the last Europeans—there being no Europeans in Europe at present." An odd conclusion, perhaps, but it saw him recognizing the category was a construct. Tate seemingly expressed an optimism about the possibility of replicating the prototype, but his words "the last Europeans" pointed to a melancholy sense of the potential end of civilized society associated with older European ideas of civilization in the time of twentieth-century crisis.[21]

I'll Take My Stand

John Crowe Ransom was the key figure in conceptualizing the "southern way of life" for the symposium. He was primarily responsible for writing the introduction, "A Statement of Principles," which came to represent the Agrarians' creed. By early 1930 he had outlined seventeen articles, adopting the structure of a church-like confession. He eventually abandoned the numbers, but he kept the content in the final draft, stating that he and his fellow adherents "all tend to support a Southern way of life against what may be called the American or prevailing way," and the contributors "agree that the best terms in which to represent the distinction are contained in the phrase Agrarian *versus* Industrial." This passage drew attention to the phrase "American way," which appeared in the same era, as Americans north and south increasingly defined ideological constructs in the face of the post–World War I sense of cultural crisis in the Western world that had resulted in new prominence for such European constructs as communism, socialism, and fascism.[22]

Later in the introductory essay, Ransom used a related term, "Americanism." He talked of it in terms of the importance of the "Cult of Science," which he labeled "an Americanism, which looks innocent and disinterested enough, but really is neither." Science took on particularly disturbing meanings in industrial society, with society investing its economic assets in the applied sciences. "Americanism," in general, had been used since the nineteenth century to suggest distinctive American traits and also loyalty to such ideals as democracy, equality, opportunity, freedom of speech, and progress. Ransom engaged only the latter in his version of Americanism, which grew out of earlier, Progressive Era meanings and was best symbolized by Fordism, or the industrial assembly line of production. The term "American way of life" would be a contested one from the Depression through the Cold War, with two major values associated with it: democracy and free enterprise business. The Agrarians wrote before these debates, though, and identified the term with "Americanism," and it became the foil for their concept of a southern way. The opening statement pointed out such evils of industrialism as "overproduction, unemployment, and a growing inequality of wealth," but industrialism's answer to solving these problems was more industrialism.[23]

Ransom evoked sectional anxieties going back to the Civil War and insisted that the Agrarians were fighting "a foreign invasion on Southern soil, which is capable of doing more devastation than was wrought when Sherman marched to the sea," as he deployed the white South's favorite symbol of Yankee evil. The opening creed identified industrialism with the centralization of not only economic power but government power. It claimed that "the true Sovietists or Communists . . . are the Industrialists themselves," who would use the government to set up an "economic super-organization, which in turn would become the government." Ransom saw communism as a menace but saw it as one growing out of "the blind drift of our industrial development," which would lead to the nation having the same economic system that violence had brought to Russia. Industrialism would lead inevitably to communism. An economic superorganization would emerge, taking power over the federal government. Ransom reflected a shared agrarian belief in 1930 that unrestrained industrial capitalism was the greatest threat to liberties in the modern United States.[24]

Ransom noted in the opening creed that the South had long been a minority region within the nation, with its "own kind of life." In recent times, New South business ideology had challenged that kind of life, he said, and more disturbing was that younger white southerners seemed removed from it. The opening agrarian creed showed, however, a willingness to move beyond region, as the group hoped to be a national movement. "Proper living" was a matter of mind and will, and it did "not depend on the local climate or geography" and was not really just southern. The southern anchoring to the ideology was nonetheless essential to the symposium being more than an abstract, theoretical statement.[25]

The creed paid considerable attention to matters of labor, religion, and the arts, and in each case, terms with spiritual meanings appeared. Labor appeared first in the context of industrialism's stress on consumption as the end that justified the evils of modern industrial work. Factory production provided more goods to consume and more time to do so, but the pace of labor was so demanding that leisure became frantic. Modern people had lost "a sense of vocation," a resonant term that suggested moderns had strayed from the sense of religious-based calling that Ransom associated with agrarianism. Religion was another key concept, and the creed defined it as submission to a God-created natural order. The industrial American way of cities and manufactured commodities had lost "the sense of nature as something mysterious and contingent." The arts depended, "like religion, on a right attitude to nature; and in particular on a free and disinterested observation of nature that occurs only in leisure." The amenities of life were prominent in the creed, listed as "manners, conversation, hospitality, sympathy, family life, romantic love—in the social exchanges which reveal and develop sensibility in human affairs"—a litany for a mannered southern way of life. These suffered under a commercial civilization, which tried to deal with their lack by funding cultural and educational efforts to "cure the poverty of the contemporary spirit." Contemporary college students in industrial-dominated societies nonetheless were in a false way of life and could not make more than "an inconsequential acquaintance with the arts and humanities transmitted to them."[26]

Most of the opening creed critically analyzed the industrial American way, but it also advocated the southern way as a variation of humanism representing the best way of life. The virtue of this southern humanism was that it was "not an abstract system, but a culture, the whole way in which we live, act, think, and feel." In discussing humanism, the creed became more specific about the Agrarians' understanding of the nature of the southern way of life. Ransom stressed that the region possessed a true humanism that had concrete manifestations "rooted in the agrarian life of the older South and of other parts of the country that shared in such a tradition." The creed distinguished itself from the era's humanist movement, identified with Irving Babbitt, by saying true humanism was "not an abstract moral 'check' derived from the classics." Instead, it rested in "the way of life itself—in its tables, chairs, portraits, festivals, laws, marriage customs." His contemporaries could not recover "our native humanism" by establishing standards of taste that might question artistic activities without being critical enough "to question the social and economic life which is their ground." Although aesthetics would be important to *I'll Take My Stand*, the Agrarians' social and economic grounding reflected broader social and cultural aspirations that encouraged them to think of their ideas as the basis for a reformist social movement.[27]

The creed spent relatively little time discussing agrarianism itself but did see an agrarian society as "one in which agriculture is the leading vocation, whether for wealth, for pleasure, or for prestige." The key issue was labor, one that touched a central concept of the southern way of life because it connected to leisure and the civilized life that could come out of it. The creed insisted that farming was labor based in intelligence and leisure and was the model for the good life. The theory of agriculture was that the culture of the soil should be economically privileged by society and engage the maximum number of workers. That sounded like an accountant, but agrarianism is better understood as a twentieth-century version of pastoralism with its Arcadian images of settled, virtuous agricultural and herding life. The individual writers had, however, very different versions of the pastoral South to emphasize, with some ennobling the region's small subsistence farmers, while others celebrated the high style of plantations. Frank Owsley put forward the yeoman as the model of the southern way of life, yet his essay also spoke highly of the "fine balls and house parties" of the Old South. In any event, images of self-sufficient farms and plantation parties hardly fit the realities of southern agriculture by the 1930s, with its troubled tenant class and emerging agribusinesses.[28]

The lead article, "Reconstructed but Unregenerate," offered other key concepts within the southern way. Ransom used the term "way of life" four times, three to refer to the southern way and once to dismiss "certain Northern industrial communities as horrible examples of a way of life we detest." This essay engaged history and place, and it noted that in the 1920s looking backward rather than forward was "out of fashion." "About the only American given to it is some unreconstructed Southerner, who persists in his regard for a certain terrain, a certain history, and a certain inherited way of living," one that linked place and people with the social and cultural system conceptualized as the southern way. Ransom made a crucial distinction between an antimaterialist Lost Cause and a sentimental Lost Cause. He admitted that the unreconstructed white southerner had "a fierce devotion to a lost cause," but he noted that even most contemporary white southerners condescendingly offered the true believer only "a little petting" in indulging such whimsy as taking the past seriously. He ridiculed the sentimental Lost Cause, upset that some people in effect tarnished the legacy of the Confederate war effort by making the South "the nearest available locus for the scenes of their sentimental songs." Ransom's key idea was that the South was unique in North America "for having founded and defended a culture which was according to the European principles of culture," and the South represented the last place in this country for those principles to survive. Ransom saw the South's civilization as not just European but specifically English because the South's Anglophile sentiment remained strong.[29]

Ransom's essay offered more concrete detail on the way of life he associated with southern agrarianism. The arts of the region were "the eighteenth century social arts of dress, conversation, manners, the table, the hunt, politics, oratory, the pulpit." These were "the arts of living and not arts of escape," a judgmental distinction with the arts in modern society. In some ways, these were folkways, and his exploration of them introduced a key concept of the southern way that other contributors would further develop. But Ransom's perspective was mostly that of an intellectual embracing advanced civilization, and he put the older southern life into the perspective of civilizations. He admitted that older southern ways did not "offer serious competition against the glory that was Greece or the grandeur that was Rome," nor did they "match the finish of the English, or any other important European civilization." Still, it was "a way of life which had been considered and authorized." Ransom rested the southern way of life's value on "the establishment having had a sufficient economic base" and thus placed the upper classes at the center of this way of life.[30]

All of these qualities contributed to Ransom's southern way's most significant quality: its spiritual character. He saw this spirituality shared through the older southern society, centralized, again, in the upper classes. The older South practiced the "European philosophy of establishment as the foundation of the life of the spirit." He used the word "squirearchy" rather than "aristocracy" to describe the upper class and harkened back to the legacy of the gentry in the early South. In one of the manifesto's few efforts to relate slavery to the southern way of life, Ransom noted that "slavery was a feature monstrous enough in theory, but, more often than not, humane in practice." Such a statement forever sullied Ransom's reputation as it justified slavery for providing the leisure to nurture antebellum southern white civilization. In contrast to his picture of classical European civilization and that of the Old South, Ransom portrayed the American way's instability and uprootedness. "Pioneering" was the term synonymous with the American way, and industrialism was the contemporary version of pioneering. Ransom nurtured the idea of a stable southern sense of place rather than the typical American idea of movement and new beginnings.[31]

Ransom recognized the problems of the southern countryside but spoke only of seemingly once-proud white southerners, those "broken-down southerners" of his age in the countryside who "were trying to live the good life on a shabby equipment" and who became "grotesque in their effort to make an art out of living when they were not decently making the living." Descendants of the Old South's squirearchy now appeared in "patched blue-jeans, sitting on ancestral fences, shotguns across their laps and hound-dogs at their feet, surveying their unkempt acres while they comment shrewdly on the ways of God." He admired their aestheticism but admitted it rested on inadequate work. It was one of the Agrarians' few references to actual problems in the contemporary rural South. Ransom did insist that the southern problem was the farmer's problem and that the farmer's decline had created a void into which industrialism had come. Ransom allowed that chambers of commerce exhibited "the formidable data of Southern progress," and New South advocates boasted of industrial recruitments. Ransom pointed as well to the human catastrophe that occurred when a southern town or rural community experienced "the cheap labor of a

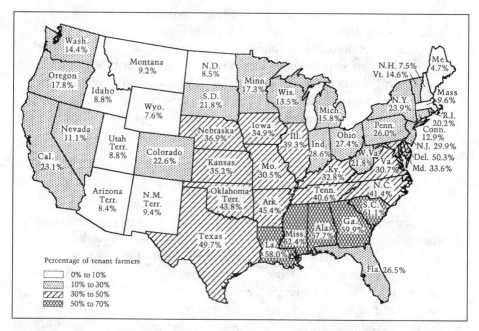

A map of farm tenancy in 1890 shows how widespread sharecropping was
in the agrarian South. In George B. Tindall, *America: A Narrative History*,
2nd ed., vol. 2 (New York: W. W. Norton, 1988).

miserable factory system." In the end, Ransom pointed to the antimaterialism
of the southern way of life he was advocating. He even allowed that in response
to the industrial money hounds "it may be necessary to revive such an antiquity as the old southern gentleman and his lady, and their scorn for the dollar-
chasers." These southern social types were not popular culture's romanticized
figures in this case but, to him, authentic southern icons who represented the
spiritual possibilities Ransom still saw in southern civilization.[32]

Donald Davidson was another of the key contributors, one who would remain an Agrarian the longest. He was more conservative and traditional than
Ransom, attuned to the specificities of southern life. His essay satirized the role
of the arts in the modern world and disputed that "they are actually cherished
in industrial civilization." Work was again a focus, as industrialism's promise
was of leisure, which one would think would benefit the enjoyment of the arts,
but "the kind of leisure provided by industrialism is a dubious benefit." The
frenzied pace of work carried over into leisure time, which became feverish and
energetic. Modern life's promise was that everyone would become materially

rich and then turn to enjoying art. "Since nice, civilized people are supposed to have art, we shall have art." The society would manufacture art to Davidson's dismay, but the conditions under which the arts had flourished from time immemorial were so different under industrialism that he felt the arts could never really flourish. Dripping with sarcasm, Davidson's words outlined the process. Literary works, chosen by the best critics money could buy, would be designated masterpieces and mailed out to hundreds of thousands "disciples of culture," while symphony orchestras were broadcast to millions over crackling radio wires.[33]

Davidson the conservative demeaned some of the proud achievements of the progressive New South. Society, he wrote, could "build immense libraries or put libraries on wheels—the flying library may be looked for eventually." Davidson especially relished lampooning popular culture as representing the worst of industrial culture. Shopgirls did not recite Shakespeare while preparing for work, but instead they read comic strips, listened to jazz records, or read confession magazines. Henry Ford's workers did not hum themes from Beethoven but thumbed through the morning paper, with its flashy pictures and easy-to-read headlines. Industrialists appealed to the lowest common denominator, and mass production, when applied to the arts, "must inevitably sacrifice quality to quantity."[34]

Davidson championed his older imagined South as a model for the arts. He noted that with Civil War battlefields "at their doorsteps, the Southern people have long cultivated a historical consciousness that permeates manners, localities, institutions, the very words and cadence of social intercourse." Davidson claimed the historical consciousness went back even farther than the nineteenth century to the colonial era. In conceptualizing the eighteenth-century South as the prototype of the modern southern way, Davidson emphasized the coherence of life in the colonial era that led into the Old South's civilization. The social inheritance from the South of the eighteenth century flowered into "a gracious civilization that, despite its defects, was actually a civilization, true and indigenous, well diffused, well established."[35]

Antebellum southern culture was not at war with its economic foundation, a key point for Agrarians in general. The manners of the people were consistent, as they did not have "to change their beliefs and temper in going from cornfield to drawing-room, from cotton rows to church or frolic." Davidson's list of commendable qualities in this southern civilization included "leisureliness, devotion to family and neighborhood, local self-sufficiency and self-government, and a capacity, up through the 'sixties, for developing leaders." Davidson granted that the historical South, "for all its ways of life did not produce much 'great' art." He praised its native architecture in old country houses and gave particular attention to the region's folk arts, which were still rich "in ballads, country songs and dances, in hymns and spirituals, in folk tales, in the folk crafts of weaving, quilting, furniture-making."[36]

Frank Owsley focused on the nineteenth-century sectional crisis, the Civil War, and Reconstruction. After the defeat and humiliation of Reconstruction, Owsley argued, the white South had retained an identity: "There appeared still to remain something which made the South different—something intangible, incomprehensible, in the realm of the spirit." Again, an Agrarian returns to spirituality as the defining feature of the southern way of life. In Owsley's view this identity led the North to a "second war of conquest, the conquest of the Southern mind, calculated to remake every Southern opinion, to impose the Northern way of life and thought upon the South, to write 'error' across the pages of Southern history which were out of keeping with the Northern legend, and to set the rising and unborn generations upon stools of everlasting repentance." Owsley echoed almost the exact words of Edward Pollard's assessment in his *Lost Cause* immediately after the Civil War. He went on to claim that the North fixed upon white southerners the stigma of treason for causing the Civil War "and thereby shook the faith of its people in their way of living and their philosophy of life." He was flying in the face of several generations of white southerners who had accepted the regional reconciliation that had become a part of the Lost Cause tradition. Owsley was indeed going back to Pollard's sensibility of threatened post–Civil War southern identity and the belligerent assertion of that identity.[37]

Owsley's historical essay asserted that the war had not been about slavery but rather the key issue of competing civilizations. He concluded that "the irrepressible conflict, then, was not between slavery and freedom, but between the industrial and commercial civilization of the North and the agrarian civilization of the South." States' rights was the "defense mechanism for its entire system of society rather than, as has been claimed, for slavery alone." In fact, he claimed, slavery was "no essential part of the agrarian civilization of the South," although white southerners under attack by abolitionists had named it as the essential issue. Owsley's conclusion was that "without slavery the economic and social life of the South would have not been radically different," an audacious denial of historical records he should have known. The "fundamental and passionate ideal for which the South stood and fell," he insisted though, was that of an agrarian society. Everything else revolved around that concept—"the old and accepted manner of life for which Egypt, Greece, Rome, England, and France had stood." He identified antebellum southern civilization with Western civilization's leading expressions and pointed out that antebellum southerners especially loved the Greeks and Romans. The classical tradition was a foundation for Old South civilization, which he insisted was a hybrid. "The Greek tradition became partly grafted upon the Anglo-Saxon and Scotch traditions of life," but the "even-poised and leisurely life of the Greeks, their oratory, their philosophy, their art—especially their architecture— appealed to the South."[38]

White southerners had preserved, Owsley insisted, the traditions of the Old World in their New World environment, and the region became "the seat of an agrarian civilization which had strength and promise for a future greatness second to none." Imagining a unified society, Owsley pictured leisure as the socially defining feature of antebellum southern civilization, as "the life of the South was leisurely and unhurried for the planter, the yeoman, or the land-less tenant," an assessment that would have surprised the latter two. Southern civilization "was a way of life, not a routine of planting and reaping merely for gain." Owsley cited a famous southerner embodying a southern agrarian sensibility in specific contrast to a northern business sensibility. He wrote that George Washington kept vigil with his horses and dogs "not as a capitalist who guards his investments, but as one who watches over his friends." This appeal-ing scenario located the site of southern civilization not in social relations but in the soil and the humane manners it nurtured.[39]

Lyle Lanier's critique on progress hit at the ideological linchpin of the New South outlook. He insisted that modern industrialism used the term "progress" "as the super-slogan, ever efficacious as a public anesthetic." He playfully noted that "the magic word" even appeared on the automobile license plates of "one of our 'advancing' states, thus recalling the charms used in primitive cultures." The term was "perhaps the most widely advertised commodity offered for gen-eral consumption in our high-powered century, a sort of universal enzyme whose presence is essential to the ready assimilation of other commodities, material and intellectual, generated by the machine age." Progress, in fact, usually meant business success. "The endless production and consumption of material goods means 'prosperity,' 'a high standard of living,' 'progress,' or any one among several other catchwords." These were all popular interpretations of the American spirit that proclaimed "a mystic faith in the industrial destiny." Lanier went deeper in inquiring about the relationship of the term "progress" to civilization, undercutting a key concept in the Victorian understanding of civilization that tied progress to material and moral advancement underpin-ning civilization. He reflected the Agrarians' embrace of Spengler's dim view of contemporary civilization and observed that Spengler "looks on industrialism and its concomitant manifestations as evidence of decay in the spirit of West-ern life." Lanier used his essay to attack such examples of decay as naturalism, positivism, materialism, economic determinism, socialism, and communism, all of which he saw eroding tradition for the sake of progress. He juxtaposed providence against progress, affirming the former.[40]

Allen Tate wrote on religion in the South, and his piece is a surprise because he was the only contributor who found fault with the Old South. He had been one of the most belligerent advocates of southern civilization. He now took "the prototype of the European tradition to be mediaeval society" and lamented that the United States had "performed wonders, considering her youth, in breaking it down." Tate's understanding of culture led him to insist that stable and civilized societies had to rest on a central faith providing discipline and commitment from its members. He concluded that the antebellum South never created a "fitting religion" for its agrarian society, and as a result its social institutions broke down after the Civil War. He claimed the social structure depended on the economic structure, and the economic conviction is the secular image of religion. Defeat in the war did not destroy the antebellum southern outlook, as that destruction came from "its lack of religion which would make her special secular system the inevitable and permanently valuable one." He contrasted, though, northern abstraction with southern understanding that its way of life rested in "a vast body of concrete fact," seen in dead Confederate bodies, for example. Modern southerners had to accept "a concrete and very unsatisfactory history," unlike the northern industrialists who saw only "mechanical formulas" that had made "a society out of abstractions." If the modern southerner had this sensibility, he or she might "conjure up some magic abstraction to spirit back to him his very concrete way of life." That way of life was nonetheless a fabricated abstraction that justified an inequitable social system.[41]

Herman C. Nixon was the Agrarian chosen to write about the economy and land. Later his interracialist views and political moderation set him apart from his mostly conservative fellow Agrarians, but they showed how a progressive could still embrace agrarianism. He wrote that "a stable agricultural civilization penetrated the South early and swiftly, leaving many nooks and corners for later development." He realized that the South's "passive indifference to industrialism" would not be enough in his age "to withstand realtors' activities and campaigns to wake up the section and over-advertise it," unless the region's traditional embrace of agriculture added a more critical self-awareness of dangers to its continuation. Nixon saw the southern way of life as what he called "the human civilization," long based on southern agriculture but now endangered, with "industrial civilization under the capitalistic system" an inadequate substitute for human values. Like the other Agrarians, Nixon endorsed the idea that the South could master industrialism because its history of post–Civil War struggle and forced antimaterialism had produced a tough-mindedness on progress. He foresaw that southern farmers could be saved "from exploitation and serfdom" if the region could master industrial processes rather than be-coming slaves to them. The South was once conquered territory, but it now needed a protest against another conquest, "a conquest of the spirit." So Nixon, despite his differing political and ideological position, shared other Agrarians' belief in the fundamental spiritual issues at stake in the preservation of agrar-ian civilization in the South.[42]

Andrew Lytle always celebrated the life of self-sufficient southern farmers. In his 1931 biography of Nathan Bedford Forrest, he wrote of the yeoman soldier who went off to the Civil War but took with him "no fine candles, but a jug of molasses, a sack of corn, and his father's musket." The young yeomen who fought for the Confederacy did so "without medieval visions" and were "plain people, the freest people in the South, whom the cotton snobs referred to as the 'pore white trash.'" Still, they went off to war "to defend their particular way of life, although they would not have spoken of it in such flat terms." Indeed, the South's plain folk developed no specific, class-based terminology of a southern way, but Lytle gave voice to their embrace of the simplest southern culture.[43]

Lytle contributed to the symposium the details of the southern way of life still at work in the Agrarians' own age. He warned that a war to the death was taking place between technology and the ordinary human functions of living. One common answer to farm problems in the early twentieth century had been to "industrialize the farm; be progressive; drop old-fashioned ways and adopt scientific methods." But under the guise of helping the farmer in such, advo-cates were telling him, in fact, to give it up and join the American mainstream. Lytle aggressively took on consumer culture, one of the growing modernist indicators in the South of the 1920s. The promoters of industrialism told the farmer that his family "deserves motor-cars, picture shows, chain-store dresses for the women-folks, and all the articles in Sears-Roebuck catalogues." Lytle used the vernacular in insisting that the South should avoid industrialism and consumerism "like a pizen snake."[44]

The South could not, Lytle insisted, embrace "pioneering," a term other Agrarians had linked to the American way of life, without damaging its regional civilization. He called industrial civilization "an aggressive state of mind," and "to such an end does bookkeeping lead. It is the numbering of a farm's re-sources." He took special aim at the good roads movement, whose highways "drive like a flying wedge and split the heart of this provincialism—which pre-fers religion to science, handicrafts to technology, the inertia of the fields to the acceleration of industry, and leisure to nervous prostration." The only ones benefitting from industrialism on the farm were "large farmers and planting corporations," with "asphalt companies, motor-car companies, oil and cement companies, engineers, contractors, bus lines, truck lines, and politicians—

not the farmer," receiving the advantages from good roads. Lytle was particularly contemptuous of "a great propaganda mill" teaching the farmer and his children "to despise the life he has led and would like to lead again." The propaganda machine included schools and universities, the press, salesmen, and agents of industrialism. It tried to uplift the farmer, demeaning his ancestors and stating that they were "not cultured because they did not appreciate the fine arts; that they were illiterate because their speech was Old English; and that the South will now come to glory, to 'cultural' glory, by a denial of its ancestry."[45]

Lytle, like Davidson, raised up folklife and saw the South as a place of charms, signs, and omens, as "folk attempts to understand and predict natural phenomena." Lytle's account lovingly recounted the midday meals, play-parties, and songs of the *Sacred Harp* songbook. He wrote that the last were songs of an agrarian people that "will bind the folk-ways which will everywhere go down before canned music and canned pleasure." Here he explicitly contrasted folk music with popular culture and testified to the tenacity and endurance of folk music. In a famous line, Lytle said, "Throw out the radio and take down the fiddle from the wall. Forsake the movies for the play-parties and the square dances."[46]

Robert Penn Warren dealt most explicitly of all the writers with issues of race. He used an image from southern African American folklore for his defense of segregation, but his essay is that of a southern moderate appealing for equal justice for Blacks within the segregated system. He admitted that Blacks often failed to get legal justice and saw this as the least they should expect. He was vague though as to social equality, as he noted that aspects of equality other than legal ones were "more subtle and confused." Insisting that the rural South was the best place for Black southerners to slowly adjust to progress, he spoke of the compensations in "this way of life for the negro and for society in general." Warren was the only contributor to the symposium to stress the centrality of African Americans to the southern way. The brunt of Warren's argument in terms of agrarianism was questioning whether industrialism could raise up Black southerners. The expectation was that industrial progress would promote African American economic independence in the South by lifting them from the "state of serfdom, ignorance and degradation." Sympathetic to the goal, Warren insisted that this hopeful view represented an exorbitant act of faith in the idea of industrialism. Admitting that industrialism in the South might contribute to the Black southerner's advancement and that of the South itself, he argued it would do so only if it grew and was "absorbed into the terms of the life it meets." Industrialism should enter the South as a citizen not a conqueror.[47]

Warren appealed as well to the enlightened self-interest of southern whites in justifying the value of labor unions because, without organized labor, industrialism would only benefit the few. Warren was also the only Agrarian to address the issue of the poor whites, and he dealt sympathetically with them. "To the Southerner, the 'poor white' in the strictest sense is a being beyond the pale of even the most generous democratic recognition; it is the negro's term, 'po' white trash,' or so much social debris." Warren's generalization reflected the feelings of most upper- and middle-class white southerners of the time, and the phrase "'beyond the pale' of democracy" is troubling today, but again, Warren was sympathetic. His striking insight was that poor whites were just as much victims of slavery as Blacks had been. Fearing that industrial development and its labor competition would trouble the waters further, he saw the only solution as recognition "that the fates of the 'poor white' and the negro are linked in a single tether."[48]

Stark Young closed *I'll Take My Stand* by affirming the urgency of arriving at "some conception of the end of living, the civilization, that will belong in the South." This issue was the region's "great, immediate problem," although critics would have pointed to, say, poverty and racial division. As did the other Agrarians, Young affirmed the southern way of life as an expression of the highest civilization. He conceptualized civilization as "the end of living," and he asked the question, "Regardless of all the progress, optimism, and noise," what must be the answer to "the civilization in the South?" He lampooned the American way of life one final time in the volume by noting that the end of living may not be "mere raw Publicity, Success, Competition, Speed and Speedways, Progress, Donations, and Hot Water, all seen with a capital letter." Bringing the focus to manners, high culture, and religion, Young saw "more fleeting and eternal things to be thought of: more grace, sweetness and time, more security in our instincts, and chance to follow our inmost nature, as Jesus meant when he said he must be about his Father's business, more of the last fine light to shine on what we do, and make the sum of it like some luminous landscape, all the parts of which are equable, distributed, and right." Young's reference to Jesus Christ was especially significant, linking the southern way of life explicitly to Christianity. Although Tate found Protestantism an inadequate religion for the Old South slave society, the Agrarians, including Tate, surely envisioned the southern way as an example of Christian civilization, embodied as well in the southern civil religion of the good society rooted in southern traditional ways.[49]

Young identified antebellum southern civilization and argued that Confederate defeat and Reconstruction did not imply "that this Southern civilization, once the fine flower of men's lives," was altogether dead. After all, he proclaimed, "the belief that the essence of the soul is its mockery of death" was the "core of our humanity." Drawing not from theory "but from an actual civilization," he emphasized that that civilization had tangible manifestations.

Young's vision was of an aristocratic, Delta variety of the southern way, appropriate to his being a Mississippian. He identified southern etiquette as the defining feature of it and remembered "people whose fathers were gentlemen" and whose servants had "good manners," including African Americans as servants in his version of the southern way of life. Young admitted that in talking about the southern way of life, he was talking of "a certain life in the old South, a life founded on land and the ownership of slaves." The yeomen had their own culture, but it was "not they who gave this civilization its peculiar stamp," he wrote, disagreeing with Owsley's point of view. Young offered a full defense of social class differences and the superiority of the South's natural planter-class leaders. The South's leadership embodied "an attitude and point of view induced by the Southern way of life that we came to mean by *aristocratic*." He labeled this attitude a sensibility that grew from "your settled connection with the land" and one's family having "maintained a certain relation to the society of the country." Young insisted that "our meaning of culture—the Southern culture of which the orators used to spout, adding a dash about chivalry and honor"—embodied gentlemanly familiar acquaintance with the classics, the poets, a respect for polish and cultivation, and "a genuine taste for oratory, whose large flowers went, perhaps, with white columns and the great white moons of the magnolia." The romanticized South loomed large here with the moonlight-and-magnolias image explicit.[50]

Young also affirmed the mannered society as the essence of the southern way. "Undoubtedly it had to do with a certain fineness of feeling, an indefinable code for yourself and others, and a certain continuity of outlook." Behaviorally, this way of life rested on the social order that came out of individual self-discipline: "You controlled yourself in order to make the society you lived in more decent, affable, and civilized and yourself more amenable and attractive." Young identified an aesthetic quality in the performance of the southern way. He argued that "the people around you were so gentle about it," as the way of life produced a "fineness and love as in itself some mode of assurance, as some guaranty of goodness." *I'll Take My Stand* mainly conceptualized the southern way as agrarianism, but civilized manners loomed large, a second concept of the southern way that was especially showcased in Young's essay.[51]

Debating *I'll Take My Stand*

I'll Take My Stand was widely reviewed, and after its publication it focused discussion about the South. Over twenty-five newspapers in the South made some mention of the book, from reviews to columns and editorials, and a score of nonsouthern publications did so as well. The editor of the *Sewanee*

Review, William S. Knickerbocker, claimed that it was "the most challenging book published in the United States since George's *Progress and Poverty,*" while Arkansas's John Temple Graves found it an "antidote to the platitudes of progress." T. S. Eliot was a literary hero to many of the Agrarians, and his review announced "that it is a sound and right reaction which impelled Mr. Allen Tate and his eleven Southerners to write their book." Some observers from within the South rejoiced at the assertion of southern traditionalism. The *Nashville Tennessean* trumpeted, "They are singing it again—Dixie, the song that has always brought its wild surge of feeling in Southern hearts." The editorial added that now it was "sung in a more thoughtful way." The *Montgomery Advertiser* praised the book's "militant Agrarianism whose followers need not be ashamed," as the book explored "a concept that had long flinched, inarticulate, before the scowls of industrialism."[52]

Many reviews, though, were unfavorable. Some pointed out that the Agrarians' views of restricting industrialism were unrealistic, since the region was already well along toward adopting that economic system. The Agrarians faced ridicule, as a columnist in the Macon, Georgia, paper called the book "a high spot in the year's hilarity." Stringfellow Barr, editor of the *Virginia Quarterly Review* and one of the most persistent critics of the Agrarians, wrote in "Shall Slavery Come South?" in October 1930 that "the traditionalists, frightened by the lengthening shadow of smokestacks, take refuge in the good ole days and in what I have called the apotheosis of the hoe." Barr condescended to the Agrarians, calling the book a "charming but impotent religion of the past" that made "idols of the defunct horse and buggy" and saying the writers "mutter impotently at the radio." This accusation of making a religion of the past was a recurring critique, one that Arthur Krock made in the *New York Times Book Review* in 1931. He asked why the region should "embalm" the remains of the Old South and preserve its "few belongings like relics at the shrine of a saint."[53]

The religious language used in such assessments reinforced, though, the centrality of spirituality to the Agrarians. Other negative reviews came down to earth to connect the Agrarians conceptualizing an agrarian South with what was happening in the contemporary rural South. The Agrarians' unrealistic assessment of the South astounded Gerald Johnson, the North Carolina journalist and protégé of Mencken, and he suggested that their embrace of agrarianism indicated that their understanding of the South had been "gleaned from the pages of Joel Chandler Harris and Thomas Nelson Page." Insisting that because the Agrarians seemed to know little of the miseries of the rural South happening "under their noses," their writings about "the fine civilization of the ante-bellum South" were suspect as well. He added that the Old South was falling into decline by the time of the Civil War "because no purely agrarian polity can maintain a fine civilization for any length of time."[54]

Indeed, the book's intellectual influence for those people thinking about the South at the time was apparent in a series of debates that took place in the years after publication. Three thousand people gathered in Richmond for the first debate, in November 1930, as John Crowe Ransom sparred with Stringfellow Barr. Ransom claimed the latter's southern identity was "a gardenia to stick in his buttonhole when he goes traveling to New York." Ransom and Donald Davidson participated in four other debates, with Ransom debating a businessman, William D. Anderson, president of the Bibb Manufacturing Company, in front of more than 1,000 people in Atlanta. The performance aspect of the Agrarians' ideology was never more apparent, as Ransom later confessed that he enjoyed nothing he did with the symposium and its issues more than these public discussions before enthusiastic, if not entirely sympathetic, audiences. Ransom and others remained frustrated that readers and reviewers often thought they were trying literally to return the South to an agricultural economy, when their intentions had been to bring public attention to what they saw as the dangers accompanying the industrialism that was coming to the South, namely the materialism, spiritual drift, and destruction of individual autonomy.[55]

Despite this excitement at intellectual engagement immediately after publication of the book, many of the leading Agrarians fell into frustration at their lack of impact. In October 1932, Davidson wrote to Tate, noting that "we like to think of ourselves as crusaders, in our mind's eye, we can see ourselves doing a kind of Pickett's charge against industrial bulwarks, only a *successful* charge this time. But we don't actually do the crusading. We merely trifle with the idea a little." He had hoped that his conceptualization of the southern way of life as agrarianism would have more impact than it did. In December of that same year, Tate wrote to Davidson that the "Agrarian Movement has degenerated into pleasant poker games on Saturday night." He added that poker was "the best agrarian game in the world," and he did not worry about that but did "object to the kind of pleasure they seem to be getting out of it." He confessed his bitter feelings about the loss of momentum. "I came back to live in the South, and I've been let down."[56]

The Thirties

Despite such frustrations, the Agrarians continued to promote their ideas in national and regional publications, planned some conferences, and attended others to push their ideas. They tried to define a more concrete and specific version of their philosophical agrarianism. The 1930s saw the Agrarians "put aside the issues of the spirit in order to alter government policies and to plan a society." A greater public policy interest led to the final act in the Agrarians' saga in the 1930s. They became involved with Seward Collins, a British editor who was publishing a conservative journal, the *American Review*. The journal advocated property and land redistribution and aspired to give voice to the concerns of small proprietors, both small farmers and small business people. Collins published the writings of conservative movements such as the British distributists and the new humanists, and the Agrarians published many of their writings of the 1930s in the journal. They downplayed now the southern dimension of their work and rarely used the term "southern way of life." As Allen Tate said, "Our purpose is to be heard, and we can't be heard now if our program is set forth as primarily sectional. That is all there is to it." He outlined a stark choice of either "writing avowedly sectional articles to be read chiefly by ourselves" or writing essays that promoted their ultimate objective of exposing the materialism and lack of spirituality in industrial modern society. Many Agrarians also wrote articles for *Who Owns America?*, which grew out of the *American Review* writings and aspired to influence policy makers on rather radical for the time land-based economic reforms that reflected their newly clarified concern for small subsistence farmers and foundational opposition to monopolistic capitalism.[57]

Collins turned out to be sympathetic to fascism, though, and the Agrarians were tainted by association with him and his writings. Writer Grace Lumpkin tangled with Collins and the Agrarians and helped expose the dark side to their writings. Lumpkin was from a prominent, Lost Cause–laced Georgia family, but, like her sister Katharine, she departed from that tradition and helped support southern radical reform efforts. The author of *To Make My Bread*, a novel about the Gastonia, North Carolina, textile strike in 1929 that leftist critics acclaimed as a valuable proletarian novel, Grace Lumpkin interviewed Collins and pointedly pushed him on his anti-Semitism and anti–African American sentiments. She went on to indict the Agrarians for their support of him and his threat of promoting American fascism. She called out Allen Tate, in particular, who responded with a mild dismissal of fascism but a vigorous attack on communism and governmental centralization as harbingers of an authoritarian state. Lumpkin wrote Tate in reply, as one southerner to another. She cited his belief that "the Southerner" must use the blunt instrument of politics to "reestablish a private, self-contained and essentially spiritual life." Such a life, she said, evoked the privileges and power that both their grandfathers had enjoyed "when slaves worked for them." She expressed genuine regret and sadness as he went "about with his butterfly net busily capturing Southern traditions." Tate felt embarrassed and defensive about the whole affair, which helped lead to the breakup of the group by 1936. By then, they rarely used the term "southern way of life."[58]

The Depression and New Deal led some of the Agrarians, most notably Herman C. Nixon, to embrace social reform, federal government activism, and interracial values, but most of the others headed increasingly rightward in their politics and feared especially the growing power of the federal government. Davidson, Owsley, and other Agrarians came to see the federal government as a threat to the segregated southern way of life. Davidson's collection of essays *Attack on Leviathan: Regionalism and Nationalism in the United States*, appearing in 1938, expressed his conviction that Confederate defeat had led to what he dubbed the "Leviathan state," a too-powerful federal government that stood for centralizing power and uniformity in American life and threatened the local particularities he so prized. That Leviathan state was, moreover, a threat to the southern way of life, which he increasingly identified not just with agrarianism but with segregation.[59]

Ransom left Vanderbilt for Kenyon College and work on the *Kenyon Review* in the late 1930s, where he cultivated his interests in aestheticism as an expression of civilization's principles and ideals. In a 1945 essay, "Art and the Human Economy," Ransom looked back on his earlier agrarian beliefs as a fantasy, a nostalgic rejection of civilization in a vain hope at going back to pastoral innocence. He saw an inherent contrast between the pastoral mode of imagination and civilization. A pastoral culture always represented a rejection of civilization, for in that world there would be "not only no effective science, invention, and scholarship, but nothing to speak of in art, e.g., Reviews and contributions to Reviews, fine poems and their exegesis." Ransom noted that since the publication of the book, most of his fellow Agrarians had left pastoralism behind and embraced aestheticism as a means to civilized values.[60]

Race and Agrarianism

The Agrarians did not question racial segregation, nor did they make a rousing defense of it in *I'll Take My Stand*, and they considered the issue a settled one, the basis of their version of southern civilization. But the book had virtually no place for African Americans in their agrarian way of life, except for a few references to servile positions in southern households. Owsley was among the worst racists in the group. He referred in his essay to cannibalism in demeaning African American equality with whites in southern society. The only member of the group in 1930 to see a place for Blacks in southern society was Robert Penn Warren, and even his essay was a defense of segregation. The Agrarians' writings in the 1930s made their hostility to Black southerners clear and connected them in the public eye with race-baiting politicians. The Agrarians wanted their South to be humane, but they could not see Black southerners with a civilized gaze. William T. Couch, director of the University of North Carolina Press, noted that the Agrarians asserted that "virtue is derived from the soil, but see no virtue in the Negro and the poor white who are closest to the soil." The Agrarian Arcadia consisted mostly of small subsistence white farmers and a culture that tolerated economic inequalities and racial discrimination.[61]

At times, the Agrarians even portrayed African Americans in minstrel terms, or else talked about what they thought of as the obsessions of northern reformers to make Blacks equal citizens in the South. Davidson's "A Sociologist in Eden" was one of the most offensive Agrarian writings on race. He objected to outside agitation, "the object of which is apparently to set the Negro up as an equal, or at least more than a subordinate member of society." Responding to calls for extending small farm ownership to more Black southerners, he insisted that this was "unattainable as long as the South remains the South." Tate's essay "A View of the Whole South," which appeared in the *American Review* in February 1934, appeared to draw a potentially violent line in the southern soil. "I argue it this way: the white race seems determined to rule the Negro race in its midst; I belong to the white race; therefore, I intend to support the white rule." He went further, addressing the ultimate weapon in the segregated southern way of life, and claimed that "lynching is a symptom of weak, inefficient rule, but you can't destroy lynching by *fiat* or social agitation." He insisted that "lynching will disappear when the white race is satisfied that its supremacy will be unquestioned in social crises." In the 1930s, the Agrarians moved from a critique of industrial America to "a jeremiad about preserving the 'organic' structure of the South," with white supremacy at the center of that structure. Race would grow ever more prominent in the late 1930s and 1940s in the definition of the southern way of life, and the Agrarians' hardening racism reflected that broader white southern development.[62]

African American educator Horace Mann Bond replied forcefully to the Agrarians' exclusion of Black southerners from their conception of the southern way of life in his essay "A Negro Looks at His South," which appeared in *Harper's Magazine* in June 1931. It began by acknowledging the "professional Southerner" was back, "boldly proclaiming the virtues of his agrarian economy, his pride in race, his scorn of lesser breeds." Bond saw this white southerner as a new incarnation of "the old, old picture of the quintessential Southron, the fine flower of Anglo-Saxon gentility, the Nordic par excellence in his dominance of the scene." He allowed that it seemed the South itself became "articulate by the self-expression" of white men and women such as the Agrarians, "and the Negro is merely a bit of back-stage scenery." In this scenario, "the white man is the Southerner, and the Negro—well, a Negro." He protested "the cavalier manner in which the accolade of Southern citizenship, or participation in the fate of the region, has been appropriated by white persons," and he proudly proclaimed that for hundreds of years his ancestors had been born in the South and had played an active role in the development of the region. He himself had lived most of his life in the South, and "all of the hope I cherish for the future is laid there," as he knew it was for the millions of African Americans in the South.[63]

The article sketched the variety of African American life in different areas of the South and the different types of Black southerners who lived in those places. Bond identified an interracial southern way of life, which was a "venerable tradition, a tangle of notions derived from daily contacts with men and women and the means of human communication." The region's culture, the books and newspapers people read, the music they heard, the radios they listened to, and the food they ate were all cultural expressions African Americans as well as whites in the South experienced. The result was "sustaining a state of mind in Negroes similar to that of whites." Bond cleverly put forward the concept of the "High Art" of racial interaction in the South and identified the methods African Americans used to finesse the Jim Crow society. He hit the Agrarians where it hurt when he insisted that, "despite the efforts of Mr. Allen Tate and his fellow 'Neo-Confederates' to extoll the gentility of the former Southern scene," he would indict the white South "on the basis of its undeveloped gentility." Bond lamented the rise of poor whites in the South to political power, and he complained that "from Savannah to San Antonio the Rotary idea is rampant." The "new type of Southern businessman" unfortunately came from the middle westerners moving to the South and bringing the materialistic ideas of "Indiana civilization"—the latter jab one the Agrarians should have appreciated.[64]

Ending his essay with a realistic note about the realities of African American life in the region, Bond recalled that he had seen "human misery and degradation in this South, which I call my own." He had also, though, strolled down Beale Street, viewed sunset from the Mississippi River Bridge in Vicksburg, and seen the "vivid color spread slowly over the swamps on the Louisiana side of the River." Such experiences had made him "realize how one may love the South and claim it as one's own," despite its flaws and the efforts of people such as the Agrarians to exclude Black southerners from their vision of the southern way of life. He asked for recognition of southern commonalities beyond ideology. "These white people, these black people, are Southerners, but what is more, they are intensely human." He was no radical, insisting that at bottom what the South needed was "the appearance of more genuine Southern white gentlemen," people who would "not be ashamed to be decent where Negroes are concerned." Bond's article was a reprimand of the Agrarians' exclusive vision of the South and a joyous proclamation of African American claims on an interracial southern way of life.[65]

Bond asserted a convincing claim on an African American southern identity and contested the Agrarians' marginalization of Black southerners. In a review of *I'll Take My Stand*, another African American intellectual, poet Sterling A.

Brown, dismissed the Agrarians as offering a warmed-over exploration of the Old South. He admitted that industrialization had its problems but saw their arguments as common ones for critics of capitalism from John Ruskin to Sinclair Lewis. Recognizing the book's evocation of a southern way of life, he questioned "just what *was* the Southern way of life." The materialism of planters belied claims that the South was nonacquisitive, and he rejected assertions of a leisurely and kind South as not ringing true to a slave society. He lampooned the "old wives tales and gentlemanly colonels musing over mint juleps" as sources for the Agrarians' flawed arguments. The book's backward-looking perspective was "ancestry worship," and he zeroed in on the Agrarians' treatment of race by noting that their stereotypical treatment of Black southerners evoked "the proverbial African woodcarving in the lumber yard." To Brown, the book was the old white man's burden not to be taken seriously.[66]

Moral and Spiritual Meanings

The moral failures of the Agrarians on race are apparent, but at the time they claimed moral high ground. They defined their southern way in opposition to the American way. The American way meant differing ideas to different groups from the Depression to the Cold War, and the values associated with free enterprise would be among the most prominent. This outlook overtook the Agrarians' communal, organic traditionalism as the defining feature of southern conservatism, and the Agrarians represented a particular, if soon dated, vision of traditionalism. More broadly, the Agrarians saw Western civilization's traditional moral and spiritual values at stake in their defense of the South. They argued that the South's antimodernism represented a last chance for the preservation of Western civilization because barbarism, to them, emerged alongside modernity. European civilization figured prominently as a model for the antebellum southern civilization they put forward as an enduring ideal. The Western civilization of their day was not their model; rather, feudal or eighteenth-century Europe provided the ideal.[67]

The Agrarians wrote out of a sense of crisis portending the impending end of civilization. Writer John Peale Bishop put it this way in a 1931 letter to Tate: "With us Western civilization ends." In one sense, the symposium's purpose had been to stop the advances of industrialism in the South, and the Agrarians drew from late nineteenth-century Lost Cause rhetoric that said Confederate defeat produced the spiritual strength to oppose American materialist ways and assert older ideas of Western civilization. In this regard, they spoke in terms of civilization and savagery. "They saw this as a crisis," notes historian Mark Malvasi, "hoping that old-fashioned, homemade, long-discredited southern ways might yet halt the threatened emergence of a new barbarism."

They identified those values as essentially spiritual and moral, and they advocated a specifically Christian civilization that would embody discipline and self-control against what Allen Tate, in his novel *The Fathers*, would term the "abyss" that lies at the edge of civilization. As a character in his novel asks, "Is not civilization the agreement, slowly arrived at, to let the abyss alone?" The Agrarians challenged such Enlightenment values as science, rationalism, and naturalism. Their Christianity was not that of the transformative spirituality of the kingdom of God on earth, which they saw as a modern expression of millennial aspirations that did not fit their view of human nature or historical reality. Their God was an orthodox one, and they saw human nature as one of sinfulness and evil. Those dangers would sink society without the discipline of religion—and the ideology of the southern way of life that represented civilized living. A later agrarian, Richard Weaver, would see the South as "the last non-materialist civilization in the Western World," and that nonmaterialism in agrarian thought was a basis for the southern civil religion's sense of mission for the South as a potentially redemptive force.[68]

In investing the concept of a southern way with the potential for moral and spiritual redemption, as seen in the ability to tame industrialism, the Agrarians affirmed the regional civil religion of the South's superiority. It echoed the southern evangelical sense of mission to preserve the South as a Zion and use that base to convert the world. By the post–World War II era, Allen Tate had left the agrarian movement and converted to Roman Catholicism. He now admitted that the Agrarians had conflated secular and sacred history, as they pictured the South as a holy nation that embodied God's will on earth. The Agrarians, Tate concluded, like their antebellum forebears, mistakenly saw the South to be "constitutionally unique among nations" and "a divinely ordained, redemptive community that would save mankind from the disappointment and torment of history." Tate saw now that his movement had, in fact, emphasized contingent and historical forces over the divine and eternal. The Agrarians had misunderstood the South as the source of social redemption and "the instrument of God's will and grace." Later, in 1953, he noted that "we were trying to find a religion in the secular, historical experience as such, particularly in the Old South." He concluded that "we were idolaters." If the Confederates had lost a supposed holy war, the Agrarians, in the end, were the South's second lost cause.[69]

The Agrarians' coinage of "the southern way of life," in any event, gave new meaning and authority to the idea of southern civilization. They invented the concept as one for modern times. Agrarians provided an assertive conservative vision of southern civilization that stressed custom, tradition, and heritage.

Timing was important. Their book came at a time when New South progressives seemed triumphant. The Agrarians kept alive the image of the South as an organic, white-dominated, pastoral, and paternalistic culture. They did not assert a ringing endorsement of white supremacy, but that concept was central to their understanding of the South as a traditional society. When Black questioning of the system became more urgent in the 1930s and afterward, some of the Agrarians allowed their racism to show. They still positioned the South as important to Western civilization, indeed, as the last chance to preserve their dated version of the civilization. Broader understandings of civilization had emerged after World War I, but white southerners, including conservative intellectuals, did not embrace this new outlook that broke the connection between Anglo-Saxon ethnicity and the highest civilization.

What did the Agrarians gain from their construction of the southern way of life? They were southern white men defending a traditional white supremacist patriarchal society that left them in positions of social authority with a status atop regional society and positioned, less securely, as aspirationally redemptive and politically powerful figures within the nation. They were, on the other hand, insecure provincial intellectuals in a modernizing society. The Agrarians were not successful in defining the southern way of life over a long term as agrarianism, but they set the framework of "modernity versus traditionalism" into the discussion of the southern way as the South began its social drama that would lead to changes in the coming decades. Their real significance was in putting forward the image of the South as a traditional society, with custom, culture, and folklore as defining features in a conservative vision. They saw moral and spiritual values defining their southern way. As the South faced internal and external challenges to its status quo, this vision would persist. The interwar years would see additional visions of a southern way, and the next two chapters examine the variety of imaginings of the southern way of life in that period.

CHAPTER FOUR

Searching for the Southern Way
in a Time of Transition

Culture, Civilization, and Way of Life
in the Interwar Years

WILLIAM T. COUCH was one of the chief intellectual architects of reform in the interwar South. As director of the University of North Carolina Press, he published works supporting a new critical attitude toward the region. They included *Culture in the South* (1934), an encyclopedic guide to the region's society and cultural expressions with contributions from an interdisciplinary group of sociologists, literary scholars, historians, journalists, and educators. Couch modeled the volume on Harold Stearns's 1922 collection of essays, *Civilization in the United States*, and sought to emphasize southern values beyond an increasingly business society's focus on wealth. "I feel that there are other values of equal, if not greater importance which ought to be defined and discussed," he wrote to John Donald Wade in February 1931. Among those values were those he still associated with the traditional folk attitudes that pervaded ordinary life in the South. Couch insisted, "The book should describe the varieties of life in the South, with emphasis on those ways of living which are most generally followed and on the influences which are changing the present patterns of life." His use of the plural "ways" revealed his goal of covering the diversity of regional experience. Couch's preface consciously sparred with the Agrarians' portrait of a singular southern way of life, critiquing one writer's view "of *the* southern spirit, another of *the* southern tradition." Couch called *I'll Take My Stand* "one of the most thoughtful books on the South published in recent years," one that showed the "fallacy of expecting a better way of life" simply from "bigger and better business," but he indicted the symposium for "the even more serious error of interpreting southern life in terms of industrialism *vs.* agrarianism" and the claims that "life on a farm is supposed to be uniquely 'southern.'" He insisted instead that life in the South was complex, varying from social class to social class and place to place. Looking at the rural South "without colored spectacles" destroyed the

Agrarians' argument. They must "have never known or imagined the misery, the long drawn-out misery, of over-work and undernourishment, of poverty and isolation, of ignorance and hopelessness."[1]

Couch's contributors did not ignore the traditions of the South, which the Agrarians had, of course, made central to their argument. Couch saw the region's cultural traditions as "strong and important," with a "measure of delight" in them. Though Allen Tate complained that the book had no comprehensive understanding of culture, Couch used the anthropological concept that saw the interrelatedness in everyday ways of behaving and thinking. He included articles on folk song, language, vernacular and fine arts, and handicrafts, but he also covered social problems, including an article on lynching. Charles Ramsdell's essay on southern history echoed the Agrarian assessment of antebellum planters whose "essential character was in its way of life and its attitude toward life." He acknowledged in the contemporary South the "new groups with 'go-getting ideals'" but claimed the old elites "did not lose their identity nor wholly change their ways of life." Ramsdell's recurrent use of the term "way of life" showed the Agrarian influence on one of the South's most respected historians.[2]

Another contributor, Broadus Mitchell, was sarcastic and unforgiving, though, in briefly talking about the failures of the Old South that the Agrarians had ennobled. Acknowledging their argument "that the way of life of the old South needed no defense, but awoke admiration" for having "developed 'culture,'" Mitchell argued that if such a culture existed, "it was so elusive that the observer today cannot find it. It did not take form in music, poetry, prose, building, works of engineering, jurisprudence, science or theology, let alone the infinitely more difficult matter of decent human comfort and independence for the average man within the South." He thus refused "to shed a tear for the passing of the old regime." Journalist Clarence Cason's article "Middle Class and Bourbon" likewise cast a critical eye on southern culture and denigrated white southern pretensions. "Why must we from time to time stultify ourselves by cautious comparisons of the southern scene with the golden ages of Greece and Rome? Southerners walking on their hind legs are abominable and should be tripped."[3]

Three of the contributors to *Culture in the South*—Wade, Donald Davidson, and Herman C. Nixon—had also written essays for *I'll Take My Stand*, and their inclusion, as well as the volume's sheer appreciation of much of southern culture, complicated the Agrarians' reaction to the book. Davidson praised the book in a letter to Allen Tate. "Anyone who reads the book carefully (especially a non-Southerner) will *not* be moved to repeat the old shibboleths about Southern civilization but must see the South as a very diverse, wholly alive section." He wrote of Couch that "though our opinions differed, I have a great deal of admiration for the book in its informative and diverse aspects and that, if the Confederate Congress were in Session (as it ought to be), he would be made a Major General at once." On the other hand, he insisted in another letter to Tate that he saw in the book "no program at all," with the Agrarians' opponents (such as Broadus Mitchell) being "thoroughly muddled people," whereas "our position, by contrast becomes convincing and very clear." He insisted that Couch's preface to the book was "an inept and vain attempt to make the book appear like an answer to *I'll Take My Stand*."[4]

Culture in the South was a revealing statement of a progressive viewpoint that emerged in the 1930s. It was critical of much in southern life yet also appreciated aspects of southern culture, especially those features rooted in regional history and folklife that made for a particular expression of a broader American reform movement in the 1930s. The Depression created a sense of crisis in the South, with the Agrarians representing one response to that crisis, but liberal reformism was another. Much of the region responded favorably to Franklin D. Roosevelt's liberal programs and supported the New Deal, at least until the end of the decade. Those years saw fundamental changes in the relationship between the South and the nation, especially to the federal government. "Regionalism" was a key new term, championed by sociologist Howard Odum, Couch, and others at the institutional center of the 1930s liberal reformism in the South, the University of North Carolina. These thinkers used the terms "way," "culture," and "civilization" relentlessly in their ambitious plans to scientifically study the South—especially the region's socioeconomic problems—and to plan for a better future. They saw the 1930s in terms of organic metaphors that lent themselves to assessing the South in its breadth and depth as a distinctive human collective, typical of thinking about civilizations and ways of life. Many of these regionalists were part of an interracial movement, a historical watershed in promoting interracial dialogue and constructive efforts at reforming Jim Crow society. A bridge to later efforts to conceptualize the southern way of life as a biracial culture in the region, their work transformed the concept of regional culture in an assertion that it expressed broader ideas of Western civilization.[5]

Writers became important intellectual figures in the region in the interwar years as well, with the Southern Literary Renaissance an expression of a new critical outlook on the South. Fiction writers, journalists, documentarians, and others engaged issues of southern cultural backwardness, and their words added to the attempt to understand the South as a distinctive culture and civilization. The range of individuals who figured in the search for understanding a southern way of life includes author William Faulkner, journalist Gerald Johnson, memoirist and reformer Katharine Du Pre Lumpkin, former Agrarian and committed interracialist Herman C. Nixon, and African American sociologist and educator Charles S. Johnson.

This chapter surveys these competing efforts to understand and shape southern cultural life and its relationship to different kinds of imagined civilizations. In the 1930s, a progressive ideology had its moment in the southern sun. Frequent engagement with terms such as "critical thinking," "poverty," "poor whites," and "folk culture" reflected a focus on the masses of people more than ever before, with New Deal programs in the face of the Depression creating the most favorable views of the federal government in the South's history. Race continued to confound the search for southern ways of life, but economic problems of the era provided the context for engaging racial issues, with the hope that solving economic problems would ease racial injustices.

Culture and Way of Life

The idea of culture became widespread in American thinking during the 1930s, and Couch's use of the concept was a timely one for contributors considering the South's relationship to tradition and modernity. Poet and cultural critic Matthew Arnold's image of culture as the highest human achievements in art and intellectual activity was ever more dated, as was the Victorian equation of culture and white supremacy. Anthropologist Franz Boas was among the leaders in a new anthropological understanding of culture that moved beyond earlier theories of societal evolution, with some cultures seen as superior and others as lesser, even savage in an early stage of evolution. Cultural hierarchies had meant racial hierarchies, but Boas and others challenged such views and turned attention to the investigation of diverse cultures, documenting how they independently developed, even as everything in cultural life was seen increasingly as interrelated.

Ruth Benedict's *Patterns of Culture*, published in 1934 (the same year as *Culture in the South*), helped popularize the idea of cultural interrelatedness. As Warren Susman noted, "Her analysis of the possibility of different cultural patterns and the way such patterns shape and account for individual behavior was part of a more general discovery of the idea itself, the sense of awareness of what it means to *be* a culture, or the search to *become* a kind of culture." He added that in the 1930s "the idea of culture was domesticated with important consequences. Americans then began thinking in terms of patterns of behavior and belief, values and life-styles, symbols and meanings."[6]

A key structural cultural element in the 1930s was "the effort to find, characterize, and adapt to an American Way of Life as distinguished from the material achievement (and the failures) of an American industrial civilization." Civilization represented technological advancements, scientific worldviews, well-organized institutions, the exercise of power, and attainment of material (financial) success. The conflict between "culture" and "civilization," between the quality of living and the material advancement of society, was anything but a new issue, but it became central in the 1930s. Progressives had, as Susman says, "valued the march of civilization and progress and had tried to make from an industrial civilization a meaningful culture or way of life." But in the 1930s "civilization itself—in its urban-industrial form—seemed increasingly the enemy." Commentators from Reinhold Niebuhr to Lewis Mumford worried "whether the civilization that had triumphed was worthy of the highest aspirations of man." The South's Howard Odum reflected this outlook and saw the region through this lens. Interest in the social sciences reflected a new cultural awareness that sought to understand the new civilization. What was new about culture in the thirties, then, was, "the more complex effort to seek and to define America as a culture and to create the patterns of a way of life worth understanding."[7]

The economic catastrophe of the decade promoted a stress on cultural pluralism within a fundamental American unity. In the 1930s, Americans were less inclined than in the Progressive Era to identify their way simply as industrialism. The Agrarians might have been happy with that turn, but a term not central to their vocabulary, "democracy," emerged as the central concept. At a 1939 forum entitled "Can We Depend Upon Youth to Follow the American Way," for example, moderator George V. Denny Jr. commented on the term: "I take it that by that phrase we mean the democratic way—the idea of 'giving everybody a chance to share in making the rules.'" The Depression era rediscovered a nation rooted in democracy and in the nation's history, symbolized by filiopietistic biographies such as Carl Sandburg's *Abraham Lincoln* and Virginian Douglas Southall Freeman's *Lee*; by the New Deal's cultural programs that documented the lives of the poor and brought American culture to communities of all sorts; and by the enormous historical popularity of historical sagas of the past such as Margaret Mitchell's *Gone with the Wind* (1936) and its film adaptation (1939). The key term in describing the American way in the 1930s, "democracy," often implied a call to action, as the nation rallied to fight the chaos of economic disaster but also reasserted the need to reform this democracy in a world where Americans faced competition from fascists, socialists, and communists.[8]

Southerners in the 1930s, African Americans as well as white commentators, were part of that effort. The term "southern way of life" was the regional equivalent of this broader American search, one that enabled a variety of southerners in the 1930s to focus new attention on their region and lead to a growth in regional self-consciousness. Many references to it were within the Agrarians' twofold framework of usage: to most people who used the term, it meant either agrarianism or tradition. In a 1940 essay, for example, Howard Mumford Jones used the concept of a southern way of life to explore whether a contrasting New England way of life existed. He discussed the Vanderbilt Agrarians with their focus on "the question of Southern values," and he saw the result as "the assumption that the Southern way of life is both valuable and defensible." Jones also saw the Chapel Hill regionalists led by sociologist Howard Odum as focusing on values in grappling with a "southern way." He admitted that, although they might not be able to "give a definition of the Southern way of life," they were "determined not merely that the Southern way of life should be improved, but also that is should be preserved."[9]

A Business Way

In the interwar years, observers often noted the coming of an "urban civilization" to the South. The businessman/industrialist became a familiar cultural figure, an icon of an emerging southern middle class. Speaking of the businessman, Claudius Murchison wrote in 1931, "In southern civilization he is for the moment the man of destiny, more achieving, more respected and more followed than preacher, politician, teacher, journalist, lawyer, or technician." In the emerging machine age "he will build the foundations upon which all these others will stand and function," a future-looking figure rather than one bound to any burdens from the past. Murchison pointed out the rural origins of most twentieth-century southern business figures, who had no specific schools for training, few journals to study, and scarce conversations with businesspeople using more modern techniques in other places. The individualistic success of this businessman had given him "a big house on the hill, a command over the amenities of life, a new prestige for his family," all seen as "a just and natural reward." In Murchison's view, the southern businessman was proud of his achievement, and "he performed it in accordance with his religion, his philosophy, and his society."[10]

The term "Atlanta spirit" embodied a vibrant economic development sentiment in the 1920s. The industrial New South had seen the maturation of textile mills, the growth of hydroelectric power, and the emergence of the petroleum industry, particularly in the region's western sections. Progressivism, meanwhile, had placed businessmen at the forefront of reform, which at that point meant a concern for government efficiency and public services. Despite the Agrarians' concerns, "progress" was a widespread term of approval in the region. The urban middle class, chambers of commerce, and Rotary Clubs represented progress, and the modern, business-oriented southern way appeared in good governments, big churches, better schools, economic development, and real estate booms.[11]

Workers developed their own understandings of a southern way of life rooted in the traditional culture of the region and their confrontation with modernity. By the 1920s, to be sure, the South was the least unionized part of the nation, and strident antiunion feelings animated people in power. The South's predominant sharecropping economy did not seem to lend itself to organizing efforts, although the Share Croppers Union and the Southern Tenant Farmers' Union would enlist tens of thousands of desperate people for a while in the 1930s. The ruthless violence and intimidation of Deep South plantation owners and the criminal justice system they controlled ultimately frustrated those efforts and left landowners dominant. Industrial workers lacked a tradition of union support. Individualistic attitudes, a large supply of cheap labor, and the antilabor policies of state and local governments, observers claimed, worked against development of a popularized union way. Evangelical religion led some journalists and academics to see a fatalism among workers that worked against protest over business practices. Still, coal miners in Kentucky and elsewhere clashed with mine owners and police, and the United Mine Workers began from there to become a major feature of life in the mountain and hill country South. Steel, rubber, oil, and tobacco workers would struggle to organize in the South. The Great Depression's economic devastation in the late 1920s and early 1930s saw a rise in strikes, though, as a way to gain economic survival in desperate times, and they became part of a southern labor consciousness.[12]

The textile industry was the South's largest one, and it saw bitter confrontations between mill owners and workers. Strikes in Henderson, North Carolina (1927), and Elizabethton, Tennessee (1929), were forerunners of a more spectacular conflict at the Loray Mill in Gastonia, North Carolina, in the spring and summer of 1929 that represented a new stage in worker alienation from bosses who had imposed work requirements aimed at achieving greater efficiency and capitalist profits at workers' expense. These abrupt changes promoted a sense that the new requirements violated many of the decades-long norms about treatment of workers and represented unreasonable exploitation of workers. Communist organizers came to the area with the National Textile Workers Union, injecting a new radicalism into communities that had traditionally been based in kin and religious networks. As always, these reformers faced opposition from bosses, sheriffs and police, and newspapers. The Gastonia paper, for example, warned that the strikers were promoting communist world revolution, irreligion, racial mixing, free love, and just about everything that sounded suspect to conservative whites. The local government effectively banned picketing and prosecuted four union members for murder in an incident that the police provoked. The textile company evicted sixty families from their mill homes.[13]

The "Rebellion of 1929" encompassed scores of strikes, but Gastonia became the primary focus of national and regional attention. Aspects of regional
culture expressed and documented a worker way of life. Ella May Wiggins, a
young mother and mill worker, was a key leader of cotton mill workers and
an organizer of the strike. Her childhood had been in the logging camps of
the southern Appalachian Mountains, and she learned the traditional ballads
of the area and later sang them at mass meetings and worker stoppages. Her
songs raised the morale of the workers, presented their case to a larger public interested in folk music, and made her into a "labor agitator"—one of the
most despised figures among conservative white southerners. She was shot and
killed while riding in the back of a truck with other strikers in September 1929,
and union members felt she had been targeted for execution. Wiggins's story
became a national one, as she was a martyr to the American labor movement,
her songs became popularized in liberal and radical circles, and ballads and
novels memorialized her and kept the saga of southern labor struggles alive.
Wiggins was not alone in using traditional southern rural music as a foundation for airing worker grievances. Florence Reese, the wife of a Harlan County,
Kentucky, organizer, wrote "Whose Side Are You On?" singing out her anger
at the brutality of deputy sheriffs toward coal mine strikers, while Aunt Molly
Jackson's "Dreadful Memories" and "I Am a Union Woman" told of the grim
lives of coal miners. Even early country music performers sang topical songs
that aired grievances against the southern industrial system, including cowboy
singer Gene Autry's tribute to a radical labor organizer, "The Death of Mother
Jones." Such songs tapped into deeply rooted southern folk traditions and converted them into union consciousness that conceptualized a way of life in the
1930s caught between traditionalism and modern capitalist exploitation.[14]

Literature also played a role in celebrating workers. Six novels focused on the
Gastonia strike. Left-wing critics praised Grace Lumpkin's *To Make My Bread*
(1932) as a worthy proletarian novel that used social realism to link racial justice to working-class women's liberation, and it won the Revolutionary Writers
Union's Maxim Gorky award. Lumpkin grew up in a Lost Cause–drenched
family in Georgia, but, like her sister Katharine Du Pre Lumpkin, she became
a reformer against the segregated southern way of life, and she embraced a
communist ideology in the 1930s. Grace Lumpkin went to Gastonia and Charlotte and heard Wiggins's songs, especially "A Southern Cotton Mill Rhyme,"
a traditional ballad that the singer used for political purposes. Lumpkin's novel
helped cement Wiggins's reputation as a traditional southerner who became
radicalized and used her music to promote social change. Historian Jacqueline Dowd Hall notes that one of the novel's contributions was showing that
a people under attack could find in their vernacular culture the inspiration

"to transform themselves through acts of political reinvention." Lumpkin paid close attention to the cotton mill song and its political meanings, while exploring the creative exchanges between commercial and traditional music and the roles of women "as organizers, artists, and cultural transformers." Hall concludes that Lumpkin demonstrated how southern working-class people "fused music and social struggle." Lumpkin became part of what Benjamin Botkin called "proletarian regionalism," a movement in the 1930s to draw from American regional cultures a respect for the nation's diversity and its contributions to an enlivened democratic heritage in the face of the trauma of the Depression. Lumpkin and other writers and musicians who captured Gastonia's cultural importance created a radical type in a new imagining of the southern way of life, described by Hall as "a poor white Southerner capable of class-conscious action and solidarity across the color line."[15]

Lost Cause and Tourism

Although Grace Lumpkin escaped her family's Lost Cause heritage, that heritage was surging in the 1920s, and it rested comfortably with the New South materialistic ideology for many white southerners and remained so in the 1930s. National respect for the Confederate heroes, the seeming national acquiescence to white racial dominance in the South, and economic interaction all promoted sectional reconciliation. One form of economic development, tourism, showed in the interwar period how the South took advantage of the marketing of the Lost Cause as a key component of southern culture. It refurbished the Lost Cause version of southern civilization for modern times in order to attract northern visitors, using the images and stories of the Old South and the Confederacy to attract travelers with dollars. One key ingredient to this development was paved roads, with over 16,000 roads connecting points across the South by 1933 and twelve well-promoted interstate highways connecting the region to the rest of the nation. They bore names reflecting the South's past, including the Dixie Highway, the Andrew Jackson, the Robert E. Lee, and the Jefferson Davis. By the mid-1930s the routes south fostered considerable business activity, including motels, restaurants and cafés, gas and garage companies, ferry operations, amusement parks, roadside stands, and overnight cabins. Tourism in the South stressed particularities based on memories of the region's past as the reason for asserting a high-style southern civilization.[16]

Charleston, at the forefront of using the South's historical imagery to market itself to tourists seeking the romantic southern way of life, established hotels catering to visitors with resonant historical names such as the Francis Marion and the Fort Sumter Hotel. The city developed brochures, advertisements in

GEN. BRAGG'S HEADQUARTERS ON MISSIONARY RIDGE, CHATTANOOGA, TENN. "ALONG THE DIXIE HIGHWAY."

The Dixie Highway represented stepped-up modernization of the South in the 1920s. Charles Reagan Wilson Collection, Archives and Special Collections, John Davis Williams Library, University of Mississippi Library, Oxford, Mississippi.

popular magazines, and promotional film and radio spots; and opened a permanent tourist bureau to coordinate its efforts. It did not highlight the city's Confederate story but opted instead to present a reconstruction of its colonial and antebellum history that emphasized "the city's colonial elegance, old-fashioned hospitality, quaint manners, nostalgic atmosphere, and purported racial harmony." The historical narrative also embraced a romanticism of the Old South, with slavery a prominent feature. Southern life in Charleston's tourist presentation expressed the highest ideals of a refined civilization. A leader in the Charleston renaissance, Alice Ravenel Huger Smith, regretted the passing of the idyllic relationship of master and slave, and she used the worst racial imagery when she wrote that slavery had secured "the dominance of the man of civilization, of morals, and education, over the absolute savage."[17]

The white Charleston elite highlighted the city's decorative arts and architecture that they saw exemplified the "refined civilization of the Old South." Antiques reached a new level of popularity in the 1920s, and Charleston became one of the nation's most popular sites for their purchase. Their aesthetic quality had social significance, as evidence of the refinement and high civilization of Charleston's aristocratic elite, a sensibility still found then in the Carolina

Low Country but vanished in a cruder modern civilization. An important step was the creation of Charleston's historic district in 1931. "Visitors to the city understandably concluded that the destruction of the civilization that had created this 'Venice of North America'" was a tragedy, not just for its residents but also for the nation. Only the tenacity of Charlestonians and their loyalty to traditions of the Old South had made it possible for modern Americans to glimpse and experience "a vanished 'way of life,'" with tourism here promoting a traditional way in the increasingly modern South.[18]

Natchez, Mississippi, was also at the forefront in using the older South to project a vanished civilization for tourists. Hosted by two competing garden clubs, the Natchez Pilgrimage began in the early 1930s. The purpose was civic improvements, especially preserving local architecture. It allowed people from all across the nation to see an Old South in person that they had seen and heard in American popular culture. Hoop-skirted white women and Blacks clothed in servant outfits welcomed visitors to historic antebellum mansions. The Confederate Pageant was the highlight, with organizers assigning demeaning roles to Blacks, donning them in the tattered garb of cotton pickers, and having them sing spirituals in the pageant. The pilgrimage epitomized how elite white southerners presented a distorted perspective on southern history that excluded all but demeaning images of African American experiences. Thus, the southern business way of life exploited the Lost Cause memory, which remained vibrant even in the changing times of the interwar years.[19]

The South promoted tourism beyond the Lost Cause. Destination tourism led to new historic districts in Savannah and Charleston, while New Orleans capitalized on its music and food. Florida has a shared Lost Cause history with other southern states, but its cultural identity often departed from theirs. The state embraced an image that harked back to the earliest symbolism of southern places as an exotic paradise—the Garden of Eden. After the Civil War, Florida became a vacation destination for travelers from the North who sought escape from cold winter weather. At first, wealthy elites discovered the historic town of St. Augustine, whose history of Spanish inheritance added to the romantic qualities that came to be associated with Florida. Henry Flagler and Henry Plant oversaw the expansion of railroads that would connect the state to cities along the Atlantic coast. Elaborate resort hotels in Tampa, Palm Beach, Miami, and Key West drew the well-off and also journalists, who popularized the state in turn-of-the-century magazines that then attracted middle-class Americans. The automobile made travel easier, and the opening of the Daytona Beach Road Course in 1902 symbolized the role of the car in Florida tourism. By the 1930s, travelers could choose from many motor courts that dotted the roadside. Further attractions would come with environmental wonders such as the Everglades and with popular culture attractions such as Cypress Gardens, snake farms, alligator parks, and monkey jungles.[20]

Still, Florida embraced Lost Cause memory with Confederate monument dedications and Rebel battle flags waving. The twenty-fourth annual Confederate veterans reunion met in Jacksonville on May 6, 1914, attracting thousands of travelers whom the city's citizens welcomed not only to hotels but to private homes. The Lost Cause as a social movement—characterized from the late nineteenth century to World War I by large crowds gathering for dedications of monuments and the celebration of such events as Confederate reunions—gradually declined after World War I. The veterans themselves had been a constant reminder to white southerners not to forget the past, but as the ranks of the veterans thinned out, white southerners had less reinforcement for remembering the war. As time went on, the religion of the Lost Cause especially lost its fervor, with ceremonies and events associated with it less likely to evoke spiritual feelings. Lost Cause activities became less and less full community events. To be sure, Confederate reunions through the 1920s were huge events for the cities hosting them, but the national Memorial Day and the Fourth of July gradually replaced Confederate Memorial Day as central community events.[21]

The region's white people continued, nonetheless, to display the individual symbols associated with the Lost Cause and more broadly "the southern tradition." Southern regional patriotism, for example, was touched easily by the playing of "Dixie." The ritual scene for the singing of the tune moved after 1920 to sporting events, as high school and college students throughout the South as late as the 1950s would sing the song and wave the Confederate battle flag to get the athletic juices flowing, including those of spectators. The setting of organized sports was representative of modern social organization and norms, and white southerners easily adapted their regional sense of tradition to this new order. By then white southerners did indeed regard the traditions of the South as being of ancient heritage.[22]

Far fewer monument dedications were taking place by the 1920s, but Lost Cause devotees celebrated the building of the Confederate memorial at Stone Mountain, Georgia. Lamar Rutherford Lipscomb, writing in 1927, was ecstatic about the scale and significance of Stone Mountain, projected at that point to have 700 carved figures, "with column after column of Confederate grey-clad infantry carved in grey and everlasting granite" and the central figures of Jefferson Davis, Robert E. Lee, and Stonewall Jackson providing gravitas for the ages. He compared it to the Sphinx of Egypt and the Colossus of Rhodes, with the Georgia carving thereby representing a scale of achievement that would "immeasurably surpass every other monument of history." The long southern ideological quest for recognition of the region's superior life would be stunningly confirmed. Lipscomb used a key term to give moral authority to the southern way enshrined on the mountain: "What a magnificent civilization will this monument present," he wrote. As other historic buildings and landmarks deteriorated or were torn down, the monument's existence offered "one shrine left for the pilgrim to come to read the chiseled history of our Southland." Nearby Atlanta might be trumpeting a modern civilization, but this sculpted Georgia outcropping was a new assertion of that Confederate worldview anchored in the nineteenth century. Its white supremacist meanings were clear, as Stone Mountain served as the site where the second Ku Klux Klan had its first ceremony.[23]

The Lost Cause of the 1930s and 1940s thus continued a trend from the early twentieth century: the nationalization of the cause. Interest in Civil War history continued to rise in the 1930s, both regionally and nationally. The memory of the Civil War came to have special meaning in the Depression years as the national mood turned inward. In part this was an attempt to understand how a country reared on a history of inevitable success could undergo such social and economic catastrophe. A new self-doubt tempered the old conviction that Americans were always victorious. Millions who had been raised on the principle that hard work and moral uprightness produced success now found the sermon untrue. A nation disillusioned by its experience in World War I and economic disaster became intrigued by the comparison with southern failure in the past. Some sixty Civil War novels appeared during the 1930s, with Margaret Mitchell's *Gone with the Wind* only the most prominent. Douglas Southall Freeman's multivolume biography of Robert E. Lee dominated dozens of nonfiction accounts of the war. Pro-southern accounts achieved new influence, with *Saturday Review* editor Bernard De Voto complaining that "the South lost the War but is in a fair way to winning the renaissance of interest in it."[24]

The adaptation of the heroic Lost Cause appeared in popular culture, another modern genre that grew in the interwar years. The merchandising of the Lost Cause was seen in regional brands such as Maxwell House coffee and Avon cosmetics. They showed a romanticized, premodern, unchanging southern society. This image appealed to white middle-class women across the nation, who bought items (think Aunt Jemima) that would symbolically represent having a Black servant in their house to help them with meals. National advertising embraced the Old South and the Lost Cause with new enthusiasm. One advertisement in the 1930s featured "hams from Ole Virginia" that were "as good as though you went to the plantation and had Mammy cook it." National liquor advertisements especially loved to embrace the appeals of the Old South. A Four Roses whiskey advertisement in 1934 said it was "soft as Southern moonlight," with a color picture of Confederate colonels sipping their mint juleps.

A fine-dining restaurant links here with quintessential "southern hospitality."
Charles Reagan Wilson Collection, Archives and Special Collections, John Davis
Williams Library, University of Mississippi Library, Oxford, Mississippi

Another Four Roses advertisement, in 1935, pictured an eager Black servant
rushing forward with his tray of juleps. The advertisement used dialect to hark
back to earlier times of servanthood: "Yes, suh, Colonel, I's comin'!" In 1934 the
Illinois Central Railroad advertised tours of the Deep South in language that
explicitly linked racism to the appeal of the Lost Cause. "Land o' Lee, where the
'white man's burden' can be laid down in the Sunny South."[25]

The same national mood that doted upon the Confederate saga of defeat
also relished a romantic image of the Confederates. The economic doldrums
of the Depression produced a widespread desire for escape. Some found solace
in popular literature and the world of Hollywood sound films. The enormous
response to Margaret Mitchell's novel *Gone with the Wind* and the film from
it suggests something of what the public sought in the popular-culture Lost
Cause. Mitchell's romantic image of the Confederacy reflected the traditions
of late nineteenth-century southern novelists. It told of a superior antebellum
life overrun in wartime by a tawdry industrial society. Growing up, Mitchell
had listened to the tales of aging Confederate veterans, admitting later that she
was ten years old before she realized the Confederacy had not won the war. She
went beyond existing southern stereotypes in her portrayal of high-spirited
Scarlett O'Hara as a "new southern woman" who was not a shrinking violet, but

she also convincingly employed the southern cavalier imagery. She reproduced the racial stereotypes of the time and even made the Klan heroic redeemers from Reconstruction. The film was so popular that it must have reinforced for viewers old white supremacy feelings. It began with words flashing across the screen that told of the end of "a civilization gone with the wind," but the racist imagery suggested that that civilization was still in the minds of many.[26]

The Lost Cause could seem trivialized by commercial exploitation and popular culture's representations, but the adaptation of the Lost Cause to modern cultural expression kept it alive for observers thinking about a collective southern civilization resting still in the past. The Lost Cause continued to provide moral authority to many white southerners thinking about their society. A good example is Douglas Southall Freeman, one of the most accomplished and famous of early twentieth-century Virginians, winner of the Pulitzer Prize, author of renowned biographies of Robert E. Lee and George Washington, and editor of the *Richmond News Leader* from 1915 to 1949. When Freeman died in 1953, Civil War historian Bruce Catton praised him for maintaining the values of the older South that had produced the admirable Lee. Catton saw Lee as "the perfect representative of a society, a kind of civilization, a way of looking at life, which no longer exists." Still, Freeman represented that same civilization. "Even though that way of life ostensibly no longer existed," writes historian Keith D. Dickson, "Catton implied that southerners like Freeman, even into the mid-twentieth century, could assume and exemplify the ideals, values, and outlook of another time." Contemporaries regarded Freeman as one of the most modern of southerners, a supporter of Progressive Era reforms, paternalistic supporter of African American uplift, and outspoken opponent of lynching. Raised in Richmond during the height of the Lost Cause commemoration, he continued to evoke the spiritual meaning of the religion of the Lost Cause long after the social and commemorative movement had ended. In a 1924 article, "Virginia: A Gentle Dominion," in the *Nation*, Freeman stressed his state's economic progress but emphasized the continuing significance of Lee and the Confederate wartime experience in promoting in Virginia the centrality of "her people's courtesy, their reserve, and their sense of values." Freeman did not use the term "southern way," but his evocation of southern manners as the heart of Virginia's culture presaged later writers, such as William Alexander Percy, who made manners the essence of the southern way.[27]

Freeman included Black southerners among his exemplars of manners because of their presence in Virginia as far back as the seventeenth century and the fact that "the manner, the beauty, the intelligence of the Negroes of Virginia so definitely exhibit the benefits of their long residence in America." But Freeman fervently supported racial segregation. For Freeman and other elite white southerners steeped in social etiquette, the southern social system rested upon what he termed in 1919 "the continued and unchallenged dominance of Southern whites." Social relationships existed within what Freeman called "the First Law of the South: a white man is a white man and must be treated as such regardless of his station." Social equality would lead to miscegenation and the resulting ruin of the region. He called racial segregation "our Southern view." Freeman helped modernize the Lost Cause culture through his use of radio to comment on current events, and his weekly *Lessons in Living* broadcast religious homilies. His influence on the community of Richmond was broad and deep through his work in community organizations, and all of his activities featured his commitment to the Lost Cause as a set of values—paternalism, patriarchy, white supremacy, and religious faith, all seen as having particular meanings in the South because of defeat in the war.[28]

Freeman represented the flourishing of popular and public history in the South. State support for archives and museums had appeared in the Progressive Era, as did the first professionally trained historians, and they had become influential opinion makers by the interwar years. One goal of this new interest in history was to inculcate good citizenship and a respect for the past as a source for an organic social unity that could bond white southerners across social classes. The "white" was crucial as popular and public history presentations of the Old South, the Lost Cause, and Reconstruction buttressed white racial privilege as the inevitable result of history. Professional historians explored the historical origins of the southern racial order and supported white public opinion's view of slavery as a benevolent institution and of racial segregation as an inevitable basis for the South's racial order. Archives collected materials only on the history of white people, and museums presented stories of only white southerners, denying any legitimacy to contrary narratives of African American history.[29]

Folklore and Popular Culture

"Folklore" was one of the most familiar descriptors of the American South in the interwar years, one familiar to Freeman and other commentators on the South. The association dated at least from the late nineteenth century, but what was new after 1920 was the rise of anthropologists and sociologists who used modern research and interpretive models to study folklife. Sociologist Howard Odum made "folk sociology" one basis for his theoretical efforts to understand the South, while African American writer Zora Neale Hurston used her training in anthropology with leading scholar Franz Boas to do extensive fieldwork in her native South. The *Journal of American Folklore* published frequent studies of the South, and collectors of oral lore and crafts roamed widely. Folklore could be a conservative force, as in *I'll Take My Stand*. Andrew Lytle's essay, for example, conveyed the ways that folk customs, rituals, oral lore, and other aspects of folklife provided the essence of southern white family and community life and anchored region-wide culture. Popular writers and scholars used folklore as a source for racist and demeaning stereotypes—such as the standard local newspaper columns that showed bumbling, lazy, or violent Black people. Progressives, though, also deployed southern folklore in the 1930s as a part of efforts to understand and celebrate American democracy and diversity during the challenge of the Great Depression. They included major studies of African American, Native American, and ethnic folklore traditions. Folklorist Benjamin Botkin saw folklore not as simply a backward-looking, premodern form of culture (as conservatives did) but rather a dynamic force that responded and adapted to modern life. Botkin hoped regional folklife could promote "cultural values derived from tradition as the liberator, not the container," of culture. African Americans themselves used folk songs, sayings, beliefs, humor, and performance to challenge the restrictions of Jim Crow society. The trickster who outwits his oppressors is a recurrent motif that offered not only a literary source of rebellion but a behavioral one in everyday life.[30]

Popular culture expanded rapidly from the 1920s onward and brought ridicule from conservative traditionalists. Popular culture offered enormous opportunities for people who once would have been trapped in tenant farming or exploitive millwork. Popular music was a prime example, producing forms that, in fact, grew often out of folk origins. Country music became identified with the South gradually. Barn dances on early radio used to be heard in the Midwest as well as in southern states, but the emergence of Nashville's Grand Ole Opry in the 1930s as the preeminent performance venue for what was then called "hillbilly music" brought increased association of the music with the South. Key Opry figure George Hays, among others, invented a country music image and performance style that demanded entertainers dress in stereotypical rube clothing and talk in vernacular regional slang. From these interwar developments, country music would become one of the most identifiable southern working-class cultural genres associated with the South, until its spread in the 1970s across the nation diminished its regional associations. The music itself from its beginnings in the rural countryside was rich with diverse, interracial meanings, with African instruments such as the banjo and musical forms such as syncopation influencing white performers and with Black southerners hearing white country sounds on the radio and adding them to their musical repertoire.[31]

Record companies, though, marketed the new popular music of white southerners and African Americans in different categories that reflected and reinforced the segregation of the South. Once known as "race music," blues music came out of rural and small-town life, but it soon adapted, like country music did, to modern technology (radio, recordings, public address systems). Black musicians made identifiable southern regional sounds, different though they might be in the east Texas of Blind Lemon Jefferson, the Mississippi Delta of Muddy Waters, or the Piedmont of the Reverend Gary Davis. American popular music in the interwar period, though, as represented by Tin Pan Alley, continued to present romanticized rural, often plantation, images of the South as a backward, if appealing, place for those busy modern Americans in other places. Blues influenced the early history of jazz that was associated with New Orleans from the second decade of the twentieth century. Freed slaves who moved to the city brought plantation songs that merged with the city's Caribbean Creole music to form the new sounds of jazz. A white group, the Original Dixieland Jazz Band, produced the first identifiably jazz recording, "The Livery Stable Blues," in 1917. Jazz in the South would be an interracial music of performers and bands, with African American influence formative as represented by trumpeter Buddy Bolden, who led the most creative jazz group. Such southern and border-south cities as Memphis, St. Louis, and Kansas City became centers for jazz during the interwar period, but New Orleans retained a long association as the southern home of jazz.[32]

By the interwar years, southerners had long been a sporting people, with hunting and fishing popular across social classes, racial groupings, and regions within the South. But in the years after 1920, organized sports rose to a new prominence that would make them among the most frequent cultural activities associated with the region. Baseball, for example, had taken deep root in small towns and cities across the region in the early twentieth century. Although no Major League Baseball franchise came into the South until after World War II, the region had popular minor league and industrial league teams in such cities as Atlanta, Nashville, Birmingham, Louisville, Memphis, and Little Rock and in mill towns, and southern college teams dominated at that level. Mel Allen and Red Barber were well-known radio announcers who spoke with notable southern accents and vernacular talk. Such major league stars as Joe Jackson, Ty Cobb, Tris Speaker, and Luke Appling evoked southern imagery, but no one surpassed Jay "Dizzy" Dean as a southern popular culture figure in the 1930s. Dean was a talented and successful pitcher for the St. Louis Cardinals (whose border-state location made them a popular team in much of the South). His colorful behavior, loquaciousness, storytelling gifts, and identification with southern rural food, music, and language made him an icon of the region in the national culture. The South's Jim Crow segregation excluded African Americans from participating in integrated organized sports, but the Negro Leagues, widespread throughout the South, reflected baseball's popularity with

Black southerners. Football would become even more popular than baseball in the South after World War II, but one saw the beginnings of that popularity in the interwar years. The turning point in the popularity of college football in the region came with the University of Alabama's victory over the University of Washington in the 1926 Rose Bowl game, as well as the Crimson Tide's invitation to play in the bowl game again the next year. Alabama beat Stanford University in the 1927 game, a triumph that led Alabama governor Bibb Graves to declare, "The hearts of all of Dixie are beating with exultant pride." He insisted that the Tide had "upheld the honor of the Southland and came back to us undefeated." Such talk showed how white southerners could unite around football triumphs in intersectional competition. An *Atlanta Journal* article made an explicit regional cultural connection, as the victorious Crimson Tide now belonged "to the whole South just like the Stone Mountain Memorial" dedicated to Confederate heroes.[33]

Howard Odum and Southern Sociology

Sports proved a lively venue for expressions of the southern way of life based in culture, but academia supported the most explicit reflections on the southern way. The South's most prominent social scientist, Howard Odum, like Freeman, grew up on stories of the Lost Cause, particularly from his two Confederate veteran grandfathers. The stories failed to nurture the romantic legend of the Confederacy in him; rather, their embittered attitudes promoted a sense of the tragic meanings for the defeated South. Odum became one of the most significant southern intellectuals of the interwar period, a modernizing social scientist whose original contribution to discussion of the southern way was to promote a new critical realism about the South, a southern self-scrutiny that had not been typical before the interwar years. Ironically, as time went on, he came to embrace a southern folk culture as the source of an enduring southern way that he argued was resistant to social change. He was an academic entrepreneur, prolific scholar, perceptive editor, and social planner, but in thinking of southern culture, civilization, and way of life, his role as an intellectual is of greatest interest. He was no original thinker, but he brought a social scientist's awareness of cultural theory and social problems of the time to the interwar South. He and his colleagues at the University of North Carolina were influential new voices in generating ideas and concepts about the South.[34]

Regionalism and folk sociology were two of his most important concepts, and after World War II Odum wrote *The Way of the South* (1947), an explicit engagement with our key concept. Odum's historical moment was the same one that produced the Agrarians, as post–World War I southern intellectuals wrestled with the coming modernity in a region that had reified tradition after the Civil War. Odum saw with unusual clarity the entire scope of the South, able "to see not only the strengths and moral virtues of southern society but the conflicts, tensions, and evils as well." He invested enormous significance in southern culture as an organizing outlook. "It seems clear," Odum insisted, "that every major problem, from farm tenancy to political democracy, is bound up with the 'culture' or 'system' of economic and social ideologies and arrangements of the region, which in turn represent the realities of recent historical development and more than the actual possibilities of the region under different conditioning and expansion." Thinking of the South's "system" of "economic and social ideologies and arrangements" led him to explore the southern way of life.[35]

Odum learned early twentieth-century organic social theory in graduate school, and he emphasized the need for balance and harmony in society. Organicism saw society as a natural organism that grew and developed in its institutions, with a properly functioning society achieving integration of social groups and institutions. When applied to the South, organicism promoted looking at the region in its totality. Culture played a crucial role in this application of organicism to the South. Franz Boas had been among the early twentieth-century leaders in defining an anthropological understanding of culture, one that assumed many cultures with their own particular logics and grounding to social functioning. Scholars should study particular folkways and customs and look for the cultural patterns that defined any society's outlook and behavior. Cultural relativism was a scholarly necessity to escape from ethnocentric preconceptions. To be sure, Odum was not immune to the Victorian-era appeals of Matthew Arnold's idea of culture as the best and finest that civilization had produced, identifying cultural patterns of the Old South that did not reflect anthropological understandings of culture but instead pointed to southern manners and breeding as the southern way. His reference to cultural patterns here reflected his primary modern anthropological understanding of the need to objectively study culture.[36]

Odum came to Chapel Hill in 1920, to head the new School of Public Welfare and the South's first department of sociology. He founded the Institute for Research in Social Science and started the *Journal of Social Forces*, and he assisted in establishing the University of North Carolina Press, which published many of the research projects from Odum's social science colleagues. The journal's series of editorials in the early 1920s criticized the shortcomings of the region. They complained of "the present coercive, intolerant, reactionary religious and intellectual tyranny" and attacked the Ku Klux Klan and the fundamentalist movement for their hypocrisy and xenophobia. Odum insisted that the time had arrived for "a sort of frank, honest, scientific, stock-taking of ourselves, giving full recognition to strong points but also to weak points and deficiencies, with a view to starting out at once upon a more creative and articulate South." Believing that the southern white masses were capable of social change, but demagogic leaders and inadequate social institutions had failed them, he wanted to bring together academic knowledge with public opinion to further social change. He called for close study of African Americans' social conditions to improve their lives without challenging racial segregation, but he wanted to reform it to achieve his broader goal of balance and harmony in a rational society. His abiding scientific critical spirit, awareness of the South's immense problems, and appreciation for the region's time of transition led him to launch his own ambitious research and to support that of others who addressed the need for sweeping changes that reflected a vision diametrically opposed to the Agrarians' southern way.[37]

After 1930, Odum worked toward defining a theory and a methodology of regionalism. Interest in American regionalism had begun to surface in the 1920s and appeared in new literary journals, poems and short stories, and "little magazines" published in Charleston, Nashville, and New Orleans as well as places outside the South, in the Midwest, New England, and the far West. The New Deal in the early and mid-1930s soon gave added impetus to increased concern for regionalism as part of a rediscovery of American democracy. Odum was a leading figure in this national network of regionalists trying to create a new civic religion around "folk liturgies" that would strengthen regional cultures around aesthetic concerns distinctive to American places and decentralize national power. Social science discussions of southern civilization and the southern way of life thus took place within the framework of regionalist ideas.[38]

Odum's "regionalism" began as a descriptive term for a large-scale assessment of the South's resources; became a term for the social rebuilding of the South and then a proposal for national planning with new regional institutional agencies exercising much power; and finally was a theory of social change, which Odum called folk sociology. The diversity of ideas he included in regionalism failed to create a new and enduring construct, but in the interwar period his regionalism was the liberal alternative to the conservative agrarianism and led Odum to put forward his own explicit use of the term "southern way."[39]

Odum's *Southern Regions of the United States* (1936) used almost 700 statistical indices for measuring regional culture, from distribution of farm income to mortality rates and what he called the "plane of living" of the region's people. The South was in the lowest realms in the nation, and Odum used the word "pathology" to suggest the seriousness of the South's situation in his assault on the romanticized legends about the region. He identified comparative differences

between the nation and the region, but he also showed socioeconomic differences within the South and differentials among races, social classes, and
twenty-seven regions within the South. Odum sought to undermine the mythic
southern view of the region's history in order to force white southerners to face
the facts, and he insisted that the antebellum era was essentially a frontier.
The planters who saw themselves as aristocrats had really just been men on
the make, and the South's problems stemmed partly from the survival of an
arrested frontier development.

Odum thus defined the problem South with impressive factual specificity.
That concept went back to the early nineteenth century, when abolitionists
from Frederick Douglass to Hinton Rowan Helper chronicled the limitations
and shortcomings of southern life, and such late nineteenth-century critics
as George Washington Cable, Walter Hines Page, and W. E. B. Du Bois, as
well as national governmental and charitable agencies, pointed to the South's
backwardness in so many socioeconomic and health categories. Odum's contribution to defining the problem South was to use social science methodology,
coming from within a leading southern university, to skewer the South's failures and to urge reform.[40]

Odum had begun his career with conventional New South racial views about
African Americans that saw them through the lens of Victorian belief in the
savagery of primitive peoples, and his early studies of African American folk
music were full of stereotypical generalizations. But he took African American
culture seriously and saw it as a foundational part of southern culture, with
the need to integrate Blacks into southern society to achieve the proper organic
functioning. In *Southern Regions* he offered a critique of the older racism, noting that modern social scientists believed that race was not "an entity in itself,
a purely physical product," but the "result of long developed folk-regional culture." He denied that African Americans were an inferior race and cited much
evidence suggesting African American capacity for intellectual accomplishment. He offered no defense of racial segregation in the book, but his limitation
in imagination appeared in his statement that it would be "asking too much
of a region to change overnight the powerful folkways of long generations."
He expressed "hard-boiled, realistic, evolutionary hope for the future" and
never abandoned his belief that American democracy of equal opportunity
and justice should apply to African Americans. He served on the Commission
on Interracial Cooperation and was president of its successor, the Southern
Regional Council, which promoted improved race relations. He lacked the social imagination and courage, though, to engage the inevitable limitations for
African Americans of racial segregation and never called for its end. In that
regard, his understanding of the southern way rested in white supremacy, as

well as in folk culture, in ways this progressive reformer of segregation could not acknowledge.[41]

By the late 1930s and 1940s, Odum's scholarly work was leading to his understanding of the southern way of life as essentially folkloric in nature. One dimension of his regionalism, folk sociology, rested on his understandings of folkways, technicways, and stateways. Most fundamental were folkways. Odum absorbed William Graham Sumner's concept of folkways, with its accumulated evidence of the tenacity and diversity of cultural mores. After Odum, the idea of cultural mores would recur in conservative opposition to social change including during the civil rights movement. Sumner's view of folkways was "a near-fatalistic and frequently racist view of the slowness of cultural change." Odum's mentor, Franklin Henry Giddings, argued that the term "mores" suggested "the folkways of a more serious sort than some others—folkways above all that have been more or less subjected to review and to criticism." Mores had conscious community support, as that community had "picked out those particular ones for more or less enforcement—not enforcement by law but enforcement by the attitude of the community, by the approval and disapproval of the neighborhood, by shunning and boycotting people not approved of, we have the mores." The reactions of the folk society become almost automatic. It was a disturbing portrait of a closed society enforcing its supposedly ancient ways, ways beyond easy change.[42]

Odum conceptualized "the folk" in general at this point as static and tenacious, like Sumner and Giddings did, but he gave the folk little specific social class and historical grounding. He spoke on the endurance of folkways in his presidential address to the American Sociological Society in 1930. Odum's main interest was in understanding the process of change from simple folk culture to advanced state civilization. A core belief was that the folk were a constant in a world of perpetual change, with the slow evolution of folkways, customs, institutions, and moral beliefs. "Technicways" was the term Odum used to describe the transitional habits and customs that developed as folk society adjusted to innovations associated with modern science and technology. Technicways quickly could overwhelm traditional folkways and the accompanying moral order supporting them. Odum developed the concept of technicways, but he did not ground it in the actual operation of power in the South, dominated by powerful agricultural and industrial forces. Finally, in Odum's conception, stateways emerged, representing governmental legislation codifying cultural ways associated with the folk. The dramatic and rapid changes to existing folkways and the moral order—changes associated with technicways—led to the need for changes in laws and increased regulation of society through stateways. Odum had learned from Giddings that folkways always defeated stateways, as

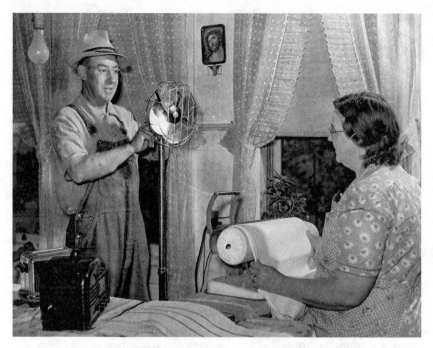

New Deal programs brought modern ways to the rural South, as in this Arthur
Rothstein photograph of electricity coming to a couple in Knox County, Tennessee.
Library of Congress, Washington, D.C.

legislation that tried to change folk customs inevitably failed. Odum's enthusiasm for social planning contradicted this belief in the mid-1930s, but by the
end of the decade he was returning to Giddings's teaching as a foundation for
his emerging concept of the southern way of life.[43]

By the late 1930s, Odum had become fearful of the growing power of technology. "Faster, faster, faster; more, more, more; bigger, bigger, bigger; new, new,
new"—he lamented that such traits were the "overpowering mode of the age."
He asked, "How much speed, bigness, science, technology for bigness' sake, for
speed's sake, for science's sake, for technology's thrills can society stand and
survive[?]" That question animated his concern as a sociologist to assist the
southern society through the cultural lag that existed between folkways and
technicways. He feared the lag could result in a "crisis, maladjustment: and if
the process goes on long enough, disintegration." Out of measuring the process
of such change and crisis, the collision between folkways and technicways, he
hoped to calculate a rate of tolerable change for societies undergoing change,
such as the South in the New Deal and World War II periods.[44]

By the 1940s, Odum focused on one aspect of culture, the folk culture, which he saw as persisting through the rise and fall of civilizations. "Culture is the cumulative processes and products of the societal achievement and denotes the quality of a folk society," he wrote. When older civilizations, such as those of Greece and Rome, passed away, new cultures arose from the folk. He saw the folk society as natural, whereas civilization was artificial. The folk had "a quality of inner consistency and unity, or spiritual and religious motivation, in contrast to the more individualistic behavior in the larger cities, on the one hand, or of their regimented behavior in the case of the most advanced totalitarian countries." Odum here, politically progressive though he was, harkened back to the old concept of the South's essential unity, seen here in its folk dimension.[45]

Civilization had, of course, long been the descriptor whose layered meanings were attached to the South, and one of Odum's contributions was to analyze civilization as part of his conceptualization of the southern way of life. Fond as he was of listing, Odum cataloged the traits of civilization that represented the essence of the state: urban life, technology, intellectualism, the concentration of power, and artificiality. Whereas folk culture had kinship tribes, clans, and political groupings, modern civilization had democracy, socialism, fascism, and communism. Odum discovered Oswald Spengler in the late 1930s and often cited his theory of the rise and fall of civilizations. Spengler saw a natural cycle of cultures, corresponding to nature's rhythms and making an analogy with childhood and youth, middle age, maturity, and finally old age. Civilizations began as agricultural and rural societies with distinctive cultures, then became villages, then industrial societies, and finally urban and technological societies. The contrast between the earlier stages of culture and the later ones of civilization appeared as machines replaced human labor, the state replaced folk custom as the source of authority, the city took the place of the country, money became the source of value, and popular sovereignty gave way to governmental power. Odum dwelled on Spengler's prophecy of the decline of contemporary civilization, and the story of the rise and fall of fascism was a recurring Odum trope, justifying his suspicions of modern civilization. The social scientist who once had identified with progress had embraced a dark and pessimistic sensibility by the end of the 1930s. He concluded that "modern society has too much civilization and not enough culture," and he urged sociologists to seek to understand how to achieve "a better balance between culture and civilization." Odum applied his theory to the South, as he saw it embodying his general outlook on culture and civilization.[46]

Odum's *The Way of the South* (1947) was the culmination of his thought on southern society. Written after World War II, it reflected his sense of the dangers of unchecked technological change and a warm appreciation of the folk character of the South. He saw "the powerful folk culture of the South, strangely unified in its complex fabric of many weavings." The region's unity, he would insist, was because, despite its diversity, "the way of the South has been and is the way of the folk, symbolic of what the people feel, think, and do, as they are conditioned by their cultural heritage and the land which Nature has given them." He identified the sources of this folk society as fourfold: nature and the frontier; the prolonged rural life nurturing "rugged individualism" and struggles with the land and climate; the remnants of frontier folk culture in isolated mountain, piney woods, and swamp country; and the African American folk culture. From the South's earliest history, he saw "the essential importance of the way of the frontier in the total way of the South."[47]

Odum was critical of the plantation South, and he lamented an unthinking aristocracy, a suspicion of education for the plain folk, an untenable attitude toward African Americans, a culture based on superficial understanding of the classics, and an exaggerated embrace of luxuries, physicality, hard drinking, and dueling—all of which counted against "the old southern civilization." He lampooned the women of the United Daughters of the Confederacy, who "preserved mass pictures of the Old South based upon romantic developments from individual incidences of beauty and glory, pictures that never were on land or sea or earth or sky." He returned to his long criticism of the South's lack of self-scrutiny from the Lost Cause mentality and pointed out how harmful the old order had been toward anyone who "brought to light facts not conducive to its glorification." Through a history of slavery, the Civil War, and Reconstruction, the South, moreover, became "so conditioned to race as class and caste that it reflected the racial situation as supreme over all others, a symbol of cultural survival and an issue of life and death."[48]

Drawing from his University of Mississippi teacher Thomas Bailey, Odum put forward the southern credo on race as foundational to his southern way. The southern racial credo was that the African American was inherently inferior to white people and could not aspire to rise above a low station in society, a defined social place below all white people. The South was a country of white dominance, and political and economic opportunities should not be given to Black people because they would lead to social equality and the mixture of the races, which was contrary to all the major premises of the southern way of life. Kept in his place, the Black man should be treated "kindly and justly." Odum recognized that "such bold and bald statements of a credo were so vivid that it was perhaps surprising to southerners." The racial credo "was in such complete contradiction" to the demands being made on the South in the name of "war and freedom and Americanism that the resulting tension and conflict were easily explainable." Odum the reformer pushed the region to move beyond its white supremacy, but he recognized its salience to understanding the rising racial ways of the post–World War II era.[49]

Religion was another fundamental factor in Odum's southern way. Early American religious conditioning had continued to shape developments in the South more than in other parts of the nation. He singled out "the emotional power of the evangelical religion among the common folk and its use as a tool of demagogic appeal in politics" as distinguishing traits of religion in the South. He saw two "elemental manifestations" of religion shaping the overall southern way of life. One was the beliefs and the faith of the evangelical groups seen in formal worship and the widespread support of churches, and the other was the power of song, with secular folk song and music reinforcing spiritual music. "The singing South, both white and Negro," was a key embodiment of "the way of the South."[50]

In his book on the southern way, Odum made his fundamental distinction between culture and civilization in regard to the South, and he saw a "practical distinction between the culture of the rural folk and the civilization of the urban center." The South was essentially the former, and the culture of its people was apparent in "the folkways of politics in the solid South and of religion, the most powerful folkways in the world"—a strident assessment in a global perspective. He evoked the mannered way he saw in "the folkways of manners and customs, of food and drink, of clothing and apparel, of housing and the other traits common to universal culture" but with particular meanings in the rural South. In the end, for Odum, "the way of the folk" was "the way of culture."[51]

Odum's writings made him a central figure in the interwar progressive critique of the South's social and economic problems, but his broader significance was seen in the network of scholars associated with him who produced critical works on the South. The social sciences flourished in the region, in research associated with Odum's institute but also at Fisk University, under the leadership of Charles S. Johnson, and at the University of Virginia's Institute for Research in Social Science. But Odum's students received the major grants to do seminal research, and their publications helped establish the discipline of sociology in the South. The South was ripe for research on such topics as sharecropping, lynchings, mill villages, Jim Crow segregation, chain gangs, and rural folk culture. Sociologist Rupert Vance became the leading authority on the cotton tenancy system and a pioneer in studying demography in the South. Journalists, other scholars, and public policy experts looked to Guy B. Johnson for insight on African American folklife and race relations. Arthur F. Raper authored a classic work on lynching and a deeply researched study of sharecroppers in the region. All three had studied under Odum and shared his desire to probe deeper into southern society than anyone had done before. Odum taught these and many other young social scientists in this period to approach the South with objectivity and a critical eye.[52]

Odum worked closely as well with William T. Couch, the director of the University of North Carolina Press, which emerged as a powerful force in publishing books that encouraged a critical approach to the region. The press published over 450 books during Couch's tenure, with 170 of them dealing with the South. Many of them were historical accounts, but the press addressed controversial contemporary social and public policy issues as well. Its lists included works on literary criticism, collections of white and Black folklore, and works by nonsoutherners who brought an outside perspective to southern problems that native white southerners did not always appreciate. The press's work that brought the most public attention—often negative—was in regional social science projects coming out of Odum's institute. Odum himself could be quite cautious by the late 1930s, but the publications he sponsored often discussed subjects that polite southerners did not usually engage. Few other southern publishing outlets existed in the interwar period, certainly so for publications critical of the region's powerful institutions and individuals. Because these books came out of a prestigious southern university, they gained credibility in many quarters that might not otherwise have been responsive to the criticisms. By the 1940s, Odum took satisfaction from what he called his "experiment in 'cultural' publishing." He noted that even though he and the press had cooperated on books that had antagonized many southerners and attracted the kind of publicity that universities usually do not like, still "we are now winning ground rapidly with our own people." He cited increased legislative appropriations for his institute and the press and the widespread use of their books throughout the South.[53]

Critical Perspectives

Odum's identification of traits of the southern way of life did not preclude his willingness to criticize fundamental features of regional culture, which was an example of one of the most important developments in southern culture between the wars—the emergence of new critical perspectives on the region. From before the Civil War, white southerners had promulgated their belief, often defensive, in the superiority of their civilization. With the end of southern white aspirations toward political independence with the defeat of the Confederacy, the perception that Reconstruction was a "tragic era" of Black rule that should never be repeated, and the turbulence of the political and social developments in the 1890s, southern whites had grasped an orthodoxy that resulted in a Solid

South that demanded white unity and Black acceptance of inferiority in an authoritarian system, one that white southerners still proclaimed as superior to other American places. This sensibility survived turn-of-the-century reform efforts and criticism by individual writers and regional and national agencies pushing to modernize the South and better incorporate it into the nation-state. World War I and the Great Migration had disturbed this orthodoxy, and the 1920s and 1930s produced new questioning of southern orthodoxy. White writers, whether journalists or fiction writers, made important contributions to this critical realism that unveiled the sordidness of southern racism, poverty, violence, and political demagoguery and undermined assertions of a long, romanticized southern life. Southern critics often saw the region now in national perspective, with the region's way of life being out of step with national values and an American civilization that they used as a counterpoint to the backwardness of southern civilization. They often undercut claims of the superior southern way of life. Thomas Wolfe's character George Webber, in *The Web and the Rock*, identified "the curse of South Carolina and its 'Southerness'—of always pretending you *used to be* so much, even though you are not now."[54]

North Carolina journalist Gerald Johnson was a protégé of the South's major nemesis of the era, H. L. Mencken, and he used his mentor's slashing style and language to indict the South, this time with a voice from inside the region. In 1923 he complained of some southerners' "swashbuckling defiance of civilization" as represented by the advanced societies of Western Europe. Events of the 1920s had fostered an image of the region as the benighted South, and Johnson pointed to the need for regional progress. South Carolina writer Du Bose Heyward had once lamented that Johnson asked too much when he expected Charleston writers to raise the cultural level of an entire section of the country, but "civilizing was expressly Johnson's purpose, and the southern writers he preferred were those—chiefly his fellow journalists—who led in examining the South's shortcomings." Johnson insisted that what those editors and their newspapers "have injected into Southern journalism is, in the last analysis, nothing but candor."[55]

In his 1924 article "Critical Attitudes, South and North," Johnson analyzed how the South had fallen behind standards of a progressive American civilization, as the Civil War had produced a "moral exile" of the South from the nation and the need for "reconstructing a shattered civilization." The "cataclysm of seventy years ago" took the South back to near frontier conditions, which were "notoriously inclement to the arts, especially the highly sophisticated art of criticism." The time was long overdue, though, for the South to develop its own internal critics if the South was to advance. Southern critics would be more effective than outsiders because, in the first place, "they have the Southern viewpoint, and can therefore be understood, and in the second place because they have the most reliable information, and therefore can most frequently spot the joints in the Southern armor." For these same reasons they could best explain the region to the nation. But to be most effective, "they must be critics, not press-agents."[56]

Southern liberal journalists of the 1920s and even earlier in some cases had been critical of the demagogues who dominated politics, the obsession with prohibition, the popularity of the Ku Klux Klan, and the spiritual excesses of religious fundamentalists, and they used the enduring descriptor of "civilization" to indict southern white behavior. They blamed the white working classes for their susceptibility to racism, superstition, intolerance, and provincialism. The effects of the Great Depression and the early actions of the New Deal refocused their critical attitudes, now more concerned with economic issues, such as the problems of the farmer and the industrial worker. They joined the battle with the Agrarians and saw their ideology as inadequate for a healthy region's way of life. With southern whites' support for the New Deal, the journalists became more hopeful about the southern masses and the possibilities for building reform upon their votes to deal with the South's problems. They came to see economic development and accompanying changes as the best way to deal with racial problems, hoping that overall economic and social advancement would lift everyone in the South. They became more critical of the New Deal by the late 1930s because of the possible effect of new federal government reforms on southern racial patterns. They continued to share many of Franklin D. Roosevelt's goals, though, and they remained important for their often-courageous criticism of southern ways they regarded as backward.[57]

Johnson's 1935 essay "The Horrible South" discussed the emergence of new fiction writers who were critical of the South in their representations and undermined any long-standing assertions of a distinguished South. Johnson pointed to Ellen Glasgow, Frances Newman, Julia Peterkin, Du Bose Heyward, Paul Green, and Howard Odum for unveiling a dark underside to traditional sentimental, romanticized portrayals of the South. He labeled T. S. Stribling, Thomas Wolfe, William Faulkner, and Erskine Caldwell as "the real equerries of Race-Head and Bloody-Bones, these are the merchants of death, hell, and the grave, these are the horror-mongers-in-chief." In terms of understandings of the South's civilization, they drove "the conservative Confederates into apoplexy" because they created a backward image of the region that undercut the Lost Cause narrative of a noble white southern people. "Dixie is full of spirited old women of both sexes," Johnson wrote, "who decline to recognize any merit in men and women who have scandalized them." Johnson insisted that thoughtful people had to acknowledge that each of the writers he mentioned had "made a contribution to the advancement of civilization in the South," and Johnson's essays themselves frequently employed differing "civilizations" to contrast advanced Western civilization with southern civilization. These writers "set down what they see, or what they honestly think they see, around them; and if what they see is dreadful, it is for the South to look at it."[58]

Johnson noted that bringing out into the open the South's problems should be seen not as a fault but rather as a necessary step in dealing with the problems. He pointed especially to Faulkner's recent novel *Sanctuary*, which had brought condemnation throughout the South. Johnson reminded readers of the southern men who had "walked through some of the scenes described in 'Sanctuary' without turning a hair, but William Faulkner screamed until he curdled the blood of half the country." Readers should ask, "Who is the more civilized Faulkner or the men who were never horrified by a real lynching half as much as they were by his description of one?" Moreover, "when is the South more civilized—when its young men view its horrors impassively, or when they are so revolted that they howl until the continent rights again?" His summary judgment again came back to the issue of civilization at stake in these writers' critical realism, in this case a specifically southern civilization. *Sanctuary* had "done well for the South in revealing the fact that there are rotting spots in our civilization that are capable of producing things so revolting that the mind recoils from their contemplation."[59]

Johnson saw the writers of his time using their critical view of the region to bring renewal. The "horrible South" that these writers portrayed "was the South that was morally, spiritually, and intellectually dead." The South since the Civil War had "fatuously regarded every form of art, literature included, as a pretty toy, but in no sense one of the driving forces of civilization." Johnson portrayed that "ghastly, cadaverous South that for forty years after the Civil War groped in the twilight region between civilization and barbarism." The New South period had been little better, though fattening itself more. The modern South's writers were "bitter muscular men with swords," but the South needed them. The "pretty literature" of the past represented in fact a South dead in mind and spirit, reeking of "tuberoses, funeral flowers," but the rigorous, earthy literature that turned a critical eye on the South was bursting with new life for the region, "smelling with the odors of the barnyard, not those of the charnel-house." Johnson's frequent use of the term "civilization" suggested the new critical realism seen by writers in the 1930s who promoted the advanced values of Western civilization, contrasted with a specifically southern civilization's corruption. The South became a rotting body that the writers were resurrecting. "Dixie, far from standing aghast, ought to hail this uproar with the triumphant shout of the Father broadcasting the return of his Prodigal Son," for her youth "was dead and is alive again, was lost and is found," using biblical references from the southern evangelical vocabulary.[60]

Johnson singled out Faulkner, and the Mississippian indeed portrayed a divided South, teetering between civilized life and backwardness. Howard Odum had lived in Lafayette County, Mississippi (home of Faulkner and the model for his mythical Yoknapatawpha County), and he confided that "I myself have known Yoknapatawpha and it is not purely imaginary fantasy. I have been close enough to Faulkner's quicksands to sense something of its terrors and have often imagined behind the cedars and columned houses, that anything could happen there." Faulkner, he said, depicted the South as a "frontier echoing both primitive and civilized heritage." Southern mythology had portrayed a heroic past, especially seen in the Lost Cause, but Faulkner excavated the southern psyche to show that the good and the bad were "all hopelessly tangled." The South here was not the bastion of "glory and innocence" such as in mythology, but "the past was now seen as a fatalistic curse upon the present that no southerners could wholly escape." Historian Daniel Singal used a resonate term, "web," that observers have often used to characterize a "southern way." He wrote that Faulkner's South was "tormented and paralyzed, trapped in an intricate web largely of its own making, which tied together sexuality, avarice, and aggression with the 'higher' facets of southern life until they were all hopelessly tangled."[61]

Faulkner created characters who stood between the civilized and primitive, as in the "tragic mulatto" typology. Charles Bon, in *Absalom, Absalom!*, is Thomas Sutpen's child, whom Sutpen refused to acknowledge because of the belief that his wife's family in Haiti had included a trace of Black blood, which tainted Bon in southern society. Sutpen had been married to the daughter of a wealthy sugar planter in Haiti, which Faulkner describes as that "halfway point between what we call the jungle and what we call civilization." Faulkner's wording suggests his view that both the jungle and civilization are constructs, but with life-or-death meaning for his characters. Such Faulkner novels as *Light in August, Absalom, Absalom!*, and *Go Down, Moses* unveil that social construction of race, not the immutable factor that southern mythology had assumed.[62]

Faulkner was the leading figure of the Southern Literary Renaissance, the flowering of creativity among southern writers that began in the 1920s, lasted for decades, and produced such other acclaimed writers as Richard Wright, Robert Penn Warren, Thomas Wolfe, Carson McCullers, Katherine Anne Porter, Jean Toomer, Zora Neale Hurston, James Weldon Johnson, Erskine Caldwell, Arna Bontemps, and Tennessee Williams, among others. Many of the Black writers were part of the Harlem Renaissance as well, a separate but closely related literary project. The writers classified as part of the Southern Literary Renaissance represented the embrace of cultural modernism, a phenomenon of the early and mid-twentieth-century Western society that would shape discussions of the southern way of life. Usually seen in cities and cosmopolitan places and characterized by aesthetic experimentation, modernism in the South spoke a regional, rural vernacular in language, setting, narrative, and character but did so with such modernist techniques as stream-of-consciousness narrative and naturalistic plots. People in the region had lived for several generations with the traumatic results of defeat in the Civil War, and self-reflections on southern traditions, history, race relations, and religion became central themes of the resulting literary expressions.

With the quickening of modernization after World War I, writers saw change coming to the region and the apparent tenuousness of regional traditions. Moving away from Victorian-era certainties, many southern writers explored such typical modernist themes as alienation, fragmentation, and marginality. They represented a generational rebellion against the older, Lost Cause narratives. Most had been born around 1900, growing up on stories of Confederate virtue and heroism, but they generally rejected the cavalier ideal—which had provided a particular southern embodiment of civilization—as dated. Instead of the Lost Cause's romantic South, these young writers explored the odd, bizarre, and eccentric, and they embraced such gothic themes as decay, terror, parody, and caricature. Critics of this southern modernism saw it as disrupting their assertions of a southern way of life resting in traditionalism, but the writers' national and international success led eventually to the old Agrarian, Donald Davidson, embracing them as a sign of southern cultural superiority—fulfilling that old dream of a southern civilization that would be both distinctive and distinguished.[63]

Poor Whites

Other writers who offered a critical perspective on southern culture helped shine a light on the region's poverty, which became a national issue in the midst of the Depression, and the discussion of it extended the late nineteenth-century's problem South discourse into the modern South. Poor whites appeared frequently in the stories and novels of the region's writers in the 1930s, the writers often representing the poor whites as beyond the pale, as southern savages. Thomas Wolfe, in *The Web and the Rock* (1939), has his protagonist George Webber repelled at the thought of them. "Without knowing why, he always wanted to smash them in the face," Webber says, and admits that he "hated everything about them." Not only were they "foully different from the people that he liked in all the qualities that made for warmth, joy, happiness, affection, friendship, and the green-gold magic of enchanted weather—he felt there was also in them a physical difference, so foul and hateful that they might be creatures of another species." Wolfe was one of the critics of southern ways, but his rhetoric portraying the South's poor whites could have been out of white supremacy's handbook in characterizations of African Americans.[64]

Few writers went as far as Wolfe in his derogatory portrayals of poor whites, but most southern white writers used representations surrounding their want and degradation. Erskine Caldwell had grown up in Georgia and seen the widespread poverty and need associated with the tenant system, and his portrayals of poor southern whites showed people dehumanized by an exploitive economic system. Literary critic Robert Brinkmeyer compared the Jeeter Lester clan in *Tobacco Road* to the idealized images of the Vanderbilt Agrarians' southern way of life, and he pointed out that Jeeter had the Agrarians' ultimate attachment to the land, unable to imagine living another way of life, despite his impoverishment. "The land has got a powerful hold on me," Jeeter says. But his unwillingness to leave his hopeless situation makes him appear "at one and the same time agrarian hero, mindless primitive, and victimized tenant farmer." Caldwell's characters are gothic figures who practice a primitive agriculture and are incapable of handling modern technology such as automobiles. Despite his derogatory characterizations, Caldwell was something of a reformer, who condemned the social and economic southern way of life that had produced these figures. He believed that the Lesters would not exist if cooperative farming and better schools were available to them. Caldwell's comic form, rooted in the antebellum southwestern humor tradition, portrayed the absurdities of their experiences in farcical terms that suggested a parody of the Agrarians' imagined southern way.[65]

The documentary genre captured a realistic side to southern rural life in the decade beyond the literary naturalism, and these themes of a fiction writer such as Caldwell exposed critical weaknesses in the region. The genre challenged the Agrarians' view but also explored the consciousness of its poor people. This was writer James Agee and photographer Walker Evans's achievement in *Let Us Now Praise Famous Men* (1941). "These children," Agee wrote after visiting pupils in a south-central Alabama town that he documented, "both of town and country, are saturated southerners, speaking dialects not very different from the negroes in *Brother Rabbit! Old Southern Tale!*" The families that they documented, named Ricketts, Woods, and Gudger, seemed the poorest, most isolated of southerners, and yet southern culture indeed saturated them, even if the Agrarians hardly mentioned poor people. People like them became national symbols during the Depression, when southern poor folk took on

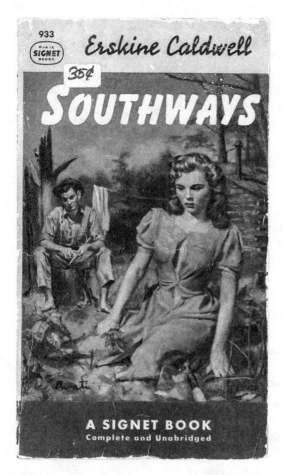

Erskine Caldwell was the South's best-selling author of the mid-twentieth century. An example of his work is this collection of fiction with a sprightly cover. Charles Reagan Wilson Collection, Archives and Special Collections, John Davis Williams Library, University of Mississippi Library, Oxford, Mississippi.

new ideological meaning for a nation itself facing hard times. Were they impoverished because of their biological degeneracy, as long portrayed in representations of the southern poor whites, or were they the product of an unjust and exploitive economic southern way of life?[66]

At the heart of the concept of a way of life was consciousness, the mindful acknowledgment of a particular way of social being. Agee spoke often in the book of human consciousness and made central to his concerns the "individual, anti-authoritative human consciousness." But he highlighted regional particularities in understanding these families. The broader human consciousness must yield to a "convergence in local place of time," and the book was a sweeping and thorough documentation of a variety of southern civilization, with Agee and Evans intentionally investigating regional consciousness and culture. In this case, the tenant was "of the depth of the working class" but also "of southern Alabamian farmers." The tenant and his family were "living in a certain house" unlike other houses, and they were "farming certain shapes and strength of land, in a certain exact vicinity." Agee portrayed the families living in a sensuous southern consciousness, as he sat on porches at night hearing the sounds of crickets, locusts, and birds, and he repeatedly evoked the sound of the whippoorwills, with "their tireless whipping of the pastoral night," although this is far from the pastoral world of the Agrarians. In discussing the Ricketts house, Agee places not only human family members there but also "the dogs, and the cats, and the hens, and the mules, and the hogs, and the cow, and the bull calf." Agee describes the Gudger dog Rowdy as "intensely of his nation, region, and class as Gudger himself."[67]

Agee captured how language defined these people and how sentences "spilled out in a cool flat drawl" as families sat on porches at night, and he identified a masculine language of southern male violence, "that slow, keen, special, almost weeping yearning terror toward brutality, in the eyes, the speech, which is peculiar to the men of the south and is in their speech." Agee dwelt on the defining heat of the place, as he walked around Birmingham and thought "that for miles and hundreds and hundreds of miles all around him in any direction he cared to think, not one human being or animal in five hundred was stirring." This climate-induced paralysis took its toll on the South's "victims and their civilization," and he saw these local people as part of a broader system he understood as a regional civilization. In observing and contemplating the specific cultural features of southern poor whites, he documented an agrarian southern way of life that one must place beside that of the Vanderbilt Agrarians, who had mostly omitted poor whites from their idealized southern way. Agee and Evans presented, though, a similar specificity of detail as the Agrarians had in exploring their southern way.[68]

Interracial Southern Way

"They say we are defending our way of life," wrote South Carolina farmer, Presbyterian layman, and social activist James McBride Dabbs in 1958. "What is our way of life? They say segregation," but he would have none of it. The "entity called the South was hammered out by black man and white man working together." The land was the setting for building a biracial community, which was at the heart of any southern way of life. This version of the southern way of life rested in the critical self-assessment seen in other areas of southern interwar intellectual life. It grew out of the South's liberal reform ethos that reached a new level of self-consciousness in the interwar era and would flourish with the end of Jim Crow segregation and the search in the 1970s for a new southern ideology reflecting a changed society. Antecedents for this interracial southern way could be found in the nineteenth century among advocates of biracial coalitions in Reconstruction and in the era of agrarian reform in the 1890s. These attempts at interracial cooperation had been limited by racial assumptions of white reformers, economic rivalries, and the chicanery of their opponents. The early twentieth century had seen progressives engaging issues of a biracial society, with the uplift philosophy associated with Booker T. Washington a main message. Interracialism then meant mostly a white paternalism that aspired at best to a civility of conversation across racial lines about making a fairer Jim Crow segregated society.[69]

In the interwar years, the interracial way took institutional shape through organizations such as the Commission on Interracial Cooperation (CIC) in 1919 and the Southern Conference for Human Welfare (SCHW) in 1938, both dealing with southern regional problems through interracial dialogues. Women's groups such as the Association of Southern Women for the Prevention of Lynching and the YWCA worked toward moderation on racial issues in the early twentieth century, fostered contacts between Black southerners and white southerners, and promoted interracial ideals. The Southern Regional Council succeeded the CIC in 1944 and thereafter served as the most effective agency for exchange of information and advocacy of interracial goals. These groups failed to call for the overthrow of racial segregation in the interwar years, but they worked for betterment of African Americans within the separate-but-equal system, and they surely planted ideas in the public mind that would one day help white and Black southerners adjust to what seemed to most white southerners in the interwar era the inconceivable end of Jim Crow laws.[70]

The concept of the interracial South came to be identified in the interwar years with southern liberals. Among the most prominent of southern leaders, they opposed race-baiting politicians, racial violence, intolerance, and bigotry, and they sometimes put themselves in harm's way with their opposition to the South's mean-spirited forces. "Backward" was an apt descriptor for the region in many ways for the southern liberals who supported New Deal reforms and generally were on the side of what reformers saw as progress at the time. They advocated African American advancement, as well as that of working-class whites, through advocacy of economic opportunity, better educational facilities, collective bargaining rights for workers, civil service reform, and improvements in the criminal justice system. Many journalists were among the liberals, although not all would have seen themselves as interracialists. Believing in the possibility of southern progress, they were quite aware of the terrible depths of white racial instincts and the violence and intimidation whites would employ. They were eloquent advocates of the free speech often circumscribed in a society that put such stress on orthodoxy. The liberals had learned the myth of Reconstruction as a disastrous historical era and could not embrace the possibility of African American political rule or true social equality, and it made them doubtful that federally sponsored racial change could work until a distant future. The nation recognized journalists' achievements, with many receiving national awards for their progressive views at the time and national foundations funding interracial work in the South. They could be eloquent in protesting lynching and other outrages against Black southerners, but overall they showed little urgency in insisting on the need for fundamental changes in the South. Most of them would not call for an end to segregation until the late 1940s or later. As Mississippian David Cohn put it, one had to accept the racial situation with "a sore heart, a troubled conscience, and a deep compassion."[71]

Despite southern liberals' criticisms of some of the South's ways, they were well socialized in southern culture. They had heard family stories of Confederate heroes and could wax eloquent on the Lost Cause; they resented northern interference in the South; and they often practiced a comfortable middle-class evangelical religion or a deep faith that would lead some of them to calls for more fundamental changes in the South than other more cautious liberals could embrace. Virginius Dabney's *Liberalism in the South* (1932) offered a primer to southern white liberal thinking. From an old Virginia family and a patrician in manner, Dabney was well known as a friend of African Americans. He spoke out forcefully for many reforms African American leaders championed, including opposing lynching, advocating repeal of the poll tax, urging an end to disfranchisement laws, and by the early 1940s embracing the end of streetcar segregation. Dismissing paternalism as an outdated form of social order, he urged whites to allow full citizenship for African Americans and to recognize that African American progress was essential for advancement of the region as a whole. He was an interracialist in believing that Blacks and whites should engage each other and work together to improve society through selective reforms. Nonetheless, he refused to abandon the color line because he feared its end would promote miscegenation, and by the 1940s he was vociferously opposing civil rights activists and lumping them with white troublemakers who stirred racial antipathies.[72]

Dabney was a supporter of the CIC, which deserves a closer look for its role in the changing consciousness in the 1920s that began to establish a newly defined concept of the southern way of life. The key figure was Will Alexander, who as a young Methodist minister in Nashville worked with southern YMCAs at the end of World War I to promote racial harmony. Postwar racial violence had shocked him and spurred him to bring together Black and white southerners to discuss racial issues, defuse local conflicts, and promote good causes. The group did not intend to challenge segregation, but the concept of allowing African Americans to voice their concerns on an equal footing with whites went well beyond Progressive Era reform groups such as the Southern Sociological Congress and the University Race Commission, neither of which allowed Black members. The CIC strategy was to mobilize elite whites and bring them together with Black leaders and to try to convince the former of the need to raise the status of Blacks, with more progressive attitudes filtering down eventually to the white masses. CIC members were from the region's cities and its growing middle class. Universities, newspapers, and churches supplied most members, with a few businessmen involved but few planters. Religion was a major influence on the work of the organization. Religious faith motivated Alexander, and CIC statements often mentioned Christian values as the source of interracialism. Prominent church leaders were active members, from all the major southern denominations.[73]

A key force in the CIC, women were led by Texan Jessie Daniel Ames, who in 1930 helped organize the CIC-funded Association of Southern Women for the Prevention of Lynching. They saw the issue of lynching in much the way Ida B. Wells and other African Americans did earlier—as a violation of civilized behavior. Southern women utilized the respect for women in the region and undercut the use of southern chivalry to justify lynching. An antilynching conference in 1920 that led to the women's group had resolved that lynching was not a deterrent to Black sexual violence and was instead a "menace to public safety" and a "triumph of anarchy" that brutalized the community in which it occurred, including especially women and children. These reformers objected to using the supposed protection of women from Black rape as justification for lynching, dismissing the "crown of chivalry which has been pressed like a crown of thorns on our heads." Willie Snow Ethridge, one of the group's founders, said southern women were going to "make war upon barbarism that has flourished in their name." Most of the organization's work was done at the local level, as respectable women worked with political leaders to prevent lynchings from occurring, a classic example of the commission's strategy of using the South's "best people" to speak against racism as a way to influence public opinion and public policy.[74]

Although scholars have shown that the Jim Crow system was never as unchallenged or immutable as once thought, interracialists experienced verbal intimidation, social ostracism, and worse for any criticism they made of the southern way of life. In 1926, Alexander told a meeting in Birmingham that he thought segregation laws were unjust, although he stopped short of calling for their repeal. Segregationists nonetheless saw his criticism as a challenge to the system. Many members of the CIC rushed to affirm that they had no desire to end segregation, as they feared loss of any influence to moderate the system. "The incident served as a warning to Southern liberals," as most of them believed that to be "identified as integrationist would negate any positive influence they might have."[75]

The CIC became decentralized in the 1920s and brought together 7,000 people of differing racial views. The group sent representatives into the countryside to talk with African American leaders about their concerns, which included the failure to use the titles "Mr." and "Mrs." in referring to Black people, pervasive Jim Crow signs, delays in mail service, inadequate public schools, and unrepaired water lines in Black sections of town. CIC representatives then worked with local officials to try to address such issues when possible and to keep open interracial lines of communication. The CIC publicized countless hate crimes, with the National Association for the Advancement of Colored People's Walter White often calling on Alexander's organization to investigate the exploitation and brutalization of tenant farmers.[76]

Although they embraced the concept of an interracial way of life, the interwar interracialists practiced only limited formal interaction within the group. Legal segregation was so pervasive in the period that it circumscribed interracial activities, but segregated Black and white committees did emerge in hundreds of counties through the South. William O. Brown, a white southerner who taught at the University of Cincinnati, noted in 1933 that the organization's meetings between "mutually ghettoized" whites and Blacks had a "farcical" aspect about them. Black southerners had little active voice in the CIC. As of 1934 the group employed only one paid African American, and no Black southerners worked in the commission's Atlanta office. Bringing together Black and white southerners could produce powerful moments of reconciliation, though. Alexander noted that at a 1921 women's meeting in Memphis, the Black women "boxed the compass pretty well for these white women about what it meant to be a Negro wife and have a Negro family in the South." As Black women entered the hall, Belle Bennett led white women in singing an old religious song, "Blest Be the Tie That Binds." Throughout the 1920s and 1930s, women's biracial cooperation in cross-racial Christian groups took root and helped progressive white women better understand conditions in the Black South. Out of such experiences would come increased discussions that promoted an interracial southern way of life.[77]

The New Deal changed the context for those promoting change in southern racial ways. Southern liberals became more emboldened and less cautious in general in working for social change. Southern New Dealers showed a new willingness to question southern racial ways and saw the federal government now as an ally for furthering efforts to assist African Americans living under the deplorable conditions that liberals recognized. Most liberals had come to see those problems as essentially economic ones, and support of New Deal programs designed to ease misery in the region would help both Black and white working people. Southern white liberals would direct or strongly influence the New Deal's major efforts that assisted African Americans in the region, including the Farm Security Administration, the National Youth Administration, the Fair Employment Practices Commission, the Works Progress Administration, and the Public Works Administration. They would write the statement that called the South "the nation's No. 1 economic problem" and justified federal government attention to the region.[78]

The CIC changed its strategy in the New Deal years and began emphasizing research and educational work as the organization gained funding from national foundations interested in the "problem South" that the work of Howard Odum had helped illuminate. In the 1930s the group gained funding from the Rosenwald Fund to support the Southern Commission on the Study of Lynching, and Arthur F. Raper, the commission's main researcher, published his investigation of every lynching that occurred in 1930 in *The Tragedy of Lynching* (1933). The Carnegie Foundation funded the Conference on Education and Race Relations, which sponsored summer workshops to promote the teaching of race relations courses in southern schools. The Rockefeller Foundation supported efforts to incorporate African Americans more fully into New Deal relief and reform programs, and Will Alexander promoted African American advisers in New Deal agencies and tried to address the needs of tenant farmers. Alexander worked with other researchers on *The Collapse of Cotton Tenancy* (1935), which criticized federal government farm policies and encouraged a federal program of long-term loans for tenants to purchase land. Alexander became head of the Farm Security Administration in 1937, charged with advancing such a plan.[79]

These efforts of the CIC contributed to turning southern public opinion against lynching and to promoting changes to assist tenant farmers suffering from the Depression and the decline of the cotton economy. A concern for respectability and caution in racial matters still limited the members' activism, though, as they saw the organization only as one to promote fairness and conciliation within a segregated society. Their belief in civility reflected a natural instinct of many in the group who had been trained well in the mannerly southern way and believed that congenial discussion of issues would avert possible racial violence better than stirring the pot of African American discontent. Their achievements were limited ones but important at the time in providing a precedent of biracial cooperation and interaction for the future and in paving the way for more activist groups. When Alexander went to work for the federal government, he became convinced of the need to end racial segregation in the South; however, his absence from the CIC contributed to its decline.[80]

The SCHW succeeded the CIC and was a product of the economic devastation of the Great Depression and the liberal reformism of the New Deal. Its members included academics, labor union leaders, journalists, and politicians, most calling themselves southern liberals. They put the need for better race relations at the top of their concerns, which also included electoral reform and promotion of social justice in general. Scholars credit Joseph Gelders, a union organizer for the International Labor Defense, and Lucy Randolph Mason, the public relations director for the Congress of Industrial Organizations, with the idea for the SCHW. They gained the moral support of Franklin D. Roosevelt, who saw the organization as a way to rally southern support for his federal government initiatives, and his wife Eleanor became an enthusiastic supporter of the SCHW and even encouraged its members to focus on such specific concerns as racial segregation, low wages, and inadequate schools. The SCHW's first meeting in Birmingham in 1938 quickly made it notorious, as its biracial nature became clear in bringing together 1,200 delegates, including 300 African Americans. In a famous scene, the meeting's first day had no segregated seating, but police chief Eugene "Bull" Connor insisted that Black people and white people sit in different areas. Eleanor Roosevelt was in attendance, and she symbolically took a seat between the two segregated sections. Such a dramatic scene was a landmark in evolving recognition of the interracial southern way of life.[81]

The SCHW was a more ambitious organization than the CIC in its racial rhetoric and activities, including supporting protests against racial incidents, circulating petitions, and lobbying. It had close ties with northern liberals, the labor movement, and the National Association for the Advancement of Colored People, each contributing to the SCHW's reputation as a radical group among many white southerners. Writer John Egerton points out that the group's members were not radicals, as their leadership was middle-class, white southern males. Charges of communist involvement plagued the organization throughout its history because its strong prolabor stance made it a convenient target for anticommunist crusaders from the 1930s into the Cold War era. Mississippi's racist senator Theodore Bilbo condemned the SCHW as a "mongrel conference" and an "un-American, communistic outfit of white Quislings" that catered to "negroes, Jews, politicians, and racketeers." He added that if he had "to name the Number One Enemy of the South today, it would be the Southern Conference for Human Welfare." The SCHW throughout the 1930s nonetheless failed to condemn segregation in forthright terms, although many of its members did so. In 1946 it did go on record against "discrimination on the grounds of race, creed, color, or national origin" and called segregation "fundamentally undemocratic, un-American, and unchristian."[82]

Organized labor was another prominent force in promoting the idea of a southern interracial way of life, and the SCHW maintained close ties with labor leaders. At the extreme edge, beginning in the 1920s communists embraced the vision of a color-blind society and made some recruits in the South. Historian Glenda Gilmore argues that in those years, individuals and organizations, like the communists, whom the larger society judged to be un-American, "took on the task of bringing the South in line with the dream of perfection, or at least as measured by the promise of equal protection of the law." Lovett Fort-Whiteman was a Dallas-born, Tuskegee-educated African American who became the first Black man to join the American Communist Party. *Time* magazine called him the "Redest of the Blacks" for his efforts at broadening communist concerns beyond the class struggle to address racism. He championed the idea of African American separatism and self-determination in the Black Belt, and communists briefly embraced the idea of an African American homeland there. Communists preached racial equality and practiced interracial interaction more deeply than perhaps any other group in the South in the 1920s and early 1930s, but they gained only modest support in North Carolina and Alabama. Socialists were surely more numerous, with youth groups such as the League of Young Southerners, the Southern Negro Youth Congress, and the League of the Youth Congress representing idealistic young people who worked across racial lines, despite the constant obstacles created by the laws and customs of segregation.[83]

The organized labor movement, like other left-leaning groups, emphasized interracialism as a necessity for the solidarity of the working class that crossed racial lines in the South. Union organizers pursued their goal of uniting Black and white workers and increasing their economic and political clout. The workforce in some industries, such as textiles, was overwhelmingly white, making cross-union alliances with biracial groups that much more difficult. The Textile Workers Strike (1934) and Operation Dixie's post–World War II union organizing efforts were both unsuccessful and weakened union appeal to many whites. Legal restrictions and white customs on race, employer resistance to union efforts, race-baiting, and unfavorable labor laws all made organizing across racial lines difficult. The Congress of Industrial Organizations nonetheless took the lead in the South in championing interracialism in such leading industries as mines, oil and gas, garment-making, and tobacco, which employed significant numbers of African American workers.[84]

Interracialism on southern ground was a complicated story. Most white workers participated in interracial unions because of economic necessity and the conviction of strength in worker unity across racial lines. Union leaders saw any cooperation as a step in the right direction and often agreed to segregated conditions in meetings and activities. In 1935 George Mitchell visited union meetings with Blacks and whites in Birmingham, and he described Black and white folk sitting apart from each other. On the platform, the Black representative was usually a preacher who opened the meeting with a prayer, and Black members spoke deferentially to whites. They addressed whites as "Brother" or "Mister," while whites called African Americans by their first names or "Brother" but not "Mister." The fewer the Black people in a particular local union, the more Jim Crow's spirit ruled. The fraternal spirit that permeated the gatherings, though, impressed Mitchell. "The interesting thing about such meetings," he wrote, "is the balance they strike between adherence to and departure from traditional Southern ways," his use of the latter words indicating how interracialism departed from the segregated southern way of life.[85]

Organized labor's efforts brought Black and white workers together more than ever before, and the unions became supporters of early civil rights efforts. Historians refer to the "long civil rights movement" that goes back to the 1930s, and organized labor was a key sector of that effort in the South. The organizational techniques, protest strategies, and foundational ideas of the 1950s civil rights movement had their origins, in many cases, in the work of organized labor. The Highlander Folk School, for example, functioned in the 1930s as a training ground for organized labor and then later became more intentionally a center for civil rights activism in the 1950s. These efforts grew out of recognition of interracialism's practical potential to bring change to the South.[86]

Lucy Randolph Mason was a key figure in negotiating interracialism in the organized labor movement and broader southern society over a forty-year career. A descendant of some of the most prominent Virginia families, she grew up the daughter of privilege but within a progressive family that was part of a lively social Christianity in Richmond. She embraced the social gospel that insisted that true Christianity demanded social justice and became a close ally of Myles Horton, a founder of the Highlander Center. She worked in public relations for the Congress of Industrial Organizations in Atlanta during the Great Depression and went on to be what John Egerton describes as the group's "troubleshooter and roving ambassador in the South." She roamed the South, preparing the way for labor organizers to safely begin their efforts in local communities, speaking disarmingly with preachers, newspapermen, sheriffs, and mill owners, as well as workers, strikers, and the unemployed. She lived out her belief in racial equality. "In my thinking," she wrote to an African American colleague on Richmond's interracial committee, "there are no inferior or superior races or nations, but only some who have had more opportunity . . . to get a running start on their brothers." She added a line that suggested a faith in civilized values that would preclude racism: "Really superior races would never exploit weaker peoples, for their superiority would rest on moral virtues." Morality for Mason was a foundation of the southern interracial way of life.[87]

Mason's faith led her to involve clergymen in organized labor's efforts. "Church people ought to do something to bring about the Kingdom of God on earth," she wrote. "That's why I am in the labor movement." On Labor Day 1937 she asked southern ministers to "speak clearly and courageously on behalf of the rights of workers to organize and bargain collectively through Representatives of their own choosing." Lambasting ministers who were "hopeless to try to educate" and others who were too "scared and ineffectual" to witness for justice, she also contested the pro-business pamphlets that promoted racial divisions and antiunion sentiment. Visits with Black union members resulted in friendships with African American leaders. She was centrally involved in Operation Dixie in the late 1940s as the Congress of Industrial Organizations intensified its union organizing efforts to bring together clergy and labor leaders. A Richmond friend described her as "a spirit consecrated, living on a plane far above that in which ordinary folk dwell." Mason's use of religious language and attempts to involve clergymen hinted at a vision of a southern civil religion that rested on egalitarian dreams for the future South.[88]

Mason praised Frank Porter Graham as an essential figure in the SCHW, and he represented a crucial presence in the interwar years in tying together the forces of organized labor, interracialism, the federal government, and the university network across the South. He served as president of the University of North Carolina for forty years beginning in 1930. He defended the freedom of the university and of students and faculty to pursue research, teaching, and outreach in controversial areas that begged for attention. The university became the most acclaimed in the region under his leadership with his scholarly integrity, concern for social engagement, and political shrewdness. He was willing to take on issues that the conservative political leadership of the state would rather have not touched, including abuses in the textile industry and religious fundamentalism's intolerance. Other southern universities looked to his leadership.[89]

An early test was in his support of the rights of organized labor. After a 1929 textile strike in North Carolina, Graham wrote a "Statement on North Carolina Industry," and he persuaded 415 other leaders in the state to defend workers' rights to collective bargaining and freedom of protest. Graham called for shorter workweeks, the end of night work, and stronger child labor legislation. He did not hide his sympathies for laboring people, sharecroppers, and the underprivileged where he found them. He realized the need for federal government efforts to address the wide-scale social problems of the South, and he became an active New Dealer. Franklin D. Roosevelt appointed him to chair the National Advisory Council on Social Security, and he served during the war on the national War Labor Board. President Harry Truman appointed him to the President's Committee on Civil Rights, which produced a seminal report on the nation's racial problems and proposals to address them. One of his defining moments, though, had come a decade or so earlier, when he had been the first chair of the SCHW. At its first conference, held in Birmingham in 1938, he delivered an opening address that appealed to the values of freedom and democracy that he saw under siege in Europe but also in the South. "The black man is the primary test of American democracy and Christianity," he told the group. "The Southern Conference for Human Welfare takes its stand here tonight for the simple thing of human freedom. Repression is the way of frightened power; freedom is the enlightened way. We take our stand for the Sermon on the Mount, the American Bill of Rights, and American democracy." His use of the term "we take our stand" draws our attention back to the 1930 Agrarian manifesto, but here Graham offers a very different vision that expresses a Christian democratic vision of reform of an unrighteous system.[90]

Religion inspired other figures who applied Christian socialism to their efforts at achieving interracial justice in the interwar South as a new embodiment of the southern way of life. Howard Kester, for example, grew up in a middle-class Virginia family and learned evangelical religion's stress on sin and salvation, but the contradiction between his religion and the racial violence he saw troubled him. He applied New Testament teachings to the South's racial issues and came to believe the race issue was a matter of Christian ethics and its solution was in a literal reading of the scriptures' teaching of human brotherhood. He and other white Christians formed the Fellowship of Southern Churchmen and practiced what they called a "prophetic evangelism" that used tent meetings long associated with revivalism and now dedicated to the message of social justice.[91]

Kester found his true cause when he joined the Southern Tenant Farmers' Union (STFU) in the mid-1930s, one of the most intriguing examples of interwar interracialism. The STFU emerged in July 1935 when a desperate group of twenty-seven Black and white sharecroppers met in Tyronza, Arkansas, a delta town north of Memphis, Tennessee. Those gathered elected a white chairman, a Black minister as vice chairman, and a holiness preacher as chaplain. A few former followers of socialist presidential candidate Norman Thomas joined the movement as organizers, along with E. B. McKinney, a popular Black preacher from nearby Marked Tree. The gospel of unionism spread rapidly in eastern Arkansas as the STFU gained 15,000 members by the end of the summer. Delta planters fought the group with all their considerable power to intimidate potential union members through a reign of terror. The union's high point was in 1938, when it had 31,000 members and national magazines and a *March of Time* newsreel had publicized the brutality used against the unionized tenant farmers. The violence and intimidation eventually halted the union's progress.[92]

The Southern Tenant Farmers' Union attempted to organize sharecroppers in
the rural South during the 1930s, but ruthless opposition from planters led to such
scenes as this eviction from the Dibble plantation near Parkin, Arkansas.
Library of Congress, Washington, D.C.

Kester was the most consistent voice for racial egalitarianism in the STFU. Its
members embraced interracialism, not out of racial enlightenment necessarily
but out of common economic grievances and the understanding that uniting
sharecroppers across racial lines offered the best hope in an otherwise impossible economic situation. The union supported Hillhouse Farm, an agricultural
cooperative in Mississippi that offered homes, land, and shares in the cooperative's profits to an equal number of Black and white farmers. This interracial
experiment was an affront to Jim Crow, but its organizers were cautious, not
using titles such as "Mr." and "Mrs." when addressing African Americans. "We
are upholding the true Christian attitude toward the races," said Presbyterian
minister Sam Franklin, "but not doing anything foolish." Newspaper editor
Jonathan Daniels visited Hillhouse and described the "queer compromise" he
saw there. The houses were in two rows, with white members living in one
row and Blacks in the other. "On the banks of the Mississippi the directors of
the cooperative are almost as sensitive to Jim Crow as it is possible for human
beings to be." Despite this caution, Hillhouse was bold in calling in 1936 for
integrated schools and forbade its members from attending labor colleges that
still practiced segregation. Work was at the center of dominant understandings

of the southern way of life, well before commentators in the 1950s used the term itself. Slavery and sharecropping were the mainstream South's answer to who would do the work of the region's plantations and farms and factories, but organized labor, including the STFU, represented the efforts of the South's working people to find ways in which an interracial way of life could bene-fit workers rather than perpetuate the status quo's advantages to planters and industrialists.[93]

Katharine Du Pre Lumpkin

A closer look at three individuals offers insights into the interracial southern way of life as such leaders defined and lived it in the interwar years. These three people were intellectual and activist leaders of the region who consciously began in this period to contest dominant racial and agrarian understandings of the southern way of life. They illuminate how individuals schooled in the orthodoxies of southern society could break away from the previous dominant ideologies of the southern way of life and reformulate the ideology into a pro-gressive one that would come to fruition generations later.

Katharine Du Pre Lumpkin underwent a dramatic change in conscious-ness that makes her perhaps the best example of an advocate for an interracial southern way of life. Her memoir *The Making of a Southerner* (1947) traced her late nineteenth-century childhood in an elite white family that was suffused with the religion of the Lost Cause. Despite defeat in the war, she wrote, "our fathers know their way was good." Southern white leaders agreed "they should keep their way of life." Her father's way embraced a totality of southern culture, but the rhetoric and language of the Confederate memory was the conceptual glue that made the South an entity to be defended. She remembered her father saying of his children, "Their mother teaches them their prayers. I teach them to love the Lost Cause." He told southern men to "let your children hear the old stories of the South; let them hear them by the fireside, in the schoolroom, everywhere, and they will preserve inviolate the sacred honor of the South." The term "sacred honor" sacralized a predominant regional value system that made defense of southern tradition a mission. Lumpkin noted that the Lost Cause was "the glamorous, distant past of our heritage," but her family and most white southerners thought "it was by no means our business merely to preserve memories." They had to "keep inviolate a way of life," and she indi-cated the foundation of that way of life was white supremacy. It was incon-ceivable "that any change could be allowed that altered the very present fact of the relation of superior white to inferior Negro." Her family understood this assumption to be "the very cornerstone of the South." Her family, the South as

a whole, embraced the centrality of white supremacy during the agrarian political turmoil of the 1890s that threatened to split whites and empower African
Americans politically.[94]

Lumpkin's racial awakening came when she was a young girl, as she heard
her father beating their Black cook for perceived impudence. "Thereafter, I was
fully aware of myself as a white, and of Negroes as Negroes." She became "self-
conscious about the many signs and symbols of my race position that had been
battering against my consciousness since virtual infancy." Of particular importance in teaching the child Katharine about the southern racial way was the
taboo of eating with African Americans, and she used the term "sin" to characterize its religious significance. Lumpkin then traces her awakening of an interracial consciousness when she leaves home for school. She saw the origins of
interracial cooperation in the South in Booker T. Washington's efforts to bring
white and Black Atlantans together after the 1906 Atlanta race riot to discuss
the causes of the violence. "Of course, the term was quite unknown as well as
inconceivable to us then. We remained ignorant of it even as first co-operative
steps were taken during the First World War." Lumpkin's awakening to an interracial way came during the Progressive Era and afterward. Her family had
left the comforts of their Georgia home when she was still a youth to move to
an impoverished up-country area of South Carolina, where the poverty she
saw broadened her mind and spirit about injustices. Her Episcopal faith was
important in giving her a vision of the scriptural basis of social justice; she
became a passionate convert to the social gospel in college and came to believe
in the kingdom of God on earth. She described this theological discovery "as
soaking into my consciousness," and an opportunity soon appeared to put her
new faith to work.[95]

Lumpkin worked with the YWCA, which employed a biracial staff, one of
whom, Miss Arthur, spoke to Katharine and other young women about Christianity and the race problem. The use of the title "Miss" was jarring to them,
as was the idea of listening to a Black woman talk about race relations, which
violated the southern racial way. But Lumpkin, looking back on it, realizes that
she and others "by sheer force of unsought circumstance" had found themselves called upon "to pluck from the Tree of Life the apple that would open our
eyes to see what was good and evil." Yet "the old Southern heritage could not
be thrust aside, even momentarily, except by something insistently strong." Its
teaching of keeping African Americans "in their place" was heretofore believed
"to be immutable and unchangeable," but the counterweight of the kingdom
of God on earth took precedence over her inherited racial beliefs. Those racial
verities had made "this tabernacle of our sacred racial beliefs untouchable."
And yet she had touched it and "nothing, not the slightest thing had happened."

This change in consciousness affected only a few white southerners, and by World War I there were few southern places where interracial discussions could take place.[96]

Lumpkin's education was another factor in her conversion to the interracial southern way. After attending Brenau College in Gainesville, Georgia, she went to Columbia University to earn a master's degree in sociology, and then she earned a doctorate in economics in 1928 at the University of Wisconsin. In graduate school she learned of the work of Howard Odum's mentor, Franklin Henry Giddings, and his "consciousness of kind" and of Herbert Spencer's social Darwinism. "It appeared that scientific minds surmised that the 'mores' were so embedded in men's social habits as to make it nearly impossible to alter them—at best taking generations of time, at worst centuries." She had grown up believing in the slowness of social change from her knowledge of the South, and now she had "a heavy sense of the authority of science confirming my own inclinations." She later learned that William Graham Sumner, who wrote of the immutability of folkways, had opposed organized efforts at worker rights, and she realized that "the author of the 'mores' himself believed enough in their possibility of change to consider it needful to put obstacles in the way." She came to understand that people such as Giddings, Spencer, and Sumner gave "a scientific name to describe what my eyes had seen, especially in our racial ways, and the solemn morality we attached to these practices which after all were but the creations of the brains of men." She discovered that the North had its own sense of racial division and observed that northerners "aped our Southern ways" and identified with white southerners' efforts to deal with the "Negro problem."[97]

In graduate school, she had an African American classmate from Georgia who was a key part of Lumpkin's conversion to the interracial way, learning from this classmate about the oppression and poverty of Blacks in a South she had grown up idealizing. When her professor had the class over for tea, it meant violating the southern racial way and committing the "grievous Southern sin" of eating with a Black person. Ironically, Lumpkin's consciousness had evolved so far by that point that she had no psychological moment of crisis as when listening to Miss Arthur, but rather "one could feel relief to have had the chance to prove that this taboo no longer held dominance over one's mind." She reflected that this taboo was not even a personal matter. "It had a large social purpose which we white Southerners had summed up as keeping the Negro in his 'place.' It was for this purpose the taboo had been made a part of our life, and on this account that it was inserted into the minds of each white generation." She came home to Georgia in the early 1920s into a turbulent post–World War I South of restless African Americans and white people determined to resist change. Her consciousness had so changed that what had seemed normal now seemed "bizarre." Lumpkin learned more about poor whites and came to work for their betterment through the organized labor movement. "I no longer used the term 'lower classes.' These were working people."[98]

Lumpkin came to understand the South was not just a traditional culture with distinctive social ways. It was an economic system, and she worked to figure out how it worked to maintain the status quo. She came to use the term "backwardness" to describe her region. Working briefly in a shoe factory to observe working conditions of long hours and low pay, she learned something of the concerns of working women. She came to realize as well how the southern economy worked, how "we were hardly more than instruments, it seemed, moved helplessly by a larger machine that ran all smaller ones at which we worked, and which was operated by some remote control, a vast over-all mechanism that was not geared to human consequences." Her grasp of capitalism's reaches led her to articulate the exploitation of workers that resulted from expanding industry's reliance on the South's cheap labor supply. She noted that in an economic sense, the mass of whites had a "place" where they were supposed to stay, but that meant that "surely wage earning whites and Negroes were, functionally speaking, not so unlike after all."[99]

Lumpkin noted that, despite her change in consciousness, for the postwar South "the old ways still mold the lives of Southern children." They still heard "as sacrosanct the old abhorrences"; "colored" and "white" signs still marked the landscape as visual enforcers of the southern way of life; and white supremacy continued as a political mantra. The Depression, the New Deal, agricultural mechanization, and the growth of the labor movement all had brought unforeseen changes to society. She recognized the limitations to deeper change as well, namely the white South's inability to confront the realities of what segregation did to African Americans and to whites as well. She took comfort that "it is not a slight thing that we strike some blows against these shackles."[100]

Herman Clarence Nixon

Herman Clarence Nixon's significance to understanding the evolving concept of the southern way of life in the interwar years is his personal movement from contributing to *I'll Take My Stand* to becoming one of the most influential southern progressive intellectuals of the time, one who saw a diverse interracial southern society that desperately needed assistance to escape social problems. Nixon's essay in the Agrarian symposium agreed with the other Agrarians that the northern economic invasion of the South after the Civil War had planted an alien industrialism in an agrarian society and had removed from national power the nation's most articulate advocates for agriculture. He dismissed the New South as insubstantial in its achievements, with New South boosters really having "no New South to boost." He wanted to promote agriculture. Acknowledging the problems with the South's tenant system, he insisted that the small family farm should remain the basic economic unit in the South. Nixon allowed that business and industry should complement farming, government should regulate excesses of free enterprise, and the region's people should retain a focus on religious values and social responsibilities. He feared the South's values under industrialism would depart from the region's traditional appreciation of humane values. Nixon believed that southern culture faced a spiritual crisis. He used the agrarian metaphor to predict the decline of Western civilization if industrialism prevailed and believed southern civilization was still a testing ground for a society's ability to master the machine. The South should not turn away from its agrarian past, he wrote, but must cultivate "its provincial soul and not sell it for a mess of industrial pottage."[101]

If Nixon seemed attuned to many of the other contributors to *I'll Take My Stand* in his agrarian philosophy, his experiences and training had already put him on a different path than Donald Davidson and other conservatives, and their paths diverged further in the 1930s. His interracialism can be traced to his childhood in Possum Trot, a small biracial farming community in north Alabama. His first awareness of racial differences came from seeing a book, *The Negro a Beast*, which some young white men were passing around. "I could not harmonize that book with Alice Lee, a Negro tenant's wife who cooked delicious blackberry pies and let me sample them freely," he recalled. "It was clear to me that she could not be a beast." Nixon realized the exploitation in the southern tenant system, but he fondly recalled an African American sharecropper who worked for four landowners over a fifty-year period without changing farms. In the end he came to rest in the farm graveyard. Possum Trot represented a vision of community that would stay with Nixon as an ideal, but he wrote of the decline of a sense of community even in Possum Trot in the face of changes in the interwar years.[102]

The sectional animosities over Populism in his childhood shaped Nixon's sensibility more than the memory of the Civil War did. Like other white southerners of his generation, he had listened to stories of Confederate war veterans and their former slaves, but experiences of people around him with late nineteenth-century agricultural depression and agrarian insurgency impressed him more than the war did. He studied with William E. Dodd, one of the first modern southern historians and an exponent of the region's democratic heritage, and his exposure to midwestern progressivism at the University of Chicago shaped his beliefs as an advocate of Woodrow Wilson's progressivism.

He recognized the problem with the colonial economy, the idea that north-eastern capitalists exploited the South in alliance with southern conservatives, leaving the region economically backward for most of its people. Nixon came to see that positive reform steps had to be taken to help the poor and have-nots or their plight would only worsen. His experiences in the 1930s and his growing involvement in reform efforts associated with the New Deal tilted his thought in new directions that led him to clarify his agrarian ideology. Nixon came to see the changing political context of the New Deal as providing an opportunity to further reforms that could preserve the humane tradition that he associated with agrarian life.[103]

Nixon would relate his evolving ideas to those of his original essay and to those of the other Agrarians after the 1930 symposium. His association with liberal newspaper editors had led to his interest in social action as being essential to building a regional community around humane values, and his appreciation of the social science work of Howard Odum led him to a confidence in regional planning, as states were too small and the nation too large at times to bring needed changes to geographical areas with common problems. Nixon wrote that his book *Forty Acres and Steel Mules* (1938) had "not only kinship but also discrepancy" with his essay for the earlier symposium. He was still proud of participating in the agrarian indictment of the American industrial system of the 1920s, he wrote, "but now I seek a broader program of agricultural reconstruction than I read into the writings which have come from most members of the group since 1930." In a letter to William T. Couch, he was more critical, writing that the Nashville Agrarians "got hold of something and fumbled the ball, for they should dare to be radical or to be considered radical in their attack on the dominance of the profit motives, in their emphasis of a good way of life (which they should emphasize for all, not just a few)." His reference to an inclusive "good way of life" made clear his interracialism in comparison with the other Agrarians. "I can not go with them in their unwillingness, as I understand them, to give the Negro a square deal; that's carrying damn-yankee-ism too far for me."[104]

In 1941 he regretted that *I'll Take My Stand* had not addressed problems associated with the South's growing population, which had put unbearable strains on the agricultural economy and society. He pointed out that the earlier symposium had given no alternative to finance capitalism for industrial activities, and it would not embrace agricultural planning he now saw as essential. It also failed to press for democratic principles in its agenda. He could praise the symposium for opposing "a standard cash-register culture, and it indicted the cult of industrial, urban, and national bigness." He combined his view of an interracial southern way of life with continuing belief in the South's humane tradition as found in agrarian society. Looking back from the vantage of 1952, he wrote that the theme of preserving the humane tradition that he identified with *I'll Take My Stand* "has as much significance for today as for the year of its first appearance." He lamented that southerners were "losing the art of living in an overpowering emphasis on developing the art of getting a living." However, by 1960 he identified the mid-1930s agrarian contributors to *Who Owns America?* as "lone-wolf individualists." He added that he had "moved on with New Deal agrarianism. I was and am a cooperative agrarian." His description here of his approach was a defining one for his ideology.[105]

Nixon's changing politics after the Vanderbilt symposium led Donald Davidson in 1935 to ask, "Hasn't he waxed a little cooperative and pink in the last year?" Nixon had indeed embraced the New Deal as a changing political circumstance that presented a new opportunity for social action to enhance humane values. He was consistent throughout his life "to the conviction that a way of life must be first and always humane to all that it touches; and when those in control exploit the political system or deny basic rights—whether to farmers or factory workers, to urban whites or blacks—a stand must be made to preserve the humane life." So Nixon came to embrace social reform politics, not only to call for more widespread land ownership and protection against commercial-industrial exploitation but also to socialize all monopolistic large-scale enterprises in the interest of farmers, laborers, and consumers. He increasingly understood the southern way as the wealthy exploiting the southern working class.[106]

Nixon was a prominent player in the institutional structure that promoted interracial reform in the 1930s South. He was one of five distinguished professors on the Southern Regional Committee beginning in 1934; he worked with Lucy Randolph Mason in the National Consumers League, helping to organize leagues across the region; and he was a member of the Federal Emergency Relief Administration state efforts through the Rural Rehabilitation Committee. He championed resettlement as a possible solution to the tenant system, visiting experimental villages in three states that gave tenants opportunities for farm ownership and new independence. More than anything, this study of farm and village life solidified his position as a cooperative agrarian and heightened his awareness of class struggle in southern society and the need to go beyond the South's traditional individualism. The Southern Policy Committee in 1938 chose Nixon as its acting chairman. Two of the Agrarians, Frank Owsley and Donald Davidson, attended the committee's first meeting and offered proposals to encourage widespread ownership of property in the South, but Nixon supported stronger cooperative measures to solve economic problems. He fought for producer and consumer cooperatives; government ownership of natural resources, public utilities, transportation, and communication systems; and establishment of insurance and credit structures on all monopolistic industries. He led his supporters to demand socialization of medical and hospital services and the abolition of the tenant system. In the late 1930s he became active in the SCHW.[107]

Several key ideas came to characterize Nixon's contribution to an interracial southern way of life. First, he always embraced the cooperative agrarian label, never rejecting "Agrarian" but coming to see it as a metaphor for community. Second, societal cooperation would promote the "good life," a term he used to describe his ideal society that represented his version of a southern civil religion. Here his original contribution to *I'll Take My Stand* remained relevant to him, as he saw the southern gentleman farmer exemplifying the humane values that he identified as a southern inheritance. He used the phrase "art of living," which meant love of the land, commitment to family, responsibility for community, disregard for materialism, need for a stable social order, sense of honor and noblesse oblige, and love of leisure. This vision was a romantic one in origin, a legacy of the Victorian South, and affirmed the organicism that Howard Odum championed. But Nixon's chief concern throughout his career was how to achieve the good life for all southerners. He came to see the need to extend these virtues beyond the narrow association of them with southern planter elites. Although he was not a militant activist for integration, he believed ending racial exploitation and political discrimination would mean inevitable incorporation of African Americans on an equal level with whites into southern society. Like other southern liberals, he believed the race problem was part of a broader dysfunctional society seen in depressed rural life, legislative malapportionment, political demagoguery, poor schools, and economic exploitation by both northern economic interests and southern power-brokers. Reform in these areas would improve race relations and free Blacks and whites to be active participants in local communities.[108]

Nixon's most significant book, *Forty Acres and Steel Mules*, sketched the exploitation that came from the colonial economy of northern industries in the South but also candidly outlined the Old South slave society as no golden age for most southerners—the yeomen, slaves, poor whites, and small slave owners. This book was the culmination of his interest in agrarianism and a summary of his thinking in the 1930s. Written in documentary style, it combined photographs and text and used 150 Farm Security Administration photographs to show a range of southern life. He took issue with Erskine Caldwell and Margaret Bourke-White's portrayal of a totally backward South in *You Have Seen Their Faces* (1938), including seven photos of confident-looking, well-dressed, smiling sharecroppers. While documenting the awful living conditions in which the poorest lived, Nixon wrote of the "health-giving elements of South-ern rural life which even ignorance and poverty can not nullify," as he por-trayed the strength of families working together on the farm, the seasonal rhythms of work, and the easy recreational activities in the countryside. He called his book "a Hillbilly's view of the South." Although a leading southern intellectual by this time, he retained a folk style in his sensibility and writing. He reminded readers of the country woman's dictum: "What I am, I am, and nobody can't make me no ammer." The first part of the book was autobiograph-ical and set the stage for the hillbilly's view. Nixon had inherited a large estate and became its manager, a position that gave him the perspective of both land-owner and tenant. He related his struggle to keep the farm out of debt while ex-perimenting to improve the quality of rural life in the surrounding area. From this experience he became convinced that "the South must face the problem of absentee ownership but not with the individualistic remedy of 'forty acres and a mule.'"[109]

The book highlighted the South's strengths and weaknesses, alternately praising and cautioning. Social and economic cooperation would be required to revitalize farm and village life and to preserve the organic character of commu-nity life. Industrial expansion should be decentralized. The concluding chapter was a warning that showed his humanism and commitment to his key concept of the good life for all, which he clarified through a litany of the South's needs. The South would never escape exploitation until it stopped the exploitation of farmers, laborers, and African Americans. The South would never, he insisted, have economic security until those groups had economic security. The South would not be highly productive until they were more productive. The South would never gain its fair share of national income until they had their share of national income. The South would not be an educated democracy until they were better schooled and brought more fully into American democracy. "The limitations of these classes are limitations on Southern communities and civ-ilization," he wrote. The use of the term "civilization" pointed to the need to extend the "good life" to the South's working people if a regional civilization was to survive and be fully developed. Historian C. Vann Woodward's review of the book called it "hillbilly realism" and praised it as a "splendid emphasis to a new realism in analyzing southern problems," but Donald Davidson also reviewed it and praised it as well.[110]

One of Nixon's key continuing ideas was of a cultural renaissance possible for the rural South. He associated this with a reaffirmation of the humane tradition that was at the heart of his version of the southern way of life that had motivated the original Agrarian manifesto and certainly remained true for him in his hopes for the region. As much as anyone, Nixon could claim intellectual and personal relationships with two strong cultural ideologies of the interwar years, agrarianism and regionalism, and he saw hope that their efforts could bring progress to the region and its interracial way of life. The two groups had "different dreams, neither of which will quite come true," but "both are interested in a better South and together they may be forerunners of a Southern renaissance." Nixon thought the South in the 1930s might emerge as a national cultural leader, "the Italy of the cultural renaissance in American civilization." This view invested the southern way of life with enormous potential creativity.[111]

Charles Johnson

Charles S. Johnson was another advocate of a southern interracial way of life. He used the term "assimilation" to suggest the need to incorporate African Americans into southern culture. His biographers describe him as a "social scientist/moderate activist," and he was one of the best known African American intellectuals of the interwar era. He made contributions to better race relations from the Harlem Renaissance to his post–World War II work at Fisk University, which he headed from 1947 to his death in 1956. His career illustrates the evolving attitudes of African American leaders in the South, who moved from having a goal of ideology-stressing accommodation—which had emerged in the late nineteenth century with Booker T. Washington—to one of assimilation. Johnson was a productive scholar of race relations, an active participant in interracial organizations, and an institutional entrepreneur of one of the nation's premier places to study race relations. He was a southerner who claimed the identity, and unlike most other African American intellectuals of the era, he stayed in the region to make his career. He had the manners associated with the South, considerable personal charm, and a reputation as a moderate leader on race relations, all of which contributed to his effectiveness in working with white southerners and northern philanthropists on interracial goals.[112]

Johnson grew up in a middle-class family in Bristol, Virginia, the son of a righteous but loving preacher father who shielded him from the worst aspects of the racial discrimination that became codified in law and practice during his turn-of-the-twentieth-century childhood. He read the literary, theological, and historical classics of Western civilization, graduated from Virginia Union College in Richmond in 1916, and went on to graduate work with one of the nation's premier sociologists, Robert Park, at the University of Chicago. Memories of worsening race relations in his youth haunted him and led him to focus his own research and institutional work on race. He remembered vividly when Jim Crow came to Bristol. He and his mother would ride the trolley to town, shop, and then stop at a soda fountain before heading home. But one day the business refused to serve them because the segregation laws had gone into effect. This traumatic event stayed in his imagination, as he noted that for southern African Americans such experiences were "the beginning of a new self-consciousness that burned."[113]

Johnson would achieve scholarly fame for his social science work, but his contributions to promoting cultural pluralism, which were expressions of his interracialism, were among his earliest achievements. He moved to New York City in 1921 as director of research for the Urban League and editor of its publication, *Opportunity*. He used his position to encourage such cultural concerns as art, literature, drama, and poetry, and he emerged as a key figure in launching the Harlem Renaissance. Along with National Association for the Advancement of Colored People leaders, he organized the White Civic Club dinner in 1924 that brought together white cultural leaders and African American creative figures. He wanted to use Black cultural achievements as a way to improve race relations through white recognition of Black talent. The annual dinners enabled aspiring Black writers, painters, and sculptors to meet white establishment figures who could assist their careers. Johnson used the dinners, writing contests, and special issues of the magazine to publicize the idea of the "New Negro," with the anthology of that title a major achievement of the Harlem Renaissance. Johnson was always an integrationist who rejected the separatism and African consciousness of Marcus Garvey in that decade, but he still encouraged Black writers who embraced the aesthetic values of African art and highlighted African civilizations of the past. Johnson saw the Harlem Renaissance he had helped launch as expressing racial consciousness, good in itself but also promoting interracialism through its contribution to cultural pluralism.[114]

Johnson's training as a sociologist led him to embrace his mentor Park's premise that African Americans were not part of a rigid caste in the United States but a minority group who had been marginalized by dominant whites. Johnson argued that "the Negro status, both social and economic, is largely one of class . . . complicated by race." He saw biracial organizations and the development of middle-class Black professionals as undermining the efforts of whites to establish a true caste system. "The Negro doctor," he said, "is more like the white doctor than he is like the Negro peasant." He identified communication as "the essence of the process of acculturation" and saw it taking place more "readily across occupational lines than between occupational levels of the same race." Increased mobility "broke down provincialism and extended social tolerance."[115]

Johnson studied the "sociology of tensions" and argued that the southern racial way of life was an unstable one, full of contradictions, blurred racial boundaries in places, and continually changing contexts. Whites exerted "terrific energy" in keeping Blacks in their stereotypical "place," and African Americans continually struggled against such categorization, all of which proved that the system was far from a natural, immutable one, as defenders of white supremacy claimed. Although he abhorred racial violence and intimidation, he insisted that social tensions were essential for African American progress; they were "the transmission belt to assimilation." Blacks pushing for social change would lead to more white resistance, but that in turn would create "that solidarity which permits the group to act." Peaceful coexistence between the powerful and the suppressed was only possible in a static society that had tried to fix racial lines permanently, and his considerable body of research piled evidence up disputing such an assumption. Near the end of World War II, he noted that "the really significant gains in race relations and in Negro development over the past century" were all "born in tension," often "accomplished by doing things regarded as not in the best interest of the Negro race or race relations."[116]

Johnson was an educator, and he stressed the centrality of education to his overall goal of assimilation of African Americans into American society and improved race relations that would promote recognition of a biracial southern way of life. Dominant whites had marginalized Black education for the masses, but Johnson believed African Americans must insist on finding ways to educate not only the young but adults as well, to prepare increasing numbers of them for professional careers that would place them in occupational worlds with white professionals and facilitate interracial dialogue. Education of white people was just as important in order to dispel stereotypes of African Americans and to show whites the realities of an unjust society. He pointed to the need to use school texts, newspapers, literature, the press, and radio broadcasts to overcome white misunderstandings of Blacks, but the best way was to do so through "direct personal contacts which run counter to stereotypical definitions." He refuted the assumptions of white southerners that they truly knew the Blacks who worked for them, especially disputing the housewife who thought she "knew her Negro maid." He saw that such misimpressions lay as the basis of the southern racial way of life and insisted that whites used the concepts of racial equality, social equality, and intermarriage to "arouse emotions of fear and hate," which drove white ideology. Meanwhile, whites had to come to terms with "the real underlying problems that caused such emotions to be triggered by mere words." He was adamant that by the interwar years it was time to examine the fears most often associated with race prejudice: the fear of "loss of status or economic security, the fear of some cosmic or remote racial degeneration through inter-marriage, and sex fears, which are at the bottom of many fears not basically racial."[117]

Johnson's scholarship in the 1930s helped pioneer the community studies research methodology that used standardized questions and interviews to document both rural and urban cultures. *Shadow of the Plantation* (1934) portrayed a near-feudalistic southern plantation system that dictated the status of the 600 Black families he studied in Macon County, Alabama. He acknowledged that preservation of traditional ways going back to slavery in the rural South had brought a certain equilibrium to the social relations across racial lines, but as Black Belt African Americans they were outside the mainstream currents of American life. But he added that these ways also promoted social disorganization. He used statistical data, qualitative observations, and the words of local people to demonstrate that economic exploitation and racial discrimination inherent in the plantation system shaped health care, folk culture, family life, and community life. His use of empirical facts and a dispassionate tone enabled him to dismantle the idea of a romantic plantation life and happy tenant farmers. Moreover, the problems inherent in the deeply rooted southern system required outside government intervention to promote needed change. The voices of the local people he presented showed a distinctive African American culture at work. *Growing Up in the Black Belt* (1941) studied some 2,000 African American young people, again using statistical data, interviews, and the results of psychological testing to present "vivid, often humorous and often wrenching personal stories by the residents themselves that give the book its depth and indelible impact."[118]

Johnson believed that World War II brought progress in race relations and provided the opportunity to confront the racial situation because of the disruption to routines the war required, increased migration out of the South, and increased urbanization. Under wartime pressures, Americans had to decide whether to "incorporate this persistently rejected group into their system of moral obligations and Christian fellowship, or revise the system itself downward to a more comfortable tolerance of permanent injustice." Wartime tensions did not mean deterioration of race relations; rather, they were "symptoms of accelerated social changes," which were "wholesome, even if their temporary racial effects are bad." Continuing to see economic problems at the base of much racial conflict, he came during the war to recognize that the racial problem in the South and nation was a moral one. He had little hope that the answer would come from segregated churches, and even his scientific academic studies of race relations had limited impact on public policy. Waiting for "time's slow solution to social ills" was not enough, and he believed in "steps that can be taken immediately to correct old ills," including government-imposed regulations to promote equal participation by minorities in the economic and political life of the nation.[119]

Johnson was a prominent participant in the institutional framework of the

interracial movement in the interwar South; indeed, he seems an essential figure as a prominent and respected southern Black leader with superb academic
credentials in studying race relations. He participated in the work of the CIC,
of the SCHW in 1938, and of the Southern Regional Council when it organized in 1944. He worked closely in the 1930s with southern white liberals,
and he believed then that the key to change in the South was benevolent segregationists, whom he hoped he could persuade to advocate the end of segregation. He rejected the accommodationist strategy of Booker T. Washington
but still thought that he could use the respect of the benevolent segregationists
for Johnson's own work to push them further toward his racial assimilation
goal. He made no direct assault on segregation in the 1930s, but one of his
friends argued that his writings and institution-building at Fisk represented
Johnson's Trojan horses inside Jim Crow, ones that one day would burst forth
in dramatic change. His strategy was to build relationships with many factions
while moving steadily toward the left without being so abrasive as to lose his
white supporters.[120]

For Johnson the World War II years had seemed a promising time in improved race relations, and he was a leader in planning the Durham Conference
in 1942, which brought together leading southern African American leaders
and produced the Durham Statement, the preamble of which said, "We are fundamentally opposed to the principle and practice of compulsory segregation
in our American society." Johnson's biographers conclude that the preamble
"reaffirmed a faith in the possibility of a way of life in the South" that was consistent with democratic principles behind the war effort.[121]

The wartime window of opportunity for major racial changes passed, and
Johnson became increasingly frustrated with the interracial ideal's limitations.
By the late 1940s, Johnson acknowledged cultural representations of African
Americans had improved and Blacks had achieved greater racial solidarity
among themselves than ever before, but he saw little comparable betterment
in overall race relations. The failed attempts to move southern white liberals to
accept desegregation disillusioned him, as he now saw that interracial committees, which might seem like signs of increasing interracial unity, were in reality
artificial ones that would not be needed if real progress were being made.[122]

In 1947, Johnson became president of Fisk University in Nashville, and he
turned it into a major center for research on southern society and African
American culture, as he championed research by African American sociologists that built on the issues and methodologies that Johnson had used in the
1930s. Johnson and his group of faculty and graduate student researchers explored the cultural anthropology of the South by focusing on deeply researched
local county case studies. At Fisk, Johnson used research as the foundation
for advocacy of social change and hoped empirical evidence would convince

policy makers of the need to combat racial discrimination. Believing in the value of democracy, he noted that even under discouraging conditions, mobilized people had the potential to bring change. Johnson believed that the more thorough the research on such issues as lynching or farm poverty, "the more the majority community, the white community, would be stirred to anger, outrage, and—what counted most—action in the form of public policy and law." Other reformers worked to promote social changes in more direct ways by the 1940s, but for an African American intellectual in the South the strategy was part of a historical progression from Booker T. Washington and W. E. B. Du Bois to Martin Luther King Jr. that prepared the way for the direct action of the civil rights movement in the 1950s. Biographer Richard Robbins concludes, "Indirection was for him a strategy, not a failing or a want of courage." It rested on cooperation with southern white liberals, who were slow to respond to his challenges to them to endorse the end of the segregated southern way of life, but by the beginning of the 1950s a considerable body of such leaders had embraced his position. Johnson and his work at Fisk represented an intellectual and institutional bridge to the early civil rights movement, which, among other achievements, championed an interracial way of life in the South.[123]

One of Johnson's most important contributions to the promotion of the interracial southern way of life came after the war through annual Race Relations Institutes at Fisk, beginning in 1945. These showed Johnson's ambitions to promote social change, with interracialism a prominent feature intellectually and logistically. They were academic in nature but aimed to reach a broad public audience and educate leaders to work in their communities for change. A pronounced international dimension appeared, with sessions dedicated to Pan-Africanism and the changing status of the underdeveloped world. Johnson included sessions on the commonalities of African American experiences with those of other American minority groups. The institutes provided a forum as well for organized labor leaders to present their case in an academic setting. The first year's registrants included eighty-one whites, fifty-five Blacks, and one Japanese, with forty-seven participants from the North and ninety working in the South. The institutes challenged southern racial etiquette through their daily living arrangements. The participants, many of whom were young white women, sat in the same classrooms with African Americans, despite Tennessee laws dictating otherwise. They lived in private rooms in the same dormitory, ate meals together, and shared entertainment activities.[124]

The first institutes brought controversy to Nashville. In addition to the living arrangements, the program upset some whites. Edwin R. Embree, the director of the Rosenwald Fund and supporter of Johnson's activities, gave a keynote address on "races and civilization" that reflected the new global context of 1940s American thought. Embree took a strong stand against imperialism and warned western nations not "to hold the East in subjection" and to continue to "treat oriental peoples as inferiors." He foresaw a shift in world power from the Atlantic to Asia. Embree spoke again at the institute in 1945, looking at race relations in a world context, and remarked that "Brazil, with an official policy of racial intermarriage, is a case of complete racial acceptance." The conservative *Nashville Banner*'s editorial "Metamorphosis" insisted that "both Western Civilization and white culture have been doing all right now for quite a number of centuries" and regretted that Embree's words suggested "racial amalgamation." The editorial concluded that Embree was an outsider to the South and that the region's racial problems could "only be SOLVED by the means" the South had worked to perfect. They would not be solved "by outside interference and agitation," ominous words for anyone pushing social change in the postwar South.[125]

Johnson reflected on the institute's value after the 1946 meeting. He saw the bringing together of community leaders in race relations as a key contribution. The resulting "cross-fertilization and mutual stimulation would be valuable even if there were no members to listen to and take part in the exchange of ideas." The institute, he insisted, was a training ground for community leaders in their hometowns. Moreover, the common experience of interracial living could "be carried back into local communities" with some of "the personal reconditioning which is an outgrowth of common experience." In particular, Johnson understood the importance of the institutes for the South as he saw the "educational value for the Southern region" in which they took place. They raised "to the level of discussion certain issues which in this area are hardly ever brought to the surface and objectively examined." The very existence of the institute was thus "a demonstration of the possibility of a kind of cooperation and integration which has been thought by many to be impossible." Despite initial unease from the Nashville establishment about the institutes' work, by the late 1940s, the Nashville mayor was welcoming participants and Johnson had assured business and other political leaders that the institutes were simply advancing interracial communication, a goal business-oriented conservatives could endorse as part of a southern interracial way of life. The institutes were significant as a cauldron of ideas, open discussions of taboo subjects in the South, presentations of social science investigations of key problems, and policy recommendations that represented a coherent agenda for racial progress in the postwar South. Johnson's Fisk thus became an institutional center that promoted the evolving interracial southern way of life on the eve of vast challenges to the segregated South—and its way of life.[126]

Beginning with World War I, the interwar years saw concentrated social change coming to a South that had developed an ideology of conservatism in the half century before that war. To be sure, the late nineteenth and early twentieth centuries were turbulent years, characterized by social, racial, political, and cultural tensions, but conservative forces had managed to dominate ideological discussion and put in place a southern system, a "southern way." In one sense, the interwar years saw a continuation of those conflicts, but the crises of two wars, the Great Depression, the New Deal, and the coming of more features of modernity made change a matter that could not be avoided. The Agrarians had claimed the initiative at the end of the 1920s in a new defense of what they then saw as endangered traditionalism, and the agrarian/industrial, southern way/American way dynamic set the tone for many reflections on the nature of southern culture, civilization, and way of life through the next decade. Claiming the term "southern way of life" gave the Agrarians a certain moral authority that those who contested their claims had to dispute. The Agrarians gave a new impetus to self-reflections on southern consciousness at the base of belief in a southern way.

In the 1930s a critical outlook emerged as a defining feature for many progressives who reflected on the South, an outlook that demanded engagement with the South's many social-economic problems to understand the nature of southern civilization. The New Deal and an expanded role for the federal government in the South represented the importance of the national context in any consideration of a southern way. Economics and social class were crucial in the 1930s and 1940s to such considerations, but it is hard still to ignore race in looking at the imaginings of the southern way of life in that period. The next chapter will grapple more directly with racial conservatives and radicals who saw the immutability of white supremacy as the singular southern way of life. We will also examine efforts of African Americans to contest the southern racial way and to assert a biracial, integrated southern civilization, but in this chapter we have seen how social scientists, white liberals, and interracialists realized the interrelatedness of race, economics, social change, and culture in a time of ideological turmoil.

CHAPTER FIVE

The Rising Racial Way

The Evolving Southern Racial Context
in the Interwar Years

THE AGRARIANS DEFINED the southern way as agrarian ideology and regional tradition, while University of North Carolina sociologist Howard Odum saw "the way of the South" as folk culture, other writers brought a variety of perspectives to southern civilization, and progressives talked of an interracial way. To most white and Black southerners in the interwar period, though, and to most visitors to the region, race relations would likely have seemed at the center of any "way" associated with the region. Commentators used "white supremacy," "the system," or more often "segregation" as words that resonated with the southern way of life. The context for race relations changed in the South during the years between the two world wars. The previous decades had seen considerable sectional reconciliation, downplaying Civil War–era conflicts, as white Americans, north and south, embraced a common white supremacy that left many white southerners believing that their social, economic, political, and legal dominance over Black southerners established in the Progressive Era had been permanently achieved. World War I had been altogether disruptive and promoted the Great Migration of Black southerners out of the region and unsettled employer-worker relationships. Black southerners who had fought overseas seemed more assertive than before they left, and a serious postwar recession left the white working and middle classes anxious about the future.

The Great Depression deepened this anxiety and raised profound questions about the future of democracy in a world of European fascism and Soviet communism. Southerners, white and Black, embraced Franklin D. Roosevelt's New Deal because of the economic resources made available to people suffering from the Depression. The New Deal replaced the "rugged individualism" of American tradition with a new cultural orientation around the idea of society, rather than a focus on the self. American culture in the 1930s explored national diversity, documented cultural traditions, and worked to strengthen democratic values. White southerners continued largely to support Roosevelt, but white conservatives became concerned by the mid-1930s with the growth of the power of the federal government and its implications for the South's segregated social system. World War II would be a watershed that brought enormous change to the South and created conditions that eroded rural agrarian life. It especially upset conventional race relations, as Black southerners challenged segregation itself more than ever before. Greater incorporation into national life and international affairs and rapid economic development finally disrupted southern patterns.[1]

This chapter focuses on the rising conservative ideology around racial issues in the late 1930s through the late 1940s. If the Depression and the New Deal had fostered progressive impulses among many southerners, the rising power of the federal government by the late 1930s and then the dislocations of World War II created anxiety over social changes for white southerners. White support for segregation was never unified, though, as some believers in white supremacy were radicals who saw little role for African Americans in the southern way of life, while others were paternalists who wanted to support the slow advance of Black southerners in their "Negro civilization." Developments in these years emboldened African Americans to press for improvements within segregation but also for the outright end of the system. Richard Wright and Zora Neale Hurston offered contrasting views on the role of African Americans in the southern way of life. These years saw the concept of the southern way of life go beyond the intellectual context that had led to its emergence with the Agrarians, and it became a political term, part of a complex of symbols and behaviors that buttressed segregation. The chapter also examines the immediate postwar period, one of experimentation and optimism before the Cold War emboldened conservatives and marginalized white progressive moderates even before the *Brown v. Board of Education* decision in 1954. Global war and the national context loomed larger than ever in efforts to convert southern ideologies into political and public policy success.

Segregation and Racial Etiquette

African American scholar and activist W. E. B. Du Bois pondered race relations in the South at the beginning of the interwar period and identified social-class status and economic competition as keys to the southern social system. Du Bois saw spirituality as an underlying issue. He speculated that white labor embraced racial hatred because "wages and prosperity are in the last analysis spiritual satisfactions." The worker received low wages if judged by food, clothes, shelter, and education, but his psychological wage was high "in the shape of the subtlest form of human flattery, social superiority over masses of other human beings." Looking specifically at one state, he observed that "Georgia bribes its white labor by giving it public bales of superiority." He saw the purpose of Jim Crow legislation as not so much to brand African Americans as inferior as it was "to flatter white labor to accept public testimony of its superiority instead of high wages and social legislation." White workers could enter railway stations from the same front door as the old aristocrats and could sit with them at the best theaters, "above and apart from 'n——s.'" Workers had titles of "Mr." and "Mrs.," which were denied to Blacks; could sit in the cleanest and best railway cars while Blacks sat isolated in dirty smokers; and could seldom lose a court case involving a Black person. The system promoted white racial solidarity, which led to mob law, "as every white man could keep Negroes 'in their places.'"[2]

Du Bois explored deeper meanings of racial segregation by placing it within the southern physical and social environment. Georgia was beautiful, but it evoked savage scenes for Du Bois: "On its beauty" rested something "disturbing and strange." He felt "a certain emptiness and monotony, a slumberous, vague, dilapidation, a repetition, an unrestraint." Beside each natural point of "poignant beauty" lay a "spiritual gloom"—"a certain brooding lies on the land," "something furtive, uncanny—at times almost a horror." He painted a gothic southern landscape, with plantations that were "homes of hatings that cringe and scream and all the world goes armed with loaded pistols to the hip; concealed, but ready—always ready." Du Bois knew the complexity of the white South well, and he saw it as a secret world, suspicious of newcomers and yet effusive in embracing them if judged unthreatening. Whites "strip their souls naked before you, there is sudden friendship and lavish hospitality." Du Bois identified "the warm human quality called 'Southern,'" but he also saw beside it "the grim fact that right here and beside you, laughing easily with you and shaking your hand cordially are men who hunt," men who had "lynched five hundred Negroes in forty years."[3]

Du Bois granted that the people of Georgia were "human and commonplace—not gods or devils." They were "people caught in the evil web of the world," using the term "web" to connect the southern way with other exploitive societal systems. Their "struggles to work and live have been complicated by hateful memories and selfish greed." Du Bois's frustration was with how little good people seemed to be able to do in dealing justly within this southern world. The interracial movement was youthful when Du Bois wrote in the 1920s, but he already saw that its members "would not dream of asking for the end of segregation." Returning to issues of spirituality, he lamented the "baffling" spiritual dilemma of the "conscientious, educated, forward-looking white man of Georgia." This type of white man was "naturally loyal to beliefs of his fathers, to what his friends never question." His difficulty was in understanding the world of African Americans. Du Bois evoked the power of social orthodoxy that discouraged progressive leadership for social change. He cited the relentless propaganda of gossip, rumors, books, newspapers, sermons, and scientific opinions, all of which restrained any questioning of the system. The white moderate must reckon with "his social status so easily lost if he is once dubbed a 'n—— lover.'" The moderate wants to see "his section take a proud place in the civilized world," but in the end Du Bois saw a "bitter fight between Georgia in 1924 and civilization." Southern whites thus aspired to the values of Western civilization, but Du Bois saw a reality far from that goal.[4]

Du Bois, a scholar, brought a sociologist's eye for status to his observations on the South. U. B. Phillips brought a historian's sense of the past and made one of the most famous considerations of southern race relations in the interwar years. He argued for the long continuity of white supremacy as the "central theme of southern history." "Southernism," he wrote in 1928, "its essence," came about because the South was "a land with a unity despite its diversity, with a people having common joys and common sorrows and, above all, as to the white folk a people with a common resolve indomitably maintained—that it shall be and remain a white man's country." Phillips used the language of civilization to explain this commitment. Going back before the Civil War, he argued that white southerners defended slavery "not only as a vested interest, but with vigor and vehemence as a guarantee of white supremacy and civilization." Non–slave owners responded just as slave owners did to a "social prompting: the white men's ways must prevail; the negroes must be kept innocuous." Phillips argued that this racial imperative kept southern whites from social class divisions, so that by 1850 "'Southern rights' had come to mean racial security, self-determination by the whites whether in or out of the Union, and all things ancillary to the assured possession of these." His version of a "southern way," though not named with that term, listed what he saw as the minimalist requirements for antebellum white southerners. Phillips followed the existing Dunning school of historiography and saw Reconstruction as a watershed in white southerners' commitment to the central theme. He insisted that ever since Reconstruction, "by Southern hypothesis, exalted into a creed, negroes in the mass were incompetent for any good political purpose and by reason of their inexperience and racial unwisdom were likely to be subversive."[5]

White supremacy was indeed manifest in numerous ways in the interwar South. Jim Crow was a legal system of public segregation. Laws dating from the 1890s and the decade after marked separate spaces for whites and African Americans, with ubiquitous "colored" and "white" signs, the most visible indicators of a southern way that was different from elsewhere. Writing in 1935, Bettie Esther Parham documented the auditory context for African Americans in a Jim Crow world of the southern way. "'To the back of the car, please;' 'This side for colored;' 'I am sorry, but we don't serve colored;' 'Side door, Sir;' 'Reserved seats for colored;' are the phrases that meet *the auditory* faculties of the southern Negro throughout his entire tenure as social beings in his community." She added that the Black person "breathes and absorbs this southern air impregnated with such phrases as he does floating microbes, and his spirit is diseased thereby." Parham highlighted the spiritual damage inherent in the southern way of life. Segregation was a "total experience of life for both blacks and whites" and emphasized the comprehensive nature of the southern racial way, "structured around racial inequality." She argued that "the unwritten rules that governed day-to-day interactions across race lines" were a form of social control but also "a script for the performative creation of culture and of 'race' itself," capturing the generative aspect of the southern way. A Black man tipped his hat to a white man, stepped aside when a white person approached on a sidewalk, and used "yes, sir," and "no, ma'am," when speaking to a white person—southerners thus performed the submission and deference underlying the southern-way-of-life ideology. Blacks did not eat at the table with whites. Whites would not touch Black people, and a handshake was especially inappropriate. More broadly, to live a Black life was to embody an inferiority; thus the expectation was that Black areas of town would be run-down, and evidence of Black immorality would confirm white assumptions of Black inferiority. White southerners expected that Black life was uncivilized because of the inherent inferiority of African Americans.[6]

The system continually reinforced white supremacy. Clerks and customers in stores always tried to assert their superiority. Social class did enter the system, as whites often recognized the "better class" of Black people and made etiquette concessions to African American lawyers, physicians, and other professionals. White southerners guarded the titles of Mr., Miss, and Mrs. as ultimate signifiers of racial status. Evidence shows African American dissatisfaction with the system, but going along with the rules did allow for a degree of security otherwise endangered. Accommodation did not always mean acquiescence to racial submission. Mississippi civil rights leader Charles Evers recalls hearing within his own family that "the white folks weren't any better than we were, Momma said, but they sure thought they were." He added, "We got it hammered into us to watch our step, to stay in our place, or to get off the street when a white woman passed." Better safe than sorry. Racial etiquette within the web of related aspects of social control suggested that white and Black southerners saw etiquette as a better solution of social conflict than the violence that was often

This 1943 John Vachon photograph shows the quintessential race relationship of the southern way of life, with Mrs. Thomas, the wife of a grocer, in her kitchen talking with her maid, in San Augustine, Texas. Library of Congress, Washington, D.C.

not far from the surface. Etiquette offered a common language for labeling status, and it enabled social interactions to take place with as little friction as possible. That was especially so in places of work, including the white house-holds that brought domestic workers and their employers together every day. The sometimes rough-and-tumble fieldwork on farms could foster personality or other conflicts, but etiquette often deflected violence. The harrowing scenes of beatings of Black servants even in twentieth-century southern memoirs indicated that etiquette sometimes failed.[7]

Social Scientists

Social scientists came to the South in the interwar years to study the social system with its complex mix of etiquette, violence, and social class competition, and they documented the southern way of life at a key moment, before postwar social changes. The University of North Carolina became the leading southern institution sponsoring sociological research in the region, and it facilitated the work of outside researchers. The university's president, Frank Porter Graham, had a national reputation as a prominent southern liberal whose institution was noted for scholarly productivity and promotion of free speech. Sociologist Howard Odum's Institute for Research in Social Science provided an organizational center for visiting scholars, and the *Journal of Social Forces* sometimes published their findings.[8]

Some researchers were northerners who saw a backward South. "Civilization" figured prominently in these outsiders' view of the region's social ways. In coming South, they entered a symbolic world where "civilization seemed thinly to veil raw social forces. They expected to see culture at work." They wanted to improve life in the region, some imagining social engineering, others hoping for moral awakenings in individuals who would then promote social change. Hortense Powdermaker had recently completed a study of life in a Melanesian village when she came to Indianola, Mississippi, for nine months of fieldwork in the fall of 1932 (with a three-month return trip in the summer of 1934). She talked of the Jim Crow arrangements in the town's railroad station, restaurants, and movie theater, and she outlined the prohibitions, warnings, and customs that undergirded racial segregation. She captured the significance of interracial interactions by comparing southern culture to that of the Pacific Islanders she had previously documented. To call a Black man "Mister," she wrote, was "to arouse the resentment, suspicion, fear, which attend the breaking of taboos and customs in any culture." When she had asked a Melanesian whether it would matter if he broke a custom such as not providing a feast for a deceased family member, his attitude was "one of complete bewilderment and strong fear at the mere suggestion." Similarly, whites not using courtesy titles for Blacks was "sensed as equally essential to the *status quo* in Mississippi." To question either was to imperil "the whole system," to "violate, weaken, endanger, the entire *status quo*."[9]

Psychologist John Dollard came to Mississippi after Powdermaker but published his book, *Caste and Class in a Southern Town* (1937), before she published hers, and his book became more influential among scholars and intellectuals. His key concept was indeed caste, which he saw defining southern white supremacy in daily life as a replacement for slavery, "as a means of maintaining the essence of the old status order in the South"—another way of suggesting a southern way of life rooted in antebellum ways. Caste was a barrier to some unwanted forms of social contact for whites, and it defined "a superior and inferior group" and regulated the interactions among people in each group. He used the social situation to reveal patterns of emotional interaction between whites and Blacks, their love, hate, jealousy, deference, and fear. Very much the participant-observer in his methodology, Dollard noted the sheer strangeness of the South to a northern visitor. He acknowledged, for example, a different cycle of time: "Morning is from when you get up until 2:00 and then 'evening' is the rest of the day." Words had different meanings than he was used to. "Can

I carry you home?" did not mean to pick someone up (as he would use the question in the North) but to "give you a ride." Language established "a strange world for northern ears."[10]

Dollard appreciated the friendliness of the white people he met, as they were as "'solid' in cordiality as in politics." He admitted to learning, after five months in Southerntown, not to shake hands with Blacks, although he confessed that he developed "the twitch of the shoulder muscles tending to put my hand forward and instantaneously the countervailing caste pressure against giving the Negro such a sign of social equality." Southern whites had no such twitch, as they had absorbed the handshake lesson in socialization. Dollard noted the importance of such cultural forms and dismissed what he called "the tendency among students of culture to consider such acts as tipping the hat, shaking hands, or using 'Mr.' as empty formalisms." He saw in the South "how severely Negroes may be punished for omitting these signs of deference," which were "anything but petrified customs." Dollard identified a depth of commitment by whites that unified them across social class lines in enforcing white supremacy, and he saw social change being far off. "The white people enforce caste rules with ominous unanimity and one is compelled by one's white-caste membership, to assist to some degree in the personal derogation of the Negro and the expression of hostile pressure against him." A corollary to white solidarity, he noted, was branding the caste traitor as a "n—— lover," which resulted in loss of some status as a white.[11]

Dollard identified economic benefits of the caste system, with Delta whites able to afford Black house servants easily. As the white Delta writer David Cohn noted, Black servants were "cheap, plentiful, and cheerful, except during cotton-picking time in the fall," when they abandoned housework to make more money in the fields than they could make in domestic work. Dollard also saw sexual advantage for white men from the southern system that gave them access to Black women while effectively forbidding Black males having contact with white women—the ultimate taboo of the system. Mixed-race offspring of white men and Black women were the subject of private gossip but only delicate public discussion. What James C. Cobb notes of the Delta was true throughout the South. "The prevention of sexual relations between black men and white women was the absolute, all-consuming obsession of white males in the Delta," he writes. They believed that Black men thought breaking the sexual color line was "tantamount to the instantaneous achievement of equality, more so than if the black man had purchased the largest plantation in the country, cast his ballot for governor, or dined in a white restaurant."[12]

Southern African American social scientist Bertram Doyle explored manners as they operated in the segregated southern way of life. Born in Alabama, he had trained with Robert Park in sociology at the University of Chicago and served as professor at Fisk University in Nashville. His book *The Etiquette of Race Relations in the South: A Study in Social Control* (1937) argued that racial etiquette was a form of social control that Black southerners had come to accept to avoid conflict and wait for eventual change. In effect, he counseled for African American adjustment to the southern system, to local customs, as the only effective way to avoid racial violence. One of the system's purposes was to assert white superiority and Black inferiority, with etiquette the daily ritual through which Black southerners acknowledged their inferiority. He overlooked such evidences of daily resistance as inefficient labor, assertive behavior, and destruction of tools on farms, but he insisted that ignoring racial etiquette was dysfunctional for African Americans. The southern way had allowed some individuals to gain security and the opportunity for limited advancement in society. His insight was that public social distance between the races made personal intimacy between Black people and white people possible, from miscegenation to amicable working relationships. Doyle did not believe that Black performances of the southern way's etiquette represented an endorsement of injustices, but neither did they represent a coded challenge to the system. The Black person, Doyle wrote, "cannot take the time to determine the class and character of every white man with whom he comes into contact; he can only observe those forms which are calculated to allow him to go his way with the least expenditure of thought and energy." Faced with the expectations by whites of racial interaction, Black southerners always "ask what is customary—not what is the law" or "what is right."[13]

Whatever practical realities racial etiquette defused, it nonetheless normalized white supremacy as whites demanded and insisted on not only deference from African Americans but also their seemingly cheerful acceptance of an inferior status. Doyle believed that racial conflict happened in areas of the South where traditional patterns broke down, where Black people were "getting out of their place," including Blacks who had become well educated and economically successful. He saw the two races as part of the same social order, though, each supplementing the other in their social roles. In addition to an interracial society, Black southerners also participated in their separate, segregated world, where they could "acquire status higher in type but separate and apart from the white people."[14]

William Alexander Percy

William Alexander Percy's memoir, *Lanterns on the Levee: Recollections of a Planter's Son* (1941), placed racial etiquette in the broader category of a mannered southern way of life. A member of an old Mississippi Delta planter family, he shared the Agrarians' sense that modernity endangered the traditional

southern way of life. Percy believed that modernity had already remade southern life, including that of the Delta. Percy wrote that "the old Southern way of
life in which I had been reared existed no more and its values were ignored or
derided." He expounded on the contrast between that way of life and its values
and the modern ways. He used five categories: African Americans, poverty,
politics, the pattern of life, and manners. Black southerners "used to be servants, now they were problems." Poverty had once represented "work with style
and dignity," but in the modern South it was "a stigma of failure." Politics had
once drawn forth people dedicated to "the study of men proud and jealous of
America's honor," but it had degenerated into "a game played by self-seekers."
Once, the South had "an accepted pattern of living," but in his age, "there was
no pattern whatsoever." Developments in manners especially revealed changes
in the southern way, as they "used to be a branch of morals" but in his age "they
were merely bad."[15]

Percy did not see the mannerly southern way as ever having been typical
of southerners in general but saw it located in the upper class and in families
like his. His family became an embodiment of the genteel manners that were
at the center of his southern way of life. His forebears had been "nice," the key
descriptor for his mannerly way. He speculated about the source for claiming
identity as post–Civil War southern aristocrats such as he believed his family
had been. He dismissed a long, pedigreed ancestry, and he did not see wealth
as responsible. "A way of life for several generations?" he asked. "A tradition of
living? . . . A style of thinking and feeling not acquired but inherited?" In the
end, he reached no conclusion as to the why but did affirm that the best people
of the South, the upper class, had the conviction of their "quality," and "the
depth of that conviction was unconscious, never talked of, never thought of."
The only people other than white southerners that he had "ever met graced with
the same informal assurance were Russian aristocrats," another doomed group.
His choice of the word "graced" was important because the defining southern-
way quality of "nice" was an inner grace, or "a mysterious spiritual blessing,"
as literary scholar Robert Brinkmeyer sees it, and the essence of this mannerly
southern way. He singled out the South's poor whites—empowered by the vote
and supportive of the social disruptions of the Ku Klux Klan—as emblematic
of the modernity that threatened the mannerly southern way of life.[16]

The Black man had a place in Percy's way of life as "the tiller of our soil,
the hewer of our wood, our servants, troubadours, and criminals," but the efforts to empower his equality in southern society threatened Percy's southern way of life. The African American's only hope for survival was "to accept
whole-heartedly that white man's mores and taboos." The fundamental one
in the South, the "one sacred taboo, assumed to be Southern, but actually and

universally Anglo-Saxon," was the "untouchability of white women by negro men." Percy remained profoundly alienated from his contemporary South: "Behind us a culture lies dying, before us the forces of the unknown industrial world gather for catastrophe." He brought readers back to the Agrarians' argument but left them with an even more apocalyptic sense of endangerment of the southern way of life.[17]

Ku Klux Klan and Fundamentalism

The sociologists offered varied perspectives on the centrality of race to the southern way of life. The early 1920s had seen the militant assertion of a radical racism through the second Ku Klux Klan but one with a certain respectability as well. Middle-class people—small-business proprietors or industrial workers and their families—were caught up in what seemed like accelerating social change in the 1920s and resented those above and below them in the social-class structure and feared what change might bring. Like the Agrarians and Howard Odum, they lived at a troubling moment, between traditional ways and modernity, and their imagining of a southern way reflected that moment. They latched on to old-time solutions that harked back to the first Klan during Reconstruction, but they made the Klan an organization with national appeal, especially in the Midwest and the Rocky Mountains—an early example of the nationalization of southern culture.[18]

Organized in Georgia in 1915, under the leadership of William J. Simmons, the Klan had a special southern character. The first Klan gathering was on Stone Mountain, Georgia, soon to be the site of a memorable memorial to the Confederacy, and the ceremony included flags, a burning cross, and a Bible open to the book of Romans, chapter 12 (which speaks of the value of sacrifice). Vigilante violence would be much more common among southern Klansmen than elsewhere and reflected a regional tolerance for violence in many forms and the tacit approval of violence by white elites and law enforcement officers in the South. Klan ideology would come to embrace many elements, but in the South, it was surely the foremost opponent in the 1920s of any racial change. Simmons spoke in Decatur, Georgia, in 1921, and the audience wildly cheered when he used a defining term in the southern way of race relations, yelling that the Klan "makes n——s get in their place and stay in their place!" Simmons made the southern spirit key. He hallowed the Reconstruction-era Klan and maintained that his order was "the reincarnation among the sons of the spirit of the fathers" who took part in the original Klan. Many Klan chapters in the South took the names of such earlier Klan leaders as Nathan Bedford Forrest and John B. Gordon. Its leaders positioned the Klan around defense of traditional Americanism, another key credo of the interwar years, by which Klansmen meant white supremacy, national and regional patriotism, conventional morality, Protestant religiosity, male fraternalism, anti-Semitism, nativism, and fears of a new menace, communism. The concern about communism came in the aftermath of the Russian Revolution in 1917 and represented the overarching anxiety among those who embraced the Klan. W. E. B. Du Bois insisted, for example, that the Klan had appeared out of fear that the "present machinery is not going to be able to keep black folks down," and one Klan article indeed complained of "the haughty ambitions and arrogant aggressiveness" of postwar African Americans.[19]

The Klan's language of sexuality offers insight on the importance of "blood" to the overall southern concept of the segregated way of life. Anxiety over white male sexual dominance was apparent in the Klan's obsessive use of such terms as the "proper blending of blood," "mongrel population," "pure and undefiled blood," and "racial pollution." Klan writings insisted that "alien" people of color and different races lusted for white women. Economics and sexuality combined in the Klan outlook, based in "the order's fealty to a vision of white petty producer households in which women and youth were dominated by adult men." Women embodied white racial identity, so that "policing the borders of white society required regulating white women's sexuality," and interracial sex became, as we have seen elsewhere in southern society, "the strongest taboo of the system."[20]

Social class was another key component in understanding the post–World War I Klan. Its ideology reflected the perspective of the small property owner. The Klan's worldview was one of reactionary populism that embraced an anti-elitism among middle-class strivers caught between capital and labor. Their outlook was not a new one in American history, as the interwar Klan groups inherited from one strain of American political culture a suspicion of Wall Street and a belief that inequality came not from the overall economic system but from laws that privileged the wealthy. The postwar economic problems energized their anxieties to fashion an ideology for a rapidly changing society. Klan spokesmen drew from classical liberalism's stress on a free economy and from republicanism's vision of the good society and the necessity for property ownership for citizenship and civic participation. Nostalgic for an imagined past of a yeoman and small-business golden age, and fearful of a future in which their American dreams seemed to be in jeopardy, they defined an ideology that they hoped would allow them to reassert their diminished political and economic power. The outlook appealed to many Americans, but it gives insight into social class, religious, gender, and racial foundations of the evolving southern segregated way of life.[21]

Evangelical Protestantism gave Klansmen a righteous language to indict the immoral, whether the wealthy who worshipped mammon and showed inadequate concern for protecting what they saw as an Anglo-Saxon-dominated polity or the immoral figures from modern society who drank, gambled, engaged in easy sex, and violated racial norms. The Klan emerged in the 1920s at the same time as fundamentalism, and the two movements overlapped, with the latter offering a spiritual anchor for the Klan's worldview. Suspicious of both democratic progressivism and governmental centralization, the Klan saw fundamentalism as a comprehensive ideology, a mass popular religious basis for social order that relied on the authority of God. Fundamentalism also gave Klansmen an apocalyptic rhetoric in regard to race relations. Their defense of segregation and other aspects of the segregated southern way of life rested in fear that any concession would empower Black people to make increasing demands that would soon lead to the toppling of white supremacy. Granting access to better schools would, for example, awaken yearnings for equality and provide skills to gain it. The use of terror was essential to the Klan prevention of Black aspirations leading to the race war they predicted. The second Klan's racial fears broadened beyond African Americans to include Jews and Roman Catholics, and the group blamed immigration for bringing racially degenerate peoples to the United States. The fear of outsiders went back to the hated abolitionists before the Civil War, but the Klan's militant racism after World War I refurbished a fear of aliens and made its characteristic dread of differentness a part of the "structure of feeling" of the interwar southern way.[22]

Respectable White Supremacy

If the Klan expressed a militant white supremacy, linked to lower-middle-class frustrations with modernity and social change, a respectable white supremacy as the foundation of a segregated southern way of life was embodied by progressive Virginia aristocrats such as newspaper editor and Pulitzer Prize–winning historian Douglas Southall Freeman, who reflected a respectable, upper-class patrician white supremacy linked to "managed race relations." Freeman used the term "the Virginia way" to refer to a segregationist southern way of life, resting in a genteel version of paternalism, suspicious of democracy and the masses, and convinced that only the better classes should rule society. A prime virtue was maintenance of stability and order in society, and its advocates rejected the rigid racial oppression and racial violence displayed in other parts of the South as destabilizing. Civility was another prime virtue, and the southern patricians embraced the ideal of harmonious relations with Black Virginians and wanted to work with upper-class Black leaders to manage the segregated society. This version of the southern way of life expressed the "mannered way" associated with people whose wealth, social position, occupations, and governmental offices gave them unusual social, political, economic, and cultural influence in the Old Dominion. To be sure, the mannered way affirmed disfranchisement and segregation and what Freeman called "the first law of the South—that a white man is a white man and must be treated as such regardless of his station."

The important point in positioning the Virginia way within discussions of the southern way of life is the class dimension. Political scientist V. O. Key noted in 1949 that leadership in Virginia was "reserved for those who can qualify as gentlemen. Rabble-rousing and Negro-baiting capacities, which in Georgia or Mississippi would be a great political asset, simply make a person as one not of the manner born." Virginia's upper class had a rosy self-image indeed, in terms of its superiority to other southerners, and they even praised Black Virginians as the elite of their race in the South. Freeman wrote that Black Virginians were blue bloods, who went back to early Virginia and absorbed the virtues of place, with their traditionalism and skills developed in interaction with whites over generations.[23]

The white Virginia elite that Freeman was a part of supported basic public services provided to Black citizens and even encouraged a measure of uplift in the Black community, in exchange for deference to white leaders. V. O. Key labeled race relations in Virginia as "perhaps the most harmonious in the South." Its style of segregation was not unique to Virginia, as its neighbor, North Carolina, symbolized a "progressive mystique" in the early twentieth century whereby elites accepted their moral responsibility to assist the needy. The stress on civility above all else prevented, however, dealing effectively with problems in the modernizing society, as civility made good manners more important than constructive action to deal with social problems.[24]

As the 1920s went on, control of the pace of social change by elites proved more difficult. The growth of cities and towns created new challenges for the segregationist order by bringing together Black and white southerners in ways beyond traditional racial etiquette in rural, face-to-face societies. Working-class whites and small property owners became ever more alienated from their supposed class superiors as they faced competition from Black people for jobs, housing, and seats on buses. African Americans also became disillusioned with the ability of white elite paternalism to address their needs, and Black leaders chafed under continued demands for deference from white elites as they increasingly supported federal lawsuits and joined the National Association for the Advancement of Colored People to assert their rights. The 1930s saw protest marches and sit-down strikes demanding Virginia provide the equal facilities and opportunities that segregation's defenders had supposedly pledged. White leaders such as Freeman came to insist that Black demands were too radical and outside the bounds of the supposed paternalist agreement with Blacks.[25]

The respectable style of white supremacy survived, nonetheless, through the 1930s, as seen in the efforts of southern politicians who, while affirming the precepts of white supremacy, did not engage in race-baiting and worked for harmonious race relations. Respectable racists such as Freeman lost ground by the time of the Depression, and that economic disaster deepened racial conflicts in the region and led to a temporary rise in lynchings, despite the long-term decline over the previous decades. Radical racism could be easily evoked through events such as the Scottsboro case. This notorious episode in southern racial injustice began in March 1931 in north Alabama with the arrest of nine African American young men accused of raping two white women on a freight train. Within only a few weeks, a jury sentenced them to death, but appeals dragged on and led to a second trial in March 1933. The case sparked national headlines because of the severity of the sentences, became a prime example for the northern media of southern barbarities in the 1930s, and evoked the usual defensiveness on the part of white southerners when attacked over racial issues. The International Labor Defense, a group associated with the Communist Party, defended the accused and thereby furthered the white South's fear at outside intervention. In 1937 a settlement led to four of the defendants being freed, while five others received long prison sentences.[26]

Agrarian writer John Gould Fletcher, a contributor to *I'll Take My Stand*, wrote a letter to the *Nation* lambasting it for what Fletcher saw as biased coverage of the Scottsboro trial. Fletcher suggested the conviction and execution of the young men would not be seen as justice in the North but would be for white southerners. "Justice is in itself an abstract matter, and as every great lawyer knows, has always to yield to the morals, the usages, the customs and conveniences of a living and functioning community." He thus framed the issue of justice in terms of the traditionalism at the heart of southern agrarianism. He went on to justify a recent lynching of four Black men in Tuscaloosa County, Alabama, in spite of his recognition that they were probably innocent. He blamed the influence of Scottsboro defense attorneys "as well as the taunts of the metropolitan press" for having "unstrung that section of the South which adjoins Scottsboro." He insisted that the South would "not suffer further dictation from the North as to what we are to do about the Negro. All that we built up again out of the ruins of Civil War and of Reconstruction is again at stake. Rather than permit our own peculiar conceptions of justice to be questioned, we will take the law into our own hands, by a resort to violence."[27]

One of Fletcher's Agrarian colleagues, Frank Owsley, wrote an article during the second trial, which he also delivered before the American Historical Association's annual meeting and argued that northerners had launched a series of crusades to destroy the South, which included abolitionism, Reconstruction, and the communist agitation of his own time. Although less incendiary than Fletcher's words—he called Black southerners "pawns" but refrained from using demeaning racial language—Owsley did insist that violence and disorder had resulted from each invasion of the South and future problems could only be averted by increasing southern autonomy. In Owsley's imagining, capitalist industrialists and communists were in an unholy alliance to conquer the South, and he saw echoes of past northern meddling in the South. "The technique of both Communists and industrialists is the same as that of the former crusaders," Owsley insisted.[28]

Race-Baiting Politicians

The Agrarians' response to Scottsboro blurred the line between radical and respectable racism as the basis of the southern way, and as the 1930s went on, that line in general could be vague. Race-baiting politicians, who became known as the Dixie Demagogues, represented an extreme in keeping radical racism alive in the South. For the southern way of life, the demagogues were important because of their mass appeal based on extreme segregated rhetoric. Individuals such as Cotton Ed Smith in South Carolina, Eugene Talmadge in Georgia, and Theodore Bilbo in Mississippi staged mass rallies, provided musical entertainment, and used compelling oratory to reach vast audiences to spread their message through southern cultural expression. They were second-generation demagogues who followed predecessors in their states, such as Ben Tillman in South Carolina and James Vardaman in Mississippi, who had helped oversee the marginalization of Black southerners in the Progressive Era. By the interwar era, African American disfranchisement, racial segregation, and all the other ways of oppressing Black people had long been in effect, and African Americans were no political threat; the demagogues continued their feverish race-baiting rhetoric by tapping into and stoking racial fears. They helped renew the association between white supremacy and the southern way of life through their identifiable southern styles.[29]

Tradition reverberated through these racist rantings. South Carolina U.S. senator Cotton Ed Smith was one of the most notable southern demagogues in the interwar years. He had stormed out of the 1936 Democratic Party national convention in Philadelphia when a Black minister took the podium to pray and again when a northern African American politician spoke. The issue for Smith was regional civilization, and he revived that hoary idea in the new context of the modernizing South. Smith insisted after the 1936 convention that "political equality means social equality, and social equality means intermarriage, and that means mongrelizing of the American race." His experience at the convention soon became known back in South Carolina as "the Phillidefy Story," and he often reprised it for effect before crowds. "I know what the people of South Carolina are interested in," he said. "White supremacy, that time-honored tradition, can no more be blotted out of the hearts of South Carolinians than can the scars which Sherman's artillery left on the State House at Columbia. And, please God, I'm tellin' it." His linkage of white supremacy with the Civil War showed the Lost Cause's continuing political viability. When Smith died in 1944, the *Columbia Record*'s eulogy noted that "he represented another epoch, another way of life."[30]

Other demagogues continued his legacy. Georgia governor Eugene Talmadge built his success on identification with rural farmers and made a populist, grassroots appeal that distanced him from social elites. Talmadge explained his racial and cultural beliefs in terms of southern tradition. Noting that his family had been in Georgia for a century and a half, he used an agrarian, southern-way-of-life pastoral image that evoked the Agrarians' ideology: "I am steeped in southern tradition and background. Neither I nor my people have ever strayed from the pasture of southern tradition. We have not even leaned against the fence." Like so many white southern Democratic politicians, Talmadge had initially supported Roosevelt and the New Deal, but he turned against them by the mid-1930s. With the rising racial consciousness of Blacks and whites during World War II, Talmadge came to rely on race-baiting in campaigning as never before. In his 1946 campaign for governor, he highlighted fears of Blacks voting as his main issue. He also inveighed against "social equality," "alien influence," and "Moscow Harlem zoot-suiters" who would go "into Atlanta's First Baptist Church" and "try to sit down right there alongside a white lady." He pledged that he would have "the N—— . . . come to the back door with his hat in his hand." Again, drawing attention to the Reconstruction memory, Talmadge urged white voters in 1946 to put aside "petty differences" and "have a solid march of white people who will go to the polls and save good old Georgia from the carpetbaggers."[31]

Mississippi's Theodore Bilbo became the most notorious of the southern demagogues. The *New York Times* identified Bilboism as a half-baked ideology, a "combination of racial hatred, Ku Klux Klanery, intimidation at the polls and a narrow parochialism to which all national interests are subordinate." He used racial terror threats to intimidate Black voters, and they were only one example of the extremity of his racial rhetoric that embarrassed even his southern congressional colleagues. Bilbo had been a Democratic Party loyalist

Eugene Talmadge was one of the South's most notorious race-baiting politicians
of the 1930s and 1940s. This photograph shows him campaigning in 1936.
Courtesy Georgia Archives, Vanishing Georgia Collection, trp321.

in the early New Deal, but he was typical of southern congressional leaders, racial moderates and radicals, who became critical of the implications of federal
government involvement in the South.[32]

Like other southern senators, Bilbo used the established political language of
states' rights, the constitutional separation of powers, and a pronounced racial
purity theme. He often combined these ideas: "We are fightin' for principles,
for our constituencies, for the sovereignty of our States, and the integrity of
the blood of the Caucasian race." After World War II, he was one of the first
white supremacists to use race as the key delineator of the term "southern way
of life." "Segregation of the races," he wrote, "was established by custom, re-
enforced by various state statutes, and this policy has remained through the
years as a definite and fixed part of the Southern way of life." The first axiom
of his racial views was the superiority of the white race, and he loved to detail
its achievements. The second axiom was that racial mixing would "destroy the
civilization that the white man had built," and while in the U.S. Senate during

the Depression and World War II, he worked to achieve a permanent separation of the races. He twice introduced bills to provide free transportation and resettlement funds to repatriate African Americans in Africa.[33]

Moderate Segregationists

More moderate politicians who did not race-bait but still embraced white supremacy without pause were important in an organized effort to preserve the racial basis of the southern way of life. Although many southern Democratic senators and congressmen originally embraced the New Deal recovery efforts, they became concerned as the decade went on about the threat to southern segregation by the growing power of the federal government and the effects of the New Deal's social programs at undermining the southern system. The late nineteenth-century architects of southern segregation had hoped they had permanently settled the South's race relations, but any such hopes disappeared in the 1930s. As African American activism gained ground, white southern political leaders began an intentional countermovement to the reform efforts of labor and civil rights activists.[34]

White supremacist leaders in the South in the 1930s spoke of "defending 'white democracy,'" and by that they meant a racial ideology and a political system. Insisting that the continuing denial of Black voting rights and maintenance of segregation were essential to the survival of a white-dominated South, they saw the region's allegiance to the Democratic Party as key to this goal. White southerners traced their politics back to Thomas Jefferson's views on constitutional government and individual freedom and rejected modern interpretations of the egalitarianism Jefferson also wrote in the Declaration of Independence. W. J. Cash called the Democratic Party in the South "the institutionalized incarnation of the will to White Supremacy." But during the 1930s the party evolved from a southern-dominated party deferential to southern white racial concerns into a multicultural party reflecting the growing African American political power in northern cities. This appalled many white southerners. When the Democratic Party changed its governing rules that in effect had given southern Democrats a veto power over nominees, southern whites saw the writing on the wall. The Democratic Party was no longer going to be the party of their grandfathers that had represented the Solid South, and they struggled to maintain southern unity and national influence amid growing anxieties over potential changes in race relations.[35]

Moderate southern segregationists included conservative businessmen, Black Belt planters, and congressional leaders. The Southern States Industrial Council formed in the early 1930s. It was made up of industrialists and businessmen

already suspicious of the New Deal's effect on southern labor relations. Southern businessmen feared that the National Labor Relations Act's codes and
regulations suggested a standardization in labor management relations across
the nation that would upset southern conditions that kept Black workers low
paid and with insecure employment. "Colored labor has always been paid less
than declared," one Alabama industrial leader said, "and for good reason." He
claimed African Americans' inefficiencies and limited capabilities justified
their lower wages; a cheap labor supply gave southern industry competitive
advantages in relation to other parts of the nation. Besides, as Tennessee textile
mill owner John Edgerton said, a segregated, racially distinct wage scale would
"preserve labor's racial purity."[36]

After the 1936 election, conservative Democrats joined with Republicans to
support a conservative manifesto that reflected a free-enterprise, fiscally restrained, states' rights agenda that would come to dominate Congress for a generation. North Carolina senator Josiah Bailey wrote the document and understood its significance for the South. Speaking at the Southern States Industrial
Council in 1938, he praised the South's "unchangeable character," its "ability to
withstand criticism," and its determination "to repel the advances of uplifters."
He evoked the fundamental connection of contemporary events to Reconstruction, likening New Deal officials to carpetbaggers. "They can't reform us, and
they can't reconstruct us." Once again, the memory of Reconstruction as a
time when savage freedmen and unprincipled northerners threatened southern
white civilization was a powerful one for a race-based southern way of life.[37]

In the 1938 midterm elections, Roosevelt campaigned against Georgia senator Walter George and South Carolina senator Cotton Ed Smith, who had
become roadblocks in his legislative efforts. They won anyway and race appeared as an issue in the campaign. Mississippian Turner Catledge wrote in the
New York Times that "white supremacy has returned as a political issue in the
South" for the first time since the late nineteenth century, and he saw increased
white anxiety over threats to segregation as the cause. The fear of rising African
American aspirations and Black political power were no longer the concerns
just of demagogues "but also of many thoughtful Southerners who had hoped
the day had come when candidates no longer could ride into office on the race
issue." That hope had rested upon the belief that white supremacy had been permanently established. The racial implications of federal government activism
"called that mythical permanency into question." Catledge worried that more
moderate politicians would be increasingly on the defensive to more radical
racial spokesmen.[38]

Georgian Richard B. Russell was one of the most important southern senators in the New Deal era, a fervent supporter of its relief and recovery efforts

and influential with Roosevelt in preventing him from being more proactive in direct support of African American civil rights. He became fearful of New Deal agencies offering opportunities for Blacks in the South that put them in positions over white people. Russell had paternalistic views of Blacks, did not use derogatory racial terms, and refused to use race as an issue in political campaigning. He also trumpeted white supremacy. When Eugene Talmadge interjected race as an issue into a campaign against Russell, he wrote Talmadge a letter pledging his fealty to segregation. "As one who was born and reared in the atmosphere of the Old South, I am willing to go as far and make as great a sacrifice to preserve and ensure white supremacy in the social, economic, and political life of our state as any man who lives within her borders." He insisted that "any southern white man worth a pinch of salt would give his all to maintain white supremacy, and it is a disgrace that some should constantly seek to drag the negro issue into our primaries, where as a matter of fact they do not in any way participate and cannot." Russell claimed African American progress had led to a new level of accomplishment that deserved praise. "The Negroes are building up a social system and a civilization of their own," he insisted, "within the social system and civilization of the South," but he was adamant that "it is separate and apart, and you cannot bring them together by law or edict." Russell thus saw the South as a site where multiple social systems and civilizations existed, in parallel relationships. He insisted that white and Black people must be strictly segregated and that Blacks make progress within their own social, economic, and political communities. His final judgment was a familiar one, seeing any integration as a step toward "mongrelization of the races." Even if Congress passed laws to promote integration, he said, "you will never be able to enforce any such system in the Southern States." Russell represented a distinctive political position within the defense of the southern way of life—a moderate who included African Americans as part of southern society, unlike extreme racists such as Talmadge, but with only a limited place for them.[39]

African Americans and the Southern Way

The interwar years witnessed dramatic changes in African American life in the nation that reflected evolving economic, social, and cultural developments coming out of modernization's impact, the reaction to the imposed restrictions on Black southerners, African American achievements in spite of those restrictions, and the attractions of the North. Between World War I and World War II, an estimated 1.5 million Black southerners left the region in response to racial segregation, disfranchisement, racial violence, and restricted job opportunities. Labor shortages in northern cities became the attraction for people looking to leave the oppressive South. The Harlem Renaissance writers put forward the "New Negro," which drew at times from southern folk culture and sometimes represented a version of the southern way of life rooted in African American rural life.[40]

African Americans who brooded over the southern way in the interwar era often portrayed the "hatred and ignorance" of a social system that oppressed them. Racial violence was a vivid concern, as it had been to Ida B. Wells and earlier African American critics of the South. Black poets often made the souvenir body parts that whites kept from lynchings into the material signifiers of the southern way. Virginia poet Anne Spencer, for example, wrote in "White Things" in 1923:

> They pyred a race of black, black men,
> And burned them to ashes white; then
> Laughing, a young one claimed a skull,
> For the skull of a black is white, not dull,
> But a glistening, awful thing.

Langston Hughes's 1922 poem "The South" showed "the lazy, laughing South, with blood on its mouth," digging in "the dead fire's ashes for a Negro's bones." Hughes wrote "Christ in Alabama" in response to the arrest of the nine African American young men in Scottsboro, Alabama, for alleged rape. The poem used a startling religious image that tied violence against African Americans to the passion of Christ: "Christ is a n——, beaten and black . . . most holy bastard of the bleeding mouth, N—— Christ. On the cross of the South." Poet Sterling A. Brown used another image of southern violence toward African Americans, the chain gang, to indict the southern system. In the poem "Southern Road," Brown portrays African Americans swinging their hammers while working on a chain gang along a southern road: "White man tells me—hunh—Damn you soul; Got no need, bebby, to be tole."[41]

Jean Toomer's *Cane* (1923) was a watershed book in the development of a New Negro literary type, and his book also portrayed the South as the setting for violence and cruelty. Every poem and vignette in the first part of the book conveyed images of violence. One short story in *Cane*, "Blood-Burning Moon," portrays the death of two men, one white and one Black, who had struggled over a Black woman. The white man, Bob Stones, desires Louisa as his mistress, so "he went in as a master should and took her. None of this sneaking. . . . Hell no, his family still owned the n——s practically." Before Stone takes Louisa, the Black male character, Tom Burwell, thinks times had changed: "White folks aint up to them tricks much nowadays. Godam better not be." But this sexual exploitation does evoke conditions under slavery, suggesting little change. In

Much paper ephemera showed demeaning and
ugly images of African Americans, but church fans
found in churches of Black people offered such
wholesome scenes as this one—a visual counterpart
to portrayals of Black life by such writers as Langston
Hughes and Jean Toomer. Charles Reagan Wilson
Collection, Archives and Special Collections, John
Davis Williams Library, University of Mississippi
Library, Oxford, Mississippi.

retaliation, Burwell kills Stone, but the white community lynches him in response. The South in *Cane* often signifies death.[42]

Violence, along with other aspects of the southern way that constrained
Black southerners, brought a broader condemnation of the region's lack of
civilized behavior. "One of the mysteries to us is, what is there to boast of in
being a southerner," wrote African American writer James Weldon Johnson in
1918. "Among so-called civilized white men, the Southerner is the most backward, the most ignorant, the most uncivilized and the most barbarous in the
world." Johnson was writing in response to H. L. Mencken's indictment of the

South and extended the Baltimore writer's undermining of white southerners' assertion of their superior culture. Johnson insisted that the South was "without scholarship, without art and without law and order; it is even without money except what it can borrow from the North." Mencken's "The Sahara of the Bozart" had praised antebellum southern culture for its achievements, but Johnson undercut that claim. "We do not think that the destruction of the old Southern Civilization or any innate inferiority of the poor white trash is the reason" for the South's uncivilized attitudes. The fundamental problem with the South was that "the mental power of the white South is being used up in holding the Negro back, and that is the reason why it does not produce either great literature or great statesmen or great wealth."[43]

African American Folk Culture

The effort to define a southern dimension of the New Negro included more elements, however, than the portrayal of southern culture as uncivilized. The "southern project" of the Harlem Renaissance saw the South as the center of African American folk culture essential to many northern Black writers in understanding the continued distinctiveness of their culture. Alain Locke argued that the New Negro appeared because "a railroad ticket and a suitcase, like a Baghdad carpet, transport[ed] the Negro peasant from the cotton field to the heart of the most complex urban civilization." Locke saw that Black writers in the interwar years were freeing themselves from the minstrel tradition and the expectations white readers had for dialect stories. Black writers now looked at southern culture with greater detachment. Poet Langston Hughes wrote in 1922 of "the magnolia-scented South, 'Beautiful like a woman, seductive as a dark-eyed whore,'" and he regretted that "I am who am black, would love her, but 'she spits in my face' and 'turns her back on me.'"[44]

The concept of the folk was essential in the New Negro construction of African American identity, and the South figured prominently in this creation. Locke extolled "those nascent centers of folk-expression" and "the migrating peasant" bringing southern Black culture north as the ultimate source of a new cultural identity. Langton Hughes was a "Southerner twice removed from the South," because, although raised in Lawrence, Kansas, his grandparents had southern ties. He grew up around southern migrants to the Midwest, and he "understood that the folk of the South were crucial to the imaginative impulse of black writers attempting to define themselves and to declare their independence from restrictive literary traditions and expectations." Music was essential in this embrace of southern rural folk culture. A line in Hughes's "Barrel House: Chicago" describes "a song that once was sung beneath the sun / In lazy far-off sunny Southern days." Music linked the South's rural Black life with the new city world of recent migrants. Writer Sterling A. Brown praised blues woman Gertrude "Ma" Rainey as a custodian of Black identity, and he urged her to "sing yo' song. . . . Git away inside us. Keep us strong." He, like Hughes, chastised the children of the Great Migration for laughing at the old country songs "born of the travail of their sires." They were "diamonds of song, deep buried beneath the torrid Dixie sun." Brown's father was a former slave who became a notable minister, and Brown learned much about the South from him. Ralph Ellison did not reach literary fame until after the Harlem Renaissance's heyday, but he understood, as well as these earlier Black writers, the importance of southern rural folk in defining African American identity. He grew up in Oklahoma City and recalled classmates going in the fall into the countryside to pick cotton. When they came back they told him about "the communion, the playing, the eating, the dancing and the singing" they experienced. He especially appreciated their jokes, "our Negro jokes—not those told about Negroes by whites," and they came back with "Negro folk stories which I had never heard before and which couldn't be found in any books I know about." Ellison paid tribute to these cultural forms that would inform his understanding of a folk-based African American southern way of life.[45]

Jean Toomer's *Cane* portrayed the explosive violence African Americans endured in the South but also embraced the warmth and richness of that folk culture Ellison would later admire. Toomer celebrated southern African American folk spirit and culture. In "November Cotton Flower," the image of the cotton flower, with "brown eyes that loved without traces of fear," symbolized the endurance of African Americans in a drought-ridden and threatening South. Charles T. Davis argues for the centrality of the southern Black folk culture— the southern Black way of life—to African American racial identity. Toomer saw "the necessity for regional connection, for the Northern black to acquire the emotional strengths that black Southerners still possess[ed], though they may be rapidly losing."[46]

Harlem Renaissance writers may have pictured a Black southern way of life based in rural folklife, but they worried over the ability of a distinctive African American identity to survive in what Alain Locke called "the most complex urban civilization." Fearing the eroding effects of urban bourgeois life on the inherited southern Black folk identity, they invited comparisons with the Vanderbilt Agrarians and their belief that the southern identity rested in rural places. Other Black intellectuals objected, however, to what they saw as admiration for primitive rural Black culture that was limiting Black advancement. They accused writers such as Hughes and Zora Neale Hurston of marketing images of Black primitivism to white audiences. This conversation among Black intellectuals got at deep issues of high culture and folk culture as the defining feature of African American identity that had been generated in a Black southern way of life but now faced challenges in northern intellectual circles.[47]

Richard Wright

Richard Wright and Zora Neale Hurston provide contrasting views of African American life under Jim Crow segregation. Wright grew up in Mississippi in a Deep South culture obsessed with racial issues and dark in its racial atrocities that shaped him; Hurston grew up in a nurturing, all-Black, small Florida town with a well-functioning African American community. The internal dynamics of Black folk culture always engaged her interest more than the racial issues that drew Wright's primary attention. Wright grew up with Black folklife and could be sympathetic to aspects of African American folk culture, but in his memoir *Black Boy* he dismissed its significance in the face of the totality of racial oppression. In her memoir *Dust Tracks on a Road* (1942), Hurston saw African American folklore as at the heart of a distinctive Black culture in the South that migrants had then transported into northern cities. Wright realized that southern culture had shaped him, but Hurston positively identified with that culture. Hurston's depiction of Black community life in the Jim Crow South showed joyous spirits, social gatherings, and a world that thrived in spite of racism, whereas Wright saw a community pathologically damaged by the segregated southern way of life.[48]

The differing outlooks between Wright and Hurston focused on issues of culture and civilization, terms they themselves often used. Wright's interest in exploring individual consciousness in authoritarian social systems led him to keen awareness of such issues, including the explicit use of "way of life." His folk history of African Americans, *Twelve Million Black Voices* (1941), conceptualized that history in such terms. "We millions of black folk who live in this land were born into Western civilization of a weird and paradoxical birth," he wrote, "victims of a deadly web of slavery that snared our naked feet" with the expansion of Western civilization "into a new World culture." Wright traced the evolution and survival of that original racist system of slavery through the continuity of "the hateful web of cotton culture." His use of the term "web" to describe the segregated southern way of life paralleled that of other observers throughout southern history. Reflecting the insights of earlier scholars on ancient African civilizations, Wright wrote that "we had our own civilization in Africa before we were captured and carried off to this land." He admitted that readers "may smile when we call the way of life we lived in Africa a 'civilization,'" but he recounted the many ways "the culture of many of our tribes was equal to that of the lands from which the slave captors came." Wright noted that the Western world into which Africans came was a "God-sanctioned civilization," and he pointed to ways that religion reinforced the materialistic motives.[49]

Pointing out that the enslaved knew no culture but one of plantation oppression, he showed how eagerly African Americans had embraced American culture when opportunities appeared to do so. "Our way of life is simple," he added, and he insisted "our unity of living" came from cooperation among Black farmworkers to do what had to be done. Wright summarily concluded that Blacks labored ceaselessly in the "mills of Western civilization, but we have never . . . become an organic part of that civilization." Instead, Blacks, north and south, went home at the end of a long day and lived within "the orbit of . . . remnants of the culture of the South," the years passing "within the web of a system we cannot beat," the term "web of a system" suggesting the totality of the southern way of life.[50]

Wright offered a detailed picture of life under the southern way of life's racial segregation. He frequently thought about "ways of life" in *Black Boy: A Record of Childhood and Youth* (1945) and later writings. He probed the consciousness of racial difference, how it emerged, how different experiences sharpened his understanding of it, and how his consciousness escaped a kind of determinism he saw at work in other African Americans who seemed to find ways to survive in the system. He tapped his memory to recall when he first learned about racial difference, at a train station in Elaine, Arkansas, where "there were two lines of people at the ticket window, a 'white' line and a 'black' line." When boarding the train, he realized whites went to one part of the train and Blacks to another. His longing to see the white part "irritated and annoyed" his mother, and his continuing questioning about race led her to slap him. It was an example of times his mother punished him for violations of racial etiquette, as she tried to prepare him for the world of the southern way of life. He attributes his eventual rebellion from southern ways to his isolation from whites as a child. "I had begun coping with the white world too late," and thus he could not "make subservience an automatic part of my behavior." He saw his everyday feelings and thoughts within the larger system, and he realized he had to "figure out how to perform each act and how to say each word in racial interaction." Wright felt he was living in an alien culture and civilization, as he constantly misread the reactions of whites around him and said and did things inappropriate for Jim Crow.[51]

After he began reading widely, Wright realized that he was developing "a yearning for a kind of consciousness, a mode of living that the way of life about me had said could not be, must not be, and upon which the penalty of death had been placed" as he identified the soul-killing results of that way of life. Like earlier writers of the Harlem Renaissance, Wright often used the term "death" to suggest the ultimate meaning of the southern way of life for Blacks. His uncle Hoskins, for example, died at the hands of whites jealous over his successful liquor business. Later, his friend Griggs told him he was too impatient. "Do you want to get killed?" he asked Wright. Wright replied, "Hell no!" Griggs's response was "Then for God's sake, learn how to live in the South." He advised him to "*think* before you act, *think* before you speak." Wright was too independent to dissemble, which required "forgetting the artificial status of race and class." Wright explored African American roles under Jim Crow, as he considered "my chances for life in the South as a Negro," and again, death figured prominently in his assessments. He could fight southern whites but could not win that way. "If I fought openly, I would die and I did not want to die." He could live the life of a "genial slave," but his experiences had "shaped me to live by my own feelings and thoughts." He could marry his friend Bess and settle into a middle-class life, but he concluded "that, too, would be the life of a slave; if I did that, I would crush to death something within me," and he would grow to hate that life.[52]

Wright speculated that he could seek escape in gambling, sex, alcohol, petty theft, or fighting his fellow Black people. Wright's conclusion was that "this was the culture from which I sprang. This was the terror from which I fled." He used the term "shocks of southern living" to describe attempts to limit him. When he became a bellboy in a Jackson, Mississippi, hotel, he came into contact with Black workers who represented possible models of behavior for surviving in the Jim Crow southern way, but "most of them were not conscious of living a special, separate, stunted way of life." Yet he knew that at some point in their socialization in the South "there had been developed in them a delicate, sensitive controlling mechanism that shut off their minds and emotions from all that the white race had said was taboo." Despite rhetoric of American opportunity, "they knew unerringly what to aspire to and what was not to aspire to," a succinct description of how the segregated southern way of life differed from the concept of the American dream.[53]

Wright found little sustenance in African American culture around him in the segregated South. Family life included persistent poverty and dysfunction, community gave him few hopeful models of behavior, and religious values and experiences meant little to him. He lacked the appreciation of the customary ways African Americans under Jim Crow used to survive their oppression. Wright brooded over "the cultural barrenness of black life" and imagined that lack as a by-product of the oppressive southern way of life. He noted that after he had "learned other ways of life," he puzzled over "the unconscious irony of those who felt that Negroes led so passional an existence!" Instead of emotional strength, he saw "our negative confusions, our flights, our fears, our frenzy under pressure." Complaining of what he saw as a shallow cultural imagination, he noted "how timid our joy, how bare our traditions, how hollow our memories, how lacking we were in those intangible sentiments that bind man to man, and how shallow was even our despair." African American culture in the South was, of course, a rich one in folkways and empowered communal values. Wright did not dwell on such features in the memoir, or perhaps his own demoralizing life under the segregated southern way of life denied him access to that culture, or perhaps he wanted to portray the darkest vision possible of life under Jim Crow to emphasize its horrors.[54]

Wright charted the illumination of his consciousness, with the term "dream" suggesting the broadening of his horizons that would eventually lead to his escape from the South and its imprisoning way of life. More than anything, reading books opened his eyes to new dreams of going north and writing books, with an appreciation of H. L. Mencken, the South's nemesis, as seminal. "I wondered what on earth this Mencken had done to call down upon him the wrath of the South." Wright came to realize the power of words and ideas, and he hungered for "new ways of looking and seeing." He concluded that the worst aspect of the southern way was its limitations on his right to feelings, an awareness that fed his visions of possibilities beyond the oppression of the southern way. Led to speculate on where "in this southern darkness" he had conceived a sense of freedom, he emphasized the importance of trying "to order my life by my feelings." The people he met demanded submission, but he dared to "consider my feelings superior to the gross environment that sought to claim me." He clutched "a dream which the state of Mississippi had spent millions of dollars to make sure that I would never feel." Moreover, he related his new understanding to a changed conceptual outlook: "a kind of consciousness, a mode of being that the way of life about me had said could not be, must not be, and upon which the penalty of death had been placed." A runaway train metaphor suggested the dangers of his new sensibility but also its exhilaration: "Somewhere in the dead of the southern night my life had switched onto the wrong track and, without my knowing it, the locomotive of my heart was rushing down a desperately steep slope, heading for a collision, heedless of the warning red lights that blinked all about me; the sirens and the bells and the screams that filled the air." The runaway railroad indicated his peril before he could actually find a way to escape.[55]

Reflecting on his "defensive living" in the South and his hope someday to understand what "living in the South had meant," he returned to the centrality of his feeling. He acknowledged that the southern way of life had marked him forever, "for my feelings had already been formed by the South, for there had been slowly instilled into my personality and consciousness, black though I was, the culture of the South." In migrating out of the region he took "a part of the South to transplant in alien soil, to see if it could grow differently, if it could drink of new and cool rains, bend in strange winds, respond to the warmth of other suns, and, perhaps, to bloom." If that happened, he hoped that out of "that southern swamp of despair and violence," light could appear even out of the "blackest of the southern night."[56]

Wright thus named aspects of the southern way of life as African Americans experienced them. The very last words of the book were a judgment on the southern way. He took with him the "hazy notion that life could be lived with dignity, that the personalities of others should not be violated, that men should be able to confront other men without fear or shame." In Wright's complicated reflection, the southern way had marked all those African Americans who had lived under it, but the African American version of southern culture still offered the potential as a basis for transcending the evils of the social system. He hoped that out of African American struggles in the South its people "might win some redeeming means." Wright used a resonant southern term here. "Redemption" at the end of Reconstruction had meant whites regaining political control of the South, and the word was a central one to the region's dominant evangelical religion. Wright saw a human, individual redemption to be possible by transcending segregation.[57]

Zora Neale Hurston

Like other figures who grappled with culture, civilization, and way of life in the interwar years, Zora Neale Hurston lived in a moment of time between tradition and modernity, through the Great Migration, the catastrophic Depression, and a world war. She brought particular perspectives to an evolving consciousness of the South's collective experience, particularly in race relations. A self-confident African American woman and a gifted fiction writer, she was also a scholar trained by one of the world's leading anthropologists and aware of modern understandings of culture. She studied the southern Black community and made use of the latest techniques in fieldwork. In some ways a part of same folk community she studied, she was also one of the accomplished writers of the Harlem Renaissance in the 1920s. She alone among the writers of the renaissance was "irrepressibly Southern in her mannerism and speech." Other Black writers would complain about her wearing the head scarf associated with slave women and of cooking soul food for their intellectual soirees, and they mocked her as a minstrel at heart. Her "audacious, down-home antics and her storytelling" made "the uncultured blacks of the South all too vivid for her cultured associates who preferred to idealize Southern folk life." A gap became evident here between the aspirational high-culture outlook of renaissance writers and the grassroots folk culture perspective that Hurston represented, a highly charged division in Black culture in the interwar years.[58]

Hurston claimed the descriptor "southerner" as part of her identity, unlike most African Americans under Jim Crow who could seldom embrace the region fully under its racial restrictions that many whites identified as the essence of the southern way of life. She saw language as the key to a southern identity, having Black origins but embracing white southernness as well. "In the first place, I was a Southerner, and had the map of Dixie on my tongue." The theater group she worked for at one point loved her idioms in conversation and teased her, in a good-natured way, about her talk. "They did not know of the way an average Southern child, white or black, is raised on simile and invective." Southerners could tell you "exactly how you walk and smell," they "furnish a picture gallery of your ancestors," and they speculate on "what your children will be like." Their speech is "full of images and flavor," essentially rural folk language, taking "their comparisons right out of the barnyard and the woods." This well-educated scholar went back and forth in her writings between formal academic prose and folk expressions and inserted colloquialisms throughout her work. She saw language, like other parts of southern Black folk culture, as empowering through the use of a distinctive voice that resisted white supremacy's southern way and avoided representations of victimized people.[59]

Hurston was significant as a native southern, well-trained anthropologist collecting African American folklore, and she offers one of the most compelling explications of folk culture's centrality in considering African American perspectives on the segregated southern way of life. From the late nineteenth century, elite southern whites had enjoyed Black songs and folktales, a part often of nostalgic, backward-looking evocations of the antebellum plantation world. Pastoral plantation literature pictured slaves as contented and docile, and the minstrel performance tradition drew from Black folklore in mixing revulsion at Black African Americans with fascination. Even state and local folklore societies and their accounts pictured Blacks as backward and primitive. Hurston's *Mules and Men*, on the other hand, depicted Black folklore as an example of everyday resistance to the limitations imposed on life in the segregated South that expressed a Black critique of southern ways, if sometimes in veiled expressions. Rather than being tradition bound, Hurston's folk are often rooted in modern life. Her informants were mostly wage laborers at lumber mills, not sharecroppers, and the second part of the book focused on New Orleans, in a city well beyond the folk traditions of agrarianism. Her sawmill storytellers recognize their white boss has excessive legal and economic power and find it "noble" when one of their own stands up to "dat cracker." Hurston's folk are not just local in their work but linked to the national economy through the symbol of the log train, which is central to their jobs, and through mail-order catalogs, the results of which appear in the dresses southern Black women wear to social activities. "*Mules and Men* represents communities that partic-ipate in modernity," literary scholar Leigh Anne Duck notes, "while deriving pleasure and substance from folk culture."[60]

Hurston's folk are not the backward folk of white folklorists of the early twentieth century. Her teacher, Franz Boas, in *The Mind of Primitive Man* (1911), had dispelled the idea of "primitive cultures" being backward ones and noted they are often as complex as Western societies in such areas as religion, music, and social activities. Folklorist John Lomax used the term "primitive" in an appreciative way to describe the songs he recorded at Parchman Prison in Mississippi. Hurston, like Lomax, believed the primitive was the basis for the "authentic" in folk culture, which people should prize. Her folk-collecting in the Caribbean, as well as the South, often evoked resonances of surviving Africanisms she treasured. "The drums throb Africa by way of Cuba, Africa by way of the British West Indies; Africa by way of Haiti and Martinique; Africa by way of Central and South America." She believed her Florida was part of an African diaspora that connected the state to the Caribbean culture.[61]

Hurston's autobiography, *Dust Tracks on a Road* (1942), is a good example of the importance of folk culture to her own life, as she recounts folktales, stories, and songs. She describes Joe Clark's store, where residents of her hometown of Eatonville sat on its porch and swapped jokes and tall tales. She first heard of Brer Rabbit and Brer Fox there, learned wordplay and innuendo, and expe-rienced joy and exhilaration she found possible even in the segregated South. In addition to drawing on Hurston's appreciation for Black folk culture, the memoir had a strong biracial theme. She tells of the white man who helped birth her and remained her companion as a child; of the two white women who visited her school and brought books that she loved; of Mrs. R. Osgood Mason, her white "godmother" and the "psychic bond between us" that Hurston saw. Her autobiography shows Hurston's awareness indeed of racism, but it has little criticism of whites, perhaps because she was dependent on the generosity of people such as Mason.[62]

Like Wright's memoir, Hurston's story focuses much attention on how living under Jim Crow influenced family life. Her family, like his, often tried to teach her the restrictions of Jim Crow society. Her grandmother had been a slave and feared Hurston's impudence. "Youse too brazen to live long," she told the young Hurston, and her father warned that "the white folks are not going to stand for it." On the other hand, her mother encouraged her aspirations, not wanting, as Hurston notes, to "squinch my spirit." Hurston had a big personality and complained of "the pigeonhole way of life" that adults often practiced in trying to halt her questioning. She was eager to grow up. "I wanted to get through high school. I had a way of life inside me and I wanted it with a want that twisted me." Her memoir did not dwell on racial issues, unlike most African American literature of the time that had pronounced concerns for social justice. In her essay "How It Feels to Be Colored Me," she did relate her racial awakening. It did not come in Eatonville but happened when she moved at age thirteen to Jacksonville to attend school. "I was not Zora of Orange County any more. I was now a little colored girl." The Jim Crow landscape made her know that. "Things were all about the town to point this out to me. Street cars and stores and then talk I heard around the school." She came to realize the implications of this new knowledge and learned it "in my heart as well as in the mirror."[63]

Despite this knowledge, she related that "I am not tragically colored. There is not a great sorrow dammed up in my soul, nor lurking behind my eyes." She proclaimed that she did not "belong to the sobbing school of Negrohood who hold that nature somehow has given them a lowdown dirty deal and whose feelings are all hurt about it." From her own experience she insisted that "the world is to the strong regardless of a little pigmentation more or less." She used a figure out of southern coastal life to make her point: "No, I do not weep at the world—I am too busy sharpening my oyster knife." She went so far as to deny the importance of the legacy of slavery for her contemporary African Americans. "Slavery is the price I paid for civilization, and the choice was not with me. It is a bully adventure and worth all that I have paid through my ancestors." A Hurston fan, writer Alice Walker noted that this statement was probably a common assumption in the early twentieth century, but to hear it "makes one's flesh crawl." Walker hit the mark in suggesting that Hurston was trying to convey that she was "a cheerful, supremely confident and extroverted little girl who assumed anyone and everyone would be delighted with her; and a passionate, nationalistic adult who exulted in her color, her 'Africanism,' and her ability to *feel*." Hurston's focus on the vitality of Black life, even under the segregated southern way of life, made her a target for Black critics of her work. Sterling A. Brown said her work did not have the "bitterness" inherent in southern Black life and labeled her work "pastoral" (which evoked the Vanderbilt Agrarians). Alain Locke said she was "too Arcadian" to be believable. She replied to such critics that she did not want to "write about the Race Problem. I was and am thoroughly sick of the subject. My interest lies in what makes a man or a woman do such-and-so, regardless of his color."[64]

Hurston's essay on the "pet Negro system" was an insightful but controversial portrayal of what she saw as one key method by which the southern way of life's racial segregation functioned. The pet Negro system afforded special privileges to African Americans who behaved as southern whites expected them to behave and thereby bonded with them. It was paternalistic, with whites deciding how to assist Blacks who worked for them, and it reinforced the white sense of superiority. Hurston began her essay with mock preaching that drew from African American folk religious tradition. "Brothers and Sisters, I take my text this morning from the Book of Dixie. I take my text and I take my time." Using language that sounds like it is out of the King James Version of the Bible, she has her preacher say, "Now it says here, 'And every white man shall be allowed to pet himself a Negro. Yea, he shall take a black man unto himself to pet and to cherish, and this same Negro shall be perfect in his sight.'"[65]

Hurston saw "more angles to this race adjustment business than are ever pointed out to the public, white, black or in-between." She claimed that the "simple race-agin-race pattern" heard in public speeches and read in writings did not reflect the actual conditions of life in the South because "the South lives and thinks in individuals." The elite white man, whom she calls "the Colonel," does favors for his Black worker whom he had grown to trust, but this attitude does not extend to the Black race in general. Southern tradition gave the Colonel his general derogatory view of the Black race, but he saw his own worker as an exception. Other whites "pull strings for the Colonel's favorites knowing that they will get the same things done for theirs." The advantages may be assistance with schooling, a decent job in the local community, bail money or minimum health care when needed, or a good word at the bank for a needed loan. In an exploitive, unjust system, such advantages are real ones, Hurston insisted, and "a lot of black folk, I'm afraid, find it mighty cozy."[66]

Blacks had their "pet whites, so to speak," as class consciousness among African Americans "is an angle to be reckoned with in the South." Black workers and middle-class business and professional people dependent on white favors "love to be associated with 'the quality' and consequently are ashamed to admit that they are working for 'strainers,'" the overly ambitious, upwardly mobile white people. African Americans in the South gained prestige derived from association with good families. Hurston noted the "well off Negro homes" and the great number of high-priced cars in more prosperous neighborhoods of African American businessmen, lawyers, doctors, and undertakers. She insisted that white southerners made "a sharp distinction between the upper-class and lower-class Negro." Such people were "living and working in the South because that is where they want to be." The businessman who had stayed in the South and not gone north knew, she argued, that segregation and discrimination took place in the North as well as the South, "with none of the human touches of the South." That last sentence suggests much about Hurston's overall favorable attitude toward the southern way of life, despite its customs that she realizes are unjust. She herself abided by Jim Crow's racial etiquette by sleeping in servant's quarters when visiting white literary friends and by using rear entrances without complaint.[67]

Hurston insisted, in the voice of her "Prophet of Dixie," that she was "not defending the system, beloved, but trying to explain it. The low-down fact is that it weaves a kind of basic fabric that tends to stabilize relations and give something to work for in adjustments." The pet Negro thus symbolizes "the web of feelings and mutual dependences spun by generations and generations of living together and natural adjustment." The southern way here, she admitted, "isn't half as pretty as the ideal adjustment of theorizers, but it's a lot more real and durable." Her use of "web of feelings" is another example of a recurring metaphor of those who have thought about the interconnectedness of life in the South, the cross-racial interdependencies of the southern way. She recognized the "dangers in the system" as too much depended "on the integrity of the Negro who benefitted to share advantages." The entire African American community was typically in need of resources, yet those resources from well-off individuals went to the personal benefit of the pet. Others in the Black community "curse him for a yellow-bellied sea-buzzard, a ground-mole and a woods-pussy call him a white-folks n——, an Uncle Tom, and a handkerchief-head and let it go at that." She argued that Black folk knew, nonetheless, the system was "too deep rooted to be changed."[68]

Hurston's politics evolved, however. World War II changed the thinking of many African American leaders, as fighting against fascism abroad gave them the context to argue for dramatic racial change in the United States. Hurston reflected that changed sensibility as well, as seen in her 1945 essay "Crazy for This Democracy." She wrote the piece for an African American audience—it appeared in *Negro Digest*—and she forthrightly came out against segregation. "I am crazy about the idea of this Democracy," she wrote. "I am all for the repeal of every Jim Crow law in the nation here and now. Not in another generation or so." Moreover, she related the urgency for repeal to her family. "The Hurstons have already been waiting sixty years for that. I want it here and now." Her sarcasm comes through in proclaiming the slowness of the nation in extending the values of democracy to its Black people. "All I want to do is to get hold of a sample of the thing, and I declare, I sure will try it." She criticized the United States and other Western governments at the end of the war for not paying more attention to the plight of Africa and Asia in the coming postwar world, a view that reflected a previously unheard social protest on her part.[69]

In the 1950s, Hurston would become more conservative and even objected to the *Brown v. Board of Education* Supreme Court decision mandating school desegregation because it devalued what African Americans had achieved in their separate communities under Jim Crow. Looked at over her career, she was a central figure in giving voice to southern African Americans who did not leave as part of the Great Migration. She explicated and gave voice to the varieties of southern culture rooted in the Black folk community and which migrants took north. Her distinctive views of southern race relations, such as the pet Negro system, suggested how people worked the margins of segregation to gain advantages, advantages that were part of socialization in a legally mandated southern way of life. Such sociologists as John Dollard and Bertram Doyle had said much the same, but Hurston's wit and bravado made her a target for Black critics wanting an orthodox presentation of the grim realities of southern life, such as those that Richard Wright represented.[70]

World War II

World War II brought substantial changes to the South and created new opportunities for the assertion of African American rights and new challenges to white defenders of the segregationist southern way of life. Federal government war efforts extended the impact of the New Deal programs in diversifying the southern economy and in creating new job opportunities for people in the South. Farmers left the land in greater numbers than in the 1930s, with mechanization emerging as a new force in reducing the need for sharecroppers and tenant farmers. Defense plants and military bases proliferated and provided job alternatives to farming in general, while federal government–mandated wage scales raised wages for southern workers. As southerners left the countryside for southern cities or midwestern, West Coast, or northeastern areas, small-town businesses declined in number, church congregations decreased, and community life suffered. The war challenged a provincialism associated with the South since the late nineteenth century as southerners joined the military and experienced new ways, not only in other American places but overseas as well. The way southerners lived was dramatically changing. Urban infrastructures could not keep up with booming population growth in places such as Mobile, Norfolk, Charleston, Pascagoula, and Beaumont. John Dos Passos noted that city life and steady wages amazed migrants to southern defense plants. A house trailer with electric lights and running water was "a dazzling luxury to a woman who's lived all her life in a cabin with half-inch chinks between the splintered boards on the floor." The effect of the war on women could be far reaching, as labor shortages allowed women the opportunity to work outside the home, gaining independence and self-sufficiency.[71]

Stories in the national press, nonetheless, played upon traditional images of backward rural folks, who stood out more than ever in new urban contexts.

In 1943, the *Washington Post* described a "large proportion" of the newcomers to shipbuilding cities along the Gulf Coast as "primitive, illiterate backwoods people" who came with "their native habits of living" and needed to learn "what it means to use gas stoves and sinks and toilets." Agnes Meyer complained that their "cultural patterns remind one of America's most primitive existence one hundred years or more ago." Southerners themselves, of all sorts, noted the social stresses in society coming from the war, as they perceived a decline in morals, condemned defense workers and cities as sources of corruption, worried about returning veterans, and feared a postwar economic depression. Such perspectives showed the stresses of southerners moving out of the Agrarians' rural southern way of life and into modern life.[72]

Between 4 million and 5 million nonsoutherners spent time in the South during the war, and they appreciated the helpfulness of individual southerners, but the "collective portrait of southerners pointed to a strange and peculiar people, every bit as ominous as the land they came from." The sense of southern difference began with the physical environment, with snakes, bugs, heat and humidity, endless rain, and other natural features that made a negative impression. A draftee from Staten Island, stationed in Louisiana, wrote of "an air of utter strangeness in the place." These visitors to the South translated the sense of a threatening, unpleasant environment to the people who inhabited it. A GI from Chicago told oral historian Studs Terkel that he had never been out of the Midwest when the war began, and his time at Fort Benning in Georgia presented "unfamiliar people with strange accents." The southerner "was an exotic creature to me." Northerners in the wartime South met the locals through exaggerated, negative, long-established images. Historian and writer William Manchester recalled his wartime stay in the South: "I looked out on shabby unpainted shacks and people in rags, all of them barefoot. No Taras, no Scarletts, no Rhetts; just Tobacco Road." Nonsouthern soldiers wrote of untutored country people and violent rednecks as the typical southerners, usually evoking outraged replies from white southerners. Nonsoutherners' observations offered perspective on the southern way of life, filled with longtime stereotypes but also firsthand experience.[73]

Although many nonsoutherners in the wartime South were prejudiced themselves, they often recorded the harshness of white southern racial behavior. Northerners often did not follow the etiquette of the segregated southern way of life, thereby touching a sensitive nerve among anxious white southerners. Northern white soldiers stationed in the region were often unhappy with small-town ways and hostility from local whites. Black soldiers were even more discontented and chafed under southern restrictions. A Black marine wrote that in his time in the South, he realized, "You ain't in the United States now.

This is North Carolina." Beyond racial conflicts, cultural issues hardened a sense of underlying, deep dissimilarities; one writer noted that northern and southern soldiers were "continually amazed at the other's inability to speak English."[74]

The coming of the war led some southerners to reflect on the region's history and character in relation to the conflict. Presbyterian lay leader, farmer, and later civil rights advocate James McBride Dabbs wrote in "Going to Win the War" (1942) that Civil War memory was still strong "when all our young men, and our old men, and our boys, too, went away to a war, and returned—those that did return—in defeat." He remembered growing up with the signs and symbols of the Lost Cause around him—his schoolmates "did not attempt to sing the 'Star-Spangled Banner,' but they did sing the 'Bonny Blue Flag.'" White southerners in the 1940s still belonged emotionally to two nations, he said: the United States, which had never lost a war, and the Confederate States, which had lost. If the war proved to be long and hard, the white southerner would not "expect war to be otherwise." He admitted that the antebellum South had been a feudalistic society, "a civilization built upon violence, or the threat of violence." Distancing himself from any defense of slavery, he insisted "that we have now come into a world where certain nations would build, not civiliza-tion, but a new barbarism upon violence." Through the South's memory of its violent origins, "we shall give them back the violence of two blows for one and shall retain something of the civilization we once built upon however unsta-ble a foundation." Dabbs harked back to the late nineteenth-century southern civilization that rested in the Lost Cause and used the old memory to inspire southerners fighting against fascism.[75]

Fascism and W. J. Cash

Fascism had loomed large through the late 1930s for American intellectuals, including many southerners, who saw disturbing analogies between Hitler's racism and that of the South. They regarded Germany as a center of high civ-ilization in Europe, and its descent into authoritarianism seemed, by the late 1930s, to threaten a new barbarism for the world. The South's system of racial segregation and its enforcement of a one-party political system came under intense scrutiny as a result of comparisons with European totalitarianism and left "the benighted South looking a good deal more benighted in the context of Fascist Italy and Nazi Germany."[76]

On the eve of American entry into the war, W. J. Cash published his sweep-ing meditation on the South, *The Mind of the South* (1941), which made explicit connections between the authoritarianism of southern culture and the bar-barism of fascism, which he saw threatening civilization itself. In the book he traced the history of the South that had produced what he saw as a cultural consciousness providing an ideological unity for the white South. He did not use the term "southern way of life" in the book, but his definition of the "southern mind" as "a fairly definite mental pattern, associated with a fairly definite social pattern," suggested he had in mind the southern way's self-consciousness and its behavioral expectations. The systematic configuration of the southern way of life appeared in his description of the southern mind as "a complex of established relationships and habits of thought, sentiments, prejudices, standards and values, and association of ideas." To Cash, the southern mind was primitive and uncritical and left itself open to irrationalism that fostered the lack of skepticism that he associated with movements such as fascism.[77]

Cash was a journalist and published articles and essays in the 1930s that showed his rising fear of fascism abroad. In "What Price Mussolini" in the *Charlotte News*, Cash wrote that fascism and Nazism were throwbacks to savage ways. The fascist countries had "fallen back into an essentially barbaric pattern—into the permanent organization of society as a military turn." He had read Oswald Spengler's *The Decline of the West*, with its pessimistic thesis on the organic development from life and vitality to decay and death that Spengler saw in all civilizations. In another 1930s essay, Cash noted that the Depression-era people he met talked "essentially the thing Spengler talks: that the world has got too complex for one man's mind to get around, that civilization is cracking down—ruin—the New Middle Ages." Whether civilization itself was in danger, Cash believed Western societies were "working toward a Big Change all around—in culture as in economic structure." He identified that change as the dominance of "the machine view of things, with its confidence that mechanical laws governed the universe," as people rejected "the old, deep, dark, mysterious humanity." Indeed, he despaired at the "dehumanization ushered in by the modern industrial state," sounding much like the Agrarians' version of the southern way of life in his critique of the change he feared coming.[78]

In a 1938 newspaper op-ed, "Spengler Comes True: Dawn for Dictators, Evening in the West," Cash insisted that the barbarism of Germany and Italy was by then fulfilling Spengler's dire insights on the decline of civilization. He had in 1936 begun connecting Nazi racial ideology and practice with the racism of the South through the similarities between Nazis and the Ku Klux Klan. He had been reading about the anthropologist Franz Boas questioning the idea of races, and he wrote that it was too late to do much for Germany in the grip of the Nazis but that "perhaps it will get some sense into the heads of some of our American Ku Kluxers who seem so hotly bent on taking us into Fascisms, willy-nilly." Elsewhere, he called Hitler "a somewhat inferior Grand Dragon Clarke."[79]

Cash did not see the southern situation as precisely the same as that of fascist Germany and Italy, but he identified extreme individualism and excited romanticism as the key traits of the primitive, uncritical southern mind that had fostered totalitarian thinking over generations as the self-conscious expression of southern civilization. Conceptually, his insight was to see the South going through a series of frontier conditions, by which he meant recurring eras of social crises that led to repeated assertions of a regional orthodoxy to provide order and stability. The early settlement of southern places, the Old South plantation world, the destruction of the Civil War and chaos during Reconstruction's efforts to remake southern society, the coming of industry, the disruptions of the post–World War I years—all these situations kept the southern cultural consciousness from moving beyond a primitive state, leaving it open to the simple solutions of authoritarianism.[80]

Cash's fertile imagination labeled several key concepts as central to the southern way of life. One was the "Proto-Dorian bond," which joined whites of all social classes in superiority over all African Americans and promoted the belief that plain white folks were true members of the South's ruling class. He saw a "vastly ego-warming and ego-expanding distinction between the white man and the black." The common white folks put their confidence in the symbol of the region's distinctiveness and success—the slave-owning planter. The Proto-Dorian bond elevated the common white "to a position comparable to that of, say, the Doric knight of ancient Sparta. Not only was he not exploited directly, he was himself made by extension a member of the dominant class." Cash's Old South had a striking similarity to the modern totalitarian state. From placing restrictions on any criticisms of slavery, it was an easy step to prohibiting any criticism of the South as not only disloyal but subversive. Emancipation did not end southern authoritarianism, as the Reconstruction South collapsed into a new frontier, a "jungle growth of poverty and ruin." Unquestioned support for the Lost Cause and a romanticized view of southern civilization now buttressed southern authoritarianism and its Proto-Dorian bond.[81]

A second of Cash's terms to note is the "Cloud-Cuckoo-Land" that he sees postbellum white southerners mentally living in, wherein all white southerners who had ever imagined their ancestors as aristocrats "would be metamorphosed with swift precision, beyond any lingering shade of doubt, into the breathing image of Marse Chan and Squire Effingham," and evoking Old South plantation images. Cash portrayed the postbellum South as virtually a martial state, with regional orthodoxy demanding absolute loyalty by whites and total deference by African Americans, with common whites again following the orders of the planters. The common white "so absolutely identified his ego with the thing called the South as to become, so to say, a perambulating South in little"—a marvelous image of what Cash imagined as a unified southern white mind. From this postwar era into the twentieth century, Cash feared the

South's antimodernism had been a threat to Western civilization, in danger
as well from European developments. Cash identified southern antimodernism as tribal and provincial, one rejecting the free intellectual play of Western
civilization at its best. Cash believed critical inquiry was the foundation for
the modern mind, and the South's suffocating orthodoxy stamped out that inquiry as it associated modernity itself with the figure of the Yankee. Cash wrote
that white southerners came to collapse scientists Darwin and Huxley, Union
generals Ben Butler and William Tecumseh Sherman, and Satan himself into
a terrifying figure that threatened their civilization. Cash had no doubt that
race was underlying this totalitarian mind control and its Cloud-Cuckoo-Land
fantasy of southern superiority, as the "consuming monomania" of the region's
way of life was to protect the purity of its blood and culture against the Black
plague threatening the white South.[82]

The coming of industry was a major force in the postbellum South, but Cash
did not believe that progress disrupted southern authoritarianism. To be sure,
southern culture faced another time of social chaos with the end of the old social patterns, people moving to towns and cities, factories and mills becoming
new sources of wealth and influence, and New South capitalists increasingly
dominating southern leadership. Cash's argument was for extreme continuity
in southern orthodoxy. The factory was simply a reconfigured plantation, with
the old paternalism surviving and the Proto-Dorian bond holding tight among
the plain whites. As Cash said, "There was no revolution in basic ideology and
no intention of relinquishing the central Southern positions and surrendering
bodily to Yankee civilization involved in the genesis of dream and program."
Although the term "southern way of life" is a twentieth-century one, Cash insisted the concept went far back in southern history and continued unchanged
in his age.[83]

Cash put forward another key concept in his understanding of the ideology
of the southern way of life—the Savage Ideal. The South's demeaning of critical
thought had long been enforced by the willingness to use intimidation and
violence against anyone who would question regional orthodoxy, a sentiment
established during Reconstruction when tolerance "was pretty well extin-
guished all along the line, and conformity made a nearly universal law." White
southerners, in his estimate, thought themselves in a life-and-death situation
during Reconstruction, one resulting in a "line between what was Southern
and what was not, etched, as it were, in fire and carried through every department of life." Cash saw how cultural memory became the basis for a prescribed
southern way, as "the ideas and loyalties of the apotheosized past fused into the
tightest coherence and endowed with all the binding emotional and intellectual
power of any tribal complex of the Belgian Congo." Southern cultural authority

then "explicitly defined in every great essential, defined in feeling down to the last detail, what one must think and say and do." Tribal indeed.[84]

Cash argued that this fanatic loyalty, the Savage Ideal, appeared in the revival of the Ku Klux Klan with the region's characteristic hates and fears embodied within "the ancient Southern pattern of high romantic histrionics, violence, and mass coercion of the scapegoat and the heretic." Connecting the Savage Ideal with Nazi Germany, he saw the Klan as a folk movement, "at least as fully as such as the Nazi movement in Germany, to which it was not without kinship." His book all along had made connections between the South and Nazi Germany's ideologies and authoritarian institutions, and his discussion of the interwar period showed his fear that the modern South was descending into a variety of Nazi savagery. The Agrarians had seen southern traditionalism as a bulwark against the instabilities of modernity, but Cash saw the traditional South as a terrifying version of modern totalitarianism underlying the southern way of life.[85]

World War II and Race Relations

Wartime conditions had created a more assertive African American community in the South, one that built on the empowerment that had come out of the Great Migration and the role of the federal government in the 1930s in at least indirectly contributing to African American economic progress. White Mississippi journalist Thomas Sancton insisted that wartime conditions exponentially increased an "aggressive negro spirit." The upending of normal social routines, new economic opportunities for African Americans, the federal government's efforts to promote a united national community in the face of foreign challenge, and the maturing of African American political leadership in northern cities all fostered opportunities for Black southerners beyond the narrow range prescribed by the segregated southern way of life. Blacks protested stereotypical racist representations and expanded their voting rolls during the war. The *Smith v. Allwright* Supreme Court decision in 1944 outlawed the white primary and opened the way for broader Black participation in party politics where the Democratic Party was the only game in the region. Black registered voters rose from 200,000 in 1940 to 600,000 in 1946, mostly in the upper South. The idealized war aims of universal freedom, the fight against a clearly racist foe, and a heightened stress on democracy all highlighted that American society had not dealt justly with Blacks. Sancton saw this change going far beyond the South, part of an American evolution, as African Americans during the war "launched a spiritual revolution"—more evidence of the importance of religiosity to the region's way-of-life construct.[86]

Southern whites clung to the idea that African Americans were a threat to the war effort, as they feared an insurrection of discontented Blacks in a time of instability. Rumors of impending, Black-inspired race riots circulated widely, with whites convinced that the Germans had organized "Swaztika Clubs" among Blacks to foster an uprising timed with an imagined Nazi invasion of the nation. "Hitler has told the Negroes he will give them the South for their help," one informant told Howard Odum during the war. Allied with this threat was the "ice pick rumor," a story that appeared across the South telling of African Americans buying up all the ice picks they could find, to be used to attack whites if a blackout presented an opportunity to attack. Less violent but even more widespread was the rumor that Black maids were subverting the South's social order to destabilize the region. Supposedly inspired by liberal first lady Eleanor Roosevelt, the "Eleanor Clubs" were made up of Black maids in white households who showed up late for work, if at all, and walked up and down the streets bumping white women off sidewalks. One story had it that the Eleanor Clubs' motto was "A white woman in the kitchen by Christmas." Little evidence supported such claims of Eleanor Clubs, the rumors of which confirmed whites' understanding of African American discontent despite public rhetoric to the contrary.[87]

White elites saw wartime Black assertiveness as an outgrowth of the New Deal's championing of Black rights. In 1942, one Mississippi Delta planter linked Eleanor Roosevelt's concerns for Black workers to efforts by the national Democratic Party to recruit African American voters, and he saw all of this as indicating trouble for the future. He predicted a time when the federal government would protect Black voters, "and we all know what that will mean in the South." Another Mississippi planter heard of an interracial meeting in 1943 and confessed that Delta whites were "sitting under the mouth of the guns" and facing their worst crisis since Reconstruction, as he drew from the white South's memory of the supposed chaotic time of Black assertiveness at the end of the Civil War. He claimed that whites were organizing vigilante groups to protect "their civilization and their way of life," and he used the intentional words to link wartime white anxieties to the defense of their entire social system resting on white racial dominance.[88]

White southerner Thomas Sancton's "Race Fear Sweeps the South," in the *New Republic* in 1943, saw the wartime white anxiety as an episode in a long southern story. From his extensive travels in the region preparing the story, he heard "talk of impending race trouble which today dominates the imaginations of Southern white people." He wrote of "an old malaise of racial fear" that settled sometimes upon "the Southern spirit." It might lie dormant, "like malaria, to return with violence in the wake of wars and great upheavals."

The "whole culture of the South"—by which he meant the segregated south-ern way of life—had been built upon the difference between white skin and Black skin, "and a war does weird things to such a culture." He related hearing "a most callous and un-Christlike kind of talk" from whites coming out of their churches, and he concluded that "the hearts of the kindest and gentlest of Southern women seem steeled against the Negro and anything affecting his well-being."[89]

White conservative intellectuals, including many of the Agrarians, became more openly racist and reactionary in the face of the stresses of war. Historian Frank Owsley had always distrusted centralized economic and political power, and he even favored the 1930s semisocialistic measures to curtail big business and restore a propertied society where small farmers and small business people would have a larger part to play. In the course of the 1930s, though, he came to fear the growing power of the federal government, which he anticipated would be used some day to overturn segregation, and he came to distrust the power of labor unions. He wrote to his fellow Agrarian Allen Tate in 1943, "I have always been *liberal* in my social views. Not any more, however. Behold in me, sire, not even a *conservative* but a *reactionary*." He admitted that he was drawn to "my friend John C. Calhoun" when thinking of states' rights. He fulminated that nothing less than the fate of constitutional democracy and "the freedom, integ-rity and self-respect of the South's white people" were at risk. Government lead-ers and politicians, of course, reinforced a continued white racial orthodoxy.[90]

White leaders long known as political moderates and supporters of improve-ments for African Americans often retreated from their moderation in the face of new Black assertiveness during the war. Conservative white observers, for example, quoted Mark Ethridge, editor of the Louisville *Courier-Journal*, as saying, "There is no power in the world—not even in all the mechanized armies of the earth, Allied and Axis—which could now force the Southern white people to the abandonment of the principle of social segregation." An-other editor, John Temple Graves, recited southern orthodoxy: "The unshak-able belief of southern whites that the problem was peculiarly their own and that attempts to force settlement from outsiders were hateful and incompetent." He pinpointed the underlying issue by insisting that southern whites had "ab-solute determination that the blood of the two races should not be confused and a mulatto population emerge." Howard Odum agreed with Graves on the fear of outside intervention and predicted that outside intervention in southern race relations would be a "tragedy of the highest order, tragedy of the Greek, as it were, because it was the innocent Negro who suffered." Mississippi Jewish writer David L. Cohn, in a 1942 essay, "How the South Feels," noted the con-ventional wisdom and found comfort in William Graham Sumner's insistence that you cannot change people's mores by law. He argued that segregation was "the most deep-seated and pervasive of the Southern mores." He agreed with Graves on the underlying issue of feared change. "It is at bottom a blood or sexual question," and he had no trepidation as to how far southern whites would go in enforcing the segregated southern way of life. Southern whites insisted, he said, that "no white in their legal jurisdiction shall marry a Negro" and "white women shall not have physical relations with Negro men except, when discovered, upon pain of death or banishment inflicted, upon one or both parties to the act."[91]

What the Negro Wants

In 1944 the University of North Carolina Press published a collection of essays entitled *What the Negro Wants* by a range of southern African American leaders boldly expressing the desire for the segregated southern way of life to end. Press director William T. Couch had commissioned the book, with historian Rayford Logan editing and picking contributors from conservatives to activists for civil rights. All of them agreed that above all else in considering race relations in the South, segregation had to end. Logan outlined a list of "irreducible fundamentals of first-class citizenship for all Negroes," including equal opportunity, equal pay, equal legal protections, equality of suffrage, and equal dignity for African Americans as well as the broader end of public segregation.[92]

The contributors to the book stressed the American context for race relations. Poet Langston Hughes began his essay by embracing "my land, America," but he confessed he was "vitally concerned about its *mores*, its democracy, and its well-being," his use of the word "mores" bringing attention to culture. He recounted his difficulties in traveling across the country, facing discrimination in securing food, accommodations, and equal treatment on railroads. He contrasted his experiences with those of immigrants to the nation who could vote and purchase tickets to concerts and lectures, whereas he could not. "Jim Crowism varies in degree from North to South, from the unified schools and free franchise in Michigan to the tumbled down colored schools and open terror of the polls of Georgia and Mississippi." He pointed out the long-standing economic color line that had characterized the entire nation. Educator Mary McLeod Bethune entitled her essay "Certain Unalienable Rights," seeing them as "the American way" in contrast to the southern way. She saw African Americans steeped in the principles of the Declaration of Independence and the memory of the Boston Tea Party's fight for American rights. Hughes complicated his account by noting that, despite racial limitations on African Americans, the advance of democratic ideals had led to greater opportunities for them.[93]

The World War II context loomed large in the collection of essays. Sterling A. Brown pointed out that discrimination in employment tarnished a war effort for the ideals of freedom. Bethune saw African Americans' wartime protests coming out of "their resentment over the mistreatment of colored men in the armed forces." Black soldiers faced limitations in joining several branches of the military, in not being assigned to positions in line with their abilities, and in the federal government's failure to protect from civilian assaults. The frustrations of Black men and women trying to secure jobs in the defense industry also provided fuel for protest. Sterling A. Brown added a telling detail: the Red Cross would not accept the blood of African Americans in the middle of a war for democracy against fascism.[94]

These leading African American figures highlighted the term "democracy," with Hughes insisting the nation should work harder to "institute a greater measure of Democracy for the eight million colored people of the South." Indeed, the southern way of life was a primary target for reform. Brown argued that African Americans wanted to be a part of that concept but did not feel welcome in claiming it. "The gravest denial of democracy and the greatest opposition to it are in the South." He expressed special disappointment in the white liberals of the region who supported greater rights for African Americans but stopped short of endorsing the end of segregation. He had heard fears that incorporating Black southerners fully into southern life would "lower the level of civilization," but he sarcastically insisted that one consequence of integration in the South "might be that civilization in such Southern cities as Atlanta, Birmingham, Memphis, and Vicksburg will decline to the level of that in unsegregated Boston, New York, Iowa City, and Seattle." He scoffed at the "false issue of social equality," especially the white fear of intermarriage—"Negroes laugh at the suggestion that crowded buses and street cars and cafeterias are marriage bureaus"—and he insisted that intermarriage was "hardly a goal that Negroes are contending for openly or yearning for secretly." The issue was a smoke screen to frighten white southerners into not conceding other rights that would endanger the "privilege and exploitation" at the heart of the southern way.[95]

What the Negro Wants contained specific ideas about what to do next. Brown saw hopeful signs that the goal of democracy was not a "doomed hope in the South," citing opposition to the poll tax, the end of the white primary, the work of southern liberals to end inequalities in the southern way, and the biracial leadership seen in wartime conferences in the South. Hughes advocated an extensive federal-government-directed program of pro-democracy education from the elementary level to the universities. He urged the military to do a better job of teaching all soldiers, especially those from the South, how to treat members of minority groups. Finally, he proposed that the government sponsor interracial teams of intellectuals and entertainers to go into the South before white audiences, "carrying messages of culture and democracy, thus off-setting the old stereotypes of the Southern mind and the Hollywood movies, and explain to the people without dialect what the war aims are about." Bethune offered a litany of specific policy goals, including protections of voter rights, the elimination of racial barriers in labor unions, realistic interracial cooperation, and a federal prohibition of lynching.[96]

Couch was stunned that all the contributors to the volume, who represented a range of African American opinion, agreed on the need for the end of segregation. He had long assumed, like most white southerners, from liberals to conservatives, that Black leaders favored maintaining the color line in education if facilities between Blacks and whites could be equalized. Couch had opposed segregation in public transportation and accommodations and focused attention on class and economic issues as being the source of racial conflict, but he did not support the end of segregation altogether. He fell back on William Graham Sumner's familiar orthodoxy on folkways representing a virtually unchangeable source of culture in the South, and he feared that Blacks liberated from the disciplines of segregation would pose a threat to white civilization in the South. He saw, though, a dramatically changed Black leadership, produced by wartime conditions, now demanding immediate equality. Another racial progressive from the 1930s who stopped short of supporting desegregation, Virginius Dabney, wrote to Couch, empathizing with him. He recalled that when Couch had commissioned the book, "you were under the delusion" that "the Negro does not want abolition of segregation, establishment of complete social equality, etc." Dabney admitted that had been his view as well at the beginning of the war, but he said he had "abandoned it completely." He realized that "the war and its slogans have roused in the breasts of our colored friends hopes and aspirations and desires which they formerly did not entertain, except in the rarest instances."[97]

Couch decided to write a "Publisher's Introduction" to the volume that allowed him to distance himself from the book. His main target was actually Gunnar Myrdal's recent book *The American Dilemma* (1944), which explored the contradiction between what Myrdal called the "American Creed" of democracy and equality, on the one hand, and on the other, American racial policies and customs, especially the public segregation and discrimination embodied in the segregated southern way of life. Myrdal, who was a Swedish social scientist, insisted that the United States had to either give up the American Creed and embrace fascism (using that term to label the southern way of life) or accept equality, which might lead to racial amalgamation. Couch claimed that Myrdal's book "was written under gross misapprehension of what such ideas as equality, freedom, democracy, human rights have meant, and of what they can be made to mean." Undoubtedly drawing from the work of his North Carolina colleague Howard Odum, Couch made a distinction between culture and civilization and acknowledged that civilization was "not the creation of any one race or people" but "the work of many over a long period of time." But a "culture" and a "civilization" were not the same thing. A culture was the total expression of a people or race in a particular area, over a long period of time, whereas a civilization was an accumulation of universal values from diverse cultures. Couch realized that it was "not possible to accept the view that any one race is perpetually superior, or that race determines culture," but he added that "it does not follow that races are equal." At any point in time, "one race may embody values higher than those embodied by any other race, and as long as it does this, a race may rightly be regarded as superior." If whites were closer to the values of high civilization than Blacks were, then the latter would represent a threat to southern white civilization.[98]

Couch praised the values of the white-dominated Western world and saw them virtually absent from Black culture. He warned African Americans that their cultural inferiority would make integration a disaster for their hopes of slow advancement as they lost out in competition with superior whites. Returning to the fundamental danger he saw in Myrdal's viewpoint, Couch insisted that values gained through Western civilization had become embodied in southern civilization, and they were "in serious danger of destruction by widespread misunderstanding of the kind represented in *An American Dilemma*." Couch soon came to realize—partly as a result of reading in the book the consistent opposition of African American writers to segregation—that his attitudes had become outdated, but such confusion about race and civilization by a leading white liberal illustrated the difficulties of ideological consensus in the face of threats to the segregated southern way of life.[99]

Interracial Movement

The interracial movement had gained ground during the late 1930s, and wartime conditions saw it advance at the same time as rising white racism. Between 1942 and 1943, a series of conferences on race relations suggested the difficulties and achievements of interracial organizing in the South. The Durham Conference in 1942 was an effort to address race relations from the perspective of southern African Americans. Out of the meeting came "A Basis for Interracial Cooperation and Development in the South: A Statement by Southern Negroes," which soon became known as the Durham Manifesto. With a mild tone and detailed policy recommendations, the signers were "fundamentally opposed to the principle and practice of compulsory segregation in our American society," but then they added that it was "both sensible and timely" to concentrate on "the current problems of racial discrimination and neglect" rather than to insist on an immediate end of segregation itself. The Durham Manifesto called for abolition of every form of racial discrimination (other than segregation), and it named the poll tax, white primary (this was before the Supreme Court decision outlawing it), police brutality, lynching, jury exclusion, employment and union membership discrimination, and inequalities in education. The manifesto saw an important role for the federal government in ensuring equal participation in all branches of the military and an end to inequalities in agricultural aid. Northern Black leaders had not been invited, and many of them saw it as acquiescence to the southern way of life because it did not press for an urgent end to segregation. Key northern leaders such as W. E. B. Du Bois and National Association for the Advancement of Colored People leader Walter White nonetheless supported the manifesto, while the southern press was favorable to the manifesto's lack of urgency about segregation itself.[100]

White liberals, led by Jessie Daniel Ames, followed up the Durham Conference with one of their own a year later in Atlanta in April 1943. Organizers invited 533 people; 115 southern moderate and liberal white leaders from business, education, journalism, and religion attended; and 292 people signed the statement that came out of the meeting. Organizers excluded virtually everyone associated with the controversial, interracial Southern Conference for Human Welfare and even New Deal officials such as Will Alexander. The Atlanta Statement endorsed the African American struggle for fairness and equity, supported the Durham Manifesto's program for change (except for its endorsement for desegregation), and praised its evolutionary methods. The conference participants stressed, as John Egerton says, "cultivating an atmosphere of cooperation, goodwill, and mutual understanding," which were familiar goals of southern white liberals. The Atlanta Statement praised the Durham Manifesto for its lack "of threat and ultimatum," and in that spirit "we gladly agree to cooperate." Egerton describes the statement as "a tepid endorsement of the black leaders."[101]

The third conference in this series was perhaps the most portentous of all, as it brought together thirty-three African American leaders and twenty-seven white leaders in Richmond, Virginia, in June of 1943 to chart the next steps in an interracial effort. The purpose, Gordon Blaine Hancock said in his major speech, was "for white and black Souths to come together and save themselves and the nation." They met in a historic location, St. Paul's Episcopal Church, cloaked in secrecy to allow honest expression of views and to avoid public harassment of an interracial gathering. Hancock said he had a "now or never feeling" about the conference, which was "one of those rare occasions of history when the clock of Destiny is striking a mighty hour." He urged white south-erners to "cease waiting for outside sources to exhort from it in the courts con-cessions that should be made without a fight." "Men must be brotherized or they will be brutalized," he lyrically told the group. Reminding the gathering that African Americans in the South had long been patient and "borne their burdens with poise and courage," he insisted that now the time had come for the South to take moral leadership and for the white South to "save the negro or itself be lost." He raised the danger of "social and economic damnation" if African American problems were not addressed. The leaders at the meeting could be "the saviors of our Nation" if they showed the "moral courage to fol-low through." Hancock attached a moral urgency to reforming the segregated southern way of life in order to save the nation itself.[102]

Hancock's passionate speech scared many whites and led to angry and fearful responses by many of them, who said he had gone too far in outlining an apoc-alyptic scenario. Howard Odum took the floor and praised Hancock's speech, and he refocused the group's attention on a long-prepared plan for a research and development organization to push southern progress and address African American concerns. It would not, however, press for immediate desegregation. Hancock doubted this plan's effectiveness for racial change, and he told Ames of his dismay at trying to find courageous white leaders to go out in front of southern opinion and call for desegregation. Out of Odum's proposal, though, came the Southern Regional Council, established in January 1944, with Odum and Fisk University sociologist Charles S. Johnson as cochairs and a board split equally between Black and white members. It would be a progressive group in opposing discriminatory public policies, albeit gradualist in approach.[103]

A few southern liberals, such as Lillian Smith, J. Wates Waring, and Will Alexander, were forthright in urging an end to segregation at that point, with Smith refusing to support the Southern Regional Council because it would not condemn the institution. She described segregation as "spiritual lynching" of Blacks and "a menace to the health and culture of our individual souls." She added (perhaps in an ironic nod to the Agrarians) that "the time has come when we must take our stand." Alexander, a founder of the Commission on Interracial Cooperation, was then active in New Deal reform agencies. In 1944 Alexander pointed to conflicting American attitudes toward Black people. On the one hand, American opinion supported Black education and believed Af-rican Americans could learn and advance, which was "a part of the American way of life" that a progressive South should embrace. In supporting education for Blacks, "we have let them in on the meaning of democracy," a key concept of the American way. On the other hand, American policy supported racial separation that kept African Americans in an inferior social position, "rooted in fear and in doubt as to whether our democratic principles will really work." He insisted that the Southern Regional Council should embrace the "abandonment of the old patterns of segregation," that is, move away from the segregated southern way of life.[104]

American Way of Life

Will Alexander's use of the term "American way of life" showed that the national context loomed larger than ever in the South. World War II brought new expressions of this counterpart to the concept of the southern way of life. The economic disaster of the Great Depression had led to reflections by a variety of Americans, including southerners, on what were core national values. The crisis in American capitalism and the threat of such ideologies as fascism and communism led to a decrease in classic American individualism and to a new stress on the ideals of majoritarian democracy and economic security as the heart of the American way. Beginning in the late 1930s, corporate leaders, businesspeople, and conservatives in general regained initiative after their loss of public trust with the Depression, and they launched public relations efforts to convince Americans that "free enterprise" lay at the heart of the American way. From the 1930s to the 1950s, different groups of Americans championed ideas of "democracy" and "freedom" as competing ideas for control of public culture and policy.[105]

Despite this contestation, World War II led to a pursuit of consensus to unify the nation ideologically against foreign enemies. The late 1930s had led to increased attention to, and usage of, the term "American way of life," which continued in the 1940s. *Harper's Magazine* in 1937 announced, for example, a $1,000 essay contest to define the term, in hope of uncovering "the essential American traditions and ideals ... so as to form a credo adapted to present and future needs." The magazine noted that communism and fascism had attained "virtually the emotional force of religion," and it hoped to define the American way so that people of differing political and economic views might all accept the ideal. The late 1930s saw ideological struggles over cultural definitions of the nation and its civil religion that fed into wartime developments. Advocates of democracy as the American way highlighted the values of cultural pluralism and inclusion of minorities in an American society that had often been represented in public culture as homogeneous. In religious terms, Catholics and Jews had often been marginalized in traditional discussions of the white

This billboard projects the idea of an American way of life as affiliated with material prosperity. Photo by Margaret Bourke-White via Shawshots / Alamy Stock Photo.

Protestant–dominated nation, but the wartime stress on consensus led to new incorporation of Catholics and Jews into discussions of national culture and contributed to the view that the United States was a Judeo-Christian nation.[106]

Those on the left—civil rights leaders, leftist intellectuals, and labor union leaders—emphasized equality as their vision of consensus that the term "American way of life" represented and hoped to promote reform in the process. From the beginning of the war, the federal government promoted national unity, and private groups called for national unity to serve their interests. Many political liberals and leftist intellectuals, labor organizers, and others who had been members of the Popular Front coalition in the 1930s saw the war as essentially a battle against fascism, a term they used to cover evils from anti-Semitism to economic injustices. They wanted to use the war effort to promote an antifascist consensus that would encourage a more democratic and egalitarian social, political, and economic order. The Congress of Industrial Organizations leadership toned down its class-conscious rhetoric to embrace the idea of workers as part of a broad civic coalition that reflected their new respectability and, hopefully, postwar influence. More moderate and conservative opinion makers used the language of consensus during the war to promote civility across lines of social class, racial grouping, ethnicity, and religious institution.[107]

On the other side of the debate on the American way were corporate leaders who used the calls for national harmony to buttress their influence on national life. The advertising world developed countless promotional materials on American life for the war effort and often advocated consumerism as what the war was all about. As one historian wrote, "Such ads suggested that Americans were fighting not for freedom of speech or religion but for a right to buy toasters, refrigerators, and Cadillacs." Many such advertisements portrayed the war as one among nations, not as a battle of ideas, downplaying especially egalitarianism. As the war went on, the selling of the nation to its people increasingly became a private matter. Companies positioned their brands for the postwar world, but in the process, they did burnish a key concept of the American way—freedom. Historian Eric Foner, in his conceptual study of American freedom, notes that what was going on grew out of a wartime stress on the concept of freedom. "Alongside ads urging Americans to grow victory gardens, purchase war bonds, and guard against revealing military secrets," he observed, "the war witnessed a burst of messages marketing advertisers' definition of freedom." The National Association of Manufacturers took the lead in bombarding the nation's people with press releases, radio broadcasts, and advertisements that attributed the wartime production achievements to "free enterprise." That organization had earlier helped popularize the term "the American way" through billboards in the late 1930s that portrayed either a happy family at a picnic, a family welcoming a father home at the end of the day, or a family taking a Sunday drive. At the top of each sign, in giant letters, was "World's Shortest Working Hours," "World's Highest Wages," or "World's Highest Standard of Living." At the bottom of the billboards was "There's no way like the American Way."[108]

Where did the South stand in the 1940s in regard to the American way of life? White southerners embraced the ideal of democracy, certainly, although for most white southerners, it was still a democracy for whites only. Racial conservatives and radicals were surely uncomfortable with much of the wartime federal government rhetoric about spreading democratic ideals. Southern newspapers denounced northern reformers who came south, the Federal Equal Protection Commission, and Eleanor Roosevelt. Reformers in the region, on the other hand, made good use of the American way's ideals of democracy, equality, and inclusion to justify social change in the South, and African Americans in particular used such rhetoric for a more assertive attack on the segregated southern way of life.[109]

Despite the wartime need for unity, some national observers omitted the South from the American way of life and isolated white southerners from national consensus. Anthropologist Margaret Mead was a pioneer in the study of national character, and her influential book *And Keep Your Powder Dry* (1942) popularized the social psychology of Americanism around democratic and pluralist ideals. She generalized about national character but specifically excluded southerners. "The generalizations in this book should be regarded as based primarily on the North, Middle West, and West," she wrote. The South's "bi-racial classification of humanity" so affected its culture, she concluded, that any attempt to generalize about both the North and the South would "be too abstract to be fruitful." She saw caste as "a directly formative element in developing standards of behavior." Southern progressives in the interwar period saw interracial folk customs as a potential source of democratic reform, but Mead's work challenged that view and saw the region as so undemocratic that it would need to be fundamentally remade after the war.[110]

The free-enterprise vision of the American way made considerable advances in the 1940s South, becoming transmogrified into a business version of the southern way, one that had distant origins in the late nineteenth-century New South movement's call for prioritizing economic development without disturbing the cultural traditions of the region. Newspaper editor John Temple Graves embraced free enterprise as having been "invented by God" but lamented the sins against it that restricted its impact, as he claimed the nation needed "freedom from all interferences—whether collectivist or laissez faire." In a traditionally poor region, the ideology of free enterprise that promised liberty and economic abundance gave its advocates considerable cachet as the war neared its end. White southerners would put their faith in the free-enterprise American way to bring prosperity and to cement in the process close ties between conservative southern business culture and national political and economic conservatives. As historian David Southern has written of the war atmosphere, "If most whites below the Potomac interpreted events as threatening the 'southern way of life,' those on the extreme right of the political spectrum throughout the nation perceived national and international trends as conspiring against the 'American way of life.'"[111]

An American Dilemma

Gunnar Myrdal's 1944 book, *An American Dilemma*, represented a new international perspective on the South, appropriate to the wartime context. He was a Swedish economist, and Americans, including Black and white southerners, assisted him in his research. Myrdal highlighted an important concept that would be a variation of the American way of life and an influential counter-point to the segregated southern way of life. He posited the American Creed, which he defined as the ideals of liberty, democracy, equality, justice, and fair play for all people. Despite the diversity of American social life, this creed held the nation together, shaped political and social behavior, and enshrined the key idea that all people were created equal and had human rights. The title of Myrdal's book, though, suggested his other key concept, the nation's dilemma of believing the American Creed as a common belief system yet discriminating against Blacks in an egregious violation of the creed.[112]

The racial situation in the United States mystified Myrdal, given what he saw as pervasive belief in the American Creed. He and his primary researcher and writer, African American leader Ralph Bunche, went on a research trip to the South. He confessed afterward to being horrified at the widespread destitution of Blacks in southern rural areas and urban slums. He found no weakening during the war in the resolve of southern whites to discriminate against African Americans in education and job opportunities and referred to the South's pathological inhumanity toward African Americans. He wondered how that pathology had been allowed by the nation for so long. He framed his argument as an American story, not just a southern one, pointing out the evidence of discrimination in the North and also the ignorance of most white northerners about conditions in the South. Northerners seemed happy to read in the press about the criminality of Blacks, who "are the happy-go-lucky children of nature who get a kick out of life which white people are too civilized to get." Show-ing that northerners embraced the same racial ideology as southern whites, he identified the northern conscience, though, as capable of being shocked when it did know of southern conditions. Myrdal aimed his book at using that con-science to promote social change. The racial problem for Myrdal was funda-mentally one of individual morality.[113]

Myrdal singled out the South's "peculiar rural structure" as an underlying factor in the southern way of life and saw it not as the traditional supportive culture of the Agrarians but a source of ineffective social control and vigilante actions. He echoed here the work of social scientists such as Odum and W. J. Cash, who stressed the holdover of the frontier heritage into the twentieth cen-tury. Disrespect for the law and public morality had long been widespread, he concluded, and the "tradition is today still part of the way of life and as such is often patriotically cherished as distinctively Southern." He thus explicitly referred to the southern way of life, and the words "patriotically cherished" picked up the southern civil religion's influence. Nonetheless, it was "certainly one of the most sinister historical heritages of the region." He pointed also to the cultural predominance of such values as individualism and romanticism,

African American day laborers waiting to be paid for cotton picking and
to purchase supplies in a plantation store on the Marcella plantation in the
Mississippi Delta. Such a scene documented sociologist Gunnar Myrdal's findings
on exploitive race relations. Library of Congress, Washington, D.C.

both of which nurtured an enduring paternalism as part of the context for
the South's segregated way of life. Myrdal's conversations with well-off white
southerners had shown him their embrace of paternalistic benevolence as the
positive side of the southern system. He described it as a social pattern that was
personal, casual, whimsical, humorous at times, sentimental, and flattering to
the ego. Myrdal recognized that southern working-class whites had embraced
the economic opportunities provided through the federal government, but they
resented the inclusion of African Americans in such social reform efforts as
labor union legislation, child labor laws, and wage-and-hours laws.[114]

Myrdal argued that changes were taking place, ones that white southerners
sometimes failed even to recognize. Religion in the South often promoted "a
feeling of equality among human beings in the South—not even excluding the
Negroes," as he recognized the religious-based interracialism of a reformist

southern way of life. Even more important was southern acceptance of the American Creed, which explained "why so many exceptions are made to the rule of excluding Negroes from voting." He impressed on readers the need to remember that "the white conservative Southerner harbors the American Creed." White southerners were allowing Black people to receive education in better schools; New Deal measures, although circumscribed in the South, still reached many Black people; and "the South, with all its traditions of inequality and illegality," was clearly headed toward social democracy. He attributed all of these developments to white southern recognition of the American Creed.[115]

Myrdal referred to "the breath-taking drama of the Southern people," a phrase that captured the power of the wartime moment for southern civilization. White southerners he talked with stressed that "customs are strong and that there is much resistance to change," but he saw that while "reality is actually dynamic in the South . . . people's ideas about reality are usually astonishingly static." White southerners' embrace of pessimistic and conservative ideas about "the 'mores' and the 'folkways'—which supposedly cannot be changed by the 'stateways'—is not only a particularly cherished notion among Southern social scientists but is something of a regional religion for a large proportion of the literate people," again recognizing the conservative southern civil religion at work. This way of thinking hampered social change, "but the material and spiritual changes under way are so momentous that they cut through these barriers." White southerners told him the poll tax would never be abolished, but Myrdal pointed out it had already been banned in three southern states. They told him African Americans would never vote because of white objections, but they increasingly were doing so in cities. The New Deal was popular in the South and made notable changes in attitudes, while long-term trends of higher educational levels for southerners portended more change. War itself was creating more change. The war was fought "for democracy, for the 'American way of life'—which is certainly not Southern traditionalism." Myrdal pointed out that "the main thing happening to the South is that it is gradually becoming *Americanized.*"[116]

Myrdal came away from his research hopeful about the possibilities of resolving the American dilemma, but race remained a challenge for advocates of consensus at the heart of the ideology of the American way of life. The stress on common national values did give African Americans new ways to make limited advancements. Black leaders claimed such concepts as individual freedom and national unity. Lawrence Reddick, the curator of the New York Public Library's Schomburg Collection, wrote during the war, for example, that "the drive for liberty, security, and for equality of opportunity is a broad struggle by and for the common man." Pointing out that Black Americans had been denied these ideals, he insisted they therefore appreciated their meaning more than any Americans. Using another concept associated with the American way of life, Reddick wrote that "the American Dream is the dream of the Negro." Horace Mann Bond, another leading African American intellectual, in "Should the Negro Care Who Wins the War?," addressed African American concerns about fighting for democracy when American society denied them that ideal. He claimed that African Americans were the quintessential Americans. "By ancestry, by birth, and by the traditions of his history, the Negro is, indeed, more 'American' than the white majority." He contrasted Black Americans with recent immigrants to the disadvantage of the latter and claimed that the long ancestry of the African American in the nation guaranteed "the purity of his national allegiance to the American ideal." Black Americans faced continuing inequalities during the war, but Black assertiveness in response led to race riots across the nation in 1943, which shocked Americans and led to new efforts at addressing racial problems to promote wartime unity.[117]

Racism and Social Class Issues

Southern conservatives came to fear the growing power of the federal government in the late 1930s, as they warned it would be used to change the segregated southern way of life. Their conception of that way of life included not only white supremacy but upper-class white economic privilege. This attitude appeared in the reaction to the Fair Employment Practices Commission, created by executive order in 1941 to deal with job discrimination in federal projects. As historian Glenn Feldman notes, the commission "struck at the very heart of the southern status quo: white supremacy *and* upper-class prerogative." In doing so, it "conjured the most emotional demons of Reconstruction memory and insult to the graven image of sectional sovereignty." White conservatives perceived the agency as questioning the southern way of life's fundamental assumption of Black inferiority and the right of business owners to decide whether or not to hire Black people and preserve a "Black wage."[118]

Horace C. Wilkinson had been a Ku Klux Klan member in the 1920s and then became a renowned progressive attorney supporting prolabor politics in Alabama. But his views shifted dramatically with a 1942 speech at a Kiwanis Club, a talk printed and widely distributed across the South. Now embracing a paternalist racial outlook, Wilkinson spoke fearfully of a coming race war. Praising the 1901 Alabama constitution, which had established white supremacy in law, Wilkinson lambasted New Deal Democrats for threatening to "destroy this glorious work" and "our way of life." His use of that term showed how the term had gone from one describing the Agrarians' intellectual concerns to one that could be used to stoke racial fears at a business club meeting.[119]

Another Alabama conservative, Jay Taylor, argued that "all dark skinned people" should not vote because they were under the control of labor bosses and antagonistic to an "American way of life." A regional variant of the American way of life became an emerging business version of the southern way of life. In the coming decades this construct would reach ascendancy as part of a new ideological combination, with the segregated southern way of life declining by the late 1960s. This southern version of the American way of life represented an updated southern civil religion, one that did not rest in the Lost Cause or the moonlight-and-magnolias Old South. It was "'the Southern Religion'—as economic, reflexively martial, and averse to public and collective solutions as it was theological." The business of southern civil religion had emerged as a New South concept in the late nineteenth century and triumphed, in a way, with the defeat of Populism's aspirations toward a more egalitarian southern Christian civilization. With modernization coming south in the twentieth century, anti-unionism undergirded the southern business civil religion. Industrial boosters saw unions leading to higher wages for workers, increased regulation to ensure worker safety, and a unified biracial workforce—all considered bad things for the low-wage southern economy and challenges to southern employers' claim to a singular, God-ordained, paternalistic authority to oversee the southern economy and society.[120]

The Congress of Industrial Organizations seemed the worst threat to the southern businessman's civil religion in the 1940s because of its biracial industrial unionism. The organization benefitted from labor law changes during the New Deal and seemed a formidable challenge to the southern business way of life by the postwar years. For a while, the union managed to convince working people to put their class-based concerns above racial divisions and struck a primal fear in southern conservatives about the preservation of the civil religion's God-sanctioned racial and class privileges. Hubert Baughn, an editor of a Deep South economic journal who had been a leading advocate of commerce and industry for the South since the 1930s, wrote in March 1944 that the Congress of Industrial Organizations was foreign to the South because its leaders embraced "social equality, not white supremacy." He termed it a "leftist, carpetbag, race-rousing outfit that endangered the South's traditions—for states' rights and white supremacy," traditions at the heart of the segregated southern way of life.[121]

Postwar Context

The years immediately after the war nonetheless provided hope for fundamental changes in the South. Returning veterans, newly enfranchised African Americans, and whites whose wartime experiences seemed to open them to support changes in the region united in backing reform efforts. Several southern states elected liberal Democratic governors, and organized labor plotted efforts for advance in the region. But by 1947 James Dombrowski, executive director of the Southern Educational Fund, reported a retreat from the forward-looking policies of the New Deal. Politicians were using the race issue to block all reforms, as a counterattack based on anticommunism and aggressive assertion of white supremacy deterred or defeated leaders speaking out for tolerance. Disillusionment with the civil rights proposals of the national Democratic Party led to the Dixiecrat movement in 1948, which would begin a new age of southern white resistance to racial changes.[122]

The South's relationship with the nation was, in one sense, closer than it had ever been, yet it was becoming an increasingly fraught relationship. Distinguished war correspondent Martha Gelhorn wrote a 1947 article, "Journey through a Peaceful Land," for the *New Republic*, and she began by noting that "for several weeks now we have been driving through the American Way of Life." At first, as she traveled through the mid-Atlantic states, "the American Way of Life looked like the tender memories of GI's, homesick songs, politicians' promises and the unattainable dream of all the homeless and hungry of Europe." Little towns were charming, "faded brick and white wood, the tall, cool trees, and life sleeping there." Along the roadsides "were places to eat, shining and comfortable, with copious—it seemed to me superb—uniform food." She contrasted such places with what she found in the South, where her descriptions sometimes seemed like the war zones she had once written about. "After Virginia," she surmised, "the American Way of Life goes largely to pot. Now it is the sandiness and the unvarying pines of North Carolina, and the Negroes." The latter reminded her of "Polish slave labor in Germany." In Rocky Mount, she found decay and superficiality: "The gutters are sodden with refuse," and at night "the young take over the streets, racing along before the brilliant show windows full of claptrap necessities, hurrying to drink more Coca-Cola." Her observations of southern cultural ways, which could charm some visitors, were disdainful. She seemed to replicate Henry Adams's much earlier dismay at the disorderliness he perceived in the South. "They shout, 'Hi, y'all' to each other, and all look alike. The older people visit from front porch to front porch." She captured the South's bigotry and provincialism in the late 1940s. "Behind their invisible barbed wire, the Negroes watch, marked by poverty and disease." She attended a movie and saw young people mocking a news story on the United Nations that had Arab and Jewish delegates, with the students making "a strange sound, something mocking, something contemptuous, unplanned, not lasting, but spontaneous."[123]

Gelhorn sometimes equated the American way with consumption and civic

engagement, and she wrote of rediscovering "the American Way of Life further down the east coast, in the coastal community of Myrtle Beach, where
she saw men walking in handkerchief-size bathing suits, beautiful and slim
and healthy, chatting away with passion about things." But generally she noted
the white southerners she met did not mention the news or know much about
current events. Stories of a lynching would have brought images in the North of
"people with blood-shot eyes and grim mouths, snarling about white honor and
keeping the n——s in their place." In Europe word of a lynching would have led
people to regard Americans "slyly or with disgust about our democracy." But in
the South, where it was happening, "no one seemed to notice it." It was not that
whites she met were hiding their opinions; "they simply did not have any." Her
observations of snatches of a southern way of life revealed a continuing negative
attitude toward that way of life.[124]

The year before Gelhorn's article, a prominent white editor from Greenville,
Mississippi, Hodding Carter, wrote an influential overview, "A Southerner
Looks at the South," for the *New York Times Magazine*. Carter raised early on
the issue of civilization and observed that "by almost every gauge by which
a culture or civilization can be measured, the South is still at the bottom—
in literacy, in crimes of violence, in productivity except for children, in social
legislation, in per capita income, in public health, in working conditions, in
housing." Its backwardness was apparent, as it was "still the happy hunting
ground for political demagogues, for racial and religious bigots, for free-lance
writers and amateur and professional crusaders." He counterbalanced this assessment by seeing hopeful "signs of ferment" that suggested some impending
dramatic changes, as "no longer is the South an unchangeable stereotype." As
evidence of change he mentioned more cash in the pockets of southerners; an
open condemnation by many southern leaders of the Ku Klux Klan; the Great
Migration and the accompanying decline in the number of African American
tenant farmers; the spread of mechanization in agriculture, reducing the need
for tenants; and the returning veterans who were bringing new perspectives,
energy, and idealism to politics and society. He granted that "the attitude of
the Southern masses has not changed much," but he saw a growing minority
of whites and Blacks pushing self-examination of the region's problems and
expressing a willingness to fight them.[125]

Although Carter saw growing political equality for African Americans in
the South, he argued the most significant postwar changes were in economics,
based largely in the "enlightened self-interest" of planters and industrialists and
the "intelligently militant Southern Negro." Granting that southern efforts toward racial advancement were more gradual than the immediate changes that
northern reformers espoused, he argued "that the old order is being challenged

and is being changed." Organized labor would be one leader of continuing change, although southern agriculturalists "abhor unionization to a degree just short of the psychotic, especially as it affects Negro labor." Southern planters and industrialists needed African American labor, though, and he believed their enlightened self-interest would lead to better wages and conditions and thereby to improved race relations. The interracial movement in southern churches, especially among the Methodists, was another hopeful sign, "especially in those spheres where appeals to economic self-interest are less telling than appeals to Christian conscience."[126]

Carter also pointed out that "the educated Southern negro is developing a consciousness of his own," often differing from the outlook of African American leaders elsewhere. Despite the Great Migration, he recognized a determination by the Black southerner to "make a place for himself in the South." He insisted that "it must be realized that there are millions of Negroes who do not want to leave the South but who want to help make the South a better place in which they can live." Their goals were "directed at securing a better deal for themselves as human beings—in education, in job opportunities, in citizenship." Carter reminded readers, though, against assuming "an uninterrupted amelioration" in the African American status in the South, as he correctly foresaw the comeback of the Ku Klux Klan and the reassertion of the racist rhetoric of politicians such as Theodore Bilbo and Eugene Talmadge in the postwar South. In the end, he concluded that "the hopeful Southerner must count heavily upon these factors"—better education and increased incomes. And he must count "upon a change in the hearts of men, within and outside the South."[127]

White southern leaders in the late nineteenth century had imagined they had fixed racial interactions through the white supremacy enshrined in Jim Crow and political disfranchisement, but the interwar years saw rising challenges to the racial underpinnings of the southern way of life. *I'll Take My Stand* had aggressively claimed the term "southern way of life" for agrarianism, and the book's writers continued to engage intellectual discussions of southern ideology in the following decade. But even many of them, including the most prominent, had moved toward endorsing white supremacy as the key to the "southern way" by World War II. White supremacy became ever more important in the cultural attitudes and behavioral expressions of what in the period was called "southernism." But the segregated southern way of life was a diverse one, with some whites defining a clear "place" for African Americans in southern society, albeit that of a secondary status; other whites were radical racists who saw no place for African Americans in southern civilization; and other whites, progressives, embraced interracialism's view of Black southerners as important constituent members of regional society, with a few even calling for an end to racial segregation. African American writings took the veil off segregated life to show its brutalities but also the possibilities for a folk-based African American southern civilization. Black leaders united in opposition to the segregated southern way of life, and they became more assertive during World War II and proclaimed the need for the nation to defeat Jim Crow at home as well as fascism abroad. The South became increasingly Americanized during the interwar years, with communication and transportation improvements tying the region to the rest of the nation more thoroughly than ever before, economic development forging relationships between southerners and nonsoutherners, and the federal government playing an ever-growing role in a region that had used the states' rights philosophy to deflect racial changes. By the late 1940s, the southern way of life and the American way of life were competing ideologies within the region, setting the stage for the crisis of southern ideology in the early 1950s.

CHAPTER SIX

Revolutions and Counterrevolutions

Challenging and Defending the Southern Way
in the Civil Rights Era

I
N 1959, APPALACHIAN WRITER Wilma Dykeman published, "What Is the Southern Way of Life?" It was a reflection by a progressive southerner on a term that had become newly popularized during the previous decade. She addressed the spasms of violence in response to the South's civil rights protests and acknowledged that the violent reactions were "outward rumblings of deep inner dislocations," including the phrase "the Southern way of life." She did not directly acknowledge the Agrarians' coinage of the term in 1930, but she showed their continuing influence in thinking about the twentieth-century South. If agrarianism was one focus for her explication of the "southern way," race was another. "To defend the Southern way of life," she wrote, one "once again campaigns with the old demagogic devices of race and fear." "To preserve the Southern way of life" organizations such as the Citizens' Councils had formed "to decide which Southerners shall define which ways in whose lives." Businessmen quaked in fear at the "invocation of this phrase," professional people became quiet, and well-intentioned outsiders "became confused." She lamented that "the loud defiant voices in the South" had been able to capture "both the physical initiative and the spiritual symbols which belong by right of both reason and tradition on the side of law and justice and humanity." Dykeman thereby vigorously asserted that the term was a spiritual symbol and was not the sole property of those who defended racial segregation. Her point would be an important theme in the history of the southern way of life from the late 1940s to the late 1960s. "At a time when the best and truest traditions of the Southern way of life could have been a stepping stone," she insisted, "it has been distorted into a millstone."[1]

Dykeman acknowledged that defense of the racial status quo had been allowed to seem the "essential fact of the Southern way of life" because issues of race stirred white southerners to public reaction. But she denied that race was the essential fact of that way of life. Antebellum southerners thought slavery was synonymous with the southern way of life, yet the end of slavery did not end the southern way, and neither would the end of racial segregation. She had foresight in suggesting that "in the future, as in the past, it may be discovered that this is too single and narrow a vision of a complex and meaningful tradition."[2] Dykeman insisted "the fundamental reality of the Southern way of life" was not segregation but its agrarianism. The dependence on the land promoted such qualities "as close family connections, a sense of continuity across generations, an awareness of place and the local, and pronounced individualism." These qualities defined the southern way of life for her, and they existed with or without the racial issue. She was a conservationist, and her portrait of the Broad River in North Carolina and Tennessee evoked the qualities associated with the southern way. The advance of industrialization in the modern world meant that in the South, "the way of life based on the land was forced to yield to that based on the factory." The region came to feel "the needs and desires of the American way as well as the Southern way." Changes in family ties, increasing liberalism in religion and higher education, exodus of people from the land— all were part of economic transformation that brought improved material lives for most people and movement toward the American way of life. But southern political behavior and social attitudes still rested "all too frequently in the rural agrarian world." When Black southerners began aggressively campaigning for racial change, that activism was the clearest threat to the old social attitudes in general and became the pretext for white protest.[3]

Dykeman saw that, in the end, "the basic change which now confronts the Southern way of life is to admit the inevitability of change itself." Black people were, she saw, entering "the mainstream of the Southern way of life," a fact that should encourage recognition of the biracial South as the heart of any southern way of life—just as the South was entering the mainstream of national life. The challenge for her moment in time was for the white southerner "to confront boldly and realistically the question of how the Southern way may be merged with the American way, without becoming submerged." She peered into the postsegregation future she could see coming to predict that "released from the bondage of an overriding concern with race and the costly toll of segregation, the best meaning of the Southern way could bring a new balance to American life: balance between the urban and the rural, between man and machine, between making a living and making a life."[4]

Historian C. Vann Woodward, writing about the same time as Dykeman, did not use the term "southern way of life" as she did, but he ruminated on the related concept of "southernism." He noted the southern white fear of social death, "the threat of becoming 'indistinguishable'" that had "haunted the mind of the South for a long time." Pointing to the Vanderbilt Agrarians, who had defended the agrarian ideology as the essence of the southern way, Woodward labeled their efforts as the South's second lost cause, the first being the defeat of slavery in the Civil War. His contemporaries in the South, he thought, in their "pursuit of the American Way and the American Standard of Living" were doing all in their "power to become what the agrarians had deplored," a simple replica of standard industrial society with no special character. "The voice of the South in the 1950's has become the voice of the chamber of commerce and Southerners appeared to be about as much absorbed in the acquirement of creature comfort and adult playthings as any other Americans."[5]

Woodward identified U. B. Phillips's concept of the South as a white man's country as a more durable idea than agrarianism, and he recognized how the defense of segregation had rallied white southerners. He foresaw, though, that identification of southernism with white supremacy would prove to be a third southern lost cause. The South of his time once again "finds itself with a morally discredited Peculiar institution on its hand," and "if Southernism is allowed to become identified with a last ditch defense of segregation, it will increasingly lose its appeal among the younger generation." He predicted that many young people would be led to "reject their entire regional identification, even the name 'Southern,' in order to dissociate themselves from the one discredited aspect." Woodward further argued that the one basis for continuing regional affiliation was the South's experiences of history, which represented a heritage apart from the American way: defeat in the Civil War in a nation with a history of military success, poverty in a nation of affluence, white supremacy in a nation of Jeffersonian egalitarianism, and sense of place in a mobile American society. Woodward himself was an active promoter of the changes of the civil rights movement, but he could not foresee how that movement would so transform the southern way.[6]

Dykeman and Woodward wrote in an era when the southern way of life, as never before, became a matter of everyday language and defining political rhetoric. The term's usage soared, a way for politicians and citizens in general to think about challenges to a social system that went back a long way. The federal government would at first play a slow but then a catalytic role in encouraging racial change in the early 1950s. In turn, those actions would activate a white supremacist resistance that would promulgate the phrase relentlessly and tie it to the most reactionary social policy and political activity. Civil rights activists challenged the segregated southern way, including the symbolism of the term and its spiritual overtones. Indeed, an American civil religion, a Black civil religion, and a southern white civil religion each read spiritual and moral significance into the events of the era, albeit with conflicting meanings.

Paralleling the struggle over the segregated southern way of life was the advance of economic modernization that diminished the centrality of agriculture and rural life to understanding the region, with the growth of cities overshadowing the southern way in towns. Observers saw urban areas and business and industry as representing the latest New South, one that often evoked optimism over the possibilities of the South escaping its social problems. Defenders of this change often coupled it, though, with continuing allegiance to the South's segregated way of life and its mannered and romanticized imagery and behavior of the southern way. By 1980, the Sunbelt mythology represented a well-emerged new business version of the southern way of life, located in economic individualism and free enterprise, suburbanization, and the celebration of "southern living."

The era of the direct-action-protest civil rights movement promoted another prominent version of the southern way of life—the biracial South. This liberal dream criticized the segregated, white supremacist southern way as un-Christian and un-American. It posited the long racial interaction of southern whites and Blacks as the essential southern way and positioned this ideology in the 1950s and 1960s as the hoped-for, postsegregation ideology for a progressive region. That ideology would, by the 1980s, compete with a reimagined southern conservatism for ideological control of the South.

Throughout the period, one cannot understand meanings of the southern way of life without considering the national image of the South. The mass media played a crucial role in publicizing events of the civil rights movement and helped to further a national consensus on the need for changes in the South by the mid-1960s. Popular culture in the two decades after World War II nurtured conflicting images of the region. The predominant one was that of the benighted South, exemplified by southern white resistance to the civil rights movement, while another portrayed a folksy South representing moral virtues and appealing values of an older America. By the 1970s the media helped to nurture a positive image of the region as a place of traditional values and folk culture, the basis for a new version of the southern way of life.[7]

Post–World War II

African American sociologist Ira De A. Reid assessed the functioning of racial segregation in the South in his 1947 article "Southern Ways," and he saw both law and custom at work to restrict Black southerners. His article is a good beginning point in considering the southern way of life just before dramatic challenges would begin from the federal government and from native southern reformers. Reid saw law as "the chief device of racial segregation in the South" as he looked at the state of Georgia, with its large African American population, for its "formidable example of 'the southern way.'" Laws on race and color determined every aspect of life. "From birth through education and marriage to death and burial," he concluded, "there are rules and regulations saying that you are born 'white' or 'colored.'" But where law ended, custom began. Throughout the region four expressions of racial separation were universal: the races could not sit together in the same compartments while traveling, they could not intermarry, they could not go to the same public schools, and they could not use the same public facilities. Beyond that, uncertainty was typical from one locale to another throughout the region. Nonetheless, Reid saw progress because of recent advances in voting strength and political power— especially in the upper South—that had helped equalize opportunities for Blacks, even if in segregated facilities. He noted that equalization of resources between the races, though, had worked to reinforce segregation rather than end it. By no means predicting the coming southern Black challenge to the segregated southern way of life, he even noted that "some colored people are in favor of doing nothing about a scheme under which they have prospered economically." Booker T. Washington's ideology of accommodation had produced a successful, if modest, Black middle class in the South, and its members represented a Black conservatism that had adjusted to southern ways. According to Reid, that middle class feared that eliminating segregation would destroy "the whole fabric of Negro life and leadership in the South."[8]

The immediate postwar years represented a brief moment when racial change nonetheless seemed possible. World War II had produced an assertive Black leadership within the South, and the continued reform spirit of the New Deal led to aggressive campaigns for organized labor and for urban efforts to improve African American living conditions and opportunities under the southern way of life. Southern liberals at the end of the war saw the possibility of a more democratic and politically empowered diverse South, where labor union workers, African Americans, and small farmers would be involved more than ever in politics and planning efforts for reform, in essence a continuation of the interracial version of the southern way of life. Mark Ethridge, publisher of the Louisville *Courier-Journal*, for example, predicted that "the swing of the post-war world *will* be to the left." Clark H. Foreman, president of the Southern Conference for Human Welfare (SCHW), admitted that conservative politics dominated the postwar South, but he saw "another South composed of the great mass of small farmers, the sharecroppers, the industrial workers, white and colored, for the most part disfranchised by the poll tax and without spokesmen" in any political or media forums.[9]

Operation Dixie, an effort by the Congress of Industrial Organizations (CIO), was a linchpin of postwar liberal hopes. Begun in the spring of 1946, the CIO effort focused on organizing such southern industries as textiles, lumber and wood products, and tobacco. The CIO was a national organization whose northern locals sent money and organizers into the South with high hopes of using southern successes to jump-start postwar union growth nationally. But southern employers, long ruthless in countering unionization efforts, pulled out all the stops to derail Operation Dixie, using their close relationships with local law enforcement and the media to promote the view that unions were anti-Christian, Yankee in the worst sense, and communistic in their ideas. The southern establishment, as represented by industrial employers, feared that unions would bring higher wages and threaten southern business's ability to recruit new industry through the perceived advantage of low-wage workers. Their efforts built on earlier efforts to portray union organizers as "outside agitators," a term applied as much to that group as to civil rights activists. According to political scientist Jasper Berry Shannon, not just financial issues were at stake for southern conservatives, because they saw the southern way of life itself in jeopardy as union organizers "question or attack values which have been set for three or four generations in the hard concrete of custom." Conservatives fattened in this postwar period, feeding off lurid portrayals of unions and emerging civil rights activism as alien to the hierarchical and paternalistic nature of the southern way of life.[10]

Changes in national political ideology led the CIO in these early years of the Cold War to adopt a vigilant anticommunist outlook, but the results divided southern liberals. The SCHW had once worked intimately with the CIO, but the union distanced itself from the SCHW when charges began proliferating that the SCHW had members who had once been communists. Senator James Eastland, in fact, held a media circus of hearings in New Orleans in 1946 designed to pin the communist label on the SCHW, and after that the labor movement became fearful that the charge of tolerating communists in allied groups would devastate their organizing work. In the end, Operation Dixie failed. It divided liberals and emboldened conservatives in the South and the nation. The Taft-Hartley Act, passed in 1947, thwarted the CIO and other union organizations both with new requirements legalizing the option of open-shop work sites (that is, not requiring union membership to hold employment) and with new certifications that union leaders had never belonged to the Communist Party. Unions had represented interracialism at its most successful in the 1930s and early 1940s, but the decline in effectiveness of unions in the late 1940s brought diminishing interracial cooperation in the workplace and alienated many white workers from the civil rights initiatives national organized labor championed.[11]

If the New Deal era had seen national efforts for economic transformation of the South, the immediate postwar years saw race emerging as the defining issue for many northerners thinking about the South. Gunnar Myrdal's influential *An American Dilemma* (1944) helped persuade postwar American liberals that race was above all a moral issue, and the South's obvious racial discrimination made it a convenient scapegoat for northerners to avoid acknowledging the discrimination in other parts of the nation. Southern liberals had always relied on support of northern progressives to further their incremental efforts at reform, which during the New Deal had focused on the economic advancement that made southern efforts central to national economic advancement. The new northern liberal agenda left southern liberals marginalized because they would not support an immediate end of segregation and were increasingly defensive at northern criticism, and southern racists targeted them as integrationist. The term "liberal" virtually disappeared, replaced now by the more tempered "moderate" to describe southern whites precariously witnessing for increased racial justice within the segregated society.[12]

White liberals and moderates had long worked in interracial organizations with Black leaders to advance reform efforts. African Americans at the end of World War II hoped for rapid social change in the South. The National Association for the Advancement of Colored People (NAACP) had long been the leading civil rights organization, and court victories such as in the *Smith v. Allwright* case (1944), which ended the white primary and brought increased Black voter participation in the upper and border South, augmented its status. In the postwar years, African Americans lived in a world parallel to that of southern whites. Public neglect of Black society had long before created "colored towns." Widespread poverty, poor housing, little indoor plumbing, and few paved roads created the issues that led to increasing Black protest in parts of the South even before the Supreme Court's *Brown v. Board of Education* decision in 1954. Black institutions under Jim Crow offered needed services the larger society ignored. Booker T. Washington's independent, if racially segregated, Black society relied on African American institutions such as churches, fraternal societies, funeral homes, newspapers, insurance companies, grocery stores, barbershops, restaurants, juke joints, and schools. Leadership and institutional sanctuaries grew out of those businesses and the professionals who served all-Black clienteles and provided a degree of distance from whites who would demean them.[13]

A vibrant African American folk culture centered on the working class and rural people, with cross-class cultural traits but clear divisions between the worlds of church and the juke joint. In 1965, Arna Bontemps wrote in "Why I Returned" about the tension between the two African American cultures within which he grew up. Bontemps's family had left Louisiana for California when he was only three. His father embraced middle-class values, while his father's uncle Buddy identified with Black folk culture. Each had complex attitudes toward the South they had left because of its racism. Bontemps remembers his father thinking of the South, "Sometimes I miss all that." The elder Bontemps admitted he might have returned to the South, except for his hopes to give his children a better life away from the southern way of life. Uncle Buddy would reply, "Folks talk a lot about California . . . but I'd a heap rather be down home than here, if it wasn't for the conditions." The term "conditions" was a down-to-earth, grassroots description of the southern way of life. Bontemps's father disapproved of Buddy's "casual and frequent use of the word n——," his love of "dialect stories, preacher stories, ghost stories, slave and master stories," and his belief "in signs and charms and mumbo jumbo." Bontemps concluded that "in their opposing attitudes towards roots my father and my great-uncle made me aware of a conflict in which every educated American Negro, and some who are not educated, must somehow take sides." A challenge for civil rights organizers would be to organize across class and urban-rural barriers to mount their direct-action protests to challenge the segregated southern way of life.[14]

Despite the segregation of the South's public life, folklife had been the site of a vibrant biracial cultural interaction that provided the foundation for a biracial southern way of life, which had been articulated in the interwar years and found fuller expression in the late 1960s and 1970s. Whites had claimed the title "southerner," and Blacks could not identify with any ideas of a southern way of life as long as whites defined it as racially separate. "Negro and white Southerners are reluctant to admit their kinship," wrote historian Lawrence Reddick in 1960, "not merely at times when it is biological, but more generally when it is regional." He emphasized, despite the stress on their differences, that "their similarities are remarkable—especially in speech, gait, food habits, and orientation toward life." He saw much of this similarity coming because "the people of Dixie are still relatively rural and folkish, encouraged in this by the open country, blue skies, and warm weather." During the civil rights years, Black people protested and white people responded, but they created in the end new understandings of the southern way of life. The region's music, food, recreational activities, and other cultural features resting in the interactions of everyday life had long provided occasions for biracial understanding but without formal acknowledgment.[15]

Race and Conservative Ideology

Public rhetoric in the South proclaimed white supremacy during World War II at the same time that progressives talked of democracy and equal rights for African Americans. In the election of 1944, for example, white southern politicians used language that incorporated the southern way of life, and in so doing they illustrated how the term transitioned from that of intellectuals such as the Agrarians and conservative thinkers in the New Deal era to that in the minds of segregationist politicians. A dread seemed to take over the thoughts of many conservatives thinking of likely postwar challenges to the southern way. Speaking of race, Texas senator Allen Drury wrote anxiously that year that white southerners were "perched on a cliff . . . above a vast and tumbled plain that stretches far away below us." He pictured in his nightmare "the South, unhappy, restless, confused, embittered, torn." In his frantic imagination he saw "discontent and bitterness, faint intimations of a coming storm like a rising wind moving through the tall grass." Part of the problem for such a south-ern Democrat was the recognition of the growing African American influence within the national Democratic Party, as the Black migration northward in the twentieth century had created African American voting blocs in cities import-ant to national Democrats' electoral hopes. This change stoked fears of a Black-influenced national party promoting racial changes that would disturb the "core of southern culture" by undermining the culture's fundamental hierarch-ical nature. Most white southerners saw that "this was civilization itself." It was "the 'Southern way of life,' something precious to preserve and protect," as a letter writer from Potts Camp, Mississippi, put it to Eleanor Roosevelt in 1944.[16]

Defenders of the segregated southern way of life that year seized the patriotic and religious symbols of southern culture, and chief among those rhetorical symbols was the southern way of life. Horace Wilkinson, for example, was a Democratic Alabama politician long associated with promoting economic rights for working-class people, but in the election year of 1944 he wrote that "our way of life is doomed" if the national Democratic Party did not change its apparent course of embracing African American interests. In a two-and-a-half-page letter to another Alabama political leader, he used the term "way of life" seven times and insisted that if that leader would assert southern white racial interests he would be "numbered among the immortals as long as there is a white race." The term "southern way of life" was one among other cultural emblems that white conservatives increasingly employed to appeal to whites.[17]

Emerging as the central focus for conservative political ideology, race created a new southern political context, replacing the economic focus that had enabled liberals to make progress in their goals during the 1930s. In January 1948 a hill country Alabama newspaper editor, Tom Abernathy, circulated to state political leaders his resolution asserting that racial segregation was essential to southern civilization and had to be defended at any cost. He called Jim Crow "the bedrock of our way of life in the South, a way of life from which we will not be driven." Observers such as Abernathy began blurring the lines between the southern way of life and the American way of life, a foundational difference for the Vanderbilt Agrarians of 1930 but now an eroding one. The wife of an Alabama minister, in a 1948 letter, condemned civil rights protests she had read about because "I can think of nothing more contrary to the American way of life than for the freedom of private industry and business to be taken away from these businesses." Private enterprise became enshrined as a new orthodoxy, combined with the patriotic embrace of the American flag and the Bible as building blocks of the modernized southern way of life appropriate to the Cold War need to counter atheistic Soviet communism. The federal government was a mixed bag in this newly emerging conservative ideological construct. The underlying concern with elite white control of Black labor—and white labor as well—was apparent in fears of federal government regulation of business through labor laws, safety regulations, employee rules, hiring guidelines, collective bargaining, and taxing of business. These concerns in the late 1940s became the basis for the emergence of the modern Republican Party that would grow ever stronger in the region.[18]

Dixiecrats

In 1946, President Harry S. Truman created the President's Committee on Civil Rights, and its report, *To Secure These Rights*, was a landmark in generating a new civil rights agenda from the federal government. The report recommended the "elimination of segregation, based on race, color, creed, or national origin, from American Life." In February 1948 the president sent proposals to Congress for a federal antilynching law, abolition of the poll tax, establishment of a permanent Fair Employment Practices Commission, and other measures that had long been liberal goals but now had stronger presidential support than ever. Later that same year Truman issued an executive order to end racial segregation in federal agencies, including the military, as white political leaders in the South reacted with disbelief at this new action of the leader of their own Democratic Party. Public opinion polls that year showed wide gaps between white southern attitudes and those of other Americans about the federal government assuming a larger role in controlling lynching, ensuring the rights of Blacks to vote, and dismantling segregation on buses and trains.[19]

The Democratic National Convention of 1948 was a startling event for white southern Democrats, who could hardly recognize the new dynamics of the party. African Americans were a prominent part of the program, and the party platform recognized civil rights goals. Grover Hall, editor of the *Montgomery Advertiser*, wrote that "the attitude of this convention toward Alabama and the South this afternoon was cold, forbidding, and contemptuous." Georgia senator Richard Russell resorted to classic language from the late nineteenth century to touch on basic southern white concepts of a racially determined society, as he railed against Truman's civil rights agenda as "a crime against civilization and a sin against nature's God." Many southern delegates left the convention, with those remaining casting their votes for Russell, but their powerlessness became obvious when Truman overwhelmingly won the nomination. Political scientist Jasper Berry Shannon wrote that southern Democrats felt betrayed "in their own household by one of their own kind, and most of all by their own polit- ical church, the Democratic party," language that hinted at the civil religious importance of the party in the South that now seemed endangered.[20]

The Dixiecrats formed a new political party in 1948 that seceded from the Democratic Party and attempted to take over the party's apparatus in south- ern states. They assumed racial issues were so paramount that southern whites would rally around their cause. The Dixiecrats hoped to leverage southern political influence and take over the national Democratic Party, so they often toned down explicit racial language to stress their states' rights message in na- tional media, but at home in the South their racial message was clear. Senator James Eastland of Mississippi said that "organized mongrel minorities," re- sponsible to the federal government, were attempting "to Harlemize the coun- try." Business groups did rally around the new party; for example, the Southern States Industrial Council and the Arkansas Free Enterprise Association gave generously and ensured that opposition to organized labor, along with defense of white supremacy, would remain a major concern of the new political effort. Their involvement reflected the emerging influence of the southern business way of life.[21]

The Dixiecrat convention in Birmingham revealed the cultural symbolism and dynamics of the party. Frank Dixon's keynote address claimed that civil rights laws proposed by President Truman would "reduce us to the status of a mongrel, inferior race, mixed in blood, our Anglo-Saxon heritage a mockery." Another speaker, William G. Carleton, observed the convention, and his de- scription captured the centrality of traditional southern cultural features to the Dixiecrats. As orators spoke with fiery flourishes, one saw "the serious up- turned faces of the 'wool-hat boys,' the 'get tough' attitude of the free-enterprise claque, the clusters of old-timers talking of the day when Wade Hampton's Red Shirts rode, the rebel yells, the strains of 'Dixie,' the Confederate uniforms and the Confederate flags, the inscrutability of the Negroes on the fringes of the audience, the frolicking of young negro boys up close to the speaker's plat- form and their joining in the applause and the fun." These references to the Lost Cause, the working class, the business class, and late nineteenth-century Redemption that ended Reconstruction all evoked a near-mystical spirit of communion with a long-standing conservative ethos around defense of white racial privilege.[22]

The Dixiecrats never became a popular movement, as the party was the ex- pression of an elite who thought they could appeal to white unity and use their understanding of the Democratic Party machinery to achieve their goals. Having constructed a political system that rested on disfranchisement of Blacks and many poor whites, they did not believe in mass politics and did not make extensive demagogic appeals to the masses of southern whites. They faced the opposition of the urban press, moderate voices, Democratic Party state regulars, and national congressmen and senators who did not want to jeopardize their powerful influence in Congress by supporting this new rebellion. Many businesses, as well as state governments, relied on federal government subsidies and did not want to endanger those. The Cold War created a context that put a premium on support of national ideals, which also worked against the Dixiecrats' noisy regional separatism. They nonetheless showed strength by carrying five states.[23]

Early 1950s

In the early 1950s, southern society seemed caught between past and present in a dramatic way that would provide a distinctive context for challenges to, and defenses of, the southern way of life. North Carolina journalist William T. Polk, in *Southern Accents: From Uncle Remus to Oak Ridge* (1953), noted that the South had long been predominantly "rural, agrarian, easy-going, poor and proud of its distinctive way of life," a use of the term "way of life" that did not refer to race in the year before the *Brown* decision. In the postwar years, however, the region was "becoming urban, industrialized, hard-working, comparatively prosperous and relatively standardized." As one scholar put it about this period before the direct-action stage of the civil rights movement, "Part of the South has adopted a new way of life the other part resisted." The result was that two Souths existed side by side in each southern state, but they were "as different as Chicago and Bangkok."[24]

The restructuring of agriculture had brought revolutionary changes to the rural countryside. A drastic decline in farm population escalated in the postwar years, as New Deal agricultural programs and wartime economic benefits and military necessities challenged agriculture's economic predominance. Mechanization, pesticides, and other changes culminated in the 1950s with the virtual vanishing of tenant farming, for so long the major agricultural activity of the South. The folk culture that had given meaning and function to everyday life for generations, and seemed to many the essence of any southern way of life, no longer seemed so pervasive.[25]

Towns were the center of the southern way of life. They saw greater economic prosperity after World War II than did rural areas, and they remained the focus of political authority. Anyone visiting them on a busy Saturday shopping day would know they remained vibrant economic sites. County seat elites retained pronounced political power in this age before redistricting broke the hold of small towns and rural areas on state political power. Planters, bankers, merchants, lawyers, and members of the old-family, plantation-based governing class exercised power at local and state levels. Owners and managers of such small businesses worked with plantation employers to keep out alternative industries that might offer higher wages for labor, whether on farms and in factories or for yardmen and maids their wives employed at home. The relationships between African American servants and white families in towns seemed to embody the southern way of life in action. Viola Goode Liddell, in her *With a Southern Accent* (1948), captured the white privilege at the heart of the segregated southern way of life. She wrote that from the post–Civil War period "every white man, high or low, could get all the help he needed to do the things which he preferred not to do himself." In areas with a large African American population, "the leisure class, which was formerly very select and elite, came to include everybody but the former slaves." Before the Civil War, southern Blacks performing menial work was defined as the essence of southern civilization. For generations whites across different classes had experienced this privilege. Liddell could already glimpse, though, "the handwriting on the wall and know that our day, as the chosen few, is about up and that it won't be long before we will be doing our own work and may be doing for others that which has long been done for us." She watched such a revolutionary change with "self-pity and dismay" as "our golden age of that fifth great freedom from menial labor [was] gradually slipping from our grasp. Nor is it likely ever to return."[26]

Conservative elites in the 1950s still saw the advantages of disfranchisement, malapportionment, and one-party politics as "proper and desirable methods for preserving the southern way of life." Town leaders reminded people of the glories of the Lost Cause, as they gathered around the ubiquitous Confederate monuments to celebrate Confederate Memorial Day in the spring. Women gathered for the social activities of the United Daughters of the Confederacy but also affirmed national history through the Daughters of the American Revolution. Their garden clubs, church societies, museum work, and school activities provided the texture for writers evoking the southern way of life in the 1950s. Old-money families had the highest social status in southern towns, but the new money associated with real estate agents, car dealers, industrial managers, and insurance agents earned status for a new middle class that sought and increasingly gained political authority. Religion was an essential feature of this town version of the southern way, with the First Baptist Church at the center of town physically and symbolically, and religion came to overlap with the new business ethos. The town landscape reminded African Americans of their humiliation in seeing "colored" and "white" signs in train depots and bus stations, in entering segregated bathrooms, watching films from balconies for Blacks while whites sat in the main sections, and using separate dressing rooms to try on clothes in department stores. Shoppers on Saturday, in from the country, would have experienced all of this separation, yet the main streets and back alleys were not segregated as the races wandered around a somewhat festive atmosphere on a day off work.[27]

Highlander Folk School and Lillian Smith

The Supreme Court rendered its *Brown v. Board of Education* decision on May 17, 1954, and declared unanimously that separate educational facilities were inherently unequal and nurtured a sense of inferiority in African American children. The decision became a new symbol of American commitment to racial equality, one of the five factors that Martin Luther King Jr. would later name as making life better for African Americans. The decision slightly validated the NAACP's legal strategy of using the federal courts to promote racial desegregation, but it led in turn to persecution and virtual banishment of the organization by Deep South state legislatures in the years after 1954. Such other civil rights groups as the Congress of Racial Equality and the Urban League had been working for over a decade to bring change and had gained modest victories in northern cities and border states. Within the South, one biracial reform group and one white intellectual were especially bold in trying to prepare white southerners to accept what they saw as coming change to the southern way of life.[28]

The Highlander Folk School was an interracial educational institution that encouraged labor organizing and civil rights activism well before the *Brown* decision. It had been founded on the Cumberland Plateau in East Tennessee in 1932. Myles Horton and Don West were white southerners who had been imbued with the social gospel theology and the Danish Folk School methodology. Serving as a school for adult education at first, it worked in local mountain counties but then became a center for training union organizers and other social activists. The school earned the suspicion and intimidation of some local people and authorities. Culture was a key component of Highlander's community organizing, as its teachers included folk singing, square dancing, and theatrical performances in their workshops, a model for later Student Nonviolent Coordinating Committee (SNCC) work. Beginning in the 1940s, Highlander integrated its workshops in defiance of Tennessee state law and in the early 1950s focused on offering residential workshops on public school desegregation. Highlander hosted such civil rights activists as Martin Luther King Jr., Ella Baker, Rosa Parks, Fannie Lou Hamer, and Bernice Johnson Reagan, and as the sit-in movement began in the early 1960s the school gathered activists together to chart directions and goals for this new stage.[29]

Martin Luther King Jr. pointed to Highlander as an important advocate for change in the South, and he was just as enthusiastic about the ideas and leadership of Lillian Smith. Born in 1897, she was one of nine children who grew up in a well-off family in Jasper, Florida. She was the daughter of a prominent business and civic leader, yet she became a leading advocate by the 1940s of a reimagined, postsegregation South. When her father lost his wealth from turpentine mills in 1915, the family moved to their summer home in north Georgia. She attended nearby Piedmont College, taught in a one-room mountain school, and helped her family manage a hotel, before leaving for musical training at a conservatory in Baltimore and then leaving the country for a three-year job teaching music in China. From 1925 to 1948, she worked with the Laurel Falls Camp for Girls, regarded as one of the most innovative institutions in the South for training young women in music, theater, and psychology. Through the camp she became friends with Paula Snelling, her lifelong partner and intellectual collaborator, publishing a magazine that became a well-known forum for progressive ideas on the South.[30]

Smith spoke from within the web of consciousness that underlay the southern way of life, and she described it in terms of such emotions as fear and anxiety. Lamenting "the placid taking for granted of a way of life, so wounding, so hideous in its effect upon the spirits of both black and white," she contested segregationists' usage of the term "southern way of life" to mean only white supremacy and disputed its supposed religious sanctions by referring to "our so-called sacred way of life." Smith's *Killers of the Dream* (1949), a prime text in understanding the emotional, rhetorical, and behavioral aspects of the southern way of life, deconstructed the horrific results of racial segregation for white souls as well as Black. She drew from her own story as an upper-class white woman, her understanding of southern history, and the psychology of white supremacy in portraying the many dimensions of the southern way of life. The book analyzed child-raising in the South and how it nurtured fear, guilt, shame, defensiveness, hypocrisy, and violence. She wrote of her loving relationship with the African American nurse who raised her, a woman who even chewed Smith's food when she was a baby and put it in Smith's mouth when she would not eat, establishing a bodily bond with her that the strictures of the southern way worked against. She referred to the "ghost relationships" between white men and Black women, white fathers and mixed-race children, and white children and Black nurses, and she insisted that these relationships haunted the South and shaped the lives and souls of white southerners.[31]

Smith remembered her mother as "the mother who taught me tenderness and love and compassion," but she was also the woman who "taught me the bleak ritual of keeping negroes in their place." Her father insisted she show no "air of superiority toward schoolmates from the mill" and reminded her that all "men are brothers," but he trained her as well in "the steel-rigid decorums I must demand of every colored male." Her incisive analysis unveiled the central paradox of the southern way of life, which aspired to combine religiosity, racism, and the notion of the South itself. By the time she had learned that "God is love, that Jesus is His Son and came to give us more abundant life, that all men are brothers with a common Father," she had also learned "that I was better than a Negro, that all black folks have their place and must be kept in it, that sex had its place and must be kept in it, that a terrifying disaster would befall the South if I ever treated a Negro as my social equal and as terrifying a disaster would befall my family if I were to have a baby outside marriage." She coined the term "race-sex-sin spiral" to describe the southern way's interconnections.[32]

Smith indicted southern segregation as a profound separation of not just the races but the human body. "They who gravely taught me to split my body from my feelings and both from my 'soul,'" she wrote, "taught me also to split my conscience from my acts and Christianity from southern tradition." As incisively as anyone, Smith explored the meanings of the sexual privilege that white men claimed as part of the ideology of the southern way of life. She believed that white women such as her mother were psychologically scarred as their husbands put them on the proverbial southern-lady pedestal, used their sexual privilege as white men to sometimes have sexual relationships with African American women, and even sometimes fathered mulatto children nearby. She saw white women facing a "sexual blankness" and interpreted their lack of sexual satisfaction, "like childbirth pangs and menstrual cramps," as not just the southern way but "God's way" and "hence if you were sensible must be accepted." Smith also was perceptive in her social class analysis of the southern way as she wrote that the southern upper class "segregated southern money from Mr. Poor White and they segregated southern mores from Mr. Rich White and they segregated southern churches from Christianity, and they segregated southern minds from honest thinking, and they segregated the Negro from everything."[33]

Smith published *Now Is the Time* (1955) as a direct response to the Supreme Court decision *Brown v. Board of Education* (1954), which mandated desegregation of public schools. The book was an intentionally planned manual to prepare white southerners to accept the end of segregation. She was a visionary who as early as 1954 foresaw a law such as the Civil Rights Act, which a decade later would end segregation. In her book, she portrayed segregation as an "un-American" and "un-Christian" system that created an "iron curtain" (drawing from Cold War imagery) behind which white southerners tried not to respond to social critics, read provocative ideas, or encourage intellectual honesty among young southerners. "It was not good form," she wrote, "to ask questions about our way of life, and we punished those who did so in quiet, subtle ways." White southerners had continued to do what their great-grandfathers had done, "to defend the morally indefensible," as she pointed to the moral issue at the heart of challenges to the southern way.[34]

Smith's influence as a southern white woman contesting the attempt to explain the southern way of life as only white supremacy was apparent when one of the original sit-in students in Greensboro, North Carolina, said he had been inspired by his reading of Gunnar Myrdal, Gandhi, and Lillian Smith. She was prescient, if a few years off, in predicting in 1951 that ten years from then "racial segregation as a legal way of life will be gone from Dixie." She looked forward to the time when the "colored" and "white" signs over doors, "which have cheapened democracy throughout the world[,] will be down," although she worried that "signs will still be nailed to a few people's minds and hearts."[35]

Brown Decision and Southern White Reaction

Smith wrote *Now Is the Time* in the aftermath of the *Brown* decision, and her book offered one path for white southerners to take to constructively carry out the court's mandate. Her publisher, however, withdrew the book before it had a chance to make much of an impact, and Smith blamed southern moderates' opposition to her commitment to the end, not reform, of segregation. Emerging civil rights activists identified *Brown* as a motivating factor in making social change seem more possible than before the decision, especially in suggesting more active support by the federal government. Certainly, it had a dramatic effect in mobilizing massive resistance to the decision among white southerners, as blatant racist expressions became more pervasive after 1954. "Talking n—— or nigra had changed from a custom to a necessity for acceptance in most circles by 1956," wrote Mississippi congressman Frank Smith, and he added that "among certain groups the loudest and the strongest talker could achieve a status otherwise unattainable." Since status was long a motivating factor in the southern way of life, this racial extremism after the decision set the tone for the coming decade of white resistance.[36]

Mississippi senator James Eastland anticipated the intensity of the southern white reaction to the court decision. "We are about to embark on a great crusade," he said. "A crusade to restore Americanism and return the control of our government to the people." The term "crusade" in this context was civil religious rhetoric, one that referenced the national context rather than just the South. He went on, though, to plant his vision of resistance squarely in the southern context. "Generations of Southerners yet unborn," he said, "will cherish our memory because they will realize that the fight we now wage will have preserved for them their untainted racial heritage, their culture, and the institutions of the Anglo-Saxon race." Eastland referenced the Civil War and Reconstruction, which led him to note that "we know what it is to fight," and he predicted "we will carry the victory." Eastland evoked the idea of the now-threatened segregated southern way of life involving issues of world destiny, race, future greatness, a crusading spirit, and racial heritage, all linked with the memory of the Confederacy and, more generally, the culture of the South.[37]

Thomas P. Brady, a circuit court judge from Brookhaven, Mississippi, produced the single most inflammatory and influential publication in the immediate aftermath of *Brown*. In *Black Monday*, he anticipated many of the arguments segregationists would employ for a decade. He framed the extended essay in both the American and southern contexts, as he wrote the book "to alert and encourage every American, irrespective of race, who loves our Constitution, our Government and our God-given American way of life." He singled out the left-wing threat he saw beneath the court decision and dedicated the book "to those who firmly believe that socialism and communism are lethal means of porridge for which our sacred birthright shall not be sold." He ranked Black Monday (the day of the court's decision) as equal in importance to July 4, 1776, when patriots signed the Declaration of Independence.[38]

If Brady wrote to broaden the segregationist defense to a national conservative audience of believers in states' rights, he was even more vehement in his racist diatribes and appeal to southern whites. The book was the "spiritual descendant of Thomas Dixon's novels" with their turn-of-the-twentieth-century lurid racial representations. "You can dress a chimpanzee, housebreak him, and teach him to use a knife and fork," Brady wrote, "but it will take countless generations of evolutionary development, if ever before you can convince him that a caterpillar or a cockroach is not a delicacy." Brady evoked the savagery of the jungle African as characteristic of African Americans. Brady referenced the idea of cultural mores as paramount in society and argued that they trump laws and thus the *Brown* decision could never be enforced. Howard Odum had said much the same, and Brady echoed Odum's ideas when he wrote that "*habits and customs* produce folkways which in turn evolve into mores." Laws "limp behind and reflect as a mirror the essence of the mores." Brady referred as well to "*sacred mores* as invulnerable to the dagger of any Brutus." With some menace, he warned that "when a law transgresses the moral and ethical sanctions and standards of the mores, invariably strife, bloodshed and revolution follow in the wake of its attempted enforcement." Brady seemed to forewarn the nation about what to expect with enforcement of school desegregation.[39]

Some southern newspapers, on the other hand, were moderate in their responses to *Brown*. The progressive Louisville *Courier-Journal* reminded readers

that "the end of the world has not come for the South or for the nation." Some
border South states and cities began complying with the decision, but most of
the region's institutions waited. A decision about integration was bad enough
for conservative white southerners, but the particular focus on the schools
waved a red flag in the face of racist ideologists. Harry Ashmore, editor of the
Arkansas Gazette, saw a coming trauma with school integration. "Interest in
the schools is universal, and it is an interest that directly involves not only the
tax-payer but his family, and therefore his emotions"—the latter term one that
identified the passion that would drive white resistance to school integration.
Ashmore added that local people who were "indifferent to all other community
affairs tend to take a proprietary interest in the schools their children attend,
or will attend, or have attended." White southerners who opposed school desegregation feared schools would become sites of interracial sex and marriage
and painted lurid pictures of rape. More commonly they imagined that racial
interaction in classrooms and school recreational activities would inevitably
bring young Black boys and young white girls into intimacy. Southern racial
identity had been constructed since the late nineteenth century around protection of white women's sexual purity, and whites saw integration threatening
that purity.[40]

The threat of school integration entered the political primaries in 1954, and
state legislatures began issuing countless laws and resolutions making the work
of the NAACP more difficult. They denounced the courts, threatened to close
schools, and planned for what to do in case integration happened. Many ordinary people thought of the decision as an abstraction, and they hoped they
would never have to confront integration. Wilma Dykeman and James Stokely,
in *Neither Black nor White* (1957), captured the underlying significance of the
Brown decision: "The rest of the world may consider the atom bomb dropped
on Hiroshima as a certain dividing point in international affairs and national
outlook, but the South uses the 1954 Supreme Court decision on school segregation as its Before and After point of no return."[41]

The Citizens' Council and Emmett Till

The most important white segregation pressure group was the Citizens' Council, whose leaders in Indianola, in the Mississippi Delta, organized in July 1954,
only two months after the court decision. Citizens' Councils spread quickly
to surrounding counties in the state and became powerful in the Deep South
states. Similar groups, such as the Defenders of State Sovereignty and Individual Liberties in Virginia, the Patriots of North Carolina, and the States'
Rights Council of Georgia, reflected a swelling of segregation sentiment in the

aftermath of *Brown*. The four-point program of the Citizens' Councils included use of the theory of interposition to interpose state authority between the federal government and local school boards; attacks on the NAACP; a national propaganda appeal to states' rights sentiment; and growth through membership drives. The Citizens' Council of America set up its headquarters in Greenwood, Mississippi, with Robert B. Patterson as executive secretary, and it published the *Citizens' Council* as its official publication, edited by William J. Simmons in Jackson. Patterson told reporter Dan Wakefield in 1955 that "there won't be any integration in Mississippi. Not now, not 100 years from now. Maybe not 6,000 years from now—maybe never." Members typically included bankers, attorneys, planters, mayors, chamber of commerce officials, and assorted school officials. Wakefield dubbed them "respectable segregationists" because of their middle- and upper-class social status. Others called them "country club Klan" or the "button-down Klan." They disdained violence, distanced themselves from the Klan, and spoke often before the Rotary, Lions, Civitan, and Kiwanis Clubs, the homes of the new business class that was rising to new status in the postwar South. Although council members officially rejected violence, they used intimidation and harsh social ostracism against whites considered to be wavering in their support of white supremacy as well as against any indication of local Blacks supporting integration. Wakefield concluded that "whether the means be a memo or a fiery cross, the end is the same—a climate of distrust and fear that breeds unsolved murders and threats of more."[42]

Wakefield was not hyperbolic, as one of the most infamous southern lynchings happened not far from the birthplace of the Citizens' Councils, in Money, Mississippi. The brutal murder of Emmett Till, in August 1955, was a pivotal moment in the emergence of a new activist stage of the civil rights movement, and it was significant in several ways for understanding the concept of the southern way of life. Such murders had not been unusual in the South for generations, but the wide publicity around Till's murder exposed the violence and cruelty of the southern way for the world to see. The bodily mutilations that Roy Bryant, his half brother J. W. Milam, and others enacted on the fourteen-year-old Till illustrated the utter power that whites assumed over any Black they deemed a threat to their way of life. Till had supposedly whistled or winked at Bryant's wife, Carolyn, and touched the ultimate taboo at the center of the southern way of life, interracial sex. Till's behavior before his kidnapping and during his torture showed that the violation of racial etiquette was a life-or-death affair. He had been brash and would not stop talking or, according to his killers, bragging; he was not the submissive "Sambo" of the white imagination.[43]

The Till murder also was significant as one of the first nationally and internationally publicized media events in an age of expanding media reach, especially through television. The *Chicago Defender* and *Jet* magazine published a photograph of Till's mangled face that brought outrage from many quarters and even appalled many white southerners, who objected, however, to publishing the photograph as well as to the brutality. The trial of the accused murderers, Bryant and Milam, was a travesty. A jury of twelve whites acquitted them after an hour of deliberation, a quick decision that illustrated the failure of the judicial system to deal with the violent, extralegal enforcement of the southern way. In William Bradford Huie's interview with Bryant and Milam, published in *Look* magazine, they admitted to the killing, including gory details. Bryant and Milam's actions also revealed the social-class dynamics of the southern way of life within the white community, as they appeared as the violent enforcers of white supremacy while the elites tolerated and even encouraged such behavior, if not publicly. Till's murder became the impetus for many African Americans in the South to become prominent members of the civil rights movement. Rosa Parks, in fact, whose failure to move to the back of the Montgomery bus set off the bus boycott there just three months after the killing, said the murder had inspired her action. Julian Bond, Stokely Carmichael, and Eldridge Cleaver all confessed to being haunted by Till's death photograph.[44]

Conservative elites, represented by the Citizens' Councils and similar groups, initiated the resistance to changing the southern way of life, but the white working and lower-middle classes made it a popular movement. Voter turnout increased throughout the 1950s, as actions of the federal government and ever-increasing Black protest made race more prominent in the thinking of these groups. The southern white working class had a long history of populist support, whether the rural reformers of the late nineteenth century or the demagogues of the twentieth, but they had also shown interest in New Deal economic reforms and unionization in the 1930s and early 1940s. The race issue now became the overwhelming topic of political discussion after *Brown*, and liberals were unable to mount an effective advocacy for their gradual reformism among the white working classes. Gallup polls in 1957 showed that the number of white southerners who believed that school desegregation was bound to happen had fallen from 55 percent in early 1956 to 43 percent in August 1957. By 1957, it seemed the segregationists were making headway in their defense of the southern way of life.[45]

Popularization of "Southern Way of Life"

As much as any group, the Citizens' Council popularized the term "southern way of life" after the *Brown* decision, using spiritual and cultural ideals to mobilize southern whites. The organization's speakers and publications frequently employed the term for an emotional appeal to whites. In an October 1955 article, "Integration Communist Inspired," D. M. Nelson insisted that members of the group were "the first citizens of our communities," who had long sacrificed "to build and preserve for us our cherished southern way of life." Thomas Waring's article in the same issue of the newspaper affirmed that the Citizens' Councils embraced "the cause of racial segregation, states rights and the Southern way of life." Waring's phrasing indicated that he saw the southern way as more than just segregation. As historian Jason Sokol wrote of this period, "'The Southern way of life' connoted magnolias and gentility, but it also carried specific implications about the region's racial order—one in which whites exercised the power, and blacks ever acquiesced." Alabama progressive Virginia Durr described the genteel and racist sides of the southern way of life in January 1955 when she said that "these people down here are so paradoxical—so gracious and kind until you hit the race question and then they are as hard as iron." The editor of the *Citizens' Council* newspaper, William J. Simmons, indicated the group's crusading spirit in the November 1959 issue when he said that "we are engaged in an all-out war to maintain our segregated way of life."[46]

After *Brown*, the term came into widespread usage in newspapers, public reports, and private correspondence. The *Jackson Daily News* in Mississippi condemned an invitation from the University of Mississippi to an Episcopal minister from Ohio because he had donated money to the NAACP. The paper proclaimed that "any man who gives aid and comfort to the NAACP is an open enemy of the Southern way of life." When the Georgia Board of Education banned textbook statements that charged whites with discrimination against Blacks, the chairman said, "There is no place in Georgia schools at any time for anything that disagrees with our way of life." That statement placed the southern way beyond any criticism.[47]

Southern segregationists asserted a timeless white unity around the phrase "southern way of life." They defended their social system by trying to enforce a rigid orthodoxy, which included suppression of dissent. The Citizens' Councils used economic intimidation against Blacks who supported desegregation or voted. Alabama Citizens' Council leaders affirmed that "we intend to make it difficult, if not impossible, for a Negro who advocated desegregation to find and hold a job, get credit, or renew a mortgage." This attitude extended to whites who questioned the racial system as well. In one speech, Georgia governor Herman Talmadge said of a white racial turncoat, "Don't let him eat at your table, don't let him trade at your filling station, and don't let him trade at your store." The Citizens' Councils compiled a list in November 1959 of seventy-four public and private associations and agencies they wanted to blacklist for supporting civil rights. Mississippi established a Sovereignty Commission in 1956, charged with investigating any threats to encroach on states' rights through desegregation, and other southern states followed suit. The Citizens' Councils gained so much power in Mississippi that one critic said that state had a "Soviet-style government with the citizens' councils paralleling the state machine in emulation of a successful Communist Party."[48]

Children were a special concern of segregationists attempting to perpetuate the idea that the southern way of life was under attack in the mid-1950s. "A Manual for Southerners" appeared in the June 1957 issue of the *Citizens' Council* newspaper, aimed at elementary school students, and it focused on the eleven essential racial differences between Blacks and whites. The article identified the Black man's arm as two inches longer than that of the white man. The jaws of Blacks and whites were shaped differently. The article identified differences between the races in the weight of brains and differences in eyes, noses, lips, cheekbones, ears, hair, and voices. The article used the term "southern way of life" and linked integrationists with communists. One section of it, "YOU CAN'T BELIEVE THE RACE-MIXERS," intoned, "The Race-Mixers are like the Communists.... These people are trying to change our way of life." A manual intended for fifth- and sixth-grade students appeared in July 1957, warning them that "the Race-Mixers even want Negroes and whites to date each other" and insisting that "they know that if the boys and girls share the school room, lunch room, dances, sports, restrooms, and playgrounds, then the boys and girls will want to date each other."[49]

Having spread their sexual and racial anxieties to southern children, segregationists recognized the need as well to appeal to nonsouthern audiences to broaden their appeal. They launched a broad media strategy to spread propaganda about the evils of integration but also the overreach of the federal government in the *Brown* decision, an argument designed to appeal to conservative sentiment in the nation. The Citizens' Councils established an education fund in December 1956 to produce media materials to spread their word and launched *Forum* in April 1957 to produce and distribute electronic news materials. The "veritable avalanche of propaganda mirrored the great vitality of the movement" and reflected its "missionary-like zeal for propagating the faith of organized resistance."[50]

Segregationist Ideology

Segregationist ideology tapped into long-held beliefs of the southern racial credo devised in the late nineteenth century by Thomas Pearce Bailey and restated by Howard Odum in the 1940s as an essential part of the "way of the South." The savagery of the African background of Black southerners loomed large in segregationist rhetoric. In July 1960, William J. Simmons, the editor of the *Citizens' Council* newspaper, wrote in "Lesson from the Congo" that that new African nation was evidence that the Black man remained a "howling savage," and he made the connection with Black southerners.[51]

Segregationists claimed to develop a systematic scientific defense of segregation, but they relied on ideas that most scientists had long moved beyond. Southern white defenders of the segregated southern way of life virtually worshipped someone such as Carleton Putnam, whose *Race and Reason* (1961) asserted the continued centrality of race to civilization. Putnam, a northerner and former airline executive and biographer of Theodore Roosevelt, had begun reading ethnography in the late 1950s, and he became a conservative polemicist who reflected older scientific views that had made race central to civilization. He relied on the contrast he saw between "a Negro settlement in the Congo" and London or Paris, drawing commonsense "conclusions regarding relative levels of character and intelligence." Governor Ross Barnett proclaimed October 26, 1961, to be "Race and Reason Day in Mississippi." The Citizens' Council magazine, the *Citizen*, devoted a whole issue to Putnam and his book and lauded his address that day as "the turning point" in the region's struggle to preserve segregation, thus revealing just how isolated segregationists were from broader intellectual trends and how unrealistic, in retrospect, they were.[52]

Fears of miscegenation, like scientific racism, had long been a staple of southern segregationists, and the *Brown* decision evoked a near-hysterical fear of race mixing in the schools leading inevitably to interracial sex. Citizens' Council spokesman Walter C. Givhan of Alabama warned that the decision would "open the bedroom doors of our white women to Negro men." The organization's newspaper had such headlines as "Mixed Marriage Will Become Commonplace," "White and Negro Marriage Is Goal," "Sex Atrocity in Massachusetts: Blacks Rape White Girl Repeatedly," and "Mixed Love in Kentucky." Historians have identified a "southern rape complex" going back to the Victorian era and located in the psyches of white men generally but especially economically insecure and sexually repressed white men, who constructed southern identity around the sexual purity of white women.[53]

Antebellum religious leaders had developed a biblical defense of slavery as part of the proslavery argument, and segregationists in the post–World War II period articulated a theology of segregation that reiterated many of the nineteenth-century arguments. In "A Christian View on Segregation," for example, the Reverend G. T. Gillespie, president emeritus of Belhaven College in Jackson, Mississippi, cited passages from Genesis, Leviticus, the Gospels, Acts, the Epistles, and Revelation to demonstrate that separation of races had divine sanction. Defenders of the segregated southern way of life could take comfort from such published sermons as "God the Original Segregationist," "Christianity and Segregation," "Is Segregation Un-Christian?" and "Christian Love and Segregation." Southern preachers ridiculed the social gospel that taught the need for a just society, and they lambasted northern churches for their role in supporting the activities of the civil rights movement and in charging white southerners with immorality over segregation. Southern Evangelicalism had long insisted that religion was only about conversion from sin, and many white ministers used that understanding to avoid involvement in promoting social reform. Laypeople controlled most southern Protestant churches, especially the Baptists, who were overwhelmingly dominant in the region. Most white Baptists wanted to avoid issues of civil rights and steer clear of controversy, and in doing so they provided a classic example of a major theme of southern evangelical history: its cultural captivity to the broader southern culture that had sanctified racial division as God ordained.[54]

The folk theology of segregation had long been rooted in blood and sex, "disseminated in everyday speech, Sunday sermons, self-published tracts, and pamphlets," which made it important as religious sanction for the normalization of the segregated southern way of life. God had created the world with different races, and humans had to accept that fact. The deacons of First Baptist Church in Jackson, Mississippi, went on record saying that "the facts of history make it plain that the development of civilization and of Christianity has rested in the hands of the white race." A South Carolina Baptist church insisted that "in integrating the races in schools, we foster miscegenation, thereby changing God's plan and destroying His handiwork." The theology of segregation promoted an obsession with purity as the basis of a God-given southern social order.[55]

Despite such pronouncements, the teaching of moderate modernist theology in seminaries and the recognition of many white southern leaders of segregation's immorality resulted in the region's denominations' general support for the *Brown* decision. The Southern Baptist Convention endorsed the *Brown* decision at its 1954 general meeting, as did Methodists and Presbyterians, and these represented the overwhelming majority of white southerners of faith. Only a few white ministers, and few of the region's most prominent ones, actively took part in the Citizens' Councils and other massive resistance organizations. The racial crisis created what newspaper editor Ralph McGill called "the agony of the southern minister," with clerics caught between "the dictates of conscience and church policy on the one hand, and the prejudices of those who 'run' the church on the other." At the local level, the conservative use of the Bible to justify the segregated southern way of life helped promote that crusading spirit that James Eastland had talked about in terms of massive resistance. A faculty member at the Baptist Mississippi College who said that "our Southern segregation way is the Christian way" explicitly identified the southern way as divinely ordained.[56]

Virulent strains of the folk religion of segregation appeared among violent defenders of racial segregation. Will D. Campbell, the renegade white Baptist minister active in the civil rights movement, remembered as a child the Ku Klux Klan leaving a Bible for the pulpit at his family's church. He warned that the real danger was "not racism per se, but that racism becomes a part of faith." He lamented that the Klan left its mark "not only on the pulpit Bible but on the minds and hearts of generations yet unborn." Campbell saw that the Klan's appeal was "essentially religious in character," and the terrible reality was that for the segregationist, "the stamp of racism has become part of his religious heritage and it is almost impossible to break through and reach him." Under Sam Bowers, another segregationist group terrorized African Americans and white sympathizers in Mississippi in the early 1960s. Bowers insisted that "a Solemn, determined spirit of Christian Reverence must be stimulated in all members" of the White Knights. Authorities believed he coordinated at least nine murders, over seventy bombings of Black churches, and 300 assaults. Convicted in 1967 for federal civil rights violations in the murder of three civil rights workers in 1964, Bowers was notable for his sense of religious mission that reflected a southern civil religion gone wild. Bowers believed God had called him to "eliminate heretics," and he made the effort to transform the defense of the southern way of life into part of a broader apocalyptic struggle. As religious historian Charles Marsh writes, "Right before his eyes, on the alluvial soil of the very heart of the Confederacy, appeared all the signs of a two-thousand-year war between the idolatrous agents of Baal and the soldiers of the one true God, the 'Galilean Jesus Christ.'" Bowers reflected the tenacious rhetoric of the South as the last bastion of imperiled faith.[57]

Religion's role in the defense of segregation was most significant for understanding how divine sanction normalized the belief that God had ordained the segregated southern way of life. Segregationists used southern history to justify "a civil religious holy war." The lines between the southern civil religion and the American civil religion became blurred as white southerners once again had come to see their cause as an American cause. The key point was that the South's evangelical dominance made it the last best hope for the nation and the world. A Southern Baptist minister saw his denomination in a peculiar position to carry out the divine will and warned that the "future of our denomination, our nation, and perhaps the world depends on our stewardship of the gospel now." Journalist Robert Sherrill wrote in 1965 that the conflict between segregation and integration in the South showed that "southerners are not just waging a political and economic war against change, but a religious war."[58]

Rebirth of the Lost Cause

This understanding led segregationists to use regional history to justify preservation of the segregated way of life. In the 1950s and 1960s, Confederate symbolism reemerged in the segregationist Lost Cause, a popular movement responding to the civil rights movement. Whether at Central High School in Little Rock in 1957, at Ole Miss in 1962, or at Selma in 1965, segregationists displayed the Confederate battle flag and played "Dixie." After the integration of Central High at bayonet point, a local official in Forest, Mississippi, told the high school band there to play "Dixie" before football games instead of "The Star-Spangled Banner." During the riot in Oxford, Mississippi, in 1962, students pulled down the Stars and Stripes from the flagpole on the University of Mississippi campus and raised the Confederate flag. This was powerful symbolism 100 years after the Civil War. The Ku Klux Klan had made that Confederate flag a central symbol in the early twentieth century, the Citizens' Councils used it in the 1950s, and in the minds of many Americans white supremacy and the flag became inextricably linked.[59]

For white southerners, the memory of the Confederacy still offered meaning and connection to the past. Newspaper editor Hodding Carter, born in 1908, noted that white southerners were typically close "to some fabulous father or grandfather, some remembering a grandmother, to whom, in our childhood and even our young manhood, the war and its aftermath was a personal, bitter, and sacred reality." Carter observed in 1950 that an audience of white southerners would politely stand for the national anthem, but "you had better stick cotton in your ears" if the band played "Dixie." When segregationists mobilized this sentiment for political resistance to desegregation, it provided vital emotional content to the defense of "southern tradition." Writer Walker Percy explained the more openly racist use of the flag: "Now when the Stars and Bars flies over a convertible or a speedboat or a citizens' meeting, what it signifies is not a theory of government but a certain attitude toward the Negro."[60]

Walker Percy identified a key phrase in the segregationist lexicon that he particularly objected to: "the southern way of life." Granting that "there was and is such a thing and it had and has nothing to do either with negroes or with a planter aristocracy" (probably thinking of "the mannered way of life"), Percy disdained in the early 1960s hearing the phrase "Southern Way of Life, because I know what is coming next. It usually means segregation and very little else." In New Orleans, he wrote, "which has a delightful way of life, the 'Southern Way of Life' usually means 'Let's Keep McDonough No. 6 Segregated.'"[61]

Defenders of the segregated southern way of life also explicitly linked the memory of Reconstruction to the post–World War II defense of the southern way. Comparing the *Brown* decision to Reconstruction, segregationists saw its supporters as new carpetbaggers and scalawags. A Charleston attorney and former politician reminded white southerners that "Reconstruction days were harsh," but despite that reality, "the basic principles for which the South fought were not destroyed." His South now faced "a similar challenge," but with "the strength of character, exhibited by the generation preceding, the dawn of a new 1876 will arrive," referring to Reconstruction's end. One insisted that white southerners could "shape their destiny and control their way of life, just as they did in the far more dangerous period of Reconstruction." Academic historians would in the 1960s revise the Reconstruction myth by showing the period had not been the failure that the Progressive Era Dunning school historians and later popular writers had supposed. They saw it instead as a period of democratic promise, valuable experiments in social integration, and the passage of constitutional amendments that now provided the basis for federal government's efforts at reform. Such new scholarly views did not enter mainstream culture immediately, but they did undercut efforts of defenders of the segregated southern way of life to use history in the post-*Brown* years to validate their racist society.[62]

American Way of Life

The term "American way of life" had emerged around 1930—the same time period as "the southern way of life." It had been a contested term from the Depression through World War II, with two meanings, democracy and free enterprise, competing for attention. World War II had reinforced the importance of the term and validated, despite the contrasting meanings, the idea that American society had a unifying ideological significance. Because materialism was a distinctive philosophical component of the Soviet enemy during the Cold War, Americans elevated respect for religion to a new authoritative position, even in a seemingly secularized society. Frances FitzGerald's study of American school textbooks of this era found that "democracy," a key term of the American way, had become simply a synonym by the 1950s for the status quo, in opposition to fascism and communism, rather than a call for social justice, as commentators in the 1930s had used the term.[63]

A leading student, and advocate, of the American way of life in the 1950s was religious sociologist Will Herberg. He wrote in 1955 that it was "at bottom a spiritual structure, a structure of ideas and ideals, of aspirations and values, of beliefs and standards." He insisted that it synthesized "all that commends itself to the American as the right, the good, and the true in actual life." Seeing expressions of the American way in a wide range of elements including "sanitary plumbing and freedom of opportunity, Coca-Cola and an intense faith in education," Herberg added an important conclusion: all were "felt as moral questions relating to the proper way of life" and indicated the spiritual nature of the concept. "The very expression 'way of life' points to its religious essence, for one's ultimate, over-all way of life is one's religion." His statement itself was an expression of American civil religion that flourished in the post-war era. Herberg saw his American way as especially significant in reconciling religion and democracy and in enabling Catholics and Jews, as well as Protestants, to be accepted in American culture.[64]

The American way of life had broad appeal in the South, with its democratic and free-enterprise components, its religiosity, and its unifying American sentiments able to reach a wide group of the region's people. Anticommunism would be especially important because it became tied in with segregationist efforts to defend the segregated southern way of life. Embracing anticommunism enabled segregationists to broaden their national appeal and place their cause in an international context. The South had few communists, in fact, with most of the national concern for internal security, espionage, and related issues focused outside the region. Nonetheless, from early on such defenders of segregation as the Citizens' Councils equated the civil rights movement with communist efforts to destroy the United States. Anticommunism bred fear and hysteria, with Joseph McCarthy's crusade a prime example, and these emotions became tangled up with race in the South. Any challenge to the southern status quo became a communist plot. Senator James Eastland held McCarthy-like hearings in New Orleans in 1954, in which he targeted former members of the reformist SCHW for not banning former communists from the group. Newspapers established special columns, such as Jack Lotto's On Your Guard in the *Jackson Daily News* in the early 1960s, that kept readers, he said, "posted on the present and future activities of the Communist Party." Liberal Mississippi congressman Frank Smith observed that young Mississippians had "been taught that only the Mississippi Way is right," and vast numbers of the state's whites believed "that any Mississippian who differs has either sold out for cash or has been a Communist all the time."[65]

The Communist Party had helped supply lawyers and resources to defend the Scottsboro boys in the 1930s from spurious charges of rape, and from then conservative white southerners equated communism with efforts to undermine the segregated southern way of life. The Citizens' Councils saw their anticommunist efforts not just as a regional struggle to preserve southern customs but as an American one to preserve their understanding of whites-only democracy and private enterprise, a view that blurred the lines between the American way and the southern way. Medford Evans became a Citizens' Council executive in the early 1960s, and one of his popular speeches was "Civil Rights and Communist Realities." He insisted that the message of the Citizens' Councils was that "since the Southern Way has become the American Way, an attack on the Southern Way is an attack on the American Way." Religion would prove to be a valuable southern contribution to national anticommunism with particular southern racial meanings. "Since God made the races, and appointed the bounds of their habitations," a Florida Baptist minister intoned, any "attempts to force racial union in social life would lead to the communist hope for producing a 'one world hybridized human,' against the Word and Will of God."[66]

Civil rights activists who questioned the segregated southern way of life challenged the inherited mental formulations of white southerners. Anticommunism gained enormous influence in the South because it helped fill a "massive conceptual gap" created in the minds of white southerners by the civil rights movement. Having long convinced themselves that the Black southerners in their midst were happy with their inferior social place, white southerners could not understand how the domestic servant who cooked their meals, the yardman who tended their gardens, or the field hands who tilled their crops could start marching for civil rights. They came to blame the dreaded communists for wanting not only world domination but also changes in the southern world.[67]

Massive Resistance

The political use of the term "massive resistance" dates from February 25, 1956, when U.S. senator Harry F. Byrd from Virginia proposed to resist school desegregation, and the term came to include many forms of resistance from thousands of legislative enactments, speeches, writings, suppressions of dissent, and ultimately the closing of public schools in several states. James J. Kilpatrick Jr., successor to Douglas Southall Freeman as editor of the *Richmond News Leader*, had laid the intellectual groundwork for massive resistance through editorials beginning in late 1955. With the Supreme Court's *Brown* decision mandating desegregation of public schools, Kilpatrick saw a "rape of the Constitution" and believed Virginia had a duty to interpose its sovereignty to halt the evil. "Interposition" thus entered the lexicon of the segregated southern way of life, or rather it reentered the South's vocabulary, because antebellum southern political philosophers had used the concept against the federal government in regard to slavery. Most of the state's newspapers followed Kilpatrick's lead in a three-month campaign for "interposition now." Editors consulted their history books to explain how the Kentucky and Virginia resolutions of the 1790s and John C. Calhoun's compact theory of the Union could justify southern states centralizing control of public schools at the state level. In early 1956 five other

Alabama governor George Wallace attempting to block integration at the
University of Alabama in 1963, in a protest during the last days of the legal
segregation of the South. Library of Congress, Washington, D.C.

state legislatures adopted interposition statutes, and by mid-1957 eight states
had such measures in place. March 1956 saw the issuance of the "Declaration of
Constitutional Principles"—better known as the Southern Manifesto—signed
by nineteen of the twenty-two senators and 82 of the 106 congressional representatives from the former Confederate states, endorsing interposition and
labeling the decision unconstitutional.[68]

Kilpatrick emerged as a major intellectual figure in the defense of the segregated southern way of life. The fight against *Brown* gave him connections
with political and intellectual conservatives across the nation, as he worked
with William F. Buckley and the *National Review,* David Lawrence and *U.S.
News and World Report,* Henry Regnery's press, and the Goldwater presidential campaign in 1964. Kilpatrick's advocacy of interposition ultimately rested
on white southerners' willingness to give up their public schools in the face
of federal government pressure to integrate. A majority of the southern states
made provisions for alternative education in the eventuality of closed schools.[69]

Segregationists used the discourse of a southern way of life in the mid-1950s
as an emotional foundation for their efforts to unite white southerners behind

resistance. Talk of a singular southern way had long been a prop for creating political unity among whites against federal government threats to segregation. In the 1950s and 1960s this effort included defining a regional orthodoxy on race and other cultural matters and then enforcing it rigidly. University of Mississippi historian James Silver traced the history of orthodoxy in his state in *Mississippi: The Closed Society* (1964) and concluded that its essence was "a never-ceasing propagation of the 'true faith' . . . with a constantly reiterated demand for loyalty to the united front, requiring that non-conformists and dissenters from the code be silenced, or, in a crisis, driven from the community." He added that the threat and reality of violence had "confirmed and enforced the image of unanimity."[70]

Although Mississippi was particularly egregious in violating civil liberties to enforce orthodox white unity, sovereignty commissions in other southern states investigated educators, Black institutions, and even religious individuals who might be inclined to question racial orthodoxy. Pat Watters, who investigated racial problems for the Southern Regional Council, wrote that "[it] was a frightening thing to go into a small city and to realize that not merely the semi-literate poor white gas station attendant, but also the bankers, the mayor, the editor, even some of the preachers, all those who are personages in such a place supported it [resistance] fervently."[71]

Popular culture also expressed the need for white southern unity and used explicitly the southern way of life as a rallying cry. The song "Move Them N——s North" was on jukeboxes, telling white listeners that "our South has been invaded by trashy liberal groups" who "don't like our southern ways." The song urged listeners that "it's time for us to make a stand / to keep our southern ways," shifting a term from the elite literary culture of the Agrarians into the world of honky-tonks. The payoff line was "It's unity that pays."[72]

Massive resistance stressed white solidarity, but national and regional events undermined segregationist efforts in the late 1950s. Although most southern whites clearly wanted to retain segregation, they did not unite on how far they would go to maintain the system or whether the southern way of life could absorb modest changes. The desegregation of Central High School in Little Rock, Arkansas, in 1957 was one landmark in massive resistance. President Dwight Eisenhower had been slow to embrace the *Brown* decision, but when Little Rock mobs threatened court-ordered desegregation, he sent in U.S. Army forces to restore order, shocking segregationist resisters. Meanwhile, a move away from interposition became apparent in its home, Virginia, as early as the fall of 1958. An open-school movement appeared, as white middle-class moderates finally began to assert their unwillingness to give up their public schools as the price for maintaining rigid segregation. The state's governor, Lindsay Almond, and its legislature passed new measures that provided for token integration, and other southern states did the same, with a more moderate position that reflected concerns for social stability, the national image of the South, business advancement, commitment to progress, and national ideals.[73]

Moderate Intellectuals, Politicians, and Neopopulists

Southern liberals had carved out an important role as intellectual critics and sometimes advocates for policy reform in the 1930s and early 1940s, but the decade after World War II found them in an increasingly precarious position between civil rights activism and segregationist resistance. Liberals saw the South's problems primarily in terms of economics, and the New Deal had embraced them and put many of them in key policy and political positions. Southern conservatism and national liberalism had come, however, to see race as overwhelmingly *the* southern issue by the time of the Dixiecrats and the emergence of the Cold War. In this context, southern liberals had little real support among the masses of middle- and working-class whites, but they were influential because they often led institutions in the South and maintained connections to northern foundations, national intellectual venues, and federal authority and patronage. They embraced regional history as a way to show their southernness, and they generally abandoned the "liberal" label in favor of the term "moderate." An especially prominent spokesperson, C. Vann Woodward, saw moderates wanting "to sting the conscience of the South into an intensified awareness of the inconsistency between creed and custom." Wanting orderly, gradual progress that would bring, one day in the far future, the end of segregation, they put their faith in rising educational levels and industrialization to end entrenched rural power and customs. With the *Brown* decision, however, their gradualism now seemed itself outdated, and African American activists became increasingly critical of their unwillingness to embrace change as the civil rights movement began a new phase.[74]

Intellectual moderates generally opposed massive resistance, as did neopopulists who based their appeal in social-class politics. Among these neopopulists were James E. Folsom, the colorful Alabama politician with strong roots in rural places, reelected governor in 1954, and Earl K. Long, who won the governorship in Louisiana in 1956. Folsom opposed his state's white Citizens' Councils, mocking them by saying, "I favor the White Citizens' Council, Black Citizens' Council, Yellow Citizens' Council, and any other color you might mention." His sympathy for the poor drove his policies, and he insisted that "as long as Negroes are held down by privation and lack of opportunity, the other poor people will be held down alongside them." In the aftermath of *Brown*, he vetoed many of the bills the state legislature passed supporting segregation and dismissed the legislature's interposition resolution as being like "a hound dog baying at the moon and claiming it's got the moon treed." Long, brother of Louisiana's landmark politician Huey Long, told one Louisiana state senator and Citizens' Council member that one day he would go home, "get up on his front porch, take off his shoes, wash his feet, look at the moon, and get close to God." When he did, Long said, "you got to recognize that n——s is human beings!" Long, like Folsom, insisted that Blacks had helped build the country and, as Long put it, "if they could fight in its army, then I'm for giving them the vote."[75]

Political moderates did offer a strategy that pushed the South toward change, but they left the region politically in the thrall of what would become a deeply rooted conservatism. Mississippi governor J. P. Coleman was progenitor of the approach of pragmatic segregationist governors. In the aftermath of *Brown*, he did not embrace massive resistance and even called the interposition measure passed by his state's legislature "poppycock." Instead, he appointed a commission to suggest peaceful, legal ways to preserve as much of segregation as possible, and he instituted measures to centralize law enforcement, modernize judicial administration, reform family law, and tighten welfare. Governors LeRoy Collins of Florida and Luther Hodges of North Carolina echoed Coleman's viewpoint and established a token acceptance of segregation that acknowledged the *Brown* decision but worked around it to improve the South's national image, promote economic development for their states, and encourage cultural growth of African Americans in the South. These pragmatic governors tried to convey a respect for Black culture, especially that of the middle class, as they praised African American institutions, traditions, and culture, even as they promoted uplift and reform of the lower classes. Their arguments emphasized that the low standards of many African Americans made integration a threat to southern whites.[76]

Culture itself became implicated in this version of pragmatic segregation. Hodges, for example, insisted that whites had an "older culture" that should be preserved, while Black southerners had a "new and rapidly developing culture" that needed to be encouraged, not placed in competitive disadvantage with that of whites. Unless southerners could, "through the good will and pride in the integrity of our respective racial cultures and way of life," separate into schools voluntarily, then progress of both racial cultures would be impeded. "Way of life" here meant acceptance of African Americans as an integral part of southern life, even though they were suffering cultural lag compared to whites. Hodges and the others did not stress African Americans' biological inferiority, as the Citizens' Councils did, but they highlighted their cultural inferiority as they cited social science data to suggest a failed moral conscience, including high rates of illiteracy, disease, and crime. Richard Ervin, a white lawyer who represented Florida in its response to *Brown*, writing of Blacks integrating previously white schools, noted that "the Southern mother doesn't see a vision of a clean scrubbed little Negro child about to embark on a great adventure." Instead, that mother "sees a symbol of the cultural lags of which she is more than just statistically aware." The pragmatic politicians replaced the angry rhetoric of massive resistance with a hopeful vision of two races voluntarily living segregated, but steadily improving, lives.[77]

The Civilized Way

The "middle way," or the "civilized way" as it was known in North Carolina, exemplified the search for a position between full desegregation and massive resistance. Businessmen and middle-class civic leaders typically took the lead in encouraging Black community and cultural development, opposing extreme rhetoric and violence, and nurturing a climate that would promote a positive national image of the South and encourage economic development. Greensboro, North Carolina, the site of the landmark first sit-in in 1961, was a progressive city located in the most forward-looking state in the South. Its civic elite included prominent attorneys, executives from the prosperous textile industry, and businessmen from the powerful insurance companies that made the city home. With a well-deserved reputation for racial tolerance, but one that rested on an aversion to conflict, the city maintained racial peace that rested on a white paternalism that insisted that "consensus offers the only way to preserve a genteel and civilized way of life." This outlook in practice often meant not giving African American leaders a true equal voice in decision-making and leaving untouched the underlying issue of public segregation. Civility was "the cornerstone of the progressive mystique, signifying courtesy, concerns about an associate's family, children and health, a personal grace that smooths contact with strangers and obscures conflict," all of which was "a way of dealing with people and problems that made good manners more important than substantial action." This was indeed a classic example of the mannered southern way of life. African Americans in the South understood and exemplified the mannered southern way, but they were also its victims, unable to penetrate the civility barrier to enable open and full discussion of problems.[78]

"The Nashville way" was a term used to describe a similar method in Tennessee's capital city. The civic elite developed slogans to advertise the nature of its progressive outlook, such as "the Athens of the South," pointing to the many colleges and universities there; "the Wall Street of the South," acknowledging the city's role as a financial and banking center; and "the Protestant Vatican," pointing to the many religious institutions located in the city. According to historian Benjamin Houston, the Nashville way "captured the self-professed style of Tennessee's capital city, where pride, provincialism, and paternalism melded in powerful ways." The city boasted of amicable race relations, with civic leaders embracing the term "moderate" to describe such attitudes, which they saw as synonymous with "progressive," "genteel," and "respectable." The moderate in Nashville, as elsewhere, was sympathetic to Black progress and aspiration but would not budge on the belief in Black inferiority and the preservation of segregation. That viewpoint of political moderates represented an upper-class, elite viewpoint stressing manners, decorum, and dislike of any threat of social unrest. The proclamations about white Nashville's "culture and pretensions of mannered graciousness," while adapting to "the best elements of progress and change," embodied "the unspoken belief that race relations could be managed, that the Southern Way of Life could adapt without sacrificing core elements."[79]

Nashville civic leaders' pragmatism led them to deal as best they could with negotiating the immediate demands of civil rights leaders without acknowledging the need for structural reforms in politics, economics, or society. This softer racial viewpoint, compared with that in the Deep South, gave civil rights leaders some leeway in their campaigns, and an identifiable Black Nashville way shaped the course of interracial relations during civil rights protests. Civil rights activist John Lewis recalled later that "something happened in Nashville that did not happen any other place in America." The city produced one of the earliest and most effective sit-ins in 1960, and in the process the young activists combined African American religious traditions with different intellectual outlooks from those of their local college training. The sit-in led them to make nonviolence not just a protest tactic but a way of life. The Nashville activists would go on to play a key role in SNCC, on the freedom rides in 1961, and at virtually every major site of civil rights protest through the mid-1960s. A *New York Herald Tribune* story in 1963 depicted Nashville as the "most desegregated in the South," with the reporters observing that the "one thing" the city could "not abide is unpleasantness." It valued "peace and quiet," contrasting it with Birmingham, which valued "separate water fountains and defiance." The reporter added, "Of course Nashville has had a long history of graciousness while Birmingham has no history at all."[80]

The Mannered Way

The concern for civility was part of the larger stress on the mannered southern way of life, an idea with deep roots in southern history. This appeal to manners received many expressions in the 1950s and 1960s, among both opponents and defenders of the segregated southern way of life. South Carolinian James McBride Dabbs, a religious lay leader and farmer, argued in *The Southern Heritage* (1958) that in the South, "manners are essential and are essentially morals." He thought moral codes, laws, and manners had been intertwined in the South with the aim of curbing individual aggressiveness and maintaining social order. White southerners such as Dabbs who wrote about manners being central to the southern way of life used such terms as "polite," "courteous," "kind," "gentle," "hospitable," and "friendly yet dignified." Noting that "manners are to be seen," Dabbs suggested that manners were a public matter of image among a group of people well known to one another. He was a prominent white supporter of the civil rights movement. Another champion of manners, James J. Kilpatrick, was an architect of massive resistance to racial desegregation. In 1962, Kilpatrick claimed that "a Southern manner, born of the Cavalier myth, persists in our own time" and was "more important than law." His examples of southern manners included "deference to women, principles of personal honor, the payment of a gentleman's debts—these are operative aspects of the Southern Way of Life." He placed race relations within this framework of manners. "This is a dual society," he wrote, "made up of white and Negro coexisting in an oddly intimate remoteness." He added that it was "a way of life that has to be experienced" and stressed manners as the behavioral aspects of the white supremacist ideology.[81]

One of the more perceptive observers of the South in these years, Georgia writer Flannery O'Connor, noted the importance of manners to the region's very identity in an interracial society. "The South has survived in the past," she wrote, "because its manners, however lopsided or inadequate they may have been, provided enough social discipline to hold us together and give us an identity." Moreover, she identified the southern African American's "elaborate manners and great formality" and suggested he had used it "superbly for his own protection and to insure his own privacy." Other observers of the time worried about how southern manners would survive with not only social changes but economic modernization, which many observers saw threatening traditional southern ways. In a letter to *Saturday Review* in 1955, Elizabeth Clay Blanford suggested, though, that new wealth in the region could actually assist in the preservation of manners. She saw that "with this new prosperity the South is very naturally restoring her own gracious way of life instead of copying the ways and customs which have evolved in other parts of the country." Reading in 1955 about a "gracious way of life" in the South gives one pause when considering the impending racial turmoil, but Blanford's words reflected the ironic, long-standing juxtaposition of differing meanings of the southern way of life.[82]

National Culture and the South

As always, understanding the concept of the southern way involves understanding northern attitudes toward southern society as well as southern beliefs. The predominant postwar image through the end of the 1960s was of a
benighted South. Anthropologist Ruth Landes, in her 1945 essay "A Northerner
Views the South," had outlined many of the South's problems that made for
this negative image and claimed that "of all the United States, the South is most
trapped by poverty and disease, illiteracy, political corruption, and a deep want
of ambition." The region had no social convictions "newer than those of Reconstruction," and she saw a backward-looking people "unable to embrace American democracy." The role of race in shaping national images of the South would
increase as the civil rights movement pursued its goals and provoked violence
from southern white extremists. National popular culture shaped attitudes
through the often-gothic works of writers such as Tennessee Williams, William
Faulkner, and Erskine Caldwell and the popular, high-profile films made from
them during the 1950s and 1960s. North Carolina writer James Street lamented
in 1955 that "the South, once seen as a Garden of Eden with good manners,"
had somehow become transformed into a never-never land, "peopled by sa-
dists, masochists, rapists, satyrs, nymphomaniacs, and necrophiles, to mention
a few of the better known types, together with assorted murderers, arsonists,
and lynchers, although it seems to draw the line at cannibalism, even during a
failure of the turnip crop." He saw the national image of the South as a "cross
between a Gothic romance and a Greek tragedy written by Freud."[83]

Some southern writers defended the region in national cultural forums.
South Carolinian Herbert Ravenal Sass, for example, had published "They
Don't Tell the Truth about the South" in the *Saturday Evening Post* in 1954,
but his article ironically corroborated the South's terrible reputation in the
national culture. He complained that "in the consciousness of the great mass
of Americans, the South has no place in the grand epic of American achievement." National history represented the South "as a barren land where neither
science nor art existed; and this barrenness continued until our own day, when
a school of Southern writers had won critical acclaim by exploiting the theme of
Southern decadence." Most of Sass's defensive and belligerent article chronicled
important contributions made by white southerners to American history. In
the end, he lamented that white southerners were so unaware of their own history, a surprising admission from a writer singing southern glories. "Martially
we are marching forward, and not even a Federal court decision aggravating
disastrously our difficult racial problem can halt our march," he wrote and

added that "our great need is in the realm of the spirit"—words that revealed a surprising weakness of the southern spirit to this defender of the southern way of life.[84]

North Carolina senator Sam Ervin Jr. published "The Case for Segregation" in *Look* to defend the segregated southern way of life. Asserting that "the vast majority of Southerners, both white and Negro," recognized social segregation as an "acceptable way of life for both races," he admitted that "the issue of racial segregation is surcharged with emotional tensions and mental misunderstandings." Segregation in the South was purely in social matters, he claimed. Interracial friendships were common, with "Southerners of either race forming warm and mutually helpful friendships with members of the other race." He denied that segregation rested in racial bigotry or prejudice and that it prevented Blacks from high achievement, pointing to African Americans operating banks, insurance companies, public transportation systems, and other businesses. Social segregation of the races was "an actual condition and not a mere theory in the south," he asserted, claiming most southerners, white and Black, saw it "as an acceptable way of life for both races."[85]

Despite southern white defenders getting their message out sometimes in national forums, the mass media played a key role in publicizing the racial struggle in the postwar South. It helped to shape American images of the South's race relations and white resistance to changes to the southern way of life. Beginning in the mid-1950s journalists and photographers came into the South to document the struggle. The nation read in newspapers and magazines about harsh southern white resistance to change, the angry rhetoric of politicians, and the violence that southern whites unleashed. The Montgomery bus boycott (1955–56) introduced the televised mass demonstration as a tactic of the civil rights movement, with the coverage generally favorable and helping to make a youthful Martin Luther King Jr. a national celebrity. The national media covered the closing of schools in Arkansas and Virginia, with images of angry white protesters at a time when network news reporting had just emerged as a key factor in national communications.[86]

Although the benighted South rested in the national psyche in these years, a secondary image was present as well—that of the folksy, down-home region, still functioning as a premodern escape for harried modern Americans who now were members in the 1950s and early 1960s of the conformist, materialistic organizational society. The positive South was no longer the moonlight-and-magnolias romantic South but that of another long theme in the nation's understanding of the region. Rustic television shows best expressed this folk image. *The Beverly Hillbillies*, for example, premiered in 1962, becoming the most popular television show in the nation through much of the decade. It showed a mountain family who struck oil, moved into a southern California mansion, but kept their quaint ways and were seemingly oblivious to the conspicuous consumption and consumer conveniences that most Americans embraced. The ridiculous loomed large in the weekly accounts of the family's adventures, but writers portrayed the often silly people as guileless folk, whom the audience cheered when the family outsmarted more sophisticated moderns. *The Andy Griffith Show*, although set in contemporary times, tried to reproduce the small-town South of the 1930s, when the star of the show had grown up in Mount Airy, North Carolina. Griffith portrayed a gentle and gregarious sheriff, notable as the opposite of such racist law enforcement figures as Birmingham's Eugene "Bull" Connor whom national news audiences were seeing go about their vicious ways. Mayberry, the fictional and mythic small southern town, was mostly white, and critics lamented its failure to include African Americans in its southern setting. The show entertained with a cast of humorous characters out of a long southern humor tradition: Barney, an incompetent deputy sheriff; Opie, the sheriff's charming son; Aunt Bee, the matriarch; and assorted oddball but lovable townsfolk. Each episode had a moral to it, as well as gentle humor and utter charm. These television shows preserved the South's appealing folk image while the benighted imagery predominated, and they be-came a bridge to a much more favorable southern image in national culture by the 1970s.[87]

The Great Debate:
Martin Luther King Jr. and Robert F. Williams

White opponents of the *Brown* decision seized the initiative in the three years after 1954, and the nation became increasingly familiar with the developing southern struggle through the media. African Americans worked in those years—before the large-scale demonstrations and protests that began in Mont-gomery in 1957—to promote racial changes in local contexts, as they tried to push along the gradual change that had begun after World War II. Voter regis-tration drives brought increasing numbers to polling places in cities and border states, and Black activists worked with schools that began token integration. Historians talk of the "long civil rights movement" and argue that its activities went back at least to the biracial labor union work of the 1930s and 1940s. The Montgomery bus boycott was a landmark in the beginning of a new stage of the African American freedom movement, the watershed moment that sustained economic pressure, direct-action protests, and court cases and could lead to public policy changes benefitting African Americans. Rosa Parks became a legendary rebel against the southern way of life for her unwillingness to give up her seat at the back of a Montgomery bus as law required. Her training at the Highlander School and her work with the NAACP had prepared her to protest segregation. The boycott began in December 1955, sparked by Parks's arrest. The idea for the boycott came from the Reverend Ed Nixon, a longtime labor organizer, and the Women's Political Council, headed by Jo Ann Robinson, a professor of English. The boycott succeeded partially because of the widespread sharing of information about alternative travel possibilities for working Black people, including many women who worked as domestics for white families. Some white women supported the boycott by providing transportation for their employees. The city government, however, remained unwilling to reform the city's transportation system, so the Montgomery Improvement Association, which led the protest, abandoned its initial call for reforms and then worked with the NAACP to file a lawsuit against the constitutionality of segregation itself. The Supreme Court invalidated the city's bus segregation, which ended in December 1956.[88]

Dr. Martin Luther King Jr. emerged at the age of twenty-seven as the leader of the Montgomery bus boycott. He became the spiritual head, symbolic presence, and rhetorical spokesman for the new stage of direct-action protest. Several key influences shaped his ideology, which became apparent in the Montgomery bus boycott, including the social gospel that stressed the social role and responsibility of religion as well as the personalism that said the dignity and value of the individual came as part of the ultimate reality of the Divine and that racial segregation degraded the individual personality.[89]

The nonviolent philosophy became the central force in King's thinking and actions and the basis for a southern way that challenged the segregated way of life. He had read Thoreau's essay on civil disobedience, studied Gandhi's thought from India, and learned from such pacifists as Glenn Smiley and Bayard Rustin about applying nonviolent methods to social justice struggles. Reflecting later that "the experience of Montgomery did more to clarify my thinking on the question of nonviolence than all of the books that I had read," he had become, as events unfolded, ever more certain of the "power of nonviolence." Protesting segregation made nonviolence "more than a method to which I gave intellectual assent; it became a commitment to a way of life." His use of the term "way of life" was surely not made without the visceral understanding of the segregated southern way of life, so King's advocacy of direct-action protest for social justice should be seen as contesting the southern white usage of "way of life."[90]

These influences of the Protestant social gospel, philosophical personalism, and Gandhian nonviolent methods gave intellectual justification for King's

Iconic image of Dr. Martin Luther King Jr. on a church fan found in African American churches and homes. Charles Reagan Wilson Collection, Archives and Special Collections, John Davis Williams Library, University of Mississippi Library, Oxford, Mississippi.

worldview that had first been nurtured in the biblically based Black church. Black theology appeared to him through sermons, songs, and stories of slavery and oppression. A central theme of individual freedom and reconciliation into a community of goodwill resonated for him from his inheritance as an African American minister. Black religious tradition emphasized the dignity and worth of all people, and God was a personal and loving God who intervened in the life of his children to enable them to "make something from nothing." King's Christian foundations pointed him to the nonviolence he embraced.[91]

King established two priorities for the civil rights movement. One was the end of the structures supporting the segregated southern way of life. Pointing to the moral issue at the heart of racial segregation, he condemned the "disease of segregation" and remembered from his childhood the "stinging darts of segregation." Recognizing the social construction of segregation, he pointed out that "white men soon came to forget that the southern social culture and all its institutions had been organized to perpetuate this rationalization" of Black inferiority. In a graphic description in *Stride toward Freedom* (1958) of the segregated southern way of life, he told of his parents having to explain segregation to him. He recalled his mother setting him on her lap and telling him about slavery and emancipation and about "the divided system of the South—the segregated schools, restaurants, theaters, housing, the white and colored signs on drinking fountains, waiting rooms, lavatories—as a social condition rather than a natural order." But she also explained that "you are as good as anyone," words that countered the degradation of the southern way of life for him and other African Americans.[92]

King saw the necessity of direct-action protest against the evils of segregation. Submitting to segregation represented cooperating with the system. Boycotts, marches, rallies, and demonstrations were essential weapons for breaking down the complacency that had taken root over generations. Because the segregated southern way of life was morally wrong, it offended the law of God, and the individual had a moral obligation to refuse to cooperate with evil. Therefore, a person had not just a legal but a moral duty to disobey unjust laws. The aim was to win freedom for African Americans but also to ensure that "through love, patience, and understanding goodwill they can call their brothers to a way of noble living." As he wrote in *Stride toward Freedom*, nonviolent resistance would awaken the "moral consciousness" of white Americans concerning segregation.[93]

King's second goal in opposing the segregated southern way of life was to awaken the African American consciousness to Black self-respect and dignity. He wrote that Rosa Parks, for example, had not been planted in the bus by some organization but, instead, refused to give up her bus seat because of "her personal sense of dignity and self-respect." Her decision not to move from the seat resulted from "the accumulated indignities of days gone by and the boundless aspirations of generations yet unborn." Depicting her as "the victim of both the forces of history and the forces of destiny," King used the operative civil religion language about the South's sense of mission, but now African Americans represented the South's emerging destiny. "She had been tracked down by the zeitgeist—the spirit of the times," he said. King thus captured the portentous meaning of the Montgomery boycott. Nonviolence had permitted the struggle to go on "with dignity and without the need to retreat."[94]

More generally, King observed in his essay "Our Struggle" (an early effort to

assess the meaning of the Montgomery boycott) that "the segregation of Negroes, with its inevitable discrimination," had nurtured aspects of inferiority
among many African Americans in the South. As a result of segregation's long
hegemony in the region, "many Negroes lost faith in themselves and came to
believe that perhaps they really were what they had been told they were—something less than men." As long as Black people would tolerate that discrimination, "racial peace could be maintained," but he added that "it was an uneasy
peace." The Black masses had reassessed their plight in the years before the
boycott, and the results had changed "the nature of the negro community"
and doomed "the social patterns of the South." For King, the Montgomery
boycott represented a revolutionary change in southern Black consciousness
that demonstrated "to the negro, North and South, that many of the stereotypes
he has held about himself and other negroes are not valid." Montgomery had
"broken the spell" and ushered in "concrete manifestations of the thinking and
action of the new negro."[95]

The "long black power movement" served, though, as a counterpoint to his
ideology. Although historians have viewed Black power as emerging in the late
1960s, it might be traced back to Marcus Garvey's Black nationalism in the
early twentieth century or, more directly, to the 1940s "march-on-Washington
movement" led by A. Philip Randolph. That movement prompted a mass African American militancy that led Franklin D. Roosevelt to sign an executive
order banning discrimination in the defense industry and to create the Fair
Employment Practices Commission. The movement was the inspiration for the
March on Washington in 1963 and Martin Luther King Jr.'s "I Have a Dream"
speech about interracial justice. The Deacons for Defense and Justice appeared
the next year in Louisiana in 1964 as advocates of armed self-defense in response to Ku Klux Klan intimidation of African Americans, and the group established more than a score of chapters in the Deep South. Stokely Carmichael
would later emerge as a leader of the Black power movement, first using the
term "Black power" at a rally in Greenwood, Mississippi, in 1968.[96]

Robert F. Williams was a key figure in the intellectual defense of armed self-
defense as part of a call for Black power going back to the late 1950s. President of
the Monroe, North Carolina, chapter of the NAACP, he participated in nonviolent direct action in 1961 to protest the segregation of a publicly funded swimming pool but also used his gun in self-defense, an action that brought condemnation from the national NAACP and from King. His extensive speeches,
writings for his newspaper, the *Crusader*, and his later broadcasts of *Radio Free
Dixie* (1962–65) from Cuba emphasized the necessity for biracial cooperation
to achieve African American freedom. He praised whites who supported the
movement, but he insisted that change would not come just from moral appeals
to white consciences. His book *Negroes with Guns* (1962) conveyed his ideology,

which stressed the economic advancement of Black Americans, Black pride, appreciation of African American culture, independent Black political protest, and armed self-defense—all of which became features of the later Black power movement in the late 1960s. He connected the Black freedom movement in the South with anticolonial movements around the world. Williams and his wife Mabel left the United States in the early 1960s for Cuba, from where he broadcast *Radio Free Dixie*, which he described on air as the "free voice of the South."[97]

Williams was an intellectual who sparred with King, including in an exchange that journalists labeled "the Great Debate," pitting nonviolence against violence in the civil rights movement. Williams supported King's nonviolence as a tactic to promote change, but he insisted on flexibility in tactics that would include armed self-defense when needed. In "The Social Organization of Nonviolence," King acknowledged that African Americans in the South should be able to defend themselves when attacked, but he strongly condemned violence in civil rights protests as dangerous and counterproductive. Williams, like King, used the language of "way of life" and "civilization." Williams was a World War II veteran, and in one interview he noted how many soldiers, white and Black, had "died to preserve the American Way of Life." He peppered his writings with references to democracy and the biracial ideal at the same time that he insisted on the recognition of African American citizenship and dignity. During the swimming pool protest in Monroe in 1961, a mob threatened Williams and other protesters, and he drew his gun in self-defense. He recalled later that an older white man yelled, "The n——s have got guns, the n——s are armed and the police can't even arrest them." Williams reflected that "the old man saw his way of life slipping away before his eyes," meaning the end of the segregated southern way of life. Violence had been the last bulwark against change for such white people, and with African American resistance to it, "white supremacy was gone with the wind," summoning the image of the end of the Old South. He used the language of civilization as well. Like Ida B. Wells, he reversed the usual imagery. "We like to think of Africa as the land of savages and jungles," he wrote, "but there are not many jungles more savage than this section of America called Dixie." Williams was a southern radical whose message of freedom included all African Americans, but his regional consciousness led him to target his message especially at the South.[98]

African American Civil Religion

Beginning with Montgomery, the civil rights movement updated the African American civil religion, as its leaders used the language of the American dream, with Blacks its new advocates. Emphasizing the hopes of Black southerners that the United States would embrace its calling to embody an ideal of brotherhood, Birmingham minister and leading civil rights activist Fred Shuttlesworth saw the nation's special role in nurturing brotherhood, for "once we got all the melting pot together here, and the hardest bit was to assimilate the blacks into it, then we could be an example to the world." The civil rights movement represented a renewal of an African American civil religion that strengthened both "a providential understanding of American history and the special role of black Americans within that history." It also highlighted the southern setting where providence would work its will. King saw the movement as an attempt to call the nation back to its essential meaning, as the Black community drove the long American dream of opportunity that the world would once again associate with the nation once the segregated southern way of life ended. As Shuttlesworth put it, "America means integration or it means nothing." In his "Letter from a Birmingham Jail," King insisted that civil rights demonstrators would "reach the goal of freedom in Birmingham and all over the nation," because African Americans had a destiny "tied up with America's destiny." They would win their freedom because "the sacred heritage of our nation and the eternal will of God are embodied in our echoing demands."[99]

The need for redemption was a key component of the African American civil religion. The theory of nonviolent protest was that suffering would lead to society's redemption, an idea that reawakened the theme in Black history of the suffering servant. King's biblical language and examples located civil rights protesters in the long line of Christian prophets and martyrs. King tried to arouse white guilt for southern injustices but then offered absolution of sorts for whites if they would provide socioeconomic justice. King understood Black moral authority from a standpoint of injustice and hoped it could be used to appeal to white conscience. The motto of King's organization after Montgomery, the Southern Christian Leadership Conference, for example, was "To Redeem the Soul of America," and King reiterated that the movement should achieve "redemption and reconciliation." To be sure, as Lewis V. Baldwin notes, "King was always somewhat ambivalent about the moral and spiritual capacity of the white South for radical and much-needed social and political change." King lamented a small but determined minority that was resorting to violence and intimidation to block change, but in the 1950s, he placed much faith in southern moderates to do the right thing and become advocates for bold change. By the early 1960s, he had lost that faith.[100]

The social gospel that spoke of the kingdom of God on earth, the personalism that saw the interconnectedness of humans as reflections of the Supreme Personality, and the Black religious tradition of hoped-for liberation and reconciliation all contributed to King's key concept: the beloved community, a term he used often but never defined in depth. "The ultimate aim of SCLC," said an early brochure of King's Southern Christian Leadership Conference, "is to foster and create the 'beloved community' in America where brotherhood is a reality." Desegregation was only the first step in achieving the beloved community, to be followed by a color-blind inclusiveness based on love and justice that would foster true brotherhood. The ideal rested on King's belief that human beings are social in nature. "We are tied together," he wrote, "in the single garment of destiny, caught in an inescapable network of mutuality." King evoked here the concept of "the web," a term long used by observers of the southern way of life to describe the interconnectedness of southern life, but King used it to evoke a radically different, progressive understanding of human interconnectedness beyond region. And yet the South provided the particular cultural context for civil rights activists to work out human connectivity beyond race. The beloved community rested on Christian love and on American democratic ideals of the nation as embodying justice, equality, and freedom. King envisioned civil rights participants as a microcosm of the beloved community, people of various backgrounds brought together in the South in a common effort for justice.[101]

The Lasting South

In the mid-1950s, at a time when the southern way of life's racial meanings had become all-pervasive and the term became widely popularized and polemicized in ways it had never been before, a book appeared that reasserted the earlier agrarian meanings of the term. Louis D. Rubin Jr. and James J. Kilpatrick modeled their edited *The Lasting South: Fourteen Southerners Look at Their Home* (1957) after *I'll Take My Stand*, with its subtitle echoing the Agrarian manifesto's twelve southerners and with its lead essay even beginning with a John Crowe Ransom quote about the backward-looking southerner. The preface asserted that the diverse group of contributors to the volume agreed that "there *is* a South, that it is possible to talk of the South, and in so doing to mean not merely a geographical grouping but a way of life and a state of mind." This assertion elevated "the southern way of life" to equivalency with W. J. Cash's by-then famous "mind of the South." Rubin's lead essay, "An Image of the South," explored the complex meanings of the southern way of life in the mid-1950s. White southerners, he wrote, "will stand in front of a sleek plate-glass window or a gaudy motel and they will talk about a 'Southern way of life,' and by that they will mean a kind of relaxed, easy-going acceptance of things, with plenty of time for leisure and with considerable family and social life." Rubin tried to distance himself from the modern trappings, but he insisted that "despite the fancy window displays and the motels, they are generally correct," as "there *is* a Southern way, a style of its own." He admitted the South had changed since the earlier Agrarians' defense of their way of life, but Rubin once again referred to a key Agrarian point about the centrality of leisure. He admitted that "it is an exasperating way of life at times, especially when there is work to be done," but he claimed that "it is the best thing about the South and in the long run, it counts for more than all the economic expansion so talked about today."[102]

Rubin sounded the alarm that "the Southern way of life is now being threat-ened, as it has not been threatened since the Civil War," as he saw even more danger in his own age than the Agrarians did in 1930. He distanced himself from political uses of the term "southern way of life" and flew in the face of the ideological warfare going on around him. Instead, he wanted to focus on "that regional quality" that was the South's "most precious possession." The book in general asserted a mannered southern way of life, although Rubin tried to distance himself from its excessive claims. He noted that "one of the most overworked clichés about the South is that which involved Gracious Living," but Rubin, in fact, embraced this image as the product of a 100-year history after Confederate defeat that had left the region bereft of material wealth and without "the opportunity to accomplish very much in a materialistic sense."[103]

Moreover, using a key term from the Agrarians' lexicon, Rubin said that the South "seldom had much room in its makeup for the pioneering spirit of America." The result was the southern interest in history, which was "seldom something conscious," but it was all around southerners "as it is perhaps not there in, say, New York City or Chicago or Detroit." He claimed that "the shock of the Civil War" was the "paramount historical fact about the South," with the Confederate memory more than anything else distinguishing the region from other areas of the nation. Southern life had been focused on agriculture before the war, but "the War fixed that way of life upon it irrevocably, strip-ping it of what capital goods it possessed, reducing it to a status of colonial dependency upon the Northeast." He saw the Civil War creating "a Solid South that acted and thought as one on all things," and he stressed white unity as well as regional distinctiveness. Rubin summoned the image of the southern community—"image," another key Agrarian term—which he saw as "likely to be a much more tightly-knit affair, much more an organized unit, than any Northern metropolis." This "complex social fabric" had led southerners "natu-rally to embrace the past, the ancestral."[104]

Rubin was slow to get around to the most pressing issue facing the South of his time, race relations, but he did admit that racial attitudes of white south-erners showed "the paralyzing effects" of a "Southern habit of worrying for the present day alone." He admitted that white supremacy had "neither changed nor yielded," despite the injustices Black southerners experienced. In the end, he diminished the centrality of the African American freedom movement against the southern way of life underway around him by insisting that racial problems were only one aspect of "the larger, over-all problem that confronts the South today." That problem was the question of how a region could keep traditional social values, based on individualism, a strong sense of community, and a pronounced historical awareness, in a modernizing world of industries and cities. Thus, he asserted another key Agrarian term, "tradition," and made the book and Rubin's essay a bridge from the earlier manifesto to the contemporary southern cultural stress on tradition as still the key to understanding the region. Rubin's picture of industrialism was right out of *I'll Take My Stand*. He lamented that factory workers were "cogs in an impersonal industrial machine." Even in the South, one was not likely to "close up shop and go fishing," as southerners were increasingly living their lives by the tempo of industrialism that measured "its days by factory whistles and its nights by television channel changes."[105]

Rubin acknowledged the material benefits the South was receiving from its new way of life in the improved roads, schools, homes, and health facilities, but he viewed "the menace of the industrial South" coming from the negative destructive impact of material gains on the distinctive and desirable features of traditional southern life. Rubin reclaimed the term "civilization" for a South that appeared benighted to many other observers, arguing that, because of its history, "the South evolved a civilization that did not place its reliance upon the material goods of life, but upon the values of individuality, self-reliance, the community arts, a life which did not allow getting and spending to interfere with leisurely, relaxed living." His summary judgment again came right out of the Agrarians' thinking of almost three decades earlier, and he once again used "way of life" as the crucial connection of the South to civilization. That earlier South embodied a lifestyle that emphasized the human relationship to nature and the inheritance of history, "a life of the spirit as well as the flesh," with "spirit" once again anchoring the southern way of life as it had for the Agrarians and many other observers of the region.[106]

The other coeditor of the book, James J. Kilpatrick, was leading the charge on resistance to school desegregation. At the time he wrote his essay "Conservatism and the South," he had proposed and developed at length the interposition argument. Kilpatrick did not include that effort, however, in choosing to examine the South's conservative intellectual tradition and its relationship to the national conservative movement in the nation, which indeed would emerge in the 1970s as at the heart of a new imagining of a suburban, middle-class way of life. He insisted that the southern states were nearly alone "in fighting this rear-guard action against the legions of Change, the armies of a supposed Enlightenment" in the rational, scientific worldview his South had long challenged. His sense of urgency and mission came through in his belief that the South represented "the last and best hope of conservatism in the American Republic." Kilpatrick laid out the essentials of conservatism in the South that represented a version of the southern way of life that drew from the earlier Agrarians: "An indwelling devotion to tradition and good manners, a resistance to industrialism, a coolness to the secularist sirens who sing of material pleasures." In addition, the political tradition of the South rested in the South's embrace of states' rights, which he saw "flourishing with fresh vitality and renewed conviction."[107]

Kilpatrick avoided discussion of race relations, except at the end of the essay, where he claimed that neither of the races in the South, "where we are accustomed by the mores of generations to thinking in terms of race[,] is yet prepared for the social intimacy in massively integrated schools." Kilpatrick understood that the nation's public opinion was increasingly against segregation, and he deplored that "what most Southerners believe to be moral, Christian and constitutional, our critics conceive to be immoral, unchristian and unconstitutional." He embraced the southern spirit for "its deep devotion to things of the spirit, as distinguished from those of the flesh."[108]

If *The Lasting South* reasserted, in some ways, the ideological arguments of the earlier Vanderbilt Agrarians, the contrasting stories of two of the original Agrarians during the struggle for civil rights reveals other agrarian legacies and limitations.[109]

During the 1950s, Donald Davidson looked back on the mockery of the South in the 1920s and claimed that the larger purpose had been the "advocacy of a collective type of government, thoroughly materialist and anti-religion in philosophy, controlling education and the arts no less than the means of production, and founded upon a dialectic that would insist on a complete break with the historic continuity of Western civilization." Naming the villain, he saw "liberalism" as the underlying challenge to the preservation of the southern way of life and to Western civilization itself. Lamenting that even chambers of commerce generally "went along with calls for southern change out of sheer opportunism," he insisted that the Agrarians had represented a sharply focused counterattack to these larger challenges. He identified "the cause of the South" as "the cause of Western civilization," a cause that still seemed relevant to Davidson in the 1950s.[110]

What motivated Davidson most was a rigorous defense of racial segregation. With the challenges to the southern racial system in the mid-1950s, Davidson became an organizer of a white resistance group, the Tennessee Federation for Constitutional Government. Davidson supported legal challenges to court decisions and certainly eschewed violence, boycotts, and intimidation. Allen Tate seemed on target when he wrote to Robert Penn Warren that "I fear his Southernism, for all its cunning and learning, is now at the level of mere White Supremacy."[111]

Davidson became agitated at Warren's increasingly pro–civil rights perspective in the 1950s. Warren's book *Segregation* (1956) came out of extensive travels through the South and interviews with many white and Black southerners. Warren and his subjects often used the term "southern way of life." He called one segregation defender "the Hillman," whose purpose was to preserve "what you might name the old Southern way, what we was raised up to." Trying to untangle motives for the defenders of segregation, he asked one if the main point was states' rights. The man responded, "Yes, in a way, but you got to fight on something you can rouse people up about, on segregation," and he identified the all-important role of emotion in catalyzing the defense of the southern way of life. One key term Warren saw among segregationists was "change," and he quoted a Black scholar who said, "It's not merely desegregation they're against so much, it's just the face of any change."[112]

About a decade later, Warren's *Who Speaks for the Negro?* (1965) became another important book focused on the southern way of life, this one exploring African American leadership in a time of social change.[113] Warren established the framework for the book by recounting the circumstances of his *I'll Take My Stand* essay on Black southerners and his changed attitude toward the essay. He had intended his essay as a humane defense of a southern way of life that would provide true equality of treatment for Black people within the southern social system, but he came to believe that "no segregation was, in the end, humane." As with the testimonies of so many white southerners who came to have doubts about the segregated southern way of life, he insisted that before his racial conversion "it never crossed my mind that anybody could do anything about it." His words revealed the power of the southern-way-of-life ideology as handed down to a sensitive white southerner imprisoned by the ideology of white supremacy who believed it to be inevitable. But unlike Davidson, Warren confronted and embraced change.[114]

Sit-Ins and Changing Regional Consciousness

Warren published his book in the mid-1960s, at the climax of the heroic-activist stage of the civil rights movement. Perhaps the key event in the movement, in terms of a changing southern consciousness, came earlier, with the student sit-ins, which began in February 1960 when four students at North Carolina

Agricultural and Technical College in Greensboro sat at a lunch counter to de-segregate it. Ella Baker, executive director of the Southern Christian Leadership Council, attributed this spontaneous protest to "the young enthusiasm and the need for action." The student protest was a very middle-class one. Students as-pired to the American dream of increased opportunity, with particular south-ern meanings as the region was economically growing and well-educated Black students wanted a part of that dream. The student sit-ins were a new tactic, and they reflected a generational shift in protest methods, as the young were show-ing impatience with the lack of progress in changing the segregated southern way of life. College campuses now joined churches as organizational centers of the Black freedom movement. Student protests and boycotts shattered the fragile racial peace of the South, with the southern elite's hope for civility before justice shattered along the way.[115]

The sit-ins were a landmark in the consciousness of both Black and white southerners regarding changes to the segregated southern way of life. For cen-turies, white southerners had engaged in the rhetorical and representational degradation of Black people, with accompanying expectations of behavioral submissiveness, enforced by intimidation and lethal violence if necessary. Fred Powledge, a North Carolina journalist, noted how racial customs had become so engrained in the white South that if whites "did notice it, it was in the way they noticed water flowing from a tap or hot weather in the summertime—it was unremarkable." The concept of the segregated southern way of life had be-come so normalized over generations as to be beyond question to many white southerners. The sit-ins were significant in empowering Black southerners, as the act of protesting gave students a sense of their own worth and effectiveness in challenging Jim Crow. The scope of the protest by 1961 discredited the white southern myth that Black southerners were happy with segregation. Black stu-dents dressed in their Sunday best and often carried college textbooks as they undertook their sit-ins at the lunch counters, and their demeanor inspired other African Americans.[116]

If Black consciousness of the possibility of social change took a giant leap forward with the sit-ins, the protests challenged white attitudes about Black people. Southern whites could not claim these college students were outside agitators, and their obvious discontent with the segregated southern way of life was hard to rationalize. Richmond editor James J. Kilpatrick, who had led the massive resistance effort in the South, was startled at the demeanor of the student protesters. He wrote an influential editorial that admired the Black students, who were "in coats, white shirts, ties, and one of them was reading Goethe, and was taking notes from a biology text." Meanwhile, a gang of white boys came to heckle—"a ragtag rabble, slack-jawed, black-jacketed, grinning fit to kill." Reflecting on the effect of the sit-ins on white southern consciousness, he admitted that "it gives one pause." Atlanta newspaper editor Ralph McGill wrote that the student protesters "have fitted none of the stereotypes. Lazy, ignorant, unclean." That was "one reason why the students in their sit-ins have produced such a revolutionary effect"; indeed, the word "revolutionary" could now be increasingly used to describe the effect of Black protest on white consciousness about Black southerners.[117]

Leslie Dunbar's 1964 article "The Changing Mind of the South: The Exposed Nerve" concluded that not until the Greensboro sit-ins "did 'the mind' of the Negro become of conscious interest to white Southerners," with the student protests leading to "an active awareness" that the "southern consensus had to include Negro values and desires." He saw it as one of the "historical markers at that dime store in Greensboro: here is where after more than three centuries, the white South and the Negro South were finally met." Calvin Trillin, who covered the South during the civil rights movement, saw the sit-ins as "the psychological turning point." As hundreds of Black college and university students risked "injury by sitting nonviolently at whites-only lunch counters, it had become more and more difficult to claim that both white and black people would be content with the Southern Way of Life if outsiders would just stop interfering."[118]

One of the most perceptive views of the relationship of the sit-ins to the southern way of life came from South Carolinian James McBride Dabbs. In "Christian Response to Racial Revolution," delivered in April 1964 at the Acworth Presbyterian Church in Acworth, Georgia, Dabbs argued that a "racial revolution" was taking place in the South, and he brought attention to the Greensboro sit-in students by echoing Kilpatrick's stress on their good manners. "Is not good manners," Dabbs asked, "the quality on which the South, justly or unjustly, has prided itself most?" And were not those students, "by this standard, good southerners?" He added that they were indeed violating racial etiquette, but "stirred by the winds of freedom which at long last had blown to them across the pages of the Bible," they saw "now no place for racial etiquette." They simply discarded it in making their revolution against the segregated southern way of life, and "perhaps the essence of this revolution is a redefinition of the great words of the South." He noted that southerners had been a "people of great words: courtesy, honor, integrity, truth, courage, love." African American protesters were making whites, he said, look at these words "and see what they mean for today," and perhaps in the process "the South will not be lost but found." Dabbs pointed out that the students came onto the pages of history not only with southern good manners but "with a religious heart" as well, again reflecting southern traditions most whites affirmed. The region had "a complex social culture, a rich web of manners, covering the surface of life, shutting off from daily view the mystery, the violence, the terror of life." He used the term "web of manners" from the traditional southern, white way-of-life lexicon, but noted its incompatibility with deeper faith.[119]

Dabbs raised up the students from the sit-ins because "these well-mannered, quiet-spirited, committed youngsters" had displayed the deep piety of the South but combined it with "a sense of social justice drawn straight from the great prophets but never stressed in the South before." The students were revolutionary in uniting the religious piety of the South with a religious demand for social justice that the white South had not made. Dabbs glimpsed God's providence and grace working through the students and applied his own Presbyterian theology to the movement. "Is this not God's most gracious Spirit giving us at last what we tried so long unsuccessfully to get?" Dabbs thus positioned the sit-in students at the forefront of contemporary efforts to understand the South's sense of mission and destiny. "As I see the racial revolution in the South, then, it is the Spirit of God working for freedom against bondage, and it is the spirit of the South discarding old evils, creating new goods." He urged his listeners to "welcome the revolution, both as Christians and as southerners—as southern Christians." To be sure, few white southerners at that point embraced Dabbs's prophetic view, but his words imbued the sit-ins with a powerful meaning as a turning point for African Americans in their struggle and for white southerners in grappling with the larger spiritual meaning of African American protest.[120]

The Civil Rights Movement in the Mid-1960s

The emergence of SNCC resulted from Ella Baker's organization of an event funded by the Southern Christian Leadership Council in April 1960 at Shaw University in Raleigh, North Carolina. Some 120 Black students and a dozen whites gathered to hear King's keynote call for nonviolent protest.

Baker was a key figure in the history of the civil rights movement, serving as the community organizer. She particularly stressed the importance of young people. "I knew that the young people were the hope of any movement," she said. By 1960, she had long dreamed of a southern youth-centered mass movement, and she nurtured young African Americans from the region, many of whom had not had the opportunity for community organizing that students from the North had. Baker was confident that the students who had started the sit-ins of their own initiative could be an example of the participatory democracy she promoted. Baker also witnessed against the sexism sometimes on display in the male-dominated, older civil rights organizations.[121]

James Lawson became a major figure in the early days of the organization, and he drew on profound knowledge of nonviolence from his time as a missionary in India observing Gandhi and from his work as a southern field secretary for the Fellowship of Reconciliation. He studied theology at Vanderbilt and trained such key SNCC organizers as Marion Barry, James Bevel, Diane Nash, and John Lewis, who played central roles in the Nashville sit-ins. SNCC's young activists brought innovative tactics, greater militancy, a heightened sense of racial consciousness, and an emphasis on work in local communities and decentralized organization. Although embracing nonviolence, some in the group contested that idea. On the one hand, John Lewis recalled that SNCC activists "believed in the philosophy and discipline of nonviolence." For many in the group it was not just a protest tactic but "a philosophy," becoming "a way of life, a way of doing things, a way of living." Lewis said that when the sit-in students went to their lunch counters, "it was like going to church" because they dressed in "church-going clothes, Sunday clothes," and sat quietly, "trying to be as dignified as possible." Lewis here links the nonviolent way of life to the southern manners and religiosity that Dabbs stressed, and he invested considerable meaning in that way of life as an alternative to the segregated southern way of life.[122]

Civil rights activist Constance Curry recalled the debates that SNCC members had about nonviolence as "argument after argument of whether or not nonviolence was a technique or a way of life." She insisted that "nonviolence as a way of life was good as an ideal, but it was something that was absolutely alien to all our backgrounds and the way that we were raised," as she pointed to the violence inherent in the segregated southern way of life. Curry had grown up the child of a well-off white family, received an excellent education at Agnes Scott College, and was an experienced worker for the National Student Association before joining SNCC. She affirmed the nonviolent way of life as a philosophy, but noted that southerners raised in a culture that was familiar with violence were disturbed by "being beaten and thrown into jail and trying to love everybody while they did it to you." In any event, "way of life" and the southern context here enriched the discussion of the concept among these young activists.[123]

The freedom rides gave SNCC an early sense of purpose. The Congress of Racial Equality had launched this initiative of integrated buses throughout the South to test whether southern states were abiding by court rulings prohibiting segregated seating on interstate transportation. White mobs attacked the freedom riders in Anniston, Alabama, and again in Birmingham. At that point,

when the Congress of Racial Equality withdrew, SNCC workers resumed the
freedom rides, which resulted in violence in Jackson, Mississippi, and New
Orleans. Other initiatives included freedom schools, which taught academic
lessons but also citizenship and helped produce new young activists, community centers, and voter registration campaigns.[124]

SNCC workers went into local African American communities to mobilize
poor and working-class people. Women such as Nash, Curry, and Jane Stem-
bridge were important leaders in the movement, and their religious faith often
empowered African American women to play active roles in SNCC projects.
Fannie Lou Hamer was one of the most extraordinary leaders working with
SNCC in her home region, the Mississippi Delta. She had picked cotton since
she was six. The daughter of sharecroppers, she was as powerless as one could
be in post–World War II America, but she was invaluable to SNCC workers
who came into the Delta in the early 1960s and found the mature, down-to-
earth, deeply religious African American woman who would be essential in
motivating other Delta Black people to register to vote. When she went to register, she lost her position on the plantation, she and her husband faced endless
financial and social intimidation, and jailors viciously beat her in the Winona,
Mississippi, county jail. But these experiences did not deter her from combat-
ting what she called the "plantation mentality" of Black people automatically
deferring to whites. Religion and music were important contributions she made
to the freedom movement that came out of southern Black culture and that
she applied now to ending the segregated southern way. A Missionary Baptist
who had regularly attended worship and Bible study in Ruleville, she grew up
with the scriptural knowledge of the Black Baptist church. Hamer could cite
scripture about characters wrestling with the devil, whom she saw in literal
terms among too many whites in the Delta. She began working for SNCC in
1963, encouraging sharecroppers to register to vote during the day and taking
an active part in the mass meetings at night in local churches. She sang from
her endless supply of spirituals and new freedom songs, and she insisted that
"singing brings out the soul."[125]

By the early 1960s, civil rights activists were on the offensive in struggles
over the southern identity in Oxford and Neshoba County, Mississippi, and in
Birmingham and Selma, Alabama. As great battlefields of southern identity
and imagination, they ranked now in the southern imagination with Shiloh,
Manassas, Antietam, and Gettysburg.[126]

Freedom Summer was another of the civil rights projects in the early 1960s
that added to the momentum for overturning the segregated southern way of
life, with Mississippi now the focus of the movement's attention. It became the
leading national news story that summer and illustrated the national media's

Fannie Lou Hamer sang spirituals, gospel songs, and freedom songs to inspire civil rights activists in the 1960s. Alabama Department of Archives and History.

centrality to the civil rights movement's successes. The national media saw race as a southern story and dispatched reporters, photographers, and camera crews to cover it. Many white southern journalists became key figures in explaining the story to the nation, and the most prestigious news forums offered a morality tale, at times, with civil rights protesters clearly a moral force and white southern resisters an enemy to the nation's democracy. Dramatic images of the region offered visual documentation of the segregated southern way of life. National press coverage became important in establishing a national consensus toward new civil rights legislation by the mid-1960s. Images of Birmingham's fire hoses and vicious police dogs attacking demonstrators were a landmark, but similar scenes from places such as Greenwood in 1964 told of coming social change. The death of three civil rights workers (James Cheney, Andrew Goodman, and Michael Schwerner) that summer, and the media's full coverage of what happened, left Mississippi exposed to the world with the vicious underpinnings of the segregated southern way of life now on public view for the nation and the world.[127]

Selma, Alabama, offered the dramatic climax to the most dramatic stage of the civil rights struggle against the southern way of life, with its violent foundations again revealed for national audiences. In January 1965, King announced a campaign to focus on advancing African Americans' right to vote in Alabama, another of the more intransigent places for civil rights workers. Civil rights activists staged several months of courthouse demonstrations, but few African Americans gained the vote. In January, over 100 Black teachers marched, with funeral directors and barbers soon following suit. On March 15, 1965, President Johnson addressed a joint session of Congress and endorsed the voting rights bill. Describing himself as "a man whose roots go deeply into southern soil" and aware of "how agonizing racial feelings are," he insisted that all Americans had to "overcome the crippling legacy of bigotry and injustice." He ended his speech with the civil rights movement anthem, saying, "We shall overcome." King proposed a Selma-to-Montgomery march that spring and hoped for the support of the federal government. Alabama governor George Wallace refused the permit for the proposed march, but demonstrators proceeded anyway, resulting in a stunning scene of Alabama state troopers' uncontrolled beatings of marchers on the Edmund Pettus Bridge in what became known as Bloody Sunday. Johnson activated the national guard, and on March 21 2,000 federal troops accompanied marchers from Selma to Montgomery. White onlookers shouted insults and waved Confederate flags that evoked once more the Lost Cause in defiance of impending social change. "The South is all gone," a man nonetheless told Assistant Attorney General John Doar. "A whole way of life is going right into memory."[128]

The Civil Rights Acts of 1964 and 1965 and the Voting Rights Act of 1965 overturned segregation laws and promoted the return of Blacks to southern politics. The end of legal segregation and voter disfranchisement in the South and the opening of economic opportunities to many Blacks throughout the nation were signal victories for the civil rights movement. Accompanying what observers called a social revolution in the South were changes fundamental to the southern way of life. The discourtesies, disrespect, and indignities of everyday life declined and became increasingly unacceptable throughout the South. As King had predicted, many protesters gained a new self-respect as participants in a collective movement, one that boosted Black pride and African American cultural awareness. The movement's victories opened the way for further activism in the late 1960s to address economic inequalities in American life, and activists moved beyond the southern context and faced the end of a national consensus on the need for civil rights reforms and an active white backlash. The southern social system had been fundamentally altered thanks to the movement.

The late 1960s and the 1970s saw a dramatic decline in the use of the term "southern way of life" as its segregated meaning virtually disappeared from public discussion. Some observers thought the concept behind the term would vanish altogether, but new ideologies emerged as Americans reimagined the South without legal segregation. The South adjusted to the end of segregation and new visions struggled to replace it—if the concept of the South and its once distinctive way of life were to survive at all.

In the years after 2019, many southern cities, towns, and college campuses removed
Confederate statues, as in this photograph of the removal of the statue from inner
campus at the University of Mississippi. Photograph by Jackson Newman.

PART III

SOUTHERN LIVING

SOUTHERN LIVING magazine began publishing its house-and-garden stories in 1966, a propitious time as the American South began its transition into a postsegregationist era, and the magazine's assertion of new southern ways growing out of older ones became a model for a new regional consciousness thereafter. Racial changes came at the same time the world economy was undergoing striking developments that moved away from older models of industrial manufacturing, embraced globalization, evolved new fluidity in managing laboring people, and relied on consumer spending to drive prosperity. In the South, regional consciousness moved from older rural-based, agricultural, historically obsessed, racially segregated assumptions into a new context, one that regional culture would soon explore and project, rooted in the past but facing the future. Part 3 assesses the elements that came to be seen as southern living. Within the flux and ephemera that came to characterize what scholars call "postmodernism" in the years after 1970, maintaining the traditions that once defined regional identity has been ever more difficult. The vanishing South has been a frequent theme of commentators who claim no South exists anymore since the conditions that gave rise to it historically have clearly evaporated.

Southern identity has been transformed and reimagined in the five decades since 1970, rather than disappearing. The growth of the middle class, movement of people to suburbs, concentration of African American and ethnic populations in larger cities, increased prosperity, stress on lifestyles, desire for authenticity despite the challenges of obtaining it, and, above all, ethic of consumption have defined the newest South. Despite a changed context for regional identity, the enduring themes of race and religion continue to play an outsized role in southern self-consciousness. Whites have used political power and economic advantages to retain as much privilege as possible within a modern, diverse southern society. With the end of the segregated South, African Americans in the region have embraced regional identities. Although critical of political and public policy attitudes of the white majority, Black southerners claim a formative role in southern identity, driving its contemporary manifestations in many ways. The term "country cosmopolitan" describes the predominant Black southern regional consciousness seen in films, fiction, memoirs, television shows, magazines, and other popular culture venues.

Religion has remained a vital force, serving as a sanctuary for southerners of all sorts who continue to support evangelical Protestant churches in greater numbers than anywhere in the world. Religious-based political issues such as school prayer, abortion, and (from a different ideological position) gay rights have stoked regional passions. Civil religious impulses still flow in the South, although now national, rather than regional, issues often bring them to attention. Racial reconciliation has been one of the most powerful movements in the contemporary South that touches the civil religious belief that the South still has a destiny: to redeem the nation from racial injustice. In the twenty-first century, the South has been the new Immigrant Belt, attracting large numbers of Latino, Asian, and Middle Eastern people who have enriched and complicated understandings of the South as well as the nation. The result has been a new multicultural southern living. Culture has become central to regional consciousness, and part 3 explores how music, literature, sports, food, and regional magazines all express a transformed and heightened southern identity.

CHAPTER SEVEN

Imagining New Ways for the South

Adjustment to Change, Economic Ways, Interracial Ways, Conservative Ways

I N SEPTEMBER 1976, *Time* magazine published a special section, "The South Today," after Georgia governor Jimmy Carter gained the Democratic Party's presidential nomination. Appearing only a decade or so after the high point of the civil rights movement and a negative image of the South in the national media in the 1960s, the issue was a glowing report of the South's progress in race relations, economic development, and preservation of a distinctive culture with much to offer the nation. The changed national attitude was apparent in the issue's essay on southern food, entitled "A Home-Grown Elegance." In the 1960s, national journalistic reports on the South would typically have referred to the South's cuisine as greasy food and overcooked vegetables served in a cheap diner to rednecks. But the 1976 view differed substantially. "Southerners quite possibly devote more time to the preparation and consumption of breakfast, lunch and dinner than any other society since Augustan Rome," the report said. It praised "the world's most abundant living larder" as the basis of the South's cuisine, which, the essay insisted, "for variety and piquancy, ranks with anything served in Florence or Provence." Educated palates, the essay beamed, would find "a Southern meal, at its diverse best, is worth the price of a ticket to Marseille or Milan." Gulf Coast shrimp, the piece said breathlessly, was as "memorable as Proustian *madeleines*." Readers must have thought, Book a flight to New Orleans.[1]

If food was a particularly revealing feature of this newest South, other forms of abundance and pleasure were foretold as well. The essay "The Good Life" opened with Sir Walter Raleigh's classic description of the Garden of Eden being found on a line of latitude that came to connect Raleigh, North Carolina, and Memphis, Tennessee, noting that ever after southerners had embraced "the concept of the idyllic South." Although romantic moonlight-and-magnolias mythology had distorted the concept beyond belief, the writer claimed that the South remained "a largely rural land of spectacular beauty and prolific

Time magazine's special issue "The South Today" in 1976 represented the region's rising national reputation in the 1970s and the ascendancy of the southern living concept. Charles Reagan Wilson Collection, Archives and Special Collections, John Davis Williams Library, University of Mississippi Library, Oxford, Mississippi.

resources for recreation and sentient delight." In an interview, writer James Dickey commented on the importance of "passing the time" in the South—"to sit on country porches and courthouse Confederate monuments and on green benches in public parks and tell each other stories, gossip and use words." Leisure loomed large in this appreciative take on an essential South of strong community bonding and outdoor sporting life. Drawing at least in part on the Agrarians' concepts and showing the continuing influence of their manifesto, the article concluded that, "despite the threats of urbanization, industrialization and pollution, Southerners have retained a vision of the good life, secular and spiritual, that may survive."[2]

The good southern life, moreover, was a biracial one, in a region that now embraced the integrated ideal. Young white political leaders understood this new reality, based on their pursuit of African American votes that were now determining elections thanks to new voter registration efforts. Democrats, especially, appreciated the vibrancy of biracial coalitions in the 1970s. Vernon Jordan, executive director of the National Urban League, said that he preferred doing business with "a converted Southerner" rather than a northern liberal. The latter was "basically paternalistic," always "looking down on you," whereas a southern white converted to racial reconciliation, "why, he would die for you."

Terry Sanford, president of Duke University, put it this way: "There was an understanding between the two peoples," which in the postsegregation time gave a common biracial background for engagement.

The special issue quoted others, however, who were not so positive about the postsegregation hope for achieving King's dream of a beloved community in the South. African American writer Jack White noted, for example, that white southerners might be taking pride in racial progress, but they had fought it at every step of the way. Several other African Americans observed that white southerners were not trying to destroy Black people, but, as one Nashville minister put it, "whites simply don't pay much attention to blacks."[3]

Time was onto a changed southern consciousness that first emerged in the 1960s and advanced in the 1970s, centered on the ideology of the biracial South. It rose to mythic level and became in that decade one of the formative myths of a reimagined regional consciousness. But the magazine also caught the continuing conservative nature of much of the southern lifestyle and an emerging conservative politics beneath the radar of the triumphant progressive Democrats. The lead article in the magazine's special section was called "The Spirit of the South," and it portrayed the region as "the last American arena with a special, nurtured identity, its own sometimes unfashionable regard for the soil, for family ties, for the authority of God and country." Despite the coming of outsiders, it remained "a redoubt of old American tenets, enshrined for centuries by the citizenry." This vision of the reimagined South blurred the lines between region and country, but old values remained the key.[4]

Time's writers also noted that "Christian revelation is a way of life in Dixie" and captured the centrality of religion to the postsegregation conservative southern ideology. The magazine singled out patriotism, respect for law and order, and family values, as well as religiosity, as key components of an ideology rooted in the past but freed from racial concerns—at least in theory. "Small-Town Soul," another essay, embraced the concept of soul as a special southern quality that captured "the Southerness of the South." The small town, the essay continued, was "the custodian of the Southern life-style." Lifestyle would indeed be the concept that anchored not only a conservative ideology that competed with the biracial ideology but an idea that appealed to many progressives as well.[5]

One other idea ran through the magazine's exploration of the South, namely the division between looking toward the past and looking toward the future. "The South," one writer said, was "particularly complex and contradictory, a mix of modern and ancient, traditional and futuristic." But the writer added that increasingly, "that conversation concerns tomorrow and not yesterday," with such examples as growing cities, economic diversity, and national influences on the newest South. C. Vann Woodward, the South's preeminent historian, prepared an essay, "The South Tomorrow," for the issue, and he wrote that, traditionally, cultural influences had gone from north to south, but recent changes suggested the South was not only becoming Americanized but was also southernizing the nation. Historians do not like to predict the future, Woodward recognized, but he speculated that the economic gap between the North and South would soon close, and he anticipated, accurately, that southern political leaders would once again dominate national politics, as in the early national period. Woodward was a liberal, and most of his projections reflected the hope that liberalism would become a stronger force in the future South, based in biracialism. But he foresaw that "much of the old distinctiveness" would be retained, including "much of the old courtesy, the antique personalism, the familial ambience, the love of place, the abhorrence of abstraction, the fear of being computerized." They were all "down-home ways" that represented the instincts of Black southerners as well as white, created "by white Southerners and Afro-Americans, during the centuries of their Southern experience." The content of this subculture, though, rested on inherited conservative values that would, as well as the biracial ideal, provide ideological ingredients for a postsegregation version of southern living.[6]

By 1976, all these concepts already framed the adjustment of the South's people to the dramatic changes not only in race relations but in economic activity as well. National attitudes toward the South had begun to shift as well, seeing the region's potential ability to push the nation toward better "human values" in race relations and, more broadly, social values of the good life. The South's adjustment to the end of Jim Crow segregation began, of course, earlier, with the economic development that raced through the region after World War II, the end of the worst white resistance to racial change, and particular ways that the region gave up its old race-based social, political, economic, and cultural systems. The story of this chapter is, then, one of the post–World War II economic advances in the region, the adjustment from the mid-1960s onward to the new federal legislation that brought social changes, and the definition of two ideological imaginings of a postsegregation South.

Economic Development

Economic development transformed the South at the same time southerners experienced the dramatic changes associated with the civil rights movement. State governments as far back as the Depression tried to diversify their economies by promoting the region as an attractive location for business and industry. Mississippi had pioneered with its Balance Agriculture with Industry project in the 1930s, and other states developed state planning agencies. They advertised the virtues of their states, assisted companies in establishing factories, trained workers, provided low-cost or free land, and gave generous tax relief for industrial development. C. Vann Woodward identified the "bulldozer revolution" as one remaking the social economy and landscape. "Hell, what we've been selling is peace and order," said one industrial promoter in Arkansas, "telling 'em what we've got down here is stability—friendly politicians who are not going to gut a business with taxes, and workers who are grateful for a job and are not going to be stirring up trouble." Mississippi editor Hodding Carter noted the varying southern attitude toward northerners. "A Northerner with new ideas might get a quick brushoff or worse, but a Northerner with a new factory deserved the best of southern hospitality." Such sentiments reflected a new regional boosterism. The booster had long been a familiar figure in southern small towns and cities, but never to the degree of cultural influence seen in the post–World War II decades. Real estate brokers, insurance agents, construction contractors, retailers, managers of public utilities, bankers, media executives, attorneys, doctors, and other professionals became the "new middle class" that increasingly influenced civic life.[7]

In 1955, *Business Week* published an extensive analysis of the southern economy called "In Dixie, the Colonel Moves Over." The issue pointed out that "just as the South is changing economically, it's also changing socially." With the social changes came "some new types of southern businessmen." The article claimed that "the leisurely businessman of stereotype" was fast vanishing. One Nashville employer said, "You don't sit under the magnolia tree sipping mint juleps any more." The magazine offered a revealing typology of southern businessmen at that point: The Old School Traditionalist had roots "planted deep in the traditions and folklore of the South," but that type was nearing retirement and would soon be a point of nostalgia. The Conservative Old School Southerner was conservative in politics and an upscale evangelical Baptist or Methodist. "He dresses quietly, drinks moderately, is a staunch family man," the story said. He was an advocate for industry for the South but "dislikes the social changes it fosters." The New School Southern Businessman, on the other hand, "might be the son of an old school type, who can and does succeed in any business environment." He operates at the national level and is at home in the East as much as in the South. The Transplanted Yankee was becoming a familiar type, one who had come south some time earlier, at first with a northern company, but liked the region and soon started a new company. The Transient Businessman was the final, and most discontented, type. He was "earmarked for bigger and better things with his company" but was not necessarily happy about spending years in the South before returning to the North to the home office.[8]

Economic development worldviews shaped the politics of postwar gover-
nors such as Sid McMath in Arkansas, Gordon Browning in Tennessee, and
Luther Hodges in North Carolina. An ethos of businesslike efficiency in government and state-sponsored infrastructure projects gained wide popularity.
"Industrialization, then, with all its advantages to the people and the state," said
Hodges, "became the number one goal of my administration." Economic development politicians promoted economic change but not racial desegregation.
They were ready to abandon rigid white supremacy if it conflicted with their
economic projects because of unfavorable national publicity over the South's
racial problems.

Sociologist Leonard Riessman observed in 1966 that the new southern
middle class represented the revolt of a modernizing bourgeoisie against an
old agrarian social elite, and he saw this new middle class as a future elite
that would inevitably gain social and political authority. Historian Numan V.
Bartley added that "the 'southern way of life' had long been an impediment
to economic progress," but by 1960 "a formidable segment of southern society
provided the basis for challenging the old regime." After the end of legal segregation and political disfranchisement in the mid-1960s, this new middle-class
elite would indeed become the South's new ruling class.[9]

A decade earlier, scholarly analysis was markedly less optimistic. Despite
undeniable economic development through the 1950s, political scientist William Nicholls, in *Southern Tradition and Regional Progress* (1960), had surveyed
the extent of southern economic change at the beginning of a new decade,
and he warned of "the possible conflicts between tradition and progress within
the greater South." He argued that areas of the South that had most departed
from the traditional values associated with the Vanderbilt Agrarians were
doing economically better than those areas that had not moved away from
traditionalism. He placed his argument in the global context, and he saw the
same conflict in such underdeveloped nations as Brazil, Turkey, and India. He
related his economic analysis to developments in race relations in the South.
"With the recent revivification in the South of traditional race antagonisms as
a result of the school integration issue," he wrote, "I completely lost any residual
belief that the South could successfully reconcile tradition and progress." He
insisted that "the South must choose between tradition and progress." He focused his attention "on those aspects of Southern tradition—as reflected in the
South's value system, its social and political structures, and its way of looking
at social and intellectual issues—which I find are serious barriers to Southern
economic development." Nicholls pointed to the South's cultural heritage as an
economic problem, and he concluded that the region's material progress had
come about "in spite of the strongly inhibiting social, political, psychological,

and philosophical elements in the Old South's cultural heritage." To complete the beginnings of economic modernization in the region, "many of those still-strong qualities of mind and spirit which have made the South distinctive must largely disappear."[10]

Nicholls cited newspaper editor Ralph McGill's observation that southern political leaders "seeking new enterprises never saw themselves as carriers of the virus which was to destroy the *status quo* in their towns" and in the process "the old 'way of life' in the South." In the early South, the qualities of individualism, appreciation of leisure, and enjoyment of the land and nature were "traits that in fact discouraged a diverse economy and the disciplined labor for industrial activity." Nicholls indicted the South's religious preoccupations as nurturing a fatalism and an inability to deal with racial relationships at the center of the South's social life, as the "South's moral leadership . . . has been found most wanting." A white southerner, Nicholls acknowledged "there is something pleasant and precious about the Southern way of life which we like, or we wouldn't be here." The southern way was not perfect, though, and he lamented the intellectual conformity that discouraged such criticism as he was offering. By the end of the 1960s, in any event, the material standard of living in the South had notably risen from the 1940s. Per capita income rose more rapidly in the decades after World War II in the South than anywhere in the nation. The South's economy by the 1960s was more urbanized, industrialized, and commercialized than it was agricultural.[11]

Southern Business Way of Life

The end of the segregated southern way of life came at the same time as the southern business way of life continued to expand. North Carolina editor Jonathan Daniels's "The Ever-Ever Land" appeared in *Harper's* in April 1965, and he saw the South looking now not so much to the past as to the future for its expanding economic identity. "Nothing is more precious in the South," he wrote, "so long supposed to be clinging to legends of the past, than myths about tomorrow." His words represented a seismic shift in attitudes. Since the Civil War, the region had "always needed the romanticized recollections of great days gone to sustain its dignity in poverty," but now it "desperately required what may be a new mythology of unequaled economic advance." Reviewing evidence of social and economic changes in the region, he warned against ignoring the reality that "the South remains the American region of lowest per capita income, least education, and most limited hope." He was skeptical of the "frayed fantasy" of "the new, new ever new South." He noted the receptivity of southerners to industrial recruiters come south. "Never before has there been

The postwar South became more modern than ever, even celebrating its role
as home to the Atomic City on this postcard. Charles Reagan Wilson Collection,
Archives and Special Collections, John Davis Williams Library,
University of Mississippi Library, Oxford, Mississippi.

such a welcoming, with bands and banquets, of carpetbaggers." Compared to
earlier efforts to recruit northern industry, "a softer Southern voice speaks in
welcome now," represented by more "golf courses and magnolia trees, crino-
lined girls and juleps on the piazza." He recognized that "cheaper labor is never
entirely concealed" and warned against ignoring those southerners in most
need and "the insistence on keeping people down." Through regional planning
efforts of the Tennessee Valley Authority and the new Research Triangle Park
in North Carolina, he glimpsed a hope for improvement in the lives of Black
and poor white southerners. At that hopeful point in time, when progressive
southerners could see the possibilities for reimagining the postsegregation
South, Daniels even allowed himself to imagine the region could fulfill a redemptive role—"the fulfillment of the American dream."[12]

Southern Airways was a good example of a new southern business representing advanced technology and claims to modernity while also trying to
represent itself in traditional southern ways. In 1968 an Atlanta advertising
company came up with a "Southern Style" campaign for the airline. As it said
in announcing the promotion, "Southern Style is folksy. This is because the
South is folksy." Employees received a card as representatives of Southern Style
and committed to "enthusiastic support to bring our customers the warm and
friendly attitude that is traditional in the South." Employees pledged, more

specifically out of southern mythology, to provide "genuine Southern Style service with emphasis on courtesy and hospitality." Those working for Southern Airways also embraced an ethic of business growth and offered themselves to "the growth of Southern Airways and to the growth of the areas we serve." How southern hospitality manifested itself in this context was through on-time flights and fast baggage handling—something passengers could easily embrace as the best of the southern way. The airline served sixty cities in the "growing South," and by 1968 it had entered northern markets. It enticed passengers in those places with, an advertisement said, "the culture of the South." Perhaps the most dramatic expression of the Southern Style campaign came at the St. Louis airport, where the airline's counter was decorated like an old southern mansion, with tall white columns that gave those boarding their flights the feeling of coming into the "big house" on a plantation. Hostesses on flights out of that city wore hoop skirts befitting the modern stewardess as a southern belle.[13]

As Daniels noted, southern business leaders identified cheap southern labor as a tangible advantage in pursuing their materialistic dreams of the southern business way of life. Chambers of commerce boasted of the lack of labor problems in southern communities, code for repressive public policies on labor unions. Workers were commodities figuring in the profit/loss tally. The white working class faced the end of the segregated southern way of life with trepidation because of the anticipated negative effect it would have on them. Releasing African Americans from the few menial employment opportunities they had traditionally been given was a great victory for them, but white workers feared the new competition. The seniority system in which whites had always had the advantage with Black workers now seemed endangered for whites. Skin color had given even the poorest of southern whites special privileges, the "wages of whiteness," over Black people, but now the rights and privileges associated with being white began eroding. "These white people never believed they were poor in the way that Negroes were poor," wrote North Carolina's Harry Golden. "White men had hope." The white working class by the late 1960s recognized that the vanishing of the southern way of life would affect them more than it did southern elites. In 1968, Raymond Wheeler of the Southern Regional Council wrote that "where desegregation has taken place, the poorer, uneducated white, least able to cope with the change, has become the most involved." Well-off neighborhoods "stay lily white, while public housing desegregated." Restaurants, movie theaters, and public swimming pools had become desegregated while country clubs, private schools, and private dining clubs remained all-white. The transition years of what some see as the end of the southern way of life thus had differing social-class results for white southerners.[14]

Economic development accelerated in the South in the 1960s, but political resistance to social change did not align with this transformation. Black southerners and their allies were driving history by the early 1960s, and white protesters against change entered a new period of resistance but one that represented the last gasp of resistance. Alabama governor George Wallace led the movement dominated by the white working and middle classes to try to use states' rights theories and a national constituency to slow racial change. In Wallace's inaugural address, delivered in Montgomery on January 14, 1963, he evoked the Confederate past as a contemporary mandate. He noted that he stood "where once Jefferson Davis stood" and that "from this Cradle of the Confederacy, this very Heart of the Great Anglo-Saxon Southland," it was appropriate "that today we should sound the drum for freedom as have our generations of forebears before us have done, time and again down through history." His rousing declaration was "I draw the line in the dust and toss the gauntlet before the feet of tyranny," as he boasted that he stood for "segregation now . . . segregation tomorrow . . . segregation forever." He praised white southerners who had helped build "this great divinely inspired system of freedom," and he thundered that as "God is our witness, Southerners will save it."[15]

Conservative James J. Kilpatrick offered a new defense of white supremacy that understood Jim Crow legal segregation was waning. In *The Southern Case for School Segregation* (1962), Kilpatrick abandoned any traditional southern white elite paternalism toward Black southerners and put the onus for southern problems on African American shoulders. He defined the South in traditional terms, and "southerner" applied only to white people. "Deference to women, principles of personal honor, the payment of a gentleman's debts—there are the operative aspects of the 'Southern Way of Life.'" Racial separation was at the center of that way of life. Recognizing that legal segregation was, to all effects, a dying concern by 1962, he defended de facto segregation as still relevant. He called it the South's "consciousness of the Negro," placing racism at the center of the way of life. Kilpatrick's book abandoned older arguments for racially determined racial segregation in favor of inflammatory attacks on African American character and morality as disqualifying them culturally for equality with white southerners. Kilpatrick was ahead of the curve in articulating a new conservative racism that spoke of a free-market engagement in which Black people could not compete and could not earn equality by merit. Not granting much to social change in this post–Jim Crow scenario, he positioned the white South for a tokenism that would avoid federal government pressures for desegregation while preserving as much of segregation as possible.[16]

National Image

The national media began to bring a new, more positive attitude to the South by the mid-1960s. With the legal basis of the segregated southern way of life ended by the Civil Rights Act of 1964 and the Voting Rights Act the following year, the South seemed to some observers to be at the beginning of a new era. *Look* magazine, one of the nation's most popular periodicals, published "The Fast-Changing South" on November 16, 1965. Two dozen editors and photographers and an artist traveled the back roads, small towns, and growing cities to produce a series of stories. Senior editor George H. Leonard said he wanted to go beyond the special reports that had been typical of national coverage of the South, including "the portentous gloom of pundits who take their cadence and their tune from Faulkner"; "the easy outrage" of reporters who failed to see the segregation in northern cities; and "the pseudo-scholarship" that lumped all southerners "into a single, unwieldy 'mind of the South' (a 'mind,' you will note, that is generally lily white)." Leonard pointed to change in the diversity of the region and the signs of an emerging new society—tall skyscrapers, well-funded arts centers, speedy interstate highways, and businessmen who had "become no less an enemy of the old order than the civil-rights worker." Highlighting as well that "there was an ugliness too, the kind you see on television screens and the other, more painful kind that afflicts the Southern heart," Leonard described his reporters facing harassment in small towns and rural places. But generally, the reporters and others received "the most touching and eager courtesy." The story recounted signs of racial progress, including integrated swimming pools, playgrounds, hotels, restaurants, and private parties. Black southerners "seemed to hold their heads higher than even five short years earlier," while white southerners "seemed more relaxed and confident." The image of the redemptive South, which would soon become a popular theme among liberals, suggested to *Look*'s reporters the "tantalizing possibility" that the South, "forced to make painful and conscious decisions about flaws not even admitted elsewhere, might solve its racial problems sooner than the rest of the nation."[17]

Another reporter for *Look*'s special issue, Fletcher Knebel, wrote on the South's changing politics, and he identified "the four R's of Dixie politics, race, registration, reapportionment and Republicans." He used the word "suddenly" to describe the onset of remarkable political changes: African American voters controlled the government of Macon County, Alabama; a Republican won a congressional seat in normally Democratic South Carolina; voters elected a Republican mayor in Hattiesburg, Mississippi, and an African American representative in the Tennessee legislature; new political authority came to the long-restricted cities; and twenty-three white southern congressmen in the House of Representatives voted for the initial passage of the voting rights bill. He saw the meaning of all these developments as a sign that the Solid South had "cracked wide open, and its boistering new politics" had become the most unpredictable in the country. The whites-only Democratic Party's long dominance and the political foundation of the southern way of life seemed to be approaching their end.[18]

By the mid-1960s observers such as those writing for *Look* saw a changing South, a place that had fought change with a vengeance but now recognized the new federal laws had created a context where segregation was no longer legal. Journalist William Emerson wrote in 1965 of "the slow, mighty shifts in the subsoils of custom, tradition, and way of life" at work in the process of school desegregation. Historian Jason Sokol characterized desegregation as "less a way of life than an experiment," which would take "years for the results to register." Supreme Court cases after *Brown* had pushed the region's people toward desegregated schools, but the court's 1969 decision in *Alexander v. Holmes* mandated immediate and thorough school desegregation. Where local communities continued to resist, courts regularly intervened.

Some white parents withdrew their children from school; by early 1970 some 400 segregation academies had enrolled over 300,000 children. But by 1973, the South had the nation's highest regional rate of high school desegregation. Willie Morris documented the integration of the Yazoo City, Mississippi, high school he had graduated from in the 1950s. In November 1970, several hundred whites, including key local leaders, signed a statement in the town newspaper backing the public schools. The school integrated in the winter of 1970, with 80 percent of whites remaining in public schools. Harold "Hardwood" Kelly, a former basketball coach and school superintendent at the time, called the change "a complete social revolution," revealing words from the ground level of southern change. Morris agreed: "An immense façade was beginning to crack," he said, and added that "if a true human revolution implies the basic restructuring of everyday life, the essential patterns of behavior toward other people, then what might be occurring here was a revolution, subtle and intensely complicated." In what was a traumatic time in Yazoo City, as throughout the South, most whites did not change their evaluation of Black inferiority, and family members often clashed over whether to accept desegregation. In Yazoo, as elsewhere, acceptance of change was often generational. Mayor Frank Myers of Americus, Georgia, claimed his children in integrated schools were leaving their racial prejudices behind. "It's gonna be our children finally who're going to deliver us out of this thing that's been going on down here ever since slavery."[19]

Culture shaped the new racial interaction in schools. Homecoming elections, cheerleading squads, and basketball lineups could lead to bitter disputes and resentments. In southern places where football was becoming a regional religion, the starting quarterback mattered, and in places where beauty queens were prime celebrities, cheerleaders dominated school life. Sports could bring people together across racial lines, as when superb athletes such as Herschel Walker in Georgia and Marcus Dupree in Mississippi became heroes to the white community despite being African American. But sports and other recreational aspects of school life could lead to conflicts as well. The songs played at school dances and the cheers at football games, for example, could be contested. Differences in African American and white understandings of style and aesthetics made for conflicts at times but also enriched new cultural expressions. The concept of "soul" became a 1970s African American contribution to broader southern culture. Again, schools were a space for Black soul to enter white minds. Thelma Barmum, the wife of a funeral director, said, "We gonna give the whites a little soul." She used another resonant word as well, saying, "We gonna give 'em some *tone*." A *Newsweek* story reported that "the blacks want more 'soul' in songs, while the whites prefer the stiffly traditional rah-rah-rah." When the team did incorporate "soul cheers," the "white girls moan that they just can't shake and shuffle like the blacks." In time, of course, they did.[20]

If schools were prime spaces where the South began transitioning from legal segregation to new arrangements, then places of public accommodation were as well. The Civil Rights Act of 1964 prohibited discrimination at government locations and any business engaging in interstate commerce—a broad rubric because supplies for restaurants, cafeterias, movie theaters, sports arenas, lunchrooms, and hotels and motels often were in an economic web of national distributers. Just before the passage of the 1964 Civil Rights Act, an Albany, Georgia, official predicted that "great changes are coming to the Southern way of life." Francis Pauley, head of the Georgia Council of Human Relations, used the key, recurring term to describe the abandonment of legal segregation when he observed that Black and white southerners ate together in public restaurants and sat together in movie theaters. "This is a revolution, whether people like it or not." Southern businessmen were at the center of this change, as they had to accommodate African Americans equally with white people. Angry scenes of conflict, loss of business, and alienation of Black and white customers alike resulted. Private clubs became one way in the late 1960s to avoid the impact of federal law. Hamburger stands, as well as other eating and drinking venues, were requiring "memberships" sometimes, which were only available to white people. John Doar, the chief of the Justice Department's Civil Rights Division, said that "you've got to prove it's a sham" to expose this attempt to avoid the civil rights law. In the first two years of the law's existence, authorities filed more than 1,600 complaints of discrimination in public accommodations in those years, although about half were eventually settled through voluntary integration. *Time* magazine concluded a report on compliance in 1966 by noting most hotels and restaurants in large southern cities did not discriminate against Black customers, but discrimination remained in smaller cities, towns, and rural areas.[21]

Food had been a powerful symbol and tangible reality of racial difference in the segregated South. The taboo of white and Black people eating together was only slightly below that of interracial sex in fearful white imaginations, so it was no surprise perhaps that restaurants became major sites of conflict as the region adjusted to the end of the segregated southern way of life. Purveyors of southern food were especially prominent in resisting the end of the southern way of food life, sometimes as prime symbols of resistance to the federal government. The American dream spoke of freedom and the opportunity to pursue social mobility, and restaurateurs, like other southern businessmen, spoke that language in lamenting that the government forced them to admit people to their businesses they did not want to serve. Lester Maddox, for example, was a white small businessman who operated a chicken restaurant in Atlanta, and in July 1964—just after the Civil Rights Act went into effect—he refused to serve African Americans who came to integrate his place. In an advertisement, he wrote that if he went to jail "it won't be Lester Maddox going to jail, nor just the Pickrick closing." Instead, it would be "freedom and liberty being placed behind bars for LIFE." Maddox saw the issue as defense of his property rights, and to keep from serving Black people, he pledged, "I'll use ax handles. I'll use guns, I'll use my fists." When sued, he went to court, but he admitted that he figured he would lose. "Our government will tell us we no longer can be free Americans," he complained, and insisted, "It's involuntary servitude; it's slavery of the first order." James Ollie McClung had owned Ollie's Barbecue in Birmingham since 1926, but in December 1964 he lost his court case that forced him to serve all potential customers. Shocked, he relied on a key concept to explain his understanding of his society: "The ownership and use of private property is basic to the American way of life." He agreed to integrate the next day, with five Black customers, one of whom allowed afterward, "We sure enjoyed Ollie's good barbecue." A Jackson, Mississippi, restaurant owner told a reporter in late 1964 that "desegregation of public accommodations does not basically alter the pattern of social life anywhere" and that's why "it has been accomplished as easily as it has."[22]

Paternalism had been an underlying linchpin of the southern way of life as far back as in talk of southern civilization before the Civil War. Southern ideology spoke of white elites having responsibility for poorer Black employees who worked for them; whites thought assisting individual Black people they knew were in need represented the underlying kindness in the segregated southern way of life, rather than being part of an exploitive system of racial control. But this key concept took a fatal hit with the new assertiveness of African Americans during the 1950s and 1960s. White planters, for example, often wrote of Black workers as being like dependent children they had to loan money to from time to time, bail them out for small scrapes with the law, and keep on the plantation in old age. A story on Louisiana planters concluded that the civil rights movement presented that "mind-set with an inescapable challenge." Planters had thought that what they did for submissive Black workers were kind acts, but civil rights assertiveness represented for the white planter "a massive rejection of the decency with which he had tried to live his life." The challenges to the segregated southern way of life coincided with the coming of agribusiness to plantation regions, and the self-image of compassionate planters soon gave way to the calculating business manager adhering to the bottom line.[23]

As Knebel had noted in his 1965 *Look* article on postsegregation southern politics, changes were dramatic in the once Solid South, none more so than the election in the late 1960s of the first Black sheriffs in the Deep South. The issue came into focus, for example, in Greene County, Alabama, where the incumbent white sheriff, Bill Lee, barely beat African American candidate Thomas Gilmore in 1966. On the scene, reporter Marshall Frady observed that "it would be hard to exaggerate the harrowing implications in those days for the rural white Southerner of a black running for sheriff of his county." The sheriff was an "absolute totem image of all authority and order out in the Southern countryside." One white man he interviewed told Frady, "Goddam, nothing could be worse than this." The man drew from his evangelical language of the ultimate battle between good and evil in predicting that "this is Armageddon." Such language perhaps justified Frady's overall conclusion about the transformative years of the 1950s and 1960s as a time when southern whites met challenges such as the first Black sheriff not as "a moral adventure" but as an "elemental tribal matter of embattlement and survival."[24]

Religion accommodated itself to the end of the segregated southern way of life. The prophetic Will D. Campbell indicted white churches and ministers for failing to provide moral leadership during the 1950s and 1960s. Campbell witnessed for racial reconciliation as one of the few southern white ministers to be involved at sites of struggle. White southern evangelical churches did not open their doors to Black worshippers in the years after racial changes took place in other areas of southern life, but neither did African Americans show interest in abandoning their profound commitments to the Black church that had been their sanctuary for so long. White denominational assemblies eschewed violence and endorsed federal court decisions promoting racial changes. The influential minister W. A. Criswell, pastor of Dallas's First Baptist Church, had called civil rights activists "infidels" in 1956, but by 1968 he decided that segregationists "do not read the Bible right" and denied that "segregation could have been or was at any time intelligently, seriously supported by the Bible." The South's dominant evangelical groups continued, though, to embrace individual salvation over social justice, an attitude that limited efforts at reconciliation.

Renegade Baptist minister Will D. Campbell was one of
the few white ministers active in civil rights protests, and
he continued prodding the hypocrisies he saw at work in
ideological concepts of the southern way of life and southern
living. Photograph by Charles Reagan Wilson.

African American churches came out of the 1960s with great moral authority
because of the leading role of many ministers, and as Black southerners made
use of new opportunities, they continued supporting their churches as not only
religious sanctuaries but social, cultural, economic, and political centers. The
end of the legally segregated southern way of life did not destroy the churches'
underpinning of southern society.[25]

White Working Class

In the 1960s transformation of the South, African Americans won civil rights,
voting rights, and a new sense of dignity and respect, while middle-class southerners benefitted from the expanding economy and their accompanying political power. On the other hand, the "working class and lower middle class remained powerless and increasingly angry, frustrated, alienated." A carpenter in

New Orleans told psychologist Robert Coles that "the rich invent clever schemes to get out of paying taxes" and the "colored come running into a city like this one, expecting money from the city every week," but meanwhile "the rest of us have big deductions taken out every week from our paychecks, and there isn't anything we can do about it." High sales taxes penalized working-class people, affordable housing was often scarce, medical care was hardly affordable for many people, the social welfare system in southern states was sparse, public transportation and other public services were limited, pay scales were low in the region, and retirement plans were modest—all legitimate grievances. The white working class and lower middle class could never really translate them into political effectiveness. They became the core constituents for George Wallace's political campaigning in the late 1960s and early 1970s, but his message was more a negative one than a positive agenda for the future and proved hard to sustain beyond Wallace himself—at least until the 1980s when the Republican Party capitalized on the white rage that Wallace had earlier tapped.[26]

The public policies of the new populist-sounding politicians, with biracial constituencies, offered some relief in the 1970s for working-class people, but many white southerners remained skeptical of the national Democratic Party that had championed Black rights and a Great Society that seemed to them a project mostly to benefit Black people. White workers suffered from automation and ever-higher educational requirements for jobs in this time period, and women seemed even more constrained. "Being a working-class woman," wrote Kathy Kahn, "means being stepped on, pushed around, overworked and underpaid." Kahn captured a sense of hopelessness for many white working-class women and lamented that their world was one in which "you have little hope that you will do anything more in life than a lot of hard work." The white working-class members often blamed African Americans rather than seeing an unfair economic system as the source of their troubles. "The government will help the n——s," said one North Carolina factory worker, "but they don't give us nothing." By the 1970s, the southern white lower-middle class was the most unhappy social group in the nation. The Harris poll found the South was the "most disenchanted part of the country," and its blue-collar and lower-middle-income groups felt the most "left out of the mainstream of American life and taken advantage of by people with power." They represented a particular, well-rooted southern life that, while not celebrated as the "southern way of life," did represent a distinctive regionally placed culture. Church and neighborhood embodied such values as charitableness, neighborliness, self-reliance, morality, religiosity, and individualism. The rising tide of the southern economy benefitted the white working class and lower-middle class so that they were far from bereft of hope and realized progress in spite of their grievances. They became in time reliable members of the Republican Party conservative coalition that would triumph in the South in the 1980s and afterward. A nostalgia for the supposed better days of the segregated southern way of life persisted among southern working-class whites long after it ended. Rural and suburban areas became centers of ongoing struggles, for example, over desegregation and schools.[27]

Ideology of the Biracial South

With the end of Jim Crow legal segregation in 1964 and of voting disfranchisement of African Americans in 1965, the southern cultural context had new realities. As a public ideology, white supremacy and the culture of the segregated southern way of life had been diminished, although they would soon morph into other forms. The Ku Klux Klan and the Citizens' Councils had been defeated, and rabble-rousing, old-time politicians had lost the battles and ultimately the massive resistance war they had proclaimed in the 1950s. The hearts of southern whites did not transform overnight on racial issues simply because of the changes the federal government mandated as a result of the pressures from their fellow Black southerners. White southerners would, however, have to adapt their public culture to a new social world. Beginning in the early 1970s, new ideologies—rooted in older precedents—came to the fore as emerging justifications for southern public life and values.

Two visions anchored the effort to think about a new southern way of life in the 1970s. One was the vision of the biracial South. This shaped the public culture of the South in unprecedented ways that would have seemed impossible to people in the South at the beginning of the 1960s. It represented a renewal of the liberal tradition, based politically in the Democratic Party that had been remade into one welcoming African Americans and maintaining close ties to the national party and federal government. The other vision of the South's future was a conservative one based in the concept of a southern business way of life, the assertion of individualism over social concerns, and an effort to preserve as much white privilege as possible despite the end of segregation. The first vision seemed triumphant through much of the 1970s, but the conservative idea of southern living would build strength in the 1970s and become dominant with the election of Ronald Reagan in 1980, the rise of the new religious Right, and the spread of some key southern cultural features nationally after that.[28]

Martin Luther King Jr.'s American dream of the beloved community grew out of many sources, but one of them was the vision of the South having a destiny, rooted in the past, of embodying the integrated, biracial South. Charles L. Black, a born-and-bred white southerner, was teaching at Yale Law School in 1957, when he outlined the legal and moral appeals that might be made to sympathetic whites to promote desegregation in the South. At the end of the essay, he revealed his longtime dream of the biracial South, formed from pondering his "relations with the many Negroes of Southern origin" that he had known. He continued: "Again and again how often we laugh at the same things, how often we pronounce the same words the same way to the amuse-ment of our hearers, judge character in the same frame of reference, mist up at the same kinds of music. I have exchanged 'good evening' with a Negro stranger on a New Haven street, and then realized (from the way he said the words) that he and I derived this universal small-town custom from the same culture." Despite such cultural affinities, white and Black people in the South, though, had failed to acknowledge these common traits that reflected a kin-ship. "My dream is simply that sight will one day clear and that each of the participants will recognize the other," Black wrote. If that happened, "if the two [races] could join and look toward the future together—something would have happened uniquely beautiful in history." The South, which had "always felt itself reserved for a high destiny, would have found it, and would come to flower at last."[29]

Black's words in 1957 expressed a mythic view of southern culture that would become in the 1970s a major ideological underpinning of a reimagined south-ern way of life. Like a good evangelist, Leslie Dunbar, executive director of the Southern Regional Council, expressed this faith even more directly in 1961 as he testified to his belief "that the South will, out of its travail and sadness and requited passion, give the world its first grand example of two races of men liv-ing together in equality and with mutual respect." Conservative southern ideol-ogy had long claimed that the segregated southern way of life was a harmonious one, the result of a hierarchical society with the races interacting under sharply prescribed rules. The deeper source of this biracial southern way of life was not in conservative thinking but in the South's liberal reform ethos. Antecedents could be found in the nineteenth century among advocates of biracial political coalitions in Reconstruction and in the era of agrarian reform in the 1890s. In the twentieth century, such organizations as the YWCA, the Commission on Interracial Cooperation, the Southern Conference for Human Welfare, and the Southern Regional Council looked at southern regional problems through an interracial lens. Organized labor promoted a biracial ideal among the South's working classes, and the Highlander Folk Center in East Tennessee worked assiduously from the 1930s to bring Black and white activists together and train them. Small numbers of southerners lived out their interracial ideals in places such as Clarence Jordan's Christian community, Koinonia, in south Georgia, and the Providence Cooperative Farm in Tchula, Mississippi.[30]

One form of southern culture, music, offered a dramatic example of the transformative possibilities of embracing biracialism at the same time the civil rights struggle advanced. The rural South had long nurtured vibrant vernacular music, not only of "whites" and "Blacks" but with influences of many ethnic groups in local areas across the region, who created musical cultures that were not pure in their African or Western elements but mixed across ethnocultural boundaries. Entertainers by the early twentieth century in the rural South, small towns, and urban areas were a part of "an invisible network composed of the shifting and overlapping itineraries of minstrel and vaudeville shows, one-night stands in small towns, street corners, brothels, juke joints, and honkytonks far removed from any tracking system." By the mid-twentieth century, with agriculture in decline and people moving off the land to towns and cities, younger people, especially, brought rural sounds to the dynamic and vibrant city life that energized their cross-racial creativity in the 1950s. At the same time the civil rights movement was rebelling against the legal and political structures of the segregated southern way of life, these young southerners, white and Black, launched a parallel cultural challenge to old southern orthodoxies. In the late 1940s, radio stations in several southern cities began mixing Black and white disc jockeys and played a variety of musical sounds, from country and blues to jazz and gospel.[31]

Sam Phillips made his recording studio in Memphis and his recording label, Sun Records, ground zero for the musical interchange. He recorded African American blues and rhythm-and-blues performers and then such white rockabilly performers as Elvis Presley, Jerry Lee Lewis, Johnny Cash, and Carl Perkins. Elvis Presley gave Phillips his first big record, recording "That's All Right," an Arthur Crudup–written blues song on one side and bluegrass king Bill Monroe's "Blue Moon of Kentucky" on the other. It was July 1954, only a few months before the Supreme Court's landmark *Brown* decision that forced white southerners to consider the end of the segregated southern way of life as a real option. Stax Studios came after Sun and was arguably as experimental as Sun had been, as it nurtured a spirit of cross-racial musical cooperation lasting until the late 1960s. Other places in the South produced musical styles that showed interracial interaction: the Macon, Georgia, of Little Richard and, later, the Allman Brothers; the New Orleans of Fats Domino and evolving jazz; Nashville's predominant country music that had come to incorporate African American musical influences; and the recording studios in Muscle Shoals, Alabama, that produced interracial studio bands that attracted the most creative rock 'n' roll performers, who witnessed in the process for biracial cultural exchange.[32]

At the forefront of the cultural rebellion against the segregated southern way of life, Elvis Presley was a young white man from Mississippi who had grown up in a shared poverty with African Americans and absorbed their culture as

The 1970s South celebrated its musical traditions, as in this publicity photograph of Booker T. and the M.G.'s in an Aston Martin (*left to right*: Duck Dunn, Al Jackson, Jr., Steve Cropper, Booker T. Jones), circa 1960. Steve Leigh Collection, Stax Museum of American Soul Music, Memphis, Tennessee.

well as that of up-country Mississippi whites and the national popular culture of radio, film, and television. He crossed the South's racial boundaries and tapped into Black cultural creativity, combined it with his own inherited folk culture, and performed to appreciative young audiences. Presley's music and cultural style appealed so much to young people that it weakened, and in some cases outright broke, the generational connection between older defenders of the segregated southern way of life and their children. It was not an overt civil rights protest but a rebellion against the orthodoxy and segregated cultural separation inherent in the southern-way-of-life concept. As writer Bobbie Ann Mason put it, Presley's style of music "appealed to the young and informed with its promises of deliverance, its rebel assault on the brutality of labor, its joyous freedom." Black Panther leader Eldridge Cleaver saw Presley sparking the social revolution of the late twentieth century because he "dared to do in the light of day what America had long been doing in the sneak thief of night—consorted on a human level with the blacks." The evidence of his engagement with African American culture is well known, from growing up in east Tupelo and hearing Black music in Shake Rag (the African American neighborhood adjacent to where his family lived), dressing as Black people dressed, and using hair cream designed for African Americans to prowling Beale Street and attending Black church services. Although some Black performers complained that he earned a great deal of money with their songs and his success raised legitimate questions of white appropriation of Black culture, still, Presley always credited Black musicians as pioneers. He undoubtedly appreciated the words of Little Richard, another leading southern musical innovator of the time: "I thank God for Elvis Presley. I thank the Lord for sending Elvis to open the door so I could walk down the road, you understand?"[33]

Elvis's significance for the southern way of life was that he helped to diminish its cultural separatism. In terms of cultural exchange, neither "white" nor "Black" American music was "pure" by the postwar era, when songs, performance styles, and audiences drew from a deep well of American national and southern regional musical cultures. Elvis's musical achievements presaged the importance of southern music as a key component in one of the most recent expressions of the southern-way-of-life concept—the idea of southern living and lifestyle in the contemporary era, with southern music a part of that vision. White arbiters of Jim Crow society lambasted Presley and other early rockers for their violations of the color line, and they used language that portrayed rock music as jungle music, the music of savages, the same language used against civil rights demonstrators. Asa E. Carter, head of the North Alabama Citizens' Council, charged that the music corrupted young white morals with its "degenerate, animalistic beats and rhythms." Robert B. Patterson, secretary of the Mississippi Citizens' Council, attended a Louis Armstrong concert at the University of Mississippi, and he wrote a friend in 1954 about how the jazzman had an interracial orchestra, addressed the white orchestra members by their first names, and hugged them. Even worse for this segregationist was the fact that he could hear "the co-eds shriek when the yellow boy soloed on his slide trombone"—this emotional reaction of white belles suggesting the music's appeal was deeper than sound.[34]

Redemptive South

Liberal reformers drew from democratic ideals to justify racial moderation and eventually the end of the segregated southern way of life, but they also relied on the South's religious culture—its evangelical character and aspirations toward salvation in a sinful world. This source was especially significant for the southern liberals in the period from 1930 to 1950 who championed not just racial moderation but the end of Jim Crow segregation altogether. Such reformers came to believe that the caste system violated basic Christian ideals of brotherhood. Reformers such as Howard Kester, Will Alexander, James Mc-Bride Dabbs, Will Campbell, and others used the language of Evangelicalism, speaking of "shame" and "guilt," in particular, to describe how their feelings were changed on racial issues. In this religious context, the southern liberals who had worked most actively before the *Brown* decision for the end of Jim Crow knew of the South's sins but thought redemption was possible. Racial healing could follow and lead to the dream of racial harmony—and the South would then redeem the nation.[35]

African Americans advanced the idea of a redemptive South, especially the ministers of the civil rights movement. In a 1961 interview, King spoke of "an intimacy of life" in the South that could become beautiful if it was "transformed in race relations from a sort of lord-servant relationship to a person-to-person relationship." Arguing that the nature of life in the region would "make it one of the finest sections of the country" once segregation ended, King said in 1963 that "when [he finds] a white southerner who has been emancipated on the issue, the Negro can't find a better friend." Claiming the descriptor of "southerner," he insisted that achieving racial justice would contribute to individual moral health, national political life, the nation's prestige in the world, and "our cultural health as a region." Like southern white liberals, King saw regional manners and informal relationships as the source of hope for achieving the dream of the biracial southern way of life in the future. King used the language of the late nineteenth-century Lost Cause as he spoke of suffering, tragedy, honor, virtue, the need of a defeated people to achieve dignity, and the search for group identity and destiny. Comparing traditional southern white values to those of Black freedom protesters in 1963, he claimed that "the virtues so long regarded as the exclusive property of the white South—gallantry, loyalty, and pride—had passed to the Negro demonstrators in the heat of the summer's battles." King rejected, as one would imagine, the Lost Cause mythology of Confederate virtue and racial purity, as he had witnessed the use of the Confederate flag and the song "Dixie" by opponents of the civil rights movement. The compensation for Black physical deprivation, for King, was a spiritual maturity—exactly the same argument white southerners had made about their defeated region in the late nineteenth century. King hoped to release "spiritual power" and "soul force" that would transform the South and, from there, the nation and the world.[36]

King's "I Have a Dream" speech in 1963 portrayed a redemptive South that would be the scene for national salvation. Reflecting a traditional southern concern for place, he argued that the nation's transformation would not be in some disembodied location, but in a specific locale, the U.S. South. The region had been the center of Black suffering and of flawed humanity, but ultimately the virtue of Black people and decent whites would lead to reconciliation. One day "on the red hills of Georgia," Black people and white people would "sit down together at the table of brotherhood." In the coming days of redemption, even the state of Mississippi, "a state sweltering with the heat of injustice, sweltering with the heat of oppression, will be transformed into an oasis of freedom and justice." By the late 1960s, King had lost much of his confidence in the white South's ability to embrace his vision, but he had succeeded earlier in transforming the civil religion of the Lost Cause into a southern civil religion resting on biracial hopes.[37]

King once acknowledged James McBride Dabbs as one of the small number of liberal white southerners who had witnessed for racial integration, and Dabbs was, indeed, another major formulator of an ideology of the biracial southern way of life. He often used that term and intentionally contested white supremacists' attempts to give it an exclusive meaning. Born in South Carolina to a family that had been in the state since the colonial era, educated both in the South at the University of South Carolina and outside of it at Clark University and Columbia University, and a soldier in France during World War I, Dabbs was, at various times, a college teacher, a leader in the southern Presbyterian Church, president of the reformist Southern Regional Council, and, for most of his life, a practicing farmer at the family plantation, Rip Raps. In a series of books and in articles in *Christian Century* and denominational journals, Dabbs brooded upon the southern past. He was prophetic in castigating "the racial sins" the white South had committed, which made understandable "the justice of its being defeated and thwarted in the Civil War." Even as he became an active supporter of the civil rights movement, he retained his influence among his fellow white southerners through the 1950s and 1960s.[38]

Dabbs explored what the southern way of life could mean and enriched the overall southern understanding of the concept. "The phrase 'way of life,'" he wrote, connoted "moral values." In a sense, he allowed, a "common American custom, say, of a 55-mile speed limit, is a way of life," but he clarified that "this is not the usual sense of the term." Instead, a way of life "is something men are inclined to defend because, presumably, it has moral values." Denying any such values in the South's racial segregation, he surmised that segregation was "rather a principle of dissociation than of association, and as such is a source, not of spiritual value, but of spiritual disvalue." Jim Crow existed to buttress "the desire of the whites for superiority." It developed "few moral implications, and is therefore but slightly a way of life." Instead, "it might more properly be

called a way of not-life," a stunning contestation in the face of the populariza-
tion of an emotionally tinged segregated southern way of life in these years. In
1958, he took issue again with defenders of that way of life. "They say we are defending our way of life," Dabbs wrote. "What is our way of life? They say segregation," but he would have none of it. Insisting there was "the Southern way of
life which men have longed for when absent and fought for when challenged,"
he claimed that segregation was not it, and he added, "It's more than hot biscuits." Like the Vanderbilt Agrarians, Dabbs rejected industrialism as a source
of values and urged southerners not to accept "the straight American religion"
and forget their past: "It seems to be sheer waste to throw away so much only
to gain—more shares in General Motors!" The South should look at its own
people and their experiences to understand the meaning of any southern way.
"Through the processes of history and the grace of God we have been made one
people," he wrote, and added that now "there is no telling what great age might
develop in the South." The region would show the way to the rest of the world.
To be sure, he saw the southern experience as a tragic one, but he believed it
had meaning, not only for southerners but for others as well. He argued that
the South had been "a pilot project learning—at terrible expense it is true, but
learning doesn't come easy—how to do within a limited area what now has to
be done if civilization is to survive." Dabbs thus placed the South once again at
the center of efforts to preserve Western civilization, but now—unlike in earlier
such expressions—he spoke for a biracial, progressive culture.[39]

The land, for Dabbs, was the setting for building a biracial community at
the heart of the southern way of life. The traits that distinguished those in the
South as southerners, he observed, "are chiefly the result of this basic productive pattern: Whites and Negroes farming, in some sense, together." Like the
Agrarians, he saw the southern farmer's work as "inwoven with his life, his life
inwoven with the family, and, through his work and his family, he is inwoven
with larger communities, even with the world, and with the universe, of which
this world is an infinitesimal part." This was the southern way of life, but "down
through the center of this rich scene, which is of course our heart, we draw a
sharp line and say: 'Segregation.'" What Dabbs described was "this real way of
life," unlike the segregated southern way.[40]

Through the working of history and the grace of God, people in the South
had been made one people. The region "was destined to show the way to the rest
of the world," as Dabbs reiterated "the religious significance of the Southerner's
experience." The South had been "God's project." Writing in the face of the segregation of the South's religious life, Dabbs insisted that the southern church
had a special responsibility to embody this understanding. The church must
"make use of the cultural similarity between the races in its attempt to unveil

the vision of the religious significance of race relations," to interpret the biracial South as God's project. Writing in 1964, he charged the southern church with recognizing "the tragedy of Southerners," which had led, through God's grace and mercy, to the creation of "a common bond between Southern Whites and Negroes." The great challenge, then, at the end of the legally segregated southern way of life, and in the decades since, has been for white southerners and Black southerners to acknowledge and embrace this understanding of their cultural similarity.[41]

Organizations of the Biracial South

The ideology of a biracial South thus received eloquent expression in the last days of Jim Crow segregation, and it became a formative one in the postseg-regation era, embodied in a number of organizations and activities. The L. Q. C. Lamar Society, formed in 1969 near Durham, North Carolina, was a good example of an organization that promoted the new outlook. Named for a Mississippi secessionist who became a post–Civil War advocate of regional reconciliation, the Lamar Society attracted a constituency of middle- and upper-middle-class professionals who advocated a vision of a still regionally distinctive South dedicated now to transcending endemic problems of racial conflict, poverty, and environmental abuse. Like the Vanderbilt Agrarians who four decades earlier had championed a conservative vision of southern tradi-tionalism in the face of modernity, members of the Lamar Society worried about the survival of a distinctive regional culture in an industrialized modern world. Unlike the Agrarians, though, these southern intellectuals and policy makers pushed for a new racial vision in the South. As writer Willie Morris said of the South in the introduction to the society's defining symposium volume, *You Can't Eat Magnolias* (1972), "Racism was the primeval obsession. No longer is this so. It will hold out in places, but it will never again shape the white South-ern consciousness." For generations, Morris wrote, racism had "misdirected the South from its other elemental problems of poverty and exploitation." He foresaw the changes in the 1960s having "a profoundly liberating effect" on the region.[42]

Alabama newspaperman H. Brandt Ayers, a founder of the Lamar Soci-ety, dismissed the continued attachment of the South to its old Lost Cause symbols, writing of the "viral weed of mythology" that had been "allowed to grow like kudzu over the South." Ayers urged southerners to embrace a differ-ent heritage, symbolized not by the White House of the Confederacy but by reverence for "the symbols of Monticello or the Hermitage—houses built by white southerners who led the nation and represented egalitarian ideals." The irony is apparent from the twenty-first century, when Jefferson and Jackson are sometimes seen as symbolizing the South's and nation's racial and imperial flaws, but it is important in understanding the 1970s transition to a different southern ideology that the idea of egalitarian democracy was becoming now central as a new myth. Ayers saw contemporary southerners within the long perspective of southern history and within the framework of evangelical culture that could witness for the possibility for redemption. "Southerners, black and white, locked together in yet another uniquely Southern experience, should be addressed with the humanity that teaches wise and just men to hate the sin, but love the sinner." Ayers also saw history overcoming the separation of the regions. The frustrations of the Vietnam War and the nation's recognition of racial problems extending beyond the South had "shattered the Yankees' innocent illusions that they have been ordained to trample out immorality and that His truth marches with them into every war."[43]

Just as the older racial myths of white supremacy rested in a weblike structure of the Democratic Party, the Ku Klux Klan, Protestant churches, state laws, and racial etiquette that virtually all white people enforced against all people of color, so now the ideology of the biracial South emerged through institutions such as the Lamar Society and its periodical *Southern Journal*; the Institute for Southern Studies in Durham and its *Southern Exposure*; the Southern Growth Policies Board; and academic regional studies centers such as the University of Mississippi's Center for the Study of Southern Culture, which the university established in 1977, with a pronounced interracial theme. African American artist Romare Bearden's painting of Black musicians adorned the cover of the latter's first annual report, a glossy publication, issued in 1980. Inside, photographs of African American blues singers and basket makers were interwoven with illustrations of white quilting ladies and people enjoying a dinner on the grounds after church. The center symbolically embraced the recognition of biracialism by picturing Alex Haley and Eudora Welty side by side in its annual report.[44]

Politics also reflected the impact of the ideology of the biracial South in the early 1970s, at a time when African Americans were becoming a major force in southern politics. The most racially obsessed states, those of the Deep South, changed from supporting pro-segregation candidates in the pre-1970 era to supporting those who did not use racial rhetoric or campaign on the segregation issue. In 1976, African Americans represented about 17 percent of the electorate in the Deep South states, and by then politicians were courting Black votes. This was not a sentimental gesture on the part of white politicians. The growing power of African American political strength led southern white politicians to acknowledge Black aspirations. As Congressman Andrew Young noted in 1976, "It used to be Southern politics was just 'n——' politics—

a question of which candidate could 'outn——' the other. Then you registered 10% to 15% in the community, and folks would start saying 'Nigra.' Later you got 35% to 40% registered, and it was amazing how quick they learned how to say 'Nee-grow.' And now that we've got 50%, 60%, 70% of the black votes registered in the South, everybody's proud to be associated with their black brothers and sisters."[45]

Progressive young governors represented the change in southern politics that would make political discourse a prime carrier of the new biracial ideology in the early 1970s. Dale Bumpers of Arkansas, Jimmy Carter in Georgia, John West in South Carolina, Reuben Askew in Florida, William Waller in Mississippi, and Edwin Edwards in Louisiana, followed by politicians such as William Winter in Mississippi and Bill Clinton in Arkansas, all promoted new interest-group politics that resulted in biracial coalitions and a new rhetoric of the South as the chosen place. They did not appeal to traditional southern defensiveness about the federal government or fears about outside agitators, nor did they throw around racial code words. Repudiating traditional southern mythology, they distanced themselves from the past and expressed hope and optimism for the future. George Busbee, elected governor of Georgia in 1974 with African American votes, stated in his inaugural address that "the politics of race has gone with the wind," using an especially evocative term in Margaret Mitchell's home state to dismiss past racial extremism. Edwin Edwards spoke to Black Louisianans in his 1972 inaugural address and pledged, "The old imaginary barriers no longer exist. My election has destroyed the old myths, and a new spirit is with us." His use of the word "spirit" suggested a metaphysical dimension to this newest South.[46]

Dramatic new images came along with the rhetoric. Eugene "Bull" Connor sang "We Shall Overcome" in a Black church while campaigning (unsuccessfully). George Wallace crowned a Black homecoming queen at the University of Alabama. The governor of Georgia, Jimmy Carter, dedicated a portrait of Martin Luther King Jr. in a prominent spot in the state capitol building. At Forrest "Fob" James's inauguration as governor of Alabama in 1979, he linked two central symbols of an emerging rhetoric of biracialism: "I believe if Robert E. Lee and Martin Luther King Jr., were here today, their cry to us—their prayer to God—would call for 'The Politics of Unselfishness'—a people together—determined to climb the highest plateau of greatness." The imagery of Lee and King praying to God together projected an explicit image of civil religion—both southern heroes blessing the region. Their photos would soon be linked in a new iconography within southern public institutions, and from 1985 to 2017 Alabama, Mississippi, and Arkansas celebrated Robert E. Lee Day and Martin Luther King Jr. Day together in a merged holiday.[47]

The revealing gestures of even segregationist politicians such as Connor and Wallace seeking the support of Black voters reflected the political aspects of a broader redefinition of the symbolic southern community in the 1970s. White southerners had shaped the imagery and meaning of previous southern mythology, and white-dominated organizations had institutionalized and promoted traditional myths. Just as Black people in the older South had been disfranchised, segregated, and exploited, so too had they been virtually powerless in influencing the South's public culture. They did not have a vote on the symbols the South's culture projected or on the civic rituals its people acted out. The process underway in the 1970s represented the beginnings of a redefinition of a new southern community, one that reflected the influence of Black southerners. Although the changed political rhetoric of a George Wallace could be attributable simply to his craven instinct for success, he was part of a broader society grappling with the need for a new ideological foundation that could buttress a sense of purpose and direction. Myths only last if they unify and can evoke feelings from a broad range of citizens, who may identify with them for different reasons. The myth of the biracial South filled the void represented by the decline of older southern myths as a time when the racial basis of power in southern society had shifted dramatically.[48]

At the heart of the ideology of the biracial South stood a moral earnestness that enabled southerners to make claims upon national idealism that were distant from the region's civil rights disgraces of the 1960s. Florida governor Reuben Askew stated the idea of southern moral superiority in 1972: "For many years now, the rest of the nation has been saying to the South that it is morally wrong to deprive any citizen of an equal opportunity in life because of his color. I think most of us have come to agree with that. But now the time has come for the rest of the nation to live up to its own stated principles." Just as the nation had "sought to bring justice to the South by mandate and court order," so now it was time for "the South to teach the same thing to other regions in a more effective way—by example."[49]

By the mid-1970s, the South had not only rejoined the nation, but it had begun to dominate it in some ways. A generation after Confederates lost their crusade against the nation, American culture embraced the Lost Cause, as southern writers became popular in American magazines, theatrical plays with southern heroes and heroines dominated American theater, and American popular music projected appealing romantic lyrics of the lazy, hazy South. Similarly, having lost their massive resistance movement, southern whites now found themselves influencing the national culture more profoundly than at any time since the late nineteenth century. Country music, evangelical Protestantism, films and television shows about southerners, southern literature—

all were in vogue. Even in politics the nation turned south, electing the first Deep South politician as president since the Civil War, Jimmy Carter. As the South shed the excesses and outrages of the segregated southern way of life, Americans found more appealing qualities that they could embrace.[50]

If southern politicians endorsed the ideology of the biracial South and the national culture became fascinated with it, Black southerners were, if anything, even more enthusiastic promoters of the ideology in the 1970s. The new ideology reflected real, dramatic changes in the region that came in the aftermath of the civil rights movement, the epochal event in the new mythology equivalent to the Civil War in the myth of the Lost Cause a century before. In 1975, the Reverend Frederick Reese, a veteran Black leader, concluded that "we've come a long way." His evidence was largely "changes in white behavior toward blacks." "Whites who wouldn't tip their hats have learned to do it. People who wouldn't say 'Mister' or 'Miss' to a black have learned to say it mighty fine. We've got black policemen, black secretaries, and we can use the public restrooms. The word 'n——' is almost out of existence." His words evoked the older South of racial etiquette that the region's public culture had finally rejected. Jessie Campbell, a Black store manager on the Mississippi Gulf Coast, insisted that race was "almost nonexistent now." He saw "a new generation of people, black and white, here" and evoked behavioral changes associated with the end of old racial ways as well as new beginnings. Campbell also pointed to economic developments that saw "there's been a pretty big rise in the standard of living of the black people." Andrew Young told a meeting of southern Black mayors that "we can't help but be people who believe in doing the impossible, because we've already done so much of it." Young, in 1974, summoned the image of the redemptive South: "I strangely think we're going to be able to deliver in the South. . . . I think the direction of this nation is going to be determined by the direction that comes from the southern part of the United States."[51]

Migration patterns suggested the demographic basis for this rhetoric. In the 1970s, for the first time, more Black people moved from the North to the South than were leaving the South for other parts of the United States. In the first three years of the 1970s, 80,000 more African Americans came to the South than left it, and in the last five years of the decade, 500,000 Black people moved to the region and reversed the historic outward migration. Writing in 1972, North Carolinian Mary E. Mebane remembered that "the names Alabama and Mississippi aroused something akin to terror." She had always viewed Black people from there "with awe" and wondered "how they could possibly have survived." The North, by contrast, "seemed the Promised Land." When Black folk from New York City came home to visit, Mebane wrote that "the men drove big cars and the women dressed in fine clothes and wore false eyelashes." But in the previous few years, she had noted that "blacks in the Northern cities were coming home, down South." Mebane admitted that "disenchantment caused by the disorder in Northern cities" was one reason that some African Americans left the North for the South, as were new job opportunities, but she concluded that "the primary reason for the influx of blacks into the South [was] the Civil Rights Acts of 1964–65." The key to the North losing "much of its allure" was the South's removal of "the overt signs of racial discrimination" and the discontinuance of "some of the most vicious racist practices."[52]

The South in the 1970s and 1980s became home to more African American elected officials than any other part of the United States. That change further contributed to the ability of southern Black people to affirm the ideology of the biracial South because of their increased potential to exercise power in the region they shared with white southerners. The South represented about 50 percent of the nation's African Americans in 1987, but it had 62 percent of elected Black officeholders. Mississippi led all states, with 548 officials in 1987, and four of the five states with the largest number of Black officeholders were in the South. Curtis M. Graves, a Black representative in the Texas legislature and a vice president of the Lamar Society, pointed out that many of these electoral successes were because of Black numerical strength, not white votes. But he looked to the biracial South for the future of Black political success in the South. "Our real strength lies in coalition politics," he wrote. He himself had been elected as a result of such a coalition. "For the first time, whites and blacks in the South are working together in mutual trust. Realizing that things in the South are not as they should be for either blacks or whites, the two groups are beginning to talk over their common problems; they are joining force to see that a better South is created."[53]

Black endorsement of the ideology of the biracial South became part of the process of African Americans redefining what "the South" meant, as they wielded not only their political power but new cultural influence as well. Literary critic Thadious Davis wrote that the return after the 1960s of African Americans to the South, both physically and spiritually, represented "a laying of a claim to a culture and to a region that, though fraught with pain and difficulty," provided a major "grounding for identity." She went further and speculated "that this return to the South is a new form of subversion—a preconscious political activity or a subconscious counteraction to the racially and culturally homogeneous 'sunbelt.'" Rather than a "nostalgic turning back to a time when there were 'good old days,'" this embrace of the South was a "gut-wrenching revisioning of specifics long obscured by synoptic cultural patterning." As part of the redefinition of "the South," Black writers tried to evoke the texture of Black culture and to understand the nature of Black history in the South—its distinct character apart from issues of white supremacy. "No one could wish for a more advantageous heritage," wrote novelist Alice Walker, "than that bequeathed to the black writer in the South: a compassion for the earth, a trust in humanity beyond our knowledge of evil, and an abiding love of justice."[54]

Ideology of the Conservative Southern Way

The second predominant postsegregation ideology came out of another variety of southern living. If the liberal, biracial southern vision emerged from the South's interracial cultural heritage, a conservative business vision of southern life came out of the South's suburban lifestyles that emerged to new prominence in the 1960s and afterward. After World War II, southerners moved to cities, made them centers of population, prosperity, and power, and drained the declining countryside and small towns of all three sources of vitality. By the 1960s, bands of suburbs, connected to inner cities by massive new highways, surrounded cities. The federal government encouraged homeownership through low-interest mortgages and by building the interstate highway system. Results of the civil rights movement added to the impetus for many whites to leave cities that African Americans had come to dominate. As businesses and schools desegregated, many whites fled to new suburbs with relatively few nonwhite families. These well-off white families who migrated to the suburbs left the cities with declining tax bases for public services and upkeep of infrastructure. By the 1970s, southern inner cities resembled those elsewhere in the nation, and observers spoke of an urban crisis growing out of high unemployment rates, crime, pollution, and the growth of a permanent underclass.[55]

White flight was a transformative social movement that left a dramatic mark on the South's politics and ideology. The federal government had helped promote suburban growth, but the suburbs became centers of conservative, antigovernment sentiment, and busing as a method of achieving school desegregation brought about a white backlash. Whites now extolled the virtues of "color-blind" language that gave new authority to freedom of choice and freedom of association. Southern suburbanites, like those elsewhere across the nation, disliked federal government programs to address urban problems, and they launched grassroots tax revolts that limited government spending for urban planning and educational programs. A movement away from the Great Society ideal—of the federal government promoting social justice and addressing economic inequality—began even before Ronald Reagan was elected president in 1980 and made greater efforts to gut Great Society programs. Conservative southern churches joined conservative political efforts to move away from what religious people came to see as the social and sexual extremism of the 1960s.

This new conservatism rooted in the suburbs had moved away from the racial basis of the traditional southern way of life. Legalized segregation was simply not the issue it had been up to 1965, with this new ideology speaking of lower taxes, neighborhood schools, less government involvement in the economy, and freedom of association. The political passion once focused on totally segregated schools and restaurants now centered on complex issues of standardized testing for students, seniority systems of new Black and older white workers, quotas, and affirmative action. Many of these ideological components, to be sure, had been a part of the massive resistance effort, whose advocates often framed it in terms of states' rights and constitutionalism in hopes of winning a national conservative audience. By the 1970s, southern conservatism was indeed in line with the national movement that would reach fruition with Reagan's policies. Southern suburbs seemed much like those elsewhere, although when *Southern Living* magazine began publishing in 1966, it highlighted how southern traditions in such areas as food, home, and gardening could be adapted to suburban living. The magazine's title became the key descriptor for evolving efforts after the end of Jim Crow segregation to define new southern ways.[56]

The suburb was the geographical center of the new conservative version of southern living in the 1970s, and the middle class was the social center. In 1930, only 15 percent of southerners worked in jobs considered middle class, but by 1980 a majority of the region's labor force was in white-collar positions. The fastest growth by then was in upper-middle-class positions, such as managers, administrators, technicians, and researchers. Most workers came from businesses that served middle-class concerns, such as insurance, finance, and real estate, as well as professions associated with the South's expanding educational, health, legal, and cultural activity. Sociologist John Shelton Reed pointed out that the repository of regional stereotypes had never included middle-class figures as distinct from the plethora of social representations associated with the plantation, the white working class, and African Americans. The "discreet charm" of the middle class had been overshadowed by "the glamor of the upper class and by the sentimental appeal of the toiling masses." Reed described the new southerner of the middle class "returning to an urban or suburban home from a managerial or professional job. Sipping bourbon while he—or she—reads *Southern Living* magazine, subvocally pronouncing the r's (as in traditional southern linguistic culture)." These middle-class southerners had reference points other than rural traditionalism as a result of education, travel, and exposure to media and cosmopolitan ideas. The new southerners, nonetheless, continued to identify with the South and its culture, from actively supporting their churches and affirming orthodox religious beliefs to endorsing conservative, free-enterprise politics. Manners, hospitality, leisure, style—by the end of the 1970s, southern Black people as well as white believed, according to public opinion surveys, that these qualities had a special resonance in the South.[57]

As with the liberal political expressions of the 1970s that represented the interracial vision of southern living, a conservative version of southern living appeared in politics. In the face of federal government laws requiring desegregation, white southern leaders accomplished "a subtle and strategic accommodation to the demands of civil rights activists and the federal government" that ensured in the process the protection of white privilege and the goals of the national conservative movement. Southern whites believed that other white Americans shared their concerns about federal government policies promoted by the national Democratic Party disproportionately benefitting African Americans, and they worked with conservatives elsewhere who believed in states' rights, constitutional government, low taxes, a strong military, and fundamentalist/evangelical religion. Rebellion against the enforced busing of schoolchildren as a way to achieve racial balance in schools was especially important in the South as a way to lead to segregation academies and church-sponsored schools, which would drain many public schools of white students (and the support of white parents). Opposition to abortion, the Equal Rights Amendment, and gay rights appeared as new causes among these southern conservatives in the 1970s, presaging the issues' centrality to the triumphant conservative political movement in the 1980s and after.[58]

The transformation of the Republican Party anchored the political expression of this conservative ideal. Much scholarship argues that southern Republicans converted white racism, which some scholars see as the real source of the Republican rise in the South, into national influence. The Dixiecrat rebellion in 1948 had drawn some white southerners away from their abiding support of the Democratic Party, and war hero Dwight Eisenhower's 1952 and 1956 presidential campaigns further eroded Democratic support in the South. The national Democrats' sponsorship of the civil rights legislation of the mid-1960s and 1964 Republican presidential candidate Barry Goldwater's opposition to the Civil Rights Act became key factors in bringing more southern whites to the Republicans. George Wallace, a volatile factor in the late-1960s southern political scene, stirred up racial antipathy between Black people and white, nationwide as well as in the South, and represented a bridge to a new political alignment around Richard Nixon. In 1968 Wallace's American Independent Party appealed to white working-class people feeling besieged by changes in the country and ignored by both major parties. Wallace won 40 percent of the southern vote among whites who were seceding from the new Democratic Party yet still uncomfortable with the idea of voting for the once-dreaded Republican Party.[59]

Parchman Farm had long been a notorious prison symbol of the South's unjust
criminal justice system, and Bill Ferris's 1975 photograph shows a work crew that was
a throwback to earlier times and a continuing expression of white racial privilege.
William R. Ferris Collection, Southern Folklife Collection, Wilson Library,
University of North Carolina at Chapel Hill.

Richard Nixon's southern strategy used coded words on racial matters to
appeal to southern whites, with particular success in presidential elections in
the decades after 1980. South Carolina political strategist Harry Dent shaped
the southern strategy to appeal to southern conservatives and help get Nixon
elected in 1968 and reelected in a 1972 landslide. Nixon issued statements in
favor of racial equality but failed to pursue policies intended to meet that goal.
He used law-and-order language that criminalized Black Americans in public
representations. The president blamed federal judges for desegregation. At the
annual Gridiron Dinner for journalists and politicians in Washington, D.C., a
newspaper reporter sang a song to the tune of "A Dixie Melody," with the lyrics
"Rock-a-bye the voters with a Southern Strategy / Don't you fuss; we won't bus
children in ol' Dixie!" The reporter was being humorous but also revealing in
singing, "We'll put George Wallace in decline / Below the Mason-Dixon Line."
The southern strategy clearly worked in draining discontented southern white

voters away from Wallace and toward the emerging Republican majority in the nation. Despite the seeming triumph of the moderate/progressive, biracially based Democratic Party in the 1970s, the South was on its way to becoming a near Solid South again, this time one devoted to the Republican Party. The party's support of white privilege and free-enterprise economic development would rest at the center of one of the most important expressions of southern living in the postsegregation South.[60]

Intellectual James J. Kilpatrick was already well known by the late 1960s for his role popularizing massive resistance in the 1950s and then devising a postsegregation plan to protect white privilege in the mid-1960s. As legal segregation collapsed, Kilpatrick and other white southerners like him looked at their personal and regional identities and considered what role race would now play in white consciousness. Kilpatrick recast agrarianism as part of a long history of southern conservatism, going back to such country-gentlemen intellectuals as John Randolph, John Taylor, and Thomas Jefferson, who all foresaw the United States as a nation of independent, property-owning farmers. In the aftermath of the civil rights movement, Kilpatrick believed he faced not only an empowered federal government but an American society, including the South, that was turning away from the sense of place, community, and social order that he believed had once defined the nation and, more recently, the region.[61]

In 1969, Kilpatrick built White Walnut Hill, a farmhouse and studio on thirty-seven acres of land on the Rappahannock River in the foothills of the Blue Ridge Mountains. He named his place Scrabble, which became a tangible and metaphorical place of sanctuary from the wicked times he found himself living through. He described the 1960s as "a decade of crime, brutality, bloodshed, blurred by tears for young men dead," and he lamented it was "the decade in which civility was lost." He related the evil winds of history even to his own place, as he wrote that "the wind rips at our Rappahannock earth built by centuries; manners, courtesy, tolerance, respect for authority—the Sixties saw these hurled in massive drifts across our roads." Offended by Watergate as well, he abandoned support for Richard Nixon. On his estate he lived the life of an old squire, loving and writing about nature's ways. He began a new syndicated column, A Conservative View, and wrote for Nation's Business; he penned hundreds of pieces about Scrabble, Virginia, and made it into "an oppositional model against an anomic America averse to self-sacrifice and building solid communities." He gloried that his Virginia place was out of American time: no liquor store, no bookstore, few public health services, modest resources for public schools, dirt roads, no hospital, and no McDonald's—only a volunteer fire department.[62]

Scrabble's people, in Kilpatrick's portrayal, lived as independent individuals in strong communities that protected the land—a case study of the Agrarian ideal in *I'll Take My Stand*. Far removed from federal authority, he lived in the memory of a racial hierarchy out of time. He looked to the same antebellum southern past as the Agrarians had and ignored its racial injustices for a romanticized image of community. Kilpatrick had been since the 1950s a southern representative of a national conservatism best represented intellectually by Russell Kirk, who himself resuscitated the classic conservative ideas of Edmund Burke to glorify traditional, organic society, based in pronounced religiosity. Kilpatrick had little use for religion but tapped into national conservatism's traditionalism and made Scrabble a new model for the postsegregation South. Agrarianism continued to be an influential idea throughout midcentury, but the triumph of industrialism and urbanization had surely made it outdated as a model by the 1970s. Kilpatrick updated it by combining localism, community focus, and individual property rights with an appreciation of free-enterprise capitalism. The Depression-era Agrarians had never tried to reconcile free-market capitalism with their ideology. If industrial capitalism was the enemy of the Agrarians' southern way of life, Kilpatrick saw federal government and liberal individualism as the threats to traditional values. He failed to see that even without a strong federal government and liberalism's policies, capitalism's relentless reach was destroying the land and communities of the South when it served economic interests. He transmuted the Agrarians' conservative values of orderly communities, rooted in the protection of the land, into "a capitalist-friendly version of republican political philosophy" that portrayed Scrabble as "a new southern Eden in an updated briar patch." Ignoring the discrimination and injustices inherent in the earlier southern social ethic, he now put forward a vision of the southern future based upon reverence for states' rights, regional identity, and the land. It also justified exploitive economic attitudes and thinly veiled disdain for African Americans. His was a proposal for cultural revitalization around updated conservatism and out of the same fear of southern white social death that had appeared at times of social change in the past.[63]

Americanization of the South, Southernization of the Nation

The election of Jimmy Carter to the U.S. presidency in 1976 was a landmark. The first president from the Deep South since the Civil War, Carter seems the expression and perhaps culmination of one stage of the interracial southern way of life. He was a political figure who combined the southern past and present and became a new symbol for the nation of a South that had changed within a decade. Carter grew up in the Georgia Black Belt, the son of a well-off farmer and a politically progressive mother. He claimed as home Plains, Georgia, a small town that appeared in national culture as almost a caricature

of an isolated southern hamlet full of eccentric characters. Carter remained anchored in the southern life he grew up with—hunting, fishing, stock car racing,
memories of the Civil War, and rock music. He championed the premier southern rock group the Allman Brothers, from Macon, as "good boys. I understand
them." Carter's embrace of evangelical Protestantism made him a typical (in
that regard) representative of his state and region and gave him a common religious vernacular as he campaigned in southern states, but it made him seem an
alien to national media covering him. But he was distant from some southern
ways, as he moved beyond the demagogic politics of such Georgia predecessors
as Eugene Talmadge, who race-baited to gain office. Carter may have grown up
on a farm, but he attended the U.S. Naval Academy and traveled to cosmopolitan places around the nation and world before returning to Plains in 1953 to
manage the family's business enterprises after his father died. He claimed the
populist label and appealed to the working classes, Black and white, by emphasizing common economic concerns. He was also, though, a technocrat, whose
politics by 1976 stressed good management, long-range planning, financial responsibility of government, and competence. When he returned to Plains, he
quickly became involved in community and civic life, served two terms in the
state legislature, and won election as governor in 1970. He became a model for
other progressive young southern Democratic governors in the 1970s and attracted a national audience disillusioned by the corruption in Washington seen
in the Watergate scandal.[64]

In 1976, *Saturday Review* proclaimed the South as "the new America," an
exemplar of the possibilities of economic development and of racial reconciliation leading to national redemption. Writer John Egerton's *The Americanization of Dixie* (1974) had captured the forces that were homogenizing the South
and made it closer to national standards. This long process accelerated in the
post–World War II years. Technological changes were especially significant,
namely the spread of air-conditioning, which tamed the worst effects of the
hot and humid climate that had so often defined the southern way of life for
southerners and outsiders. Perfected in 1939 by Willis Carrier, air-conditioning
by the 1950s cooled hospitals, banks, movie theaters, and motels. Small window
units appeared in the homes of upwardly mobile suburban homes by the 1960s,
when about 20 percent of southern homes were air-conditioned, a figure rising
to 80 percent by 1980. Air-conditioning made the increasing industrialization
of the South possible by attracting northern industries away from decaying
facilities and to new cool factories in the South. Public schools, universities,
grocery stores, department stores, city buses, sports stadiums—all these air-
conditioned places now made southern public life more bearable than before.
Private life changed as well, as southerners moved indoors, away from their

porches that had long nurtured cultural traditions of community engagement and storytelling. Air-conditioning was a taken-for-granted amenity of the suburban southern living of the 1970s and after.[65]

The spread of television also brought the South closer to national norms, lessening the region's sense of isolation from the national culture. It became more widely available beginning in the early 1950s, fascinating southerners of all races and social classes as they heard a bland national accent from television announcers far from their own language, saw the latest fashions in metropolitan areas, heard the same music as people in the rest of the nation, saw Black entertainers lauded in the national television culture, and generally witnessed people behaving in ways sometimes uncommon to traditional southern culture. The expansion of broadcast news organizations coincided with the civil rights movement, and white southerners often saw themselves as quite benighted on the evening news. Of course, southern musical traditions and lifestyles were sympathetically portrayed on television as well, and their positive portrayal of African Americans was especially significant.[66]

Transportation changes also contributed to the nationalization of southern life after World War II through the 1970s. The federal interstate highway system drew the nation's regions into the mainstream as travel times from one part of the nation to another were cut. A new roadside culture offered the same motel chains, gas stations, and fast-food franchises across the nation. The federal government also contributed to the nationalization of American life through funding for airport construction and expansion. Airports in southern cities became among the nation's leaders, and regional airline companies such as Delta Airlines and Southwest Airlines became giants in the industry. The federal government sponsored these giant infrastructure investments that appealed to the South's now economically dominant business and industrial classes and to people in the suburbs.[67]

The 1970s witnessed not only an expansion of this Americanization of Dixie but also the other side of the coin—the southernization of America. Country music radio stations appeared in the nation's largest cities, far removed from their places of rural and small-town origin. The NASCAR industry launched a major expansion beyond its traditional base in the Piedmont South into the West, Midwest, and Northeast. Television evangelists were one of the most dramatic developments in American religion in the 1970s, with ministers becoming high-profile celebrities thanks to their organizations' use of new satellite technology to broadcast their old-time religious appeals to national and even international audiences. Their faiths had been spawned in the rural South but represented high-tech presentations and sophisticated business models that generated millions of dollars. Network television shows had presented southern rural programs such as *The Andy Griffith Show* and *The Beverley Hillbillies* in the 1960s, but the 1970s witnessed the increasing identification of the region with rustic simplicity. It may have started with the televised Watergate hearings, in which North Carolina senator Sam Ervin Jr. was an appealing model of an older, grandfatherly, mannerly, Bible-quoting, honest, law-minded white southerner who charmed the nation. No matter that two decades before he had penned a defense of southern segregation; now he was a new southerner drawing from the best rural values at a time when the nation needed them.[68]

One television show, *The Waltons*, especially embodied the new respectability of white southerners coming out of a rural past that was not only southern but American. In 1971, CBS launched the show based on the writings of Virginian Earl Hamner Jr.; it attracted 40 million viewers by 1973 as part of its ten-year run. Hamner noted the show's conservative appeal in values that bridged an earlier time and a newly emerged conservative southern living located not in the countryside but in suburbs. "We are reaffirming such old-fashioned virtues as self-reliance, thrift, independence, freedom, love of God, respect for one's fellow man, an affirmation of values," which he saw as typically Virginian for two centuries but which were also quite relevant for suburban conservatives. Historian Jack Temple Kirby, himself a Virginian, noted that "Virginians of my blood and acquaintance perceive 'The Waltons' as an affirmation of their way of life, a long overdue 'true' picture of the South, and a rebuke to something vague, unsettling, urban, impersonal, criminal alien—perhaps New York." Despite the nationalization of the South, Kirby's words hinted at a continuing sectional identity rooted in the perception that conservative values especially resonated in the historic and contemporary South.[69]

Such values had particular salience in those contemporary suburban places that faced the anomie of modern life. *The Waltons* might appear timeless in a changing South, but the attitudes associated with the show had particular appeal to southerners who had modernized at a ferocious pace after World War II and experienced the impersonalization of modern bureaucracies. Observers saw the alienation of people from each other and limited community and social interactions in the suburbs compared to traditional small-town life. Growing divorce rates and soaring welfare rolls belied the politicized rhetoric of the South as the repository of family values. Conservative white southerners saw such familial dysfunction that they put forward family values as an antidote to the realities.

No writer better explored a kind of southern existentialism than Walker Percy. Percy was the nephew of Mississippi Delta poet and planter William Alexander Percy, whose 1941 memoir *Lanterns on the Levee* pronounced an end to traditional southern virtues associated with the noblesse oblige he saw in the planter class then in growing decline. William Alexander Percy adopted the young Walker Percy, who grew up in Greenville, Mississippi. His novels *The Moviegoer* (1961), *The Last Gentlemen* (1966), and *Lancelot* (1977) were set in an identifiable South yet dismissed "southern things." He told a 1974 interviewer that "old country characters are not the scene anymore; the scene is what to do with a big urban sprawl like Baton Rouge." He pondered how to write about that. "How're we gonna write about New Orleans—not the French Quarter, but Gentilly?" In Percy's essay "Random Thoughts on Southern Literature, Southern Politics, and the American Future" (1978), he complained that a "boring change is the Changing South as it is usually portrayed (say in *Southern Living*)," where the subject of a New South reminded him of the announcement of "the new Ford, the Model A, in the rotogravure section of the *Atlanta Constitution* in the 1920s." He found more momentous another change, namely that "the South has entered the mainstream of American life for the first time in perhaps 150 years." This change characterized Black and white southerners no longer having to "suffer the unique onus, the peculiar burden of race that came to be the very connotation of the word *South*." Calling race "the Great Southern Obsession," he saw this preoccupation given up but wondered what would be "the impact of this suddenly released energy?" The "astounding dimension of the recent change in the South" was that "virtues and faults of the South are the virtues and faults of the nation, no more no less." The American writer, southerner included, was now saying that "something has gone badly wrong with Americans and American life, indeed modern lifestyles, that people generally suffer a deep dislocation in their lives which has nothing to do with poverty and ignorance and discrimination." The very people who escaped *Tobacco Road*'s dysfunction had moved "to the exurbs and . . . fallen victim to the malaise." What increasingly engaged "the Southern novelist as much as his Connecticut counterpart" was no longer "the Snopeses or Popeyes, or O'Connor's crackers or Wright's black underclass," but their successful grandchildren who are "going nuts in Atlanta condominiums."[70]

Percy feared that, from the perspective of the year 2000, the Southeast "would simply have become a quaint corner of the teeming Southern rim," with the South's best writers "doing soap opera in Atlanta, our best composers country-and-western music in Nashville, our best film directors making sequels to *Walking Tall* and *Smokey and the Bandit*." He worried "whether our supreme architectural achievement will be the Superdome, our supreme cultural achievement will be the year Alabama ranked number one, the Falcons won the Superbowl, and Bobby Jones III made it a grand slam in Augusta." Alas, Percy seemed prescient, given pervasive talk of the Sunbelt in the following decade and the perpetually number one Crimson Tide—but all of his speculations were a part of the spread of southern cultural forms into the rest of the nation. Percy saw that northerners and southerners were more alike by the 1970s than at any time since the early nineteenth century, and he saw hope for common solutions to national problems, perhaps, as in the early national period, with southern politicians in the lead.[71]

———————

John Egerton explored the Americanization of Dixie and the southernization of the nation in his 1974 book, and his conclusions are sobering as one reflects upon the end of two decades of dramatic transformations but also a rising counterrevolution to social, economic, cultural, and political changes in the 1970s South. A self-professed southerner and political liberal, Egerton acknowledged the region's virtues that had grown out of a long historical experience and noted the "unique qualities," including "the moonlight and magnolias, the courtesy and kinship, the friendliness and hospitality, the importance of things personal and concrete, the sense of pace and place and space and grace and soul." But he urged readers to remember that white racism had been "the single most enduring and notorious characteristic of the South." Egerton quoted another journalist, Georgian Joseph B. Cumming Jr., who had covered the civil rights movement and in a 1972 essay noted that southern white racism was "a sort of state religion . . . a *sacred*, not a *secular*, 'way of life.'" He drew attention to the long centrality of racism to the southern way of life and to the civil religion that gave it spiritual and moral sanction. Egerton noted that the worst aspects of southern racism, "the blatant acts of cruelty and depravity," were over, but what remained was "a style and pace and form of white advantage— a more sophisticated racism—that differs little from South to North to West." The softening of the South's racial attitudes prepared the way for the final acts in the future of the Americanization of Dixie.[72]

Egerton, like other southern liberals from 1950 to 1980, foretold the end of the South. Its best qualities would vanish, he feared, as the homogenization of American life proceeded at escalating speed. From the vantage point of the end of Jim Crow segregation, one-crop farming, one-party politics, and even one-faith religion in a more pluralistic region, this thoughtful white southerner noted that "nowhere is there a clear vision of what will replace them." He saw that in the mid-1970s white liberals, as argued here as well, were the most introspective and hopeful about a future South, but Egerton saw talk of a "New South" as "too much like the New Chevy, or the New Wheaties, or even the new Nixon: the same goods in a different package." With the Americanization of the South, he lamented the loss of American diversity as well as real limitations apparent to him on the advance of equality, despite the undeniable gains of the civil rights movement. Southerners, white and African American, had long fulfilled a key American role in pointing to the nation's failure in living up to ideals, but he foresaw now a homogenized South that would give up that role. The Americanization of the South and the southernization of America said more "about fear and failure and estrangement in American society than they do about hope and achievement and reconciliation." He pessimistically listed disturbing dominant trends of the decade: "Deep divisions along race and class lines, an obsession with growth and acquisition and consumption, a headlong rush to the cities and the suburbs, diminution and waste of natural resources, institutional malfunctioning, abuse of political and economic power, increasing depersonalization, and a steady erosion of the sense of place, of community, of belonging." Many of those vanishing qualities had been concerns of the Agrarians half a century before, but Egerton spoke for a southern white liberalism with a different focus than the earlier group but with similar worries about the quality of southern life and the possibilities of obtaining a good life, and social justice, for all of the region's people. Liberalism had won many victories in the 1970s South, but the conservative counterrevolution of the 1980s and afterward would create a deep ideological division in the South, as those two ideologies would compete to find a substitute for the older southern way of life—if the region was to survive at all as a concept.[73]

CHAPTER EIGHT

Southern Living

Constructing Southern Ways
in the Contemporary Era

T HE YEARS AROUND 1980 were key ones for new expressions of what began in the early nineteenth century as southern civilization and became the southern way of life in the twentieth century. "Southern living" became the latest moniker. It adapted southern culture and society to changed post–Jim Crow contexts often more "American" than "southern." Some people still used the term "southern way of life" to describe the middle-class, suburban southern life that took deep root from the 1980s onward. *Southern Living* magazine launched in 1966 and became by 1980 the most successful southern publication and the self-proclaimed arbiter of the new southern way. Issues of style and consumption became central ones in understanding the evolving regional consciousness that centered now in suburbs and among the middle classes. Politics, society, and religion witnessed a new conservatism that emerged in the 1980s as a reaction to changes in the 1960s. Reformers seeking social justice explored the dark underside of the predominant sunny, middle-class vision of southern living. They pointed to peculiar and entrenched economic, social, cultural, and political features sometimes going back to slavery. Many progressives embraced the continued hopeful significance of the southern context, with a narrative of regional redemption of the nation based in the South's biracial culture and spiritual triumph. Culture wars have flared since then, and racial issues have taken on new guises but remain central to the newest version of the southern way of life. African American culture took a southern turn after 1980 and showed a vibrancy that bridged the gaps between an older rural culture and a modern one associated with urban ways. Authors Clifton Taulbert and Ralph Eubanks present revealing African American perspectives on racial sensibilities in the post-1980 South.

I'll Still Take My Stand

The Vanderbilt Agrarians of *I'll Take My Stand* continued to influence intellectual discussions of the South, sometimes evoking spirited responses to it. Mississippian Frank Smith's edited collection *I'll Still Take My Stand*, published in 1980 on the fiftieth anniversary of the earlier manifesto, related the volume to the earlier work. One rarely used the term "liberal" to describe Mississippi politicians in the 1950s, but Smith's opponents did so, castigating the four-term congressman from the Delta for not hewing to the politically conservative orthodoxy that defined the state. Out of political expediency, to be sure, he signed the 1957 Southern Manifesto that opposed the *Brown* decision and advocated federal support for the Delta's farmers to win their support for a while, but he came out of the liberal closet with his support for John F. Kennedy in 1960, for which his opponents maneuvered his defeat in the next election. Kennedy appointed Smith to the Tennessee Valley Authority board, and later he worked in administrative positions out of the state and taught in Virginia in the 1970s.

By 1980, he had been working for change in the region for decades, and he brought together similar figures from government, journalism, and academia for *I'll Still Take My Stand*. He described the new volume as "an attempt to delineate the South, as it exists today, for better or worse, fifty years later." Smith's preface sought to compare his book with the earlier one, whose focus on the conflict between tradition and modernity had, Smith wrote, "set a theme for Southern intellectuals which still persists." Published by little-known Yazoo Press, the volume made little impact, but its essays turn out to be engaged in 1980 with central issues of the contemporary period.[1]

Smith observed that for half a century the Agrarians "had represented the intellectual opposition to most change in southern life," zeroing in on the ongoing importance of the book for any discussion of a southern way. The contributors to *I'll Still Take My Stand*, he said, were, in comparison to the earlier group, "less conservative in politics and by no means agrarian in economics." The title of African American educator Samuel DuBois Cook's essay, "Unfinished Business: The Civil Rights Revolution in the South and the Unfinished Business of Racial and Social Justice," reflected the skepticism of most Black contributors to the volume about the acceptance of racial change in the region at the end of the 1970s. Vernon Jordan, head of the National Urban League and an Atlanta native, confessed he was "frankly troubled by some indications that this brief period of rapid change has not penetrated beneath the hard surface of age-old racial domination." Contributors generally challenged backward-looking mythologies of southern history. Long-time Tennessee progressive reformer and writer Wilma Dykeman wrote of the "infinite variety" of southern women's experience and the gap between stereotypes and realities of women's lives. University of Alabama president David Mathews engaged James Gould Fletcher's lament of mass education in *I'll Take My Stand*, with Mathews embracing public education as the chief solution to the region's problems.[2]

Steve Suitts, director of the reformist Southern Regional Council, offered one of the bleakest assessments of the South's future in the 1980 volume, as his "Where the Sunbelt Doesn't Shine" brought into the open the "forces of discrimination, poverty, and ignorance" that still plagued the "human relations among the region's inhabitants." Suitts focused on "human standards of development" and concluded that the term "Sunbelt" was something of "a bastard term—illegitimately born out of exaggerated opportunities for gross economic activity—not human development." Dreamers once had hoped that if racial segregation could be ended, "the humanness of our daily, shared lives would give the South an unparalleled advantage in achieving greatness in human relations." He saw now, though, issues of race relations being hidden in the "resentments, fear, and plain ignorance" that characterized too many public policy discussions coming out of the conservative ideology at the heart of southern living that sought to preserve white racial privilege. Suitts challenged the myth of the biracial redemptive South and predicted that "this decade may mark when both Black and White Southerners stop dreaming of that beloved community" and when law and conscience no longer brought that ideal to mind.[3]

I'll Still Take My Stand was generally a more hopeful book than that, though, one that contributed in some ways to an upbeat assessment of the new southern way of life. Emory Cunningham's "The Quality of Southern Life" gave a name to the central focus of the new concept of the southern way. Cunningham was well positioned to do so, as the longtime editor of *Southern Living* magazine, the single most important venue for the redefinition of the southern way after the end of Jim Crow segregation and the dramatic advances in the southern economy after World War II. From Alabama, he graduated from Auburn University, served as a navy pilot in World War II, and worked his way through the Progressive Farmer company to help launch and then sustain *Southern Living* for a decade and a half by the time of his 1980 essay. Cunningham claimed that attention to the South's material advancement caused some southerners to worry about the erosion of "that rich, meaningful way of life Southerners perceive to be unique." The editor of the preeminent publication about self-consciously living southern thus linked it to the term "way of life," because he wanted to reassure readers "that the quality of Southern life will not only survive, but it will flourish." He identified that "quality of Southern life" as partly "the proper respect for the region's natural advantages" and noted that "today's South is attractively wooded, enjoys an abundance of water, clean air,

and a benign climate." He highlighted an activist dimension in his vision that
relied on "thoughtful planning." "The Southern way of life" rested as well on
the human heritage of the region's people seen in the arts, music, theater, food,
sports and recreation, a love for travel, and a love of the land. Cunningham
completed his litany of this newly imagined southern way of life with "those
human qualities like Southern courtesy, respect for the work ethic, and in an
admirable and meaningful way, we are still the Bible Belt." The region should
welcome only those industries that could "enhance our Southern way of life."
Southern Living magazine had shown "in a dramatic way that our good Southern way of life, and the best of Southern tradition, cannot only go hand-in-hand
with business growth but in fact accelerate it."[4]

Southern Living

Southern Living offers the most revealing portrait of the new version of the
southern way. The magazine grew out of *Progressive Farmer* magazine, one of
those institutions that had driven the Vanderbilt Agrarians to their bourbon
to deal with their outrage at its promotion of modernization in southern agriculture. Leonidas L. Polk, a former Confederate army officer and an agricultural reformer, established the publication in 1886. He also oversaw changes in
the North Carolina Department of Agriculture and worked with the agricultural program at North Carolina's agricultural college. In 1907, Clarence Poe
became publisher, he of the dream of a great southern rural civilization that
would be racially segregated. The Agrarians saw such figures as Polk and Poe
as antithetical to their imaginings of a traditionalist South, and *Progressive
Farmer* indeed had a crusading spirit in terms of betterment for the white small
farmers who embodied enduring regional dreams of Jefferson's "God's chosen
people." But the magazine combined modern scientific agricultural teachings
with a fond appreciation of such southern farm traditions as how to preserve
not only pickles but small-farm culture as well. Eugene Butler would become
publisher of the journal after Poe, and he was president of the company when
it began publishing *Southern Living*, at a time when the South was undergoing
its dramatic and traumatic social changes associated with the end of Jim Crow
segregation. In 1980, the Progressive Farmer company became the Southern
Progress Company, and in 1985 Time, Inc., bought it for $480 million, a sale
symbolic of the magazine's notable success. Its innovative focus on middle-
class life and culture in the South would influence other publications, all of
which tried to position themselves as offering something different but comple-
mentary to *Southern Living*.[5]

The new magazine had grown out of *Progressive Farmer*'s regular house-
and-garden feature, originally called the Progressive Home and changed to

Southern Living in 1963. John Logue and Gary McCalla were part of the early editorial staff, and they remembered that the magazine started at a time when editors were defensive about their region. "Everybody was running down the South," recalled editor Emory Cunningham. "In every movie, if they had a pot-bellied sheriff, he had a Southern accent." Logue and McCalla, as well as Cunningham, resented such portrayals and felt other southern whites did as well. Older editors argued for the promotion of segregation at a time when it was being challenged and opposed whiskey advertisements just as prohibition was fading as a social policy, but they quickly left the scene after the magazine set its pattern of upbeat promotion of the modern, urban, and suburban South. The magazine long ignored African Americans in suburban southern living, seldom picturing them at all. By the early twenty-first century, the magazine had changed and incorporated Black southerners as featured celebrities, including chefs, gardeners, educators, and people in a variety of other occupations. Advertising pages prominently featured African Americans, often with biracial couples promoting products. By the second decade of the new century, the magazine highlighted women in nonstereotypical features as well.[6]

The first issue of *Southern Living* set the model for its future with regular features on cooking, gardening, and travel. Butler, who was president and editor in chief for the first issue, wrote a column entitled *Southern Living*: In Tune with Today's South, and he identified the magazine's South as "Southern and Southwestern urban and suburban families." He saw "the South's unique differences—its differences in geography and climate—in the way it works and lives—its differences in a hundred other ways." The magazine's mission, as he saw it, was to assist southern families in more enjoyable living by making better use of their growing incomes and leisure time. He spoke to southerners "who want to improve your houses, like to travel, enjoy good food, take part in community affairs, and seek to know more about the South's people and progress"—the latter a word at which the Agrarians cringed. He celebrated a superior South, one where southern readers of the magazine would "live better" than other Americans because they "use and enjoy the South's open country, its mild climate, long growing season, and relatively uncrowded highways." Natural and environmental features thus loomed large in this distinctive and distinguished South, but the magazine's early days focused as much on the region's cities as its suburbs, with Butler embracing long-range planning as the answer to problems facing a rapidly urbanizing region.[7]

Butler set an ambitious agenda for covering the South in a general-interest publication. Its early issues included curious stories for a home-and-garden magazine, such as one celebrating the warden of the Texas prison system—one of the most notorious in the nation—and a perfunctory article on a southern junior college ("one answer to the enrollment problem"). More typical of future coverage would be the first issue's cover story on the Azalea Trail, articles such as "Cornbread: The South's Own Creation" and "Winning Ways with Pork," others celebrating the wonders of Stone Mountain's carved Confederate heroes and Rock City birdhouses, four how-to-do-it articles, and one on when to install air-conditioning. Throughout the magazine's history, beginning with its initial issue, text and photographs told readers how "southerners" evoked traditions but also updated those traditions from their country and small-town origins to new urban and suburban settings. Pimento cheese is, of course, as good on a suburban patio as on a farm porch. The magazine would always avoid explicit evocation of racial segregation and of Old South plantation, Lost Cause, and benighted South imagery. Published in a New South industrial city, Birmingham, it thus carried little baggage of a romanticized South.[8]

As writer Diane Roberts observes, despite addressing a new urban and suburban audience not often targeted in earlier versions of the southern way, "*Southern Living* is still part of the South's 'performance,' representing itself as special, chosen, a favored region congratulating itself on not having the problems associated with the rest of the country." She writes that the magazine represented "a bourgeois Eden," a region "simultaneously as actual and ideal in the sunny photos, sumptuous food spreads, and gracious homes in the photographs: very like the South that tried to present itself to the richer, more powerful, industrialized North both before and after the Civil War." Circulation and advertising success gave the magazine the resources to extend its vision of the new southern way of life through house plans, instructions on making house furniture, garden designs, travel plans, and cooking schools held across the region. Its book-publishing branch, Oxmoor House, published coffee table books picturing attractive examples of southern living. These efforts reflected the growing commodification of the southern identity in general, as southern sayings and icons appeared for sale on T-shirts, bumper stickers, coffee mugs, and endless other items marketed in the magazine. *Southern Living* was a classic case of businesses promoting cultural images that do not always reflect cultural realities, as ideas of southern culture became reified. The southern living promoted by the magazine nurtured localism as well, whether the realities of urban historic preservation or environmental preservation for the region's hikers, campers, fishers, and hunters. The southern living concept in practice also promoted evolution of cultural expression. Books about the South, for example, was long a regular column, and the monthly Southern Journal was often written by prominent contemporary southern writers, a shrewd move that gave the magazine a cultural authority as an arbiter of literary taste. More recently, the magazine has extended its claim on cultural authority beyond tablescapes and garden designs by highlighting musical acts associated with the contemporary South.[9]

Southern Style

Southern style became a defining feature of belief in a distinctive southern living. In the early twenty-first century, the magazine's Oxmoor House produced *Southern Style: Easy Updates Room-by-Room Inspired by Design Ideas*, which outlined how-to-live southern design. The text defined southern style as "formal and informal, colors that soothe but don't bore, fine art but casually displayed," window treatments "that waver somewhere between frilly and masculine," and a rug with a high pedigree passed down across generations but now "the perfect spot for a lucky dog's naptime"—even the family pet was included in southern living. Alabama-born designer Richard Keith Langham, who had gained success as a designer in New York City, captured the "essence of Southern style" when he noted that "even if I'm working in the most elegant of rooms, I bear in mind creature comforts and livability." He labeled this combination "a Southern thing." Recognizing that "sweeping generalities are crazy," he offered one anyway as he insisted that "Southerners really know how to live," with "style" connected to "living." The book claimed that distinctive southern style was in line with national approaches that emphasized the simplicities of modern design, but it still affirmed that the contrasts and combinations of tradition and innovation were "the heart of Southern style" and "the hallmarks of regional charm." An Austin, Texas, designer claimed that "history and tradition should be toasted," preferably with a mint julep cup that was a handy antique. Climate, according to the book, shaped southern style, as the temperate weather in most of the South encouraged outdoor living year-round, with furniture made of wicker, rattan, cane, and bamboo providing natural links to the older South. Another designer analyzed the importance of the hearth to southern style, with the fireplace on cold days becoming the gathering place for "a lively family conversation and old-fashioned Southern storytelling," evoking hoary southern ways. Dogs, once again, occupied a favorite place in this prescriptive southern style, as paintings of hunting dogs adorned well-appointed suburban walls.[10]

Southern Living magazine itself has, of course, embodied such ideas throughout its history. Southern style is a commercialized one of much prominence in the region in general. Many retailers and blogs use the term, but the most significant is the Belk department store. In 2010, the Charlotte-based company announced a new branding and marketing campaign: "Modern.Southern. Style." Promotional features included a new logo, tagline, signage, and advertising. The use of "southern style" was part of an updated corporate identity, as well as evidence of a rising southern regional consciousness in the early twenty-first century. The company's new mission statement said it wanted "to satisfy the modern Southern lifestyle like no one else." Again, the combination of traditional and modern characterized southern living. Tim Belk, the CEO of the department store company, said that the stores would "continue to meet the needs of our traditional and classic customers," but the changes in branding and expanded fashion inventory would "attract new customers who are looking for modern, updated brands and styles." He added that "our vision is for the modern, Southern woman to count on Belk first—for her, for her family, for life." The company at that point had 305 stores in sixteen states it claimed as a southern region.[11]

Women were indeed front and center in discussions of southern style, heard finally in Darius Rucker's country music song "Southern Style." Rucker, an African American born in South Carolina, was in the popular interracial rock group Hootie and the Blowfish before becoming one of the most successful country music artists of the early twenty-first century. The song gives vivid details of southern style through its portrait of a southern, down-home young woman with "sun-kissed hair and not much makeup" and "two first names that came from grandmas on both sides," connecting to family tradition. Rucker adds a literary touch in that "she ain't ever read much Faulkner." The hard-to-read Nobel Prize winner had penetrated popular consciousness here, and people at least knew about him even if they did not actually read him. Rucker's southern woman was earthy, raised on "muddy water—southern style." The next verse identified southern style as "free and easy" and "warm and breezy." The southern woman does not believe in strangers—here is the hospitality the region enshrines—because her parents "raised her southern style."[12]

Suburban, Middle-Class, Individualist

Southern living, the contemporary southern way of life, takes place in ranch houses in the suburbs. Whereas the small town had been the locus of the southern way of life for most of the twentieth century, the suburbs emerged after World War II as new population centers, locales of social life, arbiters of cultural taste, and repositories of economic and political power. Middle-class southerners sat on patios behind their houses rather than on front porches, bringing more social isolation than they'd had in the old-time visiting space of the porch. They lived with like-minded people in subdivisions often given names to evoke the regional past, such as Tara, Twelve Oaks, Windsor, or Waverly. Barbecue grills, not pits, produced favorite regional foods, albeit with a different ambience. Familiar suburban landscape features included golf courses and country clubs, tennis courts, manicured and featureless cemeteries, and concrete swimming pools replacing the old swimming holes. Some people went to megachurches for their spiritual life, and they attended sporting events in vast new arenas nearby. The automobile loomed large in the southern suburbs, leading to sprawl, pollution, and traffic jams. The predominant southern political ideology of conservatism often militated against adequate funding for public transportation, bolstering dependence on the car. In all of this, of course, southern suburbs resembled those throughout the nation, especially in the western parts of the Sunbelt.[13]

Southern living rested on the new middle class, a group that has often not been foregrounded in discussions of the southern way of life. As much as anyone, sociologist John Shelton Reed articulated the underlying outlook of this group at the center of southern living from the early 1980s into the twenty-first century. In his autobiographical essay "The Same Old *Stand*?" he wrote of the two competing visions long structuring southern cultural ways. One was the organic, rooted in regional folk culture that shared much with other premodern societies that embodied a "traditional value orientation," which included parochialism, fatalism, authoritarianism, ethnocentrism, and categorical resistance to innovation. Urbanization and industrialization menaced these aspects of folk cultures, which characterized small towns and agrarian communities in many societies. He understood that such a value system was no longer dominant in the South and not the foundation for "a competing civilization, not the sort of thing manifestoes are made of." Here Reed references, of course, *I'll Take My Stand*, which he discovered while a student in the Northeast at the Massachusetts Institute of Technology in the early 1960s. "For a Tennessee boy," he wrote, who was having doubts "about both Massachusetts and technology, the book was a bombshell." Coming from an East Tennessee culture far from the plantation world and slavery's legacy, he realized he had never really thought about southern identity. The Agrarian manifesto, read by a Tennessean out of place in the North during the days of the civil rights movement, caused him to do so, but he came to realize that its defense of rurality and agrarian ways was surely long out of date as an accurate indicator of any dominant form of regional culture. It was no "longer a matter of defending a Southern way of life against industrialism. Increasingly that way of life *is* industrialism." What he came to prize about the book, though, was that its affection for the South itself led him to the awareness that southern identity was somewhat like the ethnic identity he saw among the northerners he met. Rejecting white supremacy as what he called "the essence" of southern living in the contemporary era, he identified his regional culture as a biracial one. He and the southern African Americans he met in the Northeast had similar accents, shared an anecdotal way of speaking, knew the same Baptist and Methodist hymns, quoted scripture in outlandish contexts, enjoyed the same foods, and shared "a good many assumptions that he couldn't quite put his finger on." As with ethnic cultures,

"the essential qualities of the group may be, finally, ineffable." Southern studies
scholars would soon distance themselves from ideas of cultural essence, but
Reed in his early work probed for ways to identify, if not an essence, then at
least the sociological norms that identified many people who claimed the title
"southerner."[14]

The second element Reed saw animating forms of regional culture historically was the "stubborn, individualist, 'I'm as good as you' outlook," a collection
of cultural themes that competed with and undermined the demands of pre-
scription, hierarchy, and organic community—all of which had characterized
I'll Take My Stand. This outlook had emerged by 1980 as the dominant one of
the new contemporary, suburban white middle-class version of southern living.
Twentieth-century economic and demographic developments had eroded the
folk culture, with the South's laissez-faire free enterprise developing relatively
"unchecked by prescriptive obligations and restraints based on family position, rank, class, or even race." Reed looked to the region's dominant religious
tradition, evangelical Protestantism, for the classic expression of individualism. In this interdenominational spiritual practice embodied by the Baptists,
Methodists, Presbyterians, and Pentecostals, the focus of spiritual life was on
sin and salvation, the conversion of the individual. This became the model
for the individualistic vision of southern living. Just as southerners worked
out their own salvation without the official institutional help of church, priest,
or sacrament, "so we have often been inclined to work out our own justice
without running off to the legislature or the courts." Respect for individualism
and self-reliance now characterized the typical southerner's economic outlook.
Middle-class white southerners, according to survey data, believed by 1980 that
African Americans should not face limited expectations through segregation
laws or discriminatory employment policies. Polling suggested southern whites
welcomed anyone as a neighbor who could afford to live in the neighborhood
and that their neighbors' children should attend the same schools as their own.
He pointed out that they were indifferent, though, to people who failed "the
sink-or-swim test of a laissez-faire economy." Reed insisted that, despite this
pronounced individualism, community survived as an ideal in the South, cush-
ioning any nascent fragmentation.[15]

Conservatism

Suburban southern living in these imaginings represented a southern version
of the American dream. Just as antebellum plain folk southerners saw rising in
society to own slaves and a plantation as the southern version of the American
dream, now white southerners could see the suburban southern lifestyle as a
new southern version of the contemporary American dream. The "whiteness"

of this dream was apparent, although it is too easy to portray the suburbs as simply an escape from an integrated post–civil rights South. For one thing, African Americans who could afford it, members of a growing Black middle class in the decades after 1980, embraced suburban living as a sign of their success, as did, later, second-generation Latino immigrants to the South. White minister Will D. Campbell saw the growth of suburbs after the civil rights movement, though, as "a time of violent resistance in many urban and suburban areas when black families, no matter how literate and genteel, tried to move into white neighborhoods." Campbell added that planning for development of such places might not be overtly color-conscious, "but perfection in community planning had not reckoned with the greatest enemy of life in community— bigotry." One saw this in schools, with "white flight" from urban areas that were becoming overwhelmingly African American by the 1980s and the white middle class abandoning public schools for private academies, church schools, and homeschooling. The laissez-faire economic and political policies of the increasingly Republican-dominated South failed to address such problems as crime, low wages, sparse social services, and poor schools.[16]

Despite predominant sunny visions of the good life of the suburbs, a considerable amount of anxiety and downright fear haunted the people in those ranch houses. *New York Times* southern correspondent Peter Applebome wrote of attending a Newt Gingrich public event in early 1994 in Cobb County, an Atlanta suburb. Gingrich admitted that the people in that county, like other suburbanites, "want safety, and they believe big cities have failed and are controlled by people who are incapable of delivering goods and services." He contrasted the "pristine work ethic of Cobb County versus the 'welfare state' values of Atlanta," which Applebome added was "a pitch as old as the South." Gingrich did not hesitate to use coded words to stir up racial animosities. African Americans in Cobb County by the 1990s were hardly a presence but Gingrich understood their symbolic value. "People in Cobb don't object to upper-middle-class neighbors who keep their lawn cut and move to the area to avoid crime," Gingrich said. "What people worry about is the bus line gradually destroying one apartment complex after another, bringing people out for public housing who have no middle-class values and whose kids as they become teenagers often are centers of robbery and where the schools collapse because the parents that live in the apartment complexes don't care that the kids don't do well in school and the whole school collapses." Gingrich thus portrayed, as Applebome puts it, "the unseen menace, horror, and decay of Atlanta, 70 percent black, just across the Chattahoochee." White suburbanites saw their world as a superior one, the achievement of the long-sought "good life," embodying what Applebome labeled "Cobb's symphony of entrepreneurial suburban virtue."[17]

The conservatism that Gingrich represented was the social philosophy that animated southern living from the 1980s, and it became the governing political philosophy of the South, allied with the growth of the Republican Party. Contemporary Republican strength built on decades of a developing realignment between white southerners and the Republican Party. Although the South had long contained pockets of populist reformism and had supported Franklin D. Roosevelt, conservatism was always a strong political sentiment, resting in the Bourbon business/landowner governing elite going back to the late nineteenth century. It feared the power of the federal government to affect race relations and elite economic and class dominance, but southern power brokers were often also firm believers in economic development and used state governments to promote that goal. Ronald Reagan's election as president in 1980 symbolized the national triumph of a conservatism well rooted in the South. No southerner, Reagan was a Sunbelt figure from California who appealed to ongoing resentment among many white Americans about race, the role of the federal government, and taxation to support public programs. He and the southern Republicans he energized branded the Democratic Party as one of criminal defendants, welfare "queens," feminists, African Americans, and others who asserted their rights coming out of the late 1960s and 1970s. The country club remained a conservative southern living space, but Reagan's appeals to the white working class and to evangelical Protestants broadened the southern Republican Party to include stock car racetracks and stained-glass-windowed worship spaces. Busing to gain racial balance in schools was a divisive issue in the 1970s, and southern Republicans lambasted it as well as the Supreme Court's ban on prayer in public schools, its sanction of abortion rights, and affirmative action policies. The religious Right became a key foundation of the Republican governing coalition. Jerry Falwell's Moral Majority had formed in Virginia in 1979, the year before Reagan's victory, and it politicized southern Evangelicals in unprecedented ways.[18]

New South for New Southerners

One group of people who represented a peculiar position in terms of contemporary ideas of the southern way of life were American migrants who came south after 1980 in significant numbers. A 1991 book, *The South for New Southerners*, offered a window on southern living at that moment in time. The authors, among the leading historians of the U.S. South, spoke a language of civilization, ways of life, and southern lifestyles. An optimistic book still in the throes of thinking about the postsegregation, economically advancing South, it rubbed traditional southern cultural ways against modernization and offered a lively blueprint of contemporary southern life for acclimating newcomers. From the beginning, the authors assumed the southern culture and lifestyle might be bewildering to many people coming from other places to the region. The book explored how doing business in the South would occur in a particular context, making it different from elsewhere. It examined white southern attitudes to the Civil War, special meanings of history in the region, boundaries of the South as a geographic and imaginary place, the rhetoric and reality of race relations, changes from rural to urban life, the myth of the southern belle and the reality of complex southern women's lives, political changes that had turned the solid Democratic South into the solid Republican South, and recent transformations of the historically poorest region into the booming Sunbelt economy.[19]

Lead editor Paul Escott, in "Getting to Know the South," used familiar words to speak of the South as a special American region, "special in its history, its character, its ways of life, and the good life it has to offer." He noted that newcomers would get questions that might befuddle, embarrass, or offend them, but, in good counseling mode, he suggested patience. When natives asked about religion, it was not so much to pry, he said, as to help incorporate the newcomer into the community. Southerners, he admitted, could be "strangely defensive" about matters such as the memory of the Confederacy, so one should choose words carefully. Escott and other authors in the volume stressed the continuing centrality of race relations in southern communities, but their agreement must have reassured northern migrants to the region that southern race relations were now not so different from those in other parts of the nation. Authors noted the inequality of wealth among whites as well as between Black and white people, but—stressing cultural ways—they argued that "living on top of a powder keg" in a mixed-race society may have encouraged the mannerly southern behavior to deflect, through tact and indirection, potential turbulent conflicts. The authors saw, as Escott put it, the "more desirable, humane traits" of the region growing out of the small-town southern context of traditional life and the weak economy that made people less consumed with the demands of a fast-paced industrial life. Newcomers doing business with southerners should listen carefully and realize that "apparently aimless pleasantries sometimes constitute the heart of a conversation as Southerners feel each other out and indirectly discover all they need to know."[20]

Another essay in the collection, "Uncle Sam's Other Province: The Transformation of the Southern Economy," dealt with a key issue in this Sunbelt-era text. Its beginning point was how economic development had led to "a good life here in the South," again utilizing a key descriptor of southern living in the contemporary era. Authors David R. Goldfield and Thomas E. Terrill admitted that salaries might still be lower in the South than elsewhere, but "the trade-off is the lifestyle" that included landscaped suburban subdivisions, easy access to mountains and beaches, and the air-conditioned comforts of home, work, and shopping. They added to that list the social relations of daily life, namely the slower pace of southern living: "Clerks at the mall take a little more time with each customer; the bank teller knows you by your first name; and the mechanics at the neighborhood filling station will fix your car and you will still have enough left over to eat for the rest of the week," all of which were advantages compared to where many newcomers came from. Indeed, they observed that what Americans sought in moving south was "not just old buildings" but a "lost lifestyle." Goldfield and Terrill's effusive conclusion was that "this is the Sunbelt, y'all—a land where prosperity has not yet driven out civility." It seemed a happy convergence of modernity and traditionalism.[21]

Religion and Southern Living

A 2006 *Washington Times* article, "Church a Way of Life in Dixie," discussed the widespread association of religiosity with the South. The Bible Belt image went back to the early twentieth century, when the national media created the image of the region's orthodox and repressive religion as part of its backwardness compared to the more secular and modern Northeast. White southerners relied on religion as a prime component of southern civilization from the early nineteenth century, and they invested divine meaning into the southern way of life in the twentieth century. Traditionally, religion in the South has prized religious experience over other aspects of religious systems, promoted missionary work to save sinners, invested extraordinary meaning in the Bible, demanded moral rigor in personal behavior, and made a very personal Jesus the center of the faith. An interdenominational religious system, embodied by the most popular groups in the region—Baptists, Methodists, and Presbyterians—dominated southern public life. Although Roman Catholics and Jews were a notable presence in some places in the South, they accommodated the Protestant consensus and preserved their faiths as sanctuaries of their ethnic and religious identities. The *Times* story cited statistics showing that southerners—Black as well as white—were still more frequent churchgoers than other Americans, and it quoted Wilfrid McClay, a scholar and evangelical Anglican at the University of Tennessee at Chattanooga, who pointed out that living in the South, "you still feel you're in a kind of Christendom," a place where "the normative assumptions are Christian and evangelical."[22]

Our initial guide to southern living—that is, the magazine—never featured religion as defining the suburban middle-class version of the southern way of life. Churches figured there as historic places to be preserved and visited as part of a satisfying trip with children. Promoters of an explicit southern living concept did not talk much about religion, but it remained a crucial foundation for those leading a southern middle-class, suburban life as well as for other southerners. Religious commitment ran parallel, in other words, to the southern living version of southern life, and it draws in the contemporary period from national as well as regional developments. The dramatic changes in the southern context in the 1960s had upended churchgoers' sense of control and order over society, and southern religious conservatives came to see not just the South but the national culture as one whose Christian foundations had fragmented and stood endangered. Southern Evangelicals had long affirmed a southern civil religion that saw sacred meanings in the regional experience, but by the late twentieth century many of them had come to accept the American civil religion that enshrined sacred meanings in national experience. The sense that that exceptionalism was endangered proved to be a powerful motivating force for southern religious conservatives organizing to promote their agenda of reversing national decay.[23]

The religious Right began its rise in the immediate aftermath of the successes of the civil rights movement and learned from the movement's organizational and ideological passions. The Moral Majority, the first prominent national religious Right organization, focused the efforts of Evangelicals and fundamentalists in the late 1970s and early 1980s by stressing a specific agenda of moral issues and an assertive patriotism. The organization found many followers in the upper South and nearby Midwest—befitting the leadership of its founder, the Virginia Baptist Jerry Falwell—but fewer in the Deep South. Even as the Moral Majority attracted supporters throughout the nation, the South was fertile territory for many other efforts by the religious Right. And when the Moral Majority collapsed at the end of the 1980s, other organizations took its place, including Christian Voice, the Religious Roundtable, the National Christian Political Action Committee, and, above all, the Christian Coalition.[24]

These parachurch groups advanced a moral agenda that defined the movement. Issues that had long been prominent for southern churches declined in significance after 1970—above all the defense of a white racial ethic and the prohibition of alcoholic beverages. They had virtually defined the churches' active social involvement in many earlier periods. Especially noteworthy was the decline of overt racism in conservative white evangelical Protestantism. Although its style and political outlook do not attract many African Americans, the white Evangelicalism that still dominates the religious South no longer openly preaches or practices racism, and white charismatics particularly embrace a spirit-filled multiracialism at times. The religious Right has often found common ground on social issues with the African American churches with which it shares so much moral belief, supporting a conservative biracial foundation for ideological southern living. Principal areas of concern for the religious Right have to do with the family and sex, but control of schools, regulation of mass culture, and policies of the federal government toward religion are also guiding interests. Prominent specific issues have been abortion, pornography, gay rights, school prayer, and the Equal Rights Amendment. The religious Right has been adept at forging alliances among Roman Catholics, Mormons, Missouri Synod Lutherans, and Orthodox Jews and even, on specific issues such as pornography, with feminists.[25]

Even as race declined as an overt divider in southern religious life, and in southern living in general, evangelical leaders did not give up their campaign against the political philosophy that had brought Jim Crow down. In a 1988 sermon to the Southern Baptist Convention (SBC), W. A. Criswell, the longtime pastor of Dallas's First Baptist Church, who had repented of his segregationist views, argued that because of "the curse of liberalism today," his opponents in the SBC claimed to be moderates, but "a skunk by any other name still stinks." He insisted that "we have lost our nation to the liberals, humanists, and atheists and infidels." When latter-day preachers such as Criswell speak of the nation, they draw on earlier images of the South as the evangelical bastion of righteousness. As religious studies scholars Carl Kell and L. Raymond Camp point out, the rhetoric of SBC presidents since Criswell "suggests that of a denominational recapture of the lost 'Southern cause.'" Gender issues have become potent items on that agenda, and the religious Right has easily, if unselfconsciously, adapted earlier racial rhetoric of keeping others "in their place." Evangelical leaders after the 1980s have affirmed an updated version of the old patriarchy that had been planted in the antebellum slave society, with women in their place at the base of the envisioned healthy society, now reimagined for a suburban middle-class population. Since 1980 SBC resolutions have affirmed that women should forever be subjected to men and have banned them from ordination to church ministry.[26]

The SBC exemplifies one of the most important developments in contemporary southern living: the diminishing support for public schools. Southern Baptists played a key role in the creation of public education in the South. The waning of support for the schools dates from the efforts to integrate them in the 1960s and the accompanying Supreme Court rulings limiting school prayer and Bible reading. School voucher programs, homeschooling, and the growth of private church schools in the 1980s exemplified the distancing of southern religious conservatives from the promise of public schooling. They lobbied state textbook committees to include creationism in addition to evolutionary science and warned darkly of schoolbooks portraying New Age religion and alternative lifestyles.[27]

The worldview of white Evangelicals in the South reflected a particular version of southern living, one rooted in the nineteenth-century southern past but representing a conservative version of the American way of life. They seek recognition of their vision of a Christian civilization that asserts that moral absolutes exist and that any honest individual can discern them. Society should affirm these moral absolutes in law, and the government should work to preserve them and to cultivate moral character in its people. The media, public educational institutions, and the federal courts are the enemies of this vision; their influence must be subdued so the tenets of the vision of a Christian civilization, which had once dominated public life, could once again be at the center not only of regional but also of national culture. Southern Evangelicals thus saw a "southern strategy" that not only focused on the South itself but involved the South's (redeemer) role in shaping the nation.[28]

Although this worldview and political agenda fired the religious Right's seeming commitment to old-time values, the middle-class, suburban living that now characterized so many of the southern faithful eroded some traditional southern church ethical concerns. Dancing had always been suspect among many southern Evangelicals, but it drew less passionate condemnations now than earlier. Many more deacons and church leaders decided it was okay to have a beer or a glass of wine, despite the ancient prohibition against demon rum. References to alcohol diminished in Southern Baptist rhetoric. The long-time opposition to divorce declined as the realities of a changing society made it hard to ignore that divorced people were everywhere in the South, and many churches began ordaining divorced men as deacons, allowed divorced men and women in Sunday School classes, and even created special programs to attract them to local congregations. The catchword had once been opposition to "worldly activities," but by the late twentieth century, the term seemed antique in the South, as southern living in everyday church life reflected a stress on individual choice rather than on compelling church social proscriptions.[29]

Politics became a battleground for the agenda of the religious Right, which allied with, and reinforced, the conservativism of the Republican Party in the South and became a bulwark of that party's national success. Richard Nixon's southern strategy foresaw appeal to religion as one way to capture southern white voters, and Ronald Reagan won the observant evangelical Protestant vote in the election of 1980. Jimmy Carter, himself a born-again Evangelical, captured some of that vote in the 1976 campaign, but Carter's success rested on Black Protestants, Catholics, secular voters, and less observant white Protestants. In the late 1970s, Republican political operatives saw the possibility of reconstituting what political scientist John C. Green calls the "white Protestant alliance" of evangelical and mainline Christian denominations in the South that had been linked for almost a century to the Democratic Party and became "a foundation of the solid South." Historically, the preservation of white supremacy combined with a view of the importance of traditional morality to undergird the southern social order. Contemporary leaders of the religious Right and the Republican Party cooperated in a new coalition of religiously observant Evangelicals, based on moral issues, and other white Protestants, based on free-market economic issues. This coalition was southern based but part of a broader national conservative movement and came to fruition with the presidential campaigns of George W. Bush in 2000 and 2004. Bush swept the eleven former Confederate states in 2000, which gave him more than half of the electoral votes he needed. States bordering the region, and with pronounced southern cultural influences, gave him another quarter of his votes. Observant evangelical Protestants were the core of the old white Protestant alliance, and they have been the driving constituency of the religious Right. Donald Trump won even more of the evangelical vote in the 2016 presidential election, despite his lack of sustained religious commitment and his clear moral turpitude. Southern religious people had long looked to being a "good man" as the defining quality in a political candidate, above and beyond ideology, but their concern at what they perceived as the endangered influence of Christian civilization led them to wholesale rejection in 2016 of that quality as a requirement for a president.[30]

Culture Wars, Civil Religion, and Megachurches

Religion was implicated in the core issues of the cultural wars of the late twentieth and early twenty-first centuries amid southern living anxieties in a new southern middle-class, suburban world. Efforts to inject religion into public life and, alternatively, to escape into new megachurches that catered to suburbanites—both showed efforts to adapt earlier religious traditions to new contexts. White Evangelicals sought to dominate the public sphere, for example, through symbolic struggles to define region and nation as embodying sacred expectations. They made social and cultural issues a defining feature of southern political life and southern living. The Confederate battle flag, with its St. Andrew's cross on a red background, was one of those prime southern symbols that had long celebrated not just the Confederacy but the entire southern way of life. It emerged first in Civil War battle, as a dramatic visual image around which troops could rally, and then became an emblem of the South's Lost Cause after the Civil War as part of a civil-religious complex that saw the Confederacy as holy. Over the years, the Ku Klux Klan displayed the flag as part of its vigilante activities, and it was a prominent icon for opponents of the civil rights movement. The Mississippi flag in the 1890s and the Georgia flag in the 1950s incorporated the image, both eras of rising white racial consciousness. Since the 1970s, African Americans and their white allies have challenged the appropriateness of such flags, as it became one of the most divisive cultural issues in the region. In 2020, Mississippi became the last southern state to change its state flag containing the battle flag image. After the mass killings at Emanuel African Methodist Episcopal Church in Charleston, South Carolina, in 2015, South Carolina removed the Confederate battle flag from the state house grounds, and Alabama governor Robert Bentley ordered the Confederate flag to be removed from state properties because it harmed economic development efforts—the driving dynamic of southern living since the 1960s.[31]

The display of the Ten Commandments in the South shows how region, nation, and religion have become intertwined in what might be considered the South's new civil religion, which puts a sacred gloss on southern living. This symbol focuses broader meanings about how evangelical Protestants and their allies believe the South must embody Christian moral expectations not just privately but in the region's public spaces. In July 2002, Roy Moore, the newly elected chief justice of the Alabama Supreme Court, directed workers to place a 5,280-pound granite monument he had designed, with the Ten Commandments and quotations from the Bible and the Founding Fathers, in the rotunda of the state judicial building in Montgomery. This act drew upon popular fervor for the state to acknowledge open religiosity, and it created a memorable firestorm in the history of civil religion in the South. Moore had claimed the Ten Commandments as his cause from his days as a state judge in Etowah County, when a hand-carved plaque of the commandments hung in his courtroom, and he later won election to the Supreme Court as the "Ten Commandments judge." In 2003, a federal district court, and later the federal circuit court of appeals in Atlanta, ordered removal of the granite monument as a violation of the First Amendment's prohibition on government establishment of religion. The court compared Moore to "those Southern governors who attempted to defy federal court orders during an earlier era," the civil rights era—with Alabama governor George Wallace in the forefront with his proclamation of states' rights. The state, regional, and national press made similar linkages that strengthened the sense that evangelical Protestant moral-religious crusading had replaced race as a defining public issue in contemporary southern living.[32]

The fundamentalist and politically conservative Protestant religious Right reflected an important dimension of the southern living concept, one that worked to preserve a traditional southern culture in a new suburban world. Such efforts were thrust into a changing context by the early twenty-first century, shaped partly by the coming of new immigrant peoples and world religions to the South. Prosperity, secularization, increasing demographic and cultural diversity, the role of the media, and technology all are obstacles to the maintenance of traditional ways in the South in general, and especially in terms of religion. If a new pluralism can be seen emerging in the recent South, a renewed sense of evangelical mission once again projects the need to preserve the South as the heartland of this religion.[33]

Megachurches are a recent development within southern and national Prot-estantism that reflect the suburban and exurban society that the southern liv-ing concept embodies. Megachurches typically have 2,000 or more attendees in combined weekend services, although some, such as Atlanta's World Changers Ministries, have congregations of 20,000 people, who meet in buildings that resemble another feature of suburban living: sports arenas. People come to hear preaching about worldly success, individual conversion, pious behavior, and respectability—a bourgeois message for middle-class people, who can combine the materialism of southern living with religious expression. The sheer size of worshipping audiences implies God's favor to believers—not only his spiritual blessing but the promise of his material blessing. Megachurches offer sanctuar-ies from the larger world by providing countless services (daycare for working families, gyms for exercise, and kitchens to cook evening meals) and ministries to targeted audiences (young singles, families with young children, the elderly, and ethnic minorities). These churches have been notable in attracting biracial middle-class worshippers, while at other times they reflect a predominantly African American religious impulse sometimes resembling the older uplift phi-losophy of teaching middle-class values to socially striving audiences.[34]

Race and Southern Living

Just as the Vanderbilt Agrarians had not discussed race as a key issue in their version of the southern way of life, despite its obvious saliency to efforts to grasp the meanings of the American South, so the architects of southern living did not make race an important issue at all. Nonetheless, as they had for the earlier writers, race relations remained of central concern, albeit hidden, for architects of southern living who did not want to rest their ideas of southern life on discredited racism. The suburbs depicted in Southern Living were, early on, more or less for whites only. There was little reference to African Ameri-cans, despite their sizable presence in the southern states. That would change as time went on, but in the early days after Jim Crow segregation ended, and certainly through the 1980s, the southern living construct represented a time of transition as white southerners worked to preserve their privileges while marginalizing African Americans from mostly white "home" venues, whether magazines, festivals, or churches. A contrary tendency toward recognizing the South as a biracial community took root and will be discussed shortly, but here the concern is to elucidate the ways whiteness continued to be attached to the concept of the southern way and southern living. No more would it be celebrated in public events, whether governors' inaugurations, legislative sessions, or school activities. But a powerful strain of southern living evoked implicitly, if not explicitly, an exclusive image of community. Often, by celebrating domestic traditions and family life in events that were semipublic and certainly those that were private, whites were able to evoke nostalgically the regional past—which, of course, had been segregated. In the time of transition after the abrupt end of legal segregation, white conservatives betrayed their anxieties of the new racial order, retreating to whites-only places, institutions, and events whenever they could.[35]

A young University of Mississippi student, who had grown up in a Memphis suburb that embodied the southern living concept, wrote in 2017 of his racism as "something I inherited." It offered a fascinating case study of how growing up in the southern living suburbs could foster a new style of polite, post–Jim Crow white supremacy. "There's no particular point that it started," he reflected, "but over the years, my surroundings introduced me to the idea that skin color could determine the character of a person, even in slight ways." Attuned to the subtle cultural ways that he learned his culture of racism, he speculated that it was "my mostly white community and the way it talked about the inner-city schools, sports teams and children as if they were holding us back." He imagined that he was taught "not by word but by action" to walk faster than usual past a Black man on the sidewalk, "the way I was taught fear." He recognized that his inherited white racism was "related to the way racist jokes, comments and conversations from older family members were constant, even if uncomfortable," aspects of his childhood. Always distancing himself from such obvious racism, he came to realize, through conversations with others at the University of Mississippi, that "the implicit biases had taken root before I finished elementary school." Writing in the student newspaper, he urged his fellow students to discuss the kinds of prejudices he recognized that he had almost unconsciously learned. The column was a rare detailing of a white middle-class suburban student's account of learning a subtle whiteness in the contemporary South but also of his ability to transcend that learning.[36]

Mississippi writer Ellen Douglas, of an old Adams County family, reflected earlier, in the 1990s, about "all the pressures to conform and live in separate worlds" that still existed, despite dramatic changes in society. She saw intermarriage as still a "threat to most white people in the South," who remained suspicious of socializing across racial lines because that could lead to romance, marriage, and children. Whites feared, she thought, the endangerment of race-based social prestige if Black people truly became equals. Her parents' generation, she felt, would not have seen it as simply loss of social or economic privileges in the face of Black assertiveness. Instead, they saw their opposition to social equality "as having a genuine moral basis," touching on the old belief in white moral superiority and Black moral inferiority. "Superiority was the genuine perception for those people," she said. "They believed it from when they were little children." She added that whites did not want to admit past injustices that now are so obvious because admitting fault would threaten their loss of authority and power.[37]

A look at Mississippi's Neshoba County Fair reveals the sometimes-painful struggles of white southerners to adjust to the rapid end of an old racial order after the late 1960s. The fair began in 1891 under the auspices of a livestock and agricultural association that has remained a private nonprofit organization that oversees the annual event each July. A 1980 *National Geographic* article by Carolyn Bennett Patterson on the fair detailed how the white participants gathered in their cabins—some of which dated back to 1893—for dinners for family and friends and went to the fairgrounds for harness racing, gospel singing, and political speeches, the result of which was to "join in tribal rites of fellowship" where "a whole way of life finds affirmation." The fair exemplified the privatization but persistence of cultural customs and ways associated with the past but shorn now of overt racial rhetoric. Whites who are an active part of the fair culture sometimes resent implications that race is involved, but it is hard to miss the absence of African Americans. The latter are present as servants sometimes, and they go to the Founder's Square for more public events. But the heart of the event is the cabin life with rather spare buildings that nonetheless foster a renowned whites-only version of southern hospitality, as visitors unknown to the families are sometimes invited in for drinks or food. Historian Trent Watts describes the cabins as the "heart of a Disneyesque 'Southland,' a racially segregated imagining of a Mississippi town." The county is nearly a third African American, but, as one Black resident of the county said of whites, "it's for them, not for us."[38]

The fair has long been associated with political rhetoric, with a range of segregationist and populist speakers. Such extreme segregation defenders as James Vardaman, Theodore Bilbo, James Eastland, and Ross Barnett were regulars and used enflamed racist language. Part of the clear transition after the 1960s for the fair was the decline of such racist language, although code words were often present, with veiled understandings of a shared white consensus. The belief in a changed Mississippi, on the other hand, has been embraced by politicians speaking at the fair, as they acknowledge the injustices of the old days, but conservatives insist that the changes of the 1960s ended racial problems. Ronald

Reagan chose the fair in the summer of 1980 for his first campaign rally after gaining the Republican nomination for the presidency. Only a decade and a half after the civil rights murders in Neshoba County, Reagan understood that southern white conservatives were a vital part of a winning national constituency. He knew as well not to use racist language, but, amid waving Confederate flags and people singing "Dixie," he spoke the language of states' rights and southern traditionalism that had long justified the southern status quo and, in this case, presaged the Reagan revolution ideology of anti–federal government, low taxes, and low services.[39]

The Neshoba County Fair is thus a telling ritual of the complicated post–Jim Crow dynamics of race relations in the South. It is an extreme example because of the long history of the event and private control of the spaces involved, but it is revealing of broad South-wide white attitudes. Race and social class have continued to be tied together in the contemporary South as well. A *New York Times* story in 2000, "How Race Is Lived in America," made that point through a case study of the Smithfield Packing Company in Bladen County, North Carolina. Whites represented most of the supervisors, Lumbee Indians native to the area did most of the skilled work, and African Americans and newly arrived Latinos worked at the dirty, low-paying slaughtering jobs. Racial tensions ran through the workplace, according to the story, among all the groups who distrusted and resented each other. Eating areas and locker rooms were self-segregated, and the lack of a common language complicated the workday. At the same time, elsewhere, the Black middle class grew throughout the years after 1980, although the recession of 2008 hit that group hard in diminishing economic reserves they had begun to accumulate. African Americans have converted their demographic dominance of southern urban areas into political, social, and cultural power, and sometimes economic power as well. They govern the South's largest cities and towns, serve in state legislatures, and represent their districts in Congress. John Lewis was as acclaimed as any southerner serving in Congress until his death in 2020, while such younger politicians as Arthur Davis in Alabama and Stacey Abrams in Georgia represented the post–civil rights leadership. African Americans are judges, city police chiefs and county sheriffs, university presidents and administrators, coaches in high school and college, hospital administrators, and managers of big and small businesses.[40]

Clifton Taulbert

One text is particularly revealing of how powerful the remnants of the segregationist southern way of life were to a prominent southern African American even a generation after the end of Jim Crow segregation; it provides another perspective on the centrality of race relations to any effort to understand contemporary southern living. In his book *The Invitation* (2014), African American writer Clifton Taulbert explores the ways that the imprisoning psychology from his Jim Crow segregated childhood survives in the mind of a successful Black businessman. Taulbert is the author of thirteen books, most of which are memoirs about his childhood in Glen Allan, Mississippi, a rural town in the Delta. A former Oklahoma banker, he is founder and director of the Building Community Institute, a company that consults on human capital development. He is a fascinating figure who uses his life story to urge more stress on community values in business and to promote social justice. His first book, *Once Upon a Time When We Were Colored* (1995), began his career as a frequent memoirist of the rural Black South. His books portray strong African American families and communities that helped Black people survive the injustices of segregation. More in the tradition of Zora Neale Hurston than Richard Wright as a commentator on southern Black life, he sees Black culture as nurturing and shows African Americans suffering from racial oppression but not defined by it. Raised by an extended family, his term for the supportive network of family and friends in his childhood is "porch people," reminiscent of Hurston's "porch" as the space for the folklife of her hometown of Eatonville, Florida.[41]

Taulbert develops a particular position in regard to the South that enables him to embrace a postsegregation South but see its shortcomings as well. "The South is this eternal place I live," he writes. "The place where I first saw the sun and admired the moon, where I first laughed and cried." The South was also "the first place I heard my own voice and the voices of others—those who loved me and those who sought to define my life by the color of my skin." Looking back on his segregated childhood, he sees skin color as the "'forever' branding that would bring into our lives the multiple lessons of race and place required for our survival." He grew up "dreaming of a better place" and used the term "southern way of life" to label the imprisoning concept that was the opposite of his dreaming. He first uses the term in the preface to his book: "I was not one of 'them,' the landed gentry who set in motion a way of life for those who looked like me—a way of living that had evolved out of slavery and dared the Emancipation to change it." Taulbert recognizes the lessons of survival he learned as a child under the southern way; the significance of his book is in showing the tenacity of those lessons long after changes had dismantled the legal structures of segregation.[42]

Taulbert's memoir recounts meeting an older white woman, Camille Davenport Sharp, during a lecture stop in a small South Carolina town. She owns a cotton-growing plantation called Rosedale, much like the one on which he grew up. Sharp invited him to spend the night at the plantation big house, where he saw many disturbing reminders of the older South—rural poverty, shotgun shacks, and bare yards. He admits that he became "overwrought by what I was seeing—the way of life of 'colored' people that hadn't changed." Taulbert thus uses the term to evoke in the twenty-first century the persistent presence of what might seem a vanished South with all of the post-1960s talk of change. He uses the imagined voice of Little Cliff, his childhood persona, who reminds Taulbert about the lessons from his childhood of the dangers of interacting with white people. Taulbert realizes that he has not forgotten "how to be colored" when he has experiences that remind him of the old way of life. He admits how much the South has changed, but that reality makes it "difficult to acknowledge and explain the lingering lessons of race and place and how they continuously invade the consciousness of many Southerners like me." His use of the term "consciousness" intentionally places his sense of the southern way as a lingering mental construct.[43]

Still, Taulbert embraces his identity as a southerner and behaves as one. Twice he sees himself as a "southern gentleman," evoking one of the most durable of southern images. He admits to using "all the Southern charm [he] could muster" to try to influence Camille Sharp, falling into calling her "Miss Camille," an old plantation nicety for white women. After a lecture in Columbia, South Carolina, Taulbert tells Miss Camille's daughter, "I guess you were right. We are Southern and in spite of everything our lives are really intertwined." Many of his experiences in the state evoke, however, bad memories of the Deep South he grew up in. As Sharp shows him the bathroom of his guest room in the plantation mansion, his mind goes back to "colored" and "white" signs on restrooms that marked rigid social boundaries. When he realizes he will be staying in the plantation house with three white women, he can't help remembering Emmett Till, the young man killed by whites for supposedly whistling at a white woman. The Lost Cause reared its head as well, as Sharp brought up the Civil War and the memory of brutalities Union troops committed occupying her family's plantation.[44]

Early on in the book, Taulbert tells readers to "remember King's beloved community ideal" and to understand "what it takes to build such a heroic place and how easy it is to allow ourselves to fall into a way of living that can be suffocating to others." Taulbert sees the failure of his generation of southerners to achieve true community. "As Southern baby boomers," he says, "most of us had not been raised to embrace a shared kinship, one that stretched across racial, social and economic lives." Thus the "incredible opportunities to build an inclusive community have been missed along the way." Throughout his time in small-town South Carolina, he sees opportunities for possible cross-racial conversations with whites, but the lessons of cautious behavior from his childhood, from Little Cliff's voice in his head, prevent him from openly raising racial topics, which are not considered polite topics for conversation throughout the South.[45]

Country Cosmopolitanism, Stankonia, and Soul

Black southerners did not embrace the concept of southern living as the magazine defined it, but they did advance from the 1970s onward an idea of the South as the locus for a worldview and identity that should be set next to the white middle-class version of southern living. Everyday interaction of people in the South and the products of corporate popular culture illustrated a "southern turn" in African American culture. Sociologist Zandria Robinson described "country cosmopolitanism" as a blend of rural values and urban sensibilities in the post–civil rights South. Southern rearing and residence came to have moral authenticity within the larger Black American culture. Country cosmopolitanism blended specifically African American remnants of traditionalism with modern outlooks, as "the class privileges of wealthier blacks, the patriarchal privileges of black men, and the sexuality privileges of heterosexuals" became common. This African American version of southern living came to the surface in the immediate post–Jim Crow segregation years, exemplified by "The South Today," a special issue of *Ebony* magazine in August 1971. The cover illustration included, on the top, a sketch of raggedy sharecroppers or enslaved Black people working in the fields and, on the bottom, a photograph of a young man and woman with Afros, kente cloths, peace necklaces, and books in hand. John H. Johnson, publisher of the magazine, argued that it was time for African Americans to take a serious look at the homeland of origin for so many Black Americans only a generation or two removed from the South. The issue portrayed Black southern living as middle class—but down-home, too. This idea coincided, of course, with the superior South imagery of the Sunbelt in the 1970s and 1980s, as middle- and upper-class Americans, across the biracial color line, portrayed the region as the home to threatened American values. Emergence of African American political power in the South and the growth in Black middle-class wealth also promoted a belief in southern Black people's superiority. Political scientist Adolph Reed complained in April 1996 about "the proliferation of nostalgia for the South" and in doing so noted the pervasiveness by then of the country cosmopolitan version of Black southern living. He saw it "in every major newspaper and excuse for a news magazine at the supermarket checkout line, in the classroom, in the local bar, across the dinner table, in cultural criticism, in foundation boardrooms and policy papers, on the talk show circuit." For critics of this construct, middle-class white and Black southerners were complicit at least in the maintenance of interracial inequalities and class iniquities because they looked back fondly on the society of what now seemed a less complicated past.[46]

White southerners from the antebellum era had asserted, often defiantly, the superior South, and now suddenly Black southerners did so as well, a sentiment aimed partly at northern Black people, who often denigrated Black southerners, and partly at white southerners, who had demeaned them for so long. One informant to a sociological study in Memphis, Tennessee, a thirty-two-year-old college student who worked at a restaurant, named ways in which the South was superior in everyday living. "We just do things better down here, you know," he said. "Bigger, Better. Better hair, Better loving, Better singing. Better churching. Better cooking. We look better, Just better. We just all around better black folks." Another interviewee cited cultural evidence of southern Black superiority. The Harlem Renaissance had been "southern stories stolen from the South made to seem like they were native to Harlem Negroes' experience." He cited the cultural achievements from southern Black communities in gospel, blues, jazz, funk, and soul. He cited Alvin Ailey's landmark choreography celebrating the rural South in *Revelations*. Ailey's work was key in the reclamation of the southern Black identity, which has been at the heart of the southern turn in Black American culture in the years since then.[47]

Ailey had gone north from Texas and become an accomplished artist in national and international contexts, and his acclaimed remembrances of the South gave a certain moral authority to southern Black claims of distinctive southern living. African Americans who had stayed in the South were not so much reclaiming the region's experiences as important ones for Black culture in the 1970s as they were reminding everyone of their struggles and triumphs, especially through the accomplishments of the civil rights movement. Culture played a key conceptual role in these claims. Southern rhythm-and-blues music had accompanied the civil rights activists in their protests, and soul music by the 1980s reminded listeners of the Black freedom struggle. It combined urban and rural motifs—the key aspect of the Black imagining of southern living. African American literature by the 1980s came to be dominated by new narratives of southern living by writers such as Alice Walker, Maya Angelou, and Ernest Gaines, whose works differed from those of most twentieth-century northern Black writers, who emphasized coming-of-age-in-the-ghetto stories. As Robinson puts it, "These narratives about black southerners vis-à-vis other forms of blackness are now as ubiquitous as narratives about white southern girls in sundresses sipping sweet tea." Critic Addison Gayle criticized the Black aesthetic movement of the 1960s for consciously erasing the Black southern experience from African American cultural memory, and he urged Black artists and

writers to "reclaim the southern experience." Soon, popular culture responded
with plays, television shows, films, and hip-hop and rap music that represented
contemporary expressions of Black southern living.[48]

Southern African Americans, to be sure, faced similar problems as Black
people in other parts of the nation, including persistent rural poverty, inadequate schools, poor health care, gentrification and urban renewal of historically
Black neighborhoods, rising rates of incarceration, bankruptcy, and teen preg-
nancy. Such racial connections made it apparent why Blacks, despite intraracial
social class differences, still embraced Black collective identity politically and
culturally. Such problems were remnants of the southern plantation economy
and the continuing failure of southern states to invest in human capital rather
than in the southern strategy of economic community development. The language of Black southern living, like the white version, was class based, with the
South positioned as a bourgeois Eden and the realities of southern living for
poor and working-class African Americans ignored.[49]

The country cosmopolitanism version of southern living was not centered in
the suburbs, as with whites, but rather in the southern urban areas that Black
southerners came to dominate by the 1980s. These "soul cities" were urban
areas that had large Black populations and divisions within Black political
power. Urban people often preserved close relationships to nearby small towns
and rural African American communities. African Americans in general, after
the demise of Jim Crow, turned south toward the imagined Black American
homeland of the rural South, and country living is, along with urban ways, the
foundation of the Black southern living concept. Disillusionment with progress
in the promised land of the North, the draw of extended families still residing
in the South, and memories of southern upbringing by those who had left the
region all promoted regionalization within Black culture. Literary critic Robert
Stepto wrote about the long-standing trope in Black intellectual life of "going
into the Black Belt" to understand the origins of Black American culture, and
the South increasingly by 1980 functioned as "home" in sometimes nostalgic
literary imaginings. The rural South had even deeper meaning as a primal connection to the distant African homeland. Alex Haley's popular *Roots* (1975)
had raised up African civilization as a noble one, launching a new interest in
genealogy among Black Americans in general. Country cosmopolitanism thus
embraced traditional rural tropes, such as home, community, family, and food,
at the same time that it modernized them.[50]

The Black rural folk culture in the South, which had taken root under segregation, now offered the possibility of distinctiveness and healing within the
American Black community and of promoting the superior Black South. Folklife became a form of social capital, distinguishing southern Black people from
other African Americans and from whites as well. Folk cures for colds, urban

Tom Rankin's photographs of spirituality in the Mississippi Delta defined a southern
visual approach to religion as an abiding part of southern rural folk culture. New Hope
Missionary Baptist Church, Estill, Mississippi, 1989. Courtesy of Tom Rankin.

gardening with old techniques, superstitions about gender relations, and, above
all, old-time religious language and behaviors that might not be rooted in denominational theologies—all could be embraced by city dwellers who might
see themselves as more sophisticated than their country cousins but still abide
by some older ways. Black southern creative people, such as filmmaker Tyler
Perry and rappers OutKast, use country cosmopolitanism to capture southern experiences and keep this version of southern living alive. It continues to
promote a Black consumer base, seen in corporate promotions that present
southern types as sellers of their products, such as Popeyes fried chicken's
Annie, who sells Louisiana's Black and Cajun cultures; Glory Foods' Shirley,
who sells canned collard greens; and the Black grandmother who endorsed the
McDonald's Southern Style Chicken Sandwich. They follow in the tradition of
such Black advertising figures as Uncle Ben and Aunt Jemima, who long enabled whites and others to have symbolic servants in their kitchens and dining
rooms. Middle-class suburban whites could live southern by consuming these
food products.[51]

Contemporary Black films suggest aspects of the Black southern living concept, again illustrating the foundational view of the superior Black South. Julie Dash's *Daughters of the Dust* (1991) began this new imagining of the Black South, using a late nineteenth-century setting to escape earlier film portrayals of victimized rural African Americans. Other films were set in the contemporary period, including Tyler Perry's *Madea's Family Reunion* (2006), his *Meet the Browns* (2008), and Malcolm D. Lee's *Welcome Home, Roscoe Jenkins* (2008). They show the South as a place for regeneration of African Americans alienated from their roots and fleeing such urban problems as drug abuse and poverty, now seen as northern. They juxtapose modern urban life in places such as Chicago's South Side ghetto with rural Black life, visually portrayed as maternal homes on the lush pastoral lands so long associated with the imagined South.[52]

Other films and television shows at the turn of the twenty-first century more directly engaged the urban side of country cosmopolitanism, as African American southern life embraced city life in ways that white society seldom did. *Jason's Lyric* (1994) portrayed Black life in Houston; *ATL* (2006) was an Atlanta story; and *Hustle and Flow* (2005) was set in Memphis. Atlanta, in particular, represents a prime imagining of the superior urban South. Popular culture's famous presentations of the city, such as in *The Real Housewives of Atlanta* and VH1's *Love and Hip Hop Atlanta*, showcase reality television's versions of Black media stars associated with the city. *Belle Collective* on the Oprah Winfrey Network portrays African American women from Jackson, Mississippi, who live out the fashion and beauty ideals often associated with white southern women. They claim that version of the southern identity, but they transform it because they are smart entrepreneurs doing quite well in the twenty-first-century economy.[53]

Although blues has had a rebirth of sorts as a part of the rediscovery of roots music, and Black gospel continues to be a true grassroots Black music in the contemporary era, hip-hop deserves special attention for its extraordinary success among young African Americans. Hip-hop artists have made the South a particular place for Black identity that demonstrates the connections between urban and rural at the heart of the country cosmopolitan version of southern living. Hip-hop artists integrate the urban and rural aspects of Black southern living into a southern Black artistic outlook; differences from Kentucky and Mississippi, Atlanta and Houston, are "subsumed under the South's regional umbrella." They can ride in rimmed LTDs and cruise through the urban worlds of Memphis, Atlanta, or New Orleans (hip-hop centers) or put on overalls and head scarves and evoke a pastoral, rural South. Afrocentric rappers Arrested Development sang "Tennessee," with an evocative video shot in Georgia. The song summoned the South as a place of healing and spirituality, saying,

Take me to another place
Take me to another land
Make me forget all that hurts me
Let me understand Your plan.

The group imagined walking the road a "forefather walked" and climbing the trees "forefathers hung from." This vision confronted the South's lynching ghosts and made southern history central to current identity. The video for Nappy Roots' "Awnaw," on the album *Watermelon, Chicken & Gritz* (2002), showed shotgun houses, tractors, trucks, pickups, and cornfields, placing these artists in the traditional rural South, with southern food an obvious theme from the album's title. But the video combines this southern traditional style with images of candy-painted Chevrolets one would expect to find in urban Memphis more than in the countryside. Erykah Badu's "Southern Girl" shows a South of "the burning church," "pocket stones" (evoking urban drug culture), "booty songs," and "finger waves that last all night long." She eats everything fried, with her tofu no exception, and gold teeth fill her "dirty mouth." The rap duo OutKast made a statement about the superiority of Black southern living in 1995 when, accepting an award for best new rap group at the Source Awards, the lead singer, André 3000, proclaimed, "The South got something to say." The "Dirty South" of hip-hop presents a gritty, sometimes raw place.[54]

OutKast defines an original hip-hop concept of southern Black consciousness: Stankonia. The group's 2000 album of that name introduced the term, which is a phonetic spelling of "stank on ya," a metaphor, as Regina Bradley writes, for speaking "the messy truth—stank—of contemporary southern black identity to power." In the album's songs, stank refers to "the musty, less-than-savory, and mispronounced aspects of southern black life." It is a counterpoint to views of southernness as racially rigid and focused only on a traumatic past unrelated to the present. Slavery, for example, is not just an oppressive part of African American history but an imaginative haunt from the past that still shapes the contemporary South. As a concept, Stankonia showed OutKast's reimagining of southern Black narratives that have concentrated on slavery, Jim Crow segregation, and the civil rights movement. It made the Black American South a conceptual and a material place where Black and southern identities intertwine; it is a dynamic space of "creative reckoning with the past, present, and future." OutKast's songs engage such issues as AIDS, poverty, and white supremacy, and they rap about these crises from a specifically southern regional perspective that insists these social problems are part of modern southern living. One song on the album, "Gasoline Dreams," contests the belief that the American dream has been accessible for many African Americans, despite

the hopefulness of civil rights rhetoric about the possibilities of equal opportunity within a changed South. Bradley insists that OutKast provides "a map
for viewing the contemporary roots of southernness: a cultural and conceptual
undertaking that is necessary to make room for newer articulations of southern
blackness" anchored in southern places away from the gaze of nonsoutherners,
such as northern hip-hop performers, who lack the sensibilities to view the
Black South as a complex social-cultural place with creative potential.[55]

Mississippi writer Kiese Laymon uses hip-hop's concept of Stankonia for
literary ends that make him a major interpreter of this new paradigm of the
southern way of life. Black southern writers have long evoked the trauma associated with their life in the South, with Richard Wright a noteworthy progenitor for Laymon. The latter evokes that trauma in the very recent times of Donald Trump and the Republican leaders who govern early twenty-first-century
Mississippi, his home state as it was Wright's. Laymon wishes he could believe
in the hopes of racial reconciliation and admits that his state's governor, Tate
Reeves, is "our white cousin by blood and culture." But he calls out Reeves and
the legislature for their unwillingness to address the socioeconomic problems
of the state's African American population, despite feeling "the daily grace
Black folks from the Deep South have offered white folks from the Deep South
in the face of unrelenting humiliation." Seeing sheer meanness around him
and the unwillingness of those political leaders to even admit they are sorry
for the state's abysmal social conditions, Laymon engages the power dynamics
that reflect systemic racism that can be traced back to slavery and then segregation. He evokes another African American literary progenitor, Ralph Ellison,
in writing about the invisibility of Black people in such a society that reflects
their marginalization.[56]

Laymon has a particular, personal, and powerful image of stank that illuminates the concept. His grandma Catherine worked for thirty years at a poultry
plant in central Mississippi doing the most unsavory of jobs—pulling the guts
out of thousands of chickens each day. Yet she took pains to always be clean and
well groomed at home. She went to work "into that plant every day, knowing
it was a laboratory for racial and gendered terror." But she wanted to be not
just the best worker at the chicken plant but "the best, most stylish, most effi-
cient worker in Mississippi." Laymon remembers staying with her as a boy and
wanting to hug her when she got home from work. "Let me wash this stank off
my hands before I hug your neck," she said, using the southern vernacular for
love. He sees that her stank "was root and residue of Black Southern poverty,
and devalued Black Southern labor, Black Southern excellence, Black Southern
imagination, and Black Southern woman magic." He concludes that "this was
the stank from whence Black Southern life, labor, and love came," and in the

process he insists that this African American perspective be included in understandings of modern southern living. His grandmother's stank made her value being fresh and, on Sundays, being the most fashionable member of the usher board at her Baptist church. Laymon's use of the Stankonia concept thus centers on personal and family experiences and is rooted in the lives of working people. He came to realize the importance of his grandmother's stank from listening to OutKast albums that "explored the inevitability of death and the possibility of new life, new movement, and new mojo."[57]

Laymon's recent, personal version of the southern way of life positions him as a young Black man growing up in the post–civil rights South. He sees his cohort of young Black southerners in tension with northern Black people, embodied by big-city rappers who disrespect southern hip-hop, which led to André's assertion of the South's role in hip-hop in 2000. Laymon writes that André understood that southerners would no longer follow the lead of New York City, "because disregarding our particular stank in favor of a stank that didn't love or respect us was like taking a broke elevator down into artistic and spiritual death"; he saw this regional perspective as one of life and death. He admitted that OutKast had created "an urban Southern stank so familiar with and indebted to the gospel, blues, jazz, rock and funk born into the rural Black South," which made Stankonia a part of the broader country cosmopolitan outlook. Laymon also places his generation of young Black southern males in tension with older southern Black people, who had lived and fought through the civil rights struggles and had high expectations for his generation. He praised OutKast, for example, for standing up "to a post–civil rights South chiding young Southern Black boys to pull up our pants and fight white supremacy with swords of respectability and narrow conceptions of excellence." He sees peers who wanted to be "divine emcees" ensconced in hip-hop culture, but their families had other plans. Laymon notes that the members of his generation were "multiple dreamers," who often did try to live up to Martin Luther King Jr.'s dream of ending the racialized southern way of life through integration and to actualize "boring dreams" of being managers, computer engineers, sergeants, and college professors; but they also aspired to being counterfeiters, racketeers, and pimps. Laymon's South is a complicated one that rubs together the respectable and disrespectable elements, as his own experience suggests there is no one cookie-cutter approach to success in the recent South when looked at from the bottom up. Still, he passionately engages the South and embraces the southern identity, as he sees the region as his home and admires that its people "have been and can be a model of transformation for the rest of the nation and the world." Laymon's Stankonia brings together the past and the present, without any burden of southern history, and he looks to the future in his novel *Long Division*, which involves time travel, past and future. The novel's title evokes a *longue durée* of Black southern life in which social and cultural issues are ongoing within a regional context.[58]

African American southern living offers another cultural feature and term that evokes religion, history, and agrarianism: soul sweetness. Soul music singer Al Green wrote "The Southern Soul" for *Southern Magazine* in 1986, and in it he presented the South as the home ground for soul. By "soul" he meant "that spirit that is inside all of us, the spirit that moves us, the spirit that keeps us aware of the Lord." But the term also meant "the music that moves us, the music that is deep down there inside of us." Born in Arkansas, he moved to Michigan and then returned south in 1970, claiming the region in his essay. "There's something here that makes it easier for that music of the soul, that feeling sort of music, to come out." He saw history as the background to a distinctive spirit in the South. Slaves "didn't have much of anything, but they had God, and when they sang, what they sang was for Him, and it had meaning, and it had feeling." He saw a "sweetness here, a Southern sweetness, that makes a sweet music." The South, he wrote, is "the home ground," the place that "can keep the real thing alive." Green's words primarily applied to African American music, but they appeared in *Southern Magazine*, implying that the "soul" sweetness he spoke about was a specifically "southern soul," part of the biracial culture that had been celebrated by some southerners since the 1970s.[59]

Fast-forward to the twenty-first century, and one hears the music of Lizz Wright, whose 2017 album *Grace* was, according to critic Giovanni Russonello, "an ode to a place, and to forgiveness," the place being the South. Growing up in a small town in Georgia where her father was musical director at her home church, Wright was by 2017 splitting time between Chicago and her house in the Blue Ridge Mountains of North Carolina. "I wanted to capture the sweetness of the South," she told Russonello, "and of my coming from it, and my experience of it." The album's songs swept across a century of music, from blues gospel composer Thomas A. Dorsey to contemporary eclectic singer k.d. lang, with such warm songs as "Stars Fell on Alabama" and Allen Toussaint's "Southern Nights," both of which evoke a sensual as well as metaphysical southern living. Recorded in the aftermath of the ugliness of Donald Trump's election in 2016 as president, Wright nonetheless wanted to find the language in songs to show "how real forgiveness and healing and openness is possible, and practical." Russonello observed that *Grace* drew "its energy straight from the soil, with acoustic and electric guitars, organ and piano locked in an earthy symbiosis." Her personal experience reinforced the album's thrust. Her house in North Carolina is on a back road, with the nearest neighbors being older white people with decidedly more conservative politics than her own. She nonetheless developed close relationships with them through shared stories and gardening, and she dedicated the album to one of those new friends, a ninety-two-year-old man. "Here I am, both a foreigner and the younger generation, moving into this area that has an incredible culture and history that is really based around being an earth steward and caring for one another," Wright said, in words that the Vanderbilt Agrarians would have cheered. Wright injected a note of African American pride and heritage into her story, though, noting that she "came from a family that has grown their own food from well into times of slavery, provided for themselves and people around them."[60]

Racial Reconciliation and National Redemption

Wright's words provide a good introduction to a major theme of southern living in the contemporary South, namely the South as a place defined by its biracial history and culture and offering the promise of racial reconciliation and redemption to the nation and the world. Martin Luther King's concept of the beloved community anchors this version of southern living that rests in uneasy conflict with the predominant conservative, middle-class, suburban-based southern living. Georgia congressman John Lewis long embodied this vision and was its main proselytizer until his death in 2020. Lewis summoned memories of his time as a beaten and bloodied civil rights activist, a part of such events as Nashville sit-ins and the march at the Edmund Pettus Bridge in Selma in 1965. "When I speak of reconciliation, I mean the ancient cry for peace and understanding," he said. That idea is "as old as the dawn of civilization," he wrote, yet the concept was still "as fresh as the rise of the sun." The key was the beloved community, where "we find compassion for others and justice for all." Like other advocates of reconciliation, Lewis pointed to the civil rights movement as the model for the hope that this "impossible dream" could advance. His story is an American one and one with international meaning, but he made it a southern story primarily by recounting how the South has changed so dramatically since his childhood in rural Alabama, "then a setting of social, economic, and political servitude akin to slavery." In that context, the civil rights activists had been "warriors in a moral revolution, a revolution of values, a revolution of ideas," with morality and ideas as key words for people who "wanted to redeem the soul of America." Fearing the memory of the movement might fade, he reminded readers that the Black freedom struggle of the 1950s and 1960s was not a "physical struggle against coldhearted authority but a moral struggle for the hearts and souls of our fellow human beings." Reminding readers as well that nonviolence was "a philosophy, a way of life, a way of living," he refurbished King's similar view of nonviolence as an alternative way

Civil rights activist John Lewis was beaten during the Selma-to-Montgomery march
in 1965, and this photograph shows him looking at an iconic image of the
scene years later. Tom William / CQ-Roll Call, Inc. via Getty Images.

of life to the segregated southern way of life. Lewis's death in the summer of
2020 silenced a powerful force for reconciliation but left an inspiring witness
for the future.[61]

In an interview for *Garden and Gun* magazine in 2015, Lewis reflected on
the South as the locus for the redemptive narrative. "I always felt growing up
that in the South there was evil but also good—so much good." Looking at the
contemporary era, he noted that "we are still in the process of becoming," and
he remained "very, very hopeful about the American South." He went even
further and asserted that "in a real sense a great deal of the South has been
redeemed," injecting a notable sense of optimism into discussions of the contemporary South. His basis for that optimism is that "people feel freer, more
complete, more whole, because of what happened in the movement." In the end,
his vision of southern living through achieving the beloved community rested
on the belief that "we are one people, one family, one house—not just the house
of black and white, but the house of the South, the house of America." Despite
setbacks, "we can create a multiracial community, a truly democratic society."

If the predominant political vision of southern living was individualism for Republican conservatives, the biracial redemptive version of southern living was of community for Democratic progressives. Lewis's faith background and language made the South a sacred ground, as he insisted that "I believe the movement happened because we were in step with the Creator."[62]

Mississippi governor William Winter has been a tenacious advocate of racial reconciliation and progressive politics. His one term as governor of Mississippi brought the landmark Education Reform Act in 1982, which became a model for other states; he served as cochair of President Bill Clinton's One America on Race project (1997–98); and the University of Mississippi established the William Winter Institute for Racial Reconciliation to promote his vision. Speaking to an assembly of southern legislators in 2004, Winter drew attention to the South as a place to achieve racial reconciliation. "I would like to believe that we who live in the South have a special insight," he said, into how racial reconciliation might be achieved, because the region's "history has been most shaped by the factors of race over three centuries." He pointed to the challenge of the twenty-first century for "southerners of both races to work to come together with the same commitment and intensity with which a generation ago so many white southerners sought to maintain segregation and so many black southerners sought to end it." The realities now, he concluded, "require us to understand our mutual interdependence," words that pointed to an underlying stress on the common good at the heart of southern racial reconciliation as the basis of a more inclusive southern living than the predominant middle-class, suburban ideal.[63]

A demanding vision of racial reconciliation in the biracial South came from community organizer John Perkins. This Mississippi-born civil rights activist left the state when he was sixteen after a policeman in Lawrence County killed his older brother, but he returned to Mississippi in 1960 and became active in the civil rights movement. In 1970 Mississippi highway patrolmen beat him senseless, and he left for California a few years later. He returned to the state in 1982 to initiate a community development program that has become an influential force for sustained change in the contemporary South. He oversaw Mendenhall Ministries beginning in 1964 and later established the Voice of Calvary in Mississippi, which included housing developments, tutoring programs, sport activities, health clinics, family counseling, legal assistance, a farming cooperative, and a Christian school. As religious studies scholar Charles Marsh notes, the community development model, in comparison with some efforts toward social justice, "is more modest, yet more enduring and more focused on pursuits in particular contexts of shared confessional or religious belief." The community development movement tries to achieve the beloved community through local projects that build community among the poor and excluded. Marsh sees the community development efforts as representing "the same spiritual vision that animated the civil rights movement," able to provide "a vital source of moral energy and social discipline for the present age."[64]

Perkins stressed the four R's of community development: relocation, redistribution, reparations, and reconciliation. Perkins thus added other components to reconciliation. Relocation referred to "incarnational evangelicalisms," such as that of Georgian Clarence Jordan at his Koinonia commune in south Georgia in the mid-twentieth century, which involved the work of a committed Christian with the poor and disfranchised. Redistribution involved sharing one's resources and talents with the poor directly in their communities to raise them up but also to support changes in public policy to promote such change. Reparations, which Perkins saw as essentially Christian, were a part of redistribution but had to be included along with immersion in the life of those in need. Racial reconciliation was thus the most genuine sign of a southern church's true Christianity. Reconciliation was not simply the result of interracial conversations that might lead to emotional release or psychological affirmation, but it resulted from the hard work of intertwined lives, with whites sharing their material resources and hard work to promote justice. This vision placed many demands on white financial resources and moral commitments and pointed to the failure of the civil rights movement to establish solidarity among white people, well-off African Americans, and the poor of all races.[65]

Although Perkins stressed the need for grassroots community development work to achieve reconciliation, conversations have been at the heart of much racial reconciliation work in the South and elsewhere. Mission Mississippi is an ecumenical group, broadly evangelical in its focus. Founded in 1992 in Jackson, it is part of a national movement among Evangelicals calling for Christians to address racial divisions through intentional interracial relationships. Mission Mississippi hosts weekly prayer breakfasts in Jackson, monthly businessmen's prayer breakfasts and women's prayer luncheons, and the Annual Governor's Prayer Luncheon; it gives restaurant discounts for two cross-racial couples eating together; and it sponsors diversity training for schools, churches, and businesses. Much of its work centers around eating together across racial lines. That was a main taboo under segregation, and the Welcome Table idea, despite the implication by some observers of seeming a minor behavioral interaction, has powerful symbolic importance as a sign of reconciliation.[66]

Mission Mississippi is one example of Mississippi's leadership in racial reconciliation efforts, growing out of its dismal racial history. The University of Mississippi founded the William Winter Institute for Racial Reconciliation in 1999, which works with local communities, businesses, schools, and nonprofits to foster projects across racial lines that can contribute to interracial under-standing. It has advocated applying the South African truth and reconciliation model—which calls for acknowledgment of past racial injustices as a prereq-uisite for racial reconciliation—to American race relations. In a 2020 book, philosopher Susan Nieman contrasted Germany's constructive efforts to deal with the memory of the Holocaust with the South's limited efforts to use the memory of slavery and Jim Crow to enact needed reform measures. At first skeptical of the work of the Winter Institute, she observed its staff at work in communities and concluded that it "made me feel more hopeful than I'd felt in years." Atlanta's Committee for Truth and Reconciliation put forward the same model. North Carolina's state government in 2000 set up a commission to investigate the Wilmington race riot in 1898, which led to a report recommend-ing economic and social compensation for descendants of the riot's victims. At the local level, countless community churches bring white and Black people together each week, and business clubs such as the Rotary and Lions gather for weekly luncheons. Middle-class and elite southerners socialize across ra-cial lines at such public occasions as sporting events, college ceremonies, gal-lery openings, and political meetings. Events with political meanings, such as school board meetings, city council meetings, and local committee hearings, can be the sites of tense cross-racial interactions, but they are part of the pro-cess of dialogue that promoters of racial reconciliation advocate. The actions of state governments and leading regional institutions have shown white south-erners willing to acknowledge past wrongs. In 2005, the U.S. Senate apologized to descendants of African Americans who had been lynched as a result of the failure to make it a federal crime in the twentieth century. In early 2007, the leg-islatures of four southern or border states passed resolutions expressing regret or apologizing for the brutalities of slavery and later racial discrimination. The SBC formally apologized to Black people in 1995 for its role in validating slav-ery and committed itself to eliminating racism. Soon, the organization would select its first African American president and begin extensive missionary work among African Americans.[67]

The prosecution of civil rights cold-case murders resulted in what became known as "atonement trials," a part of the narrative of the redemptive South. The nation from its beginning quarantined the South as the source of racist contagion, but that fiction has long been discarded. The nation now looks to the South for evidence that the nation's racism will be dissipated in the biracial South, a view that progressive southerners often affirm as well. Mississippi again led the way, with the conviction of Byron De la Beckwith in 1994 for the murder of Medgar Evers. After that case, juries voted for conviction in twenty-seven civil rights cases. In 2005, one of the most high-profile trials took place, that of the eighty-year-old Edgar Ray Killen, who had been accused of master-minding the murder of three civil rights workers in Neshoba County in June 1964. Seven former Klansmen went to prison for violating the civil rights of the murdered men. Killen sat in a wheelchair, breathing through a tube connected to an oxygen tank, as he heard his conviction on three counts of manslaughter and his sentence of sixty years in prison. In a symbolic sense, the older seg-regationist's southern way of life was on trial, seemingly on its last legs. Four years after the Killen trial, Philadelphia—county seat of Neshoba—elected a Black Pentecostal minister as mayor, even though the town was majority white. Another Deep South state, Alabama, also held similar trials. The perpetrators of the Sixteenth Street Baptist Church bombing in 1963 that killed four African American children were finally brought to justice in trials in 1977, 2001, and 2002. Writer Diane McWhorter noted that the redemption narrative is often asserted at such times to characterize the South, but "the average person in the South is not living the redemption story."[68]

Hybrid Southern Way

Race relations have long framed the story of the southern way of life, and com-mentators were ever more self-conscious in asserting the biracial cultural ideal in the contemporary South. Cultural interaction had led to hybrid expressions in music, food, and other aspects of regional culture that the region's cultural arbiters now recognized and celebrated. The long-present physical interaction that had produced a racially mixed population also promoted efforts to ac-knowledge a familial connection across racial lines. At the same time, com-mentators increasingly pointed to the hybrid nature of the southern way of life, some noting a historical grounding for it but others seeing it flourishing in the contemporary era's growth of immigration and new cultures into the region.

Ralph Eubanks's memoir *The House at the End of the Road* (2009) centers on issues of race and place and offers an additional perspective on the bira-cial South's redemptive narrative. For him, the story is within his own family, as he seeks to understand his multiracial family history and its meaning for broader southern and American society. Eubanks was director of publishing at the Library of Congress when he wrote this book as well as his earlier memoir, *Ever Is a Long Time* (2007), his story of growing up in Mississippi in the years of the civil rights movement. There he detailed the emergence of his African American identity in a race-conscious state. In his later book, he investigated his maternal grandparents, Jim and Edna Richardson. Assuming that, because his mother appeared Black and embraced an African American identity, his grandfather was Black as well, he discovered as an adolescent that his grand-father was white. Given his already-formed identity as an African American, this new knowledge at first little affected him, but the book shows how that understanding changed. Jim was a bigger-than-life local character in rural, isolated south Alabama, a white man who married a Black woman with Native American heritage, Edna, in 1914. Eubanks discovered that the Richardsons lived "as a unique family at the end of a winding sandy road in southwest Alabama in a black community. Jim moved between the black and white worlds, which the broader society of Washington County tolerated but did not completely accept."[69]

"Conversation" is a key term in the book. An older white relative told Eubanks that in Alabama "the racial die was molded, formed, and fired into black and white." Eubanks observes that "the same mindset lingers throughout Alabama whenever the topic of interracial relationships and marriage enters a conversation," as people were scared of others who "knew the cultural underpinnings of both the dominant culture and the minority culture and could move easily between the two social realms." Eubanks thus establishes a long biracial family heritage as he looks at contemporary family attitudes.[70]

Eubanks points to the one-drop rule under slavery—where any blood tie to a slave determined one's racial identity as Black—as the source of tenacious racial thinking in the South, with race and color replacing slavery after Emancipation as the basis for a classification system for oppression. The civil rights movement began the process of change, and "a generation later, the old way of life," Eubanks writes, "has been uprooted and the changes of the civil rights movement are now tenuously ingrained in the social fabric, making it easier for people to talk about the way things once were." Eubanks insists that it is time to look at his family through what unified these two branches, white and Black Richardsons, namely a common ancestry and history. He visits other white relatives, with one meeting being "a joyful occasion" but another, with distant white cousins, frustrating because they wanted him to emphasize the white side of the family. Eubanks is very much the southerner, imbued with politeness, but he comes to realize that southern etiquette could hinder necessary conversations about race. His cousin Tom was "affable and charming," but his "Southern manners would not allow him to lift the veneer of politeness to have an open discussion about the role race had played in our family history." Eubanks understands that his cousin, like most white men of his generation, "had simply never had to engage in a conversation about race."[71]

Eubanks goes from that low point, though, to consider the growing contemporary openness to accepting multiple ethnic identities. He had broadened his own sense of identity, embracing the idea that he was "a black person from a multiracial background, because that multiracial background shaped my black identity as much as my maternal relatives' decision to embrace the blackness." Coming to see the beginning of acceptance of racial ambiguity in the Obama era, he notes that "cracks are beginning to form in our sensibilities, allowing many of us to accept racial ambiguity rather than trying to categorize people firmly into one racial or ethnic group." Eubanks saw that the goal of integration influenced baby boomers, but they could not achieve it. The next generation, he predicted, would acknowledge "the familial links between black and white without shame, guilt, or embarrassment." Eubanks pinpoints a key dimension in the search for racial reconciliation in the South. When talking about race, he insists, "we must acknowledge the wounds but not allow them to overpower the conversation to the point that our talk focuses entirely on past hurts and wounds." Eubanks sees intentionality as crucial in acknowledging the burdens of the southern past.[72]

With his new understanding of the need for dialogue, Eubanks embarks on another round of visits with white relatives, to "just visit" with people, as southerners put it, and to see what comes from his conversations without an agenda. He stresses the commonalities he feels he has with white and Black Richardsons, but he learns that white and Black members of his family viewed his grandfather somewhat differently. White family members saw him as a local folk hero, while his Black relatives admired him for his fairness and ability to see beyond race. "In the eyes of many, his redemption as a man derived from his genuine desire to be seen not as a white man, but just as a man." The term "transcendence" refers to his grandfather's escape from the South's racial categorization. "Redemption" and "transcendence" in racial thinking become part of "a new lexicon of racial reconciliation, talking openly and moving beyond racial categories" in the South. Although American culture has not reached a collective fresh insight about race, Eubanks concludes that Americans have reached "a tipping point" on issues of race and identity. He predicts that a new context of expanding multiracial populations and new scientific outlooks on issues of race would change how Americans think about the subject. Eubanks closes his book by recounting taking his daughter on a trip to see her grandmother, Eubanks's mother, and in the course of their conversation he realizes "how much race lies on the periphery of the life of my children." They have "no searing recollections of being mistreated," and his daughter's world is one where "race matters less and justice and our common humanity matter more." Eubanks embodies a creole, hybrid identity for the South, one that, in fact, was there from the region's beginning in the stories of interracial cultural and biological interaction, but one that southern whites refused to embrace.[73]

———————

The years after 1980 witnessed a diminution of the overt racism in southern public and private life that had dominated discussions of the southern way of life only a generation earlier, as well as the realization that the agrarianism that

African Americans came to claim southern identities in the decades after the tipping point of the civil rights movement, including embracing the "southern charm" of beauty pageants, as in this 1980s photograph. © Greg Jensen—USA TODAY NETWORK.

had earlier structured discussions of the southern way was no longer a viable economic and societal option. Conservative and progressive visions of a newly reimagined southern way appeared around competing visions of an individualistic, competitive, middle-class, suburban southern living, on the one hand, and a biracial, redemptive southern culture, on the other. Consumerism and spirituality interweaved in imaginings of the South. By the 1980s, increased prosperity had made conspicuous materialistic consumption a defining feature of southern life, and white southerners, as well as other southerners, embraced consumerism as a behavioral expression of southern living. Spirituality took form in the contemporary era, with religiously inspired culture wars, suburban megachurches, and progressive expressions of a social gospel reform ethos competing with each other. African Americans embraced southern identity, imagined as country cosmopolitanism, that centered not on the suburbs but on Black-dominated cities and nearby rural spaces. Many differing southerners found reasons to assert a superior South, whether those living in the comfortable suburban materialistic enclaves, southern inheritors of the civil rights movement's moral triumphs who touted their "better Blackness," progressives who saw the South leading the nation toward racial reconciliation, or immigrants finding the newest South a promised land (for a while, at least). Social problems marred these hopeful visions, and the moral and social costs of free-market, individualistic public policies were all too obvious by the last decades of the twentieth century. Prosperity through the 1990s, the increased diversity of southern life, and efforts across the ideological spectrum to advocate for traditional southern virtues within an emerging South pointed toward the future as the new millennium approached. The first two decades of the twenty-first century would see a continuation of many post-1980 trends in imaginings of the southern way but in challenging new circumstances as well.

CHAPTER NINE

Into the Twenty-First Century

Multicultural Southern Living

SINCE ITS BEGINNING, the South has been home to ethnically diverse communities in particular geographic pockets. Over time these
communities have become particularly recognizable: Italians in New
Orleans, Chinese and Russian Jews in the Mississippi Delta, Vietnamese on
the Gulf Coast, Mexicans in Texas, Cubans in Florida, other Latinos in various
states, and Syrians and Lebanese in locations throughout the region. The list is
almost endless. And of course, Africans brought by the slave trade were settled
across the South. While other places in the United States might feature larger
communities with distinct ethnic and national identities, the South has long
been a multicultural place. But in the twenty-first century, a dramatic acceleration has occurred. Immigration, both legal and illegal, helped establish even
more widespread ethnic communities. The South has become the nation's new
Immigrant Belt; for example, between 2000 and 2010 Asian Americans were
the fastest-growing ethnic group in the South, increasing by 69 percent during
that period and outpacing Asian American growth in every other American
region.

The story of Korean American chef and food writer Edward Lee offers a
useful introduction to this shift. Few aspects of contemporary southern life
have been as significant for the concept of southern living as food. In the 1960s
Southern Living magazine designated traditional southern food as a symbol of
the "good life," a resonant term. But since 2000, new developments in regional
foodways have reflected the changing ideas about southern living in a multicultural South. Lee is a good example of how the South's new ethnic diversity
contributes to an emerging creole southern identity that is seeking to reconcile
old and new cultures. Lee's memoir-cookbook, *Smoke and Pickles: Recipes and
Stories from a New Southern Kitchen* (2013), describes the way he came to the
table and found acceptance through food.[1]

Lee's story begins in a working-class Korean home in Brooklyn, where
he learned to cook Asian dishes from his grandmother. He later moved into

professional cooking, but his move to Louisville in 2003 was transformative. Through "the lens of tobacco and bourbon and sorghum and horse racing and country ham," he reinvented his identity and realized that "over time, Louisville, and by extension, the American South, embraced me as an adopted son." But the move also led him to rediscover himself as a child of Korean immigrants as "all the lovely and resourceful traditions of the Southern landscape would propel me back to the kitchen of my grandmother's spicy, garlicky food."[2]

Lee pays homage to the contemporary southern food movement that embraces local sources and values food traditions. Each innovation in the cuisine "that moves it forward also pulls along with it a memory of something in the past." Lee makes a Korean-southern connection in new ways: "Like the Korean-Brooklyn kid in me tugging on a Southern apron," he notes, "I find connections where others might see contradictions." Lee's writing voice is vernacular, direct, and pithy and embraces a diverse collection of ingredients, making him a prime example of a new creolization of southern taste. Lee interweaves southern traditions with often parallel Asian ones. He plunges into southern experiences as he tells about hunting doves with friends and picking vegetables at a farm that supplies his restaurant. Southern music's Johnny Cash plays a prominent role in inspiring Lee to cook for charitable causes. Elvis Presley becomes a metaphor. We hear about the importance of the Kentucky Derby to Lee but also about attending an African American church service and afterward eating at one of Louisville's soul food restaurants.[3]

Lee embraces both sides of the region's biracial culture, but he changed that culture as well. Lee's recipes reflect the Asian-southern creolization of ingredients and cooking techniques, with smoke as the flavor that connects his childhood and adult worlds. "From the sizzling Korean grills of my childhood to the barbeque culture that permeates the South, I have always lived in an environment where food was wrapped in a comforting blanket of smokiness." He adds smokiness to any dish by using such southern ingredients as bourbon, bacon, smoked country ham, and sorghum or molasses. He shows a broad belief in the interconnections of his creole culinary world through his specific recipe for collards and kimchi: "My first vinegary, salty bite of braised collard greens was a revelation" that took him back to eating cabbage kimchi, "another precious dish that arose from poverty but has come to impress even the most sophisticated palates." These intense flavors from two cultures are distant from each other, yet "somehow they work together harmoniously, as if they belong together." This image of harmony coming from a southern kitchen shows new ethnic influences shaping a contemporary creolized version of southern culture.[4]

This final chapter explores that emerging culture. National perspectives are always important in understanding the evolving southern-way-of-life concept, but we will see they were slow in the contemporary period to recognize a multicultural southern living as represented by Edward Lee. Negative images in press coverage and nonfiction accounts revolved, instead, around older images of race, guns, and the Confederacy. More positive images came in travel pieces as writers went south with stereotypes, often qualifying them through their experiences.

The twenty-first century also has seen, though, an intensification of the culture wars. The presidency of Donald Trump represented rebellion against multicultural change in the nation in general, but the South played a prominent part. The demonization of the immigrants that were disproportionately coming to the South, the open racism toward them that seemed to hark back to southern racial attitudes, the conservative populism that politicians such as George Wallace once championed—all gave Trump's divisive politics a southern grounding. Issues surrounding the memorialization of both the Confederacy and the civil rights movement exemplified the culture wars. An emboldened neo-Confederacy movement harked back to the Lost Cause concept of southern civilization in the late nineteenth century. At the same time, the gradual idealization of the civil rights movement pushed the South toward the redemptive ideal but one that was broadened in the twenty-first century into a multicultural redemptive ideal.

Culture became a defining issue for contemporary southern living. Progressives could embrace localism and community (associated with older folk images of the South) as a counterweight to the angst of modern living. Such cultural expressions as literature and music flourished, both recognizing the region's traditions in those areas and also representing new works that critics placed in earlier categories of southern creativity. Food became perhaps the best example of multicultural southern living, with a foundation of traditional ingredients, cooking styles, and recipes combining with new ethnic influences to create hybrid foodways that embody a larger ideal of southern living. Finally, this chapter argues that regional magazines are among the best examples of the new multicultural southern living—and conveyors of it to broad audiences.

Diverse Southern Identities

Southern regional self-consciousness evolved after 2000 and became more diverse, despite the prediction that the region's identity would cease to exist. Changes in material life in the South are undeniable. Fast-food restaurants have replaced mom-and-pop cafés. Interstate highways connect the region to the nation. People in the South are as plugged into media forms and devices as much as any Americans. Population shifts have brought more African Americans, Latinos, Asians, and northern Americans into the South (making for more diversity and multiculturalism). African Americans exercise political and economic power in unprecedented ways. More people in the South live in urban areas than other places. The litany could go on. Arguments continue to appear about the vanishing South, such as Christopher Dickey's "The End of the South," which appeared in *Newsweek* in 2008.[5]

New southern studies literary scholars have taken the academic lead in arguing for a different version of the vanishing South—a "post-South" and "postmodern" sensibility. In terms of the concept of regional consciousness, new southern studies scholars have banished the "South" from their major interests. Early new southern studies works, like southern history and other scholarship in the last four decades, pointed to the constructed quality of "the South" and gave valuable readings of the narratives of southern culture. As literary scholar Martyn Bone writes, scholars in the field now, though, raise "the question whether 'region' or 'the South' is any longer a useful scale of analysis." Leigh Anne Duck proposes a "Southern studies without 'The South.'" It is puzzling why advocates of new southern studies even include the term "southern," because they have for all intents and purposes abandoned attempts to understand the regional signifier. Some people have used the idea of the South for retrograde and sometimes horrific purposes, but to not take it seriously as a category of analysis fails to confront a source of southern elite power throughout southern history and in the present. It also fails to engage how reformist southerners have mobilized the concept of the southern way of life to bring change to the region.[6]

Recent work has begun to move beyond such shortcomings. Some scholars are embracing interest in local issues, which can indeed be an important aspect for understanding the South, but without a "South" to provide context, the results seem to illuminate American issues, not particularly southern ones. The early twenty-first century is seeing a southern cultural renaissance, the emergence of a vital, reimagined southern identity, and glimpses of a coming ideological, demographic, and political transformation of the region; at the same time, however, new southern studies has missed the opportunity for sustained engagement with the historians, environmental studies scholars, religious studies scholars, ethnic studies programs, and others who are exploring this newest phase of the southern consciousness. Literary scholar Richard Gray observes that "the South is still a concept active in the everyday lives and exchanges of communities; it is still there as a determining part of their mental maps and speech acts," but one would not know it from reading much of the new southern studies literature.[7]

Social scientists, on the other hand, have produced studies throughout the contemporary period that show evidence of the survival of the southern identity as an ideological affiliation despite the material changes in the region. This perspective seems especially relevant in understanding how the southern living concept connects to earlier understandings of the conceptual South. Using interviews, focus groups, and analyses of survey data, social scientists see sociological norms still making the South a particular place on the national landscape. As one recent study concludes, people in the South today are "at least as likely to proclaim their southern identity as they ever have been." The region's dramatic social changes appear to have led many people to claim southern identity as a counterforce to the disruptions of social change. Modernization wears away at aspects of regional identification, but it also brings people together and triggers regional consciousness. Studies have shown persistence in attitudes about localism, violence, religiosity, women's issues, conservative politics, sexuality, death, manners, hospitality, food, and tolerance. Such evidence does not mean that all people in the South, or even all who identify with the region, share all these characteristics, but it does suggest norms of attitudinal and ideological grounding that are attached to the southern living concept.[8]

Perhaps the most striking aspect of attitudinal evidence about southern identity is the new diversity of subgroup identification with the South since 2000. Younger and middle-aged white people who grew up after the civil rights movement, women as well as men, still emphasize positive aspects of what they see as a vital southern culture. People living in the Deep South and people who have lived in the South a considerable time (whether natives or not) identify with the region more than those in the border South states or those recently moved south. A notable, if declining, minority of white southerners identify with a South defined by the symbols of the Old South and the Lost Cause, of patriarchal family values and hierarchical racial order. This group continues to play a dominant role in the region's conservative politics. One sees a discrepancy between the growing cultural diversity of southerners identifying with updated southern ways and with progressive politics, on the one hand, and the conservative policy positions of the dominant Republican Party, on the other.[9]

The most dramatic and significant development in the region's embrace of southern living is the growing identification of African Americans as southerners. In 1990, historian Nell Irvin Painter acknowledged that the aftermath of the civil rights movement had brought to the South "increased freedom of thought and a new flexibility of identity." Whites no longer had to see the world in categories of "Black" and "white," and African Americans were asserting new claims on the region's history. The result was Black southerners' "willingness to claim the South as their own territory and sometimes begrudging, often delighted willingness on the part of white Southerners to acknowledge this claim." By the second decade of the twenty-first century, sociological data showed that African Americans in the South were identifying as southerners as often as white people were.[10]

Of course, collective identity, with its claims on public culture, is different from individual identity, which involves people making personal choices. Older Black southerners have good reason to retain bad memories of the whites-only southern identity through most of the twentieth century. J. L. Chesnut, who had fought bitter wars of brutal race relations in the Alabama Black Belt, understandably refused to claim the identity of "southerner." In his midsixties he said, "I am hardly a Southerner in the classic sense." He added that "only white people qualify for that dubious title," and most Black Alabamians as late as the early twenty-first century probably agreed. But James Clyburn, born in South Carolina to a fundamentalist minister and a beautician, who organized civil rights marches and demonstrations and became a long-serving congressman, embraced the southern identity. In his 2014 memoir, he wrote a message to his children and grandchildren: "As Americans and South Carolinians, I hope you are as proudly black and genuinely southern as your parents and grandparents were." Mississippi-born Natasha Trethewey, who won the Pulitzer Prize in 2007 and was appointed national poet laureate in 2012, similarly told an interviewer that "my role is to establish what has always been Southern, though at other points in history it has been excluded from 'Southernness.'"[11]

The African American identification with the South could cross ideological lines. *Atlanta Journal-Constitution* columnist Cynthia Tucker insisted that "I'm a Southerner, too, as Southern as funeral home fans, collard greens and Ray Charles." She added that "my love is neither irrational nor uncritical." Tucker is a progressive in her politics, but a more conservative figure, former secretary of state Condoleezza Rice, also affirmed her southern identity. In a 2013 interview, she noted she had been born in Alabama, although she moved to Colorado when she was twelve. When asked where she is from, though, "I immediately say, 'The South.'" She credits her "strong emphasis on family, faith, and, well, food" to "my Southern roots."[12]

Chadwick Boseman, a South Carolina–born actor who starred in films about Jackie Robinson, James Brown, and Thurgood Marshall before achieving international acclaim as box-office star of the *Black Panther* film, told an interviewer that he identified as a southerner because "the Southern part of me is always going to come out." Being raised in a small town with a big family, Boseman said, gave him the strength "to deal with some of the *complications* of living in the South because I always felt like I belonged, no matter what," perhaps referring to the complications of race relations. Studies of Black attitudes suggest that African Americans who embrace the southern identity do so for much the same reason as whites do: such cultural features as perceived hospitality, good manners, pace of life, a connection to the land, and food. Boseman used an agrarian metaphor to describe the South he embraced. "There's a sense of the earth, of people being connected to people from that same earth." If agrarianism provides a shared language for Black southerners, such as Boseman, and white southerners, African Americans speak differently than whites do about southern history, politics, and race relations. They reject the Lost Cause memory, the predominant conservative politics embraced by so many white southerners, and the simplified ideas of cheery race relations, but they understand the importance of southern spaces as grounding for social and personal identities.[13]

Working-class whites also saw region as a source of their identity, but they found themselves in transition during this period. In the past, their position in the narratives of southern civilization, the southern way of life, and southern living was sometimes altogether omitted, and at other times they were portrayed as racist and ignorant villains exploited by southern power brokers. The expanding southern economy after 1980 lifted many working-class whites into the middle class. They embraced the individualistic, conservative ethos that drove the concept of southern living. In recent years, working-class southerners have become ever more visible as a part of a multicultural South. They might have left the factories and farms for jobs in the service economy—in real estate, insurance, or retail trade—and embraced the new lifestyle that magazines told them was the new southern way.

As Paul Hemphill wrote in the 1970s, the good old boys were "out in the suburbs now, living in identical houses and shopping at the K-Mart and listening to Glen Campbell (Roy Acuff and Ernest Tubb are too tacky now) and hiding their racism behind code words." He lamented the loss of "their style and spirit," which he saw traded in for "a color TV and Styrofoam beams for the den." Coming perhaps from families so long deprived of material goods, working-class whites now embraced what historian Pete Daniel called "the great American middle class and turned their sights to the accumulation of furniture, automobiles, and status." The stereotypical cars on blocks and whitewashed tires in front yards gave way to the azaleas that *Southern Living* told them how to plant. Their embrace of respectability was real, although tinctured with status anxiety that shaped their conservative politics.[14]

For those workers still in manufacturing jobs in the decades after 1970, the times were not so promising. They represented a South that the cheerful southern living concept could not include. The region sold low wages to recruit potential business. The South Carolina Department of Commerce bragged well into the twenty-first century, for example, that wages in the state were "among

the lowest in the country." Earlier, in 1984, an up-country South Carolina economic development agency refused to support a proposed Mazda plant because it would employ "over 3,000 card-carrying hymn-singing members of
the UAW," which the agency feared would have a "long-term chilling effect on
Spartanburg's orderly industrial growth." The chilling effect was on workers
looking for jobs paying higher wages. The slide of union membership continued throughout the contemporary era. Legislatures bowed to business constituencies' antiunion wishes.

Deindustrialization hit the region's workers hard as well. The once-thriving
textile industry abandoned the region for cheaper costs overseas. The North
American Free Trade Agreement (1993) enabled Mexico to use its cheap labor
to draw textile and garment industry work south of the border; it devastated
many southern small towns and left workers with few possibilities for compa-
rably paying jobs. Many working-class families relied on underpaid work that
created a high rate of the working poor in the South.[15]

No one expressed the role of the white working class in the era of southern
living more acutely than Rick Bragg. Bragg was born in 1957 into a life of outright poverty, but he found his niche as a journalist, eventually becoming a national correspondent for the *New York Times*. In 1997 he published *All Over but
the Shoutin'*, which detailed his rough childhood and how his beloved mother
saw him through it, his rise to success as a journalist, and his time as a professor
at the University of Alabama. He has long written the back-page monthly column for *Southern Living*. At first, this arrangement seemed an odd fit, as Bragg
hardly embodied the profile of the suburban, middle-class version of the new
southern way of life. The magazine gave him license, though, to write about
his own experiences and those of "my people," who told their stories to him
"of vast red fields and bitter turnip greens and harsh white whiskey like they
are rocking in some invisible chair, smooth and easy even in the terrible parts,
because the past has already done its worst." The placement of his stories in the
preeminent magazine of the new southern way of life makes the experiences of
the gritty, down-to-earth, sometime nostalgic Bragg a part of a more inclusive
southern living. One column details features of the region and is a particular
litany of southern living. Music is one part, including "the cry of a steel guitar
on a makeshift stage in the Appalachian foothills." Religion is another, as he
remembers the "hard-rock preachers in their Conway Twitty sideburns who
fling scripture with the force of a flying horseshoe at congregations who all but
levitate in the grasp of the Holy Ghost." Food is a part of it, as he evokes the
savory flavors of tomato sandwiches, oyster po' boys, and biscuits and gravy.
These are all tangible details of southern living that can be rooted in working-
class life but at which other southerners, Black and white, would likely nod in
recognition.[16]

The dinner-on-the-grounds was a food ritual of the southern white working class, as seen in this Bill Ferris photograph from Houston, Mississippi, in 1967. William R. Ferris Collection, Southern Folklife Collection, Wilson Library, University of North Carolina at Chapel Hill.

Bragg is noteworthy, above all, though, for insisting on including his social class in any talk of a southern way. He can poke at *Southern Living* magazine for its portrayal of a "perfect" turkey at Thanksgiving, which makes his mother distraught because her delicious turkey does not look like the magazine's picture. He lampoons "those delicate stores wherein ladies with big purses lean over

souvenirs of the Old South, sigh, and mumble, 'Well, ain't that just *precious.*'"
That world is not his, a world of southern romanticism, expensive T-shirts dyed
in the "honest-to-God Georgia clay" that his mother had struggled to get away
from all her life, and an "$18 box of Goo Clusters." In a 2008 column, he admit-
ted that home has always been a place where "the working people were, where
you still see a Torino every now and then, and people still use motor oil to kill
the mange."[17]

For women in the South, the contemporary era saw tensions rise between the
traditional expectations of behavior and the aspirations and new opportunities
in a modern society. A 2002 *New York Times* article, "Where a 'Southern Girl'
Is Also a Feminist," explored this underlying divided sensibility, discussing
the fourth annual Southern Girls Convention, held on the University of Georgia campus. Author Kate Zernike noted that "the ghost of Miss Scarlett" was
pervasive that weekend, with the attendees' goal being to "exorcise her white-
gloves, fiddle-dee-dee side in favor of her as-God-is-my-witness, I'll-never-be-
hungry-again side." A little bit summer camp and part political gathering, the
convention, according to one of the organizers, intended to show that "not all
Southern women are sitting around drinking sweet tea on the front porch."
That statement seemed to suggest a desire to transcend traditional stereotypes
of southern women, and indeed the reporter saw the participants wanting to
show that "it is O.K. to be feminist in the South," the assumption there being
that that sentiment had not always been true. Progressive political goals were
apparent in Georgian Natasha Murphy's observation that southern women "get
the rap for being demure and dewy-faced in the poofy dress and the big hair,"
but her group of women wanted to "change our communities" by distributing
abortion rights leaflets, participating in the Georgia Abortion Rights Action
League, and sponsoring an antirape rally. Ricci Jusis, a Georgia Tech student,
zeroed in on the need "to celebrate the South without waving the Rebel flag"
and finding "a new way to define what is a Southern woman or girl."[18]

The article seemed to reflect mostly the ambiguities of elite white women,
but working women, African American as well as white, were increasingly important figures in the southern economy as the contemporary era evolved and
familiar cultural images evolved as well. Sociologist Barbara Ellen Smith observed that traditional expectations of upright feminine behavior and morality
still shaped women's approaches to gender solidarity and protest. The service
economy that grew after 1980 relied disproportionately on women's work and
provided new opportunities for middle-class urban women with professional
training. The working poor in the service sector of retail clerks, office workers, waitresses, and others lived, though, with wages below the national average. Walmart has grown to become the behemoth of the American economy,

a small-town Arkansas company that used a low-wage strategy and low-price appeal to structure its successful economic approach. It draws intentionally from traditional southern attitudes about women service workers. At the same time, male employment in such industries as manufacturing, mining, and construction had diminished by the second decade of the twenty-first century. That change nurtured male resentment at this economic decline; hostility toward feminism yet often a necessary reliance on women's salaries; backward-looking dreams of the conventional male-dominated household; and a conservative populist political revolt that fed into Donald Trump's election as president in 2016.[19]

An interview in *Southern Living* in 2013 demonstrates how traditional southern women's roles coalesced with ones updated for the twenty-first century. Bellamy Young, an actress from Asheville, North Carolina, who had earned a modicum of popular culture fame from her role in the television show *Scandal*, told an interviewer that "being a Southern woman is a privileged tradition." It was "something that people see in you well before they hear you speak or taste your cooking," two defining aspects—language and food—of contemporary southern performance. But Young was a self-consciously vegan southerner, an identity not much identified with southern living until recently. Moreover, "I may be vegan, but my mama's buttermilk biscuits are the most delicious thing I've ever tasted." Her conclusion was that "the South is not just a geographical location—the South is a way of life."[20]

The Newest Southerners

When someone in 2003 asked esteemed sociologist and South watcher John Shelton Reed about the future of the South, he replied, "Como esta, y'all." Few changes in the contemporary South are likely to be of more long-range significance to any understanding of southern living than the arrival of Latinos in notable numbers since 1970. Although they had long been a presence in Florida, along the Gulf Coast, and in Texas, a census report showed that between 2000 and 2006 the South's Latino population nearly tripled, with most of the growth in North Carolina, South Carolina, Georgia, Alabama, Tennessee, and Arkansas.[21]

The timeline for the growth of the Latino population was significant in terms of its relationship to southern living, and it included Latinos' contributions to the region, their relationship to its culture, and the changing reaction of native white and Black southerners to them. When the new immigrants first appeared in southern places, public rhetoric was very welcoming, as observers perceived they were offering cheap labor—always a southern elite virtue—with little demanded in return. Their faith, even if often Catholic, seemed to fit the Bible Belt appreciation of religiosity, and Baptists and Pentecostals saw them as a new mission field. Latinos worked on construction crews, building the middle-class suburban houses and businesses and urban high-rises and condominiums that became symbols of southern prosperity. They worked on garden crews that beautified the houses in *Southern Living* and other regional magazines. They toiled in low-wage service industries, with the worst hours and in the most exploitive circumstances. Southern whites saw Latinos as possible replacements for the Black workers in the post–civil rights economy who fought for equal pay and opportunities. Alongside poor African Americans, Latinos worked at the most unpleasant jobs in the region's booming poultry plants and in agricultural fields, the latter of which increased in value during these early years of Latino immigration to the Deep South and Atlantic South. When the workers had wives and children, conservatives saw Latinos embodying the family values that had become a linchpin of Republican Party ideology. Latinos held privileged positions in the white southern imagination from the 1970s through the middle of the first decade of the twenty-first century, years when globalization, the shrinking federal government, and conservative and neoliberal ideologies created new economic opportunities for Latino immigrants. Latinos in those years did not become involved in labor union organizing or political organizing but did embrace the consumer culture and commodification of southern living just as white and Black southerners had done for decades.[22]

In 2000 Mike Huckabee, the Republican governor of Arkansas, attended the Cinco de Mayo Festival in downtown Little Rock, and he proclaimed to Latinos that the state had "a very special word for you today. That word is 'welcome.'" Huckabee made no reference to "illegal aliens" or "undocumented workers," terms that would later become staples of Republican Party rhetoric. The next year, in speaking to the Arkansas Baptist State Convention annual meeting, he insisted that the coming of new immigrants to the state offered his fellow Christians the chance to make amends for the "evil and wrong" done to African Americans in the past. Arkansas had one of the fastest-growing Latino populations in the nation, and Huckabee saw in this development the possibility that "God might be giving us a second chance to do right" and to "act like loving Christian people."[23]

At the same time, other native southerners saw the newcomers as unlawful, or at least unwanted, immigrants to a southern society still concerned with whiteness and order. In the 1970s and 1980s, immigrants came, often as young, single men, to work in the agricultural fields of south Georgia, the poultry plants in northwest Arkansas, and the construction crews of urban North Carolina. After 1990, more women came with their husbands to places such as

Charlotte, Atlanta, and Nashville, moving into suburbs and exurbs—into the heart of southern living middle-class culture—making use of the well-funded schools, less-expensive housing than in urban areas, and proximity to work sites. Latinos pursued the concept of the American dream and hoped that hard work and long hours would lead to progress for their families and the embrace of a consumerist vision rooted in bourgeois values. They hoped that southern people would recognize their modest goals based in economic advancement.

As many began attaining those goals, native white people and sometimes Black people increased their suspicions of the new presence in southern life. Latinos entered the closed quarters of conservative, white, suburban southern living. White homeowners, who were themselves often anxious about their social status in the new economy, resented Latinos' success and their use of such public services as public schools, health care, and even public parks. The language around the anti-immigrant ideology often evoked the old racist language of white supremacy and marked an end to the welcoming talk Mike Huckabee had embodied only a few years earlier. Huckabee himself betrayed his earlier Christian grace to become a shrill supporter of Donald Trump's anti-immigrant vitriol. People in conservative rural areas (who relied on immigrant laborers to pick their crops), small business owners in service industries, and some Christian leaders did oppose restrictive legislation against immigrants. Black-brown coalitions began to appear, and Latinos increased union activities and voter registration efforts in response to the laws.[24]

The white southern response to Latino immigration reflected ongoing anxieties about a rapidly changing South in the early twenty-first century. One 2006 *New York Times* story, "In Georgia, Newest Migrants Unsettle an Old Sense of Place," reported that "for generations, people here savored the predictable cadences of small-town living," putting the focus on "living" as the preeminent issue. Mexican migrants began coming to the small town of Pearson, Georgia, in the 1990s, a place of one traffic light, no makings for Mexican food in the grocery stores, and local people who stared at the newcomers almost in disbelief as their numbers grew. "The sudden shift is upending traditional Southern notions of race and class," the article concluded, "leaving many whites and blacks grappling with unexpected feelings of dislocation, loss and anger as they adjust to their community's evolving ethnic identity." In 1990 Latinos were 3 percent of the county's residents, but by 2004 they were 21 percent, the county's largest minority group. White businessman Elton Corbitt told the reporter that immigration threatened the very foundation of the town's life, including the quality of schools, the effectiveness of medical facilities, neighborhood life, and even the quiet nature of a small southern town that had previously been insulated from much change.[25]

An advocate for immigration rights in the state admitted that "there are people here who have real cultural concerns, who see the life they've known being submerged." But he insisted those concerns should not be the end of the discussion but a topic for negotiation and understanding. Immigrants themselves were proud to be in the community and yet felt alienated from it. Olga Contreras-Martinez had come to the United States when she was twelve. She earned her way picking fruits and vegetables in Florida and Georgia before settling in Pearson in 1993. A college graduate and American citizen, she voted regularly, savored both cheese grits and frijoles, and realized she had to negotiate the boundaries of her identities. She regarded herself as southern because she was raised in the region, and she referenced a signifier of contemporary southern women: "I'm a Latina Grits—a Latina girl raised in the South."[26]

The South through the National Lens

The national culture has long been ambivalent about the South. Sometimes commentators have cordoned it off as the source of all evil in the nation. At other times nonsouthern observers invest in southern living a spiritual and almost premodern sensibility in contrast to the bustling American way. For others, the region appears as simply backward and dumb. That contradictory quality has been apparent in national portrayals of the South in popular culture in recent years.

Television programs of the era provide insight into the diverse views of the South and its way of life. A revealing example is *Designing Women*. The popular situation comedy aired from 1986 to 1993, featuring four sassy white women and one African American man working in an Atlanta design firm. It gave the nation a very different view of the South than the headlines of the 1960s had done. The characters' southern accents and styles were positioned in an urban context with a liberal political perspective. Another show portraying more diverse views of the South was *Evening Shade* (1990–94). This gentle comedy featured Burt Reynolds as a high school football coach in Evening Shade, Arkansas, and it flashed back to a positive, somewhat nostalgic portrait of a quieter time than the contemporary world. *The Dukes of Hazzard* was set in a mythical South that contained both alligators and hills. The main characters fought for "truth, justice and wild driving." *The General Lee* was a Dodge Charger that raced through each episode, as much a character as Daisy Duke, cousins Bo and Luke, and town mayor J. D. "Boss" Hogg. Working-class southerners could identify with the show's celebration of stock car culture, but the middle-class version of southern living seemed far from this popular-culture nationally broadcast network show.[27]

Race was a major theme in television's portrayal of the South in this time period. Race has, of course, been a staple of television portrayals of the region. *In the Heat of the Night* (1988–95) brought the iconic African American detective character Virgil Tibbs back to Mississippi. In the television series he faced racism, police brutality, political corruption, and sexual harassment cases. But the series portrayed African American characters and their lives as integral to a community that was beyond the world of the segregated South and civil rights. The 1990s saw several other television series portraying stories from the civil rights era, including *I'll Fly Away* (1991–93) and *Any Day Now* (1998–2002). They reminded the national audience—and southerners themselves—that the civil rights story was a particularly southern one and a heroic one at that. The gothic South of menace and danger has been a favorite of American culture. As an interesting take on the "blood purity" racial theme, *True Blood* (2008–14) recounted the love affair between waitress Sookie Stackhouse and Bill, a 173-year-old vampire. Set in backwoods Louisiana, the series evoked all sorts of southern stereotypes, but the vampire angle added a weirdness that somehow suggested the enduring southern gothic image. *True Blood* subtly explored civil rights themes, with vampires replacing African Americans as the victims of discrimination in a society where "blood purity" meant much. In 2006, Tyler Perry's *House of Payne* presented an important, and often positive, portrayal of middle-class Black life in the Atlanta suburbs. *Frank's Place* (1987–88) and *Treme* (2010–13) chronicled Black lives and culture in New Orleans. The latter of the two drew from a well-rooted local knowledge of the city after Hurricane Katrina. Television from the 1990s reflected a wider and richer portrayal of race and African American culture, one that was nuanced by southern Blacks' embrace of southern living.[28]

One could also recount films similarly portraying the South since 1980, with cultural meanings for southern living. The eccentric characters of *Crimes of the Heart* and *Cookie's Fortune* anchored sympathetic portrayals of the biracial South, with women as central players. *Mississippi Burning* (1988) was a high-profile Hollywood film that engaged the difficult subject of the killing of three civil rights workers in 1963. It earned film industry plaudits but created controversy because of its narrative that highlighted the undercover work of the Federal Bureau of Investigation while seeming to downplay the activists themselves. *Mississippi Masala* (1992) was a revelation with its story of South Asians living in Greenwood, Mississippi, in the heart of the Delta, and interacting with the African American community there. Documentary films and independent films, both of which have been energized by the plethora of local film festivals that have emerged in the twenty-first-century South, often portray a similarly more complex South, beyond the mainstream national media images. They give voice to LGBTQ stories, for example, and present new southerners including Latinos, Asians, and other immigrants.[29]

Books, magazines, and online content flesh out the national culture's complicated portrayal of the South at the heart of the idea of southern living. One of the most outlandish critiques of southern living from the national popular culture came from Chuck Thompson in *Better Off without 'Em: A Northern Manifesto for Southern Secession* (2012). Thompson, editorial director of CNN's online news service, had written several travel memoirs and spent two years traveling the South to gather information for a polemical attack on contemporary southern culture. He went to, among other places, a church service in Mobile, Alabama, a store selling Ku Klux Klan memorabilia in South Carolina, and the Creation Museum in Kentucky. Academics appeared in the book, as did ministers, journalists, and writers. He cited polling data to buttress his arguments. With chapters on religion, politics, race, football, education, and economics, he criticized the South's backwardness in all those areas. Racism existed throughout the nation, he admitted, but he insisted it was more extreme in the South. He lambasted an educational system flawed by inadequate revenues, anti-intellectualism, and resegregation of schools. His comments about Southeastern Conference football being overrated brought the greatest ire from within the region. Overall, his observations of the region betrayed an open hostility. At one stop he watched a little girl in a museum viewing a dinosaur and insisted she did so in "silent, imbecilic awe," while at another he lamented the South's "biscuits-and-boneheads culture." Thompson was on point about many of the South's shortcomings, but his nasty tone betrayed what southerners, white and Black, have long seen as northern condescension that reinforced enduring negative stereotypes despite the notable changes in the recent South.[30]

The recurring negative national images of the South have always involved racial and, more broadly, cultural issues. This is true in the contemporary era as well. Even though so much has changed in the South, several topics still evoke visceral disdain, as seen in Thompson's book. The prevalence of guns in the South and aggressive defense of them; the evangelical conservative Protestantism that stands in opposition to many issues regarding women's rights, LGBTQ rights, and public programs aimed to assist those in need, many of whom are African American; and conservative political dominance in general all elicit responses from the national media that isolate the region from the rest of the nation and reinforce older views of the region's character.

Few topics do that as potently as the southern white embrace of the symbols of the Confederacy. Many such responses appear in national journals of opinion such as the *Atlantic, New Republic,* and *Salon.* A good example was Adam Serwer's 2017 essay "The Myth of the Kindly General Lee." In the early twentieth century, Lee had entered the pantheon of national heroes as a symbol of the nation's acceptance of the courage and heroism of Confederate and Union soldiers that blurred ideological aspects of why they fought. Critics now widely challenge that view, and the attack on Lee's character was a particularly dramatic example. Serwer insisted that Lee was not the brilliant military strategist as legend had it, nor was he a critic of the white supremacy that underlay the Confederacy. The author pointed to the massacre of African American soldiers at the battle of the Crater in 1864 by troops under Lee's command and to the rape of a young Black servant on the campus of Washington College while Lee was president there after the war. This article and others represented a pointed interpretation of the Lost Cause from outside the region, one that reinforced, in fact, successful efforts of progressive African Americans and white southerners to dismantle much of that Lost Cause public memory by the second decade of the twenty-first century.[31]

At the same time, the national culture had always found the South to be a place of escape from the complexities of modern life, and that sentiment continued in new ways in the twenty-first century. Jeremy Egner's "The South, as Seen on TV," for example, gave a positive report on a road trip through the South that included sites where producers filmed major television shows portraying the region. Its tone could not have been more different from Thompson's. Emphasizing shows that portrayed the gothic South, Egner confessed that on his trip "I ate well, drank better and zoned out on rocky-top foothills and in kudzu canyons." In addition to the Atlanta area, Egner visited Nashville, seeing the Tennessee capital city as "your cool friends' favorite city, thanks to New South cuisine and a fertile cultural scene." Music and food resonated throughout the article as what made these southern places interesting in the early twenty-first century. Egner turned to a familiar term to describe southern living: "the sense of place." He saw that quality "beguile location scouts," and his visit had been "a great way to get a sense of place." Scholars rigorously contest the idea that the South ever had a unique sense of place, but writers and observers inside the region and outside it continue to see that term resonating with the region's culture.[32]

Another travel piece in the New York Times was intriguing because Sarah Khan, a self-identified Muslim woman, wrote it after touring the country with her Muslim American friend. Her trip to Nashville included not only visiting country music sites but eating hot chicken at Hattie's, worshipping at the African American Mount Zion Baptist Church, and checking out Walmart to see what guns were selling after seeing so many "God-fearing and gun-loving bumper stickers." She wondered whether, in those parts, "Jesus himself might have drafted the Second Amendment." A trip to Memphis brought an unexpected appreciation of Graceland, a visit to the National Civil Rights Museum, and a disturbing conversation with an older white man in a doughnut shop who insisted Black people and white people had no problems in the old days. The article concluded on a positive note, though, with a hopefulness for a new multicultural South. Her Muslim friend, Nazie, a Nashville transplant, concluded that "Southern hospitality typically trumps bigotry." The southerners Nazie knew "might not agree with you, they might think Jesus needs to save you, but they believe they need to be good and kind because that's the way Jesus would have been."[33]

Since the beginning of the twenty-first century, a more multicultural version of southern living has emerged in the national media. As the region embraced the concept of southern living, these portrayals in popular media produced an image of a complicated, multicultural south that defied the definition of a monolithic southern way of life.

The South Still Remembers

In the contemporary period, the region continued its ongoing battles over the memorialization of its two central historical events, the Civil War and the civil rights movement. Together they represented a contested cross-cultural exchange. Few factors, nonetheless, have been more revealing of conservative and progressive visions of contemporary southern living than control of the public memory. The Lost Cause was an ideological foundation for post–Civil War southern civilization, and symbols and narratives of the Confederacy have been reasserted as the essence of southern history. The white resistance to racial integration revived the Lost Cause in the 1950s and 1960s. The civil rights movement challenged this mythic foundation of southern public culture, and since then, the public impact of the memory of the Confederacy has declined—but not without struggles.

The imperative among Black southerners to re-envision the South has figured in the ongoing conflicts over southern public symbols. Beginning in the 1970s, Black southerners with new authority pressured officials to remove symbols they regarded as offensive.[34]

Among the most controversial symbols were "Dixie" (the southern anthem), the Confederate battle flag, and the ubiquitous Confederate monuments found in southern spaces. Responding to threats of boycotts and other protests, most state and local governments, schools and colleges, and other institutions abandoned the intentional playing of "Dixie" at public events by the 1990s. The Confederate battle flag was perhaps even more controversial than the southern anthem because the Ku Klux Klan and other protesters against racial desegregation made the flag a visual centerpiece in their violent resistance to integration. Looking at the long period from the 1970s to now, though, the flag has virtually disappeared from the public landscape of the South. The state of Mississippi provided the most grudging resistance to abandoning these symbols, but in May 2020 the Mississippi state legislature authorized removal of the Confederate flag's St. Andrew's cross from the state flag, producing hopes among some white, as well as African American, legislators that the unexpected change could lead to more attention to the socioeconomic problems of African American communities.[35]

The Confederate battle flag evoked special passions because of its ties to both the defense of slavery and the resistance to the civil rights movement. Clyde N. Wilson, a professor of history at the University of South Carolina, spoke of the flag as "a symbol of heritage and identity" in a 1996 essay. He called advocates of the flag's continuing public display "good Americans," for whom "the flag is a symbol not of white supremacy, but of identification with their own ancestors and heritage and an affirmation of their own identity." In 1987, an Atlanta factory worker added a white working-class view that the flag "ain't got nothing to do with hating black people or any of that KKK stuff." All it meant to him was to "get the hell off my back and leave me the hell alone." In this view, the flag was a symbol of countercultural rebellion, a sentiment found both in Europe among people displaying the flag there and in the United States.[36]

Despite the steady decline in public display of the Confederate battle flag, it remained a visceral image of the culture wars into the twenty-first century, taking on a violent character in the death of nine African Americans at Emanuel African Methodist Episcopal Church in Charleston, South Carolina, in 2015. White supremacist Dylann Roof had gone to the church and was welcomed by its members before he killed them. He appeared in an online photograph with the flag, an image that ignited the ongoing South Carolina controversy over display of the flag. Republican governor Nikki Haley led a successful effort in the state after the murders to remove the flag from the state capitol grounds. One can see progress in the decline of the flag's association with southern living, but this shift has been grudging and embittering for some white southerners.[37]

While the flag continued to be a flash point in the culture wars between progressives and traditionalists, Confederate monuments became a new emotional issue in the twenty-first century. Most of the monuments had been put up between 1890 and 1960, the era of Jim Crow segregation, political disfranchisement, racial violence, and the concept of southern civilization. Big cities such as New Orleans and Memphis removed statues to Lost Cause heroes in 2017, as did colleges such as the University of Texas and the University of North Carolina at Chapel Hill (where activists tore down the Silent Sam monument at the entrance to the campus). New Orleans mayor Mitch Landrieu made the case for removal because the monuments were "not just innocent remembrances of a benign history." The monuments celebrated, he said, "a fictional, sanitized Confederacy ignoring the death, ignoring the enslavement, ignoring the terror that it actually stood for." Landrieu pointed out that the Confederates had fought against the United States of America and were therefore problematic as contemporary heroes. The removal of the Robert E. Lee statue in Charlottesville, Virginia, in 2017, brought a gathering of neo-Nazis and white supremacists to protest, leading to violence and the death of Heather Heyer, a peaceful counterdemonstrator. Monuments to four Confederate leaders were removed from Richmond's iconic Monument Avenue between July 2020 and September 2021. Historian Karen Cox argues in a *New York Times* column published on August 15, 2017, that defenders of the Lost Cause were reviving late nineteenth-century rhetoric that portrayed "the mythology of the Confederacy as a grand patriarchal civilization." This view connected a contemporary far-right version of southern living to its earlier southern civilization model. Cox revived the language of morality that has long swirled about the South, as she insisted that communities across the region had "a moral obligation to take up the cause of removing" the monuments. In *No Common Ground: Confederate Monuments and the Ongoing Fight for Racial Justice* (2021) she places the removal of monuments in the context of the Black Lives Matter movement.[38]

Defenders of the Confederate monuments saw an endangered sense of southern identity at the heart of their older version of the southern way of life. They believed a more diverse South and nation threatened them. For historian Carol Anderson, the people advocating for the preservation of Confederate monuments in public spaces believe that "they are actually oppressed and disadvantaged whenever anyone else's voice is heard, their needs addressed and their political will prevails." Karl Burkhalter, a retired racehorse trainer from a small town near Baton Rouge, came to New Orleans to protest the removal of the Jefferson Davis statue. "These monuments," he insisted, "they were a reflection of the fact that the only bit of self-esteem so many white people down here had left was tied to the sacrifices they had made for the Confederacy. I think that's what upsets so many people about the idea of removing them now." Removal of Lost Cause monuments helped ease the grievance of one southern social group but stoked that of others.[39]

Despite gradual changes in the commemoration of the Confederacy in the South, some writers and middle-class white southerners had reasserted the Lost Cause after 1980 as a "neo-Confederate movement" that has persisted. "The New Dixie Manifesto" appeared in the *Washington Post* in 1995, as the neo-Confederate movement entered the national cultural mainstream. Thomas

Fleming and Michael Hill were its authors, two of the twenty-seven people who had founded the Southern League (later renamed the League of the South) in June 1994, in Tuscaloosa, Alabama. The Southern Poverty Law Center identified that group as the "ideological core" of neo-Confederacy and classified it as a hate group. Although the group would come to be allied with some Republican politicians, it went beyond traditional American conservatism in advocating secession of fifteen southern states and the reestablishment of the Confederate States of America. "The New Dixie Manifesto" supported states' rights, local control of schooling and the end of both federal funding and regulations in southern states, Christian dominance in public life, and respect for Confederate symbols. The underlying importance of race became clear when the authors of the manifesto insisted that southern race relations were better than those in northern states.[40]

Author Tony Horwitz saw the neo-Confederate ideology drawing from "strains of Thomas Jefferson, John Calhoun, the Nashville Agrarians . . . and other thinkers who idealized Southern planters and yeoman farmers while demonizing the bankers and industrialists of the North." Horwitz concluded that this agenda was "little more than a clever glide around race and slavery, rather like the slick-tongued defense of the Southern 'way of life' made by antebellum orators." Neo-Confederates did not favor the middle-class, modern southern living that dominated the contemporary South; they rebelled against modernity and ferociously opposed rights for not only African Americans but other ethnic minorities, gays, and women.[41]

Southern Partisan magazine had appeared in 1979 and epitomized neo-Confederate ideas. Articles in the magazine explored many facets of southern white culture yet cohered in stressing the centrality of the Confederacy to southern white identity. Southerners interested in the neo-Confederate identity could join organizations such as the Confederate Society of America, the Culture of the South Association, the Southern Heritage Association, and the Sons of Confederate Veterans, one of whose chapters published the *Rebel Yell*, a newsletter with the motto "If at first you don't secede, try, try again." None of these groups was large in itself, but their significance came from their active role in Republican politics in the South and their ability to tap into the frustrations of white southerners. *New York Times* reporter Peter Applebome concluded that "the spirit of the Lost Cause" tracked well with the Republican agenda of the 1980s. John C. Calhoun's states' rights, Stonewall Jackson's messianic religiosity, praise for small government and old-time values, the pervasive undertone of race—all flashed back to the memory of the Confederacy.[42]

The commemoration of the Old South and the Lost Cause has declined, but the neo-Confederacy movement has injected a version of the older southern way of life into contemporary politics. At the same time, southerners have deepened their collective memories of the civil rights movement. Among the most significant reminders of the civil rights era are Maya Lin's dramatic memorial to the martyrs of the movement at the Southern Poverty Law Center in Montgomery; the monument to Medgar Evers in Jackson, Mississippi; the statue of the first African American student at the University of Mississippi, James Meredith; and the statue of Arthur Ashe now standing on Richmond's resonant Monument Avenue where the giant statues of Confederate leaders once stood. But perhaps one of the most significant reminders of the civil rights era is the first state-financed civil rights museum, which opened in 2017 in Jackson, Mississippi. It sits beside a prominent museum on Mississippi history in general. The *New York Times* reporter covering the opening of the museum wrote that "the new Mississippi Civil Rights Museum refuses to sugarcoat history," and the museum earned the praise of former civil rights activists for its honest portrayal of the era. Historian John E. Fleming, writing about the museum, said, "The exhibition does not shy away from the unspeakable horrors of the Jim Crow era and the atrocities that were committed in the name of preserving white supremacy."[43]

In a foreword to a book that accompanied the museum openings, *Telling Our Stories: Museum of Mississippi History and Mississippi Civil Rights Museum,* former Republican governor Haley Barbour and former African American state supreme court justice Reuben Anderson recounted the long effort to build the museums, for which the state had provided $90 million in financing, supplemented by $20 million in private donations. They identified the economic impact of the new museums, with estimates that visitors would generate $17 million dollars a year for the state. But they insisted that "education is at the core of the two museums' mission." They would be "the largest classroom in the state," and the museums quickly fulfilled that hope as schoolchildren, church groups, and others have provided a steady stream of visitors. In the introduction to the volume, Myrlie Evers, wife of civil rights martyr Medgar Evers, and former governor William Winter praised the progress of Mississippi "since the dismantling of the 'closed society'" and indicated ways the museums "capture that journey along with earlier struggles." They used their essay to point the way for the state's people "to work together to build a more just, vibrant, and healthy Mississippi for our future." Governor Phil Bryant, a conservative Republican notable for his lack of support for the agenda of African American legislators in the state, participated in its dedication. Conservatives who might not be expected to be supportive of civil rights memorialization argue that the movement addressed racial injustices and that their efforts solved all racial problems in American society, with no need for targeted programs to promote social justice in what they call a now "color-blind society."[44]

In Alabama, the National Memorial for Peace and Justice is a unique institution that commemorates not the civil rights movement but the thousands of
people lynched in the South between 1877 and 1950. Its founder, Bryan Stevenson, worked with death penalty cases for decades in Alabama, the state with the
highest per capita death penalty rate. He argues that at the heart of American
slavery was a white supremacy that was transformed after the Civil War into a
near century of lynching terror and demeaning Jim Crow segregation and later
into the contemporary high rates of incarceration of people of color. The Legacy Museum is associated with the memorial, and it documents this argument
through dramatic sculptures and oral narratives, hundreds of jars of soil from
lynching sites, and a walkway of 800 steel columns hanging from a roof and
displaying the name of each county where a lynching occurred and the name
of the person lynched.[45]

The lynching memorial evokes the trauma of African American history,
but the civil rights story generally has a more upbeat narrative. In addition
to museums, cultural tourism has also emerged as a means to draw attention
to the legacy of the civil rights movement. Civil rights trails in Alabama and
Mississippi emerged in the twenty-first century as examples of state efforts to
promote cultural tourism among African Americans and others. The National
Park Service has worked toward more inclusive history as well by commemo-
rating many African American sites in the South, including not just civil rights
movement locales but sites of slave rebellion, legal battles, Underground Railroad safe houses, historic Black colleges and universities, churches, and birth-
places of African American writers, musicians, artists, and other such figures.[46]

These civil rights trails stand in stark contrast to the traditional antebellum
plantation house tours or pilgrimages. Plantation historic places long did not
acknowledge the African American presence, and some white people continue
to see plantations as important locales for social events such as weddings. The
Behind the Big House project in Holly Springs, Mississippi, is one of many such
sites now that does acknowledge the plantation's African American presence,
however, with annual conferences that draw from a wide spectrum of the community and conduct oral history interviews with African Americans in areas
surrounding the plantation. The Whitney Plantation on Mississippi River Road
in south Louisiana is an exceptional site and the first slavery museum in the
nation. Dating back to 1752, the plantation contains 2,000 acres of land once
dedicated to raising sugarcane. New Orleans attorney John Cummings worked
fifteen years to restore the plantation to focus on the life of its enslaved workers.
The museum opened in 2014 and showcases commissioned sculptures, oral
history narratives of enslaved people, and a visual display on slave memorials
featuring the names of enslaved people who were once anonymous.[47]

At the turn of the twentieth century, Confederate veterans held reunions and parades to ensure the memory of the Lost Cause remained in the minds of future generations. Since the early 1990s, the annual bridge-crossing commemoration in Selma, Alabama, serves something of the same purpose for civil rights veterans and their followers. The Edmund Pettus Bridge was the site of one of the civil rights era's most important events, Bloody Sunday. In March 1965, civil rights protesters tried to cross the bridge only to be met by Alabama state troopers and law enforcement and be beaten back. The sight of civil rights leaders such as John Lewis, who was severely beaten that day, reenacting the march across the Edmund Pettus Bridge has attracted crowds as large as 10,000 people.

Participation by politicians has served to establish a certain credibility with African American voters. Barack Obama and Hillary Clinton both were there in 2007, and John McCain attended in 2008. Obama went to a prayer breakfast while there and said, "If it hadn't been for Selma, I wouldn't be here." In 2015, Obama said Selma was a place that symbolized "the daring of America's character." At the bridge commemoration that year, Alabama governor Robert Bentley said he hoped the occasion would show how the state had changed. "We want people in America and the world to realize that Alabama is a different place and a different state than it was 50 years ago." He was proud of the state being "as much of a colorblind state as any state in the country, and we're very proud of the advancement we've made." Jesse Jackson, in 2003, had warned, though, against the nostalgia of resting on the laurels of change and letting memorials replace the need for contemporary social action. "Beyond the bridge is crippling poverty," he noted, "people working without fair wages."[48]

Southern Living, one of the magazines that has helped shape the southern living era, was criticized in the 1960s for failing to acknowledge civil rights movement activities. The magazine's home in Birmingham was near what had been the center of movement activities. But in February 2017 editor Sid Evans wrote a column, "Powerful Memories: The South's Civil Rights Sites Are Places to Visit, Reflect, and Remember," that showed how the movement has entered centrally into the broader concept of southern living. Evans praised the work of photographer Ari Meripol, who had photographed the iconic churches, bridges, schools, and lunch counters that evoked memories of those times. "To stand in these places one day after the next was an emotional wallop," Meripol told Evans, and that was "precisely why these sites need to be preserved for future generations." Evans then recounted his own children visiting the Birmingham Civil Rights Institute, located across the street from the Sixteenth Street Baptist Church, where an explosion in September 1963 killed four Black girls. "That's a hard thing to wrap your head around if you're an adult—let alone a fourth-grade girl like my daughter—but the lessons of that horrific event become much clearer when you can stand on the steps of the church where it happened." The issue included the story "The Steps We Took" with Meripol's images and text by John Lewis. Evans wrote that "Lewis's story is a reminder of times we would rather forget, but it's also an indication of how far we've come—and how far we have to go," words that echoed African American rhetoric. The fact that the magazine highlighted the memory of the civil rights movement suggested a willingness to move beyond the commodified South its pages often present to a deeper spiritual level of the southern living concept.[49]

Culture and Diverse Southern Living

Culture itself became a defining issue of southern living in the contemporary era. Southern culture, it now became clear, had been formed in the region's rural areas over the course of hundreds of years since the original settlement of the South, with a rich folk culture seen in everything from language to religion, rituals, recreations, eating habits, and so much more. The folk culture embodied place and localism, family and kin connections, a religious worldview resting in the sin-and-salvation ethos of the long-predominant evangelical Protestantism; such gendered recreations as quilting for women and fishing and hunting for men; a pervasive musicality of songs and performances rooted in regions and spaces within the South; the crafting of pottery and other expressions of local material culture; and a storytelling inclination growing out of rural isolation. Many of the features of the southern folk culture that were apparent in rural areas and small towns until the late twentieth century were typical of peasant societies around the world, but with particular expressions in American regional terms. Local patriotism might be a common tribal feature, for example, but what one would fight and die and kill for among many white southerners was the Confederate flag, a specific symbol for a binding southern white historical experience. Racial intolerance might be a common form of xenophobia, but southern white supremacy—and sometimes the embrace of interracialism as well—grew out of the particular engagement of people from western Europe and west Africa. Two dissimilar groups of people had been brought together on southern soil to deal with each other, and Indigenous peoples, for hundreds of years and to unite their cultures in new ways, despite rank injustices in the process.[50]

The contemporary South adapts older southern cultural forms based in folk-life. City people refined the older culture through church barbecues, neighborhood music or food festivals, home tours, and concerts and craft fairs in the park—all of these were among the most familiar expressions of southern culture in urban areas. They often retained a small-town flavor. In southern

The original southerners, Native Americans, have revived traditional cultures in the twenty-first century, as seen in this man dressed as a Black Seminole for the Second Seminole War reenactment. joel zatz / Alamy Stock Photo.

cities one still hears music native to the region's places, whether jazz, bluegrass, blues, country, rhythm and blues, or soul, as well as newer southern styles such as Mississippian David Banner's Dirty South rap in Jackson or OutKast's hip-hop in Atlanta. One eats iconic southern food at urban gatherings, whether barbecue, fried chicken, or watermelon slices. The dynamism of the twenty-first-century South appears as new ethnic presences are seen in celebrations of Cinco de Mayo or the feast of Our Lady of Guadalupe, with tacos added to barbecue and fried chicken as southern urban street food. Such occasions represent the older, rural-based folk culture mingling, and merging, with the folk cultures of immigrants.[51]

Cultural expressions of many types boomed in the contemporary South. Oxmoor House, the publishing arm of *Southern Living*, published *Southern Folk Art*, a reflection that southerners were collecting folk art born in rural areas, if now displayed in suburban homes. Southern magazines, in general, became carriers of contemporary southern culture. Allison Glock's "Song of the South," for example, which appeared in *Southern Living* in September 2013, noted that "music is as much a part of the South as humidity, thanks to our Scots-Irish and African-American heritage, the church, and bourbon." Southern born, Glock had lived in the North, and she made the requisite regional comparison: up there, "music was formal," as children took music lessons from instructors using "methods." Spontaneous outbursts of "questionable pitch were not on the playlist." Down south, she rediscovered the important truth that "music here isn't so much about the song as the spirit," a key term often associated with an intangible southern way.[52]

Developments in country music revealed broader cultural trends. By the early 1980s, popular and rock music had made inroads into the mainstream country music industry, such that traditionalists were outraged when pop singer Olivia Newton-John won major industry awards for some of her cross-over hits. The claim of country music "authenticity" was always suspect, as the music had begun evolving and melding early on, when performers absorbed ethnic music into country music and electric guitars and drums appeared in the 1940s at the Grand Ole Opry. Nonetheless, the familiar dynamic between concern for tradition and the reality of change has continued to characterize country music. Neotraditionalists such as Randy Travis and Ricky Skaggs became popular in the 1980s, and later, giant crossover stars such as Garth Brooks helped define the new arena performances located in urban and suburban southern living areas by the 1990s. Country music was part of the southernization of America by the 1990s, and soon many of the leading industry stars, such as Shania Twain, were not from the South or even the United States. The television show *Nashville* showcased that city and modern country music and brought them national attention. By the early twenty-first century, a new country music outlaw such as Sturgill Simpson evoked such earlier country rebels as Waylon Jennings, Willie Nelson, Kris Kristofferson, and Johnny Cash, while young African American performers such as Mickey Guyton, Kane Brown, and Jimmie Allen made a splash in Nashville. The country music industry in the twenty-first century still remained predominantly conservative, though, in its promotion of mostly white male singers, now embodying the remnants of the South's patriarchal ways.[53]

Southern literature also showed broader trends in southern culture. *Southern Living* magazine had made writing a central part of the southern living concept from the beginning of its publication, through the Books about the South column. By the early twenty-first century, the editors published periodic memoirs by distinguished writers such as Lee Smith and Natasha Trethewey. "Southern literature" survives as a category of analysis and expectation, judging by book publishers, bookstores, book clubs, regional and national magazines and newspapers, book reviewers, and teachers from middle school to university, all of whom use the category. Writers in the southern literature genre have chronicled the region's enormous changes since the 1960s, and they draw from popular culture, with films, television shows, music, and other media venues informing their works. Long-standing forms of narrative continue to influence contemporary writers. As literary scholar James H. Justus wrote in 1997, "The storytelling cadences are distinctive."[54]

Southern literature embodies the contemporary South's embrace of a more diverse, even multicultural society. One social group that has sometimes been marginalized or stereotyped in southern writing is the white working class, but self-conscious writers from this group are among the region's more accomplished recent authors. The trailer park is a more likely setting now than Faulkner's ruined mansions. Harry Crews was the progenitor of this trend, with his memoir *A Childhood: Biography of a Place* (1978), portraying the rough South of his family, who moved from sharecropping into the demanding industrial economy of south Georgia and north Florida. The experiences of the southern poor, as their writers portray them, embody a synthesis of an underlying southern dichotomy between the awareness of human limitation, rooted in hard lives, and the possibility of transcendence, which provides inspiration for these writers. Mississippi author Larry Brown once said that he wrote "about people surviving, about people proceeding out from calamity . . . about the lost." They may be lost, but they "are aware of their need for redemption."[55]

African American writing in the years since 1980 has become more diverse than ever, as Black writers place their stories in the southern context where the land, the environment, family, folklore, religion, racial interaction with white people, and language matter. Raymond Andrews, born in 1934 in Morgan County, Georgia, as the child of sharecroppers in a tight-knit African American community, wrote of the strength of rural Black life and the complexities of interracial relationships rooted in the legacy of slavery and segregation. Ernest Gaines's achievement was a deep portrayal of south Louisiana's African American and Cajun interaction in the lives of men who work and live together in unjust situations and have long memories of plantation life. Randall Kenan was one of the most acclaimed of all southern writers, incorporating oral history, folklore, and churchly religion in his novel *A Visitation of Spirits* (1989) and his short stories in *Let the Dead Bury the Dead* (1992). The fictional locale for these tales is Tim's Creek, North Carolina, modeled after his hometown of Chinquapin in the southeastern part of the state. In an essay on the North Carolina island that his family visited and to which he returned before his death in 2020, Kenan evoked a sensibility he saw as southern: "Topsail Island and its environs are controlled by some strange Southern magic, the laws of which only the

Atlantic understands." A gay Black man, he explored through his writing the myriad identities of people caught in rapid social change, especially those in rural areas, and the tensions between Black masculinity and homosexuality.[56]

Jesmyn Ward has created a memorable fictional place, Bois Sauvage, modeled after her hometown of DeLisle, Mississippi. She glories in its heat and humidity, and its rivers and bayous give an environmental anchor to her fiction and non-fiction. She celebrates a sense of place, family, land, home, and community—a sensibility that has long been identified with the southern way of life. But unlike the whites-only world of Vanderbilt's Agrarians, Ward uses sense of place to illuminate the lives of her African American characters, for whom land is a source of independence and of a spirit strong enough to endure natural disasters or the pain of social injustice. She also populates her real and fictional landscapes with biracial relationships and cultural hybridity, reflecting a Gulf Coast culture that blends French, Spanish, Indigenous, and African influences. Yet Ward's writing is hardly sentimental. She notes that her extended family of hundreds of people who live near her sometimes frustrate her. Even more troubling is the frustration brought about by Confederate flags and conservative politics that reinforce structural inequalities. But she affirms that "this is the South and this is my blood and this is my home." Ward's acclaimed writing (she has won two National Book Awards) reminds us that African American writers in the twenty-first century have been prominent advocates of the many Souths they embrace.[57]

In the recent South, homosexuality is a frequent and open topic in literature, a significant addition to the multicultural version of southern living that has emerged in the twenty-first century, although it still evokes pushback from those with homophobic attitudes. Fannie Flagg's novel *Fried Green Tomatoes at the Whistle Stop Cafe* (1987) suggested a love relationship between two women, within a tolerant community, as the women welcomed all comers in a free atmosphere surprisingly set in the small-town South. Literary scholar Jamie Harker shows the southern context for lesbians was far more than an abject site for repression, as it was a place of resistance and reconstruction as well. Lesbian writers such as Minnie Bruce Pratt created a radical South, but the overlapping of identities could be surprising for other southern gay writers. Florence King embraced a gay identity but had a nostalgic view of southern living, while Dorothy Allison made her southern identity central to her persona, which combined gritty, working-class experiences with sexual identity. Virginian Rita Mae Brown was a self-proclaimed radical and activist, but she admired the South's talk of honor and community. "Even if I wanted to reject the Southern ways," referring to good manners, she said, "how could I. It comes in with your mother's milk." Harker concludes that for southern lesbian writers, "southern identity remained an important term of self-identification." They created a South that was "radical, queer, and free, even as some of its writers were simultaneously drawn to its reactionary pull."[58]

Globalization has made the South the center of immigration, and many writers are chronicling the stories of these new southerners who have arrived from many places. Robert Olen Butler's *A Good Scent from a Strange Mountain* (1992) pioneered a focus on Vietnamese people who fled their nation in the aftermath of the Vietnam War and made new lives on the Louisiana coast. Cynthia Shearer's *The Celestial Jukebox* (2005) portrayed the Mississippi Delta as a place for people from around the world, as Italians, Jews, and Chinese had long been there. Shearer's novel complicated the world of Black and white Mississippians, joined in contemporary times by the newest immigrants from Latin America, India, Africa, and other faraway lands. Monique Truong's *Bitter in the Mouth* (2010) tells the story of Linda Hammerick, who comes from Vietnam as a seven-year-old child to a new home with Southern Baptist parents in Boiling Springs, North Carolina. She unveils the silences and hostilities she experienced, but she grew to embrace a southern identity, seeing her lawyer father as like Atticus Finch in *To Kill a Mockingbird*. Her narrative leads to a recognition of her identity as a refugee orphan with all the trauma that entails, but she finds a home in the South—and loves North Carolina barbecue.[59]

Commentators on the South have often portrayed Florida as an outlier in understanding southern culture, but it has become a center of the twenty-first-century multicultural South. To be sure, it was a slave state, with a plantation society, and it was a part of the Confederacy; but the tropical climate, distance from other parts of the South, a prosperous tourist economy, and long-standing ties to the Caribbean made it seem not "typical" of the region. Miami now represents a new model for a South experiencing increased ethnic and cultural diversity and ties to places outside the nation. A million refugees fled Cuba from 1959 to 2000, with most settling in the Miami area, joined by other Latino immigrants from Nicaragua, Colombia, Puerto Rico, and the Dominican Republic so that Latinos represent 69 percent of the city's population. The Black population of metro Miami is 20 percent, including several hundred thousand Haitian exiles and other Black immigrants from the Caribbean. Calle Ocho (Eighth Street) and Little Havana have mambo music and salsa dancing in clubs, Cuban food in restaurants, and shops that offer dresses for quinceañeras (coming-of-age rituals for fifteen-year-old girls).[60]

Music, literature, and food from south Florida are being incorporated into discussions of southern culture. Miami's 2 Live Crew popularized dirty rap as early as the mid-1980s, and the city produced a regional hip-hop style, Miami bass, which is a subgenre of southern rap that puts together fast-paced, modern, bass-heavy electronic dance music with sustained drumbeats and sounds of funk music from the past. South Florida writers more directly than musicians engage with themes that reflect traditional southern cultural concerns but also add counternarratives to southern traditionalism and show the diversity of the American South. Poet Sandra M. Castillo, for example, came to Miami from Cuba when she was nine years old, and memories of her Cuban childhood haunt her works, which represent a sensibility rooted in loss, history, gender, language, and memory. These have also been concerns of earlier southern writers, but the content of Castillo's experiences enriches the regional understanding of those concepts.

No Cuban American writer claims a southern identity more enthusiastically than Gustavo Pérez Firmat, who came from Cuba when he was eleven years old and lived in North Carolina for twenty years before moving to New York City. His *Life on the Hyphen: The Cuban-American Way* (1994) explored hyphenated identities in the United States, but his poem "Carolina Cuban" (1985) and his short story "My Life as a Redneck" (1992) showed the twoness of ethnic and regional identities specific to the American South. How southern regional consciousness has shaped him is perhaps best seen in his book *A Cuban in Mayberry: Looking Back at America's Hometown* (2014), which combines his story of exile from Cuba with appreciation of *The Andy Griffith Show*'s presentation of home and community. He realizes well that the isolated people on the show may not have appreciated a Cuban exile showing up to disturb their homogeneity, but its idealized presentation of rootedness strikes an imaginative chord with him. Amid the racial, generational, and political turmoil of the 1960s, the show, to Firmat, touched feelings of intimacy among its characters that appealed to a wide audience that included him. The book ends with Firmat writing an imagined episode of the show, "The Lost Boy," about a young Cuban boy coming to Mayberry, whose people help him reunite with his aunt, Tia Maria, placing a Cuban experience into one of the most hypersouthern cultural expressions.[61]

Another hypersouthern cultural expression is college football. Football is a national institution, but college football has taken on a region-specific meaning. University of Alabama Crimson Tide coach Paul "Bear" Bryant became the iconic figure in southern football as it assumed new cultural meanings in the region by the 1970s. Bryant grew up on a farm in Arkansas, a figure from the older, poorer, rural South, yet he would become a part of the transition to the modern, middle-class South that celebrated southern living. He was a winner at his sport at a time when the South still had a vivid memory of debilitating poverty and of the defeat of the Confederacy. He also represented a transition out of the segregated southern way of life, as he coached during the civil rights movement and afterward. Bryant's success brought increased regional cultural investment in the sport. Legend has it that Bryant played a key role in integration in the Deep South. After the University of Southern California brought an integrated team to Birmingham in 1970 and beat Bryant's team 42–21, Bryant used the imperative of football success as a catalyst for welcoming African American recruits. According to the legend, an assistant coach said USC fullback Sam Cunningham did more for integration with that game in Alabama than Martin Luther King Jr. did in twenty years. That was an exaggeration, but the opening of college football in the Deep South to Black athletes was a landmark in race relations. As historian Harvey Jackson notes, "When Southerners put winning ahead of segregation, segregation was dead."[62]

Football coaches such as Bryant became like the Confederate generals of the late nineteenth century—figures who summon up the local identity. After the Civil War, the South obsessed over its past, and those generals had a glamour about them, even in defeat. The region's white people made them into cultural heroes symbolizing virtue and honor. Coaches later came to symbolize what people saw as the virtues of sports in the South—competitiveness, success on the national stage, and the building of character in players. The old agrarian South that produced Bryant is no more; the South is a place of a business ethic, and coaches such as another Alabama coach, Nick Saban, represent that outlook. They are CEOs in a region that now admires businesspeople as cultural heroes. The generals had lost, but the coaches win: statues of each of the five coaches who have won national college football championships for the University of Alabama rest together on a plaza outside Bryant-Denny Stadium in Tuscaloosa.[63]

College football became a legendary part of southern living because it is one of the pronounced unifiers in a region divided by racial and social class divergences. University of South Carolina coach Lou Holtz said in 1999 that football cuts across social status in the South. "I don't care if you are the governor or the paper boy or a street department worker. It's the one thing everyone has in common. 'How's our team doing?' It's the one thing that rallies everybody." The college football culture brings families and neighbors together to attend games, with tailgating around food before and after the game. This culture is not unique to the South, nor does common interest in football elide continuing class and racial divides, but southerners participate in it with enthusiasm and draw from southern culture in their rituals. The Southeastern Conference has become the sporting heartbeat of southern living, with the most successful teams in the nation for close to two decades. Average stadium capacity for the teams in the Southeastern Conference in the late 1990s was filled to 99.6 percent. The sport earns national attention, generally a source of favorable portrayals of southern living.[64]

The football culture of southern living begins with, at least, high school football, which was portrayed in the *Friday Night Lights* best-selling book, Hollywood film, and popular television program, all set in Texas. The story suggested the investment of time, talent, and money that the region's people and schools put into the sport. After the University of Alabama had won its third national championship in four years, a *New York Times* story on January 9, 2013, was headlined "Alabama Taps a Talent Pool as Deep as the South." Alabama's defensive coordinator, Kirby Smith (later head coach at the University of Georgia), noted that "our communities put more money into high school coaches than elsewhere." His conclusion was "You get what you pay for. You get better coaches, you get better players." Capitalism at work. The article quoted one fan outside the national championship game who yelled "Roll Tide." Someone asked that fan if the term was a verb or a noun. "Actually," said the fan, "it's a way of life."[65]

That term, as we have noted throughout this study, draws from deep layers of cultural religiosity, and the labeling of southern football as a religion invites consideration of that sensibility. John Allin offered one of the most incisive and witty discussions of football as a southern religion in a 1980 essay. Presiding bishop of the Episcopal Church and a native Mississippian, Allin talked about religion in the South, in general, in terms of what one might expect of Sabbath day rituals. He included priests "in brightly colored vesture and head dress" chanting choruses "led by dancers and singers," and "each petitioner" placing an offering in the box when entering "the gates of the great congregation." People gathered in "huge congregations" for "devotion all over the South." Of course, with tongue in cheek, he revealed that the priests he referenced were football coaches, the dancers and singers were the cheerleaders, and the offering box is where one turned in tickets at the stadium entrance gate. "These sabbath celebrations," he revealed, "are called football games."[66]

Allin went on to talk about "both devotees and critics alike of that which is referred to as 'the Southern way of life.'" He observed that they do not always use the term "religion," but in fact they demonstrate that "the Southern way of life" is "a religion" of sorts. He did not mean the older segregated life but the new postsegregation, contemporary southern way. "This 'way of life', southern style" described God in various ways. Allin outlined a "deist type" who believed that God created the South to be "a very special place in the world" and, gentleman that God is, "then went off to heaven." Some people in the region believed "they have been chosen and called to be 'southerners,' that there must be a proper place for everyone, and that proper relations are maintained when everyone is in their proper place." He pointed to the expressions of southern religiosity outside the church doors as well as inside, thus positioning football as central to the contemporary southern way of life and spinning out its religious overtones, although with an ironic and witty undertone.[67]

That arbiter of contemporary southern living, the magazine of that name, differentiated itself from other American house-and-garden magazines in long publishing an annual story about college football in the fall because of that sport's popularity in the region. National and regional commentators offered frequent assessments of what the sport says about the South. In 1999, Marino Casem, former Alcorn State football coach, observed, for example, that "in the East, college football is a cultural exercise. On the West Coast, it is a tourist attraction. In the Midwest, it is cannibalism. But in the South, it is religion. And Saturday is the Holy Day." Casem's comments are a valuable reminder that college football is anchored in southern Black communities as well as white. Historically Black colleges and universities have their own distinctive rituals and ceremonies around football. Discussions of southern football use terms that suggest that the southern civil religion's sense of religious mission has now devolved into worrying about a college football team; it also shows a playfulness within southern living, a playfulness that the concept and its ancestors had not much evoked.[68]

Foodways

Another cultural expression that is considered hypersouthern is its cuisine. The South's regional cuisine came to be recognized in the twenty-first century as one of the most important creative achievements of the region and a vital expression of southern living. Sandra A. Gutierrez forged a hybrid southern-Latina cultural expression through her cookbook *The New Southern-Latino Table* (2011). The book describes the contours of this hybridity and places it as part of southern living. Her story is just one example of the cultural diversity of southern living. Born in the United States to Latin American parents, Gutierrez moved to Guatemala, her parents' native country, when she was a child and "was instantly immersed in a world of melded cultures." She knew the words to two national anthems, the pledges of allegiance to the U.S. flag and the Guatemalan banner, and the histories of two nations. Attending an American school in Guatemala City, she ate in a school cafeteria that served hamburgers and tuna salad one day and *milanesas* and *panes con frijoles* the next. She sees that the family's home cooking "was also a reflection of my fused reality: we ate tamales for special occasions, huevos rancheros for birthdays, and Carolina hot dogs every chance we got." Each day brought discovery of new southern dishes as well, and she captured her emerging blended culture in language, as she writes her family motto became "hola, y'all," a good verbal expression for an emerging creole identity.[69]

Gutierrez's summary statement is that "Southern food found my soul," this last term a spiritual one long associated with southern living. She learned the light touch in making biscuits, discovered grits, and came to savor fried green tomatoes and pimento cheese. "The Latina discovered her southern belle within, and it was magic for me."[70]

Gutierrez's middle-class background may not be representative of the larger numbers of working-class Latinos who have often not had such a positive experience of southern living, and plenty of evidence suggests the hostility of native southerners in the contemporary world to the growing presence of undocumented immigrants. Gutierrez's perspective is an important one, though, for the longer-term understanding of how the Latino presence is affecting ideas about southern living, a concept that from its beginnings in the 1960s has relied on regional food in everyday life. The new influx of Latino immigrants has brought a diverse and ambitious group that includes first-generation workers as well as second- and third-generation, English-speaking Latino professionals. Latinos come from diverse national and cultural backgrounds, and when they come to the South, they are combining their culture with those of Latinos from different countries, as well as with those of southerners, Black and white. Gutierrez embraces an older model of ethnicity, the melting pot, with the South, and specifically its kitchens, as the site of a new cultural blending "shaped by a hodge-podge of flavors, an amalgamation of cultures, and an explosion of ethnic ingredients." Critics of the melting pot model see it as a loss of individual ethnic identities in the process and believe it overstates the amount of interaction that actually has happened. The melting pot metaphor came out of earlier American ethnic history, but Gutierrez is noteworthy in reclaiming the label in the face of new immigration in the twenty-first century and in seeing the South as the site of a new melting pot that promises a place where "flavors mingle without clashing."[71]

The new southern-Latino table, as she calls it, includes such blends as grits combined with roasted poblano peppers, chiles rellenos filled with pimento cheese, and pulled pork simmered in an annatto-and-citrus broth. One glimpses an emerging blend of overall culture as well as dishes.[72]

The new immigration that brought Latinos such as Sandra Gutierrez and others to the South has made southern living more diverse but diminished the concept's earlier exclusive, white, middle-class, suburban identification. Latinos, Asians, Middle Easterners, and others have created a multicultural society, one that moves beyond the traditional focus on race and the biracial South. Of course, we also now recognize better than in earlier times that the South has long been multicultural. In the colonial South, places such as Savannah and Charleston had North America's most heterogenous population, and the nineteenth century brought Catholic and Jewish immigrants to southern places, as well as diverse numbers of Protestants and the nonreligious. Although not on the scale that produced large immigrant communities in other parts of the nation, this earlier ethnic diversity created some people in the South with complex identities. Southern studies scholars increasingly use terms such as "hybrid" and "creole" to suggest an important enduring theme about the American South as a place that brought together diverse peoples in a plantation world. That plantation world rested on the exploitation of minority populations, but it still was the site of cross-cultural exchanges that produced an unintended hybridity. Defenders of southern civilization and the southern way of life, of course, did not have this in mind when they talked about the South, but nonetheless it was an ongoing current, which has surfaced in southern awareness in the contemporary era, promoted by the new immigrants' presence.[73]

The contemporary period saw changes in what southerners ate, brought on by a changing society. For example, fast food, or industrially mass-produced foods in franchised restaurants, entered the South at the same time as the civil rights movement and the growth of the southern economy and became standard fare for working-class mothers and suburban soccer moms to bring home for a hurried supper. After 1970, the pace of fast-food franchising in the South increased, with the McDonald's hamburger chain leading the way. Southern entrepreneurs marketed specifically southern foods to regional, national, and then international consumers, a major advance in the commodification of southern culture. Col. Harland Sanders became a prominent icon of southern living, with his herbed-and-spiced chicken and stereotypical "colonel" attire just ringing out "southern culture" globally. Country music singer Bill Anderson launched Po' Folks, which celebrated working-class foodways, now often known as "country" rather than as southern. Popular "all you can eat" buffets correlated with the South's striking obesity problems in the contemporary period. Gospel singer Mahalia Jackson oversaw her string of soul-food restaurants.[74]

Two central figures, among many others, in the beginnings of the southern food movement of the contemporary era were chef Edna Lewis and journalist John Egerton. Lewis grew up on a Virginia farm, and freshly grown food was a constant sustainer for her African American family. "In the South," she said, "you didn't have to be rich. There was always something good to eat." Her classic *The Taste of Country Cooking* (1976) was a landmark in the assertion of southern food as a serious cuisine. In the text, she evoked a warm agrarian sensibility long associated with the concept of a southern way of life. "I will never forget spring mornings in Virginia. A warm morning and a red sun rising behind a thick fog gave the image of a pale pink veil supported by a gentle breeze that blew our thin marquisette curtains out into the room, leaving them to fall lazily back. Being awakened by this irresistible atmosphere we would hop out of bed, clothes in hand, rush downstairs, dress in a sunny spot, and rush out to the barn to find a sweet-faced calf, baby pigs, or perhaps a colt." She summoned a distinct sense of place—that traditional, often hackneyed term that is hard to miss in Lewis's prose: "A stream, filled from the melted snows of winter, would flow quietly by us, gurgling softly and gently pulling the leaf of a fern that hung lazily from the side of its bank." After a while there, she "would return joyfully to the house for breakfast." The food she recalled from her southern childhood rested in nature and family, and she was an example of the African American creative folk from the South who identified with it. Lewis's prose sentimentalized the rural southern world, but she also conveyed a more complex view of the place. "For me the South is not just food. It is beauty, love, hate, art, poetry, and hard work. I love what is good about it. It is what makes us who we are."[75]

A 1995 story in *Newsweek* magazine highlighted Lewis's relationship with her younger friend at that point, Scott Peacock, a white southern chef. Their Horseradish Grill had opened the year before and had been widely hailed as representing a new southern cooking. American regional cooking had become a "craze" and, given that reality, wrote Laura Shapiro, "the South was bound to rise again and it has." She noted restaurants in cities across the South that embraced regional cooking above the traditional fine-dining French and Italian cuisines. The article stressed the challenges to the rise of a new southern cooking but emphasized the significance of the contribution of Lewis, who was seventy-nine at the time, and Peacock, who was thirty-three. Lewis was finishing her fourth cookbook at that point, another one on "original Southern food," and she told the reporter that "to make it you need real lard, real butter, real milk and home-cured pork." Peacock threw in that "her next book is going to come with a cow and a pig, so you can make everything in it."[76]

John Egerton was another central figure in the appearance of an organized and recognized southern food movement in the contemporary period. In *Southern Food: At Home, on the Road, in History* (1987), he wrote that "for as long as there has been a South, and people who think of themselves as Southerners, food has been central to the region's image, its personality, and its character." Food had not, though, entered into the nineteenth-century concept of southern civilization the way it had become so central in the twenty-first-century understanding of southern living. Although, he added, "accents and attitudes and life-styles may change" (the latter term tying Egerton's work to southern living), fondness for southern food remained. Egerton saw the South as having lost much of its collective identity as a separate region, and its "checkered past" had entered myth and memory, "but its food survives—diminished, perhaps, in availability and quantity, but intact in its essence and authenticity—and at its best, it may be as good as it ever was." Lamenting the "pale-imitation substi-tutes" for the best southern food such as "chicken in a sack, potatoes in a box, and biscuits in a can," he remained convinced that many individual cooks and restaurant owners "still believe in taking the time and using the right ingredi-ents and methods to prepare great old Southern dishes the way they were meant to be made." Speaking of these foods and the people preparing them, he noted that, "like Faulkner's heroes, they endure." Egerton was a pronounced liberal who did not miss the older South's racism, poverty, and other ills, but his work on southern food showed the way for others who wanted a reimagined South around the best of everyday life in the past.[77]

Egerton and over forty advocates of the study of food in the South—including this author—formed the Southern Foodways Alliance (SFA) in 1999 as an institute within the University of Mississippi's Center for the Study of Southern Culture. Founding director John T. Edge, a small staff, and an advi-sory board have coordinated academic and popular interest in southern food-ways through an annual symposium that hosts hundreds of people in Oxford, Mississippi. Its programming focuses on a common annual theme and includes summer field trips; oral history projects; a podcast; a book series through the University of Georgia Press; oratorios; folk plays; and films about, among other topics, oystermen, pit barbecues, and bartenders. The SFA evolved from an organization that celebrated the supposed authenticity of southern food to one that promoted, through studying foodways, the multicultural understanding of not only the twenty-first-century South but the past as well, and it places its work in the southern narrative of reconciliation and redemption. The group has probed questions about food and southern history and identity, asking about "who cooks, who cleans, and who earns a seat at the welcome table."[78]

A key concept in this progressive food version of southern living is indeed the "welcome table." The term, from a traditional spiritual, refers to a feast where all are welcome, but in the civil rights song "I'm Gonna Sit at the Welcome Table" it also alludes to sit-in protests at segregated lunch counters. Egerton explained its symbolic power by looking to the past. Southerners of all sorts worked together traditionally in the fields and kitchens to grow and prepare food, "but they rarely if ever sat down together to share in the fruit of the har-vest." Not only could Black people and white people not eat together—there was no welcome table then—but the patriarchy meant men ate first, with women in the kitchen serving and children off in another room. He saw foodways in the recent past unlocking "the rusty gates of race and class, age and sex." When people in the contemporary South eat now, he said, "a place at the table is like a ringside seat at the historical and ongoing drama of the region." The welcome table as a symbol of reconciliation has focused the work of the SFA. Edge notes the emotional trauma that can accompany conversations in the South about race, but "at tables piled high with country ham, buttermilk biscuits, and red-eye gravy, I've marveled as all have leaned in close to eat, to talk, to listen." Of course, as religious historian James Hudnut-Beumler observes of different religious groups who sing the old welcome table hymn, "when they all show up to eat, some will be friends and some will be strangers, according to the way they have been reckoned."[79]

"Authenticity" is a term that has been attached to the southern food movement that began by searching for iconic foods associated with the region. That term has a long history of association with the South in general. It goes back at least to the antebellum period and the appeal of plantation literature and minstrel music to northern middle- and working-class audiences, who found these genres exotic but also portraying a people and place they deemed more authentic than the complexities of other American places undergoing modernization. Later, travelers, scholars, collectors, and others saw "authentic" as the term for the South's mountain folk ballads, country blues, local-color literature, mountain crafts, and folk art. To take one example, eighth-generation Floridian Ashley Schoenith markets the authentic with her company called Heirloomed, which began by selling handmade aprons and now markets a variety of, as she said to *Okra* magazine in 2018, "history, old things and vintage pieces." Schoenith went on to add that "I try to be so authentic in what we are putting out there" and noted that the South was "truly a part of who I am," with "this way of life . . . engrained in my soul." Her use of the word "soul" shows that she sees her authentic creations as more than just a material brand: rather, they're an expression of "the spirituality associated with the region."[80]

In "An Active Authenticity," Edge reflected in 2017 on how far he had come in his conceptual approach to southern foodways. When he began writing about food, he looked for continuities with the past, as with the "oldest whole-hog barbecue joint still run by the family" or cornmeal hoecakes "cooked according to nineteenth-century techniques and served in storied quarters." He realizes that he had tried to preserve "the South in amber" and rejects such cultural conservatism in favor of new "narratives that subvert" and reflect his "aim to redefine the region." He privileges stories about immigrant cooks and writes about preferring Szechuan fried chicken to the "golden-crusted birds your gray-haired, cast-iron-skillet-wielding grandmother cooks." His version of foodways is radical foodways, aiming at "another reinvention of this beleaguered and beloved place." Edge represents the southern food movement's embodiment of a reimagined southern identity that focuses on diversity and multicultural concepts of southern living.[81]

Edge's book *The Potlikker Papers: A Food History of the Modern South* (2017) is an important text in understanding the role of food in an evolving concept of southern living in the twenty-first century. Edge reflects the contemporary understanding of the South as far from "a myth-veiled cultural monolith," and he suggests seeing the region as "an album of snapshots," "a jukebox of 45s," or "a menu of dishes." The book makes a strong statement about the contemporary food movement's move "toward paying down the debts of pleasure and sustenance owed to our forebears." Tracing the story of southern foodways over a sixty-year period, beginning with the role of food in the civil rights movement, he argues that "conversations about food have offered paths to grasp bigger truths about race and identity, gender and ethnicity, subjugation and creativity," and the contested nature of the region seen through foodways.[82]

Edge followed in the steps of well-off, well-educated, and well-traveled southerners in cities and suburban areas who had long embraced a middle-class regional identity that included appreciation for food as well as music and literature. Mississippi Delta–born Craig Claiborne used his perch as food critic at the *New York Times* in the 1980s to introduce such figures as North Carolina's Bill Neal and Louisiana's Paul Prudhomme to national audiences, and Claiborne served upscale catfish for a presidential affair. The South participated in the emergence of a new American chef culture with prominent and acclaimed celebrities such as Frank Stitt in Birmingham, Emeril Lagasse and later John Besh in New Orleans, Vivian Howard in North Carolina, Edward Lee in Louisville, and countless others whose restaurants contributed to food tourism. Women were vital to the new southern food movement, with Nathalie Dupree a singular figure in using television to showcase updated southern traditional dishes with new twists.[83]

Edge is a passionate advocate of the new hybrid South that has emerged in the twenty-first century, thanks partly to the melding of the region's notable new immigrants' cooking styles with those of the classic southern ways. After 2010, "a true new Southern cuisine flourished" because recent arrivals who came seeking jobs stayed to reinterpret chicken and fish shacks. In the process, "the Taco Circuit displaced the Chitlin Circuit, the best cooks in cities like Charlotte and Houston revealed themselves to be men from Texococo who dished cow cheek barbacoa in corn tortillas and women from Oaxaca who peddled raja tamales from street carts." As evidence, Edge cites the Chinese grocery stores in Jackson, Mississippi, which now sell Louisiana-grown rice under the Jazzmen label, "an elision of the term jasmine rice," with Louis Armstrong providing the label image. The arrival of new immigrants has not led to dissolution of the southern identity but to its reinvigoration, as the region gained "new peoples, new spices, new techniques, and new dishes"—all pointing toward "an inclusive and delicious future for the American South."[84]

Edge's expansive vision of foodways' multicultural possibilities rested in the welcome table metaphor, but that term is a contested one, with critics disputing the implication that an actual total openness across racial lines around food has somehow been achieved. African American critic Michael Twitty accused Edge in 2017 of white privilege in appropriating African American food and getting media credit and publishing and lecturing opportunities for showcasing it to the detriment of African American food advocates. This critique rested on the claim of authenticity—that only an African American could interpret food with such a pronounced Black southern origin. Twitty is an accomplished food historian, author, founder of the food blog *Afroculinaria*, and supervisor of the Southern Discomfort Tour that journeys around the South to raise awareness of racism's role in traditional southern cuisine. Reflecting on the welcome table metaphor, Edge admitted in 2018 that he had needed "to temper the hopefulness of the concept with the realities of past limitations in achieving it." He nonetheless affirmed the importance of the concept to the southern food movement's ideals and worked to provide forums for African American critics to have their say.[85]

Still, in 2020, Edge faced calls from critics to resign as director of the SFA because he had not responded as many had hoped to calls for change both in the inner-circle SFA decision-making process, to make it more diverse, and in his role as a powerful gatekeeper of southern food studies. Those demands came in the aftermath of the death of George Floyd, the protests of Black Lives Matter, and the rising sense of need for more attention to social justice throughout American society. Edge acknowledged that while concern for equity had long characterized SFA publications, meetings, and other activities, more would be required of SFA's leadership in terms of social justice, and a planning process was put in place to transition to new leadership. One of Edge's main critics, Stephen Satterfield, cofounder of a minority-owned food magazine, acknowledged the SFA had "done very good and meaningful work," but he feared it would become irrelevant in the new context without changes. Edge and the SFA had worked to nurture new food "narratives that change the South, for the better," helping to define the new progressive multicultural ideology in the first two decades of the twenty-first century. But the events around him and the organization in 2020 illustrated the complexities of achieving the lofty goals of racial reconciliation in the South during a fraught time. Some observers questioned whether racial reconciliation was enough to deal with racial inequity, but social justice has always been a prerequisite for true reconciliation. The SFA has the opportunity to advance both causes through a renewed commitment to its goals.[86]

Telling about the South Again

Eudora Welty and Zora Neale Hurston talked of the importance of storytelling to the creativity of the southern cultural renaissance in the twentieth century, and "story" remains a vibrant concept in describing the importance of creativity in this century as well. "You may have heard the news that the independent bookstore is dead, that books are dead, that maybe even reading is dead," wrote writer Ann Patchett in describing the origins of her Nashville, Tennessee, bookstore Parnassus Books. To that sentiment, she said, "Pull up a chair, friend. I have a story to tell." Lynn York, the publisher of Blair Books in Durham, North Carolina, told an interviewer in 2020 that in the South, "there are so many stories to tell, and we will never run out of talented writers bent on telling those stories." Regional book publishers have overcome the challenge of the consolidation of the book industry into a few giant northeastern publishers and from the online commercialization of bookselling represented most dramatically by Amazon. This section discusses certain venues, such as book publishing, that have helped spread ideas of multicultural southern living to popular audiences.[87]

University presses throughout the South, for example, produce titles on a wide range of topics, but they are especially important in nurturing evolving southern culture through publications on the region and the states within it. Book series at many such presses focus on race, religion, gender, social class, the environment, and other salient academic topics that express the multicultural South with interest to audiences beyond academia. The South hosts numerous independent book publishers who focus on regional topics. North Carolina's Algonquin Books began in 1983 as a bookstore but soon became iconic in its publication of, among other genres, southern fiction. Hub City Press, in Spartanburg, South Carolina, began in 1995 and publishes fiction and nonfiction that explore the multicultural recent South. Beginning in 1998, NewSouth Books, in Montgomery, Alabama, has published fiction, historical accounts, memoirs, poetry, and folklore. These presses are often part of local community art scenes, as with the Hub City Writers Project that is dedicated "to nurturing literary community in the South through the press, our independent bookshop . . . a national residency program, contests, workshops, and an annual conference, among other programs." York celebrates her Blair Books for exploring some of the foundational concerns of the multicultural South, including "new authors that are traditionally neglected in the mainstream: women, people of color, LGBTQ, and authors with disabilities." Her conclusion fits the spirit of the twenty-first-century South's cultural renaissance: "There are so many stories out there and so much to learn." Every southern state and many local communities have popular book conferences that promote southern literature and its stories.[88]

Publishers are closely connected to the independent booksellers of the South, whose stores become rich sites of storytelling often featuring southern writers. The booksellers still face the challenge of selling books in competition with

Amazon's online services and from a big-box bookstore such as Barnes and Noble. Independent booksellers are, however, not only surviving but thriving in many places. The *Southern Bookseller Review: A Book for Every Reader* works with local independent stores as part of its mission "to highlight diverse literary tastes and interests and help book lovers find their next great read." It has awarded the Southern Book Prize annually since 1999, which represents the favorites of booksellers in the region. One of the most successful bookstores is Square Books in Oxford, Mississippi. It has four stores: the main store, Off Square Books (travel books, cookbooks, used books, and remaindered books), Square Books, Jr. (children's and young people's books), and Rare Square Books (first editions). Owners Richard and Lisa Howorth founded the store in 1977, and since then it has hosted innumerable book signings, often with writers on book tours who also go to other bookstores in the region. Although the store sells a wide array of volumes, it has particularly extensive collections on southern history, literature, and music. Serving the Oxford and University of Mississippi communities, it is tied in with the work of the Center for the Study of Southern Culture and other university departments that sponsor book and author conferences that bring large numbers of literary visitors to the town and the store. The store hosts a weekly radio show with a featured author and musical performers. It has a far-flung online ordering service as well. Independent booksellers also serve other university towns, such as Flyleaf Books in Chapel Hill, North Carolina, and Ernest and Hadley in Tuscaloosa, Alabama; booming urban areas such as Decatur, Georgia, in metropolitan Atlanta, that has three bookstores; and popular tourist cities such as Asheville, North Carolina, home of Malaprop's. Stores in smaller communities are often successful as well, such as the Book Worm Bookstore in Powder Springs, Georgia, which has 30,000 books in inventory, supports book events and a book club, and uses such social media as Facebook, Instagram, Twitter, and TikTok to connect with readers. All these stores promote literacy and local and regional writers.[89]

Magazines, like books, have always played a central role in defining the southern way of life and later the southern living South. Around 1830, the southern regional identity burst forth in written expression through such new magazines as the *Southern Literary Quarterly* and the *Southern Review*. At the turn of the twentieth century, such national publications as the *Atlantic Monthly*, the *World's Work*, and *Scribner's Magazine* published the writings of southerners and nonsoutherners that explored a renewed southern consciousness. It was not surprising that in the contemporary period magazines became a main forum for examinations of the South. *Southern Living* magazine was a crucial venue for reimagining the southern way of life in the postsegregation South, and magazines have continued to reveal the evolving contours of contemporary southern living. The first issue of *Southern Magazine* appeared in October 1986, in a decade still in notable transition from an older southern way of life to a newer concept based around cultural expressions. Linton Weeks's editor's note, "On Becoming Good Friends," stressed the continuing importance of the mannered way of life, in which "good manners are more important than ever in this complex and disorienting world." He positioned the magazine as different from *Southern Living*, because southerners "have wanted a monthly magazine that explores the multidimensional South—the one beyond the well-adorned house and garden and the South we carry inside our hearts wherever we go." He promised readers a publication that celebrates the South's "quirky quintessence, but meets regional controversies and the paradoxes of what it means to be a Southerner today."[90]

The initial issue of *Southern Magazine* had some of the region's most acclaimed writers reflecting on such broad topics as the southern mind, heart, body, and soul. Willie Morris's essay grappled with whether such a thing as the South even existed anymore. "Once the albatross of race, in its more suffocating aspects, was removed, Southerners became free as never before to feel part of the broader civilization, and that is good." He used a key descriptor, "civilization," with which the South has had a long relationship. Morris suggested that to find a continuing "South" one should spend time at the ball games, the funerals, the bus stations, the courthouses, and "the bargain-rate beauty parlors and the little churches and the roadhouses and the joints near the closing hour." Morris's southern way was, thus, not in the suburbs but in the working-class culture that expressed remnants of an older rural, small-town South.[91]

The magazine would continue to advocate for social justice, as in Weeks's editor's column in the January 1987 issue that addressed the South's lack of concern for the homeless. "The South," Weeks lamented, "rejects the idea of societal responsibility"—words that unfortunately reflected the suburban southern living ideology all too well.[92]

Southern Magazine's version of southern living contained considerable whimsy. The November 1986 cover story was "White Trash Chic: Everything Old Is Nouveau Again." The writer noticed that old southern icons had become popular nationally as retro symbols, including the "old-shell-back metal chair, that used to sit on our porches and patios." Finer department stores outside the South marketed it as "the Bayou Chair" or "the Gulf Chair," with "a price tag so high it would look more at home on a LaZ-Boy." Southerners were sitting on a gold mine of "things lying around the house." The story reflected a self-conscious southern identity, urging southerners not to refute such stereotypes, not "to refute the backwater images," but to "make money off of them."[93]

Oxford American succeeded *Southern Magazine*, and with a very different focus. The magazine began publication in Oxford, Mississippi, in 1992. Marc Smirnoff was its founder, a Californian who had moved to Oxford in the mid-1980s, worked at Square Books, and became active in the town's literary scene. The magazine's subtitle gives a clue to its aspirations: "The Southern Magazine of Good Writing." It did not seek mass circulation but contributed to a key concept of southern living: a vibrant southern culture. The first music issue came in 1997, with a CD of the music discussed in the magazine, and the annual music issues covered the breadth of music in the South from blues and country to jazz, alt-country, and, more recently, rap and hip-hop. Special issues have also covered art, literature, religion, and film. If *Southern Living* had championed the bourgeois American ideal of the South, *Oxford American*'s version of southern living rested in aesthetics—and in a willingness to include articles confronting gritty and thorny social issues as well.[94]

The resurgence of the southern identity took to the internet with the *Bitter Southerner* in 2013. Its editor, Chuck Reece, wrote that the magazine would pay tribute to "great Southern musicians, chefs, farmers, artists, bartenders, scientists, innovators." Remembering when he had first moved away from the South to New York City and his accent triggered negative assumptions, he confessed that "I got pissed off. Bitter, as it were." To his New York City acquaintances, "my twang equaled 'dumb' or 'backward' or worse." He admitted that living in the South, "you sometimes fear those people are right," as with southerners who would not admit that the Civil War was about slavery and that "we still become a national laughing stock because some small town somewhere has not figured out how to hold a high school prom that includes kids of all races." He added that if you think women look good in hoop skirts or you fly the flag, "the Bitter Southerner is not for you."[95]

Reece made clear he identified with "a South that is full of people who do things that honor genuinely honorable traditions," such as drinking, cooking, reading, writing, singing, playing, and creating new things. His South was one where people faced the region's contradictions and were "determined to throw dishonorable traditions out the window." Reece highlighted his identification with a new descriptor of southern living, the phrase "the duality of the southern thing." The term came from songwriter Patterson Hood and his southern rock group, the Drive-By Truckers; Reece saw tensions in the South between "pride and shame, that eternal duality of the Southern thing."[96]

Another early twenty-first-century magazine, *Garden and Gun*, best demonstrated the state of the southern living concept as one rooted in conspicuous consumption but also in issues of craft and aesthetic values. Above all, the magazine cheered on the contemporary South's latest upscale southern living. A brochure for subscribers advertised the magazine as a way to "celebrate the good life in the South." It claimed that the magazine had "the elegance and sophistication of our great cities, and it's as down-home as our farms, hunting camps, and hand-made goods," all significant topics covered in the magazine. The brochure highlighted the South's culture, "both refined and rugged, that's all our own, from our outdoor lifestyle to the extraordinary grace of our finest homes." The use of such terms as "lifestyle," "grace," and "homes" connected the magazine to long-term cultural references. The brochure said each issue would be a "festival of all things Southern," including food and drink, land-scapes, music, art, sporting life, barbecue, bourbon, dogs, and "new twists on our timeless traditions." Although the magazine documents the prosperous, materialistic middle-class lifestyle of the South as well as any publication does, the brochure insisted that "Garden & Gun captures the soul of the South like no one else." By that, it meant the region's sense of history, its storytelling, and "the landscape we live in." The brochure asserted its claims to speaking for southern living through use of such terms as "lifestyle," "style," and "culture."[97]

The tenth-anniversary issue of *Garden and Gun* showed how it had moved beyond its initial focus on a foxhunting, elite southern living to one more in tune with the multicultural, diverse, yet regionally focused sensibility of the early twenty-first century. Its list of ten years of southern trailblazers was an eclectic group of musicians, artists, artisans, clothiers, celebrities, chefs, poets, writers, athletes, and architects. Some on the list were obvious and welcome for anyone familiar with the contemporary South's creativity, such as the Alabama Shakes' dynamite singer Brittany Howard and edgy country singer Jason Isbell, American poet laureate Natasha Trethewey, and legendary University of Tennessee women's basketball coach Pat Summitt.[98]

The list of trailblazers was wide ranging and included pop singer Beyoncé, because her 2016 album *Lemonade* paid tribute to her southern ancestry and Black womanhood while drawing from New Orleans imagery and roots music sounds. It would have been easy for a lifestyle magazine to miss the importance of writer Ta-Nehisi Coates, but *Garden and Gun* claimed him as an influential southerner. Laura Vinroot Poole is not a household celebrity even in her native South, but the magazine made the case for including her for landing "the South on the international fashion map." The tenth-anniversary issue was also sensitive to the inclusion of African Americans in southern living through its interview with Michael Boulware Moore, the CEO of the International African American Museum in Charleston, and its feature "Honor the Legacy of African Americans," written by Black social historian Jessica Harris and showcasing such items as the slave auction block in New Orleans, Harriet Tubman's shawl, a Pullman car, Chuck Berry's Cadillac, and Leah Chase's chef jacket. The issue gloried in a biracial South, something it had not highlighted in its earliest manifestation, indicating its evolution in tune with larger trends in the early twenty-first century. A playful tone often characterizes *Garden and Gun*, a welcome supplement to the earnest tone of much magazine writing about the South.[99]

The diversity of topics in new southern magazines such as *Garden and Gun* is seen also in the variety of magazines and journals now coming out of the South. *Good Grit* describes itself as the "only southern magazine capturing the authenticity of the perseverance that exists in the human spirit," and it presents uplifting stories of community engagement. *Okra* advertises its work as presenting "real southern culture." Southern Progress Corporation, which publishes *Southern Living*, also publishes *Cooking Light, Health, Coastal Living*, and *Southern Accents*. Like *Southern Living* itself, these magazines present a glowing image of an upper-middle-class South, free of controversy. *Virginia Living* began in 2002 and uses "the good life" as its brand. City magazines for Atlanta, Dallas, Charlotte, and other big cities showcase the culture of those places, while *Southern Breeze* develops the coastal lifestyle. Southern living is expressed in various niche publications for fisher people, hunters, golfers, sky-divers, hikers, and the religious faithful. Countless women's magazines such as *Houston Woman, Southern Lady*, and *Southern Beauty* highlight life for women living in a southern context. LGBTQ communities have several magazines, including *Dallas Voice, Outsmart* (Houston), *Clique Magazine* and *Southern Voice* (Atlanta), *411 Magazine* (Miami), and *Ambush* (New Orleans). Latino magazines reflect the new ethnic complexity of the South, including *Two Mundos* (Miami), *Latina Style* (Arlington, Virginia), *Hispanic Success Magazine* (Atlanta), and *Casa y Hoga* (a house magazine in Atlanta). African Americans are the audience for such publications as *Atlanta Tribune Magazine* and many others. These publications together represent a flowering of media interest in southern markets.[100]

Magazines have a robust presence on the internet, and that presence reminds us that the web has become a source for the presentation of diverse southern identities. Individual online identities can perpetuate regional-consciousness sites through web pages, chat rooms, listservs, blogs, and social networking sites all featuring multiple perspectives that claim the southern descriptor and embody a virtual southern way of life. One category of the internet South markets the South and, in the process, promotes the image of a hospitable region. A 2009 Google search for the phrase "southern hospitality" showed 2.5 million web pages and summoned timeworn images of a genteel antebellum South. Some people who respond to such sites do so to debunk such images, suggesting that online comments are open to diverse opinions on that stereotypical South.[101]

The internet South is also dominated by humor that portrays white southerners as naïve and unsophisticated, a replication of types of people going back to antebellum southwestern humor. The online *Hickophonics to English Dictionary* translates "bahs" to "boss" and "bob war" to "barbed wire." Visual images reinforce these portrayals, such as a photograph of two men hurling toilet seats as southern recreation—"redneck horseshoes." The southern version of the web expresses identities through the frequent use of such phrases as "I am a southerner" and "I am from the South." The *Southern Home Express* blog features the post "Southern Ways—Life in the South," which has Debby Mayne, the blog's Charleston founder, talking about southern ways in terms of manners, southern expressions, and the small town as still the center of this version of southern culture. Finally, people use the web to argue over politics in the region, as in the sites that proclaim white southern heritage through affirmation of the Lost Cause, which reached a crescendo in the Trump era's politics of rage that gave new attention to the Confederacy as an anti-federal government effort with continuing meaning. Hyperlinks across the web create a network of white supremacist individuals and organizations conveying vicious racist comments. On the other hand, the claims made on these sites are often contested, and African Americans use the web to disseminate the idea that southern heritage should be based on civil rights and social justice, as in the Black Lives Matter movement. The twenty-first-century South's diversity is reflected in such online LGBTQ communities as Kudzu Bears of Mississippi, Dallas Southern Pride, and Carolina Lesbian.[102]

The diverse recent media attention to the South shows a resurgence of the southern identity, focused on cultural features, in the early twenty-first century. Although talk continues of the "end of the South," southerners themselves continue to identify with southern living as an everyday reality and to tell stories about southern places and people, including African Americans. The South remains an identifiable place, although we recognize how it exemplifies American and, indeed, global realities in many ways. A telling contrast appears in the words of John Egerton in 1991 and actress Reese Witherspoon in 2015. Egerton spoke to a sense of the disappearing distinctive South: "Our freeways have come to look like the extension of the Pennsylvania Turnpike. Our airports are indistinguishable from those in the North, except that they're generally bigger (the Dallas–Fort Worth jetport is larger than the island of Manhattan)." Twenty years or so later, Witherspoon talked in an interview of being happy to have returned south, to Nashville, where she grew up. "Whenever the plane lands in Nashville, I breathe deeper. I take in the air; I don't feel the stress I feel every other place. I can live my life here. I can walk around and feel like I belong." The term she used was "home" to describe her feelings not just about Nashville but about the South. Her use of the terms "life" and "live" touch on the underlying concept of a particular way long associated with the region. In the interview, Witherspoon also discussed her new "fashion and lifestyle" brand (more resonant terms for this study of the contemporary period) called Draper James, named for her grandparents, bringing into focus family but also the commodification of southern culture. The interviewer added that "Draper James celebrates what Witherspoon sees as a renaissance in Southern style, featuring playful dresses and jewelry alongside engraved julep cups and embroidered linens." Witherspoon did not hide her goal: to sell southern style. "I feel like Southerners have their own unique sense of style, and I wanted to be a part of telling the story of what it means to be a contemporary Southern woman."[103]

The terms "southern civilization," "the southern way of life," and "southern living" have framed this volume's exploration of southern regional consciousness, and they have continued in widespread use in recent decades. Hodding Carter III, for example, in a 1996 article, "Looking Back," remembered growing up in Greenville, Mississippi, where "'our way of life' turns out to have encompassed more than the metes and bounds of institutionalized racism." The past then "was neither prologue nor even really past but was absorbed whole as explanation and justification of the present, history and life woven together by an unbroken thread of context," words that encapsulate the long history of the concept of the southern way. Carter was an older southern white progressive who still saw cultural meanings of the southern way in the 1990s. A young actress, Bellamy Young, who grew up in Asheville, North Carolina, and starred in 2013 in the television show *Scandal*, shared Carter's sentiment in 2015: "The South is not just a geographical location—the South is a way of life." Although she lived in Los Angeles, "being southern is constantly with me, in large part because I'm always on the phone with someone in North Carolina. My body is here [in L.A.], but my heart is there." Young's constant use of the phone to replenish her southern identity is revealing of how modern ways can reinforce a sense of southern living even when someone is not in the region itself. Her use of the term "being" indicates a performance and a state of existential consciousness of the South. Diane Roberts touched on a surviving less positive use of the concept, however: "The 'Southern Way of Life' may no longer mean institutionalized segregation, but it still implies backward attitudes and violence toward women, people of color—anyone and anything deemed 'foreign.'" The continued use of these concepts that have recurred throughout southern history suggests a revitalization of regional consciousness in the contemporary South.[104]

Struggles to Define Southern Living

The ideological divisions of the South seen after the civil rights movement festered for decades, with progressives and conservatives, Democrats and Republicans, and red, blue, and purple states contesting the cultural meanings of recent southern life. The long arc of history points to demographic and technological changes in southern society that suggest a diverse multicultural southern society. But politics has been the arena where these competing forces have struggled to either advance or slow social change and its significance for regional consciousness. The contest is a struggle over southern history, seen in the memorialization of the Confederacy and the civil rights movement, but it has also been a struggle over the expectations of the southern future that have engendered divisive culture wars.[105]

Think tanks and public policy commissions have been important in focusing this debate, which has implications for whose definition of southern living will shape a predominant regional identity. The John Locke Foundation, for example, was incorporated in 1989 with the mission of crafting public policy toward conservative ends in North Carolina. Like many such conservative institutions, the Locke Foundation has close ties to such national organizations as the Heritage Foundation and the American Enterprise Institute. Its research and public policy advocacy promote such issues as individual liberty, free enterprise, and limited government. Such groups often do not focus specifically on the South as much as on what they see as a traditional American individualism and a Founding Fathers' constitutionalism they believe is endangered by left-wing communitarian politics. In recent times, such think tanks push such culture war issues as abortion, gun rights, and school prayer.[106]

The most audacious conservative enterprise, and one rooted in the South, is the work of James McGill Buchanan, a Tennessee-born economist whose Center for the Study of Public Choice has spearheaded the ideas and the strategies for an antimajoritarian movement that has flourished in the early twenty-first century. Buchanan's reading of *I'll Take My Stand* gave him a vision of the good society as one where traditionalism held sway, and he particularly became a devotee of Donald Davidson, coming to embrace his vision of Leviathan (the Old Testament sea monster destroying life) embodied in the federal government dominated by liberal northeasterners. Military service in 1941 took Buchanan to New York City, which he described as "enemy territory," full of "strange beings." His advanced schooling at the University of Chicago made him a free-market libertarian. He rebelled against the *Brown v. Board of Education* decision in 1954 that mandated desegregation of public schools and led to what Buchanan saw as unprecedented changes in the interpretation of the Constitution.[107]

The University of Virginia established Buchanan's center in 1956, and it would move later to George Mason College. He developed "public choice economics," which studied how the rules of government might be changed to break the trust between governing officials and the public in order to subvert the will of the majority and protect the privileges of the well-off, who resented paying higher taxes to support government programs for a wide public constituency. He not only developed political economic arguments to "preserve a social order based on individual liberty" but also devised strategies to address the center's goals: diminish government regulation of business, lower taxes, counter the concerns of environmentalists whom he saw as a threat to industry, abolish government support for health and welfare policies that harmed the ordinary workings of labor markets, and devise policies to suppress the vote of minorities and the young. The billionaire brothers David and Charles Koch made a transformative financial gift of $10 million in 1997 to the expanded James Buchanan Center at George Mason College, and the center was a linchpin in the efforts of the last two decades to coordinate support for state legislatures and groups trying to hamper organized labor, rewrite tax codes, privatize public resources, undo environmental oversight of industry, deny climate change, and cripple public education while encouraging the growth of unregulated charter schools.[108]

Buchanan's work establishes a direct connection between the conservatism of the Vanderbilt Agrarians, the defense of white racial privilege in the 1950s when he began his institutional work, and the right-wing populism of the recent Republican Party. Progressives have supported their own network of think tanks and advocacy groups to advance their ideological concerns. North Carolina produced one of the most vibrant progressive public policy institutions, the Manpower Development Corporation, founded in 1967 as part of Governor Terry Sanford's North Carolina Fund. Sanford was a key figure in encouraging regional thinking about the transition from a rural farm economy to an industrial one and from a segregated society to an integrated workforce. The Manpower Development Corporation began as a job-training institution, but now it promotes systemic change to assist especially the poor and disadvantaged to compete in economic life. Equity and opportunity are guiding principles. The Appalachian Regional Commission came out of Lyndon Johnson's Great Society agenda and continues to address the future of mountain and hill country communities from West Virginia to north Mississippi by giving grants, publishing research, and fostering educational opportunities.[109]

Beginning in 1971, the Southern Growth Policies Board sponsored research and public policies to move the South toward greater equity in southern economic development. Former Mississippi governor William Winter chaired the board's Commission on the Future of the South, which convened in Little Rock in 1986, and he offered a sobering look at the region that has remained a blueprint for reform efforts. Winter pointed to the commission's recommendation for "the region to take a new and different road," beyond the failed hope that the South "could build a competitive economy on a foundation of low wages, minimum education, and racial discrimination." Despite the South's economic progress, the reality was the "dilemma of the two Souths"—one of luxury high-rises in booming cities that were enjoying the realization of Henry Grady's New South dreams and the other South that was mostly rural, poorly educated, unproductive, and unemployed. Though the report came out in the 1980s, the conservative dominance in southern state governments in the last two decades has hampered efforts to address the issues the report raised.[110]

The commission report urged public policies to preserve and develop natural resources and the environment, fund research and development efforts, seek foreign investment, and make commitments to underdeveloped areas of the region. Winter's agenda included the need to "preserve those qualities of the spirit that have somehow set the South apart as a special and even unique place." He stressed the values he saw at the heart of southern living, the "old verities," such as those of family and neighbors, attachment to familiar places, appreciation of the region's natural bounty, and love of the land itself. Such values appeared in other American places, but Winter claimed them as southern. He admitted such qualities were not measurable in economic terms alone, but these were "values for the shaping of the human spirit." The Southern Growth Policies Board was shut down in 2013 and its work transferred to the Southern Governors' Association, but that organization continued to spearhead efforts pointing to the need for greater equity in southern economic growth, improving the quality of rural life, addressing the problems related to continuing racial discrimination and poverty, and controlling nuclear waste.[111]

The LGBTQ identity has been a fraught one in the South, and its recent history illustrates the complex ideological contestation underway. The contemporary period has seen advances in openly gay identities but also pushback from the region's evangelical churches and Republican politicians. Most notoriously, the state of Mississippi passed House Bill 1523 in 2016, called the Religious Liberty Accommodations Act, which preserved the right of organizations and individuals with religious affiliations to discriminate against certain people if doing otherwise would compromise their faith practices. Mississippi writer Katy Simpson Smith put the issue in the context of the southern way of life: "I think we're seeing this pattern of backlash against the great social leaps we've made as a nation because there are people who inexplicably see differences as a threat to their own ways of life." Critics charged that this bill—and one in North Carolina discriminating against transgender people—was part of a new Jim Crow that legally ostracized select minorities. Historian Ted Ownby argued that both the older racial laws and the new sexuality restrictions "involved anger at distant forces, whether they were federal authorities or cultural movements." He wondered whether the Mississippi and North Carolina laws represented "a kind of massive resistance against Supreme Court decisions about same-sex marriage and adoption," while some opponents, "much as they had done under segregation, announced boycotts of states that had laws they considered hateful." In 2020, a new assault on the rights of transgender students erupted when state legislatures in North Carolina and Texas passed legislation restricting the rights of transgender students in public schools.[112]

At the same time, the contemporary period saw an advance in members of the LGBTQ community claiming both a southern and an LGBTQ identity. As Patricia Todd, an Alabama state representative, put it in 2017, "I love the South: the culture, the food, the people. It's the politics I want to change." *New York Times* columnist Frank Bruni explored what he called "America's worst (and best) places to be gay," singling out Texas in the process. He noted that "all my life I've loved Texas: those big skies, big steaks, and big attitudes," but he lamented that "Texas doesn't love me back," citing the legislature's backward laws on "adoption, gay rights, transgender rights." Bruni saw that attitudes could vary within states to the extent that Waco's lone justice of the peace would not preside over gay marriages, despite the Supreme Court decision making those marriages legal, whereas Houston had a gay mayor and was a pioneer in recognizing gay rights, and Austin was "practically Key West" on the issue. The Supreme Court ruling in *Obergefell v. Hodges* (2015) was a landmark in establishing the constitutionally guaranteed right of marriage for same-sex couples, a decision reflecting a dramatic change over the previous two decades in American public approval of LGBTQ identities.[113]

LGBTQ issues are just one of the political and sociocultural developments that have been on divergent paths in the contemporary South. The election of Donald Trump as president in 2016 exacerbated the disjunction between the conservative and progressive outlooks in the South. Ronald Reagan's political conservatism, based in states' rights, suspicion of the federal government, militarism, free enterprise, evangelical religiosity, and a barely concealed racism had taken deep root among many white southerners. George W. Bush's presidency enabled it to flourish as Republicans became not only predominant in the Solid South in presidential races but in control by the early twenty-first century of state legislatures and many statewide political offices. Barack Obama's election in 2008 came in the aftermath of the traumatic recession of that year, American fatigue at the Iraq and Afghanistan wars, and Obama's promise of change—bringing an African American Democrat to the presidency. Obama's presidency offered a possibility for the end of the Republican Solid South and the effectiveness of the Republican southern strategy, as he proved a Democrat could win Virginia, North Carolina, and Florida. In the months after Obama's victory, though, a *Washington Post* story reported on attitudes from Brinkley, Arkansas, finding small-town residents there were "wary of the president-elect's urban perspective." One farmer, a conservative Democrat speaking from the agrarian South, admitted, "I'm worried that he's not gonna understand the rural way of life." The reporter noted the problems with the "rural way of life" in Brinkley, seen in "closed-up storefronts, a population that has shrunk to 3,300, a poor education system and meager income level."[114]

Such places became breeding grounds for Donald Trump's appeal in 2016 to white rage. He was an unusual figure to appeal to white southerners—a big-city, crude businessman with little religious background. Making virtually no sectional appeal to southerners, he nonetheless reconstructed the Republican Solid South, with some of his largest margins of the popular vote in southern states. Trump's presidency drew on xenophobia, international isolationism, incivility, racism, and misogyny to intentionally stoke fears and anxieties. The Trump years were hard ones for racial reconciliation efforts. Newspaper stories recounted biracial congregations splitting, as African American religious leaders were dismayed that 81 percent of white Evangelicals had voted for Trump. White Evangelicals said they supported Trump because he appointed conservative judges and sided with conservative religious groups on legal and political issues, but their embrace of a gospel that focused on individual conversion and rejection of structural racism as the cause of social problems caused Black church people to distance themselves from white overtures for reconciliation. After becoming president, Trump pursued a southern strategy on steroids, appealing to white nationalists there and elsewhere in the nation. He praised neo-Nazis after the violence at the Confederate statue removal in Charlottesville in 2017. He criticized removal of Lost Cause monuments and unsuccessfully opposed renaming American military bases named for Confederate leaders. Critics called him the last president of the Confederacy, and it seemed appropriate in that regard that the Trump insurrection in January 2021 included the waving of the Confederate battle flag on the floor of the U.S. Capitol.[115]

Trump's support of the Confederacy and its statues and imagery occurred, though, at a time in 2020 when American racial attitudes evolved in light of recurring episodes of police brutality that led to an acceleration in the landmark removal of public reminders of the Lost Cause in the South. Virginia remains the state with more Confederate iconography than anywhere in the nation, but in 2020 eighteen monuments were removed from its capital, Richmond, stripping Monument Avenue of its central place in Lost Cause memory. After a fifteen-year debate, Mississippi, in the same year, removed the Confederate battle flag imagery from its state flag and adopted a new one altogether. NASCAR banned the flag from its racecourses. The Reverend William Barber carried on his Moral Monday movement in North Carolina, aimed at using spiritual authority to oppose racial injustice, and the death of John Lewis in 2020 reminded the South of a spiritual warrior for racial reconciliation.

The Trump years saw the opening of one of the South's most important projects dedicated to social justice: the Equal Justice Initiative, with its associated Legacy Museum: From Slavery to Mass Incarceration and the National Memorial for Peace and Justice. The initiative's organizer, Bryan Stevenson, affirmed the continuing importance of linking social justice to racial reconciliation for a story in *Southern Living* in 2019: "I just think there's something redemptive and reparatory and restorative waiting for us if we commit ourselves to truth and reconciliation." Southern magazines have featured the Montgomery project in numerous articles, attaching it to the twenty-first-century concept of southern living. "Southern" has become firmly wedded to a progressive cultural agenda represented by Stevenson's work and that of others.[116]

Sociocultural developments in the South in the twenty-first century have created a more pluralistic, multicultural region, one that is looking toward the future rather than backward as Trump's politics do. Progressive critics sometimes do, though, see continuing injustice in the South in terms of the earlier concept of the segregated southern way of life. Journalist Ron Carver captured the sentiment well in 2014 and even used the term "way of life." He recounted being harassed in the summer of 1964 by a Mississippi police chief for his work with the Student Nonviolent Coordinating Committee to end segregation and support Black voting rights: "Back in the day, the Klan did the dirty work, but the business elite set the tone through a network of White Citizen Councils." With that in mind, he "was disheartened to learn that Mississippi opinion leaders are railing even now against the folks fighting for union rights at the Nissan factory in Canton." Hearing the "echo of the old 'outside agitator' refrain" in this new struggle, he cited the writings of columnist Sid Salter, who dismissed "union organizers, local civil rights leaders and pro-union ministers as 'hired or rented guns.'" Carver concluded that Salter's words reminded him of how Salter's university, Mississippi State, was "complicit 50 years ago in preserving the South's 'way of life.'" Critics offered the phrases "new Jim Crow" to describe the region's criminal justice system that persecuted young African American men and "Juan Crow" to describe intolerance of Latino immigrants.[117]

The acceptance of multiculturalism is an aspirational ideal in the South, one that is forward looking and promises the hope of constructive change. But recent southern society's diversity is accompanied by economic exploitation associated with multinational corporations, unjust criminal justice systems supported by conservative-dominated state governments, and countless socioeconomic problems that the ideal has not addressed. Still, multiculturalism has embraced a role for diverse peoples and ideas in southern living. Progressive southerners in the twenty-first century continue to claim a multicultural, redemptive concept for southern culture. Patterson Hood is a good example of a twenty-first-century southerner whose opinions are pushing the region along toward a more diverse concept of the southern way of life. Born and raised in the north Alabama town of Florence, he grew up in one of the South's most intriguing communities. Early twentieth-century musical legend W. C. Handy was from there, as was Sam Phillips, founder of Sun Studio in Memphis, with its biracial group of musical talent in the 1950s and after. Black artists crossed racial barriers in the 1960s by recording classic rock and rhythm-and-blues music with white performers in the Muscle Shoals Rhythm Section, in which Hood's father played. In "The South's Heritage Is So Much More Than a Flag," an article Hood wrote after the killings at the Emanuel African Methodist Episcopal Church in Charleston in 2015, he began by noting, "I love the Southland." He recounted how his home country of north Alabama was thoroughly religious and politically conservative, but it also supported "a bubbling underground of progressive thought, home to a vibrant minority of freethinkers and idealists."[118]

Hood had established his reputation as an outstanding rock songwriter, and his group, the Drive-By Truckers, had recorded *Southern Rock Opera*, an album about life in the South after the civil rights movement. "The album wrestles with how to be proud of where we came from while acknowledging and condemning the worst parts of our region's history." Hood coined the resonant term "the duality of the southern thing," which has reverberated through the contemporary cultural scene for its engagement with the contradictions of southern identity. In the song of the same name, he references the Confederate flag—"Ain't about no foolish pride, ain't about no flag / Hate's the only thing that my truck would want to drag"—referring to incidents of dragging deaths of African Americans. Hood's song acknowledged the outsider stereotypes that "you think I'm dumb, maybe not too bright." But he hurled the ironic words that dissented from a right-wing conservative orthodoxy as he proclaimed, as a southerner, to be "proud of the glory, stare down the shame / duality of the Southern thing." Hood explained that in the song "The Southern Thing" each line contradicted another. "You can't just say this or that is the Southern Thing, because it encompasses all of it." He reminded readers that "Martin Luther King was absolutely a southerner, as was Robert E. Lee." Whatever "your feelings about what one or the other was supposed to have stood for, it's all connected."[119]

Hood understood his white working-class fans' religiosity well enough to frame a question to them: "Why would a people steeped in the teachings of

The rock group the Drive-By Truckers embraces the concept of a Dirty South,
a term, adopted by rap artists as well, for a gritty region. Charles Reagan Wilson
Collection, Archives and Special Collections, John Davis Williams Library,
University of Mississippi Library, Oxford, Mississippi.

Jesus Christ and the Bible want to rally around a flag that so many associate
with hatred and violence?" Truly honoring "our Southern forefathers" meant
moving beyond symbols of their time to build on "the diversity, the art and
the literary traditions we've inherited from them," succinctly stating cultural
expressions of contemporary southern life. Ending his proclamation affirma-
tively, he looked to the future, saying, "It is time for the South to—dare I say
it?—rise up and show our nation what a beautiful place our region is, and what
more it could become"—showing a redemptive sensibility.[120]

Poet Natasha Trethewey is another contemporary southerner who embraces
the South's twenty-first-century concept of a multicultural South and points to
the future. Winner of the 2007 Pulitzer Prize for Poetry, Trethewey uses her
writing to reimagine the southern past. At a time when interracial marriage

This 2008 photograph of a cell-phone-recorded baptism at the Rocky Mount Primitive Baptist Church in Panola City, Mississippi, shows an intergenerational South with old and new ways, balancing tradition and modernity. Courtesy of David Wharton.

was illegal in Mississippi, Trethewey was born in Gulfport, Mississippi, in 1966 to a father who had "white" skin and a mother who had "Black" skin. Her poetry uses this personal experience to inform her evocation of a biracial South that she claims and whose meanings she explores. She grew up in Decatur, Georgia, but spent summers with her grandmother in Mississippi and New Orleans, both of which figure prominently in her work. "Southern Pastoral" is a 2002 sonnet that portrays a recurring dream of being photographed with the Fugitive poets, in the very unagrarian Atlanta. The towering urban skyline of the city is hidden by the photographer (assisted by Robert Penn Warren), who focuses instead on "a lush pasture, green, full of soft-eyed cows." The Fugitives offer the dreamer a glass of bourbon, but she fears that if she accepts that southern drink she associates with white males, she must accept accompanying traditional expectations of women and Blacks. "Say Race," the photographer intones, and the dreamer seems "in blackface again when the flash freezes us." Trethewey is the dreamer, in effect, who presents her postmodern playful reversal of southern role-playing—she is the poet commanding, in the end, a new vision of the South that goes beyond an agrarian vision.[121]

Trethewey's *Native Guard* (2006) engages the specifics of that ultimate symbol of southern distinctiveness, defeat in the Civil War. Off the coast of Trethewey's native Gulfport, Ship Island once held a fort that had been a Union prison that housed Confederate prisoners. The second regiment of the Louisiana Native Guard—one of the Union's first Black units—protected the fort. In the title poem of the book, Trethewey enters the mind of a former slave stationed at the fort who writes letters for the illiterate and invalid Confederate prisoners of war and his fellow Union soldiers. He comes, in her portrayal, to hold a valuable memory of the Civil War experience that has been unacknowledged by historical plaques and official recognition. Other poems in the book explore her childhood as the daughter of an interracial marriage. The racial past pervades poems honoring her mother and also the overlooked history of the South. Trethewey has said that her role is "to establish what has always been Southern, though at other points in history it has been excluded from 'Southernness.'"[122]

The contemporary South since 1980 has seen notable shifts in understanding the South as a geographical place of the imagination, with a particular system of social and cultural practices. This post–Jim Crow, now-prosperous society remained tied, in some degree, to traditionalism, at the same time that powerful global and American social forces have pushed the region's people toward understanding southern living as a concept with a future. One reads little of southern civilization these days, but the southern way of life appears in the twenty-first century in all sorts of ways. Race is a long obsession that still divides people in the region, but the coming of immigrants makes for a more complex, pluralistic society. Religion continues to offer meaning and stability for people who have undergone rapid social change, yet traditional Evangelicalism has suffered decline and divisions, partly as a result of secularization and partly because of divisive culture wars. Immigrants have created a new multicultural context for religious life, with Buddhists, Hindus, Jains, and other members of world religious groups relatively new to the region now rubbing shoulders with Baptists and Methodists. The suburbs are the locus for much social life and the original generative space for the southern living concept, while urban areas and rural places anchor the country cosmopolitan concept that sees a superior South now in its Black soul, which is sometimes gritty, sometimes humorous, and sometimes sweet.

The southern turn in African American culture has given the South a new authority as a potentially progressive place in the future. The materialism of the prosperous contemporary South has led to the commodification of the region's culture and to many extravagant lifestyles that seem offensive when seen in relationship to the South's continuing social problems. The redemptive South concept offers hope for change, though, and remains anchored in the long memory of the civil rights movement, with the possibility of building on it to address remaining social problems. The danger of the concept is believing that racial redemption has been achieved when the hard process of grappling with uncomfortable racial issues from the past is well begun but far from complete. Whites too often are uncomfortable talking about racial issues, and Donald Trump gave license to extremists promoting white nationalism that has undermined efforts at regional racial reconciliation. The myth of the welcome table, though, has become deeply rooted as an aspirational ideal. A hundred years ago, white southerners created a "culture of whiteness" with demeaning representations of minority groups. The ideals of the redemptive South and the welcome table are at the front of an arc of southern history that provides very different models for the region's people.

The southern civil religion seems less vibrant now, as southern missions do not always have the moral meanings that once characterized southern ideological concepts. Having begun in the nineteenth century as a sacred support of the status quo, the southern civil religion survives in the twenty-first century among those southerners seeing the region's biracial heritage as a force for national redemption. Cultural expressions in literature, music, food, sports, and other features, meanwhile, remain as vibrant as ever—signifiers of conceptual southern ways in the twenty-first century. Except for a dwindling number of extreme white nationalists, the southern way of life is no longer a concept to fight, kill, and die for, and many critics see it trivialized by its consumerism. But it survives in expressions of everyday life—at its best a context for the pleasures of the palate, the joys of listening to music, and the insights of the region's writers. And perhaps it is now, as Pat Conroy suggested, a place to laugh before crying.

AUTHOR'S NOTE

I CAME TO THE University of Mississippi in the fall of 1981 to work on the *Encyclopedia of Southern Culture* with Bill Ferris, Ann Abadie, Sue Hart, and others at the Center for the Study of Southern Culture. The center was new then, launching its efforts with a Eudora Welty symposium only four years before. Bill, the founding director, and Ann, the associate director, oversaw the early development of the center's academic, outreach, research, and documentation projects that made it a key institution in the resurgence of regionalism in the late twentieth century.

These reflections on the center's history suggest the role of an academic institution and my own efforts in studying southern regional consciousness and culture in the contemporary period. Learning from documentary studies, which was from the beginning well rooted at the university, we have aspired to listen to the voices of the people we study and document, while advocating often as well for social and cultural change. The center's history shows how southern regional consciousness that had often been an authoritarian force could be rechanneled into one that reimagined a South of progressive values.

The *Encyclopedia of Southern Culture* became the defining interdisciplinary project for the center, published by the University of North Carolina Press in 1989, with a second edition, the twenty-four-volume *New Encyclopedia of Southern Culture*, appearing between 2006 and 2014. We studied countless reference works and settled on organizing our information into twenty-four subject areas that wove together knowledge of the region with interdisciplinary perspectives. The center's educational work drew from faculty with joint appointments, who taught in the southern studies bachelor's and master's degree programs and in home departments—an arrangement that anchored attention to interdisciplinary thinking. In our team-taught courses, I learned from some of the best scholars of the South. Anthropologist Robbie Ethridge taught me to include southeastern Native Americans when talking about the South. Photographer and documentarian Tom Rankin taught me to pay attention to Appalachian mountain ballads when thinking about the violent murders in a Cormac McCarthy novel. Literary scholar Kathryn McKee taught me close reading of southern texts, whether novels, memoirs, or films.

The center has always been a gathering spot for the exchange of knowledge on the South. University faculty who did not have joint appointments have been frequent participants in center events, and the synergy between the history and English departments was especially vital to the university's early contributions to the study of the South. To hear Charles Eagles lecture on the civil rights movement, John Neff on the Civil War, Don Kartiganer and Jay Watson on Faulkner, Jan Hawks and Elizabeth Payne on southern women's history, Zandria Robinson on African American culture in Memphis, or Adam Gussow on blues literature (to take only a few examples) gave me a breadth of knowledge on the South that was priceless and nurtured in me the intellectual outlook behind this manuscript. The annual Porter L. Fortune Jr. History Symposium, the Faulkner and Yoknapatawpha Conference, the Oxford Conference for the Book, and the Southern Music Symposium, as well as conferences on the civil rights movement and the media, science and medicine in the South, Richard Wright, and others—all exposed me to rich understandings of the South that shaped my view of the region.

In the early days, the center was an especially vibrant place (and remains so). Most of us working there were young and sassy, prizing innovation, seeing ourselves as young Turks who would have something important to say about the study of the South. Or else we just had our heads down trying to meet the next deadline, a bit less grandiose. Change was palpable in the South in those days. Mississippi had enacted landmark education reform legislation in the early 1980s, and Governor William Winter offered the kind of sustained leadership that pointed toward a promising future for an often-besieged place. Indeed, the integration of the university had occurred only two decades before I arrived. If progressive forces were emboldened in the early 1980s, remnants of the closed society remained. In pointing toward the cultural changes that had occurred in the state, I reminded a reporter that Confederate Memorial Day hardly mattered anymore, and I suggested that University of Mississippi students knew more about the singer Madonna than Robert E. Lee. In response, a university donor from Tchula, Mississippi, wrote me, and our chancellor, a rather nasty note with suggestions for my fate that would not include a raise. The center's work with African American blues music and folk culture made it a suspect institution for some in the South, but that feeling did not affect our work.

A primary premise of critical regionalist theory is that writing about a region imagines a region. When work on the encyclopedia began in the 1980s, scholars in many fields explored what the South was and where it was located. Sociologist John Shelton Reed used the yellow pages of the telephone book to document the claim of "southern" by businesses, government offices, and other institutions. Geographers charted maps of restaurants serving grits below the Mason-Dixon Line rather than the hash browns above the line, and the Bible

Belt was tangible when church membership in evangelical groups clearly delineated a South from the rest of the nation. Although one might think using phone books to gather data is outdated, along with the universality of land lines, technology turns out still to reveal "a South." Early promoters of the internet claimed its rapid communication capabilities and lack of spatial grounding would eliminate geographical and cultural identities. Instead, the South is alive and well, if diverse, in cyberspace. Do a web search for "southern way of life" and you will see a rocking chair on a porch—a traditional and contested symbol. Beyond the internet, advertisers, marketers, tourism agencies, newspapers and magazines, television stations, films, musicians, regional periodicals, and academic institutions all delineate Souths.

The South the center tried to nurture amid the demands of teaching and research was that of, in fact, many Souths. I wrote a column entitled "Many Souths" for the *Atlanta Journal-Constitution* about the encyclopedia's significance even before it appeared. Sharply departing from many earlier broad overviews of the region, we aspired toward inclusivity in our coverage. Above all, we championed a biracial perspective appropriate to the South's history and especially to that of the state of Mississippi, with the largest percentage of African Americans in the country. We stressed the region's diversity and contributed to that theme becoming central to southern studies in general. Geography anchored the encyclopedia's presentation of cultural diversity. As we wrote in the introduction, "The 'South' is found wherever southern culture is found, and that culture is located not only in the Deep South, the Upper South, and border cities, but also in 'little Dixies' (the southern parts of Ohio, Indiana, Illinois, and parts of Missouri and Oklahoma), among black Mississippians who migrated to south Chicago, among white Appalachians and black Alabamians who left the South for Detroit, and among former Okies and Arkies who settled in and around Bakersfield, California. The diaspora of southern culture is also found in the works of expatriate artists and writers." We had a major section on ethnic life and included many entries on Native Americans in the South, with even more such entries in *The New Encyclopedia of Southern Culture*. This attention presaged the flourishing scholarship on diverse groups in the last fifteen years.

Those of us working on the encyclopedia understood the South as a state of the mind, as a social and cultural construction, but we asserted that the South was still an important unit for analysis with many cultural expressions. We put ourselves back in that moment in time when talk of a disappearing South came in the face of the end of Jim Crow segregation and disfranchisement of African Americans, economic development, the end of the solid Democratic Party–dominated South, and the growing national and international influences on the region. Our documentation of so many ideas and practices associated with the South opened up new avenues for studying the region. The introduction to the volume pointed to the region's globalization, again raising the issue well before scholars began systematically to explore it.

Finally, we did not call it just an "encyclopedia of the South" but an "encyclopedia of southern culture." In that decision, we were in tune with the intellectual times. The cultural studies movement had begun in England and spread to the United States with new attention to what culture was and how it could illuminate many areas of study. We quoted the influential anthropologist Clifford Geertz and used his definition of culture as the overarching one for the volume. As he wrote, culture was "an historically transmitted pattern of meanings embodied in symbols, a system of inherited conceptions expressed in symbolic form." The study of culture would come to dominate much of the study of the South over the next generation, and the encyclopedia was in line with that development. Geertz's stress on history pointed me in all my work, including this manuscript, to analyzing the processes of cultural history.

The *Encyclopedia of Southern Culture* sold some 100,000 copies within a few years of its publication and symbolized the commodification of the South that is a major theme of contemporary southern living. To those of us involved with the volume, its success validated, more importantly, the center's mission of bringing the best scholarly knowledge about the South to broader audiences beyond the academy. We did not fear a popular audience but sought it as a way to push the South toward a more progressive outlook, beyond the academy. Many of us at the center lectured widely at conferences, symposia, and workshops and made presentations to professional, business, and governmental groups. The university funded much of the center's budget, but fundraising was a necessity to make a project such as the *Encyclopedia* a reality. Reliance on donors did not require any watering down of academic rigor. The *Encyclopedia*, for example, won the Dartmouth Award from the American Library Association as the best reference book of 1989. The oral history project of one center institute, the Southern Foodways Alliance, to give another example, won the Mississippi Historical Society's best such project of the year.

When Bill Ferris left the University of Mississippi to become director of the National Endowment for the Humanities, I became the center's director in 1998. Several initiatives after that connected with broader cultural themes in the contemporary South. The Institute for Racial Reconciliation began within the center. I chaired its first advisory board, and Susan Glisson—a graduate of the southern studies master's program and assistant director of the center—became director of the institute when the University of Mississippi named it for William Winter. The Southern Foodways Alliance, begun in 1999 as an institute within the center, has coordinated much work of a broader South-wide food movement, led by John T. Edge, another former southern studies graduate student. The Hardin

Foundation provided initial funding for the Endowment for the Future of the South, which brings together academics, government leaders, journalists, policy makers, and others to explore issues that cross lines between cultural studies and public policy.

The center has changed with the times. When I returned to teaching in 2008, I left the institution in good hands, first with Ted Ownby as director, followed by Kathryn McKee in 2019. The center's scholars and teachers have been key in pointing to globalization's impact in the region; documenting Latino culture in the South; exploring women social reformers in Appalachia; and analyzing race relations seen in slavery, Jim Crow segregation, or the new Jim Crow of mass incarceration. The center helped sponsor the early work of new southern studies scholars at a series of planning meetings, and today's center director, Kathryn McKee, coedited a key text that defined that project. A new master of fine arts degree in documentary studies and the increased production of films from the center's DocSouth project have augmented its role in that area. The center hosted the Transforming New South Identities Symposium in 2014, which resulted in a volume of papers in *Navigating Souths: Transdisciplinary Explorations of a U.S. Region* (2017). A new online peer-reviewed journal, *Study the South*, has become an important forum for interdisciplinary work on the South, and *The Mississippi Encyclopedia* (2018) has buttressed the center's scholarly and educational role within the state and beyond as a model of a state encyclopedia.

The center's broader significance, it seems to me, is as part of a resurgence of American regionalism that began in the late twentieth century and continues. Within the South, regional studies centers have been national leaders in examining how regions still function as important spaces and places. The Center for the Study of the American South, at the University of North Carolina at Chapel Hill, offers extensive programming and research activities, including its stellar periodical *Southern Cultures*. Other centers in the region include the Center for Appalachian Studies at the University of Kentucky, the Center for Southwestern Louisiana at the University of Southwest Louisiana, and the Delta Center for Culture and Learning at Delta State University. One online peer-reviewed publication, *Southern Spaces*, at Emory University, deserves mention because of its innovative explorations of the South that combine rigorous scholarship with the use of online resources in presenting research. Beyond the South, the Center for Great Plains Studies at the University of Nebraska dates to the mid-1970s. The Center for the American West at the University of Colorado and the New England studies program at the University of Southern Maine have offered curriculum and outreach activities.

I interacted with all those institutions, and in the process they reinforced my sense of the South's comparative significance with other regional cultures.

The center has always been a vigorous and energetic place with projects galore. I hope that the institution's focus on cultural work, both in academia and through outreach, has led to greater understanding and appreciation of the diversity of southern life. Certainly, the region's public culture is far more enlightened than it was even fifty years ago. This manuscript has chronicled in recent times the rise of a robust interracial movement, the empowerment of a variety of racial and ethnic minorities in unprecedented ways, and an embrace by cultural and political leaders of the South's creative culture. The dismal state of political life at the end of the second decade of the twenty-first century, on the other hand, brings a melancholy sense of the limitations of change in the South. A thinly veiled white racism remains, sometimes hidden but in the current atmosphere given more open expression and authority. I remain hopeful, though, that acknowledgment of a common multicultural narrative of the South will push the region into a brighter future.

Finally, in sketching factors that shaped this manuscript's outlook, I should mention my teaching. I directed some twenty-five PhD dissertations at the University of Mississippi and scores of master's theses in history and southern studies. Working with these young scholars kept me in touch with new research topics and disciplinary approaches. Teaching southern studies over the years meant studying the many ways people have identified with the South and claimed the southern identity. Undergraduates and university alumni often think of the academic program that way. But those of us teaching southern studies stress that this approach can encourage focusing too much on just a few groups, usually those dominant in society and often nostalgic for a supposed simpler past too often romanticized in popular culture. Nobody owned the southern identity. Southern studies also looks at the many ways people have described the region, whether defining its problems, expanding definitions of who is a southerner, or emphasizing how social and cultural changes can lead to a reimagined southern identity. It means studying all the South's people, whether or not a concern with southern identity has been crucial to them, because they have been a part of the context of southern civilization, the southern way of life, and southern living.

Teaching students and the general public through presentations at a variety of forums, editing reference works and volumes of conference and symposia papers, and researching and writing my monographs and essay collections all helped to prepare me to undertake this manuscript. Although I appreciate and draw from interdisciplinary perspectives, at heart I am a historian. In conceptual history, I found a way to trace the history of regional consciousness and culture that shows its long and complicated reach.

ACKNOWLEDGMENTS

I BEGAN WORK ON THIS BOOK in 1989 as part of a sabbatical the year I finished work on the *Encyclopedia of Southern Culture*. I wrote three chapters but then put the project aside under the press of full-time teaching and other research projects. In 2008, I returned to the manuscript, refocused it, and began sustained work on completing it. Over such a long period of time, I became indebted to many people. The University of Mississippi is an extraordinary place to be studying the American South. The university made a major commitment to that study, shortly before I came there, with the establishment of the Center for the Study of Southern Culture. Bill Ferris, its founding director, and Ann Abadie, longtime associate director, made it a vibrant institution that supported interdisciplinary teaching, faculty research, and ambitious outreach efforts. I am grateful to Bill and Ann for giving me many opportunities. I had a joint appointment in history and southern studies, and I am thankful as well to the chairs of the history department—Fred Laurenzo, Bob Haws, and Joe Ward. Bob, in particular, became a trusted adviser on many intellectual projects and a close friend. The graduate students I taught were a pleasure to work with, a source of inspiration as I heard their thoughts in class and learned from their research papers. Those who worked with me as graduate assistants and interns did much research related to this manuscript, even in long periods when I was not working on it directly. The College of Liberal Arts and the Graduate School at the university provided financial assistance some summers to help my research.

I gave papers drawing from the book's research at several academic meetings, including the Southern Historical Society, the St. George Tucker Society, the Southern American Studies Association meeting, and the Obama Institute's annual lecture at the University of Mainz as part of my work as an Obama Fellow. Alfred Hornung, the institute's director, helped arrange the latter, and that friendship deserves my recognition for our ongoing intellectual conversation.

Four historians read the entire manuscript—Ted Ownby, Richard King, Charles Eagles, and Bill Childs. They offered sage assessments with close readings, making specific corrections and clarifications that improved the manuscript. The same is true for two anonymous readers for the University of North Carolina Press, whose sharp eyes saved me from infelicities of expression and factual errors. This manuscript went through three directors at the press: Matthew Hodgson, Kate Torrey, and John Sherer. I consulted often with senior editors David Perry and Mark Simpson-Vos, who were stalwart advocates of the project, and I gained much enthusiasm to get back to work after meetings with them. In the final preparation of the manuscript, Mark gave it the thorough close reading of a most skilled editor.

I have been blessed with the deep friendships of people who have listened to my progress reports and offered words of encouragement along the way. My brother, Clifford Martin Wilson III, and I share so many attitudes and outlooks that it seemed like we have a singular worldview, and he has offered continued words of wisdom about my work. Kees and Jean Gispen are like family, and they have similarly encouraged me. Kees's rigorous sense of historical inquiry has queried my work with curiosity and probing questions. Colleagues in southern studies have been sounding boards for my discussions about this manuscript, including Kathryn McKee, David Wharton, Adam Gussow, Jodi Skipper, and Jimmy Thomas. Jimmy, in particular, earned special mention for his assistance in preparing illustrations for this work. Ted Ownby's career and mine have long been intertwined, with the many doctoral and thesis committees we served on, the conferences we worked on, and the work we did on *The Mississippi Encyclopedia*. He was the first person to read the manuscript, and his interest in it bolstered me. Jim Cobb and I began teaching at the university the same year, 1981, and we have remained close over the years with our common interest in southern history. In the last few years, our dinners at the Southern Historical Association brought frequent discussion of our manuscripts, and I valued his advice.

If colleagues have been sounding boards and sources of support, earlier mentors deserve recognition as well. Historians at the University of Texas at El Paso trained me well in historical study, especially Kenneth K. Bailey, who set me on the path studying religion in the South, and Carl T. Jackson, who taught me the intellectual and cultural history that would provide the defining historical genre for this study. William Goetzman and Robert Crunden guided work toward my doctoral work at the University of Texas at Austin and nurtured in me an understanding of the interdisciplinary study that shaped my intellectual outlook. A National Endowment for the Humanities Summer Institute with John Shelton Reed at the University of North Carolina at Chapel Hill broadened my intellectual reach and introduced me to social science research on the South. Samuel S. Hill was a mentor in my work on southern religious history and provided me a particularly admired example of a humane scholar.

Historians always rely on librarians, and I am no exception. Most of the research for this study was done at the John Davis Williams Library at the

University of Mississippi, and I especially want to thank curator Jennifer Ford and her staff at the Archives and Special Collections. I also give my thanks to librarians at the Carlos Castañeda Library and the Humanities Research Center at the University of Texas at Austin, the Southern Historical Collection and the North Carolina Collection at the University of North Carolina at Chapel Hill Library, and the Vanderbilt University Library, and to archivists at the Mississippi Valley Collection at the University of Memphis.

My wife, Marie Antoon, and I have a household that has been conducive to productive work and good times. Part of that comes from our dogs, Biscuit and Sampson, who have invariably responded with tails wagging at my discussion with them of the South's conceptual history. The same cannot be said of our cats, Scuzzer, Little Kitty, and Pepper—but then they are cats. My greatest debt is to Marie. She is my partner on life's adventures, including this book. Every afternoon we converse on wide-ranging matters, and this book became a major ongoing topic, the last few years especially. She always asked good questions and pressed me to make the book accessible to a wide audience. She offered more tangible support in her research on the endnote references. A master of the computer, she was able to locate needed material quickly and pushed the book toward completion. I dedicate this work to her with a love that has grown over the years.

NOTES

ABBREVIATIONS

JSH *Journal of Southern History*
SC *Southern Cultures*
VQR *Virginia Quarterly Review*

INTRODUCTION

1. Pat Conroy, *The Prince of Tides* (1986; repr., New York: Bantam Books, 1987), 63.

2. John B. Boles, *The South through Time: A History of an American Region* (Englewood Cliffs, N.J.: Prentice-Hall, 1995), 238–47; J. V. Ridgely, *Nineteenth-Century Southern Literature* (Lexington: University Press of Kentucky, 1980); Howard Odum, *The Way of the South: Toward the Regional Balance of America* (New York: Macmillan, 1947); Rupert B. Vance, "Beyond the Fleshpots: The Coming Culture Crisis in the South," in *Regionalism and the South: Selected Papers of Rupert Vance*, ed. John Shelton Reed and Daniel Singal (Chapel Hill: University of North Carolina Press, 1982), 252; Drew Gilpin Faust, *Creation of Confederate Nationalism: Ideology and Identity in the Civil War South* (Baton Rouge: Louisiana State University Press, 1989), 15; C. C. Goen, *Broken Churches, Broken Nation: Denominational Schisms and the Coming of the American Civil War* (Macon, Ga.: Mercer University Press, 1985), 110; James C. Cobb, *Away Down South: A History of the Southern Identity* (New York: Oxford University Press, 2005), 212.

3. Walker Percy, *The Thanatos Syndrome* (New York: Ivy Books, 1987), 64; David Harvey, *Spaces of Hope* (Berkeley: University of California Press, 2000), 67, 85; Lewis P. Simpson, *Mind and the American Civil War: A Meditation on Lost Causes* (Baton Rouge: Louisiana State University Press, 1998), 15; Willams quoted in Harvey, *Spaces of Hope*, 55.

4. W. J. Cash, *The Mind of the South* (1941; repr., New York: Alfred A. Knopf, 1978), 106; Clifford Geertz, *The Interpretation of Cultures: Selected Essays* (New York: Basic Books, 1973), 5; William Faulkner, *Light in August* (1933; repr., New York: Vintage, 1972), 56–57, 69, 80; Anthony Walton, *Mississippi: An American Journey* (New York: Alfred A. Knopf, 1996), 164.

5. Terence Ball, James Farr, and Russell L. Hanson, introduction to *Political Innovation and Conceptual Change*, ed. Terence Ball, James Farr, and Russell L. Hanson (Cambridge: Cambridge University Press, 1989), 4; Quentin Skinner, "Rhetoric and Conceptual Change," *Redescriptions: Yearbook of Political Thought, Conceptual History and Feminist Theory* 3, no. 1 (1999), 60–72. A classic example of a conceptual historical study is Eric Foner, *The Story of American Freedom* (New York: W. W. Norton, 1998).

6. Cobb, *Away Down South*; W. Fitzhugh Brundage, *The Southern Past: A Clash of Race and Memory* (Cambridge, Mass.: Belknap Press of Harvard University Press, 2005);

Martyn Bone, *Where the New World Is: Literature about the U.S. South at Global Scales* (Athens: University of Georgia Press, 2018). Scott Romine, in *The Real South: Southern Narrative in the Age of Cultural Reproduction* (Baton Rouge: Louisiana State University Press, 2008), argues that a South mechanically reproduced from mass culture characterizes the recent South and is better than a supposedly "authentic" South.

7. Douglas Reichert Powell, *Critical Realism: Connecting Politics and Culture in the American Landscape* (Chapel Hill: University of North Carolina Press, 2007), 4, 5, 6.

8. Deborah E. Barker and Kathryn McKee, eds., *American Cinema and the Southern Imaginary* (Athens: University of Georgia Press, 2011), 2; Allen Tullos, *Alabama Getaway: The Political Imaginary and the Heart of Dixie* (Athens: University of Georgia Press, 2010), 1.

9. James Silver, *The Closed Society* (New York: Harcourt, Brace and World, 1966).

10. Twelve Southerners, *I'll Take My Stand: The South and the Agrarian Tradition* (1930; repr., Baton Rouge: Louisiana State University Press, 2006); William Alexander Percy, *Lanterns on the Levee: Recollections of a Planter's Son* (New York: Alfred A. Knopf, 1941), 13, 312.

11. Charles Reagan Wilson, "The Myth of the Biracial South," in *The Southern State of Mind*, ed. Jan Gretlund (Columbia: University of South Carolina Press, 1999), 3-22.

12. Elizabeth Spencer, *Landscapes of Memory* (New York: Random House, 1998), 32, 313.

13. Walton, *Mississippi*, 58, 77-78.

14. Phillip Hammond, Amanda Porterfield, James G. Moseley, and Jonathan D. Sarna, "Forum: American Civil Religion Revisited," *Religion and American Culture* 4, no. 1 (1994), 2, 5; Arthur Remillard, *Southern Civil Religions: Imagining the Good Society in the Post-Reconstruction Era* (Athens: University of Georgia Press, 2011).

15. Hugh Jones, *The Present State of Virginia: Giving a Particular and Short Account of the Indians, English, and Negroe Inhabitants of That Colony; Shewing Their Religion, Manners, Government, Way of Living, etc., with a Description of the Country* (London, 1724), 48; *Journal of John Woolman*, quoted in Fred C. Hobson, "The Savage South," in *The Silencing of Emily Mullen and Other Essays* (Baton Rouge: Louisiana State University Press, 2005), 115-31.

16. Cobb, *Away Down South*, chaps. 1-3.

17. W. E. B. Du Bois, *Black Reconstruction: An Essay toward a History of the Part Which Black Folk Played in the Attempt to Reconstruct America, 1860-1880* (New York: Harcourt, Brace, 1935), 700-701; John Dollard, *Caste and Class in a Southern Town* (New York: Harper and Brothers, 1949).

18. Twelve Southerners, *I'll Take My Stand*; Odum, *Way of the South*.

19. Stephanie Cole and Alison M. Parker, eds., *Beyond Black and White: Race, Ethnicity, and Gender in the U.S. South and Southwest* (College Station: Texas A&M University Press, 2004).

20. "Carry on the Fight," *Meridian (Miss.) Star*, August 26, 1964; Gunnar Myrdal, *An American Dilemma: The Negro Problem and Modern Democracy* (New York: Harper and Brothers, 1944).

21. Sheryl Gay Stolberg, "Under Fire, Lott Apologizes for His Comments at Thurmond's Party," *New York Times*, December 10, 2002, A28. Diane Everett, letter to the editor, *Clarion-Ledger* (Jackson, Miss.), December 17, 2002, 8A; Duke quoted in Thomas Tweed, "Our Lady of Guadeloupe Visits the Confederate Monument: Latino and Asian

Religions in the South," in *Religion in the Contemporary South: Continuities, Changes, and Contexts*, ed. Corrie E. Norman and Don S. Ammentrout (Knoxville: University of Tennessee Press, 2005), 145.

22. Nicholas Lemann, "A Whiff of Magnolias," *Atlantic Monthly*, March 1989, 93.

23. Wilson quoted in Stephen A. Smith, *Myth, Media, and the Southern Mind* (Fayetteville: University of Arkansas Press, 1985), 91.

24. Brett Bowden, *The Empire of Civilization: The Evolution of an Imperial Idea* (Chicago: University of Chicago Press, 2009), 166; Lucien Febvre, "Civilization: Evolution of a Word and a Group of Ideas," in *A New Kind of History: From the Writings of Febvre*, ed. P. Burke (London: Routledge and Kegan Paul, 1973), 219–57.

25. Bowden, *Empire of Civilization*, 57; Winthrop D. Jordan, *White over Black: American Attitudes toward the Negro, 1550–1812* (Chapel Hill: University of North Carolina Press, 1968), 543–44.

26. Norbert Elias, *The Civilizing Process* (1978; repr., Oxford, UK: Blackwell, 1994); Bowden, *Empire of Civilization*, 26–34.

27. John Gray, *Enlightenment's Wake: Politics and Culture at the Close of the Modern Age* (London: Routledge, 1995), 123; Bowden, *Empire of Civilization*, 12, 14, 61, 75, 105.

28. Richard H. King, "Romanticism," in *Myth, Manners, and Memory*, ed. Charles Reagan Wilson, vol. 4 of *The New Encyclopedia of Southern Culture*, ed. Charles Reagan Wilson (Chapel Hill: University of North Carolina Press, 2006), 162–64; Michael O'Brien, *Rethinking the South: Essays in Intellectual History* (Baltimore: Johns Hopkins University Press, 1988); Bowden, *Empire of Civilization*, 19–34, 50–53.

29. Edward Tylor, *Primitive Culture: Research into the Development, Mythology, Philosophy, Religion, Art, and Custom* (London: John Murray, 1971); Lewis H. Morgan, *Ancient Society; or, Researches in the Lines of Human Progress from Savagery through Barbarism to Civilization* (Chicago: Kerr, 1907).

30. Gail Bederman, *Manliness and Civilization: A Cultural History of Gender and Race in the United States, 1880–1917* (Chicago: University of Chicago Press, 1995), 23.

31. R. C. Collingwood, "What 'Civilization' Means," in *New Leviathan*, ed. David Boucher (Oxford, UK: Clarendon, 1992), 486.

CHAPTER ONE

1. John Winthrop, *Winthrop's Journal, History of New England, 1630–1649*, ed. Richard S. Dunn, James Savage, and Laetitia Yeandle (Cambridge, Mass.: Belknap Press of Harvard University Press, 1996), 343; Henry Adams, *The Education of Henry Adams* (Boston: Houghton Mifflin, 1919), 47, 57, 58. Adams privately printed his memoir in 1907; Houghton Mifflin published it in 1919.

2. John Pendleton Kennedy, *Slavery: The Mere Pretext for the Rebellion; Not Its Cause* (Philadelphia: C. Sherman, Son, 1863), 5.

3. Kerry A. Trask, "Double Exposure: A Look at Southern Identity in the Eighteenth Century," *Southern Studies* 22 (Summer 1983): 153–54.

4. Beverley quoted in Trask, 153–54.

5. "Journal of Josiah Quincy," *Massachusetts Historical Society Proceedings*, vol. 49, quoted in Carl Bridenbaugh, *Myths and Realities: Societies of the Colonial South* (New York: Atheneum, 1970), 35; Trask, "Double Exposure," 147–48, 151.

6. Nicholas Cresswell, *The Journal of Nicholas Cresswell, 1774–1777* (New York: L. MacVeagh, 1924), 252–54. See also Richard Beale Davis, *Intellectual Life in the Colonial South, 1585–1763*, 3 vols. (Knoxville: University of Tennessee Press, 1978); Louis B. Wright, *The First Gentlemen of Virginia: Intellectual Qualities of the Early Colonial Ruling Class* (San Marino, Calif.: Huntington Library, 1940); and T. H. Breen, *Tobacco Culture: The Mentality of the Great Tidewater Planters on the Eve of Revolution* (Princeton, N.J.: Princeton University Press, 1985).

7. Lewis P. Simpson, "William Byrd and the South," *Early American Literature* 7 (Fall 1972): 190; "Colonel William Byrd on Slavery and Indented Servants, 1736, 1739," *American Historical Review* 1, no. 1 (1895); Kenneth Lockridge, ed., *The Diary and Life of William Byrd II of Virginia, 1674–1744* (Chapel Hill: published for the Institute of Early American History and Culture, Williamsburg, Virginia, by the University of North Carolina Press, 1989), 154; Louis B. Wright, ed., *Prose Works: Narratives of a Colonial Virginian* (Cambridge, Mass.: Belknap Press of Harvard University Press, 1966), 204.

8. Charles A. Beard and Mary R. Beard, *The American Spirit: A Study of the Idea of Civilization in the United States*, vol. 4, *The Rise of American Civilization* (New York: Macmillan, 1942), 91–100.

9. Thomas Jefferson, *Notes on the State of Virginia*, ed. William Peden (New York: W. W. Norton, 1954), 162, 164–65.

10. Jefferson, 92–107, 162–63; Winthrop D. Jordan, *White over Black: American Attitudes toward the Negro, 1550–1812* (Chapel Hill: University of North Carolina Press, 1968), 24. See also Roy Harvey Pearce, *Savagism and Civilization: A Study of the Indian and the American Mind* (Baltimore: Johns Hopkins University Press, 1953).

11. Theda Perdue and Michael Green, *The Columbia Guide to American Indians of the Southeast* (New York: Columbia University Press, 2001), 75–88.

12. Perdue and Green, 78; Mary Young, "The Cherokee Nation: Mirror of the Republic," *American Quarterly* 33 (Winter 1981): 522.

13. Young, "Cherokee Nation," 507, 517; Perdue and Green, *Columbia Guide*, 78.

14. Ethan J. Kytle and Blain Roberts, *Denmark Vesey's Garden: Slavery and Memory in the Cradle of the Confederacy* (New York: New Press, 2018); Alfred N. Hunt, *Haiti's Influence on Antebellum America: Slumbering Volcano in the Caribbean* (Baton Rouge: Louisiana State University Press, 1988).

15. Theodore Dwight Weld, *American Slavery as It Is: Testimony of a Thousand Witnesses* (1839; repr., New York: Arno, 1968), 9. See also Fred C. Hobson, "The Savage South" in *The Silencing of Emily Mullen and Other Essays* (Baton Rouge: Louisiana State University Press, 2005), 115–31.

16. David Blight, *Frederick Douglass' Civil War: Keeping Faith in Jubilee* (Baton Rouge: Louisiana State University Press, 1991), 9, 39–47.

17. David Walker, "Preamble," in *Walker's Appeal, with a Brief Sketch of His Life by Henry Highland Garnet* (New York: J. H. Tobitt, 1848), 14.

18. Quoted material in Eric Foner, *The Story of American Freedom* (New York: W. W. Norton, 1998), 138. Martin Bernal's *Black Athena: The Afroasiatic Roots of Classical Civilization* (Brunswick, N.J.: Rutgers University Press, 1987) supports these abolitionist claims, arguing that the debt that Greek culture owed to African and Middle Eastern sources was erased by nineteenth-century historians who were awash in the racism of their day.

19. James C. Cobb, *Away Down South: A History of the Southern Identity* (New York: Oxford University Press, 2005), chap. 1; John Alden, *The First South* (Baton Rouge: Louisiana State University Press, 1961), 3–32.

20. Eric L. McKitrick, *Slavery Defended: The Views of the Old South* (Englewood Cliffs, N.J.: Prentice-Hall, 1963), 12–13. Fitzhugh's stress on southern prosperity did not acknowledge the key role of the federal government in developing a financial infrastructure to support it, nor did he recognize the role of northern and international bankers and industrialists in fostering that prosperity. See Sven Beckert, *Empire of Cotton: A Global History* (New York: Alfred A. Knopf, 2014).

21. Quote in Arthur C. Cole, *The Whig Party in the South* (Washington, D.C.: American Historical Association, 1913), 174.

22. C. C. Goen, *Broken Churches, Broken Nation: Denominational Schisms and the Coming of the American Civil War* (Macon, Ga.: Mercer University Press, 1985), 1–16.

23. Jerald C. Brauer, "Regionalism and Religion in America," *Church History* 54 (September 1985): 366–78. See also Ruth H. Bloch, *Visionary Republic: Millennial Themes in American Thought, 1756–1800* (Cambridge: Cambridge University Press, 1985).

24. Robert H. Brugger, *Beverley Tucker: Heart over Head in the Old South* (Baltimore: Johns Hopkins University Press, 1978), 129–30; Paul C. Nagel, *One Nation Indivisible: The Union in American Thought, 1776–1861* (1964; repr., Westport, Conn.: Greenwood, 1980), 164–68, 184–91; Harry S. Stout, *Upon the Altar of the Nation: A Moral History of the American Civil War* (New York: Viking, 2006), 228–29, 252, 254.

25. Brantley quoted in Anne C. Loveland, *Southern Evangelicals and the Social Order, 1800–1860* (Baton Rouge: Louisiana State University Press, 1980), 260; Spratt quoted in John McCardell, *The Idea of a Southern Nation: Southern Nationalists and Southern Nationalism, 1830–1860* (New York: W. W. Norton, 1981), 135; William H. Holcombe, "The Alternative: A Separate Nationality, or the Africanization of the South," *Southern Literary Messenger*, n.s., 11 (February 1861): 84. For southern unionists, see Carl N. Degler, *The Other South: Southern Dissenters in the Nineteenth Century* (New York: Harper and Row, 1974), 99–187; and Daniel W. Crofts, *Reluctant Confederates: Upper South Unionists in the Secession Crisis* (Chapel Hill: University of North Carolina Press, 1989).

26. Michael O'Brien, *Conjectures of Order: Intellectual Life and the American South* (Chapel Hill: University of North Carolina Press, 2004), 1–20.

27. Jesse Burton Harrison, *Southern Review* 8 (February 1832): 462.

28. Russell Blaine Nye, *Society and Culture in America, 1830–1860* (New York: Harper and Row, 1974); Charles Sellers, *The Market Revolution: Jacksonian America, 1815–46* (New York: Oxford University Press, 1991).

29. Eric Lott, *Love and Theft: Blackface Minstrelsy and the American Working Class* (New York: Oxford University Press, 1993); Robert C. Toll, *Blacking Up: The Minstrel Show in Nineteenth-Century America* (New York: Oxford University Press, 1974).

30. Holmes quoted in Neal Gillespie, "The Spiritual Odyssey of George Frederick Holmes," *Journal of Southern History* 32, no. 3 (1965): 296–97; George Fitzhugh, "Southern Thought," in *The Ideology of Slavery: Proslavery Thought in the Antebellum South, 1830–1860*, ed. Drew Gilpin Faust (Baton Rouge: Louisiana State University Press, 1981), 281.

31. Drew Gilpin Faust, *A Sacred Circle: The Dilemma of the Intellectual in the Old South, 1840–1860* (Baltimore: Johns Hopkins University Press, 1977); O'Brien, *Conjectures of Order*, chaps. 4 and 5.

32. Antrobius quoted in Jessie J. Poesch, "Growth and Development of the Old South, 1830–1900," in *Painting in the South, 1564–1980* (Richmond: Virginia Museum of Fine Arts, 1983), 81–82; E. Brooks Holifield, *The Gentlemen Theologians: American Theology in Southern Culture, 1795–1860* (Durham, N.C.: Duke University Press, 1978). For the importance of periodicals, see Beth Barton Schweiger, "The Literate South: Reading before Emancipation," *Journal of the Civil War Era* 3 (September 2013): 331–59.

33. *Southern Literary Messenger* 1 (August 1834), 1. Michael O'Brien's *Conjectures of Order* is a magisterial study of antebellum southern intellectual life that proves the region's thinkers were well plugged into currents of Western thought.

34. Robert T. Handy, *A Christian America: Protestant Hopes and Historical Realities* (New York: Oxford University Press, 1971).

35. Simms quoted in David Donald, "The Proslavery Argument Reconsidered," *JSH* 37 (February 1971): 15. See also John Mayfield, *Counterfeit Gentlemen: Manhood and Humor in the Old South* (Gainesville: University Press of Florida, 2009).

36. Simms quoted in McCardell, *Idea of a Southern Nation*, 135; Frederick Law Olmsted, *The Cotton Kingdom: A Traveller's Observations on Cotton and Slavery in the American Slave States, 1853–1861* (1856; repr., New York: DaCapo, 1996), 17–18.

37. Edmund Quincy, "Where Will It End,"*Atlantic Monthly*, December 1857, 244; Theodore Parker, *Centenary Edition of the Works of Theodore Parker* (Boston: American Unitarian Association, 1907), 11: 205–6.

38. McCardell, *Idea*, 197, 160; A. B. Longstreet, *A Voice from the South: Comprising Letters from Georgia to Massachusetts, and to the Southern States* (Baltimore: Samuel E. Smith, 1848), letter 1; Kennedy, *Slavery*, 6.

39. Quote in E. Merton Coulter, ed., *The Course of the South to Secession: An Interpretation by Ulrich Bonnell Phillips* (1939; repr., New York: Hill and Wang, 1964), 141–42.

40. A large literature exists on the modernization of the nineteenth-century South. See Michael O'Brien, "Modernization and the Nineteenth-Century South," in *Rethinking the South: Essays in Intellectual History* (Baltimore: Johns Hopkins University Press, 1988), 112–28; and L. Diane Barnes, Brian Schoen, and Frank Towers, eds., *The Old South's Modern World: Slavery, Region, and Nation in the Age of Progress* (New York: Oxford University Press, 2011). The latter sees the South's centrality to national and global history as key to its antebellum history, drawing attention to the awareness of white southerners that they were part of a broader modernizing world. This study agrees with that understanding but stresses how white southerners used regional consciousness and the southern civilization construct to justify their society as offering a particular imagining of slave society facing an expansive future.

41. Drew Gilpin Faust, "The Rhetoric and Ritual of Agriculture in Antebellum South Carolina," *JSH* 45 (November 1979): 544. See also Lewis P. Simpson, "Southern Spiritual Nationalism: Notes on the Background of Modern Southern Fiction," in *The Cry of Home: Cultural Nationalism and the Modern Writer*, ed. J. Ernest Lewald (Knoxville: University of Tennessee Press, 1972), 194–203.

42. Richard Gray, *Writing the South: Ideas of an American Region* (1986; repr., Baton Rouge: Louisiana State University Press, 1997), 45–47; Simpson, "Southern Spiritual Nationalism," 189–203; Faust, "Rhetoric and Ritual," 541–68.

43. Lacy K. Ford, *Origins of Southern Radicalism: The South Carolina Upcountry, 1800–1860* (New York: Oxford University Press, 1988), 52; Kenneth S. Goldberg, *Masters and*

Statesmen: The Political Culture of American Slavery (Baltimore: Johns Hopkins University Press, 1985), vii–xi, 20–22; Daniel T. Rodgers, "Republicanism: The Career of a Concept," *Journal of American History* 79 (June 1992), 11–38.

44. Harry Watson, *Liberty and Power: The Politics of Jacksonian America* (New York: Hill and Wang, 2006).

45. Drew Gilpin Faust, *James Henry Hammond and the Old South: Design for Mastery* (Baton Rouge: Louisiana State University Press, 1982), 40–43.

46. Thomas Fleming, "Classical Tradition," in *Encyclopedia of Southern Culture*, ed. Charles Reagan Wilson (Chapel Hill: University of North Carolina Press, 1989), 4:246–48; essays in *Southern Humanities Review* 11, Special (1977).

47. Gildersleeve quoted in Fleming, "Classical Tradition," 247. See also J. Drew Harrington, "Classical Antiquity and the Proslavery Argument," *Slavery and Abolition* 10 (May 1989): 60–72.

48. "Cuba: The March of Empire and the Course of Trade," *DeBow's Review* 30 (January 1861): 41–42.

49. The definition of "south" is from Joseph T. Shipley, *Dictionary of Word Origins* (New York: Philosophical Library, 1945), 131. John Ezell, "A Southern Education for Southrons," *JSH* 17 no. 3(1951): 303–27. Matthew Guterl, *American Mediterranean: Southern Slaveholders in the Age of Emancipation* (Cambridge, Mass.: Harvard University Press, 2008), 1. See also Michael O'Brien, "Italy and the Southern Romantics," in *Rethinking the South*, 84–111.

50. Edward L. Ayers, "Honor," in *Violence*, ed. Amy Louise Wood, vol. 19 of *The New Encyclopedia of Southern Culture*, ed. Charles Reagan Wilson (Chapel Hill: University of North Carolina Press, 2011), 78–80. See also Bertram Wyatt-Brown, *Southern Honor: Ethics and Behavior in the Old South* (New York: Oxford University Press, 1982), vii–xxi, 35. Robert Elder, in *The Sacred Mirror: Evangelicalism, Honor, and Identity in the Deep South, 1790–1860* (Chapel Hill: University of North Carolina Press, 2016), argued that white southerners saw honor and faith not as opposites but intertwined, mirroring each other in efforts to manage a modernizing society.

51. Ayers, "Honor," 78–80.

52. See Donald G. Mathews, "Evangelicalism," in *Encyclopedia of Religion in the South*, ed. Samuel S. Hill (Macon, Ga.: Mercer University Press, 1984), 243–44; and Robert T. Calhoun, *Evangelicals and Conservatives in the Early South, 1740–1861* (Columbia: University of South Carolina Press, 1988).

53. Thornton Stringfellow, "A Brief Examination of Scripture Testimony on the Institution of Slavery," in Faust, *Ideology of Slavery*, 139; Thomas Smyth, *The Sin and the Curse; or, the Union, the True Source of Disunion, and Our Duty in the Present Crisis* (Charleston, S.C.: Steam Power Presses of Evans and Cogswell, 1860), 13.

54. James Henry Hammond, "Letter to an English Abolitionist," in Faust, *Ideology of Slavery*, 175, 176, 180. See also Elizabeth-Fox Genovese and Eugene D. Genovese, "Religious Ideals of Southern Slave Society," *Georgia Historical Quarterly* 70 (Spring 1986): 1–15.

55. Sigma, "Southern Individuality," *Southern Literary Messenger*, 38 (June 1864): 369, 73.

56. Michael O'Brien, "The Lineaments of Southern Romanticism," in *Rethinking the South*, 50; Richard H. King, "Romanticism," in *Myth, Manners, and Memory*, ed. Charles Reagan Wilson, vol. 4 of *The New Encyclopedia of Southern Culture*, ed. Charles Reagan

Wilson (Chapel Hill: University of North Carolina Press, 2006), 162–64; David Moltke-Hansen, "Southern Literary Horizons in Young America: Imaginative Developments of a Regional Geography," *Studies in the Literary Imagination* 42 (Summer 2009): 1–31.

57. Holcombe, "Alternative," 81–84. See also William R. Taylor, *Cavalier and Yankee: The Old South and American National Character* (New York: George Braziller, 1957); and David Moltke-Hansen, "To Civilize King Cotton's Realm: William Gilmore Simms's Chivalric Quest," in *The Field of Honor: Essays on Southern Character and American Identity*, ed. John Mayfield and Todd Hagstette (Columbia: University of South Carolina Press, 2017), 21–39.

58. Rolling G. Osterweis, *Romanticism and Nationalism in the Old South* (New Haven, Conn.: Yale University Press, 1949).

59. Thomas Dew, "Abolition of Negro Slavery"; and William Harper, "Memoir on Slavery," both in Faust, *Ideology of Slavery*, 13, 89–90. See also Drew Gilpin Faust, "Introduction: The Proslavery Argument in History," in *Ideology of Slavery*, 1–20.

60. Patrick Gerster, "Religion and Mythology," in Wilson, *Myth, Manners, and Memory*, 158–63; Thomas V. Peterson, *Ham and Japheth: The Mythic World of Whites in the Antebellum South* (Metuchen, N.J.: Scarecrow, 1978).

61. Mitchell Snay, "American Thought and Southern Distinctiveness: The Southern Clergy and the Sanctification of Slavery," *Civil War History* 35 (December 1989): 311–28; Richard T. Hughes, "A Civic Theology for the South: The Case of Benjamin M. Palmer," *Journal of Church and State* 25 (Autumn 1983): 447–68; Randy J. Sparks, "Mississippi's Apostle of Slavery: James Smylie and the Biblical Defense of Slavery," *Journal of Mississippi History* 51 (May 1989): 89–106.

62. Holcombe, "Alternative," 82, 84, 86. See also Robert E. May, *The Southern Dream of a Caribbean Empire, 1854–1861* (Baton Rouge: Louisiana State University Press, 1973).

63. The classic statement of the paternalistic argument is Eugene D. Genovese, *Roll, Jordan, Roll: The World the Slaves Made* (New York: Random House, 1972), 3–7. Recent literature stresses how slavery was embedded in the nineteenth-century expansion of capitalism. See Walter Johnson, *River of Dark Dreams: Slavery and Empire in the Cotton Kingdom* (Cambridge, Mass.: Belknap Press of Harvard University Press, 2013); Beckert, *Empire of Cotton*; Edward E. Baptist, *The Half Has Never Been Told: Slavery and the Making of American Capitalism* (New York: Basic Books, 2014); and Eugene Dattel, *Cotton and Race in the Making of America: The Human Costs of Economic Power* (Chicago: Ivan R. Dee, 2009).

64. J. D. B. DeBow, "The Non-slaveholders of the South: Their Interest in the Present Sectional Controversy Identical with That of the Slaveholders," *DeBow's Review* 30 (January 1861): 67–77. See also Eugene D. Genovese, "Yeomen Farmers in a Slaveholder's Republic," *Agricultural History* 49 (April 1975): 331–42; and Robert E. Shalhope, "Race, Class, Slavery, and the Antebellum Southern Mind," *JSH* 37 (November 1971): 557–74.

65. DeBow, "Non-slaveholders of the South," 67–77.

66. DeBow, 67–77; McKitrick, *Slavery Defended*, 122; John Hope Franklin, "The Great Confrontation: South and the Problem of Change," *JSH* 38 (February 1972): 3–20.

67. Jefferson quoted in Henry S. Randall, *The Life of Thomas Jefferson* (New York: Derby and Jackson, 1858), 1:11. See also Roger Wilkins, *Jefferson's Pillow: The Founding Fathers and the Dilemma of Black Patriotism* (Boston: Beacon, 2001).

68. Hinton Rowan Helper, *The Impending Crisis of the Union: How to Meet It* (New York: Burdick Brothers, 1857), 12, 20, 54, 185–87.

69. *Harper's Weekly* (January 1857); "Barbarism and Civilization," *Atlantic Monthly*, April 1862; Ralph Waldo Emerson, "American Civilization," *Atlantic Monthly*, April 1862; Ralph Waldo Emerson, "Address to the Citizens of Concord on the Fugitive Slave Law," in *Complete Works of Ralph Waldo Emerson*, centennial ed. (Boston: Houghton Mifflin, 1903), 11, 211–13.

70. Harper, "Memoir on Slavery," 82; "Negro and White Slavery: Wherein Do They Differ?," *Southern Quarterly Review* 4 (July 1851): 129; J. D. B. DeBow, "The Rights, Duties, and Remedies of the South," *DeBow's Review* 23 (September 1857): 225–38.

71. *DeBow's Review* 25 (July 1859); J. Quitman Moore, "The Difference of Race between the Northern and Southern People," *Southern Literary Messenger* 30 (June 1860); Holcombe, "Alternative," 84.

72. Rhett quoted in C. Vann Woodward, *The Burden of Southern History* (Baton Rouge: Louisiana State University Press, 1960), 194–95; "The Study of Nature and the Arts of Civilized Life," *DeBow's Review* 30 (May-June 1861): 603, 604.

73. Ian Binnington, *Confederate Visions: Nationalism, Symbolism, and the Imagined South in the Civil War* (Charlottesville: University of Virginia Press, 2013), 3, 7, 148; Michael T. Bernath, *Confederate Minds: The Struggle for Intellectual Independence in the Civil War South* (Chapel Hill: University of North Carolina Press, 2010).

74. Smyth quoted in James W. Silver, *Confederate Morale and Church Propaganda* (Tuscaloosa, Ala.: Confederate Publishing, 1957), 30; Peter J. Parish, "The Road Not Quite Taken: The Constitution of the Confederate States of America," in *Constitutions and National Identity*, ed. Thomas J. Barron, Owen Dudley Edwards, and Patricia Storey (Edinburgh, UK: Quadrisa, 1993); Michael Perman, *Pursuit of Unity: A Political History of the American South* (Chapel Hill: University of North Carolina Press, 2009), 98–101; Benjamin Morgan Palmer, *National Responsibility before God* (New Orleans: Price-Current Steam Book and Job, 1861), 11–13, 26–28. See also Hughes, "Civic Theology," 447–68; and William M. Robinson Jr., "A New Deal in Constitutions," *JSH* 4 (November 1938): 449–61.

75. William W. Frehling, *The South vs. the South: How Anti-Confederate Southerners Shaped the Course of the Civil War* (New York: Oxford University Press, 2001), xi–xv, 201–6; Drew Gilpin Faust, *The Creation of Confederate Nationalism: Ideology and Identity in the Civil War South* (Baton Rouge: Louisiana State University Press, 1989); Paul D. Escott, *After Secession: Jefferson Davis and the Failure of Confederate Nationalism* (Baton Rouge: Louisiana State University Press, 1978), 256–74; Lawrence Powell and Michael Wayne, "Self-Interest and the Decline of Confederate Nationalism," in *The Old South in the Crucible of War*, ed. Harry Owens and James Cooke (Jackson: University Press of Mississippi, 1983), 29–46; David Williams, Teresa Crisp Williams, and David Carlsson, *Plain Folk in a Rich Man's War: Class and Dissent in Confederate Georgia* (Gainesville: University Press of Florida, 2002), 82–88.

76. Binnington, *Confederate Visions*, 141–48.

77. "Three Victories," *Christian Index*, March 15, 1866, 46; Edward A. Pollard, *The Lost Cause: A New Southern History of the War of the Confederates* (New York: E. B. Treat, 1866), 750–52.

78. Nathaniel Hall, *The Moral Significance of the Contrasts between Slavery and Freedom* (Boston: Walker, Wise, 1864), 8–10; Emerson, "American Civilization," 507.

79. Bell Irvin Wiley, *The Life of Billy Yank: The Common Soldier of the Union* (Baton Rouge: Louisiana State University Press, 2008), 97.

80. James Russell Lowell, *The Writings of James Russell Lowell in Prose . . .* (Boston:

Houghton, Mifflin, 1890), 215–16; E. P. Whipple, "Reconstruction and Negro Suffrage," *Atlantic Monthly*, August 1865, 238–47; Jennifer Rae Greeson, *Our South: Geographic Fantasy and the Rise of National Literature* (Cambridge, Mass.: Harvard University Press, 2010), 237.

81. Holcombe, "Alternative," 81–84; Sidney Andrews, *The South since the War* (Boston: Ticknor and Fields, 1866), 22.

82. William Blair, *Cities of the Dead: Contesting the Memory of the Civil War in the South, 1865–1914* (Chapel Hill: University of North Carolina Press, 2004).

83. Eric Foner's *Reconstruction: America's Unfinished Revolution, 1863–1877* (New York: Harper and Row, 1988) remains the standard contemporary account of the immediate post–Civil War period. The historiography of Reconstruction focuses now on its failure in transitioning African Americans to freedom. Mark Wahlgren Summers, in *The Ordeal of the Reunion: A New History of Reconstruction* (Chapel Hill: University of North Carolina Press, 2014), argues that government policies were a success in their stated goals of reunifying the nation, outlawing slavery, and rejecting secession as a viable possibility in the future. Other historians explore the importance of the period for defining citizenship; promoting economic development; creating vital, if besieged, African American institutions; and pointing the nation westward. For recent overviews of new Reconstruction studies, see Luke Harlow, ed., "Forum: The Future of Reconstruction Studies," *Journal of the Civil War* 7 (March 2017); and Carole Emberton and Bruce E. Baker, eds., *Remembering Reconstruction: Struggles over the Meaning of America's Most Turbulent Era* (Baton Rouge: Louisiana State University Press, 2017). Kathryn B. McKee offers a model interdisciplinary study of Mississippi writer Sherwood Bonner in *Reading Reconstruction: Sherwood Bonner and the Literature of the Post–Civil War South* (Baton Rouge: Louisiana State University Press, 2019). For the meanings of southern civilization, the Reconstruction era represented closure of the prewar American generation's struggles to define "American civilization," which northern culture won. It was a transition era for white and Black southerners to engage over whether a common southern civilization could exist.

84. Vance quoted in Richard Current, *Northernizing the South* (Athens: University of Georgia Press, 1983), 79. See also Allen Trelease, *White Terror: The Ku Klux Klan Conspiracy and Southern Reconstruction* (New York: Harper and Row, 1971); and Lou Falkner Williams, *The Great South Carolina Ku Klux Klan Trials, 1871–1872* (Athens: University of Georgia Press, 1976).

85. Chamberlain quoted in Walter Allen, *South Carolina: A Chapter of Reconstruction in the Southern States* (New York: G. P. Putnam's Sons, 1888), 319–20. See also Nicholas Lemann, *Redemption: The Last Battle of the Civil War* (New York: Farrar, Straus and Giroux, 2006).

86. E. L. Godkin, "The White Side of the Southern Question," *Nation*, August 19, 1880, 126.

CHAPTER TWO

1. Randolph McKim, "America Summoned to a Holy War," in *For God and Country; or, The Christian Pulpit in War-Time* (1918; repr., Sydney, Australia: Wentworth, 2016), 81–83.

2. Charles Reagan Wilson, *Baptized in Blood: The Religion of the Lost Cause, 1865–1920* (Athens: University of Georgia Press, 1980), 161–82. For the historiography of the Lost

Cause, see Charles Reagan Wilson, "Preface to the 2009 Edition: The Lost Cause and the Civil Religion in Recent Historiography," in *Baptized in Blood: The Religion of the Lost Cause, 1865–1920*, 2nd ed. (Athens: University of Georgia Press, 2009), ix–xx. For the American and southern civil religions, see Arthur Remillard, *Southern Civil Religions: Imagining the Good Society in the Post-Reconstruction South* (Athens: University of Georgia Press, 2011), 1–14.

3. E. A. Pollard, *The Lost Cause Regained* (New York: G. W. Carleton, 1868), 13–14.

4. Charles Reagan Wilson, "The Religion of the Lost Cause, 1865–1920," *JSH* 46 (May 1980): 219–38; R. L. Dabney, *The New South: A Discourse* (Raleigh, N.C.: Edwards, Broughton, 1883), 15–16.

5. Bagby quoted in David Goldfield, *Still Fighting the Civil War: The American South and Southern History* (Baton Rouge: Louisiana State University Press, 2004), 21; James C. Cobb, *Away Down South: A History of the Southern Identity* (New York: Oxford University Press, 2005), 74; Thomas Nelson Page, *Social Life in Old Virginia before the War* (New York: Charles Scribner's Sons, 1897), 184–85. See also Fred C. Hobson, *Tell about the South: The Southern Rage to Explain* (Baton Rouge: Louisiana State University Press, 1983), 137–57.

6. Thomas Nelson Page, "The Want of a History of the Southern People," in *The Old South: Essays Social and Political* (New York: Charles Scribner's Sons, 1903), 253, 254–66, 269.

7. Page, 268.

8. Cobb, *Away Down South*, 78; Rollin G. Osterweis, *The Myth of the Lost Cause, 1865–1900* (Hamden, Conn.: Archon Books, 1973), 5–6.

9. David Blight, *Frederick Douglass's Civil War: Keeping Faith in Jubilee* (Baton Rouge: Louisiana State University Press, 1989), 228–31.

10. Henry Grady, *The New South: Writings and Speeches of Henry Grady*, ed. Mills Lane (Savannah, Ga.: Beehive, 1971), 107–8. See Paul M. Gaston, *The New South Creed: A Study in Southern Mythmaking* (New York: Vintage Books, 1970), 117; Albert Taylor Bledsoe, "The Origin of the Late War," *Southern Review* 1 (April 1867): 257–74; and Broadus Mitchell, *The Rise of the Cotton Mills in the South* (Baltimore: Johns Hopkins University Press, 1921), 107.

11. Albert Taylor Bledsoe, "Chivalrous Southrons," *Southern Review* 6 (July 1869): 109.

12. Broadus Mitchell's *The Rise of the Cotton Mills in the South* (107) portrays late nineteenth-century textile mill owners as the South's new cavaliers. See also James C. Cobb, *Industrialization and Southern Society, 1877–1984* (Chicago: Dorsey, 1984), 18; and Numan V. Bartley, "Politics and Ideology," in *Law and Politics*, ed. James W. Ely Jr. and Bradley G. Bond, vol. 10 of *The New Encyclopedia of Southern Culture*, ed. Charles Reagan Wilson (Chapel Hill: University of North Carolina Press, 2008), 150.

13. Mitchell, *Rise of the Cotton Mills*, 107.

14. Jacquelyn Dowd Hall, James Leloudis, Robert Korstad, Mary Murphy, Lu Ann Jones, and Christopher B. Daly, *Like a Family: The Making of a Southern Cotton Mill World* (Chapel Hill: University of North Carolina Press, 1987); David L. Carlton, *Mill and Town in South Carolina, 1880–1920* (Baton Rouge: Louisiana State University Press, 1982).

15. Richard H. Edmonds, *The South's Redemption: From Poverty to Prosperity* (Baltimore: Manufacturer's Record, 1890), 3–4; Richard H. Edmonds, *Facts about the South* (Baltimore: Manufacturer's Record, 1902), 37.

16. Edmonds quoted in Gaston, *New South Creed*, 44, 64; Wilbur Fisk Tillett, "The

White Man of the New South," *Century Magazine*, March 1887, 776; Haygood quoted in Cobb, *Away Down South*, 75.

17. Joseph Creech, *Righteous Indignation: Religion and the Populist Revolution* (Urbana: University of Illinois Press, 2010), 29, 128.

18. Creech, vii, xix.

19. Bruce Palmer, "Southern Populists Remember: The Reform Alternative to Southern Sectionalism," *Southern Studies* 17 (Summer 1978): 134, 136; Creech, *Righteous Indignation*, 102.

20. Creech, *Righteous Indignation*, 43; Robert C. McMath, *Populist Vanguard: The History of the Southern Farmers' Alliance* (Chapel Hill: University of North Carolina Press, 1975), 133–36.

21. Creech, *Righteous Indignation*, 28, 90.

22. C. Vann Woodward, *Tom Watson* (1938; repr., New York: Oxford University Press, 1963), 220.

23. John C. Green, "Believers for Bush, Godly for Gore: Religion and the 2000 Election in the South," in *The 2000 Presidential Election in the South: Partisanship and Southern Party Systems in the Twenty-First Century*, ed. Robert P. Steed and Laurence W. Morland (Westport, Conn.: Praeger, 2001), 13–15.

24. Katharine Du Pre Lumpkin, *The Making of a Southerner* (1946; repr., Athens: University of Georgia Press, 1991), 128.

25. Creech, *Righteous Indignation*, 130, 133; David S. Cecelski, ed., *Democracy Betrayed: The Wilmington Race Riot of 1898 and Its Legacy* (Chapel Hill: University of North Carolina Press, 1998).

26. S. A. Knapp, "Back to the Farm," Seaman Asahel Knapp Papers, box 2, folder 8, Southwest Collection/Special Collections, Texas Tech University, Lubbock, Texas; William L. Bowers, *The Country Life Movement in America, 1900–1920* (Washington, N.Y.: Kennikat, 1974); Natalie J. Ring, *The Problem South: Region, Empire, and the New Liberal State* (Athens: University of Georgia Press, 2012), 121–31.

27. Ring, *Problem South*, 121–31.

28. U. B. Phillips, "The Plantation as a Civilizing Factor," *Sewanee Review* 12, no. 3 (1904): 257–67.

29. Phillips, 257–67.

30. Jack Temple Kirby, "Clarence Poe's Vision of a Segregated Great Rural Civilization," *South Atlantic Quarterly* 68 (Winter 1969): 27–38.

31. Kirby, 27–38. See also Elizabeth Herbin-Triant, "Southern Segregation South Africa–Style," *Agricultural History* 87 (April 2013): 170–93.

32. J. Wayne Flynt, "Social Class in the American South: Historical Perspectives," in *Social Class*, ed. Larry J. Griffin, Peggy G. Hargis, and Charles Reagan Wilson, vol. 20 of *The New Encyclopedia of Southern Culture*, ed. Charles Reagan Wilson (Chapel Hill: University of North Carolina Press, 2012), 6–12.

33. Glenn Feldman, *Politics and Religion in the White South* (Lexington: University Press of Kentucky, 2005), 295.

34. Feldman, 296, 297.

35. Charles Reagan Wilson, "The Invention of Southern Tradition: The Writing and Ritualization of Southern History," in *Flashes of a Southern Spirit: Meanings of the Spirit in the U.S. South* (Athens: University of Georgia Press, 2011).

36. Daniel Joseph Singal, *The War Within: From Victorian to Modernist Thought in the South, 1919–1945* (Chapel Hill: University of North Carolina Press, 1982) 5, 33.

37. Lewis Henry Morgan, *Ancient Society: Researches in the Lines of Human Progress from Savagery through Barbarism to Civilization* (1877; repr., Tucson: University of Arizona Press, 1971). See also Matthew Frye Jacobson, *Barbarian Virtues: The United States Encounters Foreign Peoples at Home and Abroad, 1876–1917* (New York: Hill and Wang, 2000), 53, 144–46.

38. Jacobson, *Barbarian Virtues*, 50–51.

39. Singal, *War Within*, 32.

40. Singal, 30; John E. White, "The Backward People in the South," *Our Home Field*, May 1909, 15–17.

41. Mark M. Smith, *How Race Is Made: Slavery, Segregation, and the Senses* (Chapel Hill: University of North Carolina Press, 2006); Thomas Pearce Bailey, *Race Orthodoxy in the South, and Other Aspects of the Negro Question* (New York: Neale Publishing Company, 1914), 93; I. A. Newby, *Jim Crow's Defense: Anti-Negro Thought in America, 1900–1930* (Baton Rouge: Louisiana State University Press, 1965), 4, 27, 42.

42. Ring, *Problem South*, 91.

43. Victor I. Masters, *The Call of the South* (Atlanta: Home Mission Board of the Southern Baptist Convention, 1918), 53.

44. Charles Edward Robert, *Negro Civilization in the South: Educational, Social, and Religious Advancement of the Colored People* (Nashville: printed by the Wheeler brothers for the author, 1880), 5–6, 71, 104–5.

45. Quotes in Lawrence J. Friedman, *The White Savage: Racial Fantasies in the Postbellum South* (Englewood Cliffs, N.J.: Prentice-Hall, 1970), 22; and Stephen Kantrowitz, *Ben Tillman and the Reconstruction of White Supremacy* (Chapel Hill: University of North Carolina Press, 2000), 258–59.

46. Tillman quoted in Kantrowitz, *Ben Tillman*, 270. See also Friedman, *White Savage*, 22.

47. Thomas Dixon, *The Leopard's Spots: A Romance of the White Man's Burden—1865–1900* (New York: Doubleday, 1902), 283–84; Mary White Ovington, "Revisiting the South: Changes in Twenty-One Years," *Crisis*, April 1927, 66; Harilaos Stecopoulos, *Reconstructing the World: Southern Fictions and U.S. Imperialisms, 1898–1976* (Ithaca, N.Y.: Cornell University Press, 2018), 24. See also Jennifer Ritterhouse, *Growing Up Jim Crow: How Black and White Southerners Learned Race* (Chapel Hill: University of North Carolina Press, 2006), 74.

48. Clifton Johnson, *Highways and Byways of the South* (New York: Macmillan, 1905), 352; Grace Elizabeth Hale, *Making Whiteness: The Culture of Segregation in the South* (New York: Pantheon Books, 1998), 26; Ray Stannard Baker, *Following the Color Line: American Negro Citizenship in the Progressive Era*, ed. Dewey Grantham (1908; repr., New York: Harper Torchbooks, 1964), 31.

49. John B. Boles, *The South through Time: A History of an American Region* (Englewood Cliffs, N.J.: Prentice-Hall, 1995), 422–23.

50. Lumpkin, *Making of a Southerner*, 215; Rice quoted in Jane Dailey, Glenda Elizabeth Gilmore, and Bryant Simon, eds., *Jumpin' Jim Crow: Southern Politics from Civil War to Civil Rights* (Princeton, N.J.: Princeton University Press, 2000), 166; Charles W. Chesnutt, *The Marrow of Tradition* (1901; repr., New York: Arno, 1969), 57; Baker, *Following the*

Color Line, quoted in Hale, *Making Whiteness,* 26. See also Brian Norman and Piper Kendrix Williams, *Representing Segregation: Toward an Aesthetics of Living Jim Crow, and other Forms of Racial Division* (Albany: State University of New York Press, 2010).

51. Karen L. Cox, *Dreaming of Dixie: How the South Was Created in American Popular Culture* (Chapel Hill: University of North Carolina Press, 2011); Hale, *Making Whiteness,* 151–68; Kenneth Goings, *Mammy and Uncle Mose: Black Collectibles and American Stereotyping* (Bloomington: Indiana University Press, 1994).

52. Joan L. Silverman, "*The Birth of a Nation,*" in *Media,* ed. Allison Graham and Sharon Monteith, vol. 18 of *The New Encyclopedia of Southern Culture,* ed. Charles Reagan Wilson (Chapel Hill: University of North Carolina Press, 2011), 199–200.

53. For useful overviews of ethnic life in the South, see Celeste Ray, ed., *Ethnicity,* vol. 6 of *The New Encyclopedia of Southern Culture,* ed. Charles Reagan Wilson (Chapel Hill: University of North Carolina Press, 2007); and Mikaela M. Adams and Ted Ownby, "New Stories for a 'New South': Race-Making, Ethnic Diversity, Urbanization, and Gendered Politics," in *Reinterpreting Southern Histories: Essays in Historiography,* ed. Craig Thomas Friend and Lorrie Glover (Baton Rouge: Louisiana State University Press, 2020), 281–84.

54. Bobbie Malone, "Jews," in Ray, *Ethnicity,* 175–77; Eli Evans, *The Provincials: A Personal History of Jews in the South* (New York: Atheneum, 1976).

55. William Mark Habeeb, "Syrians and Lebanese"; Gary R. Mormino, "Italians"; and Melinda Chow, "Chinese," all in Ray, *Ethnicity,* 232–34, 171–73, 122–24; Adams and Ownby, "New Stories," 284–85; Leslie Bow, *Partly Colored: Asian Americans and Racial Anomaly in the Segregated South* (New York: New York University Press, 2010), 5.

56. James L. Peacock offers a model of the South's movement from a dual society to a pluralistic society in *Grounded Globalism: How the U.S. Embraces the World* (Athens: University of Georgia Press, 2007), 76–101. See also Stephanie Cole and Alison M. Parker, eds., *Beyond Black and White: Race, Ethnicity, and Gender in the U.S. South and Southwest* (College Station: Texas A&M University Press, 2004).

57. Theda Perdue, "The Legacy of Indian Removal," *JSH* 78 (February 2012): 3–36, quote 22.

58. Amy Louise Wood, *Lynching and Spectacle: Witnessing Racial Violence in America, 1890–1940* (Chapel Hill: University of North Carolina Press, 2009), 1–7; William I. Hair and Amy Louise Wood, "Lynching," in *Violence,* ed. Amy Louise Wood, vol. 19 of *The New Encyclopedia of Southern Culture,* ed. Charles Reagan Wilson (Chapel Hill: University of North Carolina Press, 2011), 97–103; northerner quoted in Bederman, *Manliness and Civilization,* 49; Ray Stannard Baker, "What Is a Lynching? A Study of Mob Violence, South and North," *McClure's,* January 1905, 299–314.

59. Wood, *Lynching and Spectacle,* 5–7.

60. Wood, 5–15.

61. Wood, 48.

62. Wood, 48–49, 62, 63, 64; P. L. James, *The Facts in the Case of the Horrible Murder of Myrtle Vance and Its Fearful Expiation at Paris, Texas, February 1st, 1893* (Paris, Tex.: P. L. James, 1893), 14, 149. See also Donald G. Mathews, "The Southern Rite of Human Sacrifice," *Journal of Southern Religion* 3 (August 2000), http://jsr.fsu.edu/mathews .htm.

63. Wood, *Lynching and Spectacle,* 49.

64. Masters, *Call of the South,* 73.

65. Andrew Sledd, "The Negro: Another View," *Atlantic Monthly*, August 1902, 69–71; Cobb, *Away Down South*, 97; Jennifer Ritterhouse, *Growing Up Jim Crow: How Black and White Southern Children Learned Race* (Chapel Hill: University of North Carolina Press, 2006), 76.

66. Ida B. Wells, *Crusade for Justice*, ed. Alfreda M. Duster (Chicago: University of Chicago Press, 1970), 21; Ida B. Wells-Barnett, *Southern Horrors: Lynch Law in All Its Phases*, reprinted in *On Lynchings* (Salem, N.H.: Ayer, 1987); Bederman, *Manliness and Civilization*, 58. Mia Bay discusses the concept among African Americans of white savagery in *The White Image in the Black Mind: African-American Ideas about White People, 1830–1925* (New York: Oxford University Press, 2000), 95–107.

67. Ida B. Wells, "A Sermon on Ibsen—a Coloured Woman in the Pulpit," *Christian World*, March 14, 1894, 187; Bederman, *Manliness and Civilization*, 60; Wells, *Crusade for Justice*, 101.

68. Bederman, *Manliness and Civilization*, 63, 67, 68; Wells, *Crusade for Justice*, 157–58.

69. Bederman, *Manliness and Civilization*, 70.

70. Nina Silber, *The Romance of Reunion: Northerners and the South, 1865–1900* (Chapel Hill: University of North Carolina Press, 1993); Harilaos Stecopoulos, *Reconstructing the World: Southern Fictions and U.S. Imperialisms, 1898–1976* (Ithaca, N.Y.: Cornell University Press, 2008), 18–19; Edward J. Blum, *Reforging the White Republic: Race, Religion, and American Nationalism, 1865–1898* (Baton Rouge: Louisiana State University Press, 2005).

71. J. L. Watkins, "The Future Demand for American Cotton," quoted in Ring, *Problem South*, 103; Clarence H. Poe, "The Rich Kingdom of Cotton," *World's Work*, November 1904, 548.

72. Holmes quoted in Catherine Clinton and Nina Silber, eds., *Divided Houses: Gender and the Civil War* (New York: Oxford University Press, 1993), 289; DeForest quoted in Silber, *Romance of Reunion*, 52.

73. Albion Tourgee, "The South as a Field for Fiction," *Forum*, December 1888. Jennifer Greeson explores the relationship among the South, national literature in the nineteenth century, and empire in *Our South: Geographic Fantasy and the Rise of National Literature* (Cambridge, Mass.: Harvard University Press, 2010).

74. Greeson, *Our South*, 1; Ring, *Problem South*, 44–45.

75. Ring, *Problem South*, 84, 85.

76. Ellsworth H. Huntington, *Civilization and Climate*, 3rd ed. (New Haven, Conn.: Yale University Press, 1924), 24, 35, 42–43.

77. S. A. Hamilton, "The New Race Question in the South," *Arena*, April 1902, 352–53; Alexander J. McElway, "The Child Labor Problem—a Study in Degeneracy," *Annals of the American Academy of Political and Social Science* 27 (March 1906): 55; Ring, *Problem South*, 136.

78. Henry Childs Merwin, "On Being Civilized Too Much," *Atlantic Monthly*, June 1897, 838–46.

79. Will Wallace Harney, "A Strange Land and a Peculiar People," quoted in Henry D. Shapiro, *Appalachia on Our Mind: The Southern Mountains and Mountaineers in the American Consciousness, 1870–1920* (Chapel Hill: University of North Carolina Press, 1978), 3–13; Karl Hagstrom Miller, *Segregating Sound: Inventing Folk and Pop Music in the Age of Jim Crow* (Durham, N.C.: Duke University Press, 2010). Jennifer Greeson (*Our South*, 259–68) argues that local color writings represented the national culture's invasion

of the South during Reconstruction and promoted the new creation of a specifically "southern literature."

80. E. C. Perow, "Songs and Rhymes from the South," *Journal of American Folklore* 25, no. 96 (1912): 137–38; Miller, *Segregating Sound*, 104–6.

81. Silber, *Romance of Reunion*, 78–79, 129.

82. Fox quoted in Shapiro, *Appalachia on Our Mind*, 76–80; David E. Whisnant, *All That Is Native and Fine: The Politics of Culture in an American Region* (Chapel Hill: University of North Carolina Press, 1987), 5–16.

83. Miller, *Segregating Sound*, 101–10, 118.

84. Atticus Haygood, *The New South* (1880; repr., Atlanta: Emory University Press, 1950), 10, 12.

85. George Washington Cable, *The Grandissimes: A Story of Creole Life* (1880; repr., New York: Penguin Books, 1988), 156; M. E. Junius, ed., *Critical Dialogue between Aboo and Caboo; or, a Grandissimes Ascension* (Mingo City, La.: Great Publicity House of Sam Slick Allspice, 1880), 12.

86. George Washington Cable, "Freedmen's Case in Equity," *Century Magazine*, February 1885, 409–18; George Washington Cable, "Literature in the Southern States," in *The Negro Question: A Selection of Writings on Civil Rights in the South by George W. Cable*, ed. Arlin Turner (New York: W. W. Norton, 1958), 43–44.

87. George Washington Cable, "The Silent South," *Century Magazine*, September 1885, 674–91.

88. Walter Hines Page, *The Rebuilding of Old Commonwealths: Essays toward the Training of the Forgotten Man in the Southern States* (New York: Doubleday, 1902), 121–38.

89. Walter Hines Page, *The Southerner*, ed. Scott Romine (1909; repr., Columbia: University of South Carolina Press, 2008), 108–10, 134–35; Nicholas Worth, "The Autobiography of a Southerner since the Civil War," pt. 4, *Atlantic Monthly*, October 1906, 474–75. Page's semiautobiographical novel was originally serialized in the *Atlantic Monthly* in 1906 under the pen name "Nicholas Worth," and it was published as *The Southerner* in 1909.

90. Walter Hines Page, "The Last Hold of the Southern Bully," *Forum*, November 1893, 303–14.

91. W. D. Weatherford, "How to Enlist the Welfare Agencies of the South for Improvement of Conditions among the Negroes," in *The Human Way: Addresses on Race Problems at the Southern Sociological Congress, Atlanta, 1913*, ed. James E. McCulloch (Nashville: Southern Sociological Congress, 1913), 9.

92. Weatherford, 9.

93. Mrs. J. D. Hammond, "The Test of Civilization," in McCulloch, *Human Way*, 112–17.

94. William Preston Trent, "Tendencies of Higher Life in the South," *Atlantic Monthly*, June 1897, 768, 769.

95. Robert, *Negro Civilization*, 3, 5, 82, 171.

96. Robert, 171.

97. Robert J. Norrell, *Up from History: The Life of Booker T. Washington* (Cambridge, Mass.: Belknap Press of Harvard University Press, 2009), 84, 117.

98. W. Fitzhugh Brundage, *The Southern Past: A Conflict of History and Memory* (Cambridge, Mass.: Belknap Press of Harvard University Press, 2005), 91. See also John Giggie, *After Redemption: Jim Crow and the Transformation of African American Religion in the Delta, 1875–1915* (New York: Oxford University Press, 2007), 72–75.

99. Albert J. Raboteau, "Martin Luther King, Jr., and the Tradition of Black Religious Protest," in *Religion and the Life of the Nation*, ed. Rowland A. Sherrill (Urbana: University of Illinois Press, 1990), 46–63.

100. Wilson Jeremiah Moses, *Alexander Crummell: A Study of Civilization and Discontent* (New York: Oxford University Press, 1989), 97.

101. Wilson Jeremiah Moses, ed., *Destiny and Race: Selected Writings, 1840–1898* (Amherst: University of Massachusetts Press, 1992), 287.

102. Kevin Gaines, *Uplifting the Race: Black Middle-Class Ideology and Leadership in the United States since 1890* (Chapel Hill: University of North Carolina Press, 1996); Evelyn Brooks Higginbotham, *Righteous Discontent: The Women's Movement in the Black Baptist Church, 1880–1920* (Cambridge, Mass.: Harvard University Press, 1993); Lawrence Schenbeck, *Racial Uplift and American Music, 1878–1943* (Jackson: University Press of Mississippi, 2012).

103. Booker T. Washington, *Up from Slavery: An Autobiography* (New York: Doubleday, 1901).

104. Norrell, *Up from History*, 122–27.

105. Norrell, 122–27.

106. Norrell, 122–27.

107. Norrell, 126.

108. Norrell, 126–28; Norman E. Hodges, "Booker T. Washington: We Wear the Mask," in *Black Leaders and Black Ideologies in the South: Resistance and Nonviolence* (New York: Routledge, 2005), 76–110.

109. *Tom Watson's Magazine*, June 1905, 391–93; Thomas Dixon Jr., *Saturday Evening Post*, August 1905, in Norrell, *Up from History*, 325; Villard quoted in Norrell, *Up from History*, 328.

110. David Sehat, "The Civilizing Mission of Booker T. Washington," *JSH* 73 (May 2007), 346; Booker T. Washington, "The South and Negro Education," *Southern Workman* 38 (June 1909): 330–34.

111. Norrell, *Up from History*, 196–97.

112. Booker T. Washington, speech, National Educational Association, July 16, 1884, quoted in Norrell, *Up from History*, 84; Booker T. Washington, "The Awakening of the Negro," *Atlantic Monthly*, September 1996, 326.

113. Louis R. Harlan, *Booker T. Washington: The Wizard of Tuskegee, 1901–1915* (New York: Oxford University Press, 1983), 202–5; Hodges, "Booker T. Washington," 76–110; Washington, "South and Negro Education," 330–34; John Spencer Bassett, "Stirring Up the Fires of Race Antipathy," *South Atlantic Quarterly* 2 (October 1903): 297–305.

114. John Tyler Morgan, "The Future of the American Negro," *North American Review* 139 (July 1884): 83–84.

115. Sehat, "Civilizing Mission," 324.

116. W. E. B. Du Bois, *The Souls of Black Folk*, ed. Nathan Hare and Alvin Poussaint (New York: New American Library, 1969), 35–36; David Levering Lewis, *W. E. B. Du Bois: Biography of a Race, 1868–1919* (New York: Henry Holt, 1993). Mia Bay (*White Image*, 194–202) places Du Bois in the context of civilization.

117. W. E. B. Du Bois, "Beyond the Veil in a Virginia Town," in *Against Racism: Unpublished Essays, Papers, Addresses, 1887–1961*, ed. Herbert Aptheker (Amherst: University of Massachusetts Press, 1985), 49–50.

118. W. E. B. Du Bois, "The Spirit of Modern Europe," in *The Problem of the Color Line*

at the Turn of the Twentieth Century, ed. Nathan Dimitri Chandler (New York: Fordham University Press, 2015), 139–58, quotes 141, 146, 151.

119. Du Bois, 155–56.

120. Stephanie J. Shaw, *W. E. B. Du Bois and the Souls of Black Folk* (Chapel Hill: University of North Carolina Press, 2013), 7, 29–30.

121. Shaw, 16, 26, 33, 53.

122. Shaw, 22.

123. Shaw, 22, 23.

124. Paul Oliver, *Blues Fell This Morning: The Meaning of the Blues* (New York: Horizon, 1960), 51; Neil R. McMillan, *Dark Journey: Black Mississippians in the Age of Jim Crow* (Urbana: University of Illinois Press, 1990), 265, 274. See also James R. Grossman, *Land of Hope: Chicago, Black Southerners, and the Great Migration* (Chicago: University of Chicago Press, 1989); and Isabell Wilkerson, *The Warmth of Other Suns: The Epic Story of America's Great Migration* (New York: Random House, 2010).

125. Randall K. Burkett, *Garveyism as a Religious Movement: The Institutionalization of a Black Civil Religion* (Metuchen, N.J.: Scarecrow and the American Theological Library Association, 1978), 7–9; Mary Robinson, *Grassroots Garveyism: The Universal Negro Improvement Association in the Rural South* (Chapel Hill: University of North Carolina Press, 2007); Kenneth C. Barnes, "Universal Negro Improvement Association (UNIA)," Encyclopedia of Arkansas, https://encyclopediaofarkansas.net/entries/universal -negro-improvement-association-6484/.

126. Albert Bushnell Hart, *The Southern South* (New York: D. Appleton, 1910), 218; Joel Williamson, *The Crucible of Race: Black-White Relations in the American South since Emancipation* (New York: Oxford University Press, 1984), 475.

127. Moffitt and Cotton quoted in Brundage, *Southern Past*, 29. See also Wilson, "Invention of Southern Tradition," 27–47.

128. Samuel Chiles Mitchell, preface to *The South in the Building of the Nation*, ed. Samuel Chiles Mitchell (Richmond, Va.: Southern Historical Publication Society, 1909), 10:xix, xxv, xxvii.

129. Williamson, *Crucible of Race*, 476.

130. Robert Bush, "Dr. Alderman's Symposium on the South," *Mississippi Quarterly* 27 (Winter 1973–74): 3–19.

131. Kenneth K. Bailey, *Southern White Protestantism in the Twentieth Century* (New York: Harper and Row, 1964), 6.

132. Masters, *Call of the South*, 52, 108.

133. Dewey Grantham, *The South in Modern America: A Region at Odds* (New York: HarperCollins, 1994), 84.

134. Arthur S. Link, "Woodrow Wilson: The American as Southerner," *JSH* 36 (February 1970): 3–17.

135. Link, 3–17.

136. "The Reunion in Washington," *Confederate Veteran* 25 (July 1917): 2297–98; "Address of President Woodrow Wilson," in *Reunion of the UCV . . . 1917*, ed. United Confederate Veterans (Washington, D.C.: United Confederate Veterans, 1918), 22–24.

137. Grantham, *South in Modern America*, 65.

CHAPTER THREE

1. H. L. Mencken, "The Sahara of the Bozart," in *Prejudices*, 2nd ser. (New York: Alfred A. Knopf, 1920), 136–54.

2. Mencken, 136–54.

3. George B. Tindall, "The Benighted South: Origins of a Modern Image," *VQR* 40 (Spring 1964): 281–94.

4. Paul Valery, *Variety: Paul Valery*, trans. Malcom Cowley (New York: Harcourt, Brace, 1927), 4.

5. Ezra Pound, *Selected Poems* (New York: New Directions, 1957), 64; Warren I. Susman, *Culture as History: The Transformation of American Society in the Twentieth Century* (New York: Pantheon, 1984), 105–21, quotes 109, 113.

6. Samuel Daniel Schimal Lausen and V. F. Calverton, *Sex in Civilization* (New York: Macaulay Company, 1929); David Cannadine, *The Undivided Past: Humanity beyond Our Differences* (New York: Vintage Books, 2013), 233; Frederick J. Teggart, *The Process of History* (New Haven, Conn.: Yale University Press, 1918), 6.

7. Oswald Spengler, *The Decline of the West* (New York: Alfred A. Knopf, 1918, 1922), 1:106.

8. Ransom quoted in Michael O'Brien, *The Idea of the American South, 1920–41* (Baltimore: Johns Hopkins University Press, 1979), 123; Allen Tate, "Books: Fundamentalism," review of *The Decline of the West*, vol. 1, by Oswald Spengler, *Nation*, May 12, 1926, 532, 534.

9. Calkins, Debs, and Stearns quoted in Susman, *Culture as History*, 115. See Warren I. Susman, "Culture and Civilization in the Nineteen-Twenties," in *Culture as History*, 105–21; James Truslow Adams, *Our Business Civilization: Some Aspects of American Culture* (New York: Albert and Charles Boni, 1929), 29; and Charles A. Beard and Mary R. Beard, *The Rise of American Civilization* (New York: Macmillan, 1927), 1:vii.

10. Douglas Southall Freeman, "Virginia: A Gentle Dominion," *Nation*, July 16, 1924, 68–71.

11. Paul Conkin, *Southern Agrarians* (Knoxville: University of Tennessee Press, 1988); Warren quoted in C. Vann Woodward, "Why the Southern Renaissance?," in *The Future of the Past* (New York: Macmillan, 1989), 216–17; Wolfe to his mother, May 1923, in *Thomas Wolfe's Letters to His Mother, Julia Elizabeth Wolfe*, ed. John Skally Terry (New York: Scribner's, 1943), 50.

12. Susan V. Donaldson, introduction to *I'll Take My Stand: The South and the Agrarian Tradition*, by Twelve Southerners (1930; repr., Baton Rouge: Louisiana University Press, 2006), xxxiv; Michael Kreyling, *Inventing Southern Literature* (Jackson: University Press of Mississippi, 1998), xii. Donaldson and Kreyling are among recent commentators who stress the current predominant scholarly interpretation of the Agrarians as most important for their attempt to impose a singular, conservative ideological vision of the South, focusing especially on issues of race and gender. The best overall study of the Agrarians in the context of southern history is Conkin, *Southern Agrarians*. See also Paul V. Murphy, *The Rebuke of History: The Southern Agrarians and American Conservative Thought* (Chapel Hill: University of North Carolina Press, 2001); Mark G. Malvasi, *The Unregenerate South: The Agrarian Thought of John Crowe Ransom, Allen Tate, and Donald Davidson* (Baton Rouge: Louisiana State University Press, 1997); and John J. Langdale III,

Superfluous Southerners: Cultural Conservatism and the South, 1920–1980 (Columbia: University of Missouri Press, 2012).

13. "Foreword," *Fugitive* 1 (April 1922): 2; Malvasi, *Unregenerate South*, 8; Charlotte H. Beck, *The Fugitive Legacy: A Critical History* (Baton Rouge: Louisiana State University Press, 2001). Angie Maxwell effectively connects the threads among the Fugitives, Agrarians, and New Critics in *The Indicted South: Public Criticism, Southern Inferiority, and the Politics of Whiteness* (Chapel Hill: University of North Carolina Press, 2014).

14. Ransom quoted in John T. Kneebone, *Southern Liberal Journalists and the Issue of Race, 1920–1944* (Chapel Hill: University of North Carolina Press, 1985), 56; industrial promoter quoted in Stringfellow Barr, "Shall Slavery Come South?," *VQR* 6 (October 1930): 489; Broadus Mitchell, "Fleshpots in the South," *VQR* 3 (April 1927): 171, 176.

15. Edwin Mims, *The Advancing South* (Garden City, N.Y.: Doubleday, Page, 1926); O'Brien, *Idea*, 12, 15.

16. Mencken quoted in Susan Ketchin, *The Christ-Haunted Landscape: Faith and Doubt in Southern Fiction* (Jackson: University Press of Mississippi, 1994), 347; Donald Davidson *Southern Writers in the Modern World* (Athens: University of Georgia Press, 1958), 195, 30, 40; Tate to Davidson, March 1, 1927, in *The Literary Correspondence of Donald Davidson and Allen Tate*, ed. John T. Fain and Thomas Daniel Young (Athens: University of Georgia Press, 1974), 191–92; Jeff Moran, "Scopes Trial," in *Science and Medicine*, ed. James G. Thomas Jr. and Charles Reagan Wilson, vol. 22 of *The New Encyclopedia of Southern Culture*, ed. Charles Reagan Wilson (Chapel Hill: University of North Carolina Press, 2012), 246–48.

17. John Crowe Ransom, "The South Defends Its Heritage," *Harper's Magazine*, June 1929, 108–18; John Crowe Ransom, "The South—Old or New?," *Sewanee Review* 36 (April 1928): 139–47; Conkin, *Southern Agrarians*, 48.

18. Donald Davidson, "The First Fruits of Dayton," *Forum*, June 1928, 896–907.

19. Tate to Davidson, August 10, 1929, in Fain and Young, *Literary Correspondence*, 229–33.

20. Fain and Young, 255.

21. Allen Tate, *Stonewall Jackson: The Good Soldier* (New York: Minton, Balch, 1928); Allen Tate, *Jefferson Davis: His Rise and Fall* (New York: Minton, Balch, 1929), 301–2; Tate to Davidson, August 10, 1929, in Fain and Young, *Literary Correspondence*, 229–30.

22. Twelve Southerners, "A Statement of Principles," in *I'll Take My Stand*, xxxviii; Conkin, *Southern Agrarians*, 58.

23. Twelve Southerners, "Statement of Principles," xliv; Michael Kazin and Joseph A. McCartin, *Americanism: New Perspectives on the History of an Ideal* (Chapel Hill: University of North Carolina Press, 2006), 1.

24. Twelve Southerners, "Statement of Principles," xxix, xxxix.

25. Twelve Southerners, xxxviii–xxxix.

26. Twelve Southerners, xlii, xliii.

27. Twelve Southerners, xliv.

28. Twelve Southerners, xlvi. For pastoral in the Agrarians, see Richard Gray, *Writing the South: Ideas of an American Region* (1986; repr., Baton Rouge: Louisiana State University Press, 1997), 135.

29. John Crowe Ransom, "Reconstructed but Unregenerate," in Twelve Southerners, *I'll Take My Stand*, 11–13, 6, 23.

30. Ransom, 12–14, 21, 27.

31. Ransom, 14, 21.

32. Ransom, 12–14, 16, 17, 21, 23.

33. Donald Davidson, "A Mirror for Artists," in Twelve Southerners, *I'll Take My Stand*, 28, 32, 33, 34, 47. Conservative scholar Mark Royden Winchell offers a useful corrective to much of the recent scholarship on the Agrarians in his intellectual biography of Davidson, *Where No Flag Flies: Donald Davidson and the Southern Resistance* (Columbia: University of Missouri Press, 2000).

34. Davidson, "Mirror for Artists," 32–33.

35. Davidson, 53–54.

36. Davidson, 54.

37. Frank Owsley, "The Irrepressible Conflict," in Twelve Southerners, *I'll Take My Stand*, 63, 66.

38. Owsley, 66, 70–71, 74.

39. Owsley, 71.

40. Lyle H. Lanier, "A Critique of the Philosophy of Progress," in Twelve Southerners, *I'll Take My Stand*, 122–25.

41. Allen Tate, "Remarks on the Southern Religion," in Twelve Southerners, *I'll Take My Stand*, 162–74.

42. Herman Clarence Nixon, "Whither Southern Economy?," in Twelve Southerners, *I'll Take My Stand*, 182, 199.

43. Andrew Nelson Lytle, *Bedford Forrest and His Critter Company* (1931; repr., London: Eyre and Spottiswoode, 1939), 16.

44. Andrew Nelson Lytle, "The Hind Tit," in Twelve Southerners, *I'll Take My Stand*, 204, 205, 206, 207, 234.

45. Lytle, 234, 235, 242.

46. Lytle, 224–26, 232, 244.

47. Robert Penn Warren, "The Briar Patch," in Twelve Southerners, *I'll Take My Stand*, 252, 253, 255.

48. Warren, 258.

49. Stark Young, "Not in Memoriam, but in Defense," in Twelve Southerners, *I'll Take My Stand*, 358.

50. Young, 328, 329, 336–37, 348.

51. Young, 348, 350.

52. "Making of Protest by 12 Southerners of Agrarian Tradition Issues Today: 'I'll Take My Stand,' Published by Harper's Voices Opposition to Industrialism," *Nashville Tennessean*, November 12, 1930; Knickerbocker, Graves, and Eliot quoted in Thomas Daniel Young, *Waking Their Neighbors Up: The Nashville Agrarians Rediscovered* (Athens: University of Georgia Press, 1982), 20–21.

53. Barr, "Shall Slavery Come South?," 488; Arthur Krock, "Industrialism and the Agrarian Tradition in the South," *New York Times Book Review*, January 1931, 3; Gerald W. Johnson, "The South Faces Itself," *VQR* 7 (January 1931): 157; Thomas Daniel Young, *Waking Their Neighbors Up*, 21.

54. Gerald W. Johnson, "The South Faces Itself," *VQR* 7 (January 1931): 157.

55. Thomas Daniel Young, *Gentleman in a Dustcoat* (Athens: University of Georgia Press, 1982), 219, 226; Conkin, *Southern Agrarians*, 90.

56. Tate to Davidson, October 1932 and December 10, 1932, in Fain and Young, *Literary Correspondence*, 276, 280.

57. Tate to Donald Davidson, September 28, 1935, in Fain and Young, *Literary Correspondence*, 292. Frank Owsley's "The Pillars of Agrarianism," *American Review* 4 (March 1935): 529–47, expressed an Agrarian's specific remedies to deal with the economic disaster of sharecropping and tenant farming in the South, proposing land reform and easier access to land ownership. See also Conkin, *Southern Agrarians*, 90, 106.

58. Grace Lumpkin, "From Miss Lumpkin," *New Republic*, May 27, 1936, 76; Jacqueline Dowd Hall, *Sisters and Rebels: A Struggle for the Soul of America* (New York: W. W. Norton, 2019), 359–60.

59. Donald Davidson, *Attack on Leviathan: Regionalism and Nationalism in the United States* (Chapel Hill: University of North Carolina Press, 1938). See also Edward S. Shapiro, "Frank L. Owsley and the Defense of Southern Identity," *Tennessee Historical Quarterly* 36 (Spring 1977): 75–94.

60. John Crowe Ransom, "Art and the Human Economy," *Kenyon Review* 7 (Autumn 1945): 653–55.

61. W. T. Couch, "The Agrarian Romance," *South Atlantic Quarterly* 36 (October 1937): 429.

62. Donald Davidson, "A Sociologist in Eden," *American Review* 8 (December 1936): 94–103; Allen Tate, "A View of the Whole South," *American Review* 2 (February 1934): 411–32.

63. Horace Mann Bond, "A Negro Looks at His South," *Harper's Magazine*, June 1931, 98.

64. Bond, 100, 101, 103, 106.

65. Bond, 108.

66. Sterling A. Brown, "A Romantic Defense," in *A Son's Return: Selected Essays by Sterling A. Brown*, ed. Mark A. Sanders (Boston: Northeastern University Press, 1996), 281–83.

67. Malvasi, *Unregenerate South*, 7

68. Bishop to Tate, August 25, 1931, in *The Republic of Letters: The Correspondence of John Peale Bishop and Allen Tate*, ed. Thomas Daniel Young and John J. Hindle (Lexington: University Press of Kentucky, 1981), 48; Malvasi, *Unregenerate South*, 7; Allen Tate, *The Fathers* (Chicago: Swallow, 1960), 185; Richard M. Weaver, *The Southern Tradition at Bay: A History of Postbellum Thought*, ed. George Core and Melvin E. Bradford (Washington, D.C.: Regnery Gateway, 1989), 375.

69. Tate to Donald Davidson, January 14, 1953, in Fain and Young, *Literary Correspondence*, 370.

CHAPTER FOUR

1. William T. Couch, ed., *Culture in the South* (Chapel Hill: University of North Carolina Press, 1934), vii–xi. See also Daniel Joseph Singal, *The War Within: From Victorian to Modernist Thought in the South, 1919–1945* (Chapel Hill: University of North Carolina Press, 1982), 275, 281, 282.

2. William T. Couch, preface; and Charles W. Ramsdell, "The Southern Heritage," both in Couch, *Culture in the South*, x, 15.

3. Broadus Mitchell, "A Survey of Industry"; and Clarence E. Cason, "Middle Class and Bourbon," both in Couch, *Culture in the South*, 81, 496.

4. John Tyree Fain and Thomas Daniel Young, eds., *The Literary Correspondence of Donald Davidson and Allen Tate* (Athens: University of Georgia Press, 1974), 288.

5. Sarah E. Gardner and Karen L. Cox, *Reassessing the 1930s South* (Baton Rouge: Louisiana State University Press, 2018). Gardner and Cox show how scholars and journalists, among others, challenged ideas of the South as H. L. Mencken's backward quagmire of traditionalism and put forward instead opinions of its growing modernity. The liberal regionalist support for the interracial movement gave the concept of interracialism a significant authority within southern society at the time. Their support would be part of a long interracial movement that would flourish after the 1960s. David Carleton and Peter Coclanis, in "Another 'Great Migration': From Region to Race in Southern Liberalism, 1938–1945," *SC* 3 (Winter 1997), 37–62, rightfully argue that region was more important to the regionalists than race, but cautious racial change was part of their agenda.

6. Warren I. Susman, "The Culture of the Thirties," in *Culture as History: The Transformation of American Society in the Twentieth Century* (New York: Pantheon, 1984), 153–54; Ruth Benedict, *Patterns of Culture* (New York: Penguin Books, 1934).

7. Susman, "Culture of the Thirties," 153–56.

8. Jackson Lears, *Recasting America: Culture and Politics in the Age of Cold War* (Chicago: University of Chicago Press, 1989), 41; George V. Denny Jr. et al., "Can We Depend Upon Youth to Follow the American Way," in *Conversations with Richard Wright*, ed. Kenneth Kinnaman and Michel Fabre (Jackson: University Press of Mississippi, 1993), 2; Wendy Wall, *Inventing the "American Way": The Politics of Consensus from the New Deal to Civil Rights* (New York: Oxford University Press, 2005).

9. Howard Mumford Jones, "New England Dilemma," *Atlantic Monthly*, March 1940, 460.

10. Claudius Murchison, "Captains of Southern Industry," *VQR* 7, no. 3 (1931): 387.

11. Douglas L. Fleming, "Atlanta, Its People, and the 'Atlanta Spirit,'" in *Making a New South: Race, Leadership, and Community after the Civil War*, ed. Paul A. Cimbala and Barton C. Shaw (Gainesville: University Press of Florida, 2007), 84–109; Gerald W. Johnson, "Greensboro, or What You Will," in *South-Watching: Selected Essays of Gerald W. Johnson*, ed. Fred Hobson (Chapel Hill: University of North Carolina Press, 1983), 46.

12. Catherine Fosl, "Radicalism"; and Greta de Jones, "Share Croppers Union and Southern Tenant Farmers' Union," both in *Social Class*, ed. Larry J. Griffin, Peggy G. Hargis, and Charles Reagan Wilson, vol. 20 of *The New Encyclopedia of Southern Culture*, ed. Charles Reagan Wilson (Chapel Hill: University of North Carolina Press, 2012), 222–27, 443–44.

13. John A. Salmond, *Gastonia, 1929: The Story of the Loray Mill Strike* (Chapel Hill: University of North Carolina Press, 1995).

14. Jacquelyn Dowd Hall, *Sisters and Rebels: A Struggle for the Soul of America* (New York: W. W. Norton, 2019), 258–62; Bill C. Malone, "Protest Music," in *Music*, ed. Bill C. Malone, vol. 12 of *The New Encyclopedia of Southern Culture*, ed. Charles Reagan Wilson (Chapel Hill: University of North Carolina Press, 2008), 101–5.

15. Hall, *Sisters and Rebels*, 255, 265–71; Brent D. Glass and Michael Hall, "Gastonia Strike," in *North Carolina Encyclopedia* (Chapel Hill: University of North Carolina Press, 2006).

16. W. Fitzhugh Brundage, *The Southern Past: A Clash of Race and Memory* (Cambridge, Mass.: Belknap Press of Harvard University Press, 2005), 191–92.

17. Brundage, 201, 203; Alice Ravenel Huger Smith, "Doorways, Gateways, and

Stairways of Quaint Old Charleston," *Art in America*, August 4, 1916, 296. See also Ethan J. Kytle and Blain Roberts, *Denmark Vesey's Garden: Slavery and Memory in the Cradle of the Confederacy* (New York: New Press, 2018), esp. chap. 6, "America's Most Historic City."

18. Brundage, *Southern Past*, 208.

19. Karen L. Cox, *Dreaming of Dixie: How the South Was Created in American Popular Culture* (Chapel Hill: University of North Carolina Press, 2011), 155.

20. Richard D. Starnes, ed., *Southern Journeys: Tourism, History, and Culture in the Modern South* (Tuscaloosa: University of Alabama Press, 2003); Nick Wynne, *Sunshine Paradise: A History of Florida Tourism* (Gainesville: University Press of Florida, 2011); Ken Breslauer, *Roadside Paradise: The Golden Age of Florida's Tourist Attractions: 1929-1970* (St. Petersburg: Retro Florida, 2000).

21. Charles Reagan Wilson, "'God's Project': The Southern Civil Religion, 1920–1980," in *Judgment and Grace in Dixie: Southern Faiths from Faulkner to Elvis* (Athens: University of Georgia Press, 1995), 21–23.

22. Andrew Doyle, "Turning the Tide: College Football and Southern Progressivism," *SC* 3, no. 3 (1997): 228–51.

23. Lamar Rutherford Lipscomb, "That Uncompanioned Giant in Nature Stone Mountain," *Miss Rutherford's Historical Notes* 6 (June 1927), 15, 17.

24. Cox, *Dreaming of Dixie*, 50; Bernard De Voto, "The Easy Chair," *Saturday Review of Literature*, May 22, 1937, 3; Nina Silber, *This War Ain't Over: Fighting the Civil War in New Deal America* (Chapel Hill: University of North Carolina Press, 2018).

25. Jack Temple Kirby, *Media-Made Dixie: The South in the American Imagination* (Baton Rouge: Louisiana State University Press, 1978), 75; Cox, *Dreaming of Dixie*.

26. Darden Asbury Pyron, *Southern Daughter: The Life of Margaret Mitchell* (New York: Oxford University Press, 1991); Darden Asbury Pyron and Helen Taylor, "*Gone with the Wind*," in *Media*, ed. Allison Graham and Sharon Monteith, vol. 18 of *The New Encyclopedia of Southern Culture*, ed. Charles Reagan Wilson (Chapel Hill: University of North Carolina Press, 2011), 256–59; Charles Reagan Wilson, "The Extravagant South: *Gone with the Wind* as Southern Style," *Southern Reader* 2 (Spring 1990), 16–23.

27. Douglas Southall Freeman, "Virginia: A Gentle Dominion," *Nation*, July 16, 1924, 68–71; Catton quoted in Keith D. Dickson, *Sustaining Southern Identity: Douglas Southall Freeman and Memory in the Modern South* (Baton Rouge: Louisiana State University Press, 2011), 1.

28. Freeman, "Virginia," 68–71.

29. Brundage, *Southern Past*.

30. Quote in B. A. Botkin, "Regionalism: Cult or Culture?," *English Journal* 25, no. 3 (1936): 184; B. A. Botkin, "Folk and Folklore," in Couch, *Culture in the South*, 570–93; Leigh Anne Duck, *The Nation's Region: Southern Modernism, Segregation, and U.S. Nationalism* (Athens: University of Georgia Press, 2006), 61–62; Roger Abrahams, "Phantoms of Romantic Nationalism in Folkloristics," *Journal of American Folklore* 106 (Winter 1993): 3–37.

31. Bill C. Malone, *Southern Music/American Music* (Lexington: University Press of Kentucky, 1979); Richard A. Peterson, *Creating Country Music* (Chicago: University of Chicago Press, 1997).

32. Karl Hagstrom Miller, *Segregating Sound: Inventing Folk and Pop Music in the Age of Jim Crow* (Durham, N.C.: Duke University Press, 2010); Elijah Wald, *The Blues: A Very*

Short Introduction (New York: Oxford University Press, 2010), 175–77; William J. Schaefer, "Jazz," in Malone, *Music*, 232–34.

33. John DiMeglio, "Baseball," in *Sports and Recreation*, ed. Harvey H. Jackson III, vol. 16 of *The New Encyclopedia of Southern Culture*, ed. Charles Reagan Wilson (Chapel Hill: University of North Carolina Press, 2011), 126–31; William J. Marshall, "Dizzy Dean: Baseball's Quintessential Southerner," in *The Human Tradition in the New South*, ed. James C. Klotter (Lanham, Md.: Rowman and Littlefield, 2005), 91–110; Doyle, "Turning the Tide," 36–37.

34. George Tindall, "The Significance of Howard W. Odum to Southern History: A Preliminary Estimate," *JSH* 24 (August 1958): 285–307.

35. Singal, *War Within*, 116; Howard Odum, *Southern Regions of the United States* (Chapel Hill: University of North Carolina Press, 1936), 507.

36. Singal, *War Within*, 133, 137.

37. Odum quotes in Singal, 123. See also Wayne D. Brazil, "*Social Forces* and Sectional Self-Scrutiny," in *Perspectives on the American South*, ed. Merle Black and John Shelton Reed (New York: Gordon and Breach Science, 1984), 2:73–104.

38. Robert L. Dormon's *Revolt of the Provinces: The Regionalist Movement in America, 1920–1945* (Chapel Hill: University of North Carolina Press, 1993) argues for "folk liturgies" of creative works that represented a new regional civic religion across the nation.

39. Daniel T. Rodgers, "Regionalism and the Burdens of Progress," in *Region, Race, and Reconstruction: Essays in Honor of C. Vann Woodward*, ed. J. Morgan Kousser and James M. McPherson (New York: Oxford University Press, 1982), 3–4.

40. Odum, *Southern Regions*, 227; Rodgers, "Regionalism," 10–11. See Natalie J. Ring, *The Problem South: Region, Empire, and the New Liberal State* (Athens: University of Georgia Press, 2012).

41. Odum, *Southern Regions*, 479–83.

42. William Graham Sumner, *Civilization and Society: An Account of the Development and Behavior of Human Society*, ed. Franklin Henry Giddings (New York: Holt, 1932), 50–51; Allen Tullos, *Habits of Industry: White Culture and the Transformation of the Carolina Piedmont* (Chapel Hill: University of North Carolina Press, 1989), 295; Rodgers, "Regionalism," 15–17.

43. Howard W. Odum, "Folklore and Regional Conflict as a Field of Sociological Study," *Publications of the American Sociological Society* 25, no. 2 (1931), 1–17.

44. Howard W. Odum, "The Errors of Sociology," *Social Forces* 15, no. 1 (1937): 337.

45. Howard W. Odum, "Folk Culture and Folk Society," in *Folk, Religion, and Society: Selected Papers of Howard W. Odum*, ed. Katherine Jocher, Guy B. Johnson, George L. Simpson, and Rupert B. Vance (Chapel Hill: University of North Carolina Press, 1966), 223, 225.

46. Odum, "Folk Culture," 225–28, 232–33; Howard W. Odum, "The Nature of Civilization," in Jocher et al., *Folk, Religion, and Society*, 281.

47. Howard W. Odum, *The Way of the South: Toward a Regional Balance of America* (New York: Macmillan, 1947), 61–62.

48. Odum, 136–38.

49. Odum, 49–53.

50. Odum, 163–66, 175.

51. Odum, 55, 67–68, 73, 94, 97.

52. Singal, *War Within*, 303–5.

53. Singal, 121–29.

54. Thomas Wolfe, *The Web and the Rock* (New York: Harper and Brothers, 1939), 15.

55. Hobson, *South-Watching*, 5, 106.

56. Gerald W. Johnson, "Critical Attitudes, South and North," *Journal of Social Forces* 2, no. 4 (May 1924): 575–79.

57. John T. Kneebone, *Southern Liberal Journalists and the Issue of Race, 1920–1944* (Chapel Hill: University of North Carolina Press, 1985).

58. Gerald W. Johnson, "The Horrible South," in Hobson, *South-Watching*, 29–42.

59. Johnson, 29–42.

60. Johnson, 29–42.

61. Howard W. Odum, "On Southern Literature and Southern Culture," in *Southern Renascence: The Literature of the Modern South*, ed. Louis D. Rubin and Robert D. Jacobs (1953; repr., Baltimore: Johns Hopkins University Press, 1966), 97; William Faulkner, *Flags in the Dust*, ed. Douglas Day (1929; repr., New York: Random House, 1973), 72; Singal, *War Within*, 154.

62. William Faulkner, *Absalom, Absalom!* (1936; repr., New York: Modern Library, 1951), 250.

63. Richard H. King, *A Southern Renaissance: The Cultural Awakening in the American South, 1930–1955* (New York: Oxford University Press, 1982), 3–19; David A. Davis, "Southern Modernists and Modernity," in *The Cambridge Companion to the Literature of the American South*, ed. Sharon Monteith (New York: Cambridge University Press, 2013), 88–103; John T. Matthews, "The Southern Renaissance and the Faulknerian South," in Monteith, *Cambridge Companion*, 116–31; Sarah Gardner, *Reviewing the South: The Literary Marketplace and the Southern Renaissance, 1920–1941* (New York: Cambridge University Press, 2017), 1–13; Duck, *Nation's Region*.

64. Wolfe, *Web and the Rock*, 44–45. See also Justin Mellette, *Peculiar Whiteness: Racial Anxiety and Poor Whites in Southern Literature, 1900–1965* (Jackson: University Press of Mississippi, 2021).

65. Robert H. Brinkmeyer Jr., "Marginalization and Mobility: Segregation and the Representation of Southern Poor Whites," in *Reading Southern Poverty between the Wars, 1918–1939*, ed. Richard Golden and Martin Crawford (Athens: University of Georgia Press, 2006), 231–32.

66. James Agee and Walker Evans, *Let Us Now Praise Famous Men* (Boston: Houghton Mifflin, 1941), 300. Scott L. Matthews deals with the Agee and Evans book at length in *Capturing the South: Imagining America's Most Documented Region* (Chapel Hill: University of North Carolina Press, 2018), esp. 208–16. For the documentary genre, see Allison Graham, "Film, Documentary," in Graham and Monteith, *Media*, 51–57.

67. Agee and Evans, *Let Us Now Praise*, xlvi, 11, 70, 76–77, 87, 100–107, 214.

68. Agee and Evans, 344, 391, 378–81, 391.

69. James McBride Dabbs, *The Southern Heritage* (New York: Alfred A. Knopf, 1958), 168. Mark Ellis charts the interracial movement from the 1910s through the 1930s in *Race Harmony and Black Progress: Jack Woofter and the Interracial Movement* (Bloomington: Indiana University Press, 2013).

70. John Egerton provides a thorough discussion of the leading interracial groups of the interwar period in *Speak Now against the Day: The Generation before the Civil Rights Movement in the South* (New York: Knopf, 1994), 91, 298, 210, 311–12, 333, 433, 435, 555.

See also Thomas Krueger, *And Promises to Keep: The Southern Conference for Human Welfare, 1938–1948* (Nashville: Vanderbilt University Press, 1967); and Anders Walker, "Southern Regional Council," in Griffin, Hargis, and Wilson, *Social Class*, 448–49.

71. Kneebone, *Southern Liberal Journalists*; David Cohn, "How the South Feels," *Atlantic Monthly*, January 1944, 47–51.

72. Virginius Dabney, *Liberalism in the South* (Chapel Hill: University of North Carolina Press, 1932); Virginius Dabney, "Nearer and Nearer the Precipice," *Atlantic Monthly*, January 1943, 94–100.

73. Egerton, *Speak Now*, 47–51.

74. Morton Sosna, *In Search of the Silent South: Southern Liberals and the Race Issue* (New York: Columbia University Press, 1977), 33; Willie Snow Ethridge, "Southern Women Attack Lynching," *Nation*, December 10, 1930, 650.

75. Sosna, *In Search*, 26. See also Jane Dailey, Glenda Elizabeth Gilmore, and Bryant Simon, eds., *Jumpin' Jim Crow: Southern Politics from Civil War to Civil Rights* (Princeton, N.J.: Princeton University Press, 2000).

76. Sosna, *In Search*, chap. 2.

77. Sosna, 30, 38; William O. Brown, "Interracial Cooperation: Some of Its Problems," *Opportunity* 11 (September 1933): 272–73; Alexander quoted in Paul Harvey, *Freedom's Coming: Religious Culture and the Shaping of the South from the Civil War through the Civil Rights Era* (Chapel Hill: University of North Carolina Press, 2005), 84.

78. Frank Friedel, "The South and the New Deal," in *The New Deal and the South*, ed. James C. Cobb and Michael V. Namorato (Jackson: University Press of Mississippi, 1984), 17–36; Roger Biles, *The South and the New Deal* (Lexington: University Press of Kentucky, 2006).

79. Arthur F. Raper, *The Tragedy of Lynching* (Chapel Hill: University of North Carolina Press, 1933); Charles S. Johnson, Edwin R. Embree, and Will Alexander, *The Collapse of Cotton Tenancy: Summary of Field Studies and Statistical Surveys, 1933–35* (Chapel Hill: University of North Carolina Press, 1935).

80. Egerton, *Speak Now*, 91–96.

81. Egerton, 185–97.

82. Sosna, *In Search*, 146.

83. Glenda Elizabeth Gilmore, *Defying Dixie: The Radical Roots of Civil Rights, 1919–1950* (New York: W. W. Norton, 2008), 32–36.

84. Barbara Griffith, *The Crisis of American Labor: Operation Dixie and the Defeat of the CIO* (Philadelphia: Temple University Press, 1988).

85. Mitchell quoted in Horace R. Cayton and George Mitchell, *Black Workers and the New Unions* (Chapel Hill: University of North Carolina Press, 1939), 342–68.

86. Jacquelyn Dowd Hall, "The Long Civil Rights Movement and the Political Uses of the Past," *Journal of American History* 91 (March 2005): 1233–63.

87. Mason quoted in J. Douglas Smith, *Managing White Supremacy: Race, Politics, and Citizenship in Jim Crow Virginia* (Chapel Hill: University of North Carolina Press, 2002), 207.

88. Mason quoted in Harvey, *Freedom's Coming*, 82; and J. Douglas Smith, *Managing White Supremacy*, 83.

89. William A. Link, *Frank Porter Graham: Southern Liberal Citizen of the World* (Chapel Hill: University of North Carolina Press, 2021).

90. Gilmore, *Defying Dixie*, 121–29.

91. Robert F. Martin, *Howard Kester and the Struggle for Social Justice in the South, 1904–1977* (Charlottesville: University Press of Virginia, 1991), 115–18.

92. Donald H. Grubbs, *Cry from the Cotton: The Southern Tenant Farmers' Union and the New Deal* (Chapel Hill: University of North Carolina Press, 1971); Jarod Roll, *Spirit of Rebellion: Labor and Religion in the New Cotton South* (Urbana: University of Illinois Press, 2010).

93. Franklin quoted in June Bingham, ed., *Courage to Change: An Introduction to the Life and Thought of Reinhold Niebuhr* (Lanham, N.Y.: University Press of America, 1993), 208; Jonathan Daniels, *A Southerner Discovers the South* (New York: Macmillan, 1938), 150.

94. Katharine Du Pre Lumpkin, *The Making of a Southerner* (New York: Alfred A. Knopf, 1947), 236, 121, 127–28. See also Charles Reagan Wilson, *Contesting the Southern Way of Life: Katharine Du Pre Lumpkin's Autobiography and the Progressive South during the Interwar Years* (Heidelberg, Germany: Universitatsverlag, 2019), 45–56.

95. Lumpkin, *Making of a Southerner*, 132, 133, 135, 180, 189.

96. Lumpkin, 190, 191, 193, 198.

97. Lumpkin, 192–93, 204, 202.

98. Lumpkin, 206, 207, 217.

99. Lumpkin, 218, 220, 221, 222.

100. Lumpkin, 233, 234, 235.

101. H. C. Nixon, "Whither Southern Economy," in *I'll Take My Stand: The South and the Agrarian Tradition*, by Twelve Southerners (1930; repr., Baton Rouge: Louisiana State University Press, 2006), 176–200; Nixon to Donald Davidson, January 10, 1930, quoted in Sharon Shouse, *Hillbilly Realist: Herman Clarence Nixon of Possum Trot* (Tuscaloosa: University of Alabama Press, 1986), 53–54. See also Ted Ownby, "Three Agrarianisms and the Idea of a South without Poverty," in Golden and Crawford, *Reading Southern Poverty*, 9–11; and Shouse, *Hillbilly Realist*, 58.

102. H. C. Nixon, *Possum Trot* (Norman: University of Oklahoma Press, 1941), 92; H. C. Nixon, *Lower Piedmont Country: The Uplands of the Deep South* (New York: Duell, Sloan and Pearce, 1946), xvi.

103. Shouse, *Hillbilly Realist*, 12, 71, 22, 118, 65–67, 187.

104. Nixon, *Possum Trot*, 145; H. C. Nixon, *Forty Acres and Steel Mules* (Chapel Hill: University of North Carolina Press, 1938), v; Nixon to Couch, July 23, 1934, quoted in Shouse, *Hillbilly Realist*, 74.

105. Nixon, *Possum Trot*, 147; "A Symposium: The Agrarians Today," *Shenandoah* 3 (Summer 1952): 229–30; Shouse, *Hillbilly Realist*, 30.

106. Fain and Young, *Literary Correspondence*, 292; Shouse, *Hillbilly Realist*, 67, 69.

107. Shouse, *Hillbilly Realist*, chap. 4.

108. Shouse, 187; H. C. Nixon, "Government by the People," in *Cities Are Abnormal*, ed. Elmer T. Peterson (Norman: University of Oklahoma Press, 1946), 181.

109. Nixon, *Forty Acres*, 5, 25; Erskine Caldwell and Margaret Bourke-White, *You Have Seen Their Faces* (New York: Modern Age Books, 1938); Nixon, *Lower Piedmont Country*, 115, 205; Shouse, *Hillbilly Realist*, 71–72.

110. Nixon, *Forty Acres*, 96.

111. H. C. Nixon, "The South Today: Two Schools of Southern Criticism," *Chattanooga*

(Tenn.) News, August 8, 1936; Nixon to Donald Davidson, December 8, 1929, Donald Davidson Papers, Special Collections, Vanderbilt University Library, Nashville, Tennessee.

112. Richard Robbins, *Sidelines Activist: Charles S. Johnson and the Struggle for Civil Rights* (Jackson: University Press of Mississippi, 1996); Patrick J. Gilpin and Marbeth Gasman, *Charles S. Johnson: Leadership beyond the Veil in the Age of Jim Crow* (Albany: State University of New York Press, 2003).

113. Robbins, *Sidelines Activist*, 21.

114. Robbins, 49–63.

115. Gilpin and Gasman, *Charles S. Johnson*, 61–62.

116. Gilpin and Gasman, 62–65.

117. Gilpin and Gasman, 67–69.

118. Charles Johnson, *Shadow of the Plantation* (Chicago: University of Chicago Press, 1934); Charles Johnson, *Growing Up in the Black Belt: Negro Youth in the Rural South* (Washington, D.C.: American Council of Education, 1941). See also Robbins, *Sidelines Activist*, 86.

119. Gilpin and Gasman, *Charles S. Johnson*, 64, 71.

120. Egerton, *Speak Now*, 438.

121. Robbins, *Sidelines Activist*, 130–32.

122. Egerton, *Speak Now*, 438–39.

123. Robbins, *Sidelines Activist*, 180–81.

124. Robbins, 183–200.

125. Robbins, 186.

126. Robbins, 187–88, 189–90.

CHAPTER FIVE

1. Robert McElvaine, *The Great Depression, 1929–1941* (New York: Times Books, 1984).

2. W. E. B. Du Bois, "Georgia: Invisible Empire State," in *Writing by W. E. B. Du Bois in Non-periodical Literature*, ed. Herbert Aptheker (Millwood, N.Y.: Kraus-Thomson Limited, 1982), 140–41. The article originally appeared in *Nation*, January 21, 1925, 63–67.

3. Du Bois, "Georgia," 141–42.

4. Du Bois, 142, 143, 146–47.

5. U. B. Phillips, "The Central Theme of Southern History," *American Historical Review* 34 (October 1928): 31, 32, 35, 42.

6. Bettie Esther Parham, "How the Conservative Negro Intellectual of the South Feels about Racial Segregation," *Social Forces* 14 (December 1935), 268–72; Jennifer Ritterhouse, *Growing Up Jim Crow: How Black and White Southern Children Learned Race* (Chapel Hill: University of North Carolina Press, 2006), 8–9, 44. See also Allison Davis, Burleigh Gardner, and Mary Gardner, *Deep South: A Social Anthropological Study of Caste and Class* (Chicago: University of Chicago Press, 1941), 22–23.

7. Ritterhouse, *Growing Up Jim Crow*, 47, 48; Charles Evers, *Evers* (New York: World, 1971), 29–30.

8. William A. Link, *Frank Porter Graham: Southern Liberal, Citizen of the World* (Chapel Hill: University of North Carolina Press, 2021).

9. Anne C. Rose, "Putting the South on the Psychological Map: The Impact of Region and Race on the Human Sciences during the 1930s," *JSH* 71 (May 2005): 320–56; Hortense

Powdermaker, *After Freedom: A Cultural Study of the Deep South* (1939; repr., Madison: University of Wisconsin Press, 1993), 43, 44, 45, 51.

10. John Dollard, *Caste and Class in a Southern Town*, 3rd ed. (New York: Doubleday Anchor, 1957), 2, 6–7; Rose, "Putting the South," 321–56.

11. Dollard, *Caste and Class*, 9, 10, 65, 178, 350.

12. James C. Cobb, *The Most Southern Place on Earth* (New York: Oxford University Press, 1992), 159, 153–56 (Cohn quote).

13. Bertram Doyle, *The Etiquette of Race Relations in the South: A Study in Social Control* (Chicago: University of Chicago Press, 1937), 161, 167, 170–71.

14. Doyle, 171; Charles S. Johnson, *Growing Up in the Black Belt: Negro Youth in the Rural South* (1941; repr., New York: Schocken Books, 1967), 326–27.

15. William Alexander Percy, *Lanterns on the Levee: Recollections of a Planter's Son* (1941; repr., Baton Rouge: Louisiana State University Press, 1973), 312.

16. Percy, 40–41; Robert H. Brinkmeyer Jr., *The Fourth Ghost: White Southern Writers and European Fascism, 1930–1950* (Baton Rouge: Louisiana State University Press, 2009), 111.

17. Percy, *Lanterns on the Levee*, 21, 24, 307–8.

18. Nancy MacLean, *Behind the Mask of Chivalry: The Making of the Ku Klux Klan* (New York: Oxford University Press, 1994).

19. MacLean, xv, 4–5, 128, 129, 130; W. E. B. Du Bois, "The Shape of Fear," *North American Review* 223, no.831 (1926): 301.

20. MacLean, *Behind the Mask*, 141–43.

21. MacLean, 79, 90.

22. MacLean, 91–92, 134; Kelly J. Baker, *Gospel According to the Klan: The KKK's Appeal to Protestant America, 1915–1930* (Lawrence: University of Kansas Press, 2017).

23. Douglas Southall Freeman, "Virginia: The Gentle Dominion," *Nation*, July 16, 1924, 68–71; "In the Virginia Way," *Richmond (Va.) News Leader*, February 26, 1926, 8; J. Douglas Smith, *Managing White Supremacy: Race, Politics, and Citizenship in Jim Crow Virginia* (Chapel Hill: University of North Carolina Press, 2002); V. O. Key, *Southern Politics in State and Nation* (1949; repr., Knoxville: University of Tennessee Press, 1984), 26.

24. Key, *Southern Politics*, 32; William Chafe, *Civilities and Civil Rights: Greensboro, North Carolina, and the Black Struggle for Freedom* (New York: Oxford University Press, 1980), 8.

25. J. Douglas Smith, *Managing White Supremacy*, 5–9.

26. Dan T. Carter, *Scottsboro: A Tragedy of the American South* (Baton Rouge: Louisiana State University Press, 1969); Glenda Elizabeth Gilmore, *Defying Dixie: The Radical Roots of Civil Rights, 1919–1950* (New York: W. W. Norton, 2008), 118–28.

27. John Gould Fletcher, "Is This the Voice of the South?," letter to the editor, *Nation*, December 27, 1933, 735.

28. Frank Owsley, "Scottsboro: The Third Crusade; the Sequel to Abolition and Reconstruction," *American Review* 1 (June 1933): 257–85.

29. Cal M. Logue and Howard Dorgan, eds., *The Oratory of Southern Demagogues* (Baton Rouge: Louisiana State University Press, 1981).

30. Jason Morgan Ward, *Defending White Democracy: The Making of a Segregationist Movement and the Remaking of Racial Politics, 1936–1965* (Chapel Hill: University of North Carolina Press, 2011), 1–8, 20, 27; Mary Louise Gehring, "'Cotton Ed' Smith: The

South Carolina Farmer in the U.S. Senate," in Logue and Dorgan, *Oratory of Southern Demagogues*, 144, 147.

31. Cal M. Logue, "The Coercive Prophecy of Gene Talmadge, 1926–1946," in Logue and Dorgan, *Oratory of Southern Demagogues*, 218, 224; William Anderson, *The Wild Man from Sugar Creek: The Political Career of Eugene Talmadge* (Baton Rouge: Louisiana State University Press, 1977), 22.

32. Jerry A. Hendrix, "Theodore G. Bilbo: Evangelist of Racial Purity," in Logue and Dorgan, *Oratory of Southern Demagogues*, 170, 167.

33. Hendrix, 162–63; Theodore G. Bilbo, *Take Your Choice: Separation or Mongrelization* (Poplarville, Miss.: Dream House, 1947), 45.

34. Ward, *Defending White Democracy*, 12, 24.

35. Numan V. Bartley and Bradley G. Bond, "Politics and Ideology," in *Law and Politics*, ed. James W. Ely Jr. and Bradley G. Bond, vol. 10 of *The New Encyclopedia of Southern Culture*, ed. Charles Reagan Wilson (Chapel Hill: University of North Carolina Press, 2008), 150–53; W. J. Cash, *The Mind of the South* (1941; repr., New York: Alfred A. Knopf, 1978), 132.

36. Ward, *Defending White Democracy*, 11.

37. Ward, 25.

38. Ward, 28.

39. Ward, 16; Cal M. Logue and Dwight L. Freshley, *Voice of Georgia: Speeches of Richard B. Russell, 1928–1969* (Macon, Ga.: Mercer University Press, 1997), 319.

40. David Levering Lewis, *When Harlem Was in Vogue* (New York: Penguin Books, 1997); Jeffrey O. G. Ogbar, ed., *The Harlem Renaissance Revisited: Politics, Art, and Letters* (Baltimore: Johns Hopkins University Press, 2010).

41. Anne Spencer, "White Things," in *Black Nature: Four Centuries of African American Nature Poetry*, ed. Camille J. Dungy (Athens: University of Georgia Press, 2009), 155; Langston Hughes, "The South" and "Christ in Alabama," in *The Collected Poetry of Langston Hughes*, ed. Arnold Rampersad (New York: Vintage Books, 1995), 26–27, 143; Sterling A. Brown, "Southern Road," in *Southern Road* (New York: Harcourt, Brace, 1932), 47.

42. Jean Toomer, *Cane* (1923; repr., New York: Harper and Row, 1969), 57, 59; J. Martin Favor, *Authentic Blackness: The Folk in the New Negro Renaissance* (Durham, N.C.: Duke University Press, 1999), 65. See also William M. Ramsey, "Jean Toomer's Eternal South," *Southern Literary Journal* 36 (Fall 2003): 74–89.

43. Charles Scruggs, *The Sage in Harlem: H. L. Mencken and the Black Writers of the 1920s* (Baltimore: Johns Hopkins University Press, 1984), 61, 65–66.

44. Thadious Davis, "Southern Standard-Bearers in the New Negro Renaissance," in *The History of Southern Literature*, ed. Louis D. Rubin Jr. (Baton Rouge: Louisiana State University Press, 1985), 291; Hughes quote in Arnold Ramparsad and David E. Roessel, eds., *The Collective Poems of Langston Hughes* (New York: Alfred A. Knopf, 1996), 27.

45. Thadious Davis, "Southern Standard-Bearers," 304; Ramparsad and Roessel, *Collective Poems*, 362; Nicole L. B. Furlonge, "An Instrument Blues-Tinged: Listening, Language and the Everyday in Sterling Brown's 'Ma Rainey,'" *Callalloo* 21, no. 4 (1998), 269–84; John F. Callahan, ed., *The Collective Essays of Ralph Ellison* (New York: Modern Library, 2003), 66–67.

46. Jean Toomer, "November Cotton Flower," in *Cane*, 7; Charles T. Davis, "Region

and Race as Elements within a Literary Imagination," in *The Harlem Renaissance Re-examined*, ed. Victor A. Kramer and Robert A. Russ (Troy, N.Y.: Whitson, 1997), 222.

47. James C. Cobb, *Away Down South: A History of the Southern Identity* (New York: Oxford University Press, 2005), 5–6, 147–48; Leigh Anne Duck, *The Nation's Region: Southern Modernism, Segregation, and U.S. Nationalism* (Athens: University of Georgia Press, 2006), 126–27.

48. Zora Neale Hurston, *Dust Tracks on a Road: An Autobiography* (1942; repr., New York: Harper Perennial, 1996). See also Valerie Boyd, *Wrapped in Rainbows: The Life of Zora Neale Hurston* (New York: Scribner's, 2003).

49. Richard Wright, *Twelve Million Black Voices* (New York: Thunder's Mouth, 1941), 12, 13, 18, 25, 43.

50. Wright, 48, 60.

51. Richard Wright, *Black Boy: A Record of Childhood and Youth* (New York: Harper and Brothers, 1945), 55, 215.

52. Wright, 187, 202, 203, 276.

53. Wright, 281, 283, 216–17.

54. Wright, 45.

55. Wright, 267, 274, 281, 186–87.

56. Wright, 283–84.

57. Wright, 285.

58. Thadious Davis, "Southern Standard-Bearers," 305–6.

59. Hurston, *Dust Tracks*, 135–36; Thadious Davis, "Southern Standard-Bearers," 305–6. See also Jan Cooper, "Zora Neale Hurston Was Always a Southerner Too," in *The Female Tradition in Southern Literature*, ed. Carol S. Manning (Urbana: University of Illinois Press, 1993), 57–69.

60. Zora Neale Hurston, *Mules and Men* (1935; repr., New York: Harper Perennial, 1990); Duck, *Nation's Region*, 126–32.

61. Franz Boas, *The Mind of Primitive Man* (New York: Macmillan, 1911); Marybeth Hamilton, *In Search of the Blues* (New York: Basic Books, 2008), 134; Zora Neale Hurston, *Go Gator and Muddy the Water: Writings of Zora Neale Hurston from the Federal Writers' Project*, ed. Pamela Bordelon (New York: W. W. Norton, 1999), 66–67.

62. Hurston, *Dust Tracks*, 175.

63. Hurston, 21, 32, 46, 129; Zora Neale Hurston, "How It Feels to Be Colored Me," in *I Love Myself When I Am Laughing: A Zora Neale Hurston Reader*, ed. Alice Walker (New York: Feminist, 2011), 151–54, quotes 152.

64. Hurston, "How It Feels," 152; Alice Walker, "Looking for Zora," afterword to Walker, *I Love Myself*, 150; Sterling A. Brown, *The Negro in American Fiction* (1937; repr., Port Washington, N.Y.: Kennikat, 1968), 160–61; Alain Locke, "Deep River: Deeper Sea; Retrospective Review of the Literature of the Negro for 1935," *Opportunity* 14, no. 2 (1936): 291.

65. Zora Neale Hurston, "The Pet Negro System," in Walker, *I Love Myself*, 155; Hurston, *Dust Tracks*, 233.

66. Hurston, "Pet Negro System," 155, 156.

67. Hurston, 157, 158, 159.

68. Hurston, 156, 159.

69. Zora Neale Hurston, "Crazy for This Democracy," in Walker, *I Love Myself*, 165–67.

70. Duck, *Nation's Region*, 144–45.

71. Morton Sosna, "More Important Than the Civil War? The Impact of World War II on the South," in *Perspectives on the American South: An Annual Review of Society, Politics and Culture*, ed. James C. Cobb and Charles R. Wilson (New York: Gordon and Breach, 1987), 4:145–61; John Dos Passos, "State of the Nation," *Life*, September 25, 1944, 105.

72. Agnes E. Meyer, *Journey through Chaos* (New York: Harcourt, Brace, 1944), 210.

73. Morton Sosna, "The GIs' South and the North-South Dialogue during World War II," in *Developing Dixie: Modernization in a Traditional Society*, ed. Winfred B. Moore Jr., Joseph F. Tripp, and Lyon G. Tyler Jr. (New York: Greenwood, 1988), 313, Staten Island GI quote 315; Chicago GI quoted in Studs Terkel, *"The Good War": An Oral History of World War Two* (New York: Pantheon, 1984), 39; William Manchester, *Goodbye Darkness: A Memoir of the Pacific War* (1979; repr., New York: Dell, 1982), 120.

74. Lathrophe F. Jenkins to P. L. Prattis, September 12, 1944, quoted in Sosna, "GIs' South," 319–20; Walter Bernstein, *Keep Your Head Down* (New York: Viking, 1945), 6.

75. James McBride Dabbs, "Going to Win the War," *Commonweal* 36 (April 1942): 489.

76. Robert H. Brinkmeyer Jr., *The Fourth Ghost: White Southern Writers and European Fascism, 1930–1950* (Baton Rouge: Louisiana State University Press, 2009), 3.

77. Cash, *Mind of the South*, lviii.

78. W. J. Cash, "What Price Mussolini," *Charlotte (N.C.) News*, November 11, 1935; W. J. Cash, "Holy Men Muff Chance," *American Mercury*, January 1934, 113, 115, 116; Brinkmeyer, *Fourth Ghost*, 77–79.

79. W. J. Cash, "Spengler Comes True: Dawn for Dictators, Evening in the West," *Charlotte News*, February 27, 1938; W. J. Cash, "Papa Franz Boas: He's a Testy and Aged Teuton, Who Proves that Racial Blood Streams Are as Fickle as the Waters, and as Lively," *Charlotte News*, July 12, 1936; W. J. Cash, "The Synthetic Superman: Europe's Ku Kluxers, They Invoke Nietzsche," *Charlotte News*, September 5, 1937.

80. Cash, *Mind of the South*, 35.

81. Cash, 38–39, 146. See also Brinkmeyer, *Fourth Ghost*, 85–86.

82. Cash, *Mind of the South*, 124, 113, 139, 168.

83. Cash, 179.

84. Cash, 292, 293, 296.

85. Cash, 135, 134.

86. Thomas Sancton, "Race Fear Sweeps the South," *New Republic*, January 18, 1943, 111–14.

87. Sancton, 111–14; Howard W. Odum, *Race and Rumors of Race* (Chapel Hill: University of North Carolina Press, 1943), 73–80, 81–89.

88. Cobb, *Most Southern Place*, 202.

89. Sancton, "Race Fear," 111–14.

90. Edward S. Shapiro, "Frank L. Owsley and the Defense of Southern Identity," *Tennessee Historical Quarterly* 36 (Spring 1977): 75–94.

91. Ethridge quoted in Kevin M. Kruse and Stephen Tuck, eds., *Fog of War: The Second World War and the Civil Rights Movement* (New York: Oxford University Press, 2012), 157; Graves quoted in John Edgar Tidwell and Mark A. Sanders, eds., *Sterling A. Brown's A Negro Looks at the South* (New York: Oxford University Press, 2007), 330; Odum, *Race*, 155; David L. Cohn, "How the South Feels," *Atlantic Monthly*, January 1944, 47–51.

92. Rayford Logan, ed., *What the Negro Wants* (Chapel Hill: University of North Carolina Press, 1944). See esp. Mary McLeod Bethune, "Certain Unalienable Rights," in Logan, 248.

93. Langston Hughes, "My America," in Logan, *What the Negro Wants*, 299–300; Bethune, "Certain Unalienable Rights," 250, 252.

94. Bethune, "Certain Unalienable Rights," 250–51; Sterling A. Brown, "Count Us In," in Logan, *What the Negro Wants*.

95. Hughes, "My America," 301; Brown, "Count Us In."

96. Brown, "Count Us In"; Hughes, "My America," 304–5; Bethune, "Certain Unalienable Rights," 253–55.

97. Daniel Joseph Singal, *The War Within: From Victorian to Modernist Thought in the South, 1919–1945* (Chapel Hill: University of North Carolina Press, 1982), 299.

98. William T. Couch, introduction to Logan, *What the Negro Wants*, xiii–xvi.

99. Couch, xv.

100. John Egerton, *Speak Now against the Day: The Generation before the Civil Rights Movement in the South* (New York: Alfred A. Knopf, 1994), 301–6.

101. Egerton, 307.

102. Egerton, 307–9.

103. Egerton, 309–12.

104. Lillian Smith, "Addressed to White Liberals," *New Republic*, September 1944, 331–33; Will Alexander, "Our Conflicting Racial Policies," *Harper's Magazine*, January 1945, 173–78.

105. Wendy L. Wall, *Inventing the "American Way": The Politics of Consensus from the New Deal to the Civil Rights Movement* (New York: Oxford University Press, 2008), 4–12, 209–11.

106. Wall, 15–17. The "American way of life" essays appeared in the February, March, April, and May issues of *Harper's Magazine* in 1938.

107. Wall, *Inventing the "American Way,"* 42–48, 209.

108. Wall, 34, 48–62, 121; Eric Foner, *The Story of American Freedom* (New York: W. W. Norton, 1998), 230.

109. Glenn Feldman, *The Great Melding: War, the Dixiecrat Rebellion, and the Southern Model for America's New Conservatism* (Tuscaloosa: University of Alabama Press, 2015). Feldman surveys southern white conservative political reactions of the period, while Egerton (*Speak Now*) covers the range of southern reform efforts.

110. Margaret Mead, *And Keep Your Powder Dry: An Anthropologist Looks at America* (New York: W. Morrow, 1942), 24. See also Brinkmeyer, *Fourth Ghost*, 9–11.

111. John Temple Graves, *The Fighting South* (1943; repr., Tuscaloosa: University of Alabama Press, 1985), 270–71; David Southern, *Gunnar Myrdal and Black-White Relations: The Use and Abuse of the American Dilemma, 1944–69* (Baton Rouge: Louisiana State University Press, 1994), 155; Wall, *Inventing the "American Way,"* 4–8.

112. Gunnar Myrdal, *An American Dilemma: The Negro Problem and Modern Democracy* (New York: Harper and Row, 1944).

113. Myrdal, 48.

114. Myrdal, 451.

115. Myrdal, 460, 461.

116. Myrdal, 462, 466.

117. Reddick quoted in Wall, *Inventing the "American Way,"* 76; Horace Mann Bond, "Should the Negro Care Who Wins the War?," in *Annals of the American Academy of Political and Social Science* 223 (September 1942): 81–84.

118. Feldman, *Great Melding*, 39.

119. Feldman, 39.

120. Feldman, 69.

121. Feldman, 74.

122. Numan V. Bartley, *The New South, 1945–1980: The Story of the South's Modernization* (Baton Rouge: Louisiana State University Press and the Littlefield Fund for Southern History of the University of Texas, 1995), 21–37.

123. Martha Gelhorn, "Journey through a Peaceful Land," *New Republic*, June 30, 1947, 18–21.

124. Gelhorn, 18–21.

125. Hodding Carter, "A Southerner Looks at the South," *New York Times Magazine*, July 7, 1946, 28–30.

126. Carter, 28–30.

127. Carter, 28–30.

CHAPTER SIX

1. Wilma Dykeman, "What Is the Southern Way of Life?," *Southwestern Review* 44 (Spring 1959): 163–66.

2. Dykeman, 163–64.

3. Dykeman, 164–65.

4. Dykeman, 166.

5. C. Vann Woodward, *The Burden of Southern History* (Baton Rouge: Louisiana State University Press, 1960), 12, 8, 9.

6. Woodward, 11, 12.

7. For overviews of the post–World War II South, see James C. Cobb, *The South and America since World War II* (New York: Oxford University Press, 2011), 1–22; Jennifer E. Brooks, *Defining the Peace: World War II Veterans, Race, and the Remaking of Southern Political Tradition* (Chapel Hill: University of North Carolina Press, 2004); and Neil R. McMillen, "How Mississippi's Black Veterans Remember World War II," in *Remaking Dixie: The Impact of World War II on the American South*, ed. Neil R. McMillen (Jackson: University Press of Mississippi, 1997).

8. Ira De A. Reid, "Southern Ways," *Survey Graphic* 36 (January 1947): 39–42, 48, 107–8.

9. Ethridge to Ralph W. McGill, September 7, 1944, quoted in John Temple Graves, *The Fighting South* (New York: G. P. Putnam and Sons, 1943), 125; Hodding Carter, *The South Strikes Back* (Garden City, N.J.: Doubleday, 1959), 12; Foreman quoted in Numan V. Bartley, *The New South, 1945–1980: The Story of the South's Modernization* (Baton Rouge: Louisiana State University Press and the Littlefield Fund for Southern History of the University of Texas, 1995), 24.

10. Jasper Berry Shannon, *Toward a New Politics in the South* (Knoxville: University of Tennessee Press, 1949), 51.

11. Bartley, *New South*, 45.

12. Gunnar Myrdal, *An American Dilemma: The Negro Problem and Modern*

Democracy (New York: Harper and Brothers, 1944), xli–xliii; Morton Sosna, *In Search of the Silent South: Southern Liberals and the Race Issue* (New York: Columbia University Press, 1977), 221.

13. James C. Cobb, *The South and America since World War II* (New York: Oxford University Press, 2011), 27–33.

14. Arna W. Bontemps, "Why I Returned," *Harper's Magazine*, April 1965, 308, 309.

15. L. D. Reddick, "Negro as Southerner and American," in *The Southerner as American*, ed. Charles Grier Sellers (Chapel Hill: University of North Carolina Press, 1960), 130–31.

16. Glenn Feldman, *The Great Melding: War, the Dixiecrat Rebellion and the Southern Model for America's New Conservatism* (Tuscaloosa: University of Alabama Press, 2015), 78.

17. Feldman, 93, 94, 134.

18. Feldman, 262, 267.

19. President's Committee on Civil Rights, *To Secure these Rights* (Washington, D.C.: Government Printing Office, 1947), 166.

20. Grover Hall, *Montgomery (Ala.) Advertiser*, July 15, 1948 quoted in Bartley, *New South*, 76; Russell quoted in Jason Morgan Ward, *Defending White Democracy: The Making of a Segregationist Movement and the Remaking of Racial Politics, 1936–1965* (Chapel Hill: University of North Carolina Press, 2011), 113; Shannon, *Toward a New Politics*, 79.

21. Kari Fredrickson, *The Dixiecrat Revolt and the End of the Solid South, 1932–1968* (Chapel Hill: University of North Carolina Press, 2001); Eastland quoted in Richard J. Perry, *"Race" and Racism: The Development of Modern Racism in America* (New York: Palgrave Macmillan, 2007), 82–83.

22. Bartley, *New South*, 87; William G. Carleton, "The Fate of Our Fourth Party," *Yale Review* 38, no. 3 (1949): 449–59.

23. Bartley, *New South*, 94–95; Sarah McCulloh Lemmon, "The Ideology of the 'Dixiecrat' Movement," *Social Forces* 30, no. 2 (1951): 162–71; Emile B. Ader, "Why the Dixiecrats Failed," *Journal of Politics* 15, no. 3 (1953): 356–69.

24. William T. Polk, *Southern Accents: From Uncle Remus to Oak Ridge* (New York: William Morrow, 1953), 227; Bartley, *New South*, 105.

25. Pete Daniel, *Standing at the Crossroads: Southern Life since 1900* (New York: Hill and Wang, 1986), 123.

26. Bartley, *New South*, 105; Viola Goode Liddell, *With a Southern Accent* (Tuscaloosa: University of Alabama Press, 1948), 184.

27. Bartley, *New South*, 33.

28. James C. Cobb evaluates the historiographical debate over the significance of the Supreme Court's 1954 decision in *The Brown Decision, Jim Crow, and Southern Identity* (Athens: University of Georgia Press, 2005).

29. Susan Williams, "Highlander Folk School/Highlander Research and Education Center," in *Education*, ed. Clarence Mohr, vol. 17 of *The New Encyclopedia of Southern Culture*, ed. Charles Reagan Wilson (Chapel Hill: University of North Carolina Press, 2011), 237–39.

30. Anne C. Loveland, *Lillian Smith: A Southerner Confronting the South* (Baton Rouge: Louisiana State University Press, 1986).

31. Margaret Rose Gladney and Lisa Hodgens, eds., *A Lillian Smith Reader* (Athens:

University of Georgia Press, 2016), 107, 116; Michelle Cliff, ed., *The Winner Names the Age: A Collection of Writings by Lillian Smith* (New York: W. W. Norton, 1982), 78.

32. Lillian Smith, *Killers of the Dream* (1949; repr., New York: W. W. Norton, 1995), 27, 28.

33. Smith, 27, 140, 180.

34. Lillian Smith, *Now Is the Time* (1955; repr., Jackson: University Press of Mississippi, 2004), 128, 48, 129, 75.

35. Lillian Smith, "The Walls of Segregation Are Crumbling," in Cliff, *Winner Names the Age*, 56.

36. Cobb, *Brown Decision*; Frank Smith, *Congressman from Mississippi* (New York: Pantheon, 1964), 105.

37. Eastland quoted in Joseph Crespino, *In Search of Another Country: Mississippi and the Conservative Counterrevolution* (Princeton, N.J.: Princeton University Press, 2007), 50; Numan V. Bartley, *The Rise of Massive Resistance: Race and Politics during the 1950s* (1969; repr., Baton Rouge: Louisiana State University Press, 1997), 121; James W. Silver, *Mississippi: The Closed Society* (New York: Houghton Mifflin Harcourt, 1964), 46.

38. Thomas P. Brady, *Black Monday* (Winona, Miss.: Association of Citizens' Councils, 1955), foreword, 11.

39. Brady, 12; Neil R. McMillen, *The Citizens' Councils: Organized Resistance to the Second Reconstruction, 1954–64* (Urbana: University of Illinois Press, 1994), 162.

40. *Courier-Journal* quote in William H. Chafe, *The Unfinished Journey: America since World War II*, 5th ed. (New York: Oxford University Press, 2003), 147; Harry S. Ashmore, *The Negro and the Schools* (Chapel Hill: University of North Carolina Press, 1954), 82; Ted Ownby, *Hurtin' Words: Debating Family Problems in the Twentieth-Century South* (Chapel Hill: University of North Carolina Press, 2018), 153–55.

41. Wilma Dykeman and James Stokely, *Neither Black nor White* (New York: Rinehart, 1957), 19.

42. Clayborne Carson, ed., *Reporting Civil Rights: American Journalism, 1941–1963* (New York: Library of America, 2003), 223, 224; Stephanie R. Rolph, *Resisting Equality: The Citizens' Council, 1954–1989* (Baton Rouge: Louisiana State University Press, 2018). Crespino's *In Search of Another Country* argues that the Citizens' Council movement was part of a national white racist movement that survived the days of the civil rights movement.

43. Elliott J. Gorn, *Let the People See: The Story of Emmett Till* (New York: Oxford University Press, 2018); Dave Tell, *Remembering Emmett Till* (Chicago: University of Chicago Press, 2019).

44. Emily Yellin, "Journalism (Print) and Civil Rights," in *Media*, ed. Allison Graham and Sharon Monteith, vol. 18 of *The New Encyclopedia of Southern Culture*, ed. Charles Reagan Wilson (Chapel Hill: University of North Carolina Press, 2011), 118–23.

45. Douglas Cater, "Civil War in Alabama's Citizen's Councils," quoted in McMillen, *Citizens' Councils*, 56.

46. D. M. Nelson, "Integration Communist Inspired," *Citizens' Council* (Jackson, Miss.), October 1955; Jason Sokol, *There Goes My Everything: White Southerners in the Age of Civil Rights, 1945–1975* (New York: Vintage Books, 2007), 6, 53 (Durr quote); W. J. Simmons, "The Carpetbaggers Are Coming-Again," *Citizens' Council*, November 1959, 2.

47. *Jackson (Miss.) Daily News* quoted in McMillen, *Citizens' Councils*, 244; Georgia Board of Education quoted in Michael J. Klarman, *From Jim Crow to Civil Rights: The Supreme Court and the Struggle for Racial Equality* (New York: Oxford University Press, 2004), 411.

48. Elizabeth Geyer, "The 'New' Ku Klux Klan," *Crisis*, March 1956, 140; Talmadge quoted in J. Harvey Wilkerson III, *From Brown to Bakke: The Supreme Court and School Integration, 1945–1978* (New York: Oxford University Press, 1979), 205; Bartley, *New South*, 205; "Soviet-style" quote in Bartley, *Rise of Massive Resistance*, 86.

49. "A Manual for Southerners," *Citizens' Council*, July 1957, 3; "A Manual for Southerners," *Citizens' Council*, June and July 1957, 3.

50. McMillen, *Citizens' Councils*, 39.

51. William J. Simmons, "Lesson from the Congo," *Citizens' Council*, July 1960; Brady, *Black Monday*, 2.

52. Carleton Putnam, *Race and Reason: A Yankee View* (Washington, D.C.: Public Affairs, 1961), quoted in McMillen, *Citizens' Councils*, 166.

53. Givhan quoted in "NAACP Plans Counter Action," *Jet*, December 23, 1954, 7. See also Deborah E. Barker, *Reconstructing Violence: The Southern Rape Complex in Film and Literature* (Baton Rouge: Louisiana State University Press, 2015).

54. G. T. Gillespie, *A Christian View on Segregation* (Greenwood: Association of Citizens' Councils of Mississippi, 1955), 1–13.

55. Paul Harvey, "Religion, Race, and the Right in the South, 1945–1990," in *Politics and Religion in the White South*, ed. Glenn Feldman (Lexington: University Press of Kentucky, 2005), 102–6.

56. David Chappell, "Religious Ideas of the Segregationists," *Journal of American Studies* 32, no. 2(1998): 45–72; Ralph McGill, "The Agony of the Southern Minister," *New York Times Magazine*, September 27, 1959, 116, 51, 59–60; Crespino, *In Search*, 69.

57. Campbell quoted in Sokol, *There Goes My Everything*, 101; Charles Marsh, *God's Long Summer* (Princeton, N.J.: Princeton University Press, 1997), 49.

58. Andrew Manis, *Southern Civil Religions in Conflict: Civil Rights and the Culture Wars* (Macon, Ga.: Mercer University Press, 2002), 126; Charles Reagan Wilson and Mark Silk, eds., *Religion and Public Life in the South: In the Evangelical Mode* (Walnut Creek, Calif.: AltaMira, 2005), 168–69; Mark Silk and Andrew Walsh, *One Nation, Divisible: How Regional Religious Differences Shape American Politics* (New York: Rowman and Littlefield, 2008), 67.

59. Walker Percy, "Red, White and Blue-Gray," *Commonweal*, December 22, 1961, 338; Walter Lord, *The Past That Would Not Die* (New York: Pocket Books, 1967), 31, 63, 134, 137, 178; Silver, *Mississippi*, 5; Thomas L. Connelly and Barbara L. Bellows, *God and General Longstreet: The Lost Cause and the Southern Mind* (Baton Rouge: Louisiana State University Press, 1982), 117–19; Bartley, *Rise of Massive Resistance*, third illustration.

60. Hodding Carter, *Southern Legacy* (Baton Rouge: Louisiana State University Press, 1950), 18, 23; Percy, "Red, White and Blue-Gray," 338.

61. Percy, "Red, White and Blue-Gray," 338; Erskine Caldwell, "The Deep South's Other Venerable Tradition," *New York Times Magazine*, July 11, 1965, 11.

62. Charleston attorney quoted in Wilson and Silk, *Religion and Public Life*, 169. See Bartley, *Rise of Massive Resistance*, 30; and Jack M. Bloom, *Class, Race, and the Civil Rights Movement* (Bloomington: Indiana University Press, 1987), 96.

63. Wendy L. Wall, *Inventing the "American Way": The Politics of Consensus from the New Deal to the Civil Rights Movement* (New York: Oxford University Press, 2008), 3–15; Frances FitzGerald, *America Revised: History Textbooks in the Twentieth Century* (Boston: Little, Brown, 1979); Stephen Whitfield, *The Culture of the Cold War* (Baltimore: Johns Hopkins University Press, 1991), 57.

64. Will Herberg, *Protestant-Catholic-Jew* (Garden City, N.Y.: Anchor Books, 1960, 1955), 75.

65. Wall, *Inventing the "American Way,"* 246–47; Jeff Woods, *Black Struggle, Red Scare: Segregation and Anti-Communism in the South, 1948–1968* (Baton Rouge: Louisiana State University Press, 2004), 30–31, 46–47; Jack Lotto, On Your Guard, *Jackson Daily News*, January 9, 1961, September 19, 1962; Frank Smith, *Congressman from Mississippi*, 276–77.

66. Crespino, *In Search*, 50, 51; Paul Harvey, *Freedom's Coming: Religious Culture and the Shaping of the South from the Civil War through the Civil Rights Era* (Chapel Hill: University of North Carolina Press, 2005), 234–35; Glenn Feldman, ed., *Politics and Religion in the White South* (Lexington: University Press of Kentucky, 2005), 109.

67. Sokol, *There Goes My Everything*, 85.

68. *Richmond (Va.) News Leader*, November 21, 1955; Will Hustwit, *James J. Kilpatrick: Salesman for Segregation* (Chapel Hill: University of North Carolina Press, 2013), 53; Brent J. Aucoin, "The Southern Manifesto and Opposition to Desegregation," *Arkansas Historical Quarterly* 55 (Summer 1996): 176–89.

69. Hustwit, *James J. Kilpatrick*, 85–89, 151.

70. Silver, *Mississippi*, 6.

71. Watters quoted in David R. Goldfield, *Promised Land: The South since 1945* (Arlington Heights, Ill.: Harlan Davidson, 1987), 79.

72. Johnny Rebel, "Move Them Niggers North," audiocassette of jukebox songs from northwest Florida, in Charles Reagan Wilson Collection, Archives and Special Collections, John Davis Williams Library, University of Mississippi, Oxford, Mississippi.

73. Elizabeth Jacoway, *Turn Away Thy Son: Little Rock, the Crisis That Shocked the Nation* (New York: Free Press, 2007); J. Harvie Wilkinson III, *Harry Byrd and the Changing Face of Virginia Politics, 1945–1966* (Charlottesville: University of Virginia Press, 1968), 139–54.

74. John T. Kneebone, *Southern Liberal Journalists and the Issue of Race, 1920–1944* (Chapel Hill: University of North Carolina Press, 1985), 215–31; C. Vann Woodward, *The Strange Career of Jim Crow* (1955; repr., New York: Oxford University Press, 2001), 126.

75. Folsom quoted in *Montgomery Advertiser*, March 8, 1959, and *Atlanta Journal*, January 24, 1970; Long quoted in A. J. Liebling, *The Earl of Louisiana* (Baton Rouge: Louisiana State University Press, 1960), 29–30; and in Stan Opotowsky, *The Longs of Louisiana* (New York: Dutton, 1960), 159; Anders Walker, *The Ghost of Jim Crow: How Southern Moderates Used* Brown v. Board of Education *to Stall Civil Rights* (New York: Oxford University Press, 2009), 1–7.

76. Walker, *Ghost of Jim Crow*, 1–7.

77. Walker, conclusion.

78. Benjamin Houston, *The Nashville Way: Racial Etiquette and the Struggle for Social Justice in a Southern City* (Athens: University of Georgia Press, 2012), 1–12; William Chafe, *Civilities and Civil Rights: Greensboro, North Carolina, and the Black Struggle for Freedom* (New York: Oxford University Press, 1980), 8.

79. Houston, *Nashville Way*, epilogue.

80. Houston, 5.

81. James McBride Dabbs, *The Southern Heritage* (New York: Alfred A. Knopf, 1958), 152; James Jackson Kilpatrick, *The Southern Case for School Segregation* (New York: Crowell-Collier, 1962).

82. Flannery O'Connor, *Mystery and Manners: Occasional Prose* (New York: Farrar, Straus and Giroux, 1969), 234; Elizabeth Clay Blanford, letter to the editor, *Saturday Review*, May 21, 1955, 39.

83. Ruth Landes, "A Northerner Views the South," *Social Forces* 23, no. 3 (1945), 375–79; Jack Temple Kirby, *Media-Made Dixie: The South in the American Imagination* (Athens: University of Georgia Press, 1978), 106; James Street Jr., ed., *James Street's South* (Garden City, N.Y.: Doubleday, 1955), 14–15.

84. Herbert Ravenal Sass, "They Don't Tell the Truth about the South," *Saturday Evening Post*, January 9, 1954, 67–68.

85. Sam Ervin Jr., "The Case for Segregation," *Look*, April 2, 1956, 32.

86. Gene Roberts and Hank Klibanoff, *The Race Beat: The Press, the Civil Rights Struggle, and the Awakening of a Nation* (New York: Alfred A. Knopf, 2006).

87. Kirby, *Media-Made Dixie*, 141.

88. Martin Luther King Jr. recounts the Montgomery bus boycott in *Stride toward Freedom: The Montgomery Story* (1958; repr., Boston: Beacon, 2010); Jacquelyn Dowd Hall, "The Long Civil Rights Movement and the Political Uses of the Past," *Journal of American History* 91 (March 2005): 1233–63.

89. David Garrow, *Bearing the Cross: Martin Luther King Jr. and the Southern Christian Leadership Conference* (New York: Vintage Books, 1988); Lewis V. Baldwin, *There Is a Balm in Gilead: The Cultural Roots of Martin Luther King, Jr.* (Minneapolis, Minn.: Augsburg Fortress, 1991), 2–3, 29.

90. Clayborne Carson, Tenisha Armstrong, Susan Carson, Adrienne Clay, and Kieran Taylor, eds., *The Papers of Martin Luther King, Jr.*, vol. 5, *Threshold of a New Decade, January 1959–December 1960* (Berkeley: University of California Press, 2005), 423; Martin Luther King Jr., "Pilgrimage to Nonviolence," in *A Testament of Hope: The Essential Writings of Martin Luther King, Jr.*, ed. James Melvin Washington (New York: Harper and Row, 1986), 38.

91. Lewis V. Baldwin, "Understanding Martin Luther King, Jr., within the Context of Southern Black Religious History," *Journal of Religious Studies* 13 (Fall 1987): 9–10; Clayborne Carson, Susan Carson, Susan Englander, Troy Jackson, and Gerald L. Smith, eds., *Papers of Martin Luther King, Jr.*, vol. 6, *Advocate of the Social Gospel, September 1948–March 1963* (Berkeley: University of California Press, 2007), 303.

92. King, *Stride toward Freedom*, 5.

93. King, 183, 196, 213.

94. King, 31.

95. Martin Luther King Jr., "Our Struggle," in Washington, *Testament of Hope*, 75; and in Clayborne Carson, Stewart Burns, Susan Carson, Dana Powell, and Peter Holloran, eds., *Papers of Martin Luther King, Jr.*, vol. 3, *Birth of a New Age, December 1955–December 1956* (Berkeley: University of California Press, 1997), 236.

96. Peniel E. Joseph, *The Black Power Movement: Rethinking the Civil Rights–Black Power Movement Era* (New York: Routledge, 2006); Akinyele Omowale Umoja, *We Will*

Shoot Back: Armed Resistance in the Mississippi Freedom Movement (New York: New York University Press, 2013).

97. Timothy B. Tyson, *Radio Free Dixie: Robert F. Williams and the Roots of Black Power* (1999; repr., Chapel Hill: University of North Carolina Press, 2020), 2, 251, 285; Robert F. Williams, *Negroes with Guns* (New York: Marzani and Munsell, 1962).

98. Tyson, *Radio Free Dixie*, 196–97, 255, 285–87.

99. Andrew M. Manis, "The Civil Religions of the South," in Wilson and Silk, *Religion and Public Life*, 167; Martin Luther King Jr., "Letter from a Birmingham Jail," in *The Radical King*, ed. Cornel West (Boston: Beacon Press, 2015), 127-45.

100. Lewis V. Baldwin, *The Legacy of Martin Luther King, Jr.: The Boundaries of Law, Politics, and Religion* (Notre Dame, Ind.: University of Notre Dame Press, 2002), 24.

101. David A. Bobbitt, *The Rhetoric of Redemption: Kenneth Burke's Redemption Drama and Martin Luther King's "I Have a Dream" Speech* (New York: Rowman and Littlefield, 2004), 14; Martin Luther King Jr., "Remaining Awake through a Great Revolution" (speech), June 2, 1959, Morehouse College, Atlanta, Georgia, transcript, Martin Luther King, Jr. Research and Education Institute, https://kinginstitute.stanford.edu/king-papers/documents/remaining-awake-through-great-revolution-address-morehouse-college.

102. Louis D. Rubin Jr., "An Image of the South" and preface, in *The Lasting South: Fourteen Southerners Look at Their Home*, ed. Louis D. Rubin Jr. and James J. Kilpatrick (Chicago: Henry Regnery, 1957), 1.

103. Rubin, "Image of the South," 2.

104. Rubin, 3, 7–8.

105. Rubin, 10–11, 12–13.

106. Rubin, 14.

107. James J. Kilpatrick, "Conservatism and the South," in Rubin and Kilpatrick, *Lasting South*, 188, 194–95.

108. Kilpatrick, 193, 202, 203.

109. Paul K. Conkin, *The Southern Agrarians* (Knoxville: University of Tennessee Press, 1988), 152–64.

110. Donald Davidson, *Southern Writers in the Modern World* (1958; repr., Athens: University of Georgia Press, 2010), 8, 9, 30, 38.

111. Mark Royden Winchell, *Where No Flag Flies: Donald Davidson and the Southern Resistance* (Columbia: University of Missouri Press, 2000), 17; Tate quoted in Gregory L. Schneider, *The Conservative Century: From Reaction to Revolution* (New York: Rowman and Littlefield, 2009), 84.

112. Robert Penn Warren, *Segregation: The Inner Conflict of the South* (New York: Random House, 1956), 13, 24, 32, 46.

113. Robert Penn Warren, *Who Speaks for the Negro?* (New York: Random House, 1965).

114. Warren, 10–11.

115. Adam Fairclough, *To Redeem the Soul of the Nation: The Southern Christian Leadership Conference and Martin Luther King, Jr.* (Athens: University of Georgia Press, 2001), 62.

116. Sokol, *There Goes My Everything*, 61–62; Fred Powledge, *Free at Last: The Civil Rights Movement and the People Who Made It* (Boston: Little, Brown, 1991), xix–xx, 10–11.

117. *Richmond News Leader*, February 22, 1960; Hustwit, *James J. Kilpatrick*, 109; Sokol, *There Goes My Everything*, 62.

118. Leslie Dunbar, "The Changing Mind of the South: The Exposed Nerve," *Journal of Politics* 26 (February 1964): 4–5; Calvin Trillin, "Back on the Bus," *New Yorker*, July 25, 2011, 39.

119. James McBride Dabbs, "Christian Response to Racial Revolution," in *Public Address in the Twentieth-Century South: The Evolution of a Region*, ed. Stuart Towns (Westport, Conn.: Praeger, 1999), 187–190.

120. Dabbs, 187–90.

121. J. Todd Moye, *Ella Baker: Community Organizer for Civil Rights Movement* (Lanham, Md.: Rowman and Littlefield, 2013); Barbara Ransby, *Ella Baker and the Black Freedom Movement* (Chapel Hill: University of North Carolina Press, 2003).

122. Paul Harvey, *Through the Storm, through the Night: A History of African American Christianity* (New York: Rowman and Littlefield, 2011), 174–75.

123. Curry quoted in Harvey, 174.

124. Raymond Arsenault, *Freedom Riders: 1961 and the Struggle for Racial Justice* (New York: Oxford University Press, 2005).

125. Charles Marsh, *God's Long Summer: Stories of Faith and Civil Rights* (Princeton, N.J.: Princeton University Press, 1997), 22, 26.

126. Taylor Branch, *Parting the Waters: America in the King Years; 1954–1963* (New York: Simon and Schuster, 1988).

127. Doug McAdams, *Freedom Summer* (New York: Oxford University Press, 1990), 24; Bruce Watson, *Freedom Summer: The Savage Season That Made Mississippi Burn and Made America a Democracy* (New York: Viking Penguin, 2005); Paul Hendrickson, *Sons of Mississippi: A Story of Race and Its Legacy* (New York: Vintage Books, 2003), 47; Yellin, "Journalism (Print)," 118–23; Steven Classen, "Television, Civil Rights and," in Graham, and Montieth, *Media*, 167–71.

128. Sokol, *There Goes My Everything*, 244, 246, 323; *Public Papers of the Presidents of the United States: Lyndon B. Johnson, 1965* (Washington, D.C.: Government Printing Office, 1965), 1:281–87.

CHAPTER SEVEN

1. "A Home-Grown Elegance," *Time*, September 27, 1976, 66.

2. "The Good Life," *Time*, September 27, 1976, 32–39.

3. Jordan, Sanford, and White quoted in "Away from Hate," *Time*, September 27, 1976, 48–49.

4. "The Spirit of the South," *Time*, September 27, 1976, 30.

5. "Small-Town Soul," *Time*, September 27, 1976, 56, 30.

6. "The South Today"; and C. Vann Woodward, "The South Tomorrow," both in *Time*, September 27, 1976, 29, 99.

7. C. Vann Woodward, *The Burden of Southern History*, 3rd ed. (Baton Rouge: Louisiana State University Press, 1993), 6; Harry S. Ashmore, *An Epitaph for Dixie* (New York: W. W. Norton, 1958), 119; Hodding Carter, *Southern Legacy* (Baton Rouge: Louisiana State University Press, 1950), 158.

8. "In Dixie, the Colonel Moves Over," *Business Week*, November 12, 1955, 112–24.

9. Numan V. Bartley, *The New South, 1945–1980: The Story of the South's Modernization* (Baton Rouge: Louisiana State University Press and the Littlefield Fund for Southern

History of the University of Texas, 1995), 22–23; Riessman quoted in Luther H. Hodges, *Businessman in the Statehouse: Six Years as Governor of North Carolina* (Chapel Hill: University of North Carolina Press, 1962), 32.

10. William Nicholls, *Southern Tradition and Regional Progress* (Chapel Hill: University of North Carolina Press, 1960), ix, x, 5, 15.

11. Nicholls, 157, 158, 163, 186.

12. Jonathan Daniels, "The Ever-Ever Land," *Harper's Magazine*, April 1965.

13. David Lenton Weatherford, "Route of the Aristocrats: The Regional Identity of Southern Airways, Inc." (master's thesis, University of Mississippi, 1993), 28–29, 32, 42, 48.

14. Jason Sokol, *There Goes My Everything: White Southerners in the Age of Civil Rights, 1945–1975* (New York: Vintage Books, 2007), 293; Harry Golden, untitled, *Nation*, May 20, 1968, 668; Raymond Wheeler, "The Challenge to Black and White," *New South* 24 (Winter 1969), 4.

15. "Wallace Inaugural Address, 1963," in *Public Address in the Twentieth-Century South: The Evolution of a Region*, ed. W. Stuart Towns (Westport, Conn.: Praeger, 1999), 148–52.

16. James J Kilpatrick, *The Southern Case for School Segregation* (New York: Crowell-Collier, 1962), 21, 33, 50, 71–72.

17. George H. Leonard, "The Fast-Changing South," *Look*, November 16, 1965, 34, 36.

18. Fletcher Knebel, "The Changing Face of Southern Politics," *Look*, November 16, 1965, 39.

19. Sokol, *There Goes My Everything*, 115 (Emerson quote), 172; Willie Morris, *Yazoo: Integration in a Deep Southern Town* (New York: Harper's Magazine Press, 1971), 133; Myers quoted in Marshall Frady, "A Meeting of Strangers in Americus," *Life*, February 12, 1971, 21.

20. Willie Morris, *The Courting of Marquis DuPree* (Garden City, N.Y.: Doubleday, 1983); Frady, "Meeting of Strangers," 21; *Newsweek* quoted in Sokol, *There Goes My Everything*, 180.

21. Quotes in Sokol, *There Goes My Everything*, 192, 246.

22. Quotes in Sokol, 185–91.

23. Anthony Dunbar, *The Will to Survive: A Study of a Mississippi Plantation Community Based on the Words of Its Citizens* (Atlanta: Southern Regional Council, 1969), 13.

24. Marshall Frady, "Nightwatch in Greene County," *Newsweek*, May 16, 1966, quoted in Sokol, *There Goes My Everything*, 261.

25. Will D. Campbell, *Race and the Renewal of the Church* (Philadelphia: Westminster, 1962); Merrill M. Hawkins Jr., *Will Campbell: Radical Prophet of the South* (Macon, Ga.: Mercer University Press, 1997); Criswell quoted in Sokol, *There Goes My Everything*, 106; Andrew Manis, *Southern Civil Religions in Conflict: Black and White Baptists and Civil Rights, 1947–1957* (Athens: University of Georgia Press, 1987).

26. Robert Coles, *Farewell to the South* (Boston: Little, Brown, 1963), 372; Dan T. Carter, *The Politics of Rage: The Origins of the New Conservatism and the Transformation of American Politics* (Baton Rouge: Louisiana State University Press, 2000).

27. Kathy Kahn, ed., *Hillbilly Women* (New York: Avon Books, 1973), 21; factory worker quoted in Bartley, *New South*, 279; Harris poll quoted in *Atlanta Constitution*, September 20, 1976.

28. See Stephen A. Smith, *Myth, Media, and the Southern Mind* (Fayetteville: University

of Arkansas Press, 1985); and Joseph Crespino, *In Search of Another Country: Mississippi and the Conservative Counterrevolution* (Princeton, N.J.: Princeton University Press, 2007).

29. Charles L. Black Jr., "Paths to Desegregation," *New Republic*, October 21, 1957, 15.

30. Leslie W. Dunbar, "The Annealing of the South," *VQR* 37 (Autumn 1961): 507.

31. Pete Daniel, *Standing at the Crossroads: Southern Life in the Twentieth Century* (New York: Hill and Wang, 1986).

32. Pete Daniel, *Lost Revolutions: The South in the 1950s* (Chapel Hill: University of North Carolina Press for Smithsonian National Museum of American History, Washington, D.C., 2000), 131-47.

33. Peter Guralnick, *Last Train to Memphis: The Rise of Elvis Presley* (Boston: Little, Brown, 1994); Michael Bertrand, *Race, Rock, and Elvis* (Urbana: University of Illinois Press, 2000); Bobbie Ann Mason, *Elvis Presley: A Life* (New York: Penguin Books, 2003), 35-36; Eldridge Cleaver, *Soul on Ice* (New York: Dell, 1968), 195.

34. Daniel, *Lost Revolutions*, 165-67.

35. Paul Harvey, "Social Activism," in *Religion*, ed. Samuel S. Hill, vol. 1 of *The New Encyclopedia of Southern Culture*, ed. Charles Reagan Wilson (Chapel Hill: University of North Carolina Press, 2006), 139-43.

36. Martin Luther King Jr., *The Wisdom of Martin Luther King in His Own Words* (New York: Lancer/Bill Adler Books, 1968), 23, 64, 75; Martin Luther King Jr., *Why We Can't Wait* (New York: Harper and Row, 1963), 80.

37. "Text of the Speech Dr. King Delivered 20 Years Ago Today," *New York Times*, August 28, 1983, 28.

38. James McBride Dabbs, *Who Speaks for the South* (New York: Funk and Wagnalls, 1964), 343-44. See also Robert M. Randolph, "James McBride Dabbs: Spokesman for Racial Liberalism," in *From the Old South to the New: Essays on the Transitional South*, ed. Walter J. Fraser Jr. and Winfred B. Moore Jr. (Westport, Conn.: Greenwood, 1981), 25-56.

39. James McBride Dabbs, *The Southern Heritage* (New York: Alfred A. Knopf, 1958), 24; Dabbs, *Who Speaks*, 369, 371; James McBride Dabbs, *Haunted by God: The Cultural and Religious Experience of the South* (Richmond, Va.: John Knox, 1972), 40, 134; Charles Reagan Wilson, *Judgment and Grace in Dixie: Southern Faiths from Faulkner to Elvis* (Athens: University of Georgia Press, 1980), 18-36.

40. Dabbs, *Who Speaks*, 368; James McBride Dabbs, "The Land," in *The Lasting South: Fourteen Southerners Look at Their Home*, ed. Louis D. Rubin Jr. and James J. Kilpatrick (Chicago: Henry Regnery, 1957), 78; Dabbs, *Southern Heritage*, 267-68.

41. Dabbs, *Who Speaks*, 371-73, 377.

42. Willie Morris, introduction to *You Can't Eat Magnolias*, ed. H. Brandt Ayers and Thomas H. Naylor (New York: McGraw-Hill, 1972), xi. See also Karen A. McDearman, "L.Q.C. Lamar Society," in *Myth, Manners, and Memory*, ed. Charles Reagan Wilson, vol. 4 of *The New Encyclopedia of Southern Culture*, ed. Charles Reagan Wilson (Chapel Hill: University of North Carolina Press, 2006), 242-43.

43. Ayers and Naylor, *You Can't Eat Magnolias*, 5, 19.

44. Smith, *Myth, Media*, 74-78; *Southern Journal* 1, no. 1 (1980).

45. "Out of a Cocoon," *Time*, September 27, 1976, 40.

46. Busbee and Edwards quoted in Waldo W. Braden, "The Speaking of the Deep South Governors, 1970-1980," in *A New Diversity in Contemporary Southern Rhetoric*, ed.

Calvin M. Logue and Howard Dorgan (Baton Rouge: Louisiana State University Press, 1987), 198. See also Smith, *Myth, Media*, 62–93.

47. Braden, "Speaking," 200; David R. Goldfield, *Promised Land: The South since 1945* (Arlington Heights, Ill.: Harlan Davidson, 1987), 173–74.

48. James C. Cobb, "Community and Identity: Redefining Southern Culture," *Georgia Review* 50 (Spring 1996): 9–24.

49. Askew quoted in Smith, *Myth, Media*, 89.

50. Jack Temple Kirby, *Media-Made Dixie: The South in the American Imagination* (Athens: University of Georgia Press, 1986), chaps. 8 and 9.

51. Quotes in David R. Goldfield, *Black, White, and Southern: Race Relations and Southern Culture, 1940 to the Present* (Baton Rouge: Louisiana State University Press, 1990), 220, 225–26.

52. Mary E. Mebane, "And Blacks Go South Again," *New York Times*, July 4, 1972. For the Black migration southward, see Goldfield, *Black, White, and Southern*, 221; and "Race and the South," *U.S. News and World Report*, July 23, 1990, 22.

53. Curtis M. Graves, "Beyond the Briar Patch," in Ayers and Naylor, *You Can't Eat Magnolias*, 41–42.

54. Thadious M. Davis, "Expanding the Limits: The Intersection of Race and Region," *Southern Literary Journal* 20 (Spring 1988): 6–7; Alice Walker, "The Black Writer and the Southern Experience," in *In Search of Our Mothers' Gardens: Womanist Prose* (New York: Harcourt Brace Jovanovich, 1983), 21; Patricia G. Davis, *Laying Claim: African American Cultural Memory and Southern Identity* (Tuscaloosa: University of Alabama Press, 2016), 1–18, 150–57.

55. Kevin M. Kruse, *White Flight: Atlanta and the Making of Modern Conservatism* (Princeton, N.J.: Princeton University Press, 2005); Matthew D. Lassiter, *The Silent Majority: Suburban Politics in the Sunbelt South* (Princeton, N.J.: Princeton University Press, 2006). Kruse and Lassiter argue that economic development and the rise of suburban power and influence in the South made the region more like the rest of the nation. They see an overemphasis on racism in the post–civil rights era as obscuring such broader economic and demographic trends as corporate growth, migration, and class interests.

56. Darren Grem, "Suburbanization," in *Urbanization*, ed. Wanda Rushing, vol. 15 of *The New Encyclopedia of Southern Culture*, ed. Charles Reagan Wilson (Chapel Hill: University of North Carolina Press, 2010), 155–59.

57. John Shelton Reed, *One South: An Ethnic Approach to Southern Culture* (Baton Rouge: Louisiana State University Press, 1982), 119–26; Jonathan Daniel Wells, "Middle Class, Development Of," in *Social Class*, ed. Larry J. Griffin, Peggy G. Hargis, and Charles Reagan Wilson, vol. 20 of *The New Encyclopedia of Southern Culture*, ed. Charles Reagan Wilson (Chapel Hill: University of North Carolina Press, 2012), 172–76.

58. Crespino, *In Search*, 4.

59. Earl Black and Merle Black, *The Rise of Southern Republicans* (Cambridge, Mass: Belknap Press of Harvard University Press, 2002); Marvin P. King Jr., "Republican Party," in *Law and Politics*, ed. James W. Ely Jr. and Bradley G. Bond, vol. 10 of *The New Encyclopedia of Southern Culture*, ed. Charles Reagan Wilson (Chapel Hill: University of North Carolina Press, 2008), 278–84.

60. Curtis Wilkie, *Dixie: A Personal Odyssey through Events That Shaped the Modern South* (New York: Scribner's, 2001), 201.

61. Hustwit, *James J. Kilpatrick*, 187.

62. Hustwit, 151, 187, 188, 189, 190.

63. Hustwit, 191–94.

64. Kenneth E. Morris, *Jimmy Carter: American Moralist* (Athens: University of Georgia Press, 1996); Patrick Anderson, *Electing Jimmy Carter: The Campaign of 1976* (Baton Rouge: Louisiana State University Press, 1994).

65. Horace Sutton, "The South as New America," *Saturday Review*, September 4, 1976, 8; John Egerton, *The Americanization of Dixie* (New York: Harper's Magazine Press, 1974); Raymond Arsenault, "The End of the Long Hot Summer: The Air Conditioner and Southern Culture," *JSH* 50 (November 1984): 597–628.

66. Allison Graham and Sharon Monteith, eds., *Media*, vol. 18 of *The New Encyclopedia of Southern Culture*, ed. Charles Reagan Wilson (Chapel Hill: University of North Carolina Press, 2011), 7, 174–82.

67. Raymond A. Mohl, "Expressways and Central Cities"; and Howard L. Preston, "Transportation, Mass Transit," both in Rushing, *Urbanization*, 53–59, 163–65.

68. Smith, *Myth, Media*; Sutton, "South as New America," 8.

69. Kirby, *Media-Made Dixie*, 144. Zachary J. Lechner, *The South of the Mind: American Imaginings of White Southernness, 1960–1980* (Athens: University of Georgia Press, 2018), argues that after 1970 the South was, in national culture, less a problem South and more a source of resistance for the nation to the perceived social turmoil coming out of the 1960s.

70. Walker Percy, "Random Thoughts on Southern Literature, Southern Politics, and the American Future," *Georgia Review* 32 (Fall 1978): 501, 502, 503, 509.

71. Percy, 510.

72. Quotes in Egerton, *Americanization of Dixie*, 22.

73. Egerton, 22.

CHAPTER EIGHT

1. Frank Smith, ed., *I'll Still Take My Stand: By 22 Southerners* (Vicksburg, Miss.: Yazoo, 1980), 6–8.

2. Smith, 7, 25–41, 59, 43, 49–56, 65–71.

3. Smith, 73–80.

4. Smith, 17–23.

5. John Shelton Reed, "Southern Living," in *Media*, ed. Allison Graham and Sharon Monteith, vol. 18 of *The New Encyclopedia of Southern Culture*, ed. Charles Reagan Wilson (Chapel Hill: University of North Carolina Press, 2011), 358–59; Diane Roberts, "Living Southern in *Southern Living*," in *Dixie Debates: Perspectives on Southern Culture*, ed. Richard H. King and Helen Taylor (New York: New York University Press, 1996), 85–98.

6. John Logue and Gary McCalla, *Life at "Southern Living": A Sort of Memoir* (Baton Rouge: Louisiana State University Press, 2000), 33–34.

7. Eugene Butler, "*Southern Living*: In Tune with Today's South," *Southern Living*, February 1966, 4.

8. The referenced articles are from *Southern Living* stories during its first year of publication.

9. Roberts, "Living Southern," 85–98.

10. *Southern Style: Easy Updates Room-by-Room Inspired by Design Ideas* (Birmingham, Ala.: Oxmoor House, n.d.), 11, 13, 21, 27, 30.

11. PRNewswire, "Belk, Inc. Launches New Corporate Identity: 'Modern.Southern.Style,'" news release, October 4, 2010, https://www.prnewswire.com/news-releases/belk-inc-launches-new-corporate-identity-modern-southern-style-104266688.html.

12. Darius Rucker, "Southern Style," track 4 on *Southern Style*, CD, 2015.

13. Matthew Lassiter, *The Silent Majority: Suburban Politics in the Sunbelt South* (Princeton, N.J.: Princeton University Press, 2006).

14. John Shelton Reed, "The Same Old *Stand?*" in *One South: An Ethnic Approach to Regional Culture* (Baton Rouge: Louisiana State University Press, 1982), 162, 165, 169, 171.

15. Reed, 171–73, 174, 175.

16. Will D. Campbell, *Forty Acres and a Goat: A Memoir by Will D. Campbell* (Atlanta: Peachtree, 1986), 25; Darren Grem, "Suburbanization," in *Urbanization*, ed. Wanda Rushing, vol. 15 of *The New Encyclopedia of Southern Culture*, ed. Charles Reagan Wilson (Chapel Hill: University of North Carolina Press, 2010), 155–59.

17. Peter Applebome, *Dixie Rising: How the South Is Shaping American Values, Politics, and Culture* (San Diego, Calif.: Harcourt, Brace, 1997), 44–46.

18. Numan V. Bartley and Bradley G. Bond, "Politics and Ideology," in *Law and Politics*, ed. James W. Ely Jr. and Bradley G. Bond, vol. 10 of *The New Encyclopedia of Southern Culture*, ed. Charles Reagan Wilson (Chapel Hill: University of North Carolina Press, 2008), 159–65.

19. Paul Escott and David R. Goldfield, eds., *The South for New Southerners* (Chapel Hill: University of North Carolina Press, 1991), ix–xi.

20. Escott and Goldfield, ix, 10, 12.

21. Escott and Goldfield, 135, 146.

22. Jennifer Harper, "Church a Way of Life in Dixie," *Washington (D.C.) Times*, April 29, 2006.

23. Andrew M. Manis, "The Civil Religions of the South," in *Religion and Public Life in the South: In the Evangelical Mode*, ed. Charles Reagan Wilson and Mark Silk (Walnut Creek, Calif.: AltaMira, 2005), 165–94.

24. William Martin, *With God on Our Side: The Rise of the Religious Right in America* (New York: Broadway Books, 1996).

25. Charles Reagan Wilson, "Mobilized for the New Millennium," in Wilson and Silk, *Religion and Public Life*, 195–205.

26. Carl Kell and L. Raymond Camp, *In the Name of the Father: The Rhetoric of the New Southern Baptist Convention* (Carbondale: University of Southern Illinois Press, 1999), 122.

27. Wayne Flynt, *Alabama Baptists: Southern Baptists in the Heart of Dixie* (Tuscaloosa: University of Alabama Press, 1998), 578.

28. Grant Wacker, "Searching for Norman Rockwell: Popular Evangelicalism in Contemporary America," in *The Evangelical Tradition in America*, ed. Leonard I. Sweet (Macon, Ga.: Mercer University Press, 1984), 300.

29. Flynt, *Alabama Baptists*, 579.

30. John C. Green, "Believers for Bush, Godly for Gore: Religion and the 2000 Election in the South," in *The 2000 Presidential Election in the South: Partisanship and Southern*

Party Systems in the 21st Century, ed. Robert P. Steed and Laurence W. Morland (Westport, Conn.: Praeger, 2001), 13–15. See also Samuel S. Hill, "Religion and Politics in the South," in *Religion in the South*, ed. Charles Reagan Wilson (Jackson: University Press of Mississippi, 1985), 148–49.

31. See John M. Coski, *The Confederate Battle Flag: America's Most Embattled Emblem* (Cambridge, Mass.: Belknap Press of Harvard University Press, 2005); and John Shelton Reed, "The Banner That Won't Stay Furled," *SC* 8 (Spring 2002): 94.

32. Mark Bixler, "Supporters See Chief Moore as Moral Voice in Decaying Society," *Atlanta Journal-Constitution*, August 23, 2003; Adam Liptak, "Court Orders Removal of Monument to Ten Commandments," *New York Times*, July 2, 2003.

33. Samuel S. Hill, "Religion," in *Religion*, ed. Samuel S. Hill, vol. 1 of *The New Encyclopedia of Southern Culture*, ed. Charles Reagan Wilson (Chapel Hill: University of North Carolina Press, 2006), 16–19.

34. Scott Thumma, "Megachurches," in Rushing, *Urbanization*, 107–10.

35. Pierce Lewis, e.g., characterizes *Southern Living* magazine as "relentlessly domestic and relentlessly optimistic." White southerners in such a forum expressed an innocence about broader conflicts involving long-standing racial and social class divisions in the region. See Pierce Lewis, "The Making of Vernacular Taste: The Case of *Sunset* and *Southern Living*," in *The Vernacular Garden*, ed. John Dixon Hunt and Joachim Wolschke-Bulmahn (Washington, D.C.: Dumbarton Oaks Research Library and Collection, 1993), 118.

36. Daniel Payne, "55 Years of Integration: Where Are We Now?," *Daily Mississippian* (Oxford), October 2, 2017, 2.

37. Douglas quoted in Anthony Walton, *Mississippi: An American Journey* (New York: Alfred A. Knopf, 1996), 25–26.

38. Carolyn Bennett Patterson, "Mississippi's Grand Reunion at the Neshoba County Fair," *National Geographic*, June 1980, 854; Trent Watts, *One Homogeneous People: Narratives of White Southern Identity, 1890–1920* (Knoxville: University of Tennessee Press, 2010), 140.

39. Watts, *One Homogeneous People*, 148–51.

40. Charlie Le Duff, "At a Slaughterhouse, Some Things Never Die," in *How Race Is Lived in America: Pulling Together, Pulling Apart* (New York: Holt, 2001), 97–115.

41. Clifton Taulbert, *The Invitation* (Montgomery, Ala.: NewSouth Books, 2014).

42. Taulbert, xi–xii.

43. Taulbert, 17, 40.

44. Taulbert, 11, 114–16, 122, 133.

45. Taulbert, xv, 27.

46. Zandria Robinson, *This Ain't Chicago: Race, Class, and Regional Identity in the Post-Soul South* (Chapel Hill: University of North Carolina Press, 2014), 17–18, 45; "The South Today," special issue, *Ebony*, August 1971; Adolph Reed Jr., "Romancing Jim Crow: Black Nostalgia for a Segregated Past," *Village Voice*, April 1996, 24–29.

47. Robinson, *This Ain't Chicago*, 1, 36–37.

48. Robinson, 42, 45, 49.

49. Robinson, 8–13.

50. Robinson, 5, 8, 17, 49; Robert B. Stepto, *From behind the Veil: A Study of Afro-American Narrative* (Urbana: University of Illinois Press, 1991).

51. Robinson, *This Ain't Chicago*, 17–18, 32–33, 55.

52. Robinson, 50.

53. Robinson, 55, 187.

54. Robinson, 67–69, 146–49, 162–63, 196.

55. Regina N. Bradley, *Chronicling Stankonia: The Rise of the Hip-Hop South* (Chapel Hill: University of North Carolina Press, 2021), 16, 20, 30, 31, 33.

56. Bradley, 40; Kiese Laymon, *How to Slowly Kill Yourself and Others in America*, rev. ed. (New York: Scribner's, 2020), 15–16.

57. Laymon, *How to Slowly*, 31–32.

58. Laymon, 35–36; Bradley, *Chronicling Stankonia*, 59; Ralph Eubanks, *A Place Called Mississippi: A Journey through a Real and Imagined Literary Landscape* (Portland, Ore.: Timber, 2021), 114–15.

59. Al Green, "The Southern Soul," *Southern Magazine*, October 1986, 46.

60. Giovanni Russonello, "An Ode to a Place, and to Forgiveness," *New York Times*, September 10, 2017, 108.

61. John Lewis, "Reconciliation and the Beloved Community," in *Road to Reconciliation: Conflict and Dialogue in the Twenty-First Century*, ed. Amy Benson Brown and Karen M. Poremski (Armonk, N.Y.: Sharp, 2005), 167, 169, 172.

62. John Lewis, interview by Jon Meacham, *Garden and Gun*, February/March 2015, https://gardenandgun.com/articles/gg-interview-congressman-john-lewis.

63. Charles C. Bolton, *William F. Winter and the New Mississippi: A Biography* (Jackson: University Press of Mississippi, 2013), 268.

64. Charles Marsh, *The Beloved Community: How Faith Shapes Social Justice from the Civil Rights Movement to Today* (New York: Basic Books, 2005), 5. See also Peter Slade, Charles Marsh, and Peter Goodwin Heltzel, eds., *Mobilizing for the Common Good: The Lived Theology of John M. Perkins* (Jackson: University Press of Mississippi, 2013).

65. Marsh, *Beloved Community*.

66. Peter Slade, *Open Friendship in a Closed Society: Mississippi and a Theology of Friendship* (New York: Oxford University Press, 2009).

67. Susan Nieman, *Learning from the Germans: Race and the Memory of Evil* (New York: Farrar, Straus and Giroux, 2019), 140–43, 150; Timothy J. Minchin and John A. Salmond, *After the Dream: Black and White Southerners since 1965* (Lexington: University Press of Kentucky, 2011), 273–99.

68. Jerry Mitchell, *Race against Time: A Reporter Reopens the Unsolved Murder Cases of the Civil Rights Era* (New York: Simon and Schuster, 2020); Minchin and Salmond, *After the Dream*, 264–68; McWhorter quoted in Jacob Levenson, "Divining Dixie: Is It American Country? Or a Place to Stow National Problems? A Yankee Journalist Gets Lost and Found in the South," *Columbia Journalism Review* 42 (March 2004): 13.

69. W. Ralph Eubanks, *The House at the End of the Road: The Story of Three Generations of an Interracial Family in the American South* (New York: HarperCollins, 2009), 5–19.

70. Eubanks, 45–46.

71. Eubanks, 86–98, 98, 115.

72. Eubanks, 122, 142.

73. Eubanks, 145–47, 152, 170.

CHAPTER NINE

1. Edward Lee, *Smoke and Pickles: Recipes and Stories from a New Southern Kitchen* (New York: Artisan Books, 2013), ix; Jake Grovum, "How Asian-Americans Are Changing the South," October 3, 2014, Pew Charitable Trusts, https://www.pewtrusts.org/en/research -and-analysis/blogs/stateline/2014/10/03/how-asian-americans-are-changing-the-south.

2. Lee, *Smoke and Pickles*, ix.

3. Lee, ix, xi, 188, 219, 231.

4. Lee, xi, 200.

5. Christopher Dickey, "The End of the South"; and Jon Meacham, "Just Ain't That Different Anymore," both in *Newsweek*, August 11, 2008, 23–32, 28–29.

6. Martyn Bone, *Where the New World Is: Literature about the U.S. South at Global Scales* (Athens: University of Georgia Press, 2018), 23; Leigh Anne Duck, "Southern Non-identity," *Safundi* 1 (July 2008), 329; Jon Smith, "Toward a Post-postpolitical Southern Studies: On the Limits of the 'Creating and Consuming' Paradigm," in *Creating and Consuming the American South*, ed. Martyn Bone, Brian Ward, and William Link (Gainesville: University Press of Florida, 2015), 72–94. For reactions to new southern studies scholarship, see Michael O'Brien, "Epilogue: Place as Everywhere," in *Creating Citizenship in the Nineteenth-Century South*, ed. William A. Link, Brian Ward, and Martyn Bone (Gainesville: University Press of Florida, 2013), 271–89; Richard King, "Allegories of Imperialism: Globalizing Southern Studies," *American Literary History* 23, no. 1 (2010): 148–58; and Ted Ownby, "The New Southern Studies and Rethinking the Question, 'Is There Still a South?,'" *Journal of American Studies* 49, no. 4 (2015): 871, 878. For the southern cultural renaissance, see Heath Carpenter, *The Philosopher King: T Bone Burnett and the Ethic of a Southern Cultural Renaissance* (Athens: University of Georgia Press, 2019), which usefully complicates understandings of the contemporary southern identity.

7. Richard Gray, "Inventing Communities, Imagining Places: Some Thoughts on Southern Self-fashioning," in *South to a New Place*, ed. Suzanne W. Jones and Sharon Monteith (Baton Rouge: Louisiana State University Press, 2002), xx. Bone (*Where the New World Is*, x, 20) offers a recent analysis, and defense, of new southern studies in arguing that the field now is embracing more historical context and materialist focus beyond narratives, as well as a focus on the local and global scales. Jon Smith offers a combative assessment in "Response to New Southern Studies Forum: What the New Southern Studies Does Now," *Journal of American Studies* 49, no. 4 (2015): 861–70.

8. Christopher A. Cooper and H. Gibbs Knotts, *The Resilience of Southern Identity: Why the South Still Matters in the Minds of Its People* (Chapel Hill: University of North Carolina Press, 2017), 3, 21.

9. Cooper and Knotts, 99.

10. Nell Irvin Painter, "The Rhetoric of Race Relations and Real Life," in *The South for New Southerners*, ed. Paul Escott and David R. Goldfield (Chapel Hill: University of North Carolina Press, 1991), 27, 33; Cooper and Knotts, *Resilience of Southern Identity*, 99.

11. Chesnut quoted in Allen Tullos, *Alabama Getaway: The Political Imaginary and the Heart of Dixie* (Athens: University of Georgia Press, 2011), 194; James E. Clyburn, *Blessed Assurance: Genuinely Southern, Proudly Black* (Columbia: University of South Carolina Press, 2014), 335; Joan Wylie Hall, ed., *Conversations with Natasha Trethewey* (Jackson: University Press of Mississippi, 2013), 166.

12. Cynthia Tucker, "Confederacy Lives On," *San Francisco Chronicle*, August 5, 1994; Cynthia Tucker, "South Still May Not Be the Promised Land, but It's Far Better Than Before," *Atlanta Journal-Constitution*, January 13, 1990; Tullos, *Alabama Getaway*, 194; Condoleezza Rice, "Dishing with Condoleezza Rice," interview by Jenna Bush Hager, *Southern Living*, April 2013.

13. Chadwick Boseman, "Chadwick Boseman: Man of the Hour," interview by Allison Glock, *Garden and Gun*, October/November 2017, 54.

14. Hemphill quoted in Escott and Goldfield, *South for New Southerners*, 92; Pete Daniel, *Standing at the Crossroads: Southern Life in the Twentieth Century* (New York: Hill and Wang, 1986), 229–30.

15. Daniel, *Standing at the Crossroads*, 229–30.

16. Rick Bragg, *My Southern Journey: True Stories from the Heart of the South* (New York: Time Life Books, Oxmoor House, 2015), 10–12.

17. Bragg, 44–46, 90, 156.

18. Kate Zernike, "Where a 'Southern Girl' Is Also a Feminist," *New York Times*, July 22, 2002, A14.

19. Barbara Ellen Smith, "Place and Past in the Global South," *American Literature* 78 (December 2006): 693–95; Bethany E. Moreton, *The Soul of the Service Economy: Wal-Mart and the Making of Christian Free Enterprise, 1929–1994* (Cambridge, Mass.: Harvard University Press, 2006).

20. Bellamy Young, "Paper Napkin Interview," *Southern Living*, September 2013, 68.

21. Julie M. Wiese, *Corazon de Dixie: Mexicanos in the U.S. South since 1910* (Chapel Hill: University of North Carolina Press, 2015), 11, 12–14.

22. Perla M. Guerrero, *Nuevo South: Latinas/os, Asians, and the Remaking of Place* (Austin: University of Texas Press, 2017), 178, 179.

23. Guerrero, 178–79.

24. Wiese, *Corazon de Dixie*, 12, 112–24, 210, 223–24; Guerrero, *Nuevo South*, 18.

25. Rachel L. Swans, "In Georgia, Newest Migrants Unsettle an Old Sense of Place," *New York Times*, August 4, 2006, A1.

26. Bob Moser, "White Heat," *Nation*, August 28, 2006, 11–18.

27. Christopher D. Geist, "Television Series (1940s–1980s)"; and Marsha McGee, "The Dukes of Hazzard," both in *Media*, ed. Allison Graham and Sharon Monteith, vol. 18 of *The New Encyclopedia of Southern Culture*, ed. Charles Reagan Wilson (Chapel Hill: University of North Carolina Press, 2011), 174–79, 237–38.

28. Sharon Monteith, "Television Series (1980 to Present)," in Graham and Monteith, *Media*, 179–82.

29. Gary W. McDonogh and Cindy Hing-Yak Wong, "Religion and Representations in the Filmic South," in *Images of the South: Constructing a Regional Culture on Film and Video*, ed. Karl G. Heider (Athens: University of Georgia Press, 1993), 27; and Allison Graham, "Film, Documentary"; and Nahem Yousaf, "Film, Ethnicity in," both in Graham and Monteith, *Media*, 51–57, 57–60.

30. Chuck Thompson, *Better Off without 'Em: A Northern Manifesto for Southern Secession* (New York: Simon and Schuster, 2012), 15, 30.

31. Adam Serwer, "The Myth of the Kindly General Lee," *Atlantic*, June 4, 2017.

32. Jeremy Egner, "The South, as Seen on TV," *New York Times*, December 24, 2017, TR1.

33. Sarah Khan, "Making Myself at Home," *New York Times*, October 1, 2017, TR1, 4.

34. Thadious M. Davis, "Expanding the Limits: The Intersection of Race and Region," *Southern Literary Journal* 20 (Spring 1988): 6–7; Paul Delany, "The Deep South, 30 Years Later: Touring the Sites of the Civil-Rights Struggle, a Black Visitor Finds a Changed Region," *New York Times*, February 23, 1992, 37. See also Charles Reagan Wilson, "'God's Project': The Southern Civil Religion, 1920–1980," in *Judgment and Grace in Dixie: Southern Faiths from Faulkner to Elvis* (Athens: University of Georgia Press, 1995), 18–36.

35. John Coski, *The Confederate Battle Flag: America's Most Embattled Emblem* (Cambridge, Mass.: Belknap Press of Harvard University Press, 2005). See also Charles Reagan Wilson, "Unifying the Symbols of Southern Culture," in *Judgment and Grace*, 159–63; and Kevin Thornton, "The Confederate Flag and the Meaning of Southern History," *SC* 2 (Winter 1996): 233–45.

36. Clyde N. Wilson, "The Confederate Battle Flag: A Symbol of Southern Heritage and Identity," *SC* 2 (Winter 1996): 271; W. Stuart Towns, *Enduring Legacy: Rhetoric and Ritual of the Lost Cause* (Tuscaloosa: University of Alabama Press, 2012), 138.

37. Jennifer Berry Hawes, *Grace Will Lead Us Home: The Charleston Church Massacre and the Hard, Inspiring Journey to Forgiveness* (New York: St. Martin's Press, 2019).

38. Peter Applebome, "New Orleans Mayor's Message on Race," *New York Times*, May 4, 2017; Karen Cox, "Confederate Monuments Must Fall," *New York Times*, August 16, 2017; Catherine Clinton, ed., *Confederate Statues and Memorialization* (Athens: University of Georgia Press, 2019).

39. Carol Anderson, "'They Were Not Patriots': New Orleans Removes Monument to Confederate Gen. Robert E. Lee," *New York Times*, May 19, 2017.

40. Michael Hill and Thomas H. Fleming, "The New Dixie Manifesto: States' Rights Shall Rise Again," *Washington Post*, October 29, 1995, C3; Michael Hill, "The Southern League—Hoping the South Will Rise Again," interview by Diane Roberts, *Weekend Edition*, National Public Radio, May 5, 1996; Euan Hague, Heidi Beirich, and Edward H. Sebesta, eds., *Neo-Confederacy: A Critical Introduction* (Austin: University of Texas Press, 2009), 1–19.

41. Tony Horwitz, *Confederates in the Attic: Dispatches from the Unfinished Civil War* (New York: Pantheon, 1998), 3, 5.

42. Peter Applebome, *Dixie Rising: How the South Is Shaping American Values, Politics, and Culture* (San Diego, Calif.: Harcourt, Brace, 1997), 117–20.

43. Holland Cotter, "The New Mississippi Civil Rights Museum Refuses to Sugarcoat History," *New York Times*, December 18, 2017.

44. *Telling Our Stories: Museum of Mississippi History and Mississippi Civil Rights Museum* (Jackson: University Press of Mississippi, 2017), ix–xii, 99.

45. Bryan Stevenson, *Just Mercy: A Story of Justice and Redemption* (New York: Spiegel and Grau, 2014), 3–18; Legacy Museum (website), https://museumandmemorial.eji.org/museum; Valerie Fraser Luesse, "Angels in Montgomery," *Southern Living*, February 2019, 82.

46. Claudia Dreifus, "Following the Civil Rights Trail," *New York Times*, March 11, 2020; Ron Stodgill, "Indelible Detours: The Civil Rights Trail Provides a Rewarding Start, but a Tour Can Be More Meaningful When You Don't Follow the Map," *New York Times*, August 12, 2018.

47. Ashley F. G. Norwood, "Excavating Everyday Life of Slaves Behind the Big House,"

Mississippi Today, April 22, 2017, https://mississippitoday.org/2017/04/22/holly-springs
-excavates-everyday-life-of-slaves-behind-the-big-house; Whitney Plantation (website),
www.whitneyplantation.org.

48. Nedra Pickler, "Two Rivals Mark Civil Rights Struggle, Hillary Clinton, Obama
Attend Alabama Rally," *Boston Globe*, March 5, 2007; Barack Obama, speech, March 7,
2015, Selma, Alabama, transcript, *Time*, time.com/3736357/barack-obama-selma-speech
-transcript; Peter Baker and Richard Fausset, "Obama, at Selma Memorial, Says, 'We
Know the March Is Not Yet Over,'" *New York Times*, March 7, 2015, https://www.nytimes
.com/2015/03/08/us/obama-in-selma-for-edmund-pettus-bridge-attack-anniversary.
html; Allen Tullos, *Alabama Getaway*, 258; John Lewis, "Reconciliation and the Beloved
Community," in *Road to Reconciliation: Conflict and Dialogue in the Twenty-First Century*, ed. Amy Benson Brown and Karen M. Poremski (New York: M. E. Sharp, 2005), 172.

49. Sid Evans, "Powerful Memories: The South's Civil Rights Sites Are Places to Visit,
Reflect, and Remember," *Southern Living*, February 2017, 14.

50. The twenty-four volumes of *The New Encyclopedia of Southern Culture* document
the adaptation of many cultural ways to contemporary contexts.

51. David Goldfield, "Urbanization in a Rural Culture: Suburban Cities and Cosmop-
olites," in Escott and Goldfield, *South for New Southerners*, 92.

52. Allison Glock, "Song of the South," *Southern Living*, September 2013, 72.

53. Bill C. Malone, *Southern Music/American Music* (Lexington: University Press of
Kentucky, 2003); James C. Cobb, "From Muskogee to Luckenbach: Country Music and
the Southernization of America," in *Redefining Southern Culture: Mind and Identity in
the Modern South* (Athens: University of Georgia Press, 1999), 39; Davis Peisner, "Wrangling Rough Country Beasts," *New York Times*, March 20, 2016, AR21; Ben Goad, "Hallowed Sound, Vol. 2," *Clarion-Ledger* (Jackson, Miss.), September 26, 2021, 2PE–12PE.

54. Jeffrey J. Folks and James A. Perkins, *Southern Writers at Century's End* (Lexington:
University Press of Kentucky, 1997), xi (quote); Doris Betts, "Many Souths and Broadening Scale: A Changing Southern Literature," in *The Future South: A Historical Perspective
on the Twenty-First Century* (Urbana: University of Illinois Press, 1991), 158–69.

55. Susan Ketchin, *The Christ-Haunted Landscape: Faith and Doubt in Southern Fiction*
(Jackson: University Press of Mississippi, 1994), 283 (quote); Sarah Robertson, *Poverty
Politics: Poor Whites in Contemporary Southern Writing* (Jackson: University Press of
Mississippi, 2019).

56. Fritz Gysin, "From Modernism to Postmodernism: Black Literature at the Crossroads," in *Cambridge Companion to the African American Novel*, ed. Maryemma Graham
(New York: Cambridge University Press, 2004), 139–56.

57. "Native Daughter Jesmyn Ward," *Oxford American*, Autumn 2012, 18–19; Jesmyn
Ward, "My True South: Returning Home to a Place I Love More Than I Loathe," *Time*,
August 6, 2018, 46–49; W. Ralph Eubanks, *A Place Like Mississippi: A Journey through a
Real and Imagined Literary Landscape* (Portland, Ore.: Timber, 2021), 33–41.

58. Jamie Harker, *The Lesbian South: Southern Feminists, the Women in Print Movement, and the Queer Literary Canon* (Chapel Hill: University of North Carolina Press,
2018), 5–6; Rita Mae Brown, interview by Bethanne Kelly, *Bookreporter*, April 2, 2004,
https://www.bookreporter.com/authors/rita-mae-brown/news/interview-040204.

59. Kathryn McKee, "Globalization and Southern Literature," in *Literature*, ed.
M. Thomas Inge, vol. 9 of *The New Encyclopedia of Southern Culture*, ed. Charles Reagan

Wilson (Chapel Hill: University of North Carolina Press, 2008), 82–85; Deborah Cohn, *History and Memory in the Two Souths: Recent Southern and Spanish American Fiction* (Nashville, Tenn.: Vanderbilt University Press, 1999); Jones and Monteith, *South to a New Place*. Martyn Bone, in *Where the New World Is*, offers fresh readings in a wide range of writers from the global South. See also Cinelle Barnes, ed., *A Measure of Belonging: Twenty-One Writers of Color in the New American South* (Spartanburg, S.C.: Hub City, 2020).

60. Raymond Mohl, "Miami, Florida," in *Urbanization*, ed. Wanda Rushing, vol. 15 of *The New Encyclopedia of Southern Culture*, ed. Charles Reagan Wilson (Chapel Hill: University of North Carolina Press, 2010), 217–19; Felix Masud-Piloto, "Cubans," in *Ethnicity*, ed. Celeste Ray, vol. 6 of *The New Encyclopedia of Southern Culture*, ed. Charles Reagan Wilson (Chapel Hill: University of North Carolina Press, 2007), 137–38.

61. Andria Lisle, "Hip-Hop and Rap," in *Music*, ed. Bill C. Malone, vol. 12 of *The New Encyclopedia of Southern Culture*, ed. Charles Reagan Wilson (Chapel Hill: University of North Carolina Press, 2008), 75; Gustavo Pérez Firmat, *A Cuban in Mayberry: Looking Back at America's Hometown* (Austin: University of Texas Press, 2014), 1–17, 147–51.

62. Erik Brady, "College Football's Grip on the South Stronger than Ever," *USA Today*, August 5, 2017, D2 (quote); Andrew Doyle, "Turning the Tide: College Football and Southern Progressivism," *SC*, no. 3 (1997), 28–51; Charles Reagan Wilson, "The Death of Bear Bryant: Myth and Ritual in the Modern South," in *Judgment and Grace*, 37–51.

63. Wilson, "Death of Bear Bryant," 46–49.

64. Brady, "College Football's Grip," D2.

65. Harvey Arraton, "Alabama Taps a Talent Pool as Deep as the South," *New York Times*, January 9, 2013, B13.

66. John Allin, "Religion in the South (USA)," in *I'll Still Take My Stand: By 22 Southerners*, ed. Frank E. Smith (Vicksburg, Miss.: Yazoo, 1980), 103–5. See also Eric Bain Selbo, *Game Day and God: Football, Faith, and Politics in the American South* (Macon, Ga: Mercer University Press, 2012).

67. Allin, "Religion in the South," 103–5.

68. Willie Morris, *Shifting Interludes: Selected Essays*, ed. Jack Bales (Jackson: University Press of Mississippi, 2002), 53; Mark Blaudschun, "Song of the South," *Boston Globe*, August 22, 1999, C2; Bragg, *My Southern Journey*, 13.

69. Sandra A. Gutierrez, *The New Southern-Latino Table: Recipes That Bring Together the Bold and Beloved Flavors of Latin America and the American South* (Chapel Hill: University of North Carolina Press, 2011), 1, 3.

70. Gutierrez, 3, 4.

71. Gutierrez, 4–6, 136.

72. Gutierrez, 6, 36, 39, 217.

73. Eli Evans, *The Provincials: A Personal History of Jews in the South* (New York: Atheneum, 1973); Charles H. Lippy, "Tactics for Survival: Religious Minorities," in *Religion and Public Life in the South: In the Evangelical Mode*, ed. Charles Reagan Wilson and Mark Silk (Walnut Creek, Calif.: AltaMira, 2005), 125–40. R. Bruce Brassell's *The Possible South: Documentary Films and the Limitations of Biraciality* (Jackson: University Press of Mississippi, 2015) argues that diversity is not necessarily a challenge to power relations.

74. John T. Edge, *The Potlikker Papers: A Food History of the Modern South* (New York: Penguin Books, 2017), 113–14, 117–19.

75. Edna Lewis, *The Taste of Country Cooking* (New York: Alfred A. Knopf, 1976), 3-4; Jane Lear, "What Is Southern? The Annotated Edna Lewis," in *Edna Lewis: At the Table with an American Original*, ed. Dara B. Franklin (Chapel Hill: University of North Carolina Press, 2018), 17.

76. Laura Shapiro, "Filling the Mouth of the South," *Newsweek*, December 11, 1995, 78, 80.

77. John Egerton, *Southern Food: At Home, on the Road, in History* (1987; repr., Chapel Hill: University of North Carolina Press, 1993), 2, 3, 5, 7.

78. Edge, *Potlikker Papers*, 4-5, 11; Egerton, *Southern Food*, 3-4. See also Carrie Helms Tippen, *Inventing Authenticity: How Cookbook Writers Redefine Southern Identity* (Fayetteville: University of Arkansas Press, 2018), 8-9, 163-64; and Ashli Quesinberry Stokes and Wendy Atkins-Sayre, *Consuming Identity: The Role of Food in Redefining the South* (Jackson: University Press of Mississippi, 2016).

79. John T. Edge, interview by Charles Reagan Wilson, 2018, transcript, Charles Reagan Wilson Collection, Archives and Special Collections, John Davis Williams Library, University of Mississippi, Oxford, Mississippi; Michael W. Twitty, *The Cooking Gene: A Journey through African American Culinary History in the Old South* (New York: Amistad, 2017), 407-9. See also James Hudnut-Beumler, *Strangers and Friends at the Welcome Table: Contemporary Christianities in the American South* (Chapel Hill: University of North Carolina Press, 2018), 4.

80. "Gifts: Heirloomed," *Okra*, Winter 2018, 118; W. Fitzhugh Brundage, "From Appalachian Folk to Southern Foodways: Why Americans Look to the South for Authentic Culture," in Bone, Ward, and Link, *Creating and Consuming*, 5; Jane S. Becker, *Selling Tradition: Appalachia and the Construction of an American Folk, 1930-1940* (Chapel Hill: University of North Carolina Press, 1998), 12-13, 34-38, 194-99.

81. John T. Edge, "An Active Authenticity," *Oxford American*, Summer 2017, 322-34.

82. Edge, *Potlikker Papers*, 2, 3.

83. Edge, 2, 3.

84. Edge, 10, 298, 304.

85. Edge, 86-106; Twitty, *Cooking Gene*.

86. Kim Severson, "A White Gatekeeper of Southern Food Faces Calls to Resign," *New York Times*, June 29, 2020; Jaya Saxena, "Founding Director of Influential Southern Foodways Alliance Pressured to Resign," *Eater*, June 29, 2020, www.eater.com/2020/6/29/21307584/southern-foodways-alliance-director-john-t-edge-pressured-to-resign.

87. Ann Patchett, "The Bookstore Strikes Back," Parnassus Books, www.parnassusbooks.net/bookstore-strikes-back; Lynn York, "Blair," interview by Adam Morgan, in Adam Morgan, "The Hopes and Fears of Southern Presses," *Southern Review of Books*, February 20, 2020, https://southernreviewofbooks.com/2020/02/22/southern-independent-presses-on-publishing-in-the-south.

88. York, "Blair."

89. "About the Southern Bookseller Review," *Southern Bookseller Review*, https://thesouthernbooksellerreview.org/about; Square Books (website), www.squarebooks.com.

90. Linton Weeks, Editor's Note, "On Becoming Good Friends," *Southern Magazine*, October 1986, 8.

91. Willie Morris, "Does It Still Exist?," *Southern Magazine*, October 1986, 39, 40, 43, 45, 47.

92. Linton Weeks, Editor's Note: "When the Southern Sun Goes Down," *Southern Magazine*, January 1987, 10.

93. "White Trash Chic: Everything Old Is Nouveau Again," *Southern Magazine*, November 1986, 38–40.

94. Mission statement, *Oxford American*, oxfordamerican.org/images/banners/OA2016 _mediakit_website.pdf.

95. Chuck Reece, "Why We Created the Bitter Southerner in the First Place," *Bitter Southerner*, August 6, 2013, https://bittersoutherner.com/we-are-bitter.

96. Reece.

97. "Celebrate the Good Life in the South," *Garden and Gun* subscription brochure, Charles Reagan Wilson Collection, Archives and Special Collections, John Davis Williams Library, University of Mississippi, Oxford, Mississippi. See also "The South, Sportingly: *Garden and Gun* Magazine Hunts for Well-Heeled; Lock Stock and Barrel, Magazine Devoted to Southern Way of Life," *Atlanta Journal-Constitution*, August 26, 2008; and Shawn Chandler Bingham, "Bohemian Graves, Grooves, Gardens, and Guns: The Hybrid World of Bohemian and Bourgeoisie Southern Magazines," in *The Bohemian South: Creating Counterculture from Poe to Punk* (Chapel Hill: University of North Carolina Press, 2017).

98. "Celebrate the South: The Ultimate Southern Bucket List," *Garden and Gun*, April/May 2017, 20, 46–60.

99. "Celebrate the South," 20, 46–60.

100. Sam Riley, "Magazines," in Graham and Monteith, *Media*, 130–36.

101. Derek H. Alderman, "Internet Representations of the South," in Graham and Monteith, *Media*, 114–18.

102. Alderman, 114–18; Debby Mayne, "Southern Ways—Life in the South," December 28, 2019, *Southern Home Express* (blog), southernhomeexpress.com/southern-ways.

103. John Egerton, *Shades of Gray: Dispatches from the Modern South* (Baton Rouge: Louisiana State University Press, 1991), 254–55; Reese Witherspoon, "Talking Shop with Reese Witherspoon," interview by Allison Glock, *Garden and Gun*, October/November 2015, 106.

104. Hodding Carter III, "Looking Back," *SC* 2, no. 3-4 (1996): 281, 293; Young, "Paper Napkin Interview," 68; Diane Roberts, "Stay and Resist," *Oxford American*, Fall 2016, 116–25.

105. The Center for the Study of Southern Culture's Future of the South Initiative explores connections between the humanities, economic development, and public policy in the South through such recent projects as Movement and Migration, Invisible Histories (lives of LGBTQ Mississippians), and Floodgates (climate change). "Future of the South Initiative," Center for the Study of Southern Culture, https://southernstudies.olemiss .edu/events/future-of-the-south.

106. John Locke Foundation (website), www.johnlocke.org; "Who Are We?," South Carolina Policy Foundation, https://scpolicycouncil.org/about.

107. Nancy MacLean, *Democracy in Chains: The Deep History of the Radical Right's Stealth Plan for America* (New York: Viking, 2017), xiv–xviii, 30–37.

108. MacLean, xiv–xviii, xxiii, 194–97, 230.

109. "About MDC," MDC, www.mdcinc.org/about.

110. William Winter, "Shadowboxing," *Southern Magazine*, October 1986, 67–70.

111. Winter, 67–70; Mike Randle, "Southern Growth Policies Board Shuts Down on North Carolina Governor Pat McCrory's Recommendations," *Randle Report*, September 17, 2013, http://randlereport.com/southern-growth-policies-board-shuts-down-on-n -c-gov-pat-mccrorys-recommendation/.

112. Clara Turnage, "Writers vs. Mississippi: Religious Freedom in Law," *Daily Mississippian* (Oxford), April 12, 2016, 3; Ted Ownby, Director's Column, *Southern Register*, Spring/Summer 2016, 2; Frank Bruni, "America's Worst (and Best) Places to Be Gay," *New York Times*, August 27, 2017, SR1, 3.

113. Bruni, "America's Worst," SR3; Saeed Jones, *How We Fight for Our Lives: A Memoir* (New York: Simon and Schuster, 2020); Samantha Allen, *Real Queer America: LGBT Stories from Red States* (New York: Little, Brown, 2019); Nathaniel Frank, *Awakening: How Gays and Lesbians Brought Marriage Equality to America* (Cambridge, Mass.: Belknap Press of Harvard University Press, 2017).

114. Anne Hull, "Rural Residents Unsure They're Part of Obama's America," *Washington Post*, January 16, 2009, A1.

115. Sarah Pullam Bailey, "Black and White Evangelicals Once Talked about 'Racial Reconciliation': Then Trump Came Along," *Washington Post*, August 21, 2020, https://www .washingtonpost.com/religion/2020/08/21/black-and-white-evangelicals-trump-racial -reconciliation; Nicholas Casey, "Culture Wars Reach the Pews, and Empty Them," *New York Times*, June 21, 2020, A1, 26; Eric Lutz, "Trump May as Well Be Running for President of the Confederacy," *Vanity Fair*, July 6, 2020, www.vanityfair.com/news/2020/07 /trump-may-as-well-be-running-for-president-of-the-confederacy; Paul Waldman, "Donald Trump Stands Up for the Confederacy One Last Time," *Washington Post*, November 24, 2020, https://www.washingtonpost.com/opinions/2020/11/24/donald-trump-stands-up -confederacy-one-last-time.

116. Luesse, "Angels in Montgomery," 82; "Southern Agenda: Alabama, Past Due," *Garden and Gun*, April/May 2018, 154; "National Memorial for Peace and Justice," *Local Palate*, Fall 2020, 77.

117. Ron Carver, "Anti-union Sentiment Feels Like Old South," *Clarion-Ledger*, August 23, 2014, 13A; Robert Lovato, "Juan Crow in Georgia," *Nation*, May 26, 2008, 20–24.

118. Patterson Hood, "The South's Heritage Is So Much More Than a Flag," *New York Times Magazine*, July 9, 2015, nytimes.com/2015/07/09/magazine/the-souths-heritage-is -so-much-more-than-a-flag.html.

119. Hood. Ellie Campbell places the Drive-By Truckers in the context of southern literature and popular culture in her "'Daddy, Tell Me Another Story': The Drive-By Truckers, Southern History, and Popular Culture" (master's thesis, University of Mississippi, 2006).

120. Hood, "South's Heritage."

121. Natasha Trethewey, *Native Guard* (Boston: Houghton Mifflin, 2006), 35.

122. Trethewey, 25–30; Charles Reagan Wilson, "Trethewey, Natasha," in Inge, *Literature*, 449–50.